SPORTS LAW

Simon Gardiner, BA (Hons), MA, Pg Dip,
Senior Research Fellow in Sports Law,
Anglia Polytechnic University

Alexandra Felix, LLB (Hons), LLM,
Lecturer in Law, Anglia Polytechnic University

John O'Leary, LLB (Hons), MPhil,
Lecturer in Law, Anglia Polytechnic University

Mark James, LLB (Hons), Barrister,
Lecturer in Law, Manchester Metropolitan University

Roger Welch, LLB (Hon), LLM, MPhil,
Senior Lecturer in Law, University of Portsmouth

Cavendish
Publishing
Limited

London • Sydney

First published in Great Britain 1998 by Cavendish Publishing Limited,
The Glass House, Wharton Street, London WC1X 9PX.
Telephone: 0171-278 8000 Facsimile: 0171-278 8080
e-mail: info@cavendishpublishing.com
Visit our Home Page on http://www.cavendishpublishing.com

Sports law
1. Sports – Law and legislation – England
I. Gardiner, Simon
344.2'0499

1 85941 311 0

Printed and bound in Great Britain

*To all our families, thank you for all your support
and in particular to Alexandra and Niamh,
the sports lawyers of tomorrow*

FOREWORD

The study of sports law is a relatively new worldwide phenomena. One body of thought believes that sports law does not exist *per se*. Rather, sports law study is seen merely as the application of traditional legal principles to the sports industry. A growing body of thought, however, sees the emergence of a recognisable body of statutory and case law as a subject that can be designated as a distinct legal area, namely, sports law. Whichever is the correct view, sports law traverses a broad range of legal disciplines, including contract, tort, labour, anti-trust, agency, trade regulation, criminal and administrative law, to name a few.

In essence, then, the 'sports lawyer' is the ultimate general practitioner, having to master a broad range of legal subjects in order to best serve his client. Today, lawyers off the field may be as important as managers on the field. Legal words such as 'free agency', 'rights of first refusal', 'revenue sharing' and 'luxury tax' are seen as often on the American sports pages as such statistics as 'dunks', 'assists' and 'bases on ball'. In sum, the sports industry intersects the law at every cross.

Sports law as a subject can encompass many topics, from the regulation of governing bodies to the rights of athletes; from the interrelationship between the anti-trust (competition) laws and labour laws to restrictive employment practices; from safety in sport to violence on the field; from protecting the commercial value of an athlete to ambush marketing; from providing an internal dispute resolution system to protecting both the constitutional and other inalienable rights of its participants.

In the United States, sports law as a substantive legal area received its greatest attention in the late 1960s through to the early 1980s. In *Flood v Kuhn* (1972), once again, the anti-trust exception given to baseball in 1922 was re-examined and upheld. Furthermore, in the 1970s restrictive labour practices in basketball and football in the form of the reserve clause, right of first refusal, the draft, indemnity rule, and other player restrictions were being examined in both an anti-trust and labour law context (the *Haywood, Mackie, Kapp* and *Smith* cases). The issues relative to movement of teams and 'keeping the team at home' became centre focus with respect to the City of Oakland, Los Angeles Memorial Coliseum and Oakland Raiders cases.

In addition, the player unions became more vocal and steadfast in their demands for freedom, especially freedom of movement, and labour strife in the form of strikes and lock-outs became commonplace in American professional sports. The arbitration case of 'Messerschmit – McNally' once and for all changed baseball's reserve system without the interference of a court decision. Major League Baseball adopted in 1974 what is commonly known as salary arbitration. And finally, in 1983, the general question of amateurism – in the form of whether scholarships are employment contracts, and whether or not amateur athletes are employees – became an issue in the worker's compensation case of *Rensing v Indiana State*.

Some of this legal activity may be very analogous to the *Bosman* experience of the European Community in the 1990s, when the European Court of Justice was asked to opine on the age-old transfer system, which obstructed players' freedom of movement, and to decide whether restrictions on foreign-based players were discriminatory.

As a result of this increasing sport and the law activity, the first American text books addressing sports and law issues became available in the American market place. Lionel Sobel's *Professional Sports and the Law*, and Weistart and Lowell's *The Law of Sports*, were published in the 1970s. Around 10 years later in the United Kingdom, the first edition of Edward Grayson's work, *Sport and the Law*, was published.

American law schools started to run courses that directed themselves to both the professional and amateur sports and entertainment issues. By the 1990s, most American law schools had some form of sports law course in their curriculum. Two law schools: Marquette University, based in Milwaukee, Winsconsin, in the presence of the National Sports Law Institute; and Tulane University, in New Orleans, Louisiana, have a broad range of dynamic sports law programmes, with a multitude of courses and sports law related activities, including scholarly journals.

We have witnessed a rapid worldwide growth in the 1990s, not only in the interest in sports law amongst students and lawyers, but also in the application of the existing body of law to the business of sports. No longer are the issues just American issues, but worldwide issues. Freedom of player movement; violence on the field; maximisation of revenues through venue renovation and construction; commercialisation of the athlete and ambush advertising; drug testing; international courts of arbitration, are issues and subjects that touch every country, every federation, and every governing body. As a result, law schools, as well as sports lawyers associations, now tackle issues of the industry on an international, as well as domestic, basis.

To give further credence to the substantive area of sports law, Anglia Polytechnic University established, in 1996, the Anglia Sports Law Research Centre, the first of its kind within the European Community. The centre, much like the National Sports Law Institute, acts as a sports industry resource and specialises in sports law, in the form of academic research and writing.

This book, *Sports Law*, as written by members of the Anglia Sports Law Research Centre: Simon Gardiner, Alexandra Felix, John O'Leary, Mark James and Roger Welch, is further evidence of far this field has expanded. The amount of material covered shows the importance of the subject and the increased demand for written commentary in the field of sports law worldwide.

This work is excellent for students of law and practitioners in the area of sports. The authors have focussed their commentary on sports; society and the law; the role of the State; drug use; regulation of governing bodies; sports commercialism; contracts of employment; liability and violence; sports stadiums; and safety. These topics are at the forefront of worldwide interest, and substantive comment on these issues is most necessary in order to gain a better understanding of the subject.

I extend my congratulations to Simon and the other members of the Anglia Sports Law Research Centre, not only on an institute well received, but a book that will join seminal works in the area of sports law.

Martin Greenberg
Milwaukee
November 1997

PREFACE

This book reflects of the reality of the growth of sports law in Britain as an area of academic inquiry. Up until reasonably recently, this subject has been associated primarily with the legal practicebecause of the growing number of lawyers spending considerable amounts of their professional time on sports related legal issues, and some firms having dedicated sports law practices. Over the last few years, there has been a corresponding increase in the academic study of sports law. There are currently only a few dedicated sports law courses in Britain: Anglia Polytechnic University; Kings College; London; Westminster; Warwick; and Manchester Metropolitan Universities, are among the few Law Schools offering such courses. However, sports law issues have become an important part of the curriculum in the plethora of sports studies courses that have developed in Britain in recent years.

There is clearly a growing interest in the academic study of the legal regulation of sport and now is the time to produce a book that attempts to not only provide an exposition of the growing sports law jurisprudence, but provide a full analysis and critical evaluation of its operation, reflecting the growing maturity of this legal subject.

For sport, as for society in general, legal regulation and litigation are a reality of modern life. The law has expertise and values that can contribute to the running and organisation of modern sport. Britain has, however, only quite recently recognised the crucial role that law can play in regulating sport. The creation of the British Association for Sport and the Law in 1993 was important in identifying and recognising this area of law. However, there is still much debate over the legitimacy and extent to which the law should be involved with sport. There are a number of areas where the intervention of the law is contested and there are conflicting arguments about whether the law should have a role to play in certain areas of sport.

Of course a major issue is whether this subject can be labelled 'sports law' or merely 'sport and the law'. This issue will be debated in the first chapter and although some may think it is essentially an abstract esoteric argument, it is no accident that we have titled this book, 'Sports Law'. Stating that sports law has now arrived as a legitimate legal subject reinforces the importance of the role of law in contemporary sport and the growing body of statutory and case law specific to sport.

Sport has immense cultural significance. This book has tried to analyse the legal regulation of sport clearly within the socio-cultural context of contemporary sport. The focus is, inevitably, on elite professional sport, although it should not be forgotten that the vast majority of participation in sport is on an amateur and recreational level. Football also tends to dominate the analysis of legal issues. It is, of course, Britain's number one national sport, but every attempt has been made to cover as wide a range of sports as possible. The term 'sports athlete' is used extensively throughout the book to denote an individual who participates in both team and individual sports.

This book therefore provides the first rigorous academic analysis of the role that law has in sport in Britain. It does, however, also have a practical orientation. The approach has been to develop a text and materials book with extensive extracts from primary and secondary sources. We provide detailed analysis of this material and the major issues in sports law. We believe that this will be of value to sports lawyers, sports administrators and students at sub-degree, undergraduate and postgraduate level; studying sports law, or sports studies.

We have tried to show that there are many uncertainties as to how certain areas of law are developing in sport. We have highlighted the areas of uncertainty and hope that this will lead to further research and inquiry in these areas. Sports law is an area where different types of legal research methodology – ranging from traditional library based methods to socio-legal empirical approaches – are possible. The book attempts to explain quite technical and formal bodies of law and also to put the development of sports law into a socio-economic context, in order to understand the reasons for the increasing intervention of law in sport.

This book has been a cooperative effort with five contributors. All have been involved in the growth of the sports law project at the Law School at Anglia Polytechnic University and the creation of the Anglia Sports Law Research Centre in 1996. Although two contributors have now moved to new universities, this work collectively reflects the work of the Research Centre. One strength of the book is that it does represent the work of a research group who have applied their individual interests and areas of expertise to respective areas of sports law.

The chronological development of the chapters aims to provide an unfolding account of the dominant issues in sports law. They all differ in the amount of case law and statute law discussed and applied to sport and the use of extracts of primary and secondary sources, because of the nature of the subjects involved.

Chapter 1 is written by Simon Gardiner and provides an introduction to the historical and social role that law has had in regulating sport. Some foundational material attempts to explain what we mean by sport, particularly necessary in the context of arguments supporting the need for a legal definition of sport. The causes of law's greater involvement in sport regulation are explored, including the argument that it is an obvious response to the greater professionalisation and commercialisation of modern elite sport. There is an attempt, however, to consider other reasons why law is increasingly used as a primary form of regulating sport, rather than the other forms of normative rules, primarily the internal rules of the sport itself. An attempt is made to provide a theoretical framework for understanding the role of law in modern sport.

Chapter 2 is also written by Simon Gardiner, and examines the role that the State in Britain has in regulating sport. This is both on a national level and European level with the impact of the European Commission on sport extensively evaluated. The relationship between sport and formal politics is examined. Five examples of the intervention of the law in sport are examined, compared and contrasted.

Chapter 3 is written by John O'Leary and focuses on a major issue of how national and international sports governing bodies should regulate the use and abuse of drugs in sport. The regulation of drugs in sport is highly contentious, as it is generally in society. A thorough examination is made of the different types of drugs used in sport to enhance performance and the law's role in regulation is evaluated.

Chapter 4 is written by Alexandra Felix and charts the continuing debate as to the jurisdiction of the courts in questioning the internal decisions of sporting bodies. British sports national governing bodies are essentially private organisations. This creates problems with the process of judicial review which is essentially a public law remedy. The emergence of the use of alternative dispute resolution (ADR) mechanisms in sport reflects their growing use in other areas of social life. This attempt to deal with disputes more effectively in-house and within sport itself is evaluated.

Chapter 5 is written by Simon Gardiner and examines the regulation of financial dealings in sport. The financial contours of sport have changed dramatically during the 1990s. This chapter evaluates the economic structure of contemporary sport and shows how sports athletes are becoming more financially independent and enforcing their rights through the law. A major issue examined is the clash between the values associated with financial probity generally found in business and the idiosyncratic way that financial dealings and transactions have traditionally been carried out in sport. The recent corruption scandals in sport generally, and particularly football, are examined. The move to professionalisation in a greater number of sports and in expanding parts of the world is also discussed.

Chapter 6 is written by Alexandra Felix and maps the growing development of law's role in regulating and protecting the increasingly valuable assets found within sport. Sports marketing has become an enormous industry with sponsorship and advertising deals bringing vast amounts of money into sport. The chapter considers both the legal regulation and protection that is available for these deals on a sport and event wide level and examines the protection that individual sports athletes have for the intellectual property rights they have in their own person. Finally, the role of television as the increasing bank roller of elite professional sport is examined.

Chapters 7, 8 and 9 are written by Roger Welch and focus on the role that employment law has in sport. Chapter 7 concentrates on the formation of sporting employment contracts and the rights that sports athletes enjoy. The contractual terms of sports athletes have in the past reflected the unequal position they have with club owners and sports promoters. This relationship has been subject to increased legal challenge under concepts such as restraint of trade. The 1995 decision of the European Court of Justice in *Bosman* is analysed at length and the impact that it may have on the employment position of athletes within modern sport and mechanisms such as the transfer system as a method of regulating the mobility of athletes between different employers is evaluated.

Chapter 8 focuses on the termination of employment in sport. Participation in sport at elite levels is always precarious in the context of the never-ending spectre of career breaking or ending injuries. Loss of form is always around the corner too. Sports athletes are also subject to rigorous and specific internal sporting rules as far as conduct and discipline are concerned. Disciplinary rules in a number of sports are evaluated and the dynamics of how contracts come to an end are discussed.

Chapter 9 focuses on issues of discrimination within sports employment. The primary issues will be discrimination in terms of sex, race and disability. A major social aim of sport during the recent past has been the promotion of equal opportunities for participation in sport – 'sport for all' policies. However, much of the structural discrimination found generally in the work place are found in sport and the effectiveness of the legal remedies that exist are analysed. Additionally, the sport specific programmes to counter discrimination are evaluated.

Chapters 10 and 11 are written by Mark James and provide an analysis of how the law and internal rules within sport have regulated the physical force and interaction between sports athletes that is an essential part of much sport. Excessive force can often be characterised as 'sports violence' and has been constructed as one of the major problems in contemporary sport and in need of legal regulation. Chapter 10 focuses on the issues of liability in both the criminal and civil context for sports injuries and the case law that has developed in both these areas of liability is evaluated. The distinction between legitimate and illegitimate, legal and illegal play within sport is a vital issue in terms of how liability is determined for participants, coaches and officials.

Chapter 11 focuses on the available remedies that sports athletes can use when they are injured and how perpetrators of 'sports violence' should be penalised. This is an area where there is a continuing tension concerning the competing claims of sports bodies through internal mechanisms and developing ADR procedures on the one hand, and the courts and lawyers on the other, in providing the most effective remedies. There is an emphasis in the discussion on prevention of incidents of sports violence and consequential injury ending up in the courts. For example, the development and dissemination of risk management programmes in sport are examined.

Chapter 12 is written by John O'Leary and focuses on another issue of safety in sport, that is the legal regulation of sports stadiums and participation. Sporting events attract large numbers of people and, as with any congregation of people, their regulation and control needs to be carefully managed. One of the major events in recent sporting history in Britain was the Hillsborough tragedy which led to the Taylor Report. The subsequent regulatory framework for safety is analysed in depth. The role of the civil and criminal law will be evaluated in how it directs relationships between sports spectators, participants, the police and sports organisers.

All the five authors are keen sports fans and to differing degrees are either past or current participants in a number of sports. Fandom is of course an important part of participation within the world of sport. Those who know us will be aware of our sporting allegiances: football dominates with Alex an Everton fan; Roger follows his beloved Pompey and his move to Portsmouth may have been dictated too much by 'footie' consideration rather than academic ones; John is a 'true blue' Chelsea supporter; Mark provides scouser rivalry to Alex with his love for Liverpool; and myself, an aficionado of by far the finest United team in Britain – Leeds, of course! In cricket it is myself and Roger who provide the North-South rivalry between Yorkshire and Essex respectively. We hope the foci of our sporting devotion is not too obvious in our respective commentaries.

As the individual who has acted as an informal editor for all the contributions, the blame for discrepancies in consistency of style must be laid at my door. Credit for errors unfortunately also remains with the authors.

Simon Gardiner
Chelmsford
September 1997

ACKNOWLEDGMENTS

Grateful acknowledgment is made for the following:

Bale, J, *Landscapes of Modern Sport* (1994), Leicester University Press

Barnes, J, *Sports and the Law in Canada* (1996), Toronto: Butterworths

Baldwin, R, 'Taxation of Sport' (1996) 4(3) *Sport and the Law Journal*

Bell, A, 'Dispatch from Brussels', reproduced with permission of Monitor Press Ltd, publishers of *Sports Law Administration and Practice*

Berlins, M, 'Law: The New Ball in your Court', *The Guardian*, 2 April 1996

Birley, D, *Sport and the Making of Britain* (1993), Manchester University Press

Bitel, N, 'Ambush Marketing' (1997) 5(1) *Sport and the Law Journal*

Black, J, 'Constitutionalising Self-Regulation' (1996) 59 *Modern Law Review*

Blake, A, *The Body Language: The Meaning of Modern Sport* (1996), London: Lawrence and Wishart

Boon, G (ed), *Deloitte & Touche Annual Review of Football Finance*, Deloitte & Touche, August 1997

Brearly, M, 'Cricket: Atherton Affair: The Dirt that is in all our Pockets', *The Observer*, 31 July 1994

Burrell, I and Palmer, R, 'Taxman Blows Whistle on Football's Fiddles', *The Sunday Times*, 6 June 1993

Cashmore, E, *Making Sense of Sports* (1996), London: Routledge

Chadband, I, 'A Field Fit for Lawyers: Law in Sport', *The Sunday Times*, 9 April 1995

Chaudhary, V, 'Asians can play Football, too', *The Guardian*, 17 August 1994

Downes, S and Mackay, D, *Running Scared: How Athletics lost its Innocence* (1996), Edinburgh: Mainstream Publishing

Doyle, B, 'The Anzla Dispute Resolution Service' (1995) 3(3) *Sport and the Law Journal*

Dyer, G, 'In the Noble Art, Even Failure Contains Greatness', *The Guardian*, 27 February 1995

Fitzsimons, P, *The Rugby War* (1996), Sydney: HarperSports

Ford, A, 'Whose move is this?', *The Times*, 30 July 1986

Foster, K, 'Developments in Sporting Law', in Allison, L (ed), *The Changing Politics of Sport* (1993), Manchester University Press

Gasper, T, 'Protecting Events – Catching Ambush Marketing Offside' (1994), Working Paper, University of Melbourne

Grayson, E, *Sport and the Law*, 2nd edn (1994), London: Butterworths

Hargreaves, J, *Sport, Power and Culture: A Social and Historical Analysis of Popular Sports in Britain* (1986), Cambridge: Polity Press

Hubbard, A, 'Racism in Sport: Malignant Malady that Lingers on', *The Observer*, 18 August 1996

Holt, R, *Sport and the British: A Modern History* (1989), Oxford: Clarendon Press

Leaman, O, 'Cheating and Fair Play in Sport', in Morgan, W (ed), *Sport and the Humanities: A Collection of Original Essays* (1981), Educational Research and Service, University of Tennessee

Letts, Q, 'Sports Stars Coached on Patent Law', *The Times*, 14 May 1996

Long, J, Tongue, N, Spacklen, K and Carrington, B, *What's the Difference? A Study of the Nature and Extent of Racism in Rugby League* (1995), School of Leisure and Sports Studies, Leeds Metropolitan University

Longmore, A, 'Absurd Cup Rule Obscures Football's Final Goal', *The Times*, 1 February 1994

Mason, T, *Sport in Britain* (1988), London: Faber and Faber

McVicar, J, 'Violence in Britain: The Sporting Life of Crime', *The Guardian*, 19 September 1995

Monnington, T, 'Politicians and Sport: Uses and Abuses', in Allison, L (ed), *The Changing Politics of Sport* (1992), Manchester University Press

Nazfiger, JAR, 'International Sports Law as a Process for Resolving Disputes' (1996) 45(1) *International and Comparative Law Quarterly*

Nelson, G, *Left Foot Forward* (1995), London: Headline

Parrish, R, 'Sport and the Intergovernmental Conference' (1997) 5(1) *Sport and the Law Journal*

Raja, N, 'Sports Gambling in Malaysia' (1997) 8(2) *For the Record – The Official Newsletter of the National Sports Law Institute*

Redhead, S, *Unpopular Culture: The Birth of Law and Popular Culture* (1995), Manchester University Press

Regan, T, 'Why Hunting and Trappings are Wrong' in William, J and Meier, K (eds), *Philosophical Inquiry in Sport* (1995), Champaign: Human Kinetics

Reid, R, 'Report of the FA Premier League Seminar', 8 January 1996, British Association for Sport and Law

Ryan, J, *Little Girls in Pretty Boxes* (1995), New York: Warner Books

Sheard, K, 'Aspects of Boxing in the Western Civilising Process' (1997) 32(1) *Intenational Review for the Sociology of Sport*

Stewart, N, 'Stevenage Borough FC v The Football League – A Misleading Test' (1996) 4(3) *Sport and the Law Journal*

Sutcliffe, P, 'The Noble Art?' in *Total Sport*, February 1996

Whannel, G, *Fields in Vision: Television, Sport and Cultural Transformation* (1992), London: Routledge

Williams, J, 'Support for All?', 121 *When Saturday Comes*, March 1997

Wise, A, 'Property Right in a Sports Event: Views of Different Jurisdictions' (1997) 5(1) *Sport and the Law Journal*

HarperCollins Australia for permission to reproduce extracts from Brasch, R, *How Did Sports Begin?* (1986)

The Institute for the Study and Treatment of Delinquency, King's College London, Strand, London, WC2R 2LS; e-mail: istd.enq@kcl.ac.uk; website: www.kcl.ac.uk/orgs/istd for permission to reproduce extracts from Robins, D, 'Sport and Crime Prevention: The Evidence of Research' (1996) 23 *Criminal Justice Matters*

'The European Union and Sport' (1996), European Commission

British Medical Association, *The Boxing Debate* (1993)

IAAF, *IAAF Procedural Guidelines for Doping Control 1996*

Virgin Publishing Ltd for permission for the extract taken from *Football Babylon* © Russ Williams (1996)

'Anzla News Ltd's Super League Appeal Success', *Anzsla Newsletter Update*, January 1997

There are many people who have assisted by providing formal and informal comments on the various drafts for this book and other previous sports law work carried out at Anglia that has culminated in this book. We are particularly grateful to Paul Anderson, John Barnes, Andrew Caiger, Martin Greenberg, Steve Greenfield, James Gray, Hazel Hartley, Paul Kitson, Dave McArdle, Michael Nash, Guy Osborn, Steve Redhead, David Stott, Adam Tomkins for the reviewing of drafts of sections of the book.

We would also like to thank the students on the sports law module at Anglia over the last few years who have provided many useful insights to the whole range of sports law issues.

We are grateful for support provided by the English Sports Council, the Central Council of Physical Recreation and the National Coaching Foundation.

We thank those who have allowed the inclusion of their work. We are grateful for the financial and logistical support that Anglia Polytechnic University and a number of colleagues have provided directly for the sports law project and indirectly for the book.

Every effort has been made to trace all the copyright holders but if any have been inadvertently overlooked the publishers will be pleased to make the necessary arrangement at the first opportunity.

CONTENTS

Contents

TABLE OF CASES

TABLE OF STATUTES

CHAPTER ONE

SPORT, SOCIETY AND THE LAW

The rule of law in sport is as essential for civilisation as the rule of law in society generally. Without it generally anarchy reigns. Without it in sport, chaos exists.[1]

INTRODUCTION

Sport is a truly global phenomenon. As a social activity whether it is in terms of participation as a recreational pastime, competitive playing at amateur levels or the world of elite and mainly professional level or in terms of spectating, sport assumes immense cultural significance.

Sport is going through important changes and the role that law has in regulating sport will be analysed during this chapter. Suggestions will be made concerning why legal intervention seems to have become more prominent in recent years. The chapter is divided into three sections. First, the cultural significance of sport will be evaluated. Examples of the greater legal intervention in the regulation of sport will be provided, perhaps arguably reinforcing the modern importance of sport as an area of social life. Secondly, the complex relationship between sport and society will be considered both in an historical and contemporary sense. A major question to be asked is, 'What is sport?' Lastly, an attempt will be made to provide a theoretical framework for understanding the role that law has in regulating sporting activity. The issue of whether the subject matter of this legal area and indeed this book should be described as 'sport and the law' or 'sports law' will be determined.

THE CONTEMPORY IMPORTANCE OF SPORT

Sport is very much a part of popular culture and our consumption of it is increasingly mediated through television and radio. In Britain, more sport is shown on television than ever before. Satellite television in the guise of Rupert Murdoch's BSkyB television with its three dedicated sports channels and, to a lesser extent, the other terrestrial and cable channels, has had an immense impact upon the financial contours of contemporary elite sport. Sport is a

---

1   Grayson, E, President of The British Association for Sport and Law, in his inaugural presidential address (1993) 1(1) *Sport and the Law Journal* 1.

major element on both national and local radio. Sport has also become a major part of the circulation battle between national newspapers and the number of lavish magazines on sport and recreation have multiplied. Sport books are often in the best sellers list and a number have clear literary merit and are an important part of popular culture.[2] The academic study of sport has mushroomed in the last 30 years with many university centres focusing on the scientific, philosophical, sociological, historical and legal study of sport and there is consequentially a huge volume of work.

Sport tells us much about the dynamics of social change in society. It represents a powerful political force: organisations such as Federation Internationale de Football Associations (FIFA)[3] and the International Olympic Committee (IOC)[4] are more influential than many countries:

Blake, A, *The Body Language: The Meaning of Modern Sport*

... sport is very much part of popular culture. Many people participate in it, either as amateurs or professionals and many people observe it as spectators inside stadia or by listening to the radio or watching television. At any rate, sport is continuously visible elsewhere in the world. Indeed, as this book will argue, sport is a crucial component of contemporary society, one very important way through which many of us understand our bodies, our minds and the rest of the world. This is true not only because of mass participation and observation: sport saturates the language that surrounds us. Sporting activity is reported in every newspaper; it forms an important part of the wider literary culture of magazines and books. Take the annual American journal of record, the Britannica Yearbook for 1994. In the section devoted to reviewing the previous year's events, Sports and Games forms by far the longest entry. Forty pages are devoted to reports of events from the world of sport and a further 28 pages give 'the sporting record' of performance statistics (winners, newly broken records, times and distances); both national and global events are covered, from archery through gymnastics and rodeo to wrestling. By contrast, there are only 20 pages on economic affairs and coverage of the arts is far thinner, with only four pages each on dance, music (covering both classical and popular) and publishing.

Sport is also perpetually audible and visible through the electronic media. Television and radio devote a great deal of time to sport. There are whole departments of most networks devoted to sport as current affairs, providing

---

2   Football books include Hopcraft, A, *The Football Man: People and Passions in Football* (1968), London: Penguin; Davies, H, *The Glory Years*; Davies, P, *All Played Out – The Full Story of Italia '90* (1990), London: Manadarin; Hornby, N, *Fever Pitch* (1992) London: Indigo; Hamilton, I, *Gazza Agonistes* (1993), London: Granta. A cricket masterpiece is James, C, *Beyond a Boundary* (1996), London: Serpent's Tail.

3   For discussion of role of FIFA see Duke, V and Crolley, L, *Football Nationality and the State* (1996), Harlow: Longman; Sugden, J and Tomlinson, A, 'Who Rules the People's Game? FIFA versus UEFA in the Struggle for Control of World Football' in Brown, A (ed), *Power Race, Nationality and Fandom in European Football* (1998), London: Routledge.

4   For discussion of role of IOC, see Tomlinson, A and Whannel, G (eds), *Five Ring Circus – Money, Power and Politics at the Olympic Games* (1984), London: Pluto Press and Hill, C, *Olympic Politics* (1992), Manchester University Press.

everything from the brief reporting of results on news programmes to the saturation coverage of events like the Olympics, World Cups and national championships in team sports on both mainstream and dedicated programmes and channels. Sport is arguably one of the most powerful presences within broadcasting. Both on television and radio, the principle of live coverage is often taken to mean that sporting events have priority over others. As well as driving other programming from the screen at certain times of the year, sport can instantly reshape television in a way which can only be matched by political crises or disasters involving loss of life. Unexpectedly rearranged fixtures or more routinely, late finishing matches, disrupt published broadcast schedules, to the distress of people who do not wish to stay up late or people who have programmed their video recorders to record scheduled programmes. This prioritised saturation coverage means that even those uninterested in sport or hostile to it, cannot escape its nagging presence, as an ongoing part of the 'background noise' of contemporary culture.[5]

Another perspective on the cultural significance of sport, presents a theory of the relationship between sport and culture in the context of power relations:

Hargreaves, J, *Sport, Power and Culture*

When we refer to culture in the substantive sense, then, we mean first those activities, institutions and processes that are more implicated in the systematic production and reproduction of systems of meaning and/or those not concerned mainly or immediately with economic or political processes but which instead encompass other kinds of vital activities. We are referring here to major institutions, such as religion, education, science, the arts, the media of communication, the family, leisure and recreation, as well as sports – and, in fact, to much of the routine practice of everyday life. Secondly we find it useful to employ the ethnographer's substantive sense of culture as a 'whole way of life' of a particular group of people. Culture here refers to the way different threads of similarly placed individuals' lives – work, leisure, family, religion, community, etc are woven into a fabric or tradition, consisting of customs, ways of seeing, beliefs, attitudes, values, standards, styles, ritual practices, etc giving them a definite character and identity. It is thus we speak here of working-class culture, men's and women's culture, black culture, bourgeois culture and youth culture. Cultures in this sense are profound sources of power, reproducing social divisions here, challenging and rebelling against them there, while in many ways accommodating subordinate groups to the social order. We will be at pains to develop the theme throughout this study that the function and significance of sports varies with the type of culture in question and even does so within cultures. We will be arguing that it is precisely because sport plays different roles in relation to different cultures that it is able to reproduce power relations.

We contend that, in addition, the linkages between sport and power cannot be elucidated without reference to two other forms of culture – popular culture and consumer culture. As the term implies, popular culture engages 'the

---

5   Blake, A, *The Body Language: The Meaning of Modern Sport* (1996), London: Lawrence and Wishart, pp 11–12.

people' and although, therefore, it is not the product or possession of any one specific group, popular culture does overlap to a perplexing degree with working-class culture and the culture of subordinate groups as a whole. While expressing in its content and idiom the experience of those whom it engages, like its political counterpart 'populism', it does so ambivalently, facing simultaneously in a radical and in a conservative direction – for popular culture as we know expresses a certain critical penetration of the power structure, while also manifesting a complicity in it. The long historical association between sports and popular culture, culminating in sport becoming a major component of the national popular culture is, we argue, highly significant for the character of sport Accordingly, one of our major themes will be the ambivalent relation between sport and power, exemplified best perhaps, in that mixture of respectable family entertainment, violence, rebellion and chauvinism that characterises modern day professional football.

Consumer culture, by which we mean the way of life associated with and reproduced through the operations of consumer capitalism, clearly in many ways also overlaps with working-class and popular culture, to the extent that many aspects of the latter, notably sports, seem to have been in effect appropriated by consumer culture. We will be exploring the significance of the increasing tendency of sport to become one more commodity and attempting to specify the extent to which sporting activity, as an aspect of working-class and of popular culture, remains autonomous. In particular we are rather sceptical of the notion that sport has been absorbed into a manipulated form of culture supposedly exercising a uniformly conservative influence over 'the masses'; and we will be attempting to pinpoint ways in which, as far as commodified sport is concerned, it also exhibits an ambivalent tendency to, on the one hand, accommodate subordinate groups and on the other hand, to stimulate resistance and rebellion in certain ways.[6]

Football is probably the one true global sport:[7]

Gardiner, S and Felix, A, 'Juridification of the Football Field: Strategies for Giving Law The Elbow'

The cultural significance of football is enormous. Its ubiquity as the world's premier sport provides it with a unique position. Kitchen has called football the only 'global idiom' apart from science. It is truly a global sport with the majority of the worlds nations members of the Federation Internationale de Football Associations (FIFA). The influence of FIFA should not be understated. From its Geneva headquarters it has direct contacts with many heads of State. It has in the past applied for observer status at the United Nations. The President, Joao Havalange, has largely been responsible for elevating the influence of FIFA and accommodating external pressures such as television. He was nominated for the Nobel Peace Prize in 1988. Bill Shankly's often quoted belief that football is not just an matter of life or death – it is more

---

6   Hargreaves, J, *Sport, Power and Culture: A Social and Historical Analysis of Popular Sports in Britain* (1986), Cambridge: Polity Press, pp 9–10.

7   Over two million people were estimated to have watched the 1994 World Cup final between Brazil and Italy, *The Times*, 18 July 1994.

important – may seem an exaggeration of reality but for many its influence is as profound as any fundamentalist religion. For example in 1964, during a match between Peru and Argentina in Lima, it was estimated that 318 people died in rioting that was initiated largely due to the result. The murder of the Colombian player, Andres Escobar, after his own-goal in the 1994 World Cup, displays the extreme response that can be engendered by failure.

What cannot be refuted however is the growth of football as the global game and essentially in most countries as an important element of working-class culture. As with other mass participation and spectator sports, football is highly significant in popular discourse. Both in national and international contexts, football personifies the sectarianism of class, regional and national rivalry. The mass media play a crucial role in its representation magnifying the significance of these competitive elements. Football has undergone many changes. Commercialisation has brought incremental change. Today it is increasingly commodified and developing as an integral part of the leisure industry ... In England the emergence of the Premier league or 'Premiership' as 'a whole new ball game', reflects the view of football's potential as a big money maker. Players have also been the winners with incomes changing the financial contours of the game.[8]

THE CHANGING NATURE OF SPORT

Sport plays a major role in society. It is has a significant role in the way we understand the world. Sport is currently going through major changes. These will be discussed in Chapters 1 and 2. Certainly there seems to be some dissatisfaction with what sport has become in the modern world. Some detect a loss of innocence, a fading away of the essential spirit and values of sport, that has been replaced by cynicism, gamesmanship, commercial excess.[9] It may well be however that past generations have had this same view of the deterioration of what they understand as sport and a nostalgia for a lost notion of true sport and sportsmanship. This is not just a British phenomenon. In the United States, a number of disputes, notably the baseball, strike that wiped out the second half of the 1994 season and the World Series led to widespread spectator disillusionment.[10]

In Britain sport has been subject to numerous sporting scandals during the 1990s: drug use, cheating, corruption and others. The national game, football,

---

8   Gardiner, S and Felix, A, 'Juridification of the Football Field: Strategies for Giving Law the Elbow' (1995) 5(2) *Marquette Sports Law Journal* 189, p 191.

9   See 'The Corruption of our Sporting Life', *The Sunday Times*, 18 December 1994, pp 2–20; 'Hijacking of our Dreams', *The Observer*, 9 April 1995; 'Every Little Breeze Seems to Whisper New Sleaze', *The Observer*, 19 March 1995.

10 For details see 'America's Field of Bad Dreams', *The Times*, 12 March 1995; 'Baseball Strikes in the Field of Nightmares', *The Independent on Sunday*, 26 March 1995; 'Why Sports don't Matter Anymore', *The New York Times Magazine*, 2 April 1995, p 50; Cosell, H, *What's Wrong with Sports* (1991), New York: Pocket Books.

seems to have been the most scandal bound.[11] This can be combined with a lack of success of British sports teams and individual athletes in the world theatre, perhaps crystallised with the small number of medals won at the Atlanta Olympic games in 1996.[12] An attempt will be made to evaluate these issues and others in the context of an examination of the historical development of sport.

Any cursory review of the daily newspapers reveals an increasing propensity of the law to be involved in the regulation of sport. This is not an absolutely new phenomenon: the State has been involved in regulating sporting activity for centuries, largely on grounds of policy-driven aims of prohibition. The law is intervening in sport in increasingly diverse ways and into all the interstices of the sporting world. A process that will be identified and discussed in this chapter is the increased juridification of sport, that is, that sporting relations and disputes are increasingly being understood in legal terms.

This leads to the question: does the law have a legitimate role to play in sport? This is a contentious issue. Clearly there are areas of sport where the law needs to intervene and its role is uncontroversial. However, there are areas where this intervention is contested. At various points in the book, this issue will be highlighted. It needs to be remembered that in opposition to the by-line to this chapter,[13] the law may not always be the saviour of sport and the most effective form of regulation.

The causes of this greater role of the law will be evaluated. In Chapters 5 and 6 and at other points in the book, the increasingly commercialised nature of sport, particularly at elite level, will be examined as a major reason for law's greater involvement.

It can however be argued that much sport has been commercialised and professionalised for many years. Professional football clubs have been run, sometimes badly, as commercial entities since the late 1880s. The 'amateur' cricketer, WG Grace, earned £8,835 in 1895 and an estimated £120,000 during his lifetime, equivalent today to many hundreds of thousands of pounds.[14] Nonetheless, large areas of sport have been essentially amateur or have masqueraded under this guise in terms of 'shamateurism'; athletics and rugby are two such sports. Commercialisation around sport, for example with

---

11 See 'How Soccer Sold its Soul', *The Observer*, 3 December 1995; 'Men Behaving Badly in Version of the Mad Hatter's Tea Party', *Daily Telegraph*, 21 September 1996. Also see the government 'Task Force on Football', due to report in 1998, 'True-blue Mellor is Happy to Wear Labour's Football Kit', *Daily Telegraph*, 29 July 1997, p 10.

12 See 'Our Athletes Under Cloud at Olympics', *The Sunday Times*, 4 August 1996; 'Troubled Legacy of Blighted Games', *The Observer*, 4 August 1996.

13 See n 1.

14 Holt, R, *Sport and the British: A Modern History* (1989), Oxford: Clarendon. Also see Midwinter, E, *WG Grace: His Life and Times* (1981), London: Frank Cass; and Sandiford, K, *Cricket and the Victorians* (1994), London: Frank Cass.

sponsorship, marketing and merchandising operations, have led to modern sport being a huge business.[15] The mediation of large amounts of elite sport primarily by television has helped change its financial contours.[16]

A primary question we need to ask is, what role does law play in modern sport?

THE ROLE OF LAW IN SPORT

In Britain, the crucial role that law plays in regulating sport has only recently been recognised.[17] Over the last few years a number of lawyers have begun to spend a considerable amount of their professional time on sports related legal issues and a small number of firms have sizeable sports law work loads.[18] Legal issues concerning sport are also not solely concerned with commercial law – a wide variety of sports law issues have become a part of the general discourse of sport.

The year 1996–97 saw many examples of the law's involvement in sport: the criminal trial of the footballers John Fashanu, Bruce Grobellar and Hans Seger for fraud ending in a hung jury at their first trial[19] and and acquittal at their retrial;[20] the European Court of Justice decision in *Bosman*;[21] Imran Khan's successful libel case;[22] Ben Smoldon's successful action against the

---

15 For example, the Formula One car racing industry. The owner of the holding company for Formula One, Bernie Ecclestone, earned a salary of nearly £30 million in 1995. See 'The Formula for Striking it Rich', *The Guardian*, 26 March 1997. The Chicago Bulls basketball player, Michael Jordan is estimated as being the highest paid sports athlete, making over $40 million per year. In Britain, Manchester United are the most profitable sporting club, estimated to be worth £429.85 million (*The Observer*, 27 July 1997, p 9).

16 Statistics show the increasing amount of television money. In 1987–88 football made £5 million. For television rights in the 1997–98 season it will make £243m, see 'Football's Big Question: How to Spend the Lolly', *The Independent*, 1 February 1997.

17 See Grayson, E, *Sport and the Law* (1994), London: Butterworths; Foster, K, 'Developments in Sporting Law' in Allison, L (ed), *The Changing Politics of Sport* (1993), Manchester University Press; 'When Lawyers Blow the Whistle on Sport', *The Times*, 5 December 1992, p 5; 'The Ball's in your Court', *Socialist Lawyer*, Summer 1994; 'Laws of the Game or Laws of the Land', *The Guardian*, 4 March 1995; 'A Field Fit for Lawyers', *The Sunday Times*, 9 April 1995; 'Why Sport gets its Collar Felt', *The Observer*, 17 March 1996, p 2; 'A Whole New Ball Game', *The Times*, 21 March 1996; 'Word is Law and Disorder', *The Observer*, 9 March 1997, p 9; 'Why every FC will soon need its own QC', *The Guardian*, 1 March 1997, p 20.

18 See 'Play up, play on – and win', *The Times*, 23 May 1995; 'The man at the heart of sport's legal minefield; Robert Reid QC', *The Times*, 7 August 1995, p 27; 'Legal Eagles have Landed', *The Observer*, 25 September 1995; 'A Whxle New Ball Game', *The Times*, 21 May 1996; 'Lawyers Spot a Lucrative Field of Play', *The Times*, 10 March 1997.

19 'Footballers face new trial', *The Guardian*, 5 March 1997, p 3; 'Footballers to face £750,000 retrial in match-fixing case', *The Guardian*, 7 March 1997, p 3.

20 'Soccer Stars Cleared of Match Fixing', *The Daily Telegraph*, 7 August 1997, p 1.

21 *Union Royale Belge des Societes de Football Association ASBL and Jean-Marc Bosman* Case C-415–93, 15 December 1995.

22 'Botham libel case an exercise in futility', *The Guardian*, 1 August 1996, p 9.

rugby referee for damages for his paralysing injuries;[23] the criminal conviction for assault of Duncan Ferguson;[24] and a child successfully suing a mountaineering guide for the negligent death of his father.[25] Individuals involved in sporting disputes are increasingly likely to resort to legal remedies. This may reflect a generally more litigious society.[26] Internationally the law courts have been very busy in sports law cases: the long running saga in the Australian law courts in rugby league and the Ayrton Senna manslaughter trial in Italy are examples.

Other cases have involved lawyers operating within internal mechanisms of sporting bodies: the Diane Modhal drug incident; the successful overruling of the Football Association's docking of Tottenham Hotspurs of league points for financial irregularities.[27] There are increasing incidents where the threat of legal action is raised: the Leicester City fan's attempt to sue for 'football trauma', claiming he was unable to work for two days due to a failed penalty in the FA Cup semi-final against Chelsea;[28] and the rugby union's feud with the leading English clubs.[29]

Another facet of the law's involvement in sport is the development of law that can be identified as being specific to sport. In some countries there is legislation that controls the operation of sport on a general level.[30] In Britain this has not occurred but as cases involving sporting issues have developed through the common law and partly through Acts of Parliament, a recognisable body of sports-specific law has emerged in recent years. The general law that regulates social activities and relations in all areas of social life is involved in sport in spheres such as the regulating of contracts of employment and services, revenue law taxing sport as a business and personal injuries law. In more recent times, legislation concerning the

---

23 *The Times*, 18 December 1996. Also see 'Rugby Referee Pays for Injury', *The Guardian*, 18 December 1996, p 4; 'Sport Strangled by Wrong Arm of the Law', *The Observer*, 21 April 1996, p 2; 'Awareness and Application of Rules is Paramount', *The Guardian*, 20 April 1996, p 21.

24 '£4m Footballer Loses Appeal Against Jail Term for Head-Butt', *The Times*, 12 October 1995, p 5; 'Ferguson goes Free and Returns to the Fold at Everton', *The Times*, 25 November 1995, p 43.

25 'Daniel's Victory for Father he Never Knew', *The Independent*, 21 June 1997, p 7. Also see 'Warning: the Thrill of Living is at Risk', *Daily Telegraph*, 21 June 1997, p 11.

26 See 'Trial and Trial again', *The Guardian*, 31 May 1994 on this development. But see Armstrong, N, 'The Litigation Myth' (1997) 147 *New Law Journal* 1058.

27 'Tottenham save six points but pay 1.5m', *The Times*, 7 July 1994, p 44; 'Arbiters give Tottenham new hope of Cup reprieve', *The Times*, 26 November 1994, p 48; 'FA upholds Spurs' £1.5m fine', *The Times*, 14 December 1994.

28 See 'Soccer: Distressed Leicester fan sues FA', *The Guardian*, 4 March 1997, p 24, 'So it's traumatic to be a fanatic', *The Observer*, 9 March 1997, p 28. Also see Canadian case, *Bain v Gillespie*, 357 NW 2d 47 (1984) and an action for 'referee malpractice' by a memorabilia store owner.

29 'Rugby Union: Leading clubs threaten more trouble for RFU', *The Guardian*, 27 July 1996, p 16; 'Twickenham and England's leading clubs reach deadlock in talks', *The Guardian*, 22 March 1996, p 25.

30 For examples see the Fitness and Amateur Sport Act 1961 in Canada, the Act Respecting Safety in Sports RSQ, s 3.1 in Quebec and the proposed Malaysian Sports Act 1997.

regulation of safety in sport in general and statutes concerning particular sports such as football with the Football Spectators Act 1989 and the Football Offences Act 1991 reflect the increase of legal intervention.

WHAT IS A SPORT?

A good starting point is to see sport as a human activity that exists somewhere along the continuum from work to play. There is a need to demarcate sport from recreational activities in general and games and play specifically. But an attempt at a definition reveals the dynamic and changing nature of sport. In modern elite sport, professionalisation has led to an increasing transformation of sport into a type of work with the world of 'amateur play' seemingly contracting quickly.[31] There are also a number of anomalies in the way participation in sport is described. Some sports such as football, rugby and golf are seen as being 'played' and the participants are 'players'. These are the sports most akin to work. There are other sports where it is uncommon to talk of those involved as being players; with fishing, archery and hunting the sport is not played but, in contrast to the former group, it is closer to play and leisure than work.

There are positive reasons for needing to provide definitional clarity. An activity defined as a sport has a number of financial and legal advantages. Where are the lines going to be drawn between sport, games, recreation, leisure, work and play?

SOCIAL DEFINITION

An historical examination of the development and meaning of sport provides a powerful view of what we mean by sport and its import in society. This will be carried out shortly. However, this historical perspective lacks a social context. The use of the term sport in its expansive meaning is one that is a product of modernity. The definitional problems are alluded to by Slusher when he analogises between sport and religion:

> Basically sport, like religion defies definition. In a manner it goes beyond definitive terminology. Neither has substance which can be identified. In a sense both sport and religion are beyond essence.[32]

---

31 This can be illustrated by the move away from the distinction between amateurs and gentlemen in cricket shortly after the Second World War and the recent professionalisation of rugby union.

32 Slusher, H, *Men, Sport and Existence: a Critical Analysis* (1967), Philadelphia: Lea and Febiger.

There is a considerable body of sociological and cultural literature concerning the definition of sport.[33] It is important to have a clear definitions of the concepts that are being studied. In the sociology of sport a good working definition helps an understanding of the role that sport has as a part of social life. Similarly, the study of sport and the law needs similar definitional clarity.

One approach to a clear definition of sport is to look at the level of the sporting activity. Are games or individual pursuits at elite level more likely to be termed sport than kids playing on a patch of wasteland? Do we want to develop a definition of sport that differentiates it from mere physical recreation, aesthetic and conditioning activities and informal games? Do the conditions under which people participate and engage in them inform our understanding of sport?

There are considerable problems in attempting to provide answers. For example, what of activities such as mountain climbing, which has been developed as an indoor competitive 'sport' of wall climbing, and biking, an activity that takes place within a continuum from use being purely about mobility, through use for recreational leisure, to involvement in highly competitive national and international competitions such as the Tour de France. It may also be important to consider the subjective intention and motivation of the participant; it may distinguish between involvement in sport rather than mere play or entertainment.

Using the above guidelines, can we define activities such as jogging as a sport? What about synchronised swimming, darts, fox hunting, skin diving, chess? What about hybrid sports[34] and those that are more likely to be viewed as forms of recreation and entertainment?[35] One common claim is that sport needs some notion of being a physical activity, in that there is 'the use of physical skill, physical prowess or physical exertion'.[36] Chess and other board games clearly need a minimal amount of physical effort either in terms of complex physical skills or vigorous exertion; the skills required are essentially cognitive.

Such a definitional approach emphasising physical effort would potentially include all physical activities, including sex, as a sport! In *Brown*,[37]

---

33 See Loy, J, 'The Nature of Sport: a Definitional Effort', in Loy, J and Kenyon, G, *Sport, Culture and Society: A Reader on the Sociology of Sport* (1969), New York: Macmillan; Coakley, J, *Sport in Society: Issues and Controversy* 5th edn (1994), St Louis: Mosbey Publishing; Sprietzer, E, *Social Aspects of Sport* (1967), Englewood Cliffs, New Jersey: Prentice Hall; Mandel, R, *Sport: A Cultural History* (1981), Oxford: Clarendon; and Dunning, E, *The Sociology of Sport: A Selection of Readings* (1971), Oxford: Blackwell.

34 For example, bicycle polo, octopush, a form of underwater hockey, and horseball, an amalgam of rugby, basketball and horse riding. See 'Horsing Around with a Ball', *The Times*, 21 April 21 1997.

35 Note also World Wrestling Federation (WWF), professional wrestling, ballroom dancing, dragon boat racing.

36 *Ibid*, Coakley (1994) p 13.

37 [1993] 2 All ER 75.

a case involving the legality of consensual sadomasochistic homosexual activity, an argument was expressed that the participants might have gained the protection and exemption from criminal liability from the law of assault if they could be seen as being involved 'in the course of properly conducted games or sports'.[38] The application of 'rules of play', which evidence showed often existed in sadomasochistic sex, and the policing by an official were suggested as characteristics of a would-be sport!

To distinguish sport from recreational activity, it is necessary to consider the context or conditions of the physical activity and to determine whether it needs to take place in some institutionalised situation. This can help distinguish between formally organised competitive activities compared to those in an *ad hoc* unstructured form; the distinction between a Premier League football match and a number of children kicking a football in a park. Elements that characterise the former are perhaps standardised rules, official regulatory agencies, importance of organisational and technical aspects and the learning of strategies, skills and tactics by participants.

PLAY AND DIS-PLAY

This process can be applied to the codification of the two branches of football, rugby and association, in the late 19th century. It can also be illustrated with the emergence and institutionalisation of body building, which has developed from an activity based on aesthetics and health objectives, to one being considered as a sport. Such an approach produces an essentially objective understanding of a sport. Meier[39] argues that subjective perceptions of participants are irrelevant in determining the nature of sport. Some writers however have considered that the motivations of the participants in the sport help determine its meaning. Coakley[40] claims that a 'play spirit' based on the internal motivations of the participant is an important element in determining whether the activity in question can be termed as a sport. Huizinga describes play as:

> ... a free activity standing quite consciously outside 'ordinary' life as being 'not serious' but at the same time absorbing the player intensely and utterly ... it proceeds within its own proper boundaries of time and space according to fixed rules and in an orderly manner.[41]

---

38 This exemption from liability short of grievous bodily harm (serious injury) that was consented to factually during a sporting activity was laid down in *Attorney General's Reference (No 6 of 1980)* [1981] 2 All ER 1057.

39 Meier, K, 'On the Inadequacies of Sociological Definitions of Sport' (1981) 16(2) *International Review of Sports Sociology* 79.

40 *Ibid*, Coakley (1994) p 16.

41 Huizinga, J, *Homo Ludens – a Study of the Play-Element in Culture* (1955), Boston: Beacon Press.

Stone[42] argues that sports are composed of two types of behaviour which he characterises as 'play' and 'dis-play'. Play is where the participants motivations are concerned with that individual's relationship with the activity. Dis-play on the other hand is participation being essentially concerned with spectators to the activity – the notion of a spectacle becomes more important than the sport. External motivations such as money and fame, especially if they replace the internal motivations for participating in the activity, lead to this danger. The dangers of increased commercialisation and commodification of sport together with the spectacularisation of contemporary sport are clear. Two sports where such dangers arise are boxing and wrestling:

Michener, J, *Sport in America*

In 1946, boxing and wrestling and roller derbies were taken seriously but when they began to grab the nearest dollar, the quickest laugh, the most grotesque parody of violence, their credibility was destroyed. When enough people begin laughing at the exaggerations of any sport, it is doomed.[43]

Stone, G, 'American Sports: Play and Dis-play'

Play and dis-play are precariously balanced in sport and, once that balance is upset, the whole character of sport in society may be affected. Furthermore, the spectacular element of sport may, as in the case of American professional wrestling, destroy the game. The rules cease to apply and the 'cheat' and the 'spoilsport' replace the players. Yet even here counter forces are set in motion. If we may discontinuously resume our analysis of wrestling, we would note that there is always the 'hero' who attempts to defeat the 'villain' within the moral framework of the rules of the game. It is a case of law versus outlaw, cops and robbers, the 'good guys' versus the 'bad guys'. Symbolically the destruction of the game by the spectacle has called into existence forces of revival which seek to re-establish the rules but these forces are precisely symbolic – representative. They are seldom able to destroy the spectacular components of the display. They are part of the spectacle itself.

The point may be made in another way. The spectacle is predictable and certain; the game, unpredictable and uncertain. Thus spectacular display may be reckoned from the outset of the performance. It is announced by the appearance of the performers – their physiques, costumes and gestures. On the other hand, the spectacular play is solely a function of the uncertainty of the game. The spectacular player makes the 'impossible catch' – 'outdoes himself'. He is out of character. The 'villains' and 'heroes' of the wrestling stage are in character. They are the *dramatis personae* of a pageant – an expressive drama. Consequently their roles have been predetermined. The denouement of the contest has been decided at its inception and the hero is unlikely to affect the course of events.[44]

---

42 Stone, G, 'American Sports: Play and Dis-play' (1965) 9 *Chicago Review* 83; and see also Dunning, E (ed), *The Sociology of Sport: A Selection of Readings* (1971), London: Frank Cass, p 47.

43 Michener, J, *Sports in America* (1976), New York: Fawcett Press, p 540.

44 *Ibid*, Stone (1971) p 59.

This can be illustrated by the disintegration of the professional boxing regulatory organisations and the emergence of a plethora of world titles. In professional wrestling, the emergence of the World Wrestling Federation (WWF) and the smaller rival, the World Championship Wrestling, has clearly demarcated itself from amateur wrestling still mainly played for Stone's internal reasons. WWF has become purely a spectacle where characters such as 'The Undertaker' and 'Hulk Hogan' present a slick entertainment televised through out the world in artificially created championships, 'The Royal Rumble', 'The King of the Ring' and 'Wrestle Mania'; a paradigm example of the spectacularisation of sport – content has been sacrificed for image.

Hargreaves, J, *The Autonomy of Sport: Sport, Power and Culture*

The extent to which a given cultural formation is enabled to feed the power network also depends crucially, on its own particular character, that is on those autonomous features which distinguish it from others as a specific type of cultural formation. The realm of sport encompasses a bewildering diversity of radically different kinds of activity, which defies a watertight definition – from the local hunt and pub darts match, village cricket, inter-collegiate rowing and little league football, to professionalised mass entertainment like the Football League, the Wimbledon Tennis Championships, heavyweight boxing and horse racing. Some of this activity plainly has little if any connection with power. Despite the complexity, in our view sufficient distinguishing characteristics can be identified which enable us to analyse how, in specific conditions, the sport-power relation may be constituted. First, sports to one or other degree embody an irreducible element of play. Play is a type of activity having no extrinsic purpose or end and as such it is a form of activity which enjoys a universal appeal. Sports play is not always unalloyed by other motives or considerations – financial gain, prestige, etc – and in specific instances (politicised and professional sport for example) play may be by no means the most important element. But the ludic impulse is, nevertheless, always present to some degree at least, existing in tension with disciplined organised aspects of sporting activity.

Secondly sports play tends to be highly formalised: in many cases it is governed by very elaborate codes or statutes. Sports play in this sense is far from being spontaneous: it is by convention rule orientated and to have no rules would be a contradiction in terms. Whether the rules are, in fact, being followed, is therefore an ever present issue in the conduct of sports and in this sense we could say that not only are sports rule orientated – they can be rule-obsessed. Rule-structured play, like play in general, 'suspends reality' but in this case through the acceptance of formal codes ordering the use of space, time and general behaviour. In choosing to structure their activity thus, both participants and onlookers are indulging in a form of 'play acting' and in this respect the activity can be said to be 'unserious' or set aside from normal life. Play acting is also involved in sporting activity when 'display' before an audience is one of the objectives. In addition, many sports were associated historically with the great festivals and to varying extents are still conducted in a spirit of festivity, a spirit which, by 'turning the world upside down', suspends while simultaneously challenging reality.

Thirdly sports involve some element of contest between participants. The rules which structure sporting contests, however, unlike those that structure competition and conflict in the real world, deliberately set out to equalise conditions of participation, that is, they are intended to be neutral, so that no one party to the contest has an advantage over the other(s). Since a contest within neutral rules makes the outcome inherently uncertain and in principle unpredictable, the very point of the activity is negated when either the rules are biased in favour of one or other party or when the contestants are matched unevenly, for then the outcome does indeed become predictable. The uncertainty of the contest's outcome and the attendant tension it creates lends a unique excitement to sports, compared with other activities involving play and it is probably one of the main reasons why sports become so often the subject of intense interest and emotion. Paradoxically, the deep commitment which sports often arouse also makes them deadly serious affairs as well as unserious ones.

Three other attributes of sporting activity which have received much less attention are crucial in any consideration of the sport-power relation. The play acting, contest and uncertainty elements ensure that sports are an intrinsically dramatic means of expression and an audience in addition transforms them into a form of theatre. We argue that sports fall within the province of 'the popular' and in so far as they take on the attribute of a dramatic performance they can be said to constitute a form of popular theatre, arguably the most popular contemporary form of theatre.[45]

So can we conclude on a working definition? The *European Sports Charter* provides this definition:

'Sport' means all forms of physical activity which through casual or organised participation aimed at expressing and improving physical fitness and mental well-being, forming social relationships or obtaining results in competition levels.[46]

Coakley believes:

Sports are institutionalised competitive activities that involve vigorous physical exertion or the use of relatively complex physical skills by individuals whose participation is motivated by a combination of intrinsic and extrinsic factors.[47]

Singer similarly sees sport as:

a human activity that involves specific administrative organisations and historical background of rules which define the objective and limit the pattern of human behaviour; it involves competition and/or challenge and a definite outcome primarily determined by physical skill.[48]

---

45 *Ibid*, Hargreaves (1986) pp 10–11.

46 *The European Sports Charter*, The Council of Europe.

47 *Ibid*, Coakley (1994) p 21.

48 Singer, R, *Physical Education: Foundations* (1976), New York: Holt, Rinehart and Winston.

An exact definition of sports seems to be impossible, but some common elements of the existence of rules, physical exertion and competition need to be present.

HISTORY OF SPORT

The term 'sport' derives from the French determined Middle English verb *sporten*, to divert[49] and also the Latin term *desporto*, literally 'to carry away'. The emphasis is therefore on it being a distraction, something that gives pleasure. Throughout the Middle Ages sport in England meant mainly hunting of a variety of animals. Archery, bowls and horse racing can be seen as early sports dating from the 16th century.[50] One of our main cultural and historical identifications with sport is with the original Greek Olympics held in 686 BC. Going further back in time, the earliest evidence of boxing's existence is however recorded in Ethiopian hieroglyphics around 4000 BC.

Hunting can be seen as the precursor of most modern sport. The fact that forms of it still persist today indicates its longevity. It is likely that as a sport it originally grew out of a form of play that early man took part in, especially in childhood as a training for the reality of life: the hunting and fishing way of life included the killing of animals to survive:

Brasch, R, *How Did Sports Begin?*

In the beginning, sport was a religious cult and a preparation for life. Its roots were in man's desire to gain victory over foes seen and unseen, to influence the forces of nature and to promote fertility among his crops and cattle. Sport, as a word, is an abbreviation: the shortened form of disport, a diversion and an amusement. Rooted in Latin, it literally means 'carry away' (from *desporto*). In our time millions of people, whether spectators or participants, amateurs or professionals, are carried away by the sport they love from the cares of their daily toil, their anxieties and frustrations, to a world of relaxation and emulation, excitement and thrill. However going back to the very beginning of sport as such, we find that far from being restricted, it started as part of man's history and is bound up closely with his very being. Sport was not merely a diversion or pastime but an essential feature of man's existence. An inborn impulse and a basic need caused primitive man to play games, even though it might be only hitting a stone with a branch. It eased his tension, helped him to get aggressiveness out of his system and, altogether, served as an innocuous outlet for otherwise harmful urges. After all, to hit an object was so much better than to hit a friend. Thus sport fulfilled a primary want of man and, spontaneously taken up, games catered to it, giving satisfaction and a sense of achievement and overcoming.

---

49 Webster's New Collegiate Dictionary (1995), New York: Websters Publishing.
50 *Ibid*, Grayson (1994) p 36.

Sport was a natural result of a universal love of play and man's innate desire to compete with and to excel, if not dominate, others. Another mainspring of sport was man's need effectively to defend himself, his tribe and later on, his country. In panic and fear when escaping from danger, he learned to run, jump and swim. To avoid defeat or to subdue opponents, he invented archery, judo and karate. And in order to be ready for combat, at all times he practised them and new sports evolved out of his martial training. Even football and baseball carry vestiges of battles between tribes. Muscular strength and alertness served well in the repulse or conquest of foes. Sports taught man endurance and courage, essential qualities in a fighter and man was a fighter from the very beginning. However in some parts of the world where the severity of the elements and a low protein diet endangered his life, man's healthy instinct led him to create sports for yet another reason. In cold climates, games provided vital exercise, making the blood course through the veins and keeping man warm and resistant to the hazards of nature and the harshness of the weather. Man's wish to survive, in this world and the next, explains the origin of a majority of sports. They were not deliberately invented but arose, almost inevitably, out of man's quest to exist and to overcome the countless enemies that threatened him: natural and supernatural, man and beast. He had to ward them off everywhere. Most of all, sports began as fertility magic, to ensure birth, growth and the return of spring. Therefore sport to begin with was mainly a magical rite. It tried to attain human survival by supernatural means. Numerous examples of this are at hand in ancient records and the practices of primitive races. For instance, for the Zunis, a Mexican tribe that lived in arid zones, rain was the prime necessity for life. Droughts were frequent and it was because of them that the Zunis first played games. They were convinced that these would magically bring rain for the crops.

Other primitive tribes established a fraternity of rain-making priests. The sole task of this first team of professional players was to join in games of chance which, they believed, would force nature to precipitate rain. With the approach of the whaling season, Mach Indians played a primitive type of hockey, using whalebone for ball and bat, the latter symbolising the war god's club. A hill tribe in Assam, India, arranged a regular tug of war to expel demons. The ceremony – it was not then a sport – took place at a fixed time each year. Two bands of men (the original teams) stood on opposite banks of a river, each tugging at the end of a rope stretched across the water. One team represented the forces of evil, the other those of increase in nature. On the result of the struggle depended whether trouble would haunt the tribe or the sun would shine, literally. Wrestling bouts were practised in southern Nigeria. They took the form also of a religious act to strengthen the growth of the crop by sympathetic magic. In suspense, huge crowds watched the contestants. They were not reluctant to interfere should either of the fighters show weakness, anger or fatigue, lest these deficiencies cause any ill-effect on the reproductive forces of nature. Games were highly important in winter and at the coming of spring. They were considered essential to hasten the return of the sun and ensure a fruitful season. Some of the games took place between groups of single men and women, representing the unprolific and married people, symbolising fecundity. The Wichita tribe, on the Red River of Oklahoma, conducted a sporting event very similar to modern field hockey. This, too, enacted symbolically a contest between winter and spring, to assist in the renewal of life and the conquest of the evil forces of winter. For a similar reason, some Eskimos had seasonal games. In spring, the players used a kind of cup and ball – to catch the sun. In the autumn, when the sun was going south, a sort of cat's cradle of seal gut was used to enmesh the sun and delay its departure.

Sport thus assumed even cosmic significance. Definite rules in primitive ball games were religiously observed to direct the winds, the brings of life. The two teams represented earth and sky and as no one would dare to cheat the gods, an umpire was unnecessary. No wonder that primitive man believed that sport if not divine itself, was a gift of the gods. He was firmly convinced that 'to play the game' meant to accelerate the revival of nature and the victory of vegetation. The association of games with religious worship continued from prehistoric times well into the classical period. The Olympic Games were centred on the magnificent temple of Zeus at Olympia and were played in his honour. The Python Games were closely linked with the oracle of Apollo and his shrine at Delphi. It was from those magical roots of primitive faith that our sports mainly grew. With the passing of time and frequent repetition of games, their original purpose was forgotten and people enjoyed the contests for their own sake, discovering in them a source of excitement, amusement and strength. All these pursuits can be called 'natural' sports, as they 'naturally' evolved from early rites, training for warfare and defence against threats of nature, whether of the animate or inanimate kind. Equally prominent in this class are sports now taken up for mere pleasure, which developed out of man's search for sustenance: hunting for food, catching fish, rowing and sailing across rivers and the sea. In the practice of these skills, he acquired as well a liking for them, independent of their primary aim and pursued them even after their original purpose no longer applied. A means to an end here became an end in itself. And that is how hunting, angling, yachting and shooting became sports. There is no doubt that the present day probing of outer space sooner or later will create a modern 20th (or 21st) century sport, perhaps called cosmonauts. Finally, of course, there are those sports which do not constitute relics of man's previous preoccupation with his fate or which are not the by-products of vital tasks. They were artificially created and from the very beginning designed as sports and nothing else. New technological advance may account for the origin of such sports as car racing and flying. Mostly, the motive was to present a new type of exercise, demanding different skills and a novel kind of recreation when older games could not be played or, for one reason or another, had lost their appeal. In one case, however, ten pin bowling, a new sport was devised simply as a legal subterfuge. And yet, unconsciously, even the latest of sports continues to answer some of the identical needs that had urged our ancestors in the dim past to play games.

Some of the earliest statutes emphasised the power and agility of man. Sporting pictures adorned the walls of Egyptian temples. The Pharaohs and their nobles enjoyed sport, not merely as spectators but as participants. A hieroglyphic inscription lauds Pharaoh Amenophis II as a perfect athlete – 'strong of arm', 'long of stride', 'a skilled charioteer', an efficient oarsman and a powerful archer. Gradually, sport soon became part and parcel of man's social life. Even the Bible, though interested mainly in the spiritual aspect of existence, could not ignore sporting activities altogether. Hebrew Scripture mentions the use of the sling and the bow. Some authorities have even suggested that it contains certain allusions to weightlifting, either as a test of strength or a means to toughen one's muscles (Zechariah XII:3). Contests and tournaments were known and with them, the selection of champions. The New Testament abounds in references to games and St Paul, especially, aware of how much they belonged to everyday life, makes frequent metaphorical use of them. In the Epistle to the Corinthians, for instance, he recalls the spirit of contest to illustrate the strenuous and glorious issue of the Christian fight. Foot races, boxing and wrestling alike supplied him with memorable phrases to express essential lessons. Paul thus speaks of man's wrestling against the powers of darkness, his fighting the good fight and finishing the race. Describing his mission and the task of the faithful Christian, he could say: 'I do not run aimlessly, I do not box as one beating the air but I pommel my body to subdue it.' A notable passage in the Epistle to the Hebrews compares the vast multitude of men and women who have borne testimony to their faith in God, to the enormous crowd of spectators at a foot race in which the contestant discards all unnecessary encumbrance. He needs patience to go forward perseveringly and to gain the prize conferred by the umpire, who judges all. The terminology of sports has its own story. The word 'game' recalls an Old English and Teutonic term that referred to 'participation' and a 'gathering' for fun. The scoring of points is linked with primitive methods of counting and recording. 'Score' is derived from an Old Norse word for 'notch'. Notches made on a stick served to register the correct number of hits, wins or killings. Score also came to indicate units of 20. In earliest days, dents were cut into pieces of wood to mark every 20, possibly, first of all, when sheep were being counted. Originally, 'umpire' – from the Latin *non par* – described an 'odd' man who was called upon to settle differences. Amateurs (from the Latin *amare*, 'to love') played for the love of the game. Civilisation has been defined as what man does with his leisure time. Its wise use for the practice of sports has had its beneficial effect not only on his physical health and the promotion of numerous skills but on his moral character. All sports, irrespective of their origin, developed in man faculties that have enriched his life manifold. They trained him in endurance, hard work and vigorous self control, gave him stamina and the will to do his best, no matter what. Some of the greatest lessons of life have come out of the world of sport. They have taught man to be undaunted by any challenge. Athletics, from the Greek, embodies the 'prize' (*athlon*) awarded to the winning contestant. Yet, failing to gain it, the true sportsman also knows how to take defeat. He will always be ready to try again and strive to attain what has never before been achieved. Sports, not least, have had their impact on the social ethics of man. Not accidentally do we speak of 'playing the game', it 'not being cricket', to 'abide by the rules of the game' or 'hitting below the belt' and being a 'spoilsport'.[51]

---

51 Brasch, R, *How Did Sports Begin?* (1986), Sydney: Angus and Robinson, pp 1–5.

Derek Birley in his two volumes on the history of sport, *Sport and the Making of Britain* and *Land of Sport and Glory – Sport and British Society 1887–1910*, believes that the Celts which came to Britain around 1000 BC developed boar hunting as a form of military sport. This could be seen as the birth of hunting as a recognisable sport. Birley also speculates that the Romans brought with them ball games and chariot racing. During the Dark Ages until the Norman Conquest, he provides some scant evidence of other developing sports; swimming running, archery and horse racing. He also chronicles early prohibition of sport: hunting was limited to the ruling classes and certain areas of land; the church tried to control the misuse of holy days, eg in 747 AD the Council of Clofeshoh in the North of England forbade sports and horse racing on Rogation Days.

Below are a number of extracts from *Sport and the Making of Britain* which chart both the origins and development of recognisable sports and their control and prohibition by the State. Greater State control appeared with the coming of the Normans:

> In Normandy bloodthirsty fights between barons and knights had long been a menace that defied control ... But the melees and skirmishes that were rife on the continent were held in check by the force of William and his judicious distribution of largesse (clemency).[52]

Restrictions on hunting that had been in force before the Norman Conquest continued, especially amongst the 'lower orders' with only rabbit and the wolf open to 'hunting for all'. The law has consistently controlled hunting rights on private land to the modern age. Formal jousting however became a common event. Sport became not only exclusive to rural life and with the first meaningful urbanisation towards the end of the 12th century, new sporting forms developed:

> Shrove Tuesday, the great carnival before Lent, was a special day for schoolboys. In the morning, on receipt of his cock-penny, the master would cancel lessons so that his pupils could match the fighting cocks they had trained for the occasion. This educational custom survived for many years and its passing was bemoaned by traditionalists. Cock fighting itself remained a fashionable and popular diversion, declining in reputation as the squeamish middle classes grew in influence but still an attraction to the raffish, rich and poor alike, in the 19th century.

> For the medieval students of London and their counterparts in industry the holiday was not over. After lunch they went to play 'the famous game of Ball' (*ad ludum Pilae celebrem*) on a level ground near the city (probably Smithfield). Scholars from every place of learning and workers in the various occupations town played their own games of Ball, whilst older men, fathers and rich men from the city on horseback, watched the young men's contests, being young along with them in their own way, showing a natural excitement at so much action and sharing in the uninhibited pleasures of youth.

---

52 Birley, D, *Sport and the Making of Britain* (1993), Manchester University Press, p 16.

We are told no more about these games but they may have included football which was so prominent in the later history of Shrove Tuesday sport. Annual tussles, village against village with the ball being captured and carried home in triumph or married versus single, with the ball provided by newly weds, were part of ancient manorial custom. They were tolerated and even encouraged by parish clergy, some of whom provided the ball, as part of the pre-Lenten carnival, a good way of letting off steam. Lords of the manor were often hosts at the celebrations. And later, in more urban communities, Shrove Tuesday football matches were sponsored by the various craft gilds with special reference to the initiation of apprentices.[53]

Control of urban sporting activity began in the 13th century:

London needed special attention. In 1285 after years of political dissidence, corruption and violent crime Edward I manoeuvred the civic authorities into a situation where he could impose direct rule on the city. He immediately banned tournaments and sword play. The statute, referring to 'fools who delight in their folly', prohibited the teaching of swordsmanship in the city on pain of 40 days' imprisonment. It did not close the fashionable fencing schools but it drove them underground, confirming their reputation as hotbeds of drinking, gambling and brawling. Nothing of course could prevent sword fights when it was the right and duty of every freeman to bear arms. Military swords were too cumbersome for pedestrian use and the classes obliged to go on foot carried staves for protection and support, especially in the country or on journeys. Daggers, of varying length, were widely used, either openly or concealed. In a ball game, probably football, at Ukham, Northumberland on Trinity Sunday 1280, Henry de Ellington was accidentally killed when, jostling for the ball, he impaled himself on another player's knife. But ball games could be dangerous even without knives. Three years earlier a 10 year old boy killed a 12 year old companion by hitting him on the ear after a clash of sticks in a hockey game (*ad pilam ludendo altercantes*). And there was growing fear of public nuisance especially in towns. In 1303 an Oxford student from Salisbury was killed – allegedly by Irish fellow students – whilst playing football in the High. By 1314, calling for restraint during Edward II's forthcoming absence in the resumed wars with the Scots, the Lord Mayor of London issued a proclamation on the King's behalf forbidding rumpuses with large footballs (*rageries de grosses pelotes de pee* in Norman French) in the public fields.[54]

The curb on civilian sports continued. In 1369 the King sent his sheriffs throughout England a list of the games they were to ban. As well as cock fighting these included *jactus lapidem, lignum et ferrum*, throwing stone, wood and iron. Casting the stone we have already encountered in Fitzstephen's account of London amenities. Such tests of strength were amongst the earliest and most basic of sports: reputedly early Irish and Scottish chieftains would keep a rock or two by their doors for the purpose. Throwing a lump of iron (called a *diskos*) was one of the events in Patroclus's funeral games in *The Iliad*

---

53 *Ibid*, pp 20–21.
54 *Ibid*, p 32.

when iron working was part of the new technology and *jactus ferrum* no doubt included contests with shot, discus or quoit.

Similarly, throwing wood could include tossing the caber (Celtic for beam) or the more domesticated (English) axle tree. The chances are, however, that the terms also embraced bowling and skittles and such variants as *loggats, kayles* and *doish,* prohibited by name in later statutes. Bowls itself was traced back to the 13th century by Joseph Strutt, who illustrates three types: players trying to hit each other's bowl, bowling at small cones and bowling to a jack in the modern manner.

The other main category of prohibitions was that of games *ad pilam manualem, pedalem et baculoream, et cambucam:* handball, football, dub ball and cambuck. This last, also called cammock, may have been, as a contemporary commentator believed, a game in which a small wooden ball was propelled forward with a curved stick or mallet (and thus an ancestor of golf, pall mall and croquet); or, equally likely, an early form of hockey, also known as bandy, shinty, hurling and *camogie,* games that were played with the bent or knobbed stick from which cammock got its name. From the law enforcement point of view, of course, it did not matter if the categories were overlapping: overlap was better than underlap. Thus *pila baculorea,* club ball or stickball, could also refer to the hockey group of games. Club ball, however, was the term later used to denote the rounders-type game illustrated in early manuscripts and believed by Strutt (but not his later editors) to be the source of cricket.

The two remaining games in the prohibition were to cause the authorities great concern over the years. Football, *pila pedalis,* was banned, as Strutt put it 'not, perhaps from any particular objection to the sport in itself but because it co-operated, with other favourite amusements, to impede the progress of archery'. Handball, *pilamanualis,* no doubt took many forms about which the same could be said. The kind that caused most trouble later, however, was the French game *jeu de paume,* later known as tennis, played in an open quadrangular space, making use of surrounding roofs buttresses and grilles.[55]

In the late 14th century, hunting restrictions increased:

Parliament had been given a fright and clamped down even harder on the peasants. In 1388 hunting laws were introduced which applied not just in the royal forest but throughout the land. Noting that 'artificers and labourers and servants and grooms' were in the habit of keeping 'greyhounds and other dogs' and that 'on holy days, when good Christian people be at Church' they went hunting 'in parks, warrens and coneyries of lords and others, to the very great destruction of the same', the new law forbade, on pain of a year's imprisonment, laymen with holdings worth less than forty shillings and clerics with benefices less than ten pounds a year to keep greyhounds or other hunting dogs or to use 'ferrets, hayes, rees, hare pipes, cords and other engines to take or destroy the deer, hares or coneys'. The legislation also renewed the ban on 'importune games' with particular reference to the servant and labourer

---

55   *Ibid,* pp 35–37.

class, forbidding all ball games whether handball or football, together with quoits, dice and casting the stone.[56]

Henry IV and V regularly renewed Edward's III's ban on popular sports, with new Acts in 1401, 1409, 1410 and 1414 and they tried to apply the same disciplinary standards to the upper classes of society as to the lower orders.[57]

During the reign of Henry VIII, with the war with France continuing, prohibitions against sport were made in 1526 in order to boost the war effort against France:

Two years later with peace restored Wolsey introduced a revised measure which whilst equally draconian was more socially selective. It gave the county commissioners appointed under his 1526 legislation power to enter private houses in search of illicit crossbows and handguns and to enter hostelries, inns and alehouses to '"take and burn" tables, dice, cards, bowls, closhes, tennis balls' and other instruments of the devil. Tennis was forbidden only if courts were not properly conducted: similarly bowls was condemned 'because the alleys are in operation in conjunction with saloons or dissolute places' which denied it the status of a true sport.[58]

Animal sports continued to be popular:

The death of Henry VIII left a power vacuum. Then the pendulum swung between the extreme Protestantism of the boy Edward VI (1547–53), who completed his father's asset-stripping of the Roman church by dissolving the chantries and the avenging Catholicism of his equally pious half sister Mary who burnt at the stake some 300 enemies of the faith. There was no apparent conflict between religious belief and personal cruelty.

At Christmas 1550 the saintly Edward had publicly rebuked Mary for popish practices like 'conjured bread and water': then after dinner on the feast of the Epiphany he watched a bear baiting with the 17 year old Princess Elizabeth. When, as Queen, Mary was persuaded by her devious Philip of Spain to visit Elizabeth at her country house at Hatfield she was treated to a bear baiting, with which 'their highnesses were right well content'. And when Elizabeth herself became Queen in 1558 it was natural entertainment she offered to foreign ambassadors would include bear baiting.

The royal family had its own private bear gardens but there were public bear gardens in London of which the most famous was behind the Globe Theatre, Bankside. Because of their cost bears were usually kept alive (it was the dogs that died) but as they grew battle-scarred they could expect no mercy; as a German visitor pointed out: 'to this entertainment there often follows that of whipping a blind bear, which is performed by five or six men, standing in a circle with whips, which they exercise upon him without any mercy'.

Bulls were more readily available and expendable, though if they fought well they too might be retained for further service. They could do a lot of damage

---

56 *Ibid*, p 38.
57 *Ibid*, p 41.
58 *Ibid*, pp 56–57.

with their fearsome horns and the trick was for the bulldog to get in underneath and grab the muzzle, the dewlap or 'the pendant glands'. If it got a hold it clung on and either tore the flesh away and fell or had to be pulled off, with the aid of flour blown up the nostrils to make it let go. This tenacity so inspired the populace that the bulldog became an emblem of the British character. There was a convenient superstition that bulls needed to be baited to improve the taste of beef and in some parts of the country bylaws required this to be done.[59]

The masses were excluded from gentleman's sports:

Tudor licensing laws were much concerned with keeping out 'men of base condition' from fashionable games like tennis and bowls. In 1592 Thomas Bedingfield, seeking permission to keep houses in London and Westminster for dice, cards, tables, bowls and tennis, proposed exemplary rules: no play before noon on weekdays or during hours of religious service on Sundays, no swearing or blaspheming and 'none but noblemen, gentlemen and merchants or such as shall be entered in the Book of Subsidies at £10 in land or goods'.[60]

In the late 16th century, common concerns on how the working masses spent their leisure time became prominent:

Yet it was old religious allegiances that brought sport to the centre of the political stage requiring the intervention of the King himself. There was a new twist to the old concern about the way the lower orders spent their leisure time. Now that archery practice had ceased to be thought desirable they were supposed to spend it reading the Bible or thinking improving thoughts. Catholic magistrates generally allowed games-playing after divine service but this was thought outrageous and provocative in Puritan circles, which were widening all the time. In Edinburgh games sic as gof had been banned all day on the Sabbath since 1592. On a tombstone at Llanfair church, South Wales, appeared the warning:

> Who ever hear on Sunday
>
> will practis playing at Ball
>
> It may be before Monday
>
> The Devil will Have you all.

In 1607 young men of Aberdeen were arraigned for profaning the Sabbath by 'drinking, playing football, dancing and roving from parish to parish'. At Guisborough, Yorkshire, in 1616 a man was charged with 'making a banquet for football players' on a Sunday.

The question for Puritans, as expressed by Stubbes, was whether 'the playing at foot ball, reding of mery bookes and such like delectations' profaned the Sabbath day. They had only one answer. But Puritanism was essentially a middle class movement. A day of quiet contemplation each week was all very well for those who had leisure on weekdays for more exciting activities but a

---

59 *Ibid*, pp 62–64.

60 *Ibid*, p 68.

bit hard on the average man in the fields. Matters came to a head in Lancashire, a county of extremes. Many of the aristocracy and their rustic followers clung obstinately to the old faith but Puritanism was also strong. Sunday sport was an inevitable source of conflict. In 1616 the Manchester justices banned 'piping, dancing, bowling, bear and bull baiting' or any other 'profanation' at any time on the Sabbath and similar restrictions were imposed in surrounding districts.

The following year as James was returning from Scotland a party of Lancashire villagers met him at Myerscough with a petition complaining about the attempt to ban their customary amusements. The King made an impromptu speech promising them protection. They took him at his word and the following Sunday there were complaints from churchgoers in the vicinity that their worship had been disturbed by music, piping, dancing, shouting and laughter outside. The outcome was a declaration drawn up on the King's instructions by the local bishop to be read from pulpits throughout Lancashire. It was a rambling document but it answered the purpose, which was compromise. The King rebuked certain 'Puritans and precise people' for interfering with the people's 'lawful recreations' and ordained that after divine service on Sundays and other holy days piping, dancing, archery, 'leaping and vaulting and other harmless recreations were to be allowed'. Yet he maintained existing legislation which forbade bear and bull baiting and interludes on Sundays and bowling 'for the meaner sort of people' at all times.

James was so impressed by the success of his Solomon-like judgment in Lancashire that in 1618 he ordered an expanded version to be read in every pulpit in England and Scotland, adding approval of May games, Whitsun ales, Morris dances and the like 'in due and convenient time' to his bounty. James's Book of Sports, as it came to be known, was a setback for extreme Puritanism. Its arguments, taken at face value, were hard to counter – the people would turn from the church if it allowed them no amusement; they would be 'less able for war'; if denied sport they would spend more time in the alehouse. Most telling of all when would 'the common people have leave to exercise if not upon Sundays and holy days, seeing they must apply their labour and win their living in all working days?'[61]

In the 17th century, a more moderate approach to team sports and games seemed to be supported:

> It was 1667 before new laws 'for the better observation of the Lord's Day' were enacted and they were not specifically directed at sport ... Indeed when in 1664 a law was passed against 'deceitful, disorderly and excessive gaming' the preamble declared that, properly used, games were innocent and moderate recreations: it was when they were misused that they promoted idleness and dissolute living and circumventing, deceiving, cozening and debauchery of many of the younger set.[62]

---

61   *Ibid*, pp 79–80.
62   *Ibid*, p 91.

Violence against animals continued to be a sport:

> Bears, which had higher social status and did not toss dogs about, were in shorter supply. Bulls were therefore the standard fare, not only for baits but for rustic variants such as the traditional bull running at Stamford and the bizarre goings on at Tutford. The lowest level of baiting was of badgers, all that could be afforded in some country districts. The connoisseur's sport was cock fighting. Charles Cotton grew lyrical:
>
> > Cocking is a great sport or pastime so full of delight and pleasure that I know not any game ... to be preferred before it and since the Fighting Cock hath gained so great an estimation among the gentry in respect of this noble recreation I shall here propose it before all the other games of which I have afore succinctly dismissed.
>
> Fighting cocks had metal spurs tied to their heels, often of silver, fashioned by expert craftsmen, proud to engrave their name on each pair. Cockspur Street in London took its name from this sophisticated craft. Huge sums were wagered on choice birds by the highest in the land.[63]

Public demonstrations of violence against the criminal classes were very violent and very visible and this was reflected in continued enjoyment of blood sports during the early 18th century:

> Hanging and whipping were greatly enjoyed as public spectacles and what the literary set saw as cruelty in sport enthusiasts saw as a desirable emblem of virility. Thus cock fighting was proclaimed a valuable way of diverting the English gentry from effeminate dancing, whoring and drinking 'which are three evils grown almost epidemical' and a more manly occupation than 'to run whooting after a poor, timorous hare'. Its ancient lineage was generally cited in its favour and at least one writer, a Scottish fencing master, cited Aristotle, with salacious intent.[64]

The distinction between the way football and cricket were viewed by the State was clear:

> ... opposition to football grew, not only for its lack of decorum but for fear of what it bred, idleness and what it could conceal, subversives. In England, football was sometimes a symbol of resistance to authority or to change ... In East Anglia, which had its own popular variant, campball, it frequently marked objections to Fenland drainage schemes or enclosures ... Amidst this turmoil cricket was better suited both to gambling and to the preservation of the social order.[65]

Field sports were going through a period of transition in the mid 18th century, with shooting becoming more popular. Grouse, pheasants and the like began to be protected:

---

63 *Ibid*, p 94.
64 *Ibid*, p 106.
65 *Ibid*, p 115.

The notion of game as property fitted well into the modern scheme of things. Thirty two game laws were enacted in George III's reign and gamekeepers proliferated. Despite this – or perhaps because of it – poaching was rife. When the law made it illegal to buy and sell game both poachers and gamekeepers found it profitable to sell a few brace on the side. Animal predators, as ever, were a serious problem. Farmers' enemies, especially if they were edible like hares and rabbits, were more likely to be snared than shot but for bigger nuisances, like the fox, either shooting or stopping up their earths and digging them out was common.[66]

The preceding extracts show that the State has been involved in regulating sport for centuries.[67] Historically this has revolved around a number of issues: the control of land and the rights to hunting has been a perennial issue dividing clearly on class grounds between the aristocracy, landowners and the masses. The needs of war dictated the legitimacy of many sporting activities until the late middle-ages. The maintenance of order has been a major concern, both in nationalistic terms with alarm of foreign influence being attained by certain sports and secondly the disorder implicit in may team sports. The spectre of the mob, the uncontrollable rabble, was a constant fear. The dysfunctional effects of gambling on sport has also clearly been an increasing concern.

It is certainly possible to speculate which of the above continue to be current concerns: the debate about fox hunting and the use of land;[68] the influx of 'foreign players' in a number of sports continues;[69] the regulation of sports crowds especially in the context of football hooliganism; restriction on sports gambling, are just a few.

---

66   *Ibid*, p 131.

67   For other historical perspectives on sport, particularly of the 19th and 20th century see Holt, R, *Sport and the British: a Modern History* (1989), Oxford: Clarendon Press; Mangan, J, *Athleticism in the Victorian and Edwardian Public School* (1981), Cambridge University Press; Mason, T, *Sport in Britain* (1988), London: Faber and Faber and Mason, T (ed), *Sport in Britain: a Social History* (1989), Cambridge University Press; Vamplew, W, *Pay up and Play the Game* (1989), Cambridge University Press. On specific sports see Vamplew, W, *The Turf: a Social and Economic History of Horse Racing* (1976), London: Frank Cass; Walvin, J, *The Peoples Game: a Social History of British Football* (1975), London: Allen Lane; Murray, B, *Football: a History of the World Game* (1994), London: Scholar Press; Taylor, R and Ward, A, *Kicking and Screaming: An Oral History of Football in England* (1995), London: Robson Books and the BBC television series of same name (1995); Brookes, C, *English Cricket: The Game and its Players Through the Ages* (1978), London: Frank Cass; *Sporting Fever*, BBC television (1996).

68   See Chapter 2.

69   A debate raged in the 1970s and 1980s concerning the large number of 'foreign players' in English cricket and the adverse impact that it was having on the performance of the English Test team led to current regulations that limit this to one per team. It can be speculated whether the increased cosmopolitan nature of British football will lead to similar concerns in the future.

THE VICTORIAN AGE

The early years of Queen Victoria's reign began a period of the modernising of sport in a number of ways including the regulation of blood sports:

Cock fighting became illegal in 1849 but it continued nevertheless, especially outside the range of the metropolitan police. In the capital there were two compensatory vogues in the sporting inns. One was ratting. Perhaps the most famous rat pit was that of Jeremy Shaw, an expugilist, where the turnover was between 300 and 700 rats a week and where handling rats dead and alive was a mark of virility. The dogs pitted against them were often little bigger than the rats: Henry Mayhew, the journalist, described the two lb wonder, Tiny, who wore a lady's bracelet as a collar and had killed 200 rats. Another London attraction was dog fighting; in some hostelries there were contests every night and for some it was the sole topic of conversation. George Borrow recalled the scorn of a dog fancier when the topic of religion came up: 'Religion, indeed! If it were not for the rascally law my pit would fill better on Sundays than any other time. Who would go to church when they could come to my pit? Religion! why the parsons themselves come to my pit'.[70]

Barnes, J, *Sports and the Law in Canada*

In the late 18th century, Britain began to change into the urban industrial society that would eventually produce modem organised sport. Before this time, sport bore the badges of 'Merrie Englande': landed society had its field sports, horse racing and cricket; the common people had rural folk games; and both classes patronised prize fights for their attractive combination of gore and gambling. The initial phase of the industrial revolution was then accompanied by a campaign against the lower class traditions as puritanism affected the urban middle class. From the 1780s to the 1840s, State intervention in popular play was usually 'penal and restrictive'. The traditional folk sports were associated with taverns and with seasonal fairs and holidays; typical events included local versions of riotous football, smock races, greasy poles, pugilism and animal baiting. These customary festivities had pagan roots and brought associated problems of disorder, gambling' and intemperance but they enjoyed the patronage of rural squires. Their slow decline occurred as public land was lost to enclosure and as authorities responded to the demands of evangelicals and industrial employers. The new morality called for personal salvation, seriousness, domesticity and a disciplined workforce. Such recreation as respectable reformers allowed had to be self-improving and 'rational'. Local magistrates and national legislators moved to ban fairs, street football and lower class cruel sports and sought to promote Sunday observance; employers meanwhile cut the number of holidays. Many traditional forms of play nevertheless survived and popular interest remained to be recaptured by the controlled and standardised sports of a later generation.

By the 1850s, the stage was set for the Victorian reconstruction of sport. A positive games ethic first developed in the elite public schools, which had

---

70   *Ibid*, Birley (1993) p 208.

recently undergone moral renewal through the supposed influence of Thomas Arnold of Rugby. The reformed schools catered to the new upper middle class by assimilating their sons into the gentlemanly traditions of the aristocracy. Arnold's successors first promoted organised games to discipline boys' spare time and instil the manly virtues of courage, fair play and character but games soon became an end in themselves. The athletic culture then spread because it appealed to those shades of dominant Victorian opinion that saw sports as an effective means of preparing leaders. Educators and 'Sparto-Christians' found a favourable link with the ancient Greeks. Traditionalists and the Tory establishment saw sports as patriotic activities imbued with heroism and chivalry and serving as a training ground for military service and empire building. Social Darwinians and the commercial middle-class appreciated the notional 'equality' of sports, where success goes to the healthy, industrious competitor who struggles for the survival of the fittest. The Victorians found the ultimate attraction in sport's capacity to distinguish the social classes and separate the sexes. Sport was useful in class conciliation but aristocratic patronage and the new code of amateurism ensured exclusivity. Medical myths, aesthetics and decency limited women's exercises to appropriate feminine pursuits. In codifying games, the society pursued goals that were also central to the movement to restructure criminal law: the new sports and the new criminal law both sought to instil character and responsibility and looked to maintain disciplinary controls based on age, class and sex.

Conditions were now right for the growth of approved sports. Legitimate physical recreation emerged as cities provided parks and facilities and as 'muscular Christians', driven by an ideal of public service, began to incorporate lower class participation. These social missionaries had their greatest conversion when working men adopted the newly codified version of football (soccer). Rule structures and elite governing bodies began to emerge in the 1860s and 1870s: the Football Association in 1863, the Amateur Athletic Club in 1865, boxing's Queensbery Rules in 1867, the Rugby Union in 1871 and the Wimbledon Lawn Tennis Tournament in 1877. Cricket was revitalised as a spectacle during the 1870s by the county championship and the exploits of WG Grace. The new games were suited to urban constraints of time and space and were seen as useful remedies for the problems of 'health, morality and discipline that affected city life'. They also conformed to the Victorian tendency to measure, regulate, structure and improve. Playing and watching were made possible by advances in transportation and by the more regular pattern of work and leisure time in industrial society. General interest in standardised sports was spread through the new system of public education and through communications technology and the popular press. By the 1880s, sports became important forms of mass entertainment. Soccer, in particular, emerged as a commercial spectacle played by professionals and offering a regular schedule of games through the Football League.

British traditions of class, religion and commerce thus found a way to tame and approve popular sports. The final vision of terraces packed with spectators was not exactly what the early reformers had had in mind but sports were now at least incorporated into the moral order: they had shifted from being the crimes of the idle to become well-drilled, respectable recreation that safely preserved class distinctions. The rationalised sports were capable of worldwide diffusion, so that they came to transcend all cultures. The British duly spread their games and in the 1890s an Anglophile French aristocrat revived the Olympics. North America in the 19th century offered especially strong possibilities: with their serious, clean, profitable Protestantism, sports seemed American to the core.[71]

During the Victorian era sport became increasingly codified with the formal rules of the major British sports being initiated. National governing bodies that exist today in their original or modified form were originated.[72] Team sports became an important part of social life, both in terms of playing and spectating. The first concerns about spectator hooliganism, particularly in football were raised. Concern also continued about the propensity of gambling and betting on sport.

The importance of sport in society grew considerably during this period. The concept of 'muscular Christianity' became a powerful cipher of the time: sport could be used as means of purifying the body by participation in rational recreation. This form of Christian socialism and social engineering was used as form of social control. Hand in hand with the codification of sport, attempts were made to increasingly codify and control society.

In Chapter 2, the contemporary role of the State in sport will be examined and further parallels with the past drawn.

SOCIOLOGY OF SPORT

The role of sport in society needs explanation: traditional sociological theories develop competing perspectives:[73]

Coakley, J, *Sport in Society: Issues and Controversies*

Sociology provides a number of theoretical frameworks that can be used to understand the relationship between sport and society and each takes us in a different direction ... we focused on four of those frameworks: functionalism, conflict theory, critical theory and symbolic interactionism. The purpose of this chapter was to show that each framework has something to offer, helping us understand sport as a social phenomena. For example functionalist theory offers an explanation for positive consequences associated with sport involvement in the lives of both athletes and spectators. Conflict theory

---

71 Barnes, J, *Sports and the Law in Canada* (1996), Toronto: Butterworths, pp 4–7.

72 These include the Amateur Boxing Association in 1880, the Amateur Athletics Association in 1880, Football Association in 1863, Rugby Football Union in 1871, Amateur Swimming Association in 1886, English Football League in 1888, Scottish Football League in 1891 and the Rugby League in 1894.

73 For both general reading and explanation of both general and specific theories see: *ibid*, n 33, Coakley (1994); *ibid*, n 6, Hargreaves (1986); Jarvie, G and Maguire, J, *Sport and Leisure in Social Thought* (1994), London: Routledge, p 179; Cashmore, E, *Making Sense of Sport* (1996), 2nd edn, London: Routledge.

identifies serious problems in sports and offers explanations of how and why players and spectators are oppressed and exploited for economic purposes. Critical theory suggests that sports are connected with social relations in complex and diverse ways and that sports change as power and resources shift and as there are changes in social, political and economic relations in society. Social interactionism suggests that an understanding of sport requires an understanding of the meanings, identities and interaction associated with sport involvement.

It is also useful to realise that each theoretical perspective has its own weaknesses. Functionalist theory leads to exaggerated accounts of the positive consequences of sports and sport participation; it mistakenly assumes that there are no conflicts of interests between groups within society; and it ignores powerful historical and economic factors that have influenced social events and social relationships. Conflict theory is deterministic, it overemphasises the importance of economic factors in society and it focuses most of its attention on top-level spectator sports, which make up only a part of sport in any society. Critical theory provides no explicit guidelines for determining when sports are sources of opposition to the interests of powerful groups within society and it is only beginning to generate research on the everyday experiences of people involved in struggles to define and organise sport in particular ways. Symbolic interactionism does a poor job relating what goes on in sports with general patterns of social inequality in society a whole and it generally ignores the body and physical experiences when it considers the self and issues of identity ... Which theory or theoretical framework will lead us to the truth about sports?[74]

Coakley's account of the main theoretical perspectives identifies functionalism,[75] conflict theory,[76] critical theory[77] and symbolic interactionism.[78] There is not enough space to discuss any of these in detail beyond how they are described above. They all have some validity in understanding sport as a social phenomenon and particular theoretical perspectives are used as the basis of research methodology for individual researchers' own projects within this discipline.

The descriptions of the various areas of sports law in this book clearly are not atheoretical although there is a dominant ideology in Western jurisprudence of legal positivism, in seeing law as autonomous and separate from political values. These alternative sociological theoretical perspectives

---

74 *Ibid*, Coakley (1994) pp 49–50.

75 See Uschen, G, *The Interdependence of Sport and Culture*, in Loy, J *et al* (eds), *Sport, Culture and Society* (1981), Philadelphia: Lea and Febiger; Wohl, A, 'Sport and Social Development' (1979) 14(3) *International Review of Sport Sociology* 5–18.

76 See Hammond, D, *Foul Play: A Class Analysis of Sport* (1993), London: Ubique.

77 See *ibid*, n 6, Hargreaves (1986); Messner, M, *Power at Play: Sports and the Problem of Masculinity* (1992), Boston: Beacon Press; Donnelly, P (ed), 'British Cultural Studies and Sport' (1992) Special Issue of 9(2) *Sociology of Sport Journal*.

78 Coakley, J and White, A, 'Making Decisions: Gender and Sport Participation amongst British Adolescents' (1992) 9(1) *Sociology of Sport Journal* 20.

are applied to the study of the sociology of law as they are to the sociology of sport. Law is a political instrument. It is not value free, it is not democratic in terms of its construction. It reflects power relations in society and changes as social, political and economic relations shift in society. Law is not a neutral mechanism, separate from societal values.

The use of law in regulating sport needs therefore to be understood in the context and recognition of it being used in a contingent and ideological way. Critical theory is probably the theoretical perspective which is the most plausible in the subsequent theoretical explanation of law's intervention in sport. The concept of 'hegemony', largely introduced by the Italian Marxist, Antonio Gramsci,[79] and developed in the sport context by John Hargreaves, is central to this theoretical view. What it characterises 'is the achievement of consent or agreement' to dominant ideologies in society, those determined by the groups who hold social, economic and political power and promoted as being in the interests of the whole of society. Sport as an immensely powerful cultural institution is seen as helping carrying out this process.

FEMINIST THERORIES OF SPORT

Coakley also recognises feminist theories as a form of critical theory becoming more important in the study of sport:

Coakley, J, *Sport in Society: Issues and Controversies*

Feminists describe sports as 'gendered' activities. The fact that organised sports were developed to emphasise competition, efficiency and performance ranking systems and to devalue supportiveness and caring contributions to the 'gendered' character. To say that sports are 'gendered' activities and to say that sports organisations are 'gendered' structures means that they have been socially constructed out of the values and experiences of men.[80]

Jarvie, G and Maguire, J, *Feminist Thought in Sport and Leisure in Social Thought*

It might be suggested that some or all of the following concerns have been central to many feminist accounts of sport and leisure: (a) to consider the structures which have historically exploited, devalued and often oppressed women; (b) to consider various strategies which are committed to changing the condition of women; (c) to adopt a critical perspective towards intellectual traditions and methods which have ignored or justified women's oppression; (d) to explain women's involvement in and alienation from different sport and leisure contexts and practices; and (e) to highlight the engendered nature of sport and leisure organisation, bureaucracies and hierarchies.[81]

---

79 Gramsci, A, *The Prison Notebooks* (1971), London: Lawrence and Wishart.

80 *Ibid,* Coakley (1994) p 38.

81 *Ibid,* Jarvie and Maguire (1994) p 179.

Although there are many varieties of feminist methodology: liberal, radical, black and post-modern, the focus has been on why women are devalued in sport. Areas of inquiry include levels of participation in sport; legitimate use of the female body; barriers to participation and consumption; biological myths surrounding performance.[82] The law has provided some provision for challenging sex discrimination in sport and this will be considered in Chapter 9.

FIGURATIONAL THEORY

One applied theoretical position that has been massively influential on the British sociology of sport movement is that of Figuration as espoused by Norbert Elias and developed by Eric Dunning. Elias argues that British society since the late Middle Ages has become increasingly codified with rules and norms gradually being introduced to govern human activity.

Blake, A, *The Body Language: The Meaning of Modern Sport*

Since the 1950s the so-called 'figurative sociology', the work of Norbert Elias and his followers, has become influential. Elias has always been interested in sports and his theories have always been applied to sports as much as to other aspects of society. The argument ... involves a particular interpretation of history. Here is the outline of the argument. Elias and friends argue that since the Middle Ages, western society has become more 'civilised', by which they mean better behaved, more temperate and less violent. Medieval sport was a violent part of a violent society: aristocratic tournaments, wild boar hunting and quarterstaff fighting could all involve the serious injury, even death, of the participants. They claim that new forms of public disciple which were first practised at medieval courts spread down the social scale. First the ruling elite became less military and more political and learned. In Britain, castles were gradually replaced by magnificent but indefensible, country houses, as the ruling classes gave up the civil wars and rebellions which had been routine in high politics before their apex, the 17th century civil war. After this point, disagreements amongst gentlemen increasingly tended to take the form of parliamentary debate. At the same time, the gentlemanly elite began to set up the first nationally organised sports, cricket and horse racing. Then the middle classes sought to emulate the aristocracy and gentry, by gaining a classical education; sure enough the school system expanded massively during the 19th century and sure enough the universities set up the next wave of nationally organised sports, the newly rationalised games such as soccer and rugby. The values expressed in the ways that these games were taught and played – values such as public restraint and fair play within the rules – then spread to

---

82 See Tomlison, A (ed), *Gender, Sport and Leisure* (1995), University of Brighton; Hargreaves, J, *Sporting Females: Critical Issues in the History and Sociology of Women's Sport* (1994), London: Routledge; Humberstone, B (ed), *Researching Women and Sport* (1997), London: Macmillan Press.

those who took up the team sports with such enthusiasm, the skilled working class ... Sport is an example of the 'civilising process' in two ways. As well as providing a very necessary public arena for the display of public emotions, it displays or demonstrates, the containing and disciplining of public violence. However violent they appear, Elias and followers argue, the new team sports show how high the threshold of public toleration of resistance has risen since the time of the Roman gladiatorial arena or the medieval tournament, in which people quite routinely killed others in front of cheering crowds.[83]

Elias presents an historical view of sport having increasingly become codified, regulated and a part of civil society. This presents a very specific view of history and one that can be contended. As Blake argues:

> Elias and company offer a vision of 'progress' that is deeply Eurocentric, elitist (claiming that change spreads from the top of the social scale downwards) and masculinised. Many people would argue that the replacement of public confrontation and uprising by parliamentary discourse has merely disempowered people. In other words, by following rules, which conveniently protected the lives and property of an elite, we have gravely damaged the potential for radical social change.[84]

Elias uses the term 'sportisation' to refer to a process in the course of which the framework of rules applying to sport becomes stricter, including those rules attempting to provide for fairness and equal chances to win for all. The rules become more precise, more explicit and more differentiated and supervision of rule-observance becomes more efficient. In the course of the same process, self-control and self-discipline reach a new level, while in the games contests themselves a balance is established between the possibility of attaining a high level of combat-tension and reasonable protection against injury. Rules are therefore a development to attain competition – seen, of course, as an integral part of sport.

Figurational theory is therefore useful to use at a time when the law is increasingly regulatory law and adding to the codifying and civilising process.[85] Sport has clearly become more rule-bound and is now challenged by the rules of law. Can the law's involvement counter the claim of increased civilisation of sport as supported by figurational theory especially in areas such as sports violence and drug abuse? Or is the law's involvement a part of the 'civilising process'? Or in fact are conflict or critical theories more persuasive of law being used as a mechanism of control?

---

83   *Ibid*, Blake (1996) pp 48–49.

84   *Ibid*, pp 49–50.

85   See Agozino, B, 'Football and the Civilizing Process: Penal Discourse and the Ethic of Collective Responsibility in Sports Law' (1996) 24 *International Journal of the Sociology of Law* 163–88.

TENTATIVE THEORY OF LEGAL REGULATION OF SPORTS: DOES SPORT NEED THE LAW?

The emergence of the law in regulating sport has been examined. An attempt has been made to do this in the historical, cultural and sociological context of sport. This discussion is necessarily incomplete. The study of the social phenomenon of sport is vast and multifaceted. The rest of the chapter will attempt to provide some competing perspectives on the reason for this legal development and suggest a theoretical framework for the contemporary involvement of law in sport. The commercial reasons for law's greater presence have already been briefly noted. They are very important and a significant influence. It may be too simplistic to see law's intervention as being purely due to increasing commercialisation; doing so may hide some of the other causal reasons for the greater role of the law in sport. The relationship between greater legal regulation and the commercialisation of sport will be dealt with at length later in the book.

The interaction of sports internal rules and the influence of the law is also important. Sport as a social practice is highly rule-bound. Individual sports are regulated by their own constitutional rule book and adjudication machinery. The volume of rules varies between different sports. Some are particularly multifarious. Rules in sport exist for both its organisation and playing. Explicit codes of ethics are also relatively new developments as largely informal but written normative statements. Sport is also surrounded by strategies and practices that are not explicitly stated and recorded but partly amount to the 'working culture' of particular sports. The internal rules of sport need to be examined before the role of the law in sport can be fully evaluated.

Parameters of Laws' Intervention

Edward Grayson, acknowledged as the 'founding father' of British sports law, has argued strongly for the involvement of law in the operation of sport. His early writings[86] culminating in the book *Sport and the Law*, the first edition of which was published in 1987,[87] have been crucial in identifying and

---

86   Grayson, E (1969) *Police Review*, 19 November; 'On the Field of Play' (1971) *New Law Journal* 413, 10 June; 'The Day Sport Died' (1988) *New Law Journal* 9, 8 January; *The Sport and the Law* (1987), London: Butterworths; 'Keeping Sport Alive' (1990) *New Law Journal* 12, 12 January; 'Foul Play' (1991) *New Law Journal* 742, 31 May; (with Bond, C) 'Making Foul Play a Crime' (1993) *Solicitors Journal* 693, 16 July; and 'Drake's Drum Beat for Sporting Remedies/Injuries' (1994) *New Law Journal* 1094, 5 August.

87   Grayson, E, *Sport and the Law*, 2nd edn (1994), London: Butterworths.

recognising this area of law. The creation of the British Association for Sport and the Law in 1993 has crystallised both the professional and practical importance and academic relevance of the study of sports law. Internationally, particularly in North America, sports law has been identified for a significantly longer period of time.[88]

There are many ethical issues to be determined in sport and the law has a role to play in helping provide solutions but the laws' intervention itself provides ethical issues: does the law have a role to play or not? If intervention is seen as legitimate, then to what extent? There are many issues of policy too, where the law is use as an instrument to prohibit and regulate sports activity.

The regulation of violence is an example. A full discussion on this topic is found later in the book but it is an area where the legitimacy of the law's involvement is contended. There are precedents suggested that the sports field is not a private area where the law cannot intervene, as reinforced by the statement that 'the law of the land never stops at the touchline'. Support for the intervention of law is often predicated on belief that sport is more violent today than in the past.[89] There is a counter belief that the most effective mechanism for controlling violence on the sports field and providing effective punishment and compensatory remedies is more likely to come from National Governing Bodies' internal mechanisms or quasi-legal alternative dispute resolution machinery: the view that sports administrators are the best arbiters for disputes that arise rather than lawyers.

Grayson, E and Bond, C, 'Making Foul Play a Crime'

If a person intentionally or recklessly causes harm to another in order to prevent them from reaching a ball or for the reason of sheer thuggery, then these actions are in breach of the criminal law. Clearly the administrators of sport have failed to control this evil within their own sports. The concept that sporting supervisory bodies should usurp the power of the courts and the system of British justice cannot be supported by any cogent argument. Why should offenders who commit a crime within their game not be punished for their villainy ... the law of the land never stops at the touch line.[90]

---

88 See Weiller, P and Roberts, G, *Cases and Materials and Problems on Sports and the Law* (1995), St Paul's: West Publishing; Yasser, R, McCurdy, J and Gopleruid, C, *Sports Law: Cases and Materials*, 2nd edn (1994), Cincinnati: Anderson; Greenberg, M, *Sports Law Practice* (1993), Charlottsville: Mitchie Co.

89 The view that contemporary sport is more violent than in the past is contentious. For socio-cultural explanations for an increase in sports violence see Smith, M, *Violence and Sport* (1983), Toronto: Butterworths; Gruneau, R and Whitson, D, *Hockey Night in Canada* (1993), Toronto: Garamond; Messner, M, *Power at Play: Sports and the Problems of Masculinity* (1992), Boston: Beacon Press; Young, K, 'Violence in the Workplace of Professional Sport from Victimological and Cultural Studies Perspectives' (1991) 26 *International Review for the Sociology of Sport* and 'Violence, Risk and Liability in Male Sports Culture' (1993) 10 *Sociology of Sport Journal* 373. There is also medical evidence, see 'Injury cost of not so violent rugby', *The Guardian*, 9 June 1995.

90 Grayson, E and Bond, C, 'Making Foul Play a Crime' (1993) *Solicitors Journal* 693, 16 July.

A counter argument can be developed:

Gardiner, S and Felix, A, 'Juridification of the Football Field: Strategies for Giving Law the Elbow'

Grayson, one of the few writers on law and sport issues in Britain, in a series of articles has consistently argued that 'law does not stop at the touchline'. He believes that it is axiomatic that both the civil and the criminal law should be involved in incidents such as the Fashanu-Mabbutt one. There is clearly a distinction to be made between the punitive nature of the criminal law and the compensatory character of the civil law. The criminal law's involvement is more contentious. Grayson argues that the criminal law should be actively involved in the regulation of violence on the sports field and should be prioritised over the intervention of the appropriate supervisory body of the sport in question. Using a similar argument as with football hooliganism, Grayson believes that violence is much more prevalent today on the sports field than in the past and uses this to support his argument for legal intervention. We unequivocally disagree with his analysis. He harks back with nostalgia to times when those playing contact sports merely played the game and winning was a minor peripheral issue. This mythologised view is reinforced by his support for Corinthian values, where for example if a penalty was awarded against a team, the goalkeeper would step aside and allow an unhindered shot at goal. This distortion of the reality of the past only confirms an overtly bourgeois and reactionary analysis of the place of sport and specifically football in social history. Grayson believes that the law will save sport from the violence of today.[91]

As far the general role of the law in regulating sport goes:

I have always opposed people who seek to bring too much law into sport. I believe very much that sport should govern itself on the field of play.[92]

Two extracts from the press, the first on sports violence and the second on general sport issues, indicate common perceptions concerning the general appropriateness of legal intervention in sport:

Berlins, M, 'Law: The New Ball in Your Court'

Will the law of the land kick sport's rule book into touch? Marcel Berlins keeps score of sportsmen's retaliation off the pitch.

The paralysed rugby forward Ben Smoldon's claim for compensation for his injuries is the latest in the fast growing fashion of bringing sporting incidents into the courts. Criminal prosecutions or civil claims arising from clashes on the field of play were, until recently, relatively rare. They are now becoming commonplace. The principle that fighting and foul play between participants should be dealt with by the sporting authorities is being quickly eroded. But is the law of the land too protective of those who play rough sports?

---

91 Gardiner, S and Felix, A, 'Juridification of the Football Field: Strategies for Giving Law the Elbow' (1995) 5(2) *Marquette Sports Law Journal* 189.

92 Ted Croker, former Chief Executive of the English Football Association, *The Times*, 21 September 1992 and quoted in Grayson (1994).

Last October Duncan Ferguson, a Scottish international footballer now at Everton, was sentenced to three months in prison for head butting during a game in 1994, when Ferguson was playing for Rangers. Rejecting his appeal, Scotland's most senior judge, Lord Hope, commented 'It has to be made clear to players' that such criminal acts cannot be tolerated on the field of play any more than they can be tolerated in any place in this country'. The footballing establishment was shocked. Everton manager Joe Royle summed up 'We all see events on football pitches every week and they are a lot worse than what Duncan finds himself imprisoned with hardened criminals for'.

Five weeks ago the rugby world expressed equal disappointment when Simon Devereux, a player with Gloucester, was sentenced to nine months' jail for punching an opponent, breaking his jaw in three places. 'Warnings have been given to all sportsmen, particularly in rugby, that unlawful punching cannot be tolerated,' the judge said. Several rugby players have been jailed for violence on the pitch but the length of sentence was a shock. The concern of sporting bodies over the apparent rise in criminal prosecutions is exceeded by worries over the growth in civil claims for compensation.

There is nothing new in players suing over their injuries. Usually the amounts awarded have been low (though in 1994 one footballer was paid £70,000 in an out of court settlement). But the stakes are getting higher and more and more players are realising that they may be able to make money out of their misfortunes. In 1994, the former Chelsea footballer Paul Elliott sued fellow professional Dean Saunders, then with Liverpool, for damages for having ended his career by shattering his knee in a tussle for the ball. A deliberate or at least reckless act, Elliott argued. Unintentional, Saunders responded. The judge, after watching the video and hearing expert witnesses on both sides, decided against Elliott. Had he won, the damages might have exceeded £1 million. But even though he lost, the case caused consternation. It seems inevitable that a similar case will be decided the other way, attracting a rush of hopefuls to court. The spectre of litigation mania among high earning sportsmen reaching for their lawyers the moment they realise they have been injured is constantly present.

Ben Smoldon's law suit has raised a new horror, that of referees being made legally liable for the consequences of their decisions and their control of the game. Smoldon claims that his injuries were caused partly by the referee's failure to take the necessary action to stop scrums collapsing. The principle of referee responsibility, once established, would not be limited to football and rugby. A boxing referee could be made legally liable for not stopping a fight sooner and allowing a boxer to sustain serious damage. A cricketing umpire might be sued if he allows a fast bowler to bowl aggressively and injure a tail-end batsman. Smoldon's case has not yet been decided but whichever way it goes, a new, unwelcome element has entered sports litigation.

But should the law of the land lend itself to being used by sportsmen to resolve issues that should be better handled within their sport? Are we nannying rough sports with too much legal attention? If you choose to play a bodily contact sport in which you know lots of people get injured, should you be entitled to come running to the courts when you get a bloody nose? There is a famous legal maxim, *volenti non fit injuria* – no [legal] wrong is done to one who consents. But where does consent stop? The easy answer is to say that a player consents to be a victim of conduct within the rules of the game. But that would be unrealistic. The strict rules of any sport involving physical contact are never rigidly adhered to. So the test has to be wider, perhaps this: a player consents to be the victim of behaviour within the usual conduct parameters of that sport – and that includes not just the rules of the game but also behaviour which is illegal by the rules but happens often enough to be a normal part of the game. Under such a test, far fewer cases would reach court. It would mean that a football player in effect agrees to be cynically tripped after he has passed the ball and a rugby forward consents to being at the receiving end of the occasional punch thrown in the heat of battle. Scarcely a rugby game today does not contain a flare-up with fisticuffs. It has become the new norm. It is not realistic for a rugby player to say 'I quite accept the risk of a bit of violence within the hothouse of the scrum but I draw the line at being punched'.

This argument applies to criminal prosecutions as well. Why should the State bother to prosecute in the courts a player who has biffed someone who has consented to it, by choosing to play a rough contact sport in which he knows tempers are often lost, punches thrown, heads butted and kicked? Leave it to the sporting authorities to ban dirty and overly violent players, for life if necessary. Lord Hope went too far, in Ferguson's case, in saying that the law treated criminal acts on the sporting field in the same way as those elsewhere. There is a world of difference between a head butt on an innocent person in the street and a head butt on a sportsman who has chosen to participate in a sport known for its violent tendencies. The law should step back and leave the lads to beat each other up.[93]

Chadband, I, 'A Field Fit For Lawyers: Law in Sport'

Win or lose on the field of play, what really counts these days is success in the legal battle. Ian Chadband investigates the way the tentacles of the law are threatening to strangle sport's ability to control its own affairs.

It came to light last week that a former weight lifter, Roland Schmidt, plans to go to court in June on an extraordinary quest. He is demanding compensation because he insists that years of steroid use in the old drug-infested East German sports regime caused him to grow what resembled a pair of female breasts.

Schmidt, who was left with scars after undergoing surgery to remove the fatty tissue from his chest, maintains he was never made aware of the side effects of steroid use and a court in Dresden will have to decide if he can claim damages from the doctors who gave him the drugs and whether Germany's health ministry is liable for injustices perpetrated in the now defunct GDR. It is difficult to know whether to laugh or cry about this bizarre case. Yet those who have closely chronicled the crazy spiral of legal conflicts in sport will be surprised by nothing. It was probably only a matter of time before the logical conclusion to this increasingly alarming disfigurement of sport under a pile of litigation would be the unedifying sight of a drugs cheat trying to sue those who made him cheat.

---

93   Berlins, M, 'Law: The New Ball In Your Court', *The Guardian*, 2 April 1996, p 13.

Yet the Schmidt case was just the tip of the iceberg in a week when, reading the sports pages, you could have been forgiven for feeling you had chanced instead upon a law journal. On Sunday, Liz McColgan's London Marathon comeback was marked with talk of a possible medical negligence claim; on Monday, in the USA, there was the latest courtroom turn in the baseball strike; on Wednesday, in Germany, came Katrin Krabbe's bid for massive damages against her national and international athletics federations; by Friday, attention had turned to Desmond Haynes's move to sue the West Indies Cricket Board of Control over its decision to declare him ineligible for the current Test series against Australia.

While Australian rugby league authorities were promising a challenge to the breakaway super league amid mutterings that the sport was ready to plunge into a Packer-style crisis, there were suggestions that their English rugby union counterparts would face similar problems over plans to limit the number of foreigners competing in their clubs' championship. Meanwhile, an obscure Belgian footballer, Jean-Marc Bosman, was outlining his plans to cause a football revolution with his visit to the European Court of Justice. This was not an untypical week on sport's fastest growing, most contentious playing field, where lawyers are the key personnel. Following the Cantona story, future attractions coming to a tribunal near you soon will be Diane Modahl's drugs appeal hearing, the outcome of three Welsh rebel football clubs' High Court battle with the FA of Wales and more developments in the Premier League's bungs inquiry. Sport seems to be tottering out of one legal whirlwind and into another.

If sport has suddenly become particularly litigious, it is, perhaps, inevitable. Society itself is more litigious. Maybe the only surprise is that, in a multibillion pound entertainment business, it has taken so long for the rewards finally to trickle down to the performers and so long for them to realise their power. We now have a breed of financially able, legally clued up competitors who have no second thoughts about challenging the people running their sport, the administrators whose word, a generation ago, was gospel. More alarming, though, is that many of those administrators do not appear to have made the same leap into the 1990s. If there is a common thread running through many of the disputes infesting sport, it is the failure of sports governing bodies to uphold and enforce their own creaking rule books. According to Edward Grayson, the doyen of sports lawyers, 'Sport is effectively losing control of its own destiny'. The Corinthian ideal has been overtaken by what has become a billion-dollar industry, while its rulers have retained outmoded philosophies and values which do not sit easily alongside the necessities of business.

Tottenham's appearance in today's FA Cup semi-final is a reminder of that apparent impotence. If the FA could have their ruling to drum Spurs out of the competition for financial irregularities so embarrassingly overturned on a legal challenge, then what hope is there for less professionally administered and influential governing bodies? David Dixon, a solicitor and secretary of the Commonwealth Games Federation, insists that the growing threat of litigation has prompted a new awareness among British sports organisations about the critical importance of following correct legal procedures and being more conscious about the rights of individual performers. If so, then some sports are clearly learning slower than others. 'If sport were better administered, then there would be far fewer high-profile disputes,' said Stephen Townley, a leading British sports commerce lawyer who advises international sports bodies on how to restructure their rules to that end. His alarming estimate is that there are about 60 very vulnerable federations with far from watertight regulations.

The lawyers' input is more crucial than ever before. In the USA, it is no coincidence that the commissioners of the four major sports American football, baseball, ice hockey and basketball are all attorneys. Grayson can envisage a time when Britain's leading sports will also be run by lawyers, 'though not without a good deal of resistance from the traditional administrators'. The Premier League, which, to facilitate its hasty creation, effectively took the old Football League rule book as the blueprint for its own constitution, has quickly discovered, in the wake of the George Graham case, that it was inadequate in key areas. The loopholes have quickly been closed. 'I am rapidly having to become a legal expert,' said its chief executive, Rick Parry. Parry is just one of many administrators tired of the perception of sport running out of control, constantly engaged in high-cost, high-profile High Court battles. But in an era when there is really no such thing as sports law but rather a bewilderingly wide variety of specialist legal disciplines which are constantly being brought to bear on the sporting arena, the key question is whether sport is really fit and able to police itself with any degree of competence.

Those who run the Swiss based Court of Arbitration for Sport (CAS) believe it can. Last week, hundreds of administrators worldwide descended on Monte Carlo to hear details of the fledgling organisation which purports to be sport's first global independent court and which talks of becoming the ultimate arbiter in disputes, a body whose decisions will prove final, binding and enforceable and will help to keep sport out of the civil courts. That, at least, is the dream; many believe it is just a pipe dream, that CAS is only a reinvention of the International Olympic Committee's arbitration court which for a decade had the same ambitions but proved, for the most part, anonymous and insignificant. But CAS is a different animal, insists its Secretary General, Jean-Philippe Rochat. For a start, the IOC has relinquished control, the one factor which caused so many sports organisations to mistrust the old court; now the Lausanne based CAS is administered and financed by an international council comprised of members selected by a wide range of international federations, national Olympic committees and even athletes themselves. The arbitrators are trained lawyers with experience of sport. CAS is gaining crucial backing from international federations, even if, as Townley believes, it may be as much to do with arm-twisting as genuine enthusiasm. By next year's Atlanta Games, Rochat believes all Olympic sports will have made the amendments to their rules which will effectively compel them and their athletes to use CAS as the ultimate arbiter. But would CAS's verdicts be worthless should an athlete decide to challenge them in the courts? Rochat points to an important precedent in 1992, when a German horseman, under suspension from the international equestrian federation, failed in his bid to have the ban overturned by the IOC court. He then took his case to Switzerland's highest appeal court, which again found against him, ruling that he was bound by his federation's agreement to have disputes settled by the IOC's arbitration. While an arbitration decision in Switzerland may be liable to attack in another country's civil court, courts are reluctant to interfere if a sports organisation has followed its procedures rigidly and exhausted its own appeal process. Perhaps, then, CAS could be a significant step forward for sport but only if competitors learn to trust in its fairness and efficacy.

Many others also remain unconvinced that a tribunal based in Switzerland and dominated by Swiss lawyers can hope to dispense justice any more quickly or cheaply than a civil court. Rochat counters that CAS is encouraging the establishment of national courts which will be charged with resolving purely domestic disputes. By the end of the year, the planned British Sports Arbitration Panel should be in place. 'It could mean that disputes are resolved cheaply, quickly and cost effectively by persons expert in sport,' said BSAP's architect, Charles Woodhouse, legal adviser to the British Athletic Federation. Arbitration courts like these may never be a panacea for sport's headaches, just as fashioning a perfect rule book will never be a guarantee for a governing body against a courtroom challenge but if there is a will from those who play as much as from those who administer, such courts could yet point the way forward if sport is to regain some semblance of control in an ever more hazardous legal minefield.

Six Case Histories where Sport entered a Legal Minefield

Alan Sugar

In May 1994, the Football Association charged Tottenham Hotspurs with 34 breaches of FA and Football League rules involving irregular payments to players. The offences took place under a previous regime and before Sugar, the Amstrad computer tycoon, became the club's principal shareholder and chairman. Hoping for leniency, Tottenham pleaded guilty to the charges at the first FA hearing in June and were horrified when they were fined £600,000, had 12 Premier League points deducted and were expelled from the FA Cup. In July, Sugar faced an FA appeal hearing without his lawyers. The result: the fine increased to £1.5 million, the points lost reduced to six and the Cup ban upheld. Five months later, an arbitration tribunal comprising two barristers and a former appeal court judge heard submissions from Sugar's lawyers and decided the FA had been 'irrational' in penalising Spurs other than by a fine and overturned both punishments. It was a legal humiliation for the FA with worrying implications for their ability to govern the game.

Diane Modahl

The most controversial doping case in the history of British athletics appears to have plenty of mileage still in it. Banned for four years for failing a drugs test last June but still protesting her innocence, Modahl may have her appeal to the British Athletic Federation heard next month. If the ban is upheld, Modahl's husband, Vicente, has said she would bypass the final appeal to an IAAF arbitration panel and go to the courts. But whether a British court would hear the case without her first having exhausted the sport's own international appeals procedure remains open to question. If Modahl had her day in court, at least the evidence could be heard by everybody. After her disciplinary hearing behind closed doors, her lawyers' request that her appeal to BAF be held in public was turned down. Her experience illustrates athletics' drawn-out judicial process. If she loses her appeal and then goes to the IAAF, the evidence would have been heard three times before a final verdict. No wonder a visit to the courts might be preferable.

Bud Selig

When the 232 day baseball strike ended a week ago, it was not because either owners or players had triumphed. True, the US district court judge Sonia Sotomayor had signalled that Bud Selig, the acting commissioner and the owners were for the high jump by upholding an injunction ordering them to restore the collective bargaining agreement. The ruling gave the major league players the excuse they needed to call off their action, which has cost the game hundreds of millions of dollars, forced thousands of support staff to be made redundant and soured America on its national pastime. But Sotomayor's ruling effectively sends the dispute back to square one; the two sides are still hopelessly divided on the main issue the owners' desire to cut costs by instituting a salary cap. And though the owners' legal team failed last Monday to get the injunction lifted, they have since issued dire warnings that 'major league baseball will likely suffer its second consecutive year of no play-offs and no World Series'. A return to court seems assured.

Jean-Marc Bosman

Bosman, a Belgian footballer with RFC Liege, wanted to move but could not because his club demanded an exorbitant transfer fee. Without a transfer tribunal to turn to, Bosman took his case to the European Court of Justice, claiming £300,000 against the Belgian FA, UEFA and RFC Liege for restraint of trade. The case will be heard in Luxembourg on 20 June. Bosman's lawyers will argue that under European Union law, footballers should be entitled to the same freedom of movement as any other EU workers. They are seeking an end to transfer fees and to UEFA's restrictions on foreign players. 'I am going to explode the transfer system,' Bosman says. 'If I win, it means a catastrophe for UEFA. It will be as big as the fall of the Berlin wall'. Some in British football worry that if Bosman is successful, small clubs who depend on selling players to bigger clubs could be forced out of business. Gordon Taylor, the chief executive of the Professional Footballers Association, has warned that 'if football ignores the Bosman judgment it will do so at its peril'.

Butch Reynolds

This case, more than any other, sent shock waves through the bigger sports federations and prompted Olympic chiefs to erect unprecedented new legal safeguards in time for next year's Atlanta Games. In 1992, a US federal judge in Ohio awarded the world 400m record holder $26 million (about £16 million) damages after ruling that athletics' ruling body, the IAAF, was wrong to ban him for two years for failing a drugs test in 1990. The federations breathed a sigh of relief more than a year later when a US appeal court ruled that the Ohio judge had no jurisdiction over the IAAF. Primo Nebiolo, the IAAF president, hailed the verdict as 'an important precedent for the authority of international sports bodies'. But a harsh lesson had been learned. Before Atlanta, all competitors will have to sign a declaration tying them to use the Court of Arbitration for Sport to settle any disputes. It will effectively prevent them from running off to the US courts to seek the sort of telephone numbers awarded to Reynolds.

George Graham

The sacked Arsenal manager will have a chance to clear his name of bung allegations at an FA hearing on 20 April. Graham claims to have lost more than £1 million as a result of his dismissal and is adamant that he will be vindicated. Graham was dismissed on 21 February after revelations that he had received unsolicited gifts amounting to £425,000 from Rune Hauge, a Norwegian agent. The payments followed the transfers of John Jensen and Pal Lydersen. During his eight and a half years at Arsenal, Graham, who is untrained in accountancy or business, bought 24 players at a cost of some £23 million and sold 22 for about £13 million. The Premier League has left it to the FA to deal with such matters. A Premier League inquiry into illegal transfer payments has still not reached a conclusion after more than 18 months, in part because the League has lacked the power under its constitution to bring miscreants to book. But under a proposed set of new regulations, the League will have its own disciplinary and punishment procedure without having to rely on the FA.[94]

Due to Edward Grayson's influence on this debate, a number of extracts from his work are important. He argues:

To create a level of awareness among all readers of the extent to which ... the law can and should come to the help of sport; and indeed, how sport with its high profile and image can come to the help of the law. For sport without rules and their control creates chaos. Society without laws and their enforcement means anarchy.[95]

Supporting Corinthian values, Grayson argues that:

... if sport and its rulers cannot or will not try to preserve that Corinthian tradition, which the citations throughout ... and the inspiration for this book demonstrate is an ideal realistically and recognised and capable of attainment to aim for, if not always achieved, then the courts can and will do it for them, through the law of the land at both criminal and civil levels and certainly if adequate compensation is required.[96]

Grayson sees that the essential amateur Corinthian values are the epitome of sportsmanship and are an increasingly dissipating ethos in modern sport. The view that these were in fact the dominant values in sporting history has already been questioned. Much of sport in the past has been violent, secular, partisan and competitive. Sportsmanship is clearly a positive virtue as far as participation in sport is concerned. Players of the post-war era such as

---

94 Chadband, I, 'A Field Fit for Lawyers: Law in Sport', *The Sunday Times*, 9 April 1995, pp 2–14.

95 *Ibid*, Grayson (1994) p vii.

96 *Ibid*, Grayson (1994) p xxxvi.

footballers Bobby Charlton and Gary Lineker and cricketers Dennis Compton[97] and David Gower can be closely associated with it.[98] Grayson uses cricketers such as GO Smith and CB Fry and the Corinthian cricket and football teams to support the view that sport was played with absolute adherence to the letter and spirit of the rules.[99] The one fact that these sportsmen and teams shared in the early 1900s was their upper-class background of public school education and privilege. Grayson believes it was their background and professional lives as doctors, lawyers(!) and schoolmasters that provide them with this outlook on sport. He presents a view of the past where sport was purely played for the love of participation.

Gamesmanship and shamateurism[100] in sports history have already been identified and will be discussed later in the context of examples of 'cheating' in cricket. Much of modern sport continues to be played for precisely this reason. However as already explained, participation in sport has other motivations and especially at the elite level, the nature of sport is much more complex. Grayson clearly supports the argument that modern sporting bodies cannot be trusted to uphold these values and that the rule(s) of law is needed. Commenting on the reasons for writing *Sport and the Law*, he once again stresses that dispute resolution should not be left to sports administrators:

Grayson, E, *Sport and the Law*

Many within both sport and the law could not see any need for bringing the law into sport believing, with the author, that it ought always to be enjoyed for fun and, at times, as a spectators' entertainment. Indeed they were generally hostile to such a position. For whatever the true meaning and the position of sport in society may be, if ever all of its elements can be defined, too many thought that sport was cocooned in a world of its own, sealed off from reality and the rule of law. The vagaries and limitations upon human conduct and contact however, preclude such idealism in an ever-growing intensively competitive and commercially orientated sporting climate. Thus the creation of a book which explored that theme required justification, notwithstanding the existence for over a century of intervention by the courts and of Parliament, in relation to specific sporting issues. I was placed in a defensive position six years ago in 1988 in order to justify the subject of sport and the law. That defence was against a combination of abuse, ignorance, ridicule and hostility linked to the arrogance of feudalism based on an absence of awareness of the past which has permeated so much of sporting administration and still lingers

---

97 On Compton's death in 1997, see 'Cricketing Cavalier who Dazzled a Nation', *Daily Telegraph*, 24 April 1997.

98 Also see 'Professional Touch from the Last Corinthian', *Daily Telegraph*, 26 April 1997 on the rugby player, Lawrence Dallaglio.

99 See Grayson, E, *Corinthian and Cricketers – And Towards a New Sporting Era* (1996), Harefield: Yore Publications. Also see 'Casuals Stroll on Defiantly', *The Observer*, 19 January 1997.

100 WG Grace is a good example. Not only was he paid very well for his services, he was infamous for his tactics of gamesmanship, see Midwinter, E, *WG Grace: His Life and Times* (1981), London: Frank Cass.

again. The intervening six years, however, have changed all that. Indeed, anyone who seeks to challenge the need for law to partner sport for the benefit of each discipline in 1994 should examine his or her conscience ... today no-one can argue that the subject of sport and law does not exist.[101]

Wither sport and the law: what direction should sport take today? Whatever route is taken, the rule of law, on and off the field, alone can and must guide it within a rapidly revolving social setting whose pace can hardly match the kaleidoscopic changes daily imposed upon the public mind and eye.[102]

Foster, K, 'Developments in Sporting Law'

This increasing proliferation of cases of police involvement in violent play on the field is not untypical. It is just one of many examples which illustrate an accelerating trend towards increased legal intervention in sport and a decline in the myth of sport as an autonomous and separate sphere where the law has no place.

This myth of sporting autonomy has been used as an argument against legal intervention in sport; a view expressed as recently as 1986 by a judge declaring that 'sport would be better served if there was not running litigation at repeated intervals by people seeking to challenge the decisions of the ruling bodies'. But this concept of sporting autonomy is a mix of different ideas. At a cultural level, it is that sport has values which are divorced from those which law is normally seen as regulating. Sport and games are seen as mere amusements, ways of passing the time for pleasure. As a private use of time, it is clearly within civil society and outside the concerns of the State. Team games as well can be seen as supporting communal and cooperative values, celebrating and rewarding cooperation and allowing harmless competition and conflict by not giving rise to the disputes of social and economic interests which the legal process is best suited to resolving and adjudicating.

But 'sporting autonomy' can also be used as a concept to describe the view that sport and the law are separate realms, where the kind of social relations involved are not amenable to being reconstructed into legal relations. Legal norms are fixed rules which prescribe rights and duties; relationships within the social world of sport are not seen in this way. The two discourses have no common language and no links between them; there is no mechanism for communication between the different norms. The result is that law is seen as an inappropriate form of controlling the social norms of sport.

Another meaning of 'sporting autonomy' refers to the debate as to the extent of State and legal intervention into sporting affairs. The principal tensions centre on viewing sport as an economic activity, as big business, against seeing sport as a leisure pastime where citizens have their free time to use as they wish. Governing bodies in sport need to be regulated and accountable, it is argued, because they control large economic resources. Whether that regulation is best achieved by voluntary self-regulation or external legal regulation becomes the focus of debate. On the whole, there has to date been a preference for

---

101 *Ibid,* Grayson (1994) pp xxxi–ii.
102 *Ibid,* Grayson (1994) p 418.

voluntary regulation but in some sports legislative frameworks have been created for the sport's administration where self-regulation is considered inappropriate, horse racing being the most obvious example.

Against legal intervention, there is the view that sport is a pursuit for pleasure, not profit. In this area of private activity, legal intervention is inappropriate and unnecessary. As a private use of time, it is pre-eminently within civil society and outside the concerns of the State. At worst, any necessary regulation can be left to voluntary consensual organisations who are private clubs with no need for legal control nor accountability.[103]

This argument provides a 'turf war' in terms of the right to govern: international and national governing bodies and sports administrators or lawyers and the courts? In Britain there has been increasing concern about the ineffectiveness of sports administrators in the modern commercialised world of sport. Although this may well not be a new phenomenon, a new era of sports management seems to be dawning. The move to professionalisation in Rugby Union was accompanied by Will Carling's description of the English Rugby Union Committee as '57 old farts running Rugby Union'.[104] The English Football Association has also been seen as out of touch with the realities of modern sport.

The organisation of English cricket has gone through changes, with the Test and County Cricket Board becoming the English and Welsh Cricket Board in 1997. Major criticisms have been voiced over the years as to the lack of vision for the future of the game. Now with the appointment of Lord MacLaurin, ex-chairman of the Tesco supermarket chain, the hope is that a more rational plan for the future of cricket will be developed.[105] In athletics similar disharmony has reigned:

Downes, S and Mackay, D, *Running Scared: How Athletics Lost its Innocence*

Until 1990, British athletics was organised by 16 different governing bodies in a confusing *miasma* of administration, full of duplication, as well as conflicting and contradicting interests. The AAA (Amateur Athletics Association), the oldest athletics body in the world, which still governed the affairs of men's athletics in clubs throughout England, was the richest and most powerful and was not alone in its reluctance to cede its independence and authority to a new group. But after 30 years of debate, wrangling, consultation reports and more discussion, the sport finally, if somewhat reluctantly, came together under the umbrella of a single federation, the BAF (British Athletics Federation), in 1991.[106]

---

103 Foster, K, 'Developments in Sporting Law' in Allison, L (ed), *The Changing Politics of Sport* (1993), Manchester University Press.

104 See 'Last Stand of the Farts', *Fair Game*, Channel 4 Television, 18 June 1996.

105 See England and Wales Cricket Board, *Raising the Standard*, August 1997.

106 Downes, S and Mackay, D, *Running Scared: How Athletics Lost its Innocence* (1996), London: Mainstream Publishing Project, pp 29–30.

Yet the new federation has not been immune from disaster and internal strife. Malcolm Jones, the first Chief Executive lasted little over a year in the position; his successor Peter Radford's reign has not been without controversy over issues such as drug use, appearance money and National Lottery funding.[107]

Often disputes within the administrative structure of sports have been disputes between competing governing bodies or internal power struggles or between governing bodies and players associations as to the right to administer. What do lawyers have to offer to improve sports administration? In the United States, lawyers have been actively involved in running and regulating sport for some time.[108] The big four professional team sports in the USA, American football, basketball, baseball and ice hockey have lawyers as commissioners or presidents of their respective national associations.[109] There is big money to be earned: David Stern, the Commissioner of the National Basketball Association earns over £26 million per year.[110] Not surprisingly the head of the new professional US Soccer Federation is also a lawyer, Alan Rothenberg.

Lawyers clearly have qualities to offer: rational thinking, objectivity, foresight and development of preventive methods.[111] British sport may be learning from the United States. The Chairman of the Welsh Rugby Union and the International Rugby Union Board is Vernon Pugh QC.[112] The second chief executive of the English Premier League is a lawyer, Peter Leaver QC. An acknowledgment from sports governing bodies that legal expertise has a role to play in sports administration.[113]

---

107 See 'Fed up Athletics Chief in Shock Resignation', *The Observer*, 19 January 1997; *ibid*, Downes and Mackay (1996) and 'One Track Mind', *The Guardian*, 28 June 1996 on details of these controversies.

108 Judge Landis was commissioner of baseball from 1920–44, Clarence Cambell, a lawyer, was the National Hockey League President from 1946–77. See Kaplan, J, 'The Most Fun They've Ever Had: Lawyers in the World of Pro Sports' (1992) 78 *American Bar Association Journal* 56 and Shulruff, L, 'The Football Lawyers' (1985) 71 *The American Bar Association Journal* 45.

109 See 'Student Note' (1990) 67 *Denver University Law Review* 109.

110 '£26m For Sport's Best Paid Officer', *Daily Telegraph*, 15 February 1996.

111 Common qualities discussed by lawyers generally and recounted in a series of interviews with leading sports lawyers in Britain in 1994 by author. Generally, on lawyers qualities and values see Cotterrell, R, *The Sociology of Law: An Introduction*, 2nd edn (1992), London: Butterworths.

112 'Pugh Playing a Blinder', *The Observer*, 28 June 1996.

113 See 'Why every FC will soon need its own QC', *The Guardian*, 1 March 1997, p 20.

SPORT: A NEED FOR A LEGAL DEFINITION[114]

There is no legal definition under English law.[115] The Law Commission Consultation Paper,[116] concerning the issue of criminal liability for injury caused by participation in recognised sport, has raised the issue of how a sport is to be defined. The most likely criteria that the Law Commission suggests are those concerning safety and risk of injury.[117] The existence of rules that deal with these issues within a sport and the absence of wider political, ethical or moral reasons why the sport should not exist may provide us with some vague definition but one that is imprecise. This may well make it difficult to define developing activities as sports in the future. The Law Commission proposes that criminal liability for sporting injuries should be so constructed that:

> ... a person should not be guilty of an offence of causing injury if he or she caused the relevant injury in the course of playing or practising a recognised sport in accordance with its rules.[118]

Liability is therefore to be only possible outside the rules of a particular sport. The Law Commission identifies the need to produce a corresponding definition of what is a 'lawful sport'[119] so that the internal rules or regulations of such a sport can be verified or recognised. This they see as particularly important in the context of what they call 'martial arts activities', a number of which have failed to be recognised as sports.

The Sports Council believes that a lawful sporting activity is one:

> ... with a reasonably responsible attitude to minimising risks of harm ... unless Parliament takes the view that it is so dangerous that it should be outlawed.[120]

The Sports Council however already have a set of recognition criteria for sports. They have a number of statutory duties that require it to identify sports: deciding those sports that should be associated with and developed; to advise local authorities and other bodies on those activities they should promote; advise on safety in sport; to evaluate competence of organising and

---

114 See Gardiner, S, 'Sport: A Need For A Legal Definition?' (1996) 4(2) *Sport and the Law Journal* 31 for a fuller discussion.

115 This has created some difficulty. In the Commons Registration Act 1965, which indicates provides registration for land which can be used by that local inhabitants to indulge in 'lawful sports and pastimes'. There is no definition in the act of a lawful sport. See Samuels, A, 'Getting Greens Registered' (1995) *Solicitors Journal* 948.

116 The Law Commission Consultation Paper No 139 *Criminal Law: Consent in the Criminal Law* (1995), London: HMSO.

117 *Ibid*, para 13.11.

118 *Ibid*, Law Commission 1995, para 12.68.

119 *Ibid*, Law Commission 1995, para 13.1.

120 *Ibid*, Law Commission 1995, para 13.6.

supervising sporting bodies; and evaluate the financial support to be given to a sport by the Council. The process of recognition is twofold. The sporting activity is first recognised and then the sports organisational structure needs to be recognised in terms of competency to administer any government funds it may receive. The sport governing body 'must maintain and demonstrate an agreed level of management and financial accountability'.[121] The Sports Council uses the following criteria:

Sports Council, 'Recognition of Activities and Governing Bodies'

Physical skills: does the activity involve physical skills? Are physical skills important and for successful participation? Can they be developed or are they inherent in the individual?

Physical Effort: does the activity involve physical effort? Is it important for successful participation? How important are any mechanical or other aids in comparison to skills and physical effort?

Accessibility: is participation available to all sections of the community and not overtly restricted for reasons of cost, gender or on any other grounds?

Rules and Organisations: is there an established structure to the activity with rules and, where appropriate, organised competitions nationally and/or internationally?

Strategy and Tactics: are there strategies and tactics within the framework of the rules? Is developing and employing an awareness of them important for successful participation?

Essential Purpose: what is the essential purpose of the activity? Is it some form of physical recreation a means to another, more basic purpose?

Physical Challenge: does the activity present a physical and/or mental challenge to the participant whether against himself/herself, others to the environment?

Risk: does the activity involve any degree of risk? Is this level acceptable? What safeguards are employed by those taking part to minimise any risk?

Uniqueness: is this a unique activity or is it a variation of another, more similar activity that is already recognised?

Other Considerations: are there any political, moral or other ethical considerations which might prohibit the Sports Council from recognising the activity?[122]

These criteria can be divided into two basic groups, those that are to demarcate a physical sport from a recreation, hobby or pastime and those that are based on safety and ethical considerations together with the legitimate structure of the sports organisation. In terms of sports being given recognition for protection from the involvement of the criminal law, the second grouping

---

121 Sports Council, 'Recognition of Activities and Governing Bodies', *Sports Council Paper SC* (93) 68, para 4.3.

122 *Ibid*, Law Commission 1995, paras 1.1–1.10.

of criteria would seem to be the most important. The Law Commission suggests that the new UK Sports Council[123] would be the obvious choice as the appropriate recognition body for determining a 'legal sport' in consultation with other sporting bodies including existing sports governing bodies, local authorities and the Central Council of Physical Recreation.

In the context of eligibility for National Lottery funding, the Sports Council has been looking at definition and recognition of sports. It has ruled that camping and caravanning are no longer sports but rambling, caving and life-saving are. Some controversy was caused when darts was deselected as a sport for this purpose.[124] Recognition also has other financial implications including exemption from VAT. The Sports Council considered that darts involved insufficient physical activity by the participants. The British Darts Organisation believed that they have been singled out due to snobbery:

> They wrote to us and said that they do not simply decide what is and is not a sport but 'identify sports and governing bodies with which they want to be associated'. They are really saying that they do not want to be associated with fat blokes with fags in their mouth but that is such an outdated image of the sport.[125]

HISTORY OF RULES OF SPORT

Rules are needed for individual specific sports to be played. The historical development of them has been outlined above. They can generally be divided into those having the goal of ensuring safety and those regulating the dynamics of play.

In boxing the rules developed to codify prize-fighting in the 18th century were motivated by safety:

> That a square of a Yard be chalked in the middle of the Stage; and on every fresh set-to after a fall or being parted from the rails, each Second is to bring his Man to the side of the square and place him opposite to the other and till they are fairly set-to at the Lines, it shall not be lawful for one to strike at the other.[126]

These are the first, crude rules set down in print to govern boxing. Written by Jack Broughton in 1743 – two years after he had killed George Stevenson in a prize-ring in Tottenham Court Road, his patron the Duke of Cumberland a horrified spectator. They are couched in language that reflects the peculiarly

---

123 The UK Sports Council has been formed in addition to separate Sports Councils for England, Wales, Scotland and Northern Ireland since 1996.
124 See 'When Octopussy Comes to Shove H'appeny, it isn't Croquet', *The Observer*, 18 February 1996; 'When is a Sport not a Sport?', *Daily Telegraph*, 27 February 1996.
125 'Darts Swept from the Board', *The Guardian*, 14 February 1996.
126 'Sportsview: Why they can't close school of hard knocks', *The Observer*, 29 October 1995, p 10.

muscular decency of the times. These rules were further codified in 1867 under the auspices of the Marquis of Queensbery. As noted earlier, the late 1800s saw the formal codification of many sports.

The combinations of safety rules and the rules determining the mechanics of play can be termed as the 'constitutive rules':

Simon, R, *Fair Play: Sports, Values and Society*

If players were unaware of such rules or made no attempt to follow them they logically could not be playing basketball (although minimal modifications might be acceptable in informal play or other special contexts). Constitutive rules should be distinguished sharply from rules of strategy such as 'dribble only if there is no faster way of advancing the ball up the court'. Rules of strategy are general suggestions as to how to play the game well; constitutive rules determine what counts as a permissible move within the game itself.[127]

Rules of strategy are therefore separate from the constitutive rules of the game or sport. They may be formally written though in coaching manuals, etc or they may be informal rules, ones that can be seen as a part of the working culture of the sport. This relationship between the formal rules and informal culture of the sport can help determine when the law intervenes:

Gardiner, S, 'The Law and the Sports Field'

The reality is that in contact sports there is a continued risk of injury. The rules of sport are designed to avoid serious injury. They are a crucial guide in determining criminal liability. In the absence of proof of intent or recklessness to injure, participants who cause injury within the reasonable application of the rules of the sport can rely on the victim's consent to potential harm. An injury caused due to an illegal tackle that amounts to a foul within the rules of the sport is also likely to be seen as consensual. It may be contrary to the rules of the game but may well be inside the 'code of conduct' or 'working culture' of the sport. Consent is not limited solely by the formal rules in contact sports.[128]

The informality of the working culture of sport can be exploited illegitimately especially perhaps in the context of the winner-takes-all mentality of modern sport. The spectre of cheating is raised. Increasingly in sport, codes or charters of ethical behaviour and fair play have been developed, stressing the need to play fairly. These can have many targets: the use of violence; drug abuse; exploitation of young athletes. They target not only sports participants but administrators, coaches, spectators, etc. In terms of sports participants, though, they encourage ethical behaviour within the general context of the sport being played. It provides a balance to the legitimacy of participation beyond the exact application of the rules but within the working culture. Two examples can be provided by way of illustration:

---

127 Simon, R, *Fair Play: Sports, Values and Society* (1991), Boulder: Westview Press, pp 14–15.
128 Gardiner, S, 'The Law and the Sportsfield' (1994) *Criminal Law Review* 513, 514.

Council of Europe, 'Fair Play – The Winning Way Code of Sports Ethics'

AIMS

The basic principle of the Code of Sports Ethics is that ethical considerations leading to fair play are integral and not optional, elements of all sports activity, sports policy and management and apply to all levels of ability and commitment, including recreational as well as competitive sport.

The Code provides a sound ethical framework to combat the pressures in modern day society which appear to be undermining the traditional foundations of sport – foundations built on fair play and sportsmanship and on the voluntary movement

The primary concern and focus is fair play for children and young people, in the recognition that children and young people of today are the adult participants and sporting stars of tomorrow. The Code is also aimed at the institutions and adults who have a direct or indirect influence on young people's involvement and participation in sport ...

DEFINING FAIR PLAY

Fair play is defined as much more than playing within the rules. It incorporates the concepts of friendship, respect for others and always playing in the right spirit. Fair play is defined as a way of thinking, not just a way of behaving. It incorporates issues concerned with the elimination of cheating, gamesmanship, doping, violence (both physical and verbal), exploitation, unequal opportunities excessive commercialisation and corruption.

Fair play is a positive concept. Sport is a cultural activity which, practised fairly, enriches society and the friendship between nations. Sport is also recognised as an activity which, played fairly, offers the individual the opportunity of self-knowledge, self-expression and fulfilment; personal achievement, skill acquisition and demonstration of ability; social interaction, enjoyment, good health and well-being. Sport promotes involvement and responsibility in society with its wide range of clubs and leaders working voluntarily. In addition, responsible involvement in some activities can help to promote sensitivity to the environment ...

SPORTS AND SPORTS-RELATED ORGANISATIONS

Sports and sports-related organisations have the following responsibilities in setting a proper context for fair play:

- to publish clear guidelines on what is considered to be ethical or unethical behaviour and ensure that, at all levels of participation and involvement, consistent and appropriate incentives and/or sanctions are applied;

- to ensure that all decisions are made in accordance with a code of ethics for their sport which reflects the European Code;

- to raise the awareness of fair play within their sphere of influence through the use of campaigns, awards, educational material and training opportunities. They must also monitor and evaluate the impact of such initiative;

- to establish systems which reward fair play and personal levels of achievement in addition to competitive success;

− to provide help and support to the media to promote good behaviour ...

Sport is governed by a set of rules and, often unwritten principles of behaviour which usually come under the banner of Fair Play. Sadly, it is often these principles which are not strictly adhered to in a range of sports. The Council of Europe's Code of Sports Ethics is a valuable reminder of the need to demonstrate and practise ethical behaviour in sport.[129]

A second example comes from the world of surfing:

British Surfing Association, 'Code of Conduct for Surfers'

All surfers must be able to swim at least 50 metres in open water.

Ensure that you are covered by Public Liability Insurance for surfing.

Keep your surfing equipment in good condition.

Always wear a surf leash to prevent you from losing your surfboard (or body board). For you your board is a safety device, for others it may be a lethal weapon.

Have consideration for other water users including anglers.

Never surf alone or immediately after eating a meal.

Never mix surfing with alcohol or drugs.

Always wear a wetsuit when surfing in Britain.

If you are new to the sport never hire a surfboard without first having a surfing lesson (given by a qualified instructor)

Be considerate of other beach users especially when carrying your board to and from the water.

When possible use a lifeguard patrolled beach. Obey the lifeguard's instructions and be prepared to assist them if required.

Where possible surf in a recognised surfing area (eg in between the black and white checked flags).

When paddling out avoid surfers who are riding waves.

When taking a wave see that you are clear of other surfers. Remember, if someone else is already riding the wave you must not take off.

Be environmentally friendly. Always leave the beach and other areas as you would wish to find them.[130]

So the formal rules of sport (of the variety that have been discussed) have developed very much as a product of modernity. As John Bale argues they have produced an increasingly uniform activity:

---

129 Council of Europe: 'Fair play – the Winning Way Code of Sports Ethics' (1996) *Sports Council leaflet.*

130 British Surfing Association, Code of Conduct for Surfers. For more information contact BSA, Champions Yard Penzance, Cornwall TR18 2SS.

Bale, J, *Landscapes of Modern Sport*

It is a plausible claim that 'the first laws ever to be voluntarily embraced by men (*sic*) from a variety of cultures and backgrounds are the laws of sports' and these laws are crucial to the contents of this book. Without laws which were accepted over large areas, inter-regional competition was difficult if not impossible and the laws of sports were drawn up to make competition between geographically dispersed teams more meaningful. To enforce these laws, national (or in large countries, regional) bureaucracies (ie sports associations) were set up. In western nations the cumulative frequency curves for the growth of such associations display a pattern of initially slow but subsequently rapid (late 19th century) growth, characteristic of many cultural innovations.

As sports diffused internationally the formation of national governing bodies was followed by similar global organisations but western sports did not simply take root in virgin soil; they were often firmly implanted – sometimes ruthlessly – by imperialists, while in other cases indigenous elites sought to imitate their masters in order to gain social acceptance. Such sports colonisation was at the expense of indigenous movement cultures and as cultural imperialism swept the globe, sports played their part in westernising the landscapes of the colonies – tennis courts and golf courses, race tracks and football pitches becoming permanent features of the cultural environment while evidence of indigenous games often became relict features of the landscape. The laws drawn up by the sports bureaucracies almost always included the spatial parameters within which the sporting action was to take place. It is this explicitly spatial character of the globally applied rules of sport which has such an important impact on the sports environment since it facilitates global 'body trading', permitting people from different cultures to make sense of the sports landscape by encouraging 'sameness' wherever it might be in the world. Although the 'globalisation' of culture is not the same as its 'homogenisation', the globally enforced rules of sport encourage sameness, homogenisation and placelessness to an extent not so commonly found in such global common denominators as tourism, leisure or work. Even if one was to accept the rather unconventional view that modern sport is essentially the same as its antecedents in that each are 'the ritual sacrifice of physical energy', the modernity of sport (in the sense that word is used in this book) is demonstrated by its standardised spatial and environmental forms. Today, a squash court or a running track is essentially the same whether it is in London or in Lagos. Sports, therefore, are versions of what Appadurai calls 'technoscapes', each having roots in number of multinational organisations (sports' governing bodies) which, with the help of modern technology insist on certain standardised landscapes within which sport is allowed to take place.[131]

Bale shows how sport has become more uniform wherever it is played through the development of rules as far as play and the increasingly standardised spatial dimensions of play, eg football pitches need to be within

---

131 Bale, J, *Landscapes of Modern Sport* (1994), Leicester University Press.

certain size limits, international boxing rings need to meet a number of criteria on surface and size and lastly, environmental factors such as wind velocity need to be inside certain parameters for the validity of international records in athletics. He shows how certain sports facilities are increasingly regulating environmental factors, the SkyDome in Toronto with its retractable roof, for example. He uses the terms 'placelessness' to describe this process of increasing standardisation of the places that sport is played. As he says:

> The modern sports landscape can be described as tending towards placelessness in its geographical sense of places looking and feeling alike with 'dictated and standardised values'.[132]

Interestingly this is one of the complaints concerning the introduction of all seater football stadiums since the Taylor Report after the Hillsborough disaster – grounds have become too soulless without recognisable ends and lacking the atmosphere of old. What Bale certainly shows in his geographical examination of sport, is the increasing importance of the rule framework of sport.

RULE CHANGES

Another issue is to what extent and frequency the rules of games should be modified. One argument is that changes are merely tinkering and are often carried out with the aim of short-term expediency. This is often to placate external pressures such as sponsors and television and may run the danger of curbing excellence of participants. An example are the changes in the rules of Formula One motor racing largely to curb the past dominance of the Williams team.[133] Similarly the constant changes in cricket to the short pitch delivery rules have been carried out to control the dominance of the West Indies over the last 20 years[134] The opposing argument is that rule changes are needed to secure the integrity of modern support in the context of the commodification and globalisation of sport. New variants of a traditional sport are periodically introduced, such as one day cricket in 1963. Coaches and players are under increasing pressure to succeed and therefore exploit the limitations of existing rules. Rule changes are then required to try to re-establish the vitality and balance in a particular sport. New skills and strategies then develop to confront the new rules. This allows the sport to be dynamic and reflects the character of rules as being both certain and being pliant.

---

132 *Ibid*, Bale (1994) pp 94–95.

133 'Do not Change the Balls or Tinker with the Rules Please', *The Times*, 6 July 1994, p 42; 'Law-makers Struggle to Keep Pace with the Law-breakers', *The Guardian*, 16 September 1994; 'Scots Urge IB to Speed up Game', *The Guardian*, 4 October 1994; 'The Dangers of Playing for Time-out', *The Independent on Sunday*, 9 April 1995; 'FIFA to Hit Taller Keepers by Moving the Goalpost', *The Guardian*, 3 January 1996.

134 'Bouncer Law is Changed', *The Guardian*, 7 July 1994.

Rules certainly do have an elasticity and together with the players 'working culture', are only part of the regulation of the sport. Without this acknowledgment and the ability to modify rules, sport are subject to predictability and ossification. But in most sports, rule changes have significantly accelerated in the last 30 years. Increasing external pressures may well be the cause. Too many changes can be counterproductive and damage the balance of sports. Some sports such as American Gridiron have numerous and complex rules. Others such as football have a simplicity that is derived from a small number of rules. Rule changes are made for these reasons: to promote safety, assist the fluidity of the game and to allow the skilful to shine. Some are not fundamental changes in the rules but different interpretations of existing ones. There is however a danger that rule changes in sport are developing an increasingly sanitised game for mass global consumption

There is a complex interaction between the playing rules and the officials that enforce them. At particular points in time, governing bodies instruct referees or umpires to enforce the rules more or less strictly.[135] This can lead to disquiet from players and more or less formal infringements and fouls during the game.[136] The statistics may indicate a fall or increase in foul play but it is unlikely to be primarily about changes in the style of play, becoming more violent for example. It is much more about official attitudes towards actual and potential perpetrators during the game. Increasingly the human vulnerability of officials is being questioned. A number of sports are increasingly using various forms of technology to aid officials in coming to decisions. In sports such as horse racing and athletics, cameras have been used for many years. In tennis, some line decisions are determined electronically. The use of video cameras as an aid to the officials or as a final arbiter is starting to be used in sports such as cricket and rugby league in Britain. There are interesting issues concerning whether this undermines the official's authority and makes a game too clinical or whether human error needs to be minimised as mush as possible when a wrong decision may have an enormous financial cost.[137]

Some rule creations and changes, as with the law itself, can also be clearly dysfunctional and sometimes utterly bizarre:

Longmore, A, 'Absurd Cup Rule Obscures Football's Final Goal'

The law, they say, is an ass and more of an ass in sport than most walks of life but not even the bigwigs at the Football Association could have concocted a rule so daft that both sides ended a competitive cup match attacking their own goals, the farcical situation that occurred at the end of a recent match between

---

135 'UEFA Orders Referees to Stay Tough', *The Guardian*, 11 June 1996, p 22.

136 'Referees Must Go With The Flow', *The Observer*, 18 September 1994, p 6.

137 See Gardiner, S, 'The Third Eye: Video Ajudication in Sport' (1997) 5(3) *Sport and the Law Journal* 20.

Barbados and Grenada in the final group match of the Shell Caribbean Cup.

Needing to beat Grenada by two clear goals to qualify for the finals in Trinidad and Tobago, Barbados had established a 2–0 lead midway through the second half and were seemingly well in control of the game. However an own goal by a Bajan defender made the score 2–1 and brought a new ruling into play, which led to farce. Under the new rule, devised by the competition committee to ensure a result, a match decided by sudden death in extra time was deemed to be the equivalent of a 2–0 victory. With three minutes remaining, the score still 2–1 and Grenada about to qualify for the finals in April, Barbados realised that their only chance lay in taking the match to sudden death. They stopped attacking their opponents' goal and turned on their own. In the 87th minute, two Barbadian defenders, Sealy and Stoute, exchanged passes before Sealy hammered the ball past his own goalkeeper for the equaliser.

The Grenada players, momentarily stunned by the goal, realised too late what was happening and immediately started to attack their own goal as well to stop sudden death. Sealy, though, had anticipated the response and stood beside the Grenada goalkeeper as the Bajans defended their opponents' goal. Grenada were unable to score at either end, the match ended 2–2 after 90 minutes and, after four minutes of extra time, Thorne scored the winner for Barbados amid scenes of celebration and laughter in the National Stadium in Bridgetown.

James Clarkson, the Grenadian coach, provided an unusual variation on the disappointed manager's speech: 'I feel cheated,' he said. 'The person who came up with these rules must be a candidate for the madhouse. The game should never be played with so many players on the field confused. Our players did not even know which direction to attack. Our goal or their goal. I have never seen this happen before. In football, you are supposed to score against the opponents to win, not for them,' he added. Nobody should tell the organising committee of the World Cup. They might get ideas.[138]

CHEATING AND SPORTSMANSHIP

Is the above example and the actions of the Barbadian team an example of cheating? The issue of cheating and its regulation in perhaps the two main sporting contexts of violence and drugs will be discussed later in the book. The distinction of how governing bodies in sport seem to deal more harshly with drug abuse compared with excessive violence is of interest.[139]

---

138 Longmore, A, 'Absurd Cup Rule Obscures Football's Final Goal', *The Times*, 1 February 1994, p 44.

139 James, M and O'Leary, J, 'Comparing Private Law Making and Criminal Implications of Cheating in Sport', unpublished conference paper, *Socio-Legal Studies Conference*, University of Cardiff, March 1996.

But what do we mean by 'cheating'? It is invariably seen as actions that are contrary to the rules of the sport; but can it be reconciled with the working culture of the sport; when does the law have a role play in regulating it? Leaman has attempted to define cheating:

Leaman, O, 'Cheating and Fair Play in Sport'

It is not as easy as it might initially be thought to define cheating in sport and it is just as difficult to specify precisely what is wrong morally with such behaviour and why fair play should be prized. In this article I intend to try to throw some light on the notions of both cheating and fair play and to suggest that stronger arguments than those so far produced in the literature are required to condemn the former and approve the latter.

Let us try to deal first with the definitional problem of what sorts of behaviour constitute cheating and come to the ethical issue later. Gunther Luschen boldly starts his essay on cheating in sport with this definition:

> Cheating in sport is the act through which the manifestly or latently agreed upon conditions for winning such a contest are changed in favour of one side. As a result, the principle of equality of chance beyond differences of skill and strategy is violated.

A problem with this definition is that it omits any consideration of intention. After all, if a player unwittingly breaks the rules and thereby gains an unfair advantage he will not necessarily have cheated. For example, if a boxer has a forbidden substance applied to bodily damage without his knowledge, then he has not cheated even though the rules have been broken to his advantage. Were he to be penalised or disqualified, it would not be because of his cheating but due to the rules having been broken by those who attend to him in the intervals.

A superior account of cheating is then provided by Peter McIntosh, who claims that:

> Cheating ... need be no more than breaking the rules with the intention of not being found out ... Cheating, however, implies an intention to beat the system even although the penalty, if the offender is found out, may still be acceptable.

But McIntosh next claims that:

> This definition, however, is too simple. It is not always the written or even the unwritten rule that is broken; tacit assumptions which one contestant knows that the other contestant acts upon may be rejected in order to gain an advantage. A more satisfactory definition is that of Luschen.

McIntosh's adaptation of Luschen's account makes possible the useful distinction between intending to deceive, which he calls cheating and breaking the rules without having that intention. He concludes that 'Cheating is an offence against the principles of justice as well as against a particular rule or norm of behaviour'.

If people undertake to play a game, then they may be taken to have understood and agreed to the rules of the game and the principle upon which any fair victory in the game must rest ... Yet what are 'the rules of the game' to which players supposedly commit themselves when they enter a game? If we look at the ways in which some sports are played it becomes evident that the rules of the game involve following the formal rules in so far as it is to the advantage of one's own side and breaking them when that is perceived, perhaps wrongly, to be to the side's advantage, where the possibility of suffering a penalty is taken into account. The existence of an authority in games enshrines cheating in the structure of the game; the authority is there to ensure that cheating does not interfere with the principle of fairness in a game. He is there to regulate cheating so that it does not benefit one side more than the other except where one side is more skilful at cheating than the other and to see that the amount of cheating which takes place is not so great as to change the general form of a particular game. That is, the formal rules of the game must in general be adhered to by all players since otherwise in a clear non-moral sense the game is not being played. But if we are profitably to discuss the notion of the rules of the game and of cheating and fair play, we must address ourselves to the ways in which players and spectators perceive those rules rather than to an abstract idea of the rules themselves. The next step is to determine what notion of fair play is applicable within the context of the ways in which players actually participate in sporting activities. An injection of realism into philosophical discussions of cheating and fair play in sport is long overdue.[140]

Cheating is therefore a complex philosophical phenomenon.[141] Three examples from the cricket world will be used to illustrate this concept.

Bodyline

Holt, R, *Sport and the British: A Modern History*

All this brings us to 1932 and the 'bodyline' tour. The bones of the business can be set out quite simply. After being soundly beaten by Australia in England in 1930 mainly as a result of the remarkable batting of Bradman, whose 334 at Headingley broke the existing Test record, England had to find a way to contain the 'Don' and win back the Ashes. The England captain, Douglas Jardine, for all his Oxford amateurism, was a grim competitor. Like some of his Australian critics, he did not believe simply in 'playing the game for its own sake' and being a 'good loser'. Jardine had only one advantage in comparison to Bradman's Australia. He had a formidable pace attack at his disposal in the form of Larwood, Voce, Bowes and Allen. To be able to draw upon four fast bowlers was extremely rare in the days when spin was still regarded as essential for a balanced side. The fact that Harold Larwood was possibly the

---

140 Leaman, O, 'Cheating and Fair Play in Sport' in Morgan, W (ed), *Sport and the Humanities: A Collection of Original Essays* (1981), Educational Research and Service, University of Tennessee, pp 25–30.

141 See Luschen, G, 'Cheating in Sport', in Landers, D (ed), *Social Problems in Athletics* (1977), Urbana: University of Illinois Press; McIntosh, P, *Fair Play: Ethics in Sport and Education* (1994), London: Heinemann; Meier, W and K (eds), 'Part IV – Fair Play, Sportsmanship and Cheating' in *Philosophical Inquiry in Sport*, 2nd edn (1995), Champaign: Human Kenetics; Simon, R, *Fair Play: Sports Values and Society* (1991), Boulder: Westview Press.

fastest bowler of all time gave Jardine a potentially strong hand to play. It was the way he played that hand which caused the trouble.

Bradman had proved a magnificent player of spin bowling. If he had any weakness at all it was perhaps a tendency to play too much off the back foot and to hook the high fast ball on the line of the body. Whether the 'bodyline' assault was coldly premeditated by Jardine or it was Larwood himself who hit upon it while bowling to a momentarily nervous Bradman during the 1930 series may never be fully resolved. What is more important is that both captain and bowler were determined to use intimidatory bowling to unsettle Bradman. Larwood always claimed it was a fair tactic but it was precisely the legitimacy of playing this way which was at the heart of the controversy. Though he was slightly built, mentally Larwood was a tough professional, an ex-miner, who believed the batsmen who got the glory had to be able to take punishment and show courage when it was needed. Jardine also felt intimidatory bowling was legitimate. He set a leg-side field and waited for a simple catch as the batsman tried to protect himself from a sharply bouncing ball aimed at the upper body and an unprotected head. In brief, the tactic seemed to work. Bradman's test average slumped from over a hundred to a mere 50 – still well ahead of the rest – but England regained the Ashes.

The real trouble came in the third Test at Adelaide when the Australian captain was felled by a short pitched but straight ball from Larwood. What really incensed the crowd was Jardine's switch to a full leg-field immediately after the accident. Later the Australian wicket keeper Oldfield was struck on the head, again from a straight delivery from Larwood and the crowd roared angry abuse at the England team. Jardine, who was believed to loathe Australians and to enjoy baiting them by his supercilious attitude, silk handkerchief and Harlequin cap, was the main target. When drinks were brought out, a voice from the crowd was heard to shout, 'Don't give him a drink, let the bastard die of thirst'. Jardine had been barracked in the earlier 1928–29 tour of Australia and was said to have deeply resented it. He had even requested that spectators be forbidden to attend net sessions. At the end of the day's play the England manager, 'Plum' Warner, who had been born in Australia and captained several successful pre-war tours, went to enquire about the injuries after the game and received what has since become the best known rebuke in the history of the game: 'Of two teams out there,' said Woodfull, 'one is playing cricket, the other is making no effort to play cricket'. There are several versions of the precise form of words he used but the message was unmistakable and Warner left deeply hurt. Privately he urged Jardine to desist from the tactic but without success. 'Not cricket?' roared the Australian popular press and matters became much worse when the Australian Cricket Board surprisingly made public a telegram they sent to the MCC which read 'Bodyline bowling has assumed such proportions to menace the best interests of the game ... in our opinion it is unsportsmanlike'. To have been a fly on the wall of the Long Room at Lord's when this arrived would have been a rare treat. The MCC have diplomatically 'lost' the records of their discussions but their icy reply insisting the 'unsportsmanlike' be withdrawn and offering to cancel the tour is well known. By implication the Australian cricketing authorities and public were questioning the good faith of the British in the common morality that bound them together ... the MCC could not contemplate the public humiliation of accepting that their side was 'not playing the game'. So the MCC had to stick by its man for the duration of the series and the Australians withdrew the word 'unsportsmanlike'. But in the time honoured traditions of the British establishment Jardine was quietly ditched despite his success and Larwood was never selected for England again.[142]

At this time in the 1930s this style of bowling was labelled as cheating. It would be interesting to see whether it would be viewed in the same way in modern cricket.

Ball tampering I: Dirt in the pocket

The second example comes from a Test match against South Africa in 1994, when the England cricket captain, Mike Atherton, was fined £2,000 by the Test and County Cricket Board after he admitted not telling the whole truth over 'ball tampering' allegations. Atherton was seen on television putting his hands in his pockets and apparently rubbing something on the ball. Atherton said that he had dirt in his pockets, which he was using to dry his fingers on a clammy day. There is nothing wrong with this – but it would be illegal to use it on the ball contrary to the Laws of Cricket and law 42(5):

Law 42 Unfair Play

(5) Any member of the fielding side may polish the ball provided that such polishing wastes no time and that no artificial substance is used. No one shall rub the ball on the ground or use any artificial substance or take any action to alter the condition of the ball. In the event of a contravention of this Law, the Umpires, after consultation, shall change the ball for one of similar condition in that in use prior to the contravention. This Law does not prevent a member of the fielding side from drying a wet ball or removing mud from the ball.[143]

On the face of it the act was the time-honoured behaviour of a man doing something illegal to make the ball swing. However Atherton, when challenged by the match referee Peter Burge to explain his actions, said he was drying his hands in his pockets and did not mention the dirt in there. With reference to the rule, a number of questions were left unanswered. Did Atherton rub dirt on the ball? What is an artificial substance? This raised interesting issues of interpretation:

Fraser, D, 'Balls, Bribes and Bails: the Jurisprudence of Salim Malik'

The case of Michael Atherton with its legal, interpretative difficulties may well be more accurately classified as a case of 'perjury' or perversion of the course

---

142 Holt, R, *Sport and the British: A Modern History* (1989), Oxford: Clarendon Press, p 233, by permission of Oxford University Press. See Le Quesne, L, *The Bodyline Controversy* (1983), London: Macmillan, for further discussion of the bodyline strategy.

143 MCC, The Laws of Cricket (1980 Code).

of justice' rather than as a case of 'ball tampering'. Nonetheless it remains true that it originally started off as what appeared to be a clear-cut case of 'ball tampering' and remains classified as such by many observers of the game. Whatever jurisprudential taxonomy one decides to apply in this case, however, it is clear that it was treated by all concerned, almost from the outset, as something different from a 'Pakistani ball tampering case'. It serves as a classic example of the way in which the apparently neutral discourses and practices surrounding the legal and ethical issues in question actually serve to establish a dual system of legal rules and ultimately of 'justice'. This epistemological and juridical duality is confirmed by recent events.[144]

Fraser goes on to recount how Atherton's misdemeanours were largely forgotten when he batted for almost 15 hours to save the Test against South Africa at Johannesburg in the return series in 1995. 'Atherton was treated as a hero of the great colonial struggles of yore.'[145]

Brearley, M, 'Cricket: Atherton Affair: The Dirt that is in all our Pockets'

'Unfamiliar action', as the Test and County Cricket Board statement put it, it certainly was. I had never heard of a cricketer pocketing dirt to dry his hands. What is less clear is whether, in the same statement's second quaint phrase, 'there was nothing untoward', this strange little incident contains, concealed in pockets about its person, several dubious psychological substances. The poets were right to see 'a World in a Grain of Sand' and 'fear in a handful of dust'! These issues touch us all. Are we not all inclined, to some degree, to be both over-suspicious and naive; to be self-righteous and to turn a blind eye? Do we not all have deep-seated responses to the possible downfall of the Great and the Good, ranging from horror to salacious triumph? This pocketful of dirt – does it epitomise the dirt we all carry, usually hidden, however white our gear?

In a society where cricket is supposedly synonymous with fair play, is the burden of expectation on England's captain too great? What, too, is the role of the cricket Establishment? Have they done all they could to be seen to be both fair and stringent? Do we have one standard for our own and another for others? (And this can work both ways: we can condemn our own man, like Caesar's wife, simply for being suspected – which in a world of lascivious suspiciousness may be simply unjust – or we may refuse to believe that one of us is dishonest while assuming dishonesty in, say, a Pakistani bowler.) And what, exactly, was Michael Atherton up to? If dishonest, he seemed so unconcerned; if honest, so disinclined to come clean.

First, the evidence; and then, as the Michelin guides have it, a little history. I start with the sequences shown on television news on Monday. To my eyes, Atherton looks like a man taking a little pinch of snuff from his pocket; instead of sniffing it, he appears to drop it on the ball. The stuff looks like fine, grey

144 Fraser, D, 'Balls, Bribes and Bails: the Jurisprudence of Salim Malik', *Law and Popular Culture Research Group Working papers* (1995), Manchester Metropolitan University, p 12. Also see Fraser, D, *The Man in White is Always Right: Cricket and the Law* (1993), London: Blackwell.
145 *Ibid*, Fraser (1995) p 12.

dust. He then polishes the ball and hands it to the bowler, Gough, who takes it with finger and thumb, presumably touching only the seam, gingerly, as if the rest of the ball were made of china. When questioned about what had happened, Atherton at first failed to mention the dirt in his pocket. Later he said that he had used it to dry his hands but that he didn't apply it to the ball. The umpires stated that the condition of the ball had not been altered. Later, Illingworth fined him £1,000 for doing whatever he was doing with the ball and £1,000 for not coming clean about the dirt with the match referee. I gather that Atherton had picked up the dust from the footholes not long before.

Now for the history. In England the traditional way of interfering with the ball has been to raise its seam with the nail. This practice is not, I think, endemic but it is certainly not rare. Seam picking goes on because English pitches often permit movement and the slightly raised seam makes such movement slightly more likely. Most professionals would tend to shrug their shoulders at a minor degree of seam raising. They would also be angered by the few who have gone further and more substantially and systematically altered the seam. From time to time umpires are instructed to check the condition of the ball frequently. Such spot checks eradicate the habit for the time being. Overseas the ball moves off the seam less and the likelier form of minor cheating has been to put skin cream or lip salve on the ball and thereby heighten the polish. This helps orthodox swing, that is, swing where the bowler delivers the ball with its shiny half on the side from which the ball is to swing; this shinier side meets less resistance and travels faster through the air. Sweat, a natural substance, is permitted for this purpose.

More recently, in Pakistan, where the ball tends to get roughened by the bare ground quicker than elsewhere, a new technique – reverse swing – has been developed. Apparently the essential requirement for this is an oldish ball whose non-shiny side is kept dry; hence the need for dry hands. For some reason reverse swing usually means in-swing. In Gough, England now have a bowler capable of doing this. Reverse swing can transform the game, since, as the innings goes on, it can make batting suddenly much harder rather than, as one would usually expect, easier. It also means that there is less need for spin bowlers, who usually do most of their work with the old ball. I first encountered this sharp, old ball in-swing batting against Sarfraz Nawaz in Karachi in 1972 but had no idea how he did it. Keeping the rough side dry is not the only aid to reverse swing. Bowlers have been accused of lifting the quarter-seam and scuffing and gouging the rough side. This, if practised, is ball tampering writ large. But I find it hard to understand why regular spot checks don't rule out such practices.

If I am right, that Atherton put a pinch of dust on the ball, then it is not true that he was using it only to dry his hands. (And wouldn't he need to dry both hands, not only his right hand? Why not two pockets of dirt?) However, the umpires say the ball's condition was not altered and I see no reason to doubt this. The fine dust was probably used only to dry sweat from the ball. Moreover, the law does not say that no substances may be applied to the ball, only artificial ones. Presumably the intention was to rule out all substances except sweat; but dust, though perhaps artificial in contrast to sweat, is not artificial in contrast to sun cream. Nowadays, the ball may not be rubbed in the dirt but the laws don't explicitly rule out dirt being rubbed in the ball. (As far as gravediggers are concerned, the man going to the water is a different matter from the water coming to the man: Hamlet Act V Scene 1.)[146]

Ball tampering II: In the High Court

The legitimacy of ball tampering has become an on-going debate within the cricket world.[147] The third and last example, the libel action by ex-English test cricketers Ian Botham and Allan Lamb, against the accusations of the ex-Pakistani test cricketer Imran Khan, had a complex underlying narrative concerning cheating. The dispute which resulted in the costly High Court action can be traced back to the summer of 1992, when the Pakistan cricket team arrived in England and allegations of cheating were being made against them. The 1992 series, which Pakistan won 2–1, was described in court as savage and ugly, with accusations of cheating being made by the tabloid press against Pakistan's two fast bowlers, Wasim Akram and Waqar Younis. There were headlines like 'Paki cheats' and claims that the two Pakistan bowlers, had regularly been tampering with the ball, by either picking the seam or scratching it on one side, to make it swing more than it should. Some even suggested that this contributed to their World Cup win against England months earlier.

The controversy resurfaced in 1994 when Imran admitted in a biography that he had scratched a ball with a bottle top while playing for Sussex in a county match. Imran claimed in court that he was merely trying to highlight the unacceptable face of ball tampering which he claimed had gone on in English cricket for years. Picking the seam with your fingers or applying a bit of grease to one side of the ball was 'tacitly accepted' but using outside agents like bottle tops was overstepping the limit. 'That is what I would call cheating,' Imran confessed while giving evidence during the trial.

Lamb and Botham responded swiftly to the Imran biography. In May 1994, Lamb contributed an article to *The Sun* newspaper in which Imran was accused of cheating and teaching Younis and Akram how to tamper with the ball. This was followed by an article in the *Daily Mirror* in which Botham called for a full investigation into Imran's ball tampering and demanded his resignation from the International Cricket Conference. Less than a week later, Imran, who by now had retired from Test cricket and was concentrating on building a cancer hospital in his native Lahore, responded by giving an interview to *The Sun*. Headlined 'World's greatest bowlers have all doctored the ball' he once again claimed that ball tampering was an accepted part of English cricket.

---

146 Brearley, M, 'Cricket: Atherton Affair: The Dirt that is in all our Pockets', *The Observer*, 31 July 1994, p 10; also see 'Cheating Art That's Not Just Cricket', *The Observer*, 31 July 1994.

147 Khan, I, 'ICC Need to Come to Grips with Laws', *Daily Telegraph*, 24 January 1996.

With England-Pakistan cricket relations at an all-time low, matters deteriorated when extracts from an interview given by Imran to *India Today* magazine appeared in the British press. He was quoted as calling Botham and Lamb racists, claiming that their approach to the whole issue of ball tampering was 'irrational' because they were lower-class and uneducated. It was this interview that led Botham and Lamb to bring their libel action against Imran while Botham alone was suing him for *The Sun* article, claiming that Imran had called him a cheat. At times the trial became bogged down with technical details of what happens to a cricket ball when it is scratched, has its seam picked or lip salve is applied. The issue of what constitutes cheating in cricket became crucial and the darker side of cricket was publicly exposed, with successive players, including England captain Mike Atherton and ex-test cricketer and television commentator, Geoffrey Boycott, admitting that ball tampering was part and parcel of the game. At the end of the day it was a tussle between two cricket giants with egos to match who refused to back down once heated words were exchanged over what is cheating in their sport.

This was the second time Lamb had been in a libel action. He was fined £5,000 by the Test and County Cricket Board after accusing Pakistani bowlers of ball tampering in 1992. The following year he was sued for libel by former Northamptonshire and Pakistani paceman Sarfraz Nawaz. The case was settled out of court but effectively ended his England career after 79 Tests, three as captain.[148]

In which of these situations can cheating be identified? Are the actions cheating when institutionalised over a period into the working culture of the particular sport.[149] Do these examples illustrate the inadequacies of the internal rules of sport and maybe the need for the law to intervene or does it in fact identify the flexibility of rules and the real problems of precise interpretation? This would seem to present a good example of rule scepticism, identified with the American jurisprudential movement, the American Realists, most prominent in the first half of this century, with its emphasis on the inherent problem of reducing law into a precise form of a set of rules. The American Realists promote scepticism concerning the possibility to make exact interpretations of legal or non-legal rules. The Atherton example is a good illustration of this problem. This scepticism may well provide caution to the view that the law can provide exact solutions to the problems of sport.

---

148 See 'Judge Raises Finger To Expansive Boycott', *The Guardian*, 27 July 1996, p 3 and 'Botham libel case: an exercise in futility', *The Guardian*, 1 August 1996, p 9. For other sporting libel cases see *Tolley v Fry* [1931] AC 333 (HL), *Williams v Reason* [1988] 1 WLR 96 (CA) (both concerning allegations of shamateurism).

149 See 'Par for the Courts', *The Guardian*, 28 April 1994 concerning cheating in golf and Greenberg, M and Gray, J, 'The Legal Aspects of the Tonya Harding Figure Skating Eligibility Controversy' (1994) 2(2) *Sport and the Law Journal* 16.

So a question needs to be asked: where the formal rules of sport and the informal working culture (an amalgam of (il)legitimate strategy and codes of ethics) are ineffective, does the law of the land have a role to play? An attempt will be made to provide an answer in the following section.

JURIDIFICATION OF SPORT

The argument as to whether sport needs law is one that has been discussed. Certainly in the past, sport has been seen as an area of social life that was removed from normal everyday life and as such should be treated as a separate area largely excluded from legal intervention. There are two types of legal intervention that need to be evaluated. One is government intervention through legislative and quasi-legislative action: the implementation of policy; the other is direct legal intervention via lawyers and the courts: the application of the existing substantive law.

The first method has been highlighted in the historical extracts showing that the State has always been involved in intervention in sport. Chapter 2 will consider the State's contemporary policy in sport. Although an explanation of why the law has a greater role in sport encompasses this first issue, it is the second method of legal intervention, the application of existing law and discrete 'sports law' by lawyers and the courts into the world of sport, where complex and varied causes are found and opinion differs as to the appropriateness of this greater intervention.

Both sport's informal and formal rules are subject to change which creates a dynamic relationship with new tactics being developed by sports coaches and participants.[150] This is the context within which the rules of law operate. The consequential tripartite amalgam of normative rules, sport rules/sport's working culture and the law, leads to many issues of demarcation.

A major issue with the intervention of the law into new 'sporting arenas' is the dangers of juridification, where what are intrinsically social relationships between humans within a 'social field' become imbued with legal values and become understood as constituting a legal relationship – social norms become legal norms.[151] If a dispute then befalls the parties, a legal remedy is seen as a primary remedy. This will invariably change the nature and perception of the dispute and the relational connection between the parties.

---

150 See 'Do not Change the Balls or Tinker with the Rules Please', *The Times*, 6 July 1994.

151 See Bourdieu, P, 'The Force of Law: Towards a Sociology of the Juridical Field' (1987) 38 *Hastings Law Review* 814.

Foster, K, 'Developments in Sporting Law'

Juridification ... at a simple level, it merely reproduces the traditional idea of private and public realms, with private areas increasingly being subject to public or judicial control, a move from voluntarism to legalism. But it offers also a more complex version which stresses the interaction as legal norms are used to reorder the power relations within the social arena.[152]

Sport is not alone as being a social field that has increasingly become legally regulated. The family has increasingly become regulated by the law; examples include the development of remedies for domestic violence particularly against women; the recognition of child abuse as a real social problem and the initiation of the Child Support Agency to bring to account errant fathers. There may be criticism of how the law actually works in these and connected areas but few would argue that the family should not be subject to this legal regulation. That law should never be involved in regulating sport is clearly absurd. The question is when and to what extent it should be involved, that is there are very debatable issues.

An important part of this process is the ability of lawyers to develop new areas of work. The involvement of lawyers in sport can be compared with their involvement in other environments where their participation is contested. As Bankowski and Mungham argue concerning tribunals of both a legal and a wider quasi-legal nature:

The creation and maintenance of legal problems by lawyers follows a ... pattern ... when 'proper' becomes synonymous with 'legal' and 'paid' then there is created a pressure to abandon extra-legal means of dispute settlement in favour of legal ones.[153]

Similarly Flood and Caiger in their examination of lawyers' rivalry with non-lawyers to control arbitration mechanisms in the construction industry argue:

Lawyers are in a strong position to effect colonisation because of their power over the discourse of legalism. They have the power of appropriation.[154]

The danger is that the law too easily becomes the primary regulatory mechanism to be used to provide remedies. However it is increasingly argued, particularly by Alan Hunt, that law is best understood in contemporary society, not in the classic formulation of English jurisprudence as a collection or model of rules but as a form of 'governance' or regulation. He stresses that this occurs not only through law but other quasi-legal and non-legal mechanisms:

---

152 *Ibid*, Foster (1993) p 108.

153 Bankowski, Z and Mungham, G, *Images of Law* (1976), London: Routledge, p 62.

154 Flood, J and Caiger, A, 'Lawyers and Arbitration: The Juridification of Construction Disputes' (1993) 56(3) *Modern Law Review* 412.

Hunt, A, 'Law as a Constitutive Mode of Regulation'

The model of law as regulation can be seen as a shift towards public law that focuses on the varied means whereby extensive fields of social life are made subject to regulatory intervention ... we should recognise the diversity of legal phenomena and avoid falling into the presumption of a unitary entity 'the law' ... On the one hand law exists as an increasingly detailed and particularistic regulation of ever more specific situations and relations in which any boundary between law and non-law is difficult if not impossible to identify. On the other hand this important recognition of the diversification and pluralisation of law and regulation should not lead us to forget about the role that law plays as the medium of an ever-expanding State.[155]

This view fits in with the interaction of law with the internal sporting rules. The reluctance of the courts until quite recently to judicially review sporting bodies internal rule-based decisions perhaps indicates the contrary view that sport should govern themselves and are separate from the law of the land. Law's increased intervention in sport in recent years provides the mix of legal and quasi-legal regulation.

Hunt uses the work of the French philosopher Michel Foucault[156] as the basis of some of his study of the sociology of governance. He sees Foucault's contention that though law was important in the pre-modern world as a form of control, in modern society (from the end of the 18th century), law has largely given way to 'governance' and 'policing', a more complex multidimensional form of regulation. One of Foucault's most persistent influences on political philosophy are his ideas on discipline and surveillance, in that increasingly the State uses bodies of knowledge to intervene as a form of power. As Hunt says:

... the picture that he is taken to have painted is of ever extending and ever more intrusive mechanisms of power that insert themselves into every nook and cranny of social and personal life.[157]

One aim of this for Foucault is the stated aim for increasing 'normalisation' and the search for new sites of disciplinary intervention. Can sport be seen as one of these sites needing regulation? Of course, some of the sociological perspectives discussed earlier see sport itself as a form of social control. In a wider context, Steve Redhead sees the law's intervention in popular culture generally (sport arguably being a part of this culture) as closely associated with the regulation of social activities that are considered to be morally reprehensible, a threat to social order.[158] The earlier historical extracts showed

155 Hunt, A, 'Law as a Consitutive Mode of Regulation', in *Explorations in Law and Society: Towards a Constitutive Theory of Law* (1993), London: Routledge, p 307.

156 Foucault, M, *Discipline and Punish: The Birth of the Prison* (1977), London: Penguin.

157 *Ibid*, Hunt (1993) p 288.

158 Also see Stanley, C, *Urban Excess and the Law: Capital Culture and Desire* (1996), London: Cavendish Publishing.

how this has occurred particularly concerning team sports, especially those seen as the wrong type, notably football and the control of the crowd. Redhead sees the regulation of football as a clear example. The work of Geoffrey Pearson[159] is pertinent with his focus on the State's control of football and surrounding culture by its construction as something that was a threat and should be feared, what Pearson calls 'respectable fears'. This construction of social problems has also been termed 'moral panics'.[160] Although football has persistently been subject to such condemnation, Redhead sees that much of popular culture has been censured since the end of the last century:

Redhead, S, *Unpopular Culture: The Birth of Law and Popular Culture*

The whole field of 'law and popular culture' (or law and 'play' to coin another phrase) is of increasing scholarly interest in the field of legal, social and cultural studies, not least in the massive body of regulatory instruments (court cases and statutes, local authority bylaws) now in place which require interpretation and application. In Britain, for instance, such laws seem to be literally everywhere. For example, consider the following Bills: the Entertainment (Increased Penalties) Act 1990 (dubbed the 'Bright' Bill or 'Acid House' Bill in the press) and its attack on the organisation of what have been called pay parties or legal or illegal 'raves'; the Football Spectators Act 1989 and its abortive compulsory identity card scheme to combat soccer hooliganism with its introduction of new measures to stop soccer fans travelling abroad and ban convicted offenders attending designated matches; the Football (Offences) Act 1991 with its attempt to outlaw racist abuse, pitch invasions and other 'hooligan' activity at domestic soccer matches; the strengthening of licensing laws to close down certain clubs through the Licensing Act 1988; the calls for changes in the environmental and other laws to curb the noise of all night dance parties and the nuisance of the 1990s folk devils such as 'New Age travellers' and 'ravers' in various parts of town and countryside ... the moral panics about ecstasy (MDMA), LSD, cannabis and other 'recreational' (as defined by users) drug taking amongst large swathes of late 20th century global youth. These regulatory regimes all exhibit familiar features of the relationship between law, market and the State in the 1990s and illustrate contemporary attempts to regulate, discipline and police popular culture in the late 20th century which apply generally to many countries outside the national boundaries from where specific examples are drawn. Indeed such boundaries are part of the problem, as technologies and other changes make control on such border/lines almost impossible. But these aspects of legal discourse are for some commentators plainly what might be termed more or less 'repressive' in that they are seen to be part of a larger network of what many theorists persist, even in the 1990s, in calling 'social control' through criminal justice and penal systems which have in the past been theorised as part of the 'law and order control culture'. In the cruder, over-simplified versions of this conception, the State, through law, is seen as

---

159 See Pearson, G, *Hooligan: A History of Respectable Fears* (1983), London: Macmillan.

160 See Cohen, S, for an explanation and analysis of moral panics in *Folk Devils and Moral Panics: The Creation of Mod Rockers* (1972), London: MacGibbon and Kee.

capable only of acting negatively – or repressively – against a group, class individual. Power is conceived in much of this mode of theorising as a thing, an instrument, which is wielded by one group, class or individual against another ... such theorisation of legal discourse and agency is often unsatisfactory – though Foucauldian alternative theorisations of the productivity of power can be equally problematic – especially when it is focusing on new instances of folk devils, moral panics or law and order campaigns.[161]

Moral panics can therefore be seen as having justified some legal intervention in sport. Their creation in popular culture and sport are produced by a complex amalgam of social pressures, the media having a central role in their amplification. Recent social examples are the allegations of satanic abuse, dangerous dogs, the widespread problem of road rage. Redhead presents a number that have justified State intervention in regulating popular culture. In sport, football has been the most prone to this effect.[162] The consequence is 'panic' law that is invariably ineffective and feckless. It fits in with the wider regulatory view of law colonising new social fields and expanding its sphere of influence.

COMPETING THEORIES

Two theoretical models of law's intervention have been presented. They may not necessarily be oppositional and can be potentially complementary.

The first model is that the law's involvement is an extension along the road of the civilising process in sport in addition to the internal constitutive sports rules. The law is providing a functional role in the context of the modern commercial complexity of sport. This fits in with a functionalist perspective on sport and society.

The second model is the law as a form of regulatory power, a form of control. Intervention is often legitimised in the context of the creation of moral panics.

Which is the most persuasive? One point can be made: the phenomenon of the greater activity of lawyers in sport is one that can fit into both models. A cynical view is that lawyers will always follow where there is work and where money can be made.

161 Redhead, S, *Unpopular Culture: The Birth of Law and Popular Culture* (1995), Manchester University Press, pp 7–8.

162 See Greenfield, S and Osborn, G, 'Criminalising Football Supporters: Ticket Touts and the Criminal Justice and Public Order Act 1994' (1995) 3(3) *Sport and the Law Journal* 36; Greenfield, S and Osborn, G, 'After the Act; The (Re)construction and Regulation of Football Fandom' (1996) 1(1) *Journal of Civil Liberties* 7; Greenfield, S and Osborn, G, 'When the Whites Go Marching In? Racism and Resistance in English Football' (1996) 6(2) *Marquette Sports Law Journal* 315; Gardiner, S, 'Eric Cantona: Sport, Racism and the Limits of the Law' in McDonald, I and Carrington, B (eds), *Land of Hope and Glory? Racism and British Sport*, Leicester University Press (forthcoming 1998).

SPORT AND THE LAW OR SPORTS LAW?

In the context of the increasing body of law that has been specifically developed for sport generally and sports such as football in particular, the last section in this chapter will consider whether there is any such identified legal subject known as 'sports law' or whether it is more accurate to talk of merely a relationship of 'sport and the law':

Grayson, E, *Sport and the Law*

No subject exists which jurisprudentially can be called sports law. As a soundbite headline, shorthand description, it has no juridical foundation; for common law and equity creates no concept of law exclusively relating to sport. Each area of law applicable to sport does not differ from how it is found in any other social or jurisprudential category ... When sport hits the legal and political buffers, conventional and ordinary principles affecting the nature of the appropriate sporting issue concerned including parliamentary legislation are triggered into action.[163]

Woodhouse, C, 'The Lawyer in Sport: Some Reflections'

I have often said there is no such thing as sports law. Instead it is the application to sport situations of disciplines such as contract law, administrative law (disciplinary procedures), competition law, intellectual property law, defamation and employment law ... I hope the next generation of sports lawyers will enjoy it as much as I have over the past 25 years. But do remember there is no such thing as sports law.[164]

Barnes, J, *Sports and the Law in Canada*

Sports law deals with State interests and the resolution of conflicts according to general legal norms. Sports maintain internal rules and structures to regulate play and organise competition. In sports law, the wider legal system impinges on this traditionally private sphere and subjects the politics of the sports game to the politics of the law game. The result is a double drama as the deep human concern for play combines with the concern for social justice. Sports law addresses basic ethical issues of freedom, fairness, equality, safety and economic security. The subject matter of sports law includes State control and subsidy of sport, rights of access, disciplinary powers and procedures, commercial and property rights, employment relations and compensation for injuries. Sports law is grounded in the material dimensions of sport and includes a study of the life and times of its heroic practitioners.

State interest in sport and recreation has a long history and there are early Canadian instances of civil litigation and prosecutions for violent play but the flowering of sports law dates from the 1970s when a 'daily barrage of socio-legal crises' began to fill newspaper sports pages. Law, politics and finance

---

163 *Ibid*, Grayson (1994) p xxxvii.
164 Woodhouse, C, 'The Lawyer in Sport: Some Reflections' (1996) 4(3) *Sport and the Law Journal* 14.

have since become prominent features of sports culture and various factors explain this trend: sports now offer lucrative commercial rewards so that participants look to protect their economic interests through legal and industrial relations processes; governments have addressed social problems in sport and have been involved in sports administration; and sports have been affected by emancipation movements seeking wider recognition of legal and constitutional rights. Sports management has always relied on legal power to control the enterprise and retain the prime slice of the pie. Conflict has grown as the underpaid, the injured and the excluded have acquired remedies and gained the organisational strength necessary to further claims. The legal profession has been happy to appropriate this conflict.

The most familiar court battles occurred in the North American professional sports leagues. Some disputes involved the community interests affected by the establishment or relocation of team franchises but most cases dealt with the rights and freedoms of players. Litigation in the United States has partly emancipated professional athletes from restraints that limit them in selling their services to the highest bidder. The formation of rival leagues first offered alternative markets and anti-trust actions and collective bargaining then brought further mobility and prosperity. These developments inevitably affected Canadian members of American based leagues and the new freedoms served as models for Canadian athletes. Litigation has not, however, been limited to the major leagues. Sports organisations at all levels in Canada have been forced to respond to members who are more willing to seek judicial remedies and question restrictive regulations and disciplinary powers.

After a quarter century of intense conflict, litigation fatigue may now have set in and there is some yearning to revert to a lost 'pre-legal' ideal. The dissatisfaction with sports law reveals itself in public impatience over labour disputes and the lofty levels of professional salaries but a more concrete threat comes from the excesses of the war on drugs. Some feel that general legal principles should not intrude unduly into the sports world and that athletes' rights can only go so far.[165]

Opie, H, 'Sports Associations and their Legal Environment'

'Sports law' is one of those fields of law which is applied law as opposed to pure or theoretical law. Rather than being a discipline with a common legal theme such as criminal law, equity or contract law, sports law is concerned with how law in general interacts with the activity known as sport. Hence, the label applied law. Yet there is an increasing body of law which is specific to sport. This produces debate among scholars over whether one should use the term sports law, which indicates a legal discipline in its own right or 'sport and law' which reflects the multifarious and applied nature of the field. No doubt the general public would regard this as one of those sterile debates which are so attractive to inhabitants of ivory towers – if the public bothered to think about it!

---

165 Barnes, J, *Sports and the Law in Canada* (1996), Toronto: Butterworths, pp 2–3.

Sport and the law is not the only field of law to be debated in this way. As new fields of law emerge it is almost customary for them to undergo this debate until they have been around long enough to establish themselves. This leads to an important observation: namely systematic attention to sport and law is a relatively new phenomenon in Australia. It is certainly something which has occurred only during the last 15 years. It is rare to find any seminar papers or learned articles on the topic prior to that period. Those which existed were regarded or presented almost as curiosities at their time of publication. There seems to have always been court cases concerning sport but these were isolated and are insignificant compared with the variety and volume of court proceedings that are to be observed today. A contributing factor to this prior inactivity is that in some fields of law the courts pursued a policy of non-intervention by holding that sport disputes were private matters which did not raise justiciable issues. Any informed observer will realise that the position is vastly different today. What has produced this change?[166]

These four accounts present alternative views on this issue: sport and the law or sports law. Grayson believes there is no such identifiable area of sports law. Woodhouse agrees. In a qualified way Barnes agrees, stating that 'there is really no distinct 'sports law' but the proliferation of sports legislation, litigation and arbitral decisions has led to some special doctrine'.[167] Opie believes that it is possible to see a recognisable sports law, an applied area of law and notes the debate concerning whether an 'identifiable legal subject' exists has occurred in other developing and burgeoning areas.

This last position is a strong one. The development of this subject area of law's involvement in sport is part of a process that has happened to all legal areas in the past. Labour or employment law is a subject area that has only achieved relatively recent recognition. It has its origins in contract law in the employment context but no one would doubt that with the plethora of legislation during the post-war era regulating the workplace, it has become a subject area in its own right. Passing through various incarnations such as industrial law, it is now a mature legal subject.

The process by which legal areas are identified, constituted and named is a complex one and often to some extent arbitrary. There is no official recognition procedure. It is a process of legal practitioners and academics recognising the growing application of law to a new area of social life. Computer law is a good example to analogise with sports law. It is a relatively new legal subject, where specific laws dealing with this new technology are recent developments. In Britain two pieces of legislation, The Data Protection Act 1984 concerning access to information on computers and the Computer Misuse Act 1990 concerning criminalisation of unauthorised access to computer systems, have developed due to the inadequacies of the existing law to effectively regulate. As far as unauthorised access to computers or hacking,

---

166 Opie, H, 'Sports Associations and their Legal Environment' in McGregor-Lowndes, M, Fletcher, K and Sievers, S (eds), *Legal Issues for Non-Profit Associations* (1996), Sydney: LBC Information Services, pp 74–94.

167 *Ibid*, Barnes (1996) p 2, n 4.

as it is commonly known, unsuccessful attempts had been made to apply the law of criminal damage to penalise such activities. The need for new legislation was overwhelmingly supported.

A significant body of computer law has developed. It falls into the 'applied law' classification that Opie describes. The development of legal areas which involves essentially the application of pure legal areas in the context of a human activity, in this case sport, move from a loose association such as sport and the law to a more recognisable body of law such as sports law. It is true to say that it is largely an amalgam of interrelated legal disciplines involving such areas as contract, taxation, employment, competition and criminal law but dedicated legislation and case law has developed and will continue to do so. As an area of academic study and extensive practitioner involvement, the time is right to accept that a new legal area has been born – sports law.

CONCLUSION

Opie believes that there are a number of main reasons for law's growing importance in sport: its increasing commercialisation has led to more professional sports participants and a vast importance as an advertising medium; greater governmental intervention and consequential legislation; and less acceptance of injury and violence. Certainly within the commercialised world of contemporary sport where large amounts of money have become available to sports administrators through sponsorship and the selling of television rights, all areas of law are involved in the regulation of sport. As with most areas of social life, legal regulation and litigation are here to stay as a reality of modern life. The law's involvement is often predicated on the argument that the expertise and values found within law can contribute to the running and organisation of modern sport.

Both Barnes and Opie provide clear commercial reasons, amongst others, for law's greater involvement in the US and Australia. There does seem to be a strong complementary relationship between greater regulation of sport by the law and its increased commercialisation and commodification. This has happened in the sense of increased marketability of sport in terms of advertising and sponsorship together with greater professionalisation of sport. The enormous changes in the world of rugby are a good illustration of the latter. Rugby Union has moved from a notional amateur status to a professional one since the end of 1995. Rugby league has been re-packaged to suite the demands of television. Both of these events have led to many legal issues and large amounts of litigation, both in Britain and abroad. The concept of commercialisation and commodification of modern sport will be discussed in detail in Chapters 5 and 6.

To conclude, this chapter has shown that in Britain and elsewhere, there are also other reasons for law's intervention in sport. The legal regulation of sport reflects the increase to regulate generally, with interaction between different levels of normative rules. Sports law is an area on the periphery of the legal domain and as such, the law's role in regulating sport is open to continual analysis, debate and evaluation. Lawyers have seen sport as a social field ripe for colonisation and exploitation. Finally, many 'problems' in sport such as drug use and violence are presented as 'moral panics' in need of legal regulation.

CHAPTER TWO

SPORT AND THE ROLE OF THE STATE IN BRITAIN

INTRODUCTION

Compared with a number of other European countries, the State's involvement in sport in Britain is fairly minimal. The history of legal prohibition of certain types of sport has been chronicled earlier – with the State playing a reasonably active role. In promoting and effectively managing sport, the State has played a very passive role. It is sad to report that one of the most obvious examples of direct State intervention in sport in Britain has been in response to a number of sports stadium disasters (almost all concerning football) that have occurred during the last 50 years with official reports after the 1946 disaster at Bolton where 33 spectators died, the 1972 disaster at Ibrox in Glasgow where 66 died, the Bradford fire in 1985 where 55 died, and most notably the 1989 report, the Taylor Report on the Hillsborough disaster where 96 Liverpool supporters died. It was not until this last report that the British government acted positively to legislate as far as sports stadium safety is concerned.

In light of the lack of success in recent years for Britain's national sporting teams and the sporadic accomplishment of individual sports men and women, especially highlighted by the poor performance by British sportsmen and women in the 1996 Atlanta Olympics, the debate concerning how the State can play a more effective role in sport has gained considerable immediacy. Increasing pressure has been brought on the State to provide greater financial and material assistance to British sport.

This chapter will initially consider the framework of the State's intervention in sport in Britain. The State has a number of different roles in sport. This can be through various methods including financial support. The role of bodies such as the Sports Council will be discussed. The regulatory framework within the international and the increasingly influential European context will be examined.

Sport as a form of social policy being used to fight crime will be considered and the relationship between sport and formal and informal politics will be examined. The State can regulate and it can also prohibit sport. A number of different sports issues will be considered and the argument of how the State should intervene through social policy and legal methods will be evaluated.

FRAMEWORK OF SPORT IN BRITAIN

Until the Second World War, other than Acts of prohibition of some sporting activity, there was virtually no direct State involvement in the framework and organisation of sport. All that existed were a number of private federations for particular sports, many for the major sports, having their origins at the end of the 19th century. These organisations were on the whole controlled by establishment figures who had close connections with the politically powerful. One significant development was the creation of what is now the Central Council of Physical Recreation (CCPR) in 1935, initiated as a non-governmental voluntary organisation, an 'umbrella body' of sporting organisations funded from private sources.

In 1957 the CCPR appointed a committee to report on 'the future of sporting administration in promoting the general welfare of the community'. The subsequent Wolfenden Report in 1960 ended with 57 paragraphs of conclusions and recommendations. It indirectly led to other key developments in the State intervention of sport: the appointment of a Minster of Sport in 1962 and the birth of the Sports Council in 1966.

Today the CCPR and the Sports Council are the two main organisations enforcing sports policy in Britain.[1] There are a number of other bodies that are worthy of mention. A British Sports Forum has been in existence since the early 1990s. There are organisations such as the National Coaching Foundation which provides educational and advisory services for coaches in all sports. In addition to the many sports organisations under the umbrella of the CCPR, there is the British Olympic Association, founded in 1905, which is the National Olympic Committee for Britain.

The legal structure and form of the large number of British sports federations and governing bodies needs also to be explained. They are essentially private bodies and have no statutory base. The ability of the courts to question their decisions will be discussed later. They have constitutions that indicate the relationship between the organisation and individual leagues, clubs and players in any particular sport. There is a great deal of variety between different governing bodies, but they share some common elements, especially the need to conform to the requirements of international sporting federations.

---

1 See Hargreaves, J, *Sport, Power and Culture* (1986), London: Polity Press for an analysis of the operation of these bodies and State intervention in general.

The Central Council of Physical Recreation

The CCPR, as the representative body of many British sports governing bodies, has as its modern aims:

- to constitute a standing forum of national governing and representative bodies of sport and physical recreation;
- to collectively, or through special groups where appropriate, formulate and promote measures to improve and develop sport;
- to support the work of the specialist sports bodies and to bring them together with other interested organisations;
- to act as a consultative body to the Sports Council.[2]

The day to day work of the CCPR includes representing its members interests concerning general sporting issues; analysing issues in areas such as the financing of sport and the impact of European policy; mounting campaigns in areas such as sport and drugs and fair play in sport; liaising with central and local government; advising on legal matters; liaising with the media; offering financial management and advice; providing insurance; encouraging international contacts; providing information; obtaining sponsorship for sport; serving professional sport through the Institute of Professional Sport; promoting sport in the community; and organising charity.[3] In early 1997, the CCPR produced a Manifesto for Sport in the run-up to the General Election. It claimed that:

> If improvements are to be achieved for British sports then a much closer partnership needs to be established between government – local and national – and the governing and representative bodies of sport in developing national and local strategies.[4]

The Sports Council

The Sports Council has gone through a number of changes since its inception in 1966. In contrast to the CCPR, it is a publicly funded official advisory body to the government. Since 1972, the structure was modified with the creation of the Great Britain Sports Council and three additional Councils for the other parts of the United Kingdom (Scotland, Wales and Northern Ireland) with extended powers. At the end of 1996, The Great Britain Sports Council was divided into the UK Sports Council and the English Sports Council, with the

2 'CCPR Memorandum of Association' (1972), London: Central Council of Physical Recreation.

3 *The CCPR: What it Does and How it Operates* (1995), London: Central Council of Physical Recreation.

4 *A Manifesto for Sport: A Sporting Future* (1997), London: Central Council of Physical Recreation.

three other home country sports councils continuing unchanged. They are all national, non-departmental public bodies (sometimes known as quangos), which receive funding from, and are accountable to, the Department of Culture, Media and Sport, the renamed Department of National Heritage since the 1997 General Election. There is a Secretary of State for this Department and a Parliamentary Under-Secretary of State, known as the Minister for Sport. The House of Commons scrutinises the work of the United Kingdom Sports Council and the English Sports Council via the relevant Select Committee and the Public Accounts Committee.

UK Sports Council

The UK Sports Council has a small staff and acts as a co-ordinating body for the four home country Sports Councils (England, Northern Ireland, Scotland and Wales).[5] It deals with areas of common interest at UK level. These include:

- preparation of a strategy for UK sport;
- international relations, including attracting major events to the UK, work with the Council of Europe and marketing of UK sports expertise abroad;
- performance and excellence issues at UK level including co-ordination of the proposed British Academy of Sport;
- doping control including services to governing bodies and educational programmes.

English Sports Council

The English Sports Council focuses on three main policy areas. These are:

Young people. The English Sports Council, in partnership with the Youth Sports Trust and others, targets resources through the National Junior Sports Programme to schemes which support youth sports whether in schools, through partnerships between schools and sports bodies or with youth agencies.

Development of excellence. The English Sports Council works to develop performance and excellence in sport through support to governing bodies of sport, the six National Sports Centres and the proposed British Sports Academy.[6]

National Lottery. The English Sports Council distributes grants from the Lottery Sports Fund and provides advice to applicants on sports facility planning, design and management. From March 1997, lottery funds have been

---

5   See its guide, 'Sport and Legislation in the UK', 2nd edn (1996), London: The UK Sports Council.

6   See, *England, the Sporting Nation: a Strategy, Consultation Document* (1997), London: The English Sports Council ESC/646/2M/2/97.

available for revenue grants to individuals as well as capital grants for facilities.[7]

All English Sports Council work, including the promotion of women in sport, sport for people with disabilities and sustainable sport in the countryside is developed as an integral part of the above policy priorities. There are 10 regional offices in England delivering the Council's policies and programmes.

Whereas the main emphasis during the 1970s, 1980s and early 1990s was on promoting a 'sport for all' policy,[8] in the past, the Sports Councils had as their prime objectives:

> ... to encourage mass participation in sport and to promote excellence in sporting achievement. These aims are interlocked. The greater the number of people participating in sport the more chance of excellence emerging. The higher the achievements of the top performers, the greater the number of those who will be inspired to emulate them.[9]

There have also been specific programmes targeting women,[10] ethnic minorities,[11] the disabled[12] and children.[13] Since the mid-1990s, there has been a shift towards promoting excellence in sport with the government indicating a more pro-active role in sport. The then Department of National Heritage published a discussion paper in 1995:

Major, J, 'Introduction to Sport: Raising the Game'

Some people say that sport is a peripheral and minor concern. I profoundly disagree. It enriches the lives of the thousands of millions of people of all ages around the world who enjoy it. Sport is a central part of Britain's National Heritage. We invented the majority of the world's great sports. And most of those we did not invent, we codified and helped to popularise throughout the world. It could be argued that 19th century Britain was the cradle of a leisure revolution every bit as significant as the agricultural and industrial revolutions we launched in the century before.

Sport is a binding force between generations and across borders. But, by a miraculous paradox, it is at the same time one of the defining characteristics of nationhood and of local pride. We should cherish it for both those reasons.

---

7   See 'Guide to the Lottery Sports Fund' (1996), London: The Sports Council SC/605/12M/6/96.

8   *Sport in the Nineties: New Horizons* (1993), London: The Sports Council SC/1970/15M/9/93.

9   The Great Britain Sports Council Royal Charter 1972.

10 *Women and Sport* (1994), London: The Sports Council SC/285/10M/3/94 and 'The Brighton Declaration' (1994), London: The Sports Council.

11 *Black and Ethnic Minorities and Sport: Policy and Objectives* (1994), London: The Sports Council SXC/213/10M/6/94.

12 *People with Disabilities and Sport: Policy and Current/Planned Action* (1993), London: The Sports Council.

13 *Young People and Sport: Policy and Frameworks for Action* (1993), London: The Sports Council.

In this initiative I put perhaps highest priority on plans to help all our schools improve their sport. Sport is open to all ages – but it is most open to those who learn to love when they are young. Competitive sport teaches valuable lessons which last for life. Every game delivers both a winner and a loser. Sportsmen must learn to be both. Sport only thrives if both parties play by the rules, and accept the results with good grace. It is one of the best means of learning how to live alongside others and make a contribution as part of a team. It improves health and opens the door to new friendships.

But this is not to be too dispassionate about sport. Above all, it produces pure enjoyment for those who play and those who watch. Frankly, for me, it needs no other recommendation than that.

... Finally, I want to help our best sportsmen and women make the very best of their talents. I take as much pride as anyone in seeing them lead the world. I did not want to see them having to go abroad to learn how to exploit their talents. That is why our new proposals include ideas to improve talent spotting and talent support right here at home. With the help of the National Lottery we will create a new British Academy of Sport with world class facilities, to help sporting stars, and will support it by a developing network of regional and sports academics to bring on the best.[14]

The document supports a more specific role for sport in schools,[15] colleges and universities and a move to supporting excellence in sport more rigorously. The debate about the exact formulation of the new British Academy of Sport has not been without controversy.[16] The tangible success of this approach of supporting excellence in Australia with the National Institute of Sport in Canberra has been used as an example of how the State should support modern sport. This has been a debate concerning the appropriate balance between the selective supporting of sporting excellence and the more general supporting of 'sport for all' policies.[17]

The first policy briefing of the newly formed English Sports Council reflects this shift of emphasis:

English Sports Council: 'Policy Briefing'

We aim to lead the development of sport in England by influencing and serving the public, private and commercial sectors. Our aim is:

– more people involved in sport;
– more places to play sport;
– higher standards of performance in sport, leading to more medals.

14 *Sport: Raising the Game* (1995), London: Department of Heritage.
15 One subsequent policy implemented has been the *School Community Sport Initiative* (1996), London: English Sports Council SC/626R/9M/10/96.
16 Hawkey, I, 'A £100m School for Scandal', *The Sunday Times*, 23 February 1997.
17 Concerning debate see *Sport: Raising the Game* (1995); *Creating Excellence in British Sport: Labour's Proposals for a British Academy of Sport* (1994), London: The Labour Party; *All to Play For* (1992), London: Liberal Democrats; Allison, L, 'Sport for the Best, not All', *The Guardian*, 29 September 1994; 'Sport for All: In Pursuit of Excellence', *The Guardian*, 14 March 1995.

The English Sports Council is committed to playing the major part in realising a national vision to make England the sporting nation. Our core purpose is to put English sport on a sure footing through working with sports bodies, local authorities and the private sector.[18]

SPORT AND CRIME

Sport can be seen as an increasingly important part of cultural life that needs to be supported and cultivated by the State. Financial support is vital, but perhaps changes in ethos and attitudes are more important. John Major supported the positive aspects of sport in terms of providing a general education to the ways of the world. He considered the playing of competitive sport by the young as particularly important for later life. Connected to this are the social policy claims made for sport as an effective tool for fighting social problems such as crime and juvenile delinquency. There is a competing view of the relationship between sport and crime:

McVicar, J, 'Violence in Britain: This sporting life of crime'

Despite this upsurge of concern about violence in sport, playing these games continues to be seen as character building; an assumption reinforced by John Major's recent governmental commitment to promoting excellence in sport. Doubtless he wants to incorporate it in his English vision of village greens and early morning mists. Yet one of the most glaring links between sport and violence is the way so many in organised crime began as useful sportsmen and continue to show an avid interest in sport throughout their criminal career.

This connection receives scant attention from social scientists, lawyers, sports administrators or government officials; yet go into any prison gymnasium and who is in the thick of the action? Not rapists – except Mike Tyson – but robbers, gangsters and others who figure in the criminal pecking order. Similar observations can be made at any big fight or in the stands at Highbury where north London's leading criminal family and their favoured hit man can be seen cheering on Arsenal. I was reminded of all this by two recent books by our great men of crime. In *Memoirs Of A Life Of Crime*, Mad Frankie Fraser talks about his lifelong obsession with boxing and football (he played park football into his 50s). Now in his mid 70s, Frank is a regular at Highbury and is ringside at all the big fights. And this love and involvement in sport is virtually the norm among heavy-duty professional criminals. Take the latest piece of – forgive me for mentioning the name – Kray memorabilia, *The Krays' Lieutenant* by Albert Donaghue. In this, one of the twins' old henchmen talks about Ronnie and Reggie being like 'two hunting dogs' as they sniffed out victims for their brainless mayhem; but their taste and capacity for violence had been honed during their long careers as amateur and professional boxers.

---

18 English Sports Council: Policy Briefing No 1 Ref No 0660 (March 1997), London: The English Sports Council. Also see *Sport: Raising the Game – The First Year Report* (1996), London: Department of National Heritage.

Obviously, an apprenticeship in sport is neither sufficient nor necessary for graduating into organised crime. But, given other factors, a solid grounding in sport can and often does make crime an attractive proposition. What factors? Well, first, this relationship applies almost solely to males: organised crime, like physical sport, is virtually a male preserve. Secondly sport and crime tend to coalesce only at the bottom of society. Sportsmen from higher up the social scale often develop – for example, through playing rugby – a hypermasculine identity but other circumstantial factors, such as family background, education and their social networks, militate against this being conducive to a life of crime. Finally, the sporting apprenticeship should not be too successful, as that is likely to catapult the athlete into a sporting career, diverting him from the temptations of crime. If Ronnie and Reggie Kray had been champion boxers, they would almost certainly not have become murderers, nor, as a consequence, spent most of their lives in prison.

What is it about physical sports, though, that helps equip the young plebeian male for a life of crime? What qualities does it impart that make him better at crime and more likely to choose it as a career? (Incidentally, career criminals are nothing to do with the stage army of petty criminals who clog the courts and overcrowd the prisons. These inadequates invariably have disturbed upbringings that render them incapable of playing anything organised or disciplined; they are neither good at sport or crime.) Contact sports, which are premised on mock war or combat, are not solely about orchestrating warrior virtues but the latter are clearly by-products of boxing, rugby, football and so on. Even if some don't teach a youngster how to look after himself, they all increase his strength and speed, his physical prowess. Males from the lowest level of society, though, find such qualities far more useful than their more socially privileged peers because violence, and its threat, figures far more in the regulation of their social life than it does on other social levels. Violent skills, even familiarity with violence, fitness, strength and so on, are also functional in the commission of crime. They confer, as it were, occupational advantages on the career criminal. Moreover, a capacity or potential for violence is also important in regulating relationships between criminals. Career criminals are enmeshed in a network of criminal relationships, the integrity of which rests upon their nature and content being hidden from the police. Thus all enduring criminal groups develop a prohibition against cooperating with law enforcement officials and others, such as journalists, who would be likely to pass on information to the police. This is the cornerstone of the criminal way of life.[19]

Robins, D, 'Sport and crime prevention: the evidence of research'

The idea that engaging in sports and outdoor activities has a morally redemptive quality was very popular with Victorian social reformers. Bold claims are sometimes made today. But how effective are sports and outdoor pursuits in crime prevention?

---

19 McVicar, J, 'Violence in Britain: This sporting life of crime', *The Guardian*, 19 September 1995, p 6.

Mistaken assumptions

The assumption that participation in sport or the provision of sports facilities affects levels of delinquency, is made in the absence of any supporting evidence. Coalter (1987), in his review of the literature on the subject commissioned by the Scottish Sports Council felt 'unable to conclude a correlation between high level of sports participation/low level of delinquency holds good in the UK'. Mason and Wilson alluded to the myriad of variables that have to be taken into account before the relation between sport and delinquency can be ascertained. My own (1990) study concluded that there is no sound theoretical basis for the use of sport and outdoor adventure activities to combat or prevent juvenile crime.

The view that participation in sport has little effect is shared by many of those who work professionally with offenders. Many are deeply sceptical of sport as prevention. But the power of the sports lobby is strong. Not for the first time, the findings of the researchers and the experiences of the practitioners are at odds with the decisions of the policy makers.

Sport as prevention

The use of sports, games and rigorous PE sessions are just as much the core feature of today's 'young offender institutions' as they were of the borstals. The use of outdoor adventure in treatment programmes for youth at risk is also commonplace. Considerable amounts of public funds and private charitable donations are deployed in this direction. When asked to propose solutions for young offenders who for the most part are destined to spend their lives trying to survive in the jungles of the cities, politicians of all political persuasions will evoke windswept rock faces and speak of Challenges Overcome and Lessons Learnt. Even Britain's leading expert on young offenders, Professor David Farrington of Cambridge University, has invoked the supporting, and discredited, safety valve theory expounded by the Victorians by suggesting that 'if offending is linked to boredom, excitement seeking and impulsiveness then it might be reduced by some kinds of community or recreational programmes that provide socially approved opportunities for excitement and risk-taking'. For your average tearaway a socially approved 'buzz' is a contradiction in terms. This sort of thinking also implies that the best way to handle hyped up, manic and self destructive kids, is to give them more and better opportunities to 'act out'.

The belief in 'sport as prevention' also occurs in community development capital programmes aimed at improving sport and recreational facilities in deprived areas. This approach aims to reduce delinquency rates by encouraging a positive use of leisure time. There is of course nothing objectionable about greater investment in sport and recreational provision in these areas. But it cannot be stressed enough that there is no evidence of concomitant reductions in juvenile crime following such developments. On the contrary, gleaming sports centres have become the foci for young people's negative projections and the targets for violent attacks.

Failed dreams

In October 1990 the French high rise suburb of Vaulx en Velins was engulfed in a week of bloody clashes between police and local youths, during which new community facilities were set on fire and destroyed. Immediately before the disturbances a brand new sports centre, including a gymnasium and a swimming pool, had been opened in a euphoric mood of self-congratulation. A climbing wall inaugurated a few days earlier had been seen as the culmination of a successful programme based on the idea of providing constructive sports pursuits for people with time on their hands. At the height of the disturbances, several hundred riot police had to be deployed to protect the sports centre.

Some new treatment programmes attempt to blend the joys of sport and outdoor adventure with group confrontation therapy techniques. Sending 'bad boys' up mountains to find themselves, confronting childhood trauma with more trauma in group therapy: these are the alternatives to the customary verbal beating by the magistrate followed by the custodial sentence. I have found that advocates of such programmes are often propelled by a sort of aggressive optimism which acts as a defence against the hopelessness felt when confronting the destructive nihilism of criminalised youth. (Of course this is preferable to the attitude adopted by the present Home Secretary, Mr Michael Howard. He appears to be driven purely by a need to punish children.)

Policy makers and criminal justice professionals need to be reminded of the essential futility of sports and outdoor pursuits, the fact that they make no direct contribution to the wealth of the community, or to a fairer society. At the risk of sounding old fashioned, to privilege such programmes is to denigrate more cerebral activities. Intellectual qualities – a sceptical, questioning attitude towards authority and convention, broadening horizons, acquiring a more educated view of society – are not required. The old socialist belief in the educational, and intellectual, advance of working-class youth has been abandoned.

There is no evidence that participation in physical endeavour based programmes, whether punitive or 'liberal', prevents criminality. But another incontrovertible fact is that sports and games are massively popular. A staggering three million people play football on a regular basis. Every youth worker and prison officer knows that football is a priceless lowest common denominator of activity designed to hold the attention of young men who are otherwise uncooperative, and who have successfully resisted the lessons of the classroom. The sad consequence of the failure to find real educational solutions for young offenders is that the purely instrumental aspects of sport become the main rationale for provision.[20]

---

20   Robins, D, 'Sport and crime prevention: the evidence of research' (1996) 23 *Criminal Justice Matters* 26 Spring. Also see Coalter, F, *Sport and Delinquency* (1987) Unpublished; Mason, G and Wilson, P, *Sport Recreation and Juvenile Crime* (1988) Australian Institute of Criminology; Robins, D, *Sport as Prevention* (1990), Oxford Centre for Criminal Research; Farrington, D, 'Implications of criminal career research for the prevention of offending' (1990) 13 *Journal of Adolesence* 93; Jones, V, 'Football and Crime Prevention' and Dulop, D, 'Can Sport Reduce Crime Amongst Young People?' both (1996) 23 *Criminal Justice Matters* 24 Spring.

The view that sport can be the magical cure for juvenile crime is naive. Participation in sporting endeavour can of course be a positive channelling of energies and can help teach positive values about life. It is unlikely to have any impact upon the underlying social reasons for criminality. The causes of crime are highly complex and contested. Sport has a role to play in helping fight crime, but one has to be realistic about its limitations.

SPORT AND POLITICS

Within both the national and the international community, the relationship between sport and formal politics is complex. The argument that sport is apolitical in the sense of being neutral and value-free in terms of cultural values was considered in Chapter 1. The argument that sport is separate from formal politics is one that is considered now. There are many examples where sport has become a part of the political arena and has been 'used' for political ends:

Monnington, T, 'Politicians and Sport: Uses and Abuses'

The characteristic forceful intervention of Mrs Thatcher in policy implementation, which was much in evidence during the passage of the Football Spectators Bill, had been similarly apparent earlier in her administration in 1980, again in the sports arena. The major debate in international politics in 1980 was the Soviet Union's actions in Afghanistan. It was not only the intervention of that country in the domestic affairs of another sovereign State, but also the reported atrocities perpetrated there that aroused international concern. Direct action was impossible by either the British or American governments. In an endeavour to cause as much embarrassment to the Soviet government as possible the Carter administration in the USA implemented a boycott of the forthcoming Olympic Games in Moscow that summer. Mrs Thatcher intervened personally in support of the American Games boycott and called on British athletes and the British Olympic Association to boycott the Games also.

The very limited success of this British boycott is again well documented history, but its significance less so. The real diplomatic value of the American boycott in influencing the government of the USSR, according to a study by J H Frey, was minimal. He revealed that analysis of top level contacts between the USA and USSR governments around the time of the Moscow Games made no reference to the boycott. The use of sport in this context was more for media and public consumption.

The consequence for the British political scene was not only an early indication of Thatcher's tendency to become involved directly in a wide range of policy matters, but also her willingness to ride roughshod over the heads of her ministers. The then Minister for Sport, Hector Munroe, was not even called to speak in the House of Commons debate on the Moscow Olympics, held in March 1980.

For Mrs Thatcher her intervention into the sporting arena proved to be a political disaster. Although she was not prepared to go as far as Jimmy Carter in withdrawing the British competitors from the Games, she did consider seizing the passports of British competitors until advised as to the likely illegality of such an action. Attempts to persuade the British Olympic Association to refuse to send a team met with a frosty response.

Threats of dismissal were even made to members of the British team who were public employees if they chose to take their holidays at a time that would allow them to travel to Moscow for the Games. Several of the athletes faced with this threat resigned from their jobs rather than acquiesce to this overt pressure. In the end, with only a limited number of enforced absences, a British team attended the Games, competing under the Olympic flag. For the British government and Mrs Thatcher in particular the entire incident was an embarrassment; an example of political naivety and a failed attempt to bring British sport into the Cold War political arena.

Five years later, when the Heysel Stadium incident was debated in Cabinet, it was Mrs Thatcher and her senior ministers who were involved, not Colin Moynihan. Moynihan had, as Macfarlane suggested, 'become a member of the smallest and most unimportant trade union in the House, the Trade Union of Ministers with special responsibility for Sport'.

The forceful diplomatic stand that Mrs Thatcher took with respect to the Soviet intervention into Afghanistan and her support for the American boycott of the Moscow Olympics contrasts with her position on South Africa. She maintained the support of the British government for the Gleneagles Agreement signed by Callaghan in 1977, which discouraged sporting links with South Africa. But she has often been criticised as selective in her isolation policy with respect to that country by maintaining diplomatic and trade links. Sport was apparently an easy public policy weapon, without any real diplomatic or political recoil, to express the British government's opposition to another country's conduct in its domestic affairs.

Mrs Thatcher's reluctance to take such a firm stand over sporting contacts with South Africa as she had with respect to the USSR in 1980, along with her obvious eagerness to avoid bringing South Africa to its knees through the imposition of economic sanctions, alienated many of the member nations of the British Commonwealth. The policy consequence for many of these nations was the boycott of the 1986 Commonwealth Games in Edinburgh. Mrs Thatcher was held to be personally responsible for their absence from the Games.

There are several other areas where sport has experienced the consequences of 'Thatcherism'. These have occurred when reforms such as compulsory competitive tendering, local management of schools, the 'opting-out' of schools from local authority control and actual local authority restructuring have been implemented. In addition, the current debate over the national curriculum in physical education bears the imprint of Thatcherism. But it is important to appreciate a subtle, yet important, difference here. Sport is affected in these instances as a consequence of policy, rather than being used as an instrument of policy implementation.

A final consideration must be the relationship of Mrs Thatcher to the Sports Council. She came to power with a 'New Right' ideological belief that government 'quangos' (quasi-autonomous non-governmental organisations) should be curtailed in power and number. The reality was that after 11 years in office the importance of such bodies was not significantly reduced. In particular, the Sports Council remained in existence, with an enhanced role and a much increased grant from government. However, it too did not remain isolated from the tentacles of Thatcherism. Increasingly, the Council was subjected to 'clientism' as successive Ministers for Sport, closely directed by Mrs Thatcher, more rigidly interpreted the Council's Royal Charter and regarded the body as an 'executive arm of government'. In particular the Council increasingly mirrored the government's stance on the role of sport in the maintenance of public order. A coincidental policy match or an example of the guiding hand of government? Have the most appropriate policy initiatives for sport that the Sports Council should have been pursuing, been compromised or stifled as a result of government interference?

The hand of Thatcher with respect to sport, despite her apparent indifference to the activity itself, was clearly evident during her Premiership. Sport was used and perhaps abused in a very distinctive manner. The jury remains out, however, still considering its verdict on the consequences of her policies for sport.

Thus two highly visible politicians, Margaret Thatcher and Ronald Reagan have in their own particular manner utilised sport as a valuable medium to further their own political objectives. They both left office when their finest hours were perhaps already behind them. But they have left a political legacy that is both significant in terms of policy successes as well as failures, and also in terms of style. The 'Gipper' and the 'Iron lady' have assured themselves a place in the annals of both political, as well as sporting, history.[21]

Gardiner, S and Felix, A, 'Juridification of the Football Field: Strategies for Giving Law the Elbow'

The relationship between sport and formal politics is however conversely best categorised as one that 'lacks invisibility'. Although sport in general, and football in particular, have been projected as autonomous from political values, they have been used both in terms of liberation and the soliciting of legitimacy. The role of sport in the war against apartheid in South Africa cannot be overstated. Conversely there are a number of examples of the role sport has played in deception and distortion of political reality. The Brazilian national football team has been used to symbolise harmony and well-being in general life. The 'beautiful game' can be easily used to promote the beautiful life. In 1970 the winning of the World Cup was used to distract concern away from the injustices of military rule. Today similarly the exploits of Romario, Babeto *et al* and the winning of another World Cup have been used to attempt to deflect national and international concern away from the infanticide being

---

21 Monnington, T, 'Politicians and Sport: Uses and Abuses' in Allison, L (ed), *The Changing Politics of Sport* (1992), Manchester University Press, p 128.

practised by the 'Justiceros' vigilante squads. Ironically, one sure way for street kids to escape the likelihood of an early death is to excel at football.[22]

Largely due to sport's immense cultural importance, politicians are prone to see sport as a powerful political tool. Of course this does not always have negative connotations. Sport can be used to support very positive values of community and cooperation. It can also show disapproval. The sports boycott of South Africa during the apartheid era played an important role within the general political and economic boycott. Sport has increasingly been seen as an area of human activity with which the European Union should be involved, mainly because of its commercial structure, but also because of its cultural significance and ability to transcend national barriers.

EUROPE AND SPORT

There are a number of European sporting bodies, the football body UEFA for example, that have great power. In addition, as with all areas of social life, a variety of European institutions are increasingly influencing sport. The European Commission are probably the most important such institution. But there are others.

Council of Europe

The Council of Europe, the European cultural inter-governmental institution, comprises the majority of European countries. Situated in Strasbourg and sharing a site with the European Parliament of the European Union when in session, it is best known for its Human Rights Convention. It also does useful work in a number of areas such as the environment, education and local government. The Council of Europe has a directorate with sole responsibility for sport. Through this directorate, the European Ministers responsible for sport meet every three years to draw up guidelines for the Council of Europe's sports policy and to discuss problems arising in international sport. If required, they also hold informal European Ministers meetings within the three year cycle.

The Steering Committee for the Development of Sport consists of national governmental and non-governmental officials and prepares and implements the ministers' decisions. It decides the annual work programme and organises seminars and workshops on sports-related issues. It meets annually in February/March. Two full Conventions, the Convention on Anti-Doping and the Convention on Spectator Violence at Sports Events have been drawn up:

---

22 Gardiner, S and Felix, A, 'Juridification of the Sportsfield: Strategies for Giving Law the Elbow' (1995) 5(2) *Marquette Sports Law Journal* 189, pp 194–95.

Walker, G, 'Conventions of the Council of Europe on Sport'

One of the most significant texts drawn up by the Council of Europe in the field of sport is that known as the 'European Sport for All' Charter. Adopted at the First Conference of European Ministers responsible for sport at Brussels in 1975 and later (1976) as a Resolution of the Committee of Ministers of the Council of Europe it has had an impact on national and international sports policies disproportionate to its status as a recommendation to governments. This text has not only provided the basis for broadening the idea of sport, including all the forms of physical activity at all levels of ability, but has also brought together government and non-government sports organisations, especially at national level. It has also provided a connection as an expression of Western democratic and liberal values during difficult times and is now the heart of sports co-operation in all the existing and new members of the committee for the development of sport.

It is important to stress that the New European Sports Charter which is being drawn up for the forthcoming conference of the Ministers for Sports, will be built on the solid foundations of the 1975 charter which is still a valid text.

The two sports conventions of the Council of Europe were not the fruit of hazard, the chance result of political opportunism. They exist because they are the logical consequences of a whole series of relevant initiatives going back, in the case of spectator violence, to 1977, and in the case of doping to 1967. This is a pedigree which is priceless.

European Convention concerning spectator violence and misbehaviour at sports events and especially football matches

Spectator violence had already been a topic debated among the Ministers for Sport of the Council of Europe. In 1984, at their request, the Committee of Ministers adopted Recommendation R(84)19 concerning the decrease in spectator violence. The week of the Bradford fire, the Ministers for Sport agreed to evaluate the impact of the Recommendation. The Parliamentary Assembly suggested that a convention might be suitable. The difficulty was not political but of a practical nature.

How were legitimate, indeed urgent, public concerns to be conciliated with the private nature of a football match? The answer was to request that UEFA co-operate with the Ministers in order to address the subject. UEFA's response was rapid and effective. Ever since the drawing up of the Convention in May and June 1985, UEFA has been closely associated with the Council of Europe in all matters pertaining to the control of hooliganism and safety.

The Convention established a Standing Committee to monitor its implementation. This Standing Committee, in which UEFA is constantly represented, has developed a complete body of doctrine and courses of action which form a series of measures simultaneously applied to the 21 contracting parties of the Convention.

The anti-doping convention

The extensive study on doping in sport which was carried out in the Council of Europe from the start of the 1980s provided the knowledge and experience which formed the basis for the text of the Convention. The CDDS had already developed and refined a steady cooperation with the international sports organisations.

The Anti-Doping Convention Monitoring Group's main achievements in the two meetings it has held so far have been to amend the reference list of banned substances and methods of the Convention so that it corresponds with the valid IOC list, thus ensuring that the banned lists of both sport and government are identical. The Convention entered into force two years ago and 13 States have ratified it with another 11 as signatories, many of whom, including Spain, are actively pursuing the ratification process at national level.

Some conclusions

For sport, support of public authorities is given within the context of a legal instrument, with clearly marked and agreed boundaries. For government, the organisers of sports events are made aware of public concerns and their decisions take account of, and are complementary to, the measures which public authorities put in place to enable large-scale sports events to be organised.

International laws developed through the Council of Europe are already having an impact upon international sport. It remains to be seen how far this impact will go, and what results it will have.

Sport and sportspeople are as much subject to the law as any other field of human endeavour. Sport is reluctant to recognise this fact. The beginnings of a change are apparent in the way the two Conventions were prepared and are now put into operation.[23]

European Non-Governmental Sports Organisation (ENGSO)

The European Non-Governmental Sports Organisation (ENGSO) was formerly the NGO Club. It was established in the early 1970s as a club of professional Secretaries General of European national sports confederations or their representatives around the time when the Council of Europe was becoming more involved in sport.

In 1990 the name was changed to ENGSO in order to reflect more properly the changing role of the organisation. Slightly amended aims and objectives were adopted in the light of recent political developments in Europe. Certain Central and Eastern European nation States which have established sports confederations have been admitted to the membership.

According to the ENGSO terms of reference, established in Liechtenstein in 1990, 'the aim of ENGSO is to improve sport in the member countries by:

- sharing information on national sports development;
- discussing current sports political issues;
- seeking common positions on sports issues, and 'marketing these positions'.

---

23 Walker, G, 'Conventions of the Council of Europe on Sport' in *Congres Internacional Del Dret Il'Esport Proceedings*, Barcelona, March 1992.

Association of European National Olympic Committees (AENOC)

The aims of the Association of European National Olympic Committees (AENOC) are to further the Olympic ideals throughout Europe, including the education of youth through sport, the promotion of cooperation between individual European National Olympic Committees (NOCS) through research, study and the exchange of information and also the development in Europe of 'Olympic Solidarity' programmes in collaboration with the IOC. The British Olympic Association is the official UK representation.

European Sports Conference (ESC)

The European Sports Conference was born out of the 'Ostpolitik' phase of the Cold War in the early 1970s. It meets every two years in a different country and provides a forum for sports administrators from both East and West Europe to discuss issues of mutual interest. Whilst each Conference has had a specific theme, considerable emphasis was always given to the unofficial bilateral negotiations between Member States which takes place during the Conference. In recent years, the ESC has instituted a number of working groups. One group established a European Sports Charter; other subjects have included anti-doping strategies and scientific work and cooperation.

European Commission

There has been some debate concerning whether the European Commission should be actively involved in the regulation of sport. Most people would argue that it is different from areas of economic activity such as agriculture and the Common Agricultural Policy. The European Commission have however acknowledged that sport is big business and the general provisions of the Treaty of Rome should apply to sport, ie the four freedoms underpinning the single market – free movement of individuals, goods, capital and services.[24]

In a paper entitled The European Community and Sport,[25] the European Commission has defined its overall approach to relations with the world of sport. For sports federations, this paper provides the first reference framework defining the scope of Community action. Far from being the end of the line, it marks the starting point for a constructive dialogue which will allow for the specific characteristics of sport and enable it to find its place in the definition of a new European citizenship.

---

24 'The European Community and Sport' (1992) Commission of the European Communities 2/1992.

25 Commission communication to the Council and Parliament, SEC(91) 1438 of 31 July 1991.

The creation of the single market in 1992 has had serious consequences for European sport. Sport has become an industry and many aspects of sporting activities are now covered by Community law and are subject to the legal and institutional imperatives of the Community. A number of rulings by the European Court of Justice have long since spelled out the relationship between sport and the Community. This was first laid down in *Walrave and Koch v Union Cycliste Internationale*,[26] which ruled that sport, at professional not amateur level, falls within the Treaty of Rome:

Walrave and Koch v Union Cycliste Internationale Case 36/74

Having regard to the objectives of the Community, the practice of sport is subject to Community Law only as far as it constitutes an economic activity within the meaning of Article 2 of the Treaty.

This has clearly been reinforced by the *Bosman* case.[27] The European Parliament has also taken an interest in the role that sport could play in creating European citizenship. The European Commission has set up a specialised unit to serve as a focal point for Community action located within the Directorate General X.

The Community has developed a communications campaign centred on sporting events with a Community dimension, such as the European Yacht Race, the Philadelphia-Nieuwpoort Constitution Race to mark the 30th anniversary of the Treaty of Rome and the 200th anniversary of the United States Constitution, the European Youth Olympics and the European Community Swimming Championships. Since 1987, the Commission has been associated with a wide range of events, including sport for the disabled and sport for all, under the slogan 'A frontier-free Community, open to the world'.

The importance of sport to European Commission is recognised in the following extract.

'European Union and Sport'

Sport is one of the most widely practised human activities. Whether it be for money or pleasure, regularly or occasionally, millions of people in the European Union take part in various forms of sporting activity. Some practise individual pursuits such as fishing, running and cycling. Others prefer team games whether they be football, rugby or basketball.

Sport can improve an individual's physical well-being. It helps to develop a range of personal skills useful in daily life, like stamina and teamwork. Sport brings a lot of people into organisations and associations where they are actively involved in cultural networks and exercise democratic responsibility. It bridges national and cultural divides, helps the social integration of the

---

26 Case 36/74 [1974] ECR 1405; [1975] 1 CMLR 320. However *Dona v Mantero*, Case 13/76 [1976] 2 CMLR 578; [1976] ECR 1333 was more cautious in the application of the Treaty of Rome, ruling that it was not applicable to national sporting associations.

27 For further discussion of the case, *Union Royale Belge des Societes de Football Association ASBL and Jean-Marc Bosman* Case C-415/93 15 December 1995, see Chapters 5 and 7.

disabled and brings people together as players and spectators alike. In short, it is an excellent way to promote international understanding – a goal strongly supported by the European Union.

But professional sport is also a serious economic business. Millions of ECUs and thousands of jobs are at stake. Financial interest is not just focused on the result on the football pitch or in the sports stadium itself, but also in broadcasting rights, product endorsement and scores of other downstream activities.

The European Union has no intention of meddling in different sports just for the sake of it. It neither wants to duplicate what is already being done, nor try to do what can be better accomplished at national and regional levels. But it can use its influence to bring together people involved in sport to exchange ideas and promote best practice. It can encourage specific activities like sports for people with disabilities. It can also ensure that where sport is a genuine economic activity, EU rules are fully implemented. In short, a vast swathe of EU activity directly impinges on the sporting world.

Sport and statistics

Sport is both a major leisure activity and a creator of employment.

About 125 million EU citizens take part in one sport or another – equivalent to more than one person in every four. Their expenditure is equal to some 2% of household spending and has considerable potential for growth.

A detailed study in Germany shows that there are 85,000 sports clubs and organisations in the country, that some 700,000 jobs are dependent on sport and that sport provides about 1.4% of the nation's GNP.

France has calculated that 15,000 jobs could be created in the sports sector by the end of the century.

Sport frequently means savings in medical services.

Research shows that men average 10 minutes a day of sport during the week and 15 minutes at weekends. For women the figures are five minutes and six minutes.

There are noticeable differences within the Union. Swedish women on average spend eight and a half minutes on sport every day. In Greece the figure is less than one minute.

European Union support for sport

The European Union's involvement in sport is no new endeavour. It goes back several years and continues to expand. Out of a total of 24 separate European Commission departments, 20 deal on a regular basis with policies which have a direct interest for the sporting world. These activities range from the free movement of people to sports funding and taxation.

The Union's competition rules, for instance, can have a direct bearing on television broadcasting rights. Union legislation on advertising has implications for the financing of sporting events. The creation of a single European insurance market opens up the possibility of buying insurance policies against sporting injuries from companies established in other Member States.

As the Union fights to bring down unemployment, the sports sector is one area where new jobs could be created and where the EU can use its support for infrastructure investments, new technology and education and exchange programmes to good effect. Job opportunities now exist for experts in new sports, in the growth in sport-related clinics, sanatoria and new spa businesses and in the growing interest shown by people seeking to stay healthy as they grow older.

The sporting goods sector, whether it be clothing, equipment or toys, is a good example of the close relationship which now exists between the industry and the Union.

The sector employs around 40,000 people in the 15 Member States and manufacturers must keep abreast of EU moves to harmonise standards, protect intellectual property rights and enforce competition policy. Their activities will also be affected by the volume of sporting goods the Union allows to be imported from various developing countries and by legislation on aspects of design and manufacturing norms, misleading advertising and user instructions.

The Commission's main interest in sport is in constructing an active and permanent dialogue with all those involved on issues of common interest. Information flows in both directions. The Union needs to be aware of the concerns and opinions of the sports world when preparing new EU rules, while sports authorities must be well-informed on Union developments which will affect their activities.

Since 1991, a key meeting place for this dialogue has been the annual European Sports Forum ensuring better co-ordination between the world of sport and the Commission. It brings together people involved in sport from national ministries and non-governmental organisations as well as officials from international and European federations. Typical themes discussed are: health and safety issues, educational funds, the sports sector as a job creator and whether a specific article on sport should be included in the revised Maastricht Treaty.

These multilateral contacts are reinforced with bilateral meetings between the Commission and European and national sports organisations. The practice has grown up of holding biannual meetings of European sports directors to consider how to improve cooperation even further.

The European Parliament also plays a key role in providing a bridge between sport and the Union. The main responsibility for fostering these contacts lies with the Parliament's Committee on Culture, Youth, Education and the Media. But since 1992, a cross-party intergroup of MEPs has met regularly to examine the implications of developments in the Union on sport.

The point of view of the European Parliament

Sport today is no longer regarded as secondary and pointless activity, as used to be the case. It is an integral part of education and culture. It has a prime economic role to play. It arouses passions – some healthy, others less so – and it can involve enormous sums of money. Cases concerning sport are even coming before the highest courts. There are few other activities which can equal sport's function for integrating people into society. In March 1996, when the European Parliament was setting its priorities for the Intergovernmental Conference, it stated that 'sport must be included in the European Treaty, in the context of education, training and employment policy, as well as cultural policy. The Union should encourage in particular transnational initiatives, while respecting national sporting identities'.

A key player in the extensive two-way information flow is a special help desk in the Commission: Sport Info Europe. It can help people both inside and outside the institution find the information they need from the Commission's various departments and acts as a useful channel to funnel data and ideas to policy makers. It can be contacted by telephone on (32 2) 29 69 258 and by fax on (32 2) 29 57 747.

The Union's aim is 'sport for all'. In 1996 it had a budget of ECU 3.5 million' to meet this challenge. It has devoted special attention to two specific programmes.

Eurathlon was launched by the Commission in 1995 with the clear remit of providing a framework for EU subsidies to different sports. Its overall objective is to use sport as a vehicle for better understanding between people and in so doing to break down social barriers and promote health education. Many of the schemes have a specific purpose such as tackling unemployment, racism and violence or promoting equality of opportunity between men and women. Others develop training programmes for managers and sportspeople and encourage sport exchanges.

In its first year, the programme had an ECU 700,000 budget and backed over 80 projects selected by independent juries in a score of sports. In 1996 it supported 175 projects covering 50 different sports ranging from athletics and roller skating to fencing, volleyball, rowing and parachuting. The single most popular sport represented was football. The projects all involved individuals, sportsmen or administrators from at least three EU countries.

Sports for people with disabilities is a clear reflection of the Union's belief that all citizens in the EU should have the same opportunities, regardless of their background or abilities. About 10% of the Union's population – over 36 million individuals – have some form of disability whether physical, mental or sensory.

The range of activities supported by the Union in the programme bears testament to the spirit, dedication and skills of individuals who have overcome personal tragedy to hold their own in a variety of sporting arena. High profile events include Winter Paralympic Games in Lillehammer, European Wheelchair Basketball Championships, European Athletics Championships for the Blind and the 1996 Paralympic Games in Atlanta. But other activities are also encouraged. The programme has also seen almost 80 people with heart transplants running in the annual Brussels 20 kilometre road race, scores of disabled sportsmen participate in a 1,500 kilometre relay on the Paris to Santiago de Compostella pilgrim route and a congress in Germany for over 400 delegates on rehabilitation by sport.

Other initiatives include:

- a joint campaign with the Council of Europe in the fight against drugs in sport. The 'Clean Sport Guide' is a comprehensive information and education pack for athletes, teachers, coaches and doctors;
- measures to end restrictions on the temporary import of sports equipment for competitions or other events;
- specific legislation on animals used in sport such as horses, dogs and pigeons.

European law and sport

Realisation that European law with its emphasis on the free movement of people and cardinal principle of non-discrimination on grounds of nationality also applies to economic activities such as professional sports struck home with a landmark ruling by the European Court of Justice (ECJ) in December 1995. The case involved football and a professional Belgian player, Jean-Marc Bosman.

The *Bosman* case

Jean-Marc Bosman was a professional Belgian football player, who previously played for RC Liège. In 1990 he was in dispute with his club, which was then in the Belgian first division, and was suspended for the 1990–91 season. The player brought legal action against the club – and later against the Belgian Football Federation and the European Football Association UEFA – on the grounds that UEFA-FIFA transfer rules had prevented his move to the French club, US Dunkerque.

The Belgian footballer attacked the rule of transfer fees being paid by a club when a player's contract has expired. He also called into question the widespread practice of limiting the number of other EU nationals in a side to three players plus two others considered assimilated because they had played in the country for an uninterrupted period of five years (the 3+2 rule).

The European Court of Justice based its reasoning on Article 48 of the Treaty of Rome and its guarantee of the right of free movement for people within the Union. It ruled that transfer fees (except when they applied to transfers within a Member State) directly affected a footballer's access to the employment market in another EU country. They were therefore an obstacle to the free movement of workers, and illegal under the Treaty.

The Court also ruled against any limit on the number of other EU players who could be fielded in a club team on the grounds that it could restrict a footballer's chances of being employed by a club in another Member State. The exclusion of foreign players, however, is still permitted in matches between national football teams.

After considering the consequences of the historic judgment, UEFA accepted the ruling in February 1996 and began to adapt its rules.

But it has far wider repercussions. The ruling confirmed unequivocally that the Union's fundamental principles, aimed at removing obstacles which prevent workers or employees from plying their skills in another Member State, also apply to professional sports. Transfer fees once a contract has expired, are now considered to be such an illegal obstacle.

The case is already having a major impact on football as the sport comes to terms with the demise of the transfer system between Member States (although it may continue within a Member State).

The implications will spread to other sports whether they be hockey, rugby, basketball or judo. Sporting associations and administrators may also have to consider the complex structures which frequently exist between professional, semi-professional and amateur players. The ruling means changes to the sporting world, not just in the 15 EU Member States, but also in Norway, Iceland and Liechtenstein, which are linked to it through the European Economic Area.

The *Bosman* case is the most high profile example of the impact of the European Union on sport. But it was by no means a unique illustration.

The Union's competition policy rules were applied for the first time to ticket sales for sporting events in 1990. As football fans prepared for the World Cup, the European Commission ruled that the arrangement whereby one tour operator had the exclusive rights to sell entry tickets as part of a package tour to the world's premier soccer competition was an exclusive distribution agreement that restricted competition to the detriment of football fans. Supporters now have a choice between several distributors when they wish to buy tickets or package tours for football matches, athletics events or other major sporting occasions.

European law also ensures that sports instructors who have trained and received professionally recognised qualifications in one EU Member State can have these accepted in another without taking a further series of tests. This mutual recognition system, for example, is designed to allow qualified tennis instructors trained in the United Kingdom or Austria to teach tennis players in France or Italy.

EU legislation on trans-frontier broadcasting, much of which involves sports programmes, lays down requirements for television advertising and sponsorship. These ban any advertising of tobacco products at sporting events. Moves are now afoot to establish EU-wide rules for satellite broadcasting and cable retransmission.

The Union is also keeping a close eye on the arrangements for exclusive broadcasting rights for sporting events and the development of pay television channels to ensure that the general interest of viewers is protected. In 1996 the European Court of First Instance in Luxembourg annulled a decision allowing the European Broadcasting Union with its 67 public broadcast members exclusive rights to broadcast sporting events.

Hooliganism

Unfortunately, sport, particularly football, can also have its antisocial, dangerous side with the violent behaviour of small groups of supporters spoiling the enjoyment and endangering the lives of the majority. As the Union's provisions on the free movement of people make it easier to travel from one EU country to another, so the phenomenon is spreading. The Union is increasingly considering ways of preventing such hooliganism especially as preparations are put in place for the 1998 World Cup finals in France.

In March 1996 EU governments adopted a joint strategy. It involves the exchange of information on known troublemakers, assessment of the global risks involved, details of travel arrangements to away fixtures and a network of liaison officers on hooliganism. The measures have to strike a balance between protecting public order and respecting individual rights and EU rules on freedom of movement and non-discrimination on the basis of nationality.

The European Parliament has also identified the need for a co-ordinated EU approach on ticket sales, the consumption of alcohol at sports grounds and the design and safety of sports areas. It has organised meetings with representatives from football associations, police federations and others involved in the sport to work out effective measures.

The future

As the last few years have shown, the European Union has an ever increasing impact on sport. In the future it will continue to use its resources to encourage specific sporting activities. It will also act as a referee to ensure that EU rules are applied correctly to enable everyone to be treated fairly and enjoy the same opportunities. As the Union prepares for enlargement, sport will be a useful bridge between the peoples of existing and future Member States. For all these reasons it is important that the dialogue and contacts between the Union and the sporting world be well co-ordinated and as frank and constructive as possible.[28]

It seems that there is a good chance that in the not too distant future sport will be more centrally a part of European Union policy:

Parrish, R, 'Sport and the Intergovernmental Conference'

The preceding analysis presupposes that sport has certain values worthy of protection. Sport operates in an independent and non-governmental environment and to apply the EU's internal market logic rigidly to it may risk losing sight of sports socio-economic and indeed integrationist qualities. Sport can have a role to play in the binding of emerging nations and indeed international organisations. It can contribute to unification, identity, recognition and respect for other countries and cultures. Sport also promotes health benefits, self-actualisation needs and the development of individual and group value systems. Furthermore, sport can improve race relations, suppress asocial behaviour, provide opportunity for underprivileged and unemployed and contribute to economic growth and opportunity.

The central concern of many European sporting associations is to ensure action by the EU in sport is limited and that sport no longer becomes the unintended victim of policy externalities emanating from elsewhere. Paradoxically, this can only be achieved through closer links with the EU. A number of options to secure these objectives have emerged.

---

28 'The European Union and Sport' (1996) European Commission.

Improved consultation links

The first option lies in clarifying sport's current ambiguous status within the EU. Formally, sport falls within the competency of Directorate General X (DGX – Information, Communication, Culture and Audio-Visual). In the wake of the Bosman ruling and with the issue of television rights on the agenda, DGIV (Competition) and DGXV (Internal Market) have also become significant players. Indeed, 18 out of the 23 DGs in the European Commission have some responsibility over matters relevant to sport. This fragmentation may serve to restrict access to the European policy process by sports interest groups. In order to provide some co-ordination of information, the European Sports Forum was established by the Commission in 1991 to meet annually allowing a discussion forum between EU officials and members of Europe's sporting world. As a result of one such meeting in 1993, the 'Sports Sector' was created within DGX to provide a similar link. Through this link in DGX, 'Sports Info Europe' provides a further information service to facilitate dialogue between the EU and the sports world.

The strengthening and extension of such links will prove beneficial for interested sports groups but this strategy affords sport no extra treaty protection. This approach therefore needs to be used in conjunction will other possible strategies.

Sport and Article 3

One such complementary strategy would be to include sport in the list of community activities outlined in Article 3 of the EU Treaty. Used in conjunction with Article 235, the 'catch-all' article, this would permit action by the EU in sports matters if it was felt appropriate for the attainment of one of the objectives of the treaty. Acting unanimously, on a proposal from the European Commission and after consultation with the European Parliament, the Council of Ministers could take appropriate measures. Improved consultation and co-ordinating mechanisms at Commission level would facilitate interest group input into the policy process but this strategy grants sport no specific safeguards and it fails to prevent the possibility of harmonisation measures being adopted. Neither would it ensure sport being taken into account in the formulation of other EU policies.

A statement by the European Council

A further option lies in the persuasive powers of so called 'soft law'. The European Council could declare a special status for sport and this would be referred to every time the EU takes initiatives in that area. Soft law can prove a powerful force and a useful benchmark which may well shift the area from the margins of Community competency to mainstream EU decision making. This development has occurred in the field of vocational training and was a strategy adopted at Maastricht with regards animal welfare. If sufficient pressure mounts to include sport in the EU Treaty, this may prove the preferred option of the Member States as a method of dealing with the issue without incorporating binding measures.

Sport and Article 128 (Culture)

A further alternative lies in explicitly linking sport with culture and incorporating it into Article 128 of the EU Treaty dealing with culture. The assumption underlying this approach is that sport can be equated with culture. This analogy was rejected by the European Court of Justice when considering the *Bosman* case. Sport may share with culture similar features but the two are very different. The contribution to the development and consolidation of emerging nations in cultural terms came more through the intellectual pursuits of art, music and literature than sport. Although sport and culture clearly cannot be divorced from the political, economic and legal environments in which they operate, sport as a mass movement has been influenced more by these features and has increasingly detached itself or been detached from culture. The result has been sport being viewed as simply one of many economic activities. Although the cultural option provides a useful model, the differences are such as to warrant a separation. This has led to interest in a similar incorporation, this time with Article 126, Education, Vocational Training and Youth. The same type of problems would however be evident here.

A separate Article for sport

Having a separate article for sport appears to be the favoured option of a number of European sporting groups. This method would achieve the twin objectives of ENGSO (the European Non-Governmental Sports Organisations) and the EOC (the European Olympic Committee) of limiting the action of the EU by prohibiting any harmonisation whilst securing the right for sport to be taken into account in the framing of other EU policies. Furthermore, by ensuring that the codecision procedure applies (Article 189b), the widest possible consultation would be guaranteed. The European Sports Forum would provide the most suitable consultative body which the Commission would consult at the initiation stage. This would require a commitment on the part of the Commission to adopt such mandatory consultation. This commitment was forthcoming by the Commission with regards to the consumer protection and vocational training policies.

Conclusions

The *Bosman* ruling created both 'demand' and 'supply' side pressures for greater EU involvement in sport. On the demand side, many European sporting associations have been converted to the idea of limiting EU involvement in sport by paradoxically fostering closer links. On the supply side, the ruling created opportunities for those actors that could deliver on such demands, ie the EU institutions and officials who recognised the possible benefits of extending their scope in this area.

European sporting groups generally hope to secure three objectives from their demands. First, they hope to ensure that sport is taken into account when other EU activities are being framed. Secondly, they hope to restrict EU involvement in sport, particularly ruling out harmonisation, by allowing the EU some involvement. Finally, the insertion of an article for sport in a new treaty would ensure some binding protection and thus created a more stable environment for sport to operate. These are the possible benefits. The likely risks are unclear and largely depend on the strategy adopted. However it seems clear that if an article for sport is inserted into a revised treaty, professional sportsmen and women would not receive other treaty bound protections, such as freedom of movement and freedom from discrimination.

The 'supply' side actors have been slow to respond to these demands, further highlighting the often patchy and unco-ordinated response of the EU's decision making machinery. In the immediate aftermath of Bosman, Belgian Prime Minister Jean Luc Dehaene declared his public support for sport to be treated as a special case. Since then little has been heard. Luxembourg have also come out in favour whilst France opposes an insertion. The recent Irish Presidency of the EU reported no interest in the proposal and as such ignored the issue in its Dublin draft treaty. The European Commission would normally be expected to seize on such demands to widen their own policy remit, but thus far have kept quiet for fear of sparking inter DG rivalry over who would claim competency. This has left the European Parliament as the main arena for discussion, with much work already having been carried out through its Sports Intergroup. With this degree of support from the main supply side actors it seems unlikely that sport will be included in the new treaty. If it is, it will be inserted at the very last minute. In the meantime sports professionals are increasingly showing a determination to break with tradition and settle disputes in the courts. *Bosman* is of course the best example of this and others are following his lead. Currently, the Christelle Deiliege and Jyri Lehtonen cases are challenging the right of national and international sports federations to limit and decide who participates in international sports events and the legality of transfer deadline rules. As case law builds up, sport will increasingly find itself shackled, as any other economic activity, to the logic of the internal market.[29]

The European Union recognises two things. First the huge financial reality of sport as big business.[30] It can no longer be protected and excluded from the application of the treaty provisions of the Union. There is a belief that both sports administrators and organisers and players and athletes should be subject to and be able to avail themselves of European law. Secondly the political value of sport is being identified. Sport is seen as being able to achieve integration within the 'New Europe' in a way that other institutions cannot. The European Commission in the surrounding issues of the Bosman case suggested that the development of a European football team might be a long term goal. At a time of political pressure from some Member States for greater unification, sport may be seen as one of the neutral mechanisms to sell the European dream. A number of various European sporting initiatives have been discussed above. Although not initiated by the European Commission, and predating it by many years, we have already been integrated in golfing

---

29   Parrish, R, 'Sport and the Intergovernmental Conference' (1997) 5(1) *Sport and the Law Journal* 32–33.

30   See study by Coopers and Lybrand for DGX, 'The Impact of European Union Activities on Sport' (1995) European Commission. Also see Miller, F, 'The EC Commission Final Report on the Impact of European Activity in Sport' (1994) 2(2) *Sport and the Law Journal* 8.

terms: the dramatic victory of the European team over the USA in the Ryder Cup in 1995 was followed by millions. As a rare event of a 'supra-national' team being widely supported, it helped reinforce the notion of being European.

To what extent there is a general transference of being European into the general consciousness and popular culture is another question. Together with the Bosman decision, the Europeanisation of our sporting teams and the nationality of players in national leagues seems likely to increase.[31] These seem to be the very conditions in sport under which the spectre of extreme nationalism is raised. Sport can be a unifying factor, but it clearly is also the arena where 'difference' in numerous ways, importantly in terms of nationality, is highly visible.

INTERNATIONAL SPORTS LAW

Sports law issues are increasingly international in nature. There are a number of international sports bodies that have been noted: the Federation Internationale de Football Associations (FIFA), the International Olympic Committee (IOC) and the International Amateur Athletic Federation (IAAF). Sports disputes often involve relationships between individual athletes, national and international bodies. Arbitration and mediation mechanisms, most notably the Court of Arbitration for Sport in Switzerland, dedicated to resolving sports disputes, often involve international issues. Issues of jurisdiction therefore become vital. The development of international sports law is becoming a practical necessity.

Nazfiger, JAR, 'International Sports Law as a Process for Resolving Disputes'

International sports law is more than a static set of rules and principles: it is better described as a process for avoiding and resolving disputes. Recent cases highlight its significance. The *Swiss Equestrian* case, decided by the Swiss Federal Tribunal, demonstrates the efficacy of using this process in cases involving issues of eligibility for competition. By contrast, the *Reynolds* case, decided by US federal courts, shows the folly of ignoring non-judicial remedies prescribed by international sports law. As a result, *Reynolds* became a sort of Dickensian struggle involving three years of litigation and some nine decisions before the case was finally dismissed. The courts could have, and should have, reached the same result by simply enforcing decisions of the appropriate international sports federation and the arbitral tribunal that had upheld the federation's decision. The *Harding* case, which was also decided in the United States, demonstrates that adjudication outside the prescribed process of international sports law is fundamentally unstable.

---

31 See Foster, K, *Games Without Frontiers: Free Movement in Sport* (1995) (unpublished draft with author). He argues that European integration will only be understandable to the average person when it becomes recognisable as a part of popular culture.

Several cases from English courts, to be discussed later in this article, suggest appropriate parameters for judicial review and the role of national law. The message is clear: national courts should be cautious about resolving disputes arising out of international sports activity. Judicial review is appropriate primarily when decisions of sports bodies either arrogate jurisdiction from other sports bodies to the injury of individual athletes or seriously threaten fundamental rights of athletes including that of due process or natural justice.

Introduction

International sports law provides a dynamic, though still incomplete, process to avoid, manage and resolve disputes among athletes, national sports bodies, international sports organisations and governments. This process is distinctive although it incorporates rules and procedures drawn from more general regimes of private and public law and operates within a structure of established institutions, including arbitral bodies and national courts.

Among the most difficult issues of international sports law today, perhaps the most difficult is the role of national courts. Some would argue that they are too intrusive in the sports arena. Others would argue the opposite: that courts should be more active in protecting the rights of athletes and the best interests of organised sports. Fundamental questions of jurisdiction, choice of law and enforcement of judgments cry out for answers. For example: are decisions by international sports bodies non-reviewable by national courts? On the other hand, may courts simply ignore such decisions? If not, to what extent are they controlling?

Identifying the various fora for resolving international sports disputes, and the relationships between them, is essential in answering such questions. These fora include national sports bodies, international sports federations, Olympic bodies, arbitral tribunals and the courts. Although each has its own process for resolving disputes, they are interrelated. Sports bodies often provide, under national law, for arbitration of disputes by established tribunals. Gradually, a distinctive *lex specialis* is emerging from a line of arbitral decisions. Standard rules and procedures for avoiding disputes are also emerging within the process of international sports law. A good example is the anti-doping resolution adopted by the International Olympic Committee (IOC) and the Association of Summer Olympic International Federations (ASOIF). It standardises rules and procedures for conducting unannounced tests for doping and provides for technical cooperation among sports bodies responsible for carrying out the tests. The resolution thus establishes a comprehensive means, governed by the IOC, for bringing international sports law to bear on a particularly serious threat to fair play.

The Olympic Movement, though non-governmental, is at the heart of the legal process. Its Charter and the decisions of its governing bodies, especially the IOC, define a broad range of customary practice that applies to both amateur and professional activity. This law addresses political issues affecting sports, eligibility of athletes, racial and gender discrimination against athletes, commercialisation of sports and professionalism. Misunderstanding the central role of the Olympic Movement in training and competition leads to confusion about the legal significance of decisions by international federations, each governing a particular sport, and other sports organisations, generally at national and local levels.

It is, however, difficult to define a single hierarchy of authority and jurisdiction in this process. Trying to resolve the jurisdictional issues – who gets to do what to whom and when? – can be as complicated as it is essential. Relationships between organisations and their dispute resolution processes vary, as do interpretations of rules and principles among different legal systems. Even so, it is possible to identify ... trends, constituting a growing State practice, for avoiding, managing and resolving disputes.[32]

Conclusion

A comparison of the *Reynolds* and *Swiss Equestrian* cases, both decided by national courts, demonstrates the efficacy of international sports law. It can be instrumental in blending natural institutions into a single process of justice that avoids judicial complexity. Although courts can be expected to address the most serious issues of due process and public interest, judicial abstention is advisable in most disputes between individual athletes, on the one hand, and designated sports bodies and organisations, on the other. Unless injunctive relief is absolutely necessary to prevent gross injustice to individual athletes or the public, adjudication is especially doubtful under the kind of time constraints that made the Reynolds and Harding cases so exciting but perilous on the eve of major competition.

The excitement of sports competition is best left to the sports arena, not the courtroom. Fortunately, the Federal Appeals Court in *Reynolds,* after the case had stumbled along for nearly four years, reached the right result of dismissing the action. Moreover, the consistent arrogance of the district court may have been an anomaly. Another court in the United States is perhaps more typical in finding 'most unfortunate the increasing frequency with which sporting events are resolved in the courtroom'.

Decisions of English courts, particularly *Greig v Insole* (1981), *Reel v Holder* (1978) and *Cowley v Heatley* (1986), hint at the bounds of judicial review. Despite the willingness of national courts to review issues of procedural fairness and fundamental public interest, they properly view adjudication as only a last resort for resolving international disputes. Normative trends thus confirm a growing commitment of national legal systems to the special processes of international sports law. The Court of Arbitration for Sport, in particular, is assuming a central position for avoiding, managing and resolving international disputes. What remains is for the legal profession throughout the world to take international sports law seriously.[33]

---

32 Nazfiger, JAR, 'International Sports Law as a Process for Resolving Disputes' (1996) 45(1) *International and Comparative Law Quarterly* 130–32 .

33 *Ibid*, pp 148–49.

SPORT AND PUBLIC POLICY

Contemporary State Regulation in Sport

The major role of the State in sport continues to be regulating and prohibiting sporting activities and peripheral issues concerning spectators. The question is not straightforward: to regulate or not to regulate, or perhaps prohibit? There are complex surrounding issues that are not easily reconciled. The legitimacy of the State in protecting individuals from certain activities can be explained in terms of 'paternalism' where essentially the State acts as a parent, guiding behaviour. This has its origins in the ideas of the legal philosopher, John Stuart Mill,[34] where human activities can be justifiably regulated or prohibited when they cause 'harm' to others or to oneself. The work of Mill will be discussed at greater length in the context of how drug use in sport should be regulated or prohibited.

The counter view is the belief that the State is too interventionist in people's lives – the nannying State is the cry. This view develops a libertarian approach that essentially argues people should be able to do what they want, in this case, in the sporting context. The ban on handguns in the wake of the Dunblane tragedy would be a good example.[35] This move had wide public support, but those who take part in the sport of shooting, have vociferously decried this move as an over-reaction and denial of their rights.

Before the approach to the use of drugs in sport is considered at length, five other areas of State involvement in sport will be examined:

- the regulation of boxing and martial arts;
- sports involving animals, including so called blood sports;
- the regulation of children's activity centres;
- racism in sport;
- protection of child athletes from abuse.

These areas are a disparate collection of areas of controversy and 'perceived problems' that exist in contemporary sport. The first two areas deal with activities, boxing and fox hunting, where there is strong public opinion that the State should ban them. There is however sizeable support for their continuation. The third area is where a regulatory framework has been implemented for activity centres for children, mainly due to the Lyme Bay canoeing tragedy. The fourth area evaluates what role the law should have in regulating spectator racism in sport. The last area concerns how a more effective legal and non-legal regulatory framework can safeguard children participating in sports from abuse of all forms.

---

34 Mill, JS, *On Liberty*, Everyman Edition (1962), London: Fontana.
35 See the Firearms (Amendment) Act 1997.

In all these areas of sporting activity, the role of the law will be considered. It is vital to bear in mind the discussion in chapter one concerning the role of the law in regulating areas of social life. The law increasingly operates together with other normative rules such as codes of practice and any existing internal rules, in this case, sports rules. The major area of contention is whether the law can be an effective mode of regulation. It can have positive results, but it is not always the best way of providing solutions to perceived problems.

THE REGULATION OF BOXING AND MARTIAL ARTS

Boxing: The Noble Art?

Boxing holds a curious position in English law. This will be discussed in detail later, but legal authority suggests that only sparring (practising) between boxers is lawful; actual boxing has no specific legal precedent and seems to be treated as an anomaly.[36] What is clear, is that its legality and legitimacy has been constantly debated over the last few years instigated by the deaths and critical injuries to a number of boxers in professional bouts. A number of Private Members' Bills have been initiated in Parliament to attempt to ban boxing.[37] There have also been numerous internal changes within boxing to promote safety. In amateur boxing, headguards have been worn for a number of years. In 1982 the number of rounds in professional fights was reduced from 15 to 12 by the world's two main boxing authorities. This followed the death of the South Korean lightweight Duk Koo Kim after he was knocked out in the 14th round of a fight against the American Ray Mancini. In Britain, the deaths of Steve Watts, Bradley Stone[38] and James Murray[39] and the serious brain-damage of Michael Watson[40] and Gerald McClellan[41] has led intermittently to the same polarised opinion about whether boxing can be justified within contemporary society.

For supporters of boxing, the sport is about bravery and determination in the face of extreme physical danger. Boxing is seen as the noble art, the epitome of man's instinct to fight, a way of teaching self-discipline. The history of sport discussed in Chapter 1 indicates that boxing can be seen as a

---

36 For a detailed discussion see Gunn, M and Omerod, D, 'The Legality of Boxing' (1995) 15(2) *Legal Studies* and Pannick, D, QC, 'What's so special about boxing?' *The Times*, 14 March 1995, p 31.

37 See Parpworth, N, 'Parliament and the Boxing Bill' (1996) 4(1) *Sport and the Law Journal* 24.

38 See 'Boxer's life in danger after bout', *The Guardian*, 28 April 1994.

39 See 'Your son is brain dead, surgeon tells boxer's parents', *The Observer*, 15 October 1995, p 3.

40 See 'Boxing: Board bows before surgeon's advice', *The Guardian*, 17 October 1991, p 20.

41 'Near-tragedy brings fresh calls for ban on boxing', *The Guardian*, 27 February 1995, p 3.

continuum of the need for man to be able to fight to survive. This supportive view, mainly from those involved in boxing, tends to minimise the risk of boxing compared with other sports such as mountaineering and rock-climbing.[42]

Opponents say that a civilised society should not tolerate this organised brutality, however brave and heroic it might appear.[43] Professional boxing, in contrast to the highly regulated amateur game, is banned in Sweden, Norway and Iceland. Increasingly there is a middle ground of opinion that has started to question the legitimacy of boxing as it is currently organised. Greater safety and regulation are seen as a necessary development by almost everyone, especially in the professional game.

A number of extracts will help evaluate these competing perspectives on the legitimacy of boxing:

Sutcliffe, S, 'The Noble Art?'

James Murray's death last year polarised opinion about the future of boxing. A disciplined forum for innate aggression or unreformable barbarism inviting brain damage and worse? Phil Sutcliffe takes the temperature on sport's bitterest debate.

Dr Helen Grant is one of a handful of specialists who have looked inside the skull of a dead boxer. An expert on diseases of the nervous system, in 1986 she examined Steve Watt, who collapsed and went into a coma after being stopped in the 10th round of a Southern area title fight. 'He died, as Bradley Stone did last year, and Michael Watson and Gerald McClellan nearly did, of an acute bleed from a severed vein which led to rapid accumulation of blood squashing the brain stem down against the base of the skull. Although he was treated in hospital for a couple of days, it was clear that he had been brain dead in the ambulance'.

But the fatal injury was not all Grant saw when she examined Watt's brain. 'There were about 20 lesions in his brain from that fight and hundreds of scars from old lesions. Each one was about the size of a cherry. Such lesions heal after about six weeks. But the scars represent lost brain cells. In addition, the septum dividing the two ventricle (main cavities) was torn away; that was also old damage. Steve Watt was 29. He had been boxing for 10 years, I think. In my opinion, he was on the slippery slope to punch-drunk syndrome. The only logical place to hold a boxing match is in the operating theatre of a neurosurgical hospital,' she concludes. 'But major traumas are not the main point. It is the long term diminution of the man's ability that is awful. If you

---

42 Statistics discussed in a Parliamentary debate on a Private Members' Bill in 1991, stated that between 1969 and 1980 in Britain, compared to two deaths in professional boxing, there were 93 in mountaineering and rock climbing, Hansard, 4 December 1991 at col 293.

43 See 'Boxing: That dangerous game', *The Guardian*, 15 March 1994, p 11; 'Noble art has no defence', *The Observer*, 8 May 1994, p 8; 'Boxing looks to get a bit more clever', *The Guardian*, 25 October 1995, p 27; 'Pros and plenty of cons in boxing', *The Guardian*, 20 October 1995, p 25; 'Boxing: Doctors say ban is best safety measure', *The Guardian*, 25 October 1995, p 27; 'Sportsview: Why they can't close school of hard knocks', *The Observer*, 29 October 1995, p 10. Also see 'Boxing – Ban It?', *Panorama*, BBC Television, 25 October 1995.

take part in boxing for long, a great deal of your grey matter bites the dust, that is what it amounts to. I say that with every respect for boxers. I think they are the bravest people in the world.'

In 1982, prompted by concern over the hazards of dementia pugilistica and recurring ring fatalities, the British Medical Association (BMA), representing 80% of doctors, called for the abolition of boxing, professional and amateur. Their argument was that any punch to the head causes the soft tissue of the brain to 'swirl' in what by some evolutionary aberration is the skull's 'inhospitable environment' of internal bumps and ragged edges: damage is therefore inevitable and cumulative even where not traumatic. Ever since, the BMA has been an energetic and persuasively credible focus for the campaign against the sport in the UK. So began the latest phase of the boxing debate, a sporadic war of words in which a new volley is fired after every tragedy – most recently when James Murray died on 17 October last year. But the entrenched battle lines never move. They cannot. As presented, it is a for or against issue. To box or not to box.

Both combatants summon up science to state their case. The BMA is keen on the Haslar report which 'finds evidence of brain impairment among amateur boxers in the armed forces'. Boxing counters with the Butler report which found 'no evidence of cumulative effect'. Then both sides will quote the John Hopkins University Stewart Study of 'central nervous system function in US amateur boxers', the biggest research project ever undertaken on the sport. It notes an association between a large number of bouts and 'diminished performance in selected cognitive domains', as the BMA points out. Yet it also says that 'none of the changes we have observed to date, however, are clinically significant' – delighting the International Amateur Boxing Association so much that they published the whole report in a booklet of encouraging medical evidence 'to offensively counteract the permanent and unfounded attacks on Olympic style boxing'.

To the layman watching this ultimately pathetic ping-pong of tentative conclusions and prudent reservations, it soon becomes plain that the scientific jury is still out. Then a further cogent thought occurs: while both sides are keen to establish a hard-fact justification for their enthusiasms, that is not the heart of the debate at all. Nobody significant on the pro-boxing side denies the risk of brain damage. They would dispute only matters of quantity and degree. What really counts for both sides is their own gut feelings about common sense, decency and civilised behaviour.

BMA spokeswoman Dr Fleur Fisher insists that the anti-boxing campaign is scientific, not moral or emotional, yet she moves on to say 'it is difficult for doctors to see trauma inflicted on that most exquisite computer, the brain, and not take action. It would be unethical for us not to speak up. It is bizarre that it is utterly ungentlemanly to hit a man in the balls and OK to hit him in the brain. I see Nigel Benn fighting, psyched up, I think 'Oooh' (cry of pain and frustration), you recognise the bravery, the determination but, in that McClellan fight, you see his head bouncing around, you are in agony watching it, thinking what the cost could be. After the Murray tragedy I watched the boxing world go through mourning in a state of denial, still trying to say it's a wonderful sport'.

Nicky Piper, chair of the Professional Boxers Association (PBA), the fighters' trade union, does say 'it is a wonderful sport. It is the oldest of all sports. It is man's instinct to want to fight and it is far better done in a civilised form with rules and controls. It comes down to knowing the risks, freedom of choice, making your own decision'. 'Boxing really does teach discipline,' adds Dr Adrian Whiteson, chief medical officer of the British Boxing Board of Control and chair of the World Boxing Council's medical commission. 'Diet, not smoking, very little drink, certainly no drugs, getting up early in the morning to do your roadwork, training, sparring. To do all this properly adds up to being true to yourself. Then it gives people from underprivileged areas – I know it sounds trite – a chance to better themselves.'

That is a traditional line Fisher particularly detests: 'What a terrible slur on our society if boxing was the only way that the enormous force of character in a young man like James Murray could have shone through'. Thus the spirit and substance of the stand-off between the BMA and the boxing world. It is impossible to say whether the feud has stimulated or set back progress to reduce the level of risk to boxers. Perhaps its value has been as a sort of moral background music accompanying more practical developments. But despite Fisher's assertion that 'the issue has moved' and that boxing is 'just unacceptable to society' in the aftermath of Murray's death, it is interesting to note that none of the three main political parties currently supports abolition.

For anyone who seriously cares about boxers, the realities of the sport's future are surely all about improving safety. The measures recommended by the medical panel convened by the Board after Bradley Stone's death in April 1994, will obviously help, despite the remaining grey areas which worry Nicky Piper and the PBA – for instance, qualified anaesthetists not compulsory at ringside 'because they are not necessarily the best people for a war situation', says Whiteson and electrolyte drinks between rounds still banned in face of the venerable addiction to plain water.

Probably the most important rule change arose from a relatively recent realisation that pre-fight dehydration to make the weight could have deadly effects because, as well as weakening the body, it actually shrinks and therefore 'loosens' the brain. Conversely, rehydrating rapidly by slinging down three or four pints of water in half an hour can cause cerebral swelling. Basically, a dehydrated fighter is a disaster waiting to happen. In response, weigh-ins have been brought forward to at least 24 hours in advance of the fight. That has been followed up by introducing a sequence of weight checks through the fortnight ahead of major championships. If a boxer is outside carefully calculated parameters at any stage the bout will be cancelled or postponed. Enforced conscientiously, this could all but guarantee that boxers operate in their natural divisions.

Some of the best ideas are still being worked on. St John's Ambulance are devising a boxing-specific first-aid course which will then be compulsory for all trainers. A government department is researching the possibility of reducing the impact of punches by altering glove materials and design. The World Boxing Council will probably back a British inspired study of psychometric testing – which hopefully would reveal mental malfunction even earlier than a scan would visually reveal an abnormality.

However Piper is very pleased that the Board is now championing annual and post-stoppage MRI (Magnetic Resonance Imaging) scans, replacing the cruder CT. MRI shows 'the architecture of the brain'. While the BMA stresses that it can only pick up damage already done – 'When the boxer is already doomed' by Dr Grant's reckoning – Whiteson says that it will enable the Board to withdraw boxers' licences at the first sign of anything amiss. His guiding principle, after all, is damage limitation because damage elimination is impossible without closing the sport down.

All the same, Whiteson has a militant warning for Piper about the coming of MRI scans and then psychometric testing: 'When we tell a boxer he has to stop, he must accept it and the PBA have to agree with us too, no going to law to get his licence back'. 'It is not a simple situation for us,' says Piper, diplomatically. 'I think if a test shows a problem we would invariably recommend the boxer to accept the Board's decision. But we are here to represent our members and we would have to take each case individually.' Whiteson won't wear any such ambivalence. 'You cannot ride two horses on this one,' he says, then raises the stakes a little further. 'Anyway when these test results start to come in the PBA may get the biggest shock of their lives. Who knows? Some of the biggest names may find they're not boxing any more.' It is a hint of the future that might give even the BMA their first and last laugh out of boxing. *Reductio ad absurdum pugilisticum*: the Board's safety measures could become so exacting that they have to refuse all professional boxers a licence, thereby delivering the *quietus* to a sport which, in truth, the abolitionists have barely laid a glove on.

If British boxing is to survive through the 21st century, it will have to bind itself together better than ever and, paradoxically, the sport's foot soldiers – the boxers – are going to have to lead the way. In one important detail government help is needed. For the 'official' sport to prosper, professional and amateur, and secure the safety standards developed at such cost, unlicensed boxing with its unsupervised and dangerous conditions must be made illegal.[44]

Boxing can be subject to Elias's 'civilising process' discussed earlier in Chapter 1. Perhaps the increased safety provisions in recent years are an extension of a continuing regulatory approach to boxing that has been going on since the mid-19th century when pugilism, or prize-fighting, where the winner took all, was a popular 'sport'. The facets of this regulatory approach are outlined below:

Sheard, K, 'Civilising Developments in Boxing'

There is little doubt that the pugilists of the 18th and 19th centuries would have difficulty recognising the boxing of today as being the same activity as the prize-fighting of their own time. In the intervening period the rules governing the sport have become increasingly complex, the bureaucratic organisations controlling it have become more powerful, and the law of the land has become more intrusive, more protective, than ever before. The violence of boxing has been controlled and contained. Prize-fighting, like fox

---

44 Sutcliffe, P, 'The Noble Art?' in *Total Sport*, February 1996, pp 92–94.

hunting, can be said to have gone through a 'sportisation' process as it metamorphosed into boxing.

Using the framework developed by Dunning ... the modern sport of boxing can be said to have become more 'civilised' by a number of interrelated processes which include the following:

(1) Boxing in the early period of its development – ie from approximately the mid-17th to the early decades of the 19th century – was by present standards an extremely violent, brutal and bloody activity. However this aspect of the sport has since become increasingly regulated by a complex set of formal written rules. These rules not only define and control the sorts of violence which are permitted, but also outlaw violence in certain forms. The type of violent blow permitted and the areas of the body allowed to be attacked have been carefully delineated. Thus in the early stages of the sport's development it was possible to use a variety of what we would now call 'wrestling' holds to subdue an opponent. For example, the 'cross-buttock' throw, in which the opponent could be thrown over one's hip to the ground, was allowed. This could then be followed by a leap upon the fallen adversary, smashing one's knees into his exposed ribcage. Eyes could be gouged, hair pulled, and the testicles attacked. The nature of the punch, and the shape of the fist, have also been more carefully defined. The 'target' must be hit with the knuckle part of the hand. Hitting with an open glove – 'slapping' – is not allowed, possibly because it once permitted one's opponent to be injured by the lacing of the glove. 'Straight finger' blows to the eyes are also banned.

(2) The rules also allow for penalties to be imposed upon boxers who infringe these rules. For example, points may be lost by boxers who hit 'below the belt', use the head illegally, or who receive constant warnings for holding and hitting. As early as 1838, under the London Prize Ring Rules, if a fighter went down deliberately without being hit or thrown – thus allowing him to rest for a while or corruptly 'throw' the fight – he could be disqualified and thus prevented from gaining any pecuniary or other advantage from the ploy. Under modern conditions champions who refuse to defend their titles within a specified time period, or who turn up to defend their titles overweight, may have the titles taken from them.

(3) Weight divisions have been introduced in an attempt to equalise conditions for all boxers. In the early days of the prize-ring, there were no weight divisions and men fought each other irrespective of poundage. It was not until the 1880s, after the widespread adoption of the Queensbery Rules of 1865, that a real effort was made to standardise weight divisions both in Britain and the United States. This innovation, of course, allowed boxing skill to have a greater impact upon the outcome of a contest than extra poundage or extra reach.

(4) Boxing has also been civilised by having restrictions placed upon the length of contests and the length of 'rounds'. These restrictions differ according to the experience of the boxers and the nature of the contest, for example whether or not a fight is for a title or whether it is an amateur or a professional fight. Most professional championship contests in Britain now

follow the lead given by the European Boxing Union and are fought over 12 rounds. In America until relatively recently the stipulated 'distance' was 15 rounds. And before this – in both the US and Britain – the usual distance was twenty rounds of three minutes each. By contrast, prior to the 1860s, a round ended with a fall, and fights would be fought to a finish or until one of the fighters could not continue for any reason. In Britain, the largest number of rounds to be fought under this system was the 276 fought between Jack Jones and Patsy Tunney, in Cheshire in 1825

(5) Physical protection has been introduced to protect boxers from the permitted and accidental violence they can inflict upon each other. For example, padded gloves, gum shields, headguards and groin protectors have all been introduced over the years. Gloves are claimed to have been first introduced in 1747, by Jack Broughton, an ex-prize-fighter, early 'entrepreneur' and boxing tutor, and supposed originator of the first code of written rules governing the 'sport' of boxing.[45]

The British Medical Association has been the most vociferous campaigners for the abolition of boxing. Their arguments are primarily on medical grounds, not only as far as the risk of traumatic tragedy is concerned, but also in terms of cumulative damage that almost inevitably occurs during any prolonged boxing career:

British Medical Association, *The Boxing Debate*

During the course of a boxing match, the contestants receive a variable number of blows to the upper torso, arms and head. These blows land on the target with widely differing degrees of force. The lightest may be a mere flick of a glove and the heaviest, may be as much as half a ton, which has been likened to being hit by a 12 lb padded wooden mallet travelling at 20 miles per hour. A considerable amount of energy is therefore applied to the target area when significant punches hit a boxer. In the case of the torso and arms, the bony structures are covered by skin, fat and well-developed muscles, all of which absorb energy in much the same way as the crumple zone on the front of a car absorbs much of the force of impact in a collision. Although there may be superficial bruising, usually little damage is done to underlying structures. In the case of the head, however, the skin is taught over the underlying skull and its bony projections, such as the eye sockets. There is limited energy absorption and the greater amount of the force of the blow is transmitted directly to the skull and its contents, the brain. Occasionally, over bony projections, especially round the eyes, the skin may split producing the familiar 'cut'.

Training, experience and skill may enable a boxer to reduce the force received from the blows of their opponent. The boxer learns to move away from the blow, 'riding the punch' as it is called, diverting much of the force of the blow so that it glances off the side of the head, forearm or gloves. Strong muscles in the shoulders, upper chest, and neck, may reduce the resulting movement of the head when struck and, as mentioned later, this may reduce the damage to

---

45 Sheard, K, 'Aspects of boxing in the western civilising process' (1997) 32(1) *International Review for the Sociology of Sport* 35–36.

the brain. In spite of all these defensive measures a boxer will receive significant punches in all but the most one-sided contest. Increased and more scientifically based training will increase the weight of the punches delivered by a particular boxer in the same way that modern training improves all athletic performance. The effect of media interest, especially television, is to emphasise the importance of the heavy blow, the knock-out punch. This is exemplified by the regular slow motion analysis of such punches that television provides. Professional boxers may therefore be encouraged to concentrate on heavy punching rather than skilful defence. Such trends and effects nullify the benefits of fitness and training and increase the risk to an individual boxer.

... The brain and the eye are delicate and vital organs with a limited ability to repair damage received. Deformation of the eye due to blows sustained in boxing frequently leads to retinal tears and sight-threatening damage to other structures of the eye, including the drainage angle and the lens. Retinal detachments more or less inevitably develop following retinal tears if these are not accurately diagnosed and subjected to expert treatment. In young, non-myopic patients, however, there may be a considerable delay between a retinal tear occurring and the onset of retinal detachment. Retinal damage associated with boxing injuries is frequently so severe that treatment taxes the skills of even the most experienced of retinal surgeons. Very major surgical procedures may be required to save sight and a satisfactory outcome cannot be guaranteed. Cataract may also not develop for some time after concussive injury to the lens of the eye. The force upon the brain due to the blows received in a boxing bout leads to movement of the brain within the skull and it is this movement that leads to damage to nerves, blood vessels and tissue. After an initial heavy punch that results in cerebral damage the brain is increasingly susceptible to further damage. Fortunately the brain has a certain amount of reserve capacity so that damage to its delicate structures may go unnoticed for some time. However any process that further reduces the reserve capacity of the brain, ageing for example, may lead to the damage received through boxing becoming apparent. Little can be done to protect the brain from the damage received in a boxing bout and there is only a minimal amount that can be achieved through rapid treatment of injury. Boxing may therefore result in damage to the brain. Such damage may be cumulative and, unfortunately, once it has occurred there is no means by which lost capacity can be regained.[46]

The danger that if boxing is banned, it will inevitably go underground is also often raised with the spectre of an increase in prize-fighting being the consequence.[47] Unlicensed boxing or prize-fighting continues to occur.[48] Although not yet found in Britain, in certain States in America a new form of

---

46   *The Boxing Debate* (1993), London: British Medical Association, pp 11–12, 28–29

47   See Parpworth, N, 'Boxing and Prize Fighting: The Indistinguishable Distinguished?' (1994) 2(1) *Sport and the Law Journal* 5; Jones, R, 'A Deviant Sports Career: Towards a Sociology of Unlicensed Boxing' (1997) 21(1) *Journal of Sport and Social Issue* 37–52; *ibid*, n 47, Sheard, K (1997); 'Raw Scrap from Boxing's Underbelly', *The Guardian*, 23 May 1997, p 6; 'How Bare-Knuckled Savagery became a Noble Art', *The Times*, 30 June 1997.

48   Darling, A, 'You cannot beat a good right hander', *Total Sport*, August 1997.

unregulated boxing, 'extreme fighting', has been commercially promoted. It is a form of fighting where two bare-knuckled combatants are pitted against each other in a ring until only one is left standing. There are no rounds, no time-outs and no holds barred – just a lot of punching, kicking, choking, nose pinching, ear yanking and groin kneeing. Only eye gouging and biting are forbidden.[49]

Sheard, K, 'Aspects of boxing in the western "civilising process"'

Donnelly's belief that, if banned, boxing as we now know it would be driven underground is valid. Indeed, such a ban would probably have all sorts of unintended and unanticipated consequences. Boxers fighting under such circumstances might be at greater risk than they are at present. Donnelly's claim that 'the sport may, under present social conditions, be defensible' might also be concurred with. However it is doubtful whether the 'dominant class' or 'culture' is deterred from legislative action by a fear that death or serious injury might befall a few working-class young men. The debate, as Donnelly implicitly recognises, is primarily about the morality of boxing and the 'bad example' which it sets, and not the pain and suffering it causes. If boxing were to be made illegal and pushed behind the scenes as prize-fighting was in the nineteenth century – and even if it continued to exist in a subterranean way – this would indeed be a reflection of greater 'civilisation' as the term is used here.[50]

The fight between Nigel Benn and Gerald McCellan in 1995 that left McCellan with severe brain damage, was universally seen as a brutal fight where the protagonists went to the absolute brink. As many are, the bout was built up as a grudge fight.[51] This fight perhaps crystallised the debate about the continued legitimacy of boxing in the context of an activity between two humans that has an essential natural link to our drive to survive.

Dyer, G, 'In the Noble Art, Even Failure Contains Greatness'

A couple of years ago, discussing boxing with an acquaintance, I was taking my usual line that boxing was an art form and so forth. If you ever see people fighting in the street it is ugly, hideous. In the ring, however, with the complex of rules governing what can and cannot be done, what begins in ugliness can become magnificent. Ban boxing and you ban the possibility of there being events like the Leonard-Hagler or Ali-Foreman fights. The history of the century would be impoverished without them. 'But what you want to see,' interrupted my acquaintance, 'is two blokes beating the shit out of each other'. There is no refuting this claim. Since then, although I have continued to follow boxing, I accept that everything else one might say about the sport is predicated on this brutal truth. By these terms Saturday's encounter between

---

49 'Extra time: Knuckles for two, dinner for one', *The Guardian*, 17 November 1995, p 26.
50 *Ibid*, n 47, Sheard (1997) p 54. Also see Donnelly, P, 'On Boxing: Notes on the Past, Present and Future of a Sport in Transition' (1989) 7(4) *Current Psychology: Research and Reviews* 331.
51 'Hype That Stirs Bad Blood', *The Independent on Sunday*, 5 March 1995.

Nigel Benn and Gerald McClellan was pretty much the ideal fight: two blokes smashing the shit out of each other.

My acquaintance, I should add, was speaking not as a critic of boxing but as a fan. Boxers do not fight for their fans. They do it for themselves. Nor, despite what Chris Eubank is always saying, do they box just for the money, any more than Martin Amis wrote his new novel for the money. Marvin Hagler said that if, when he died, his head was opened up all you would find would be a boxing glove because that is all there was in his life: boxing. Boxers box to prove something, to make their mark on the world, to become themselves. The price is often high but, as Robert Redford's film *Quiz Show* demonstrates, people will ruin themselves for more paltry things than a world boxing title. Besides, all sorts of activities take our lives away. A lifetime of factory work almost killed my father. First it wore him down and then, when he was exhausted, it came close to killing him. Ban factories and then ban boxing. As for the arts, music, painting and writing, they devour people. Greatness rarely comes cheap. Failure costs even more. Jazz begins with Buddy Bolden who, as Jelly Roll Morton said, 'went crazy because he really blew his brains out through the trumpet' ...

As with Bolden so with boxers: they remind us how far most of us fall short of living our lives to the full. Anyone with any desire to live would gladly have traded places with McClellan, knowing what might happen. Benn was nervous, frightened before the fight. To stand any chance of beating McClellan he had to overcome not simply his opponent but himself. This ex-squaddie thereby achieved what for Nietzsche was the highest possible affirmation: to go to meet what was simultaneously your greatest desire and your greatest fear. McClellan used up his life in 30 minutes on Saturday, bringing to bear every fibre of his being, everything he had been born with, everything he had learned. In sport we often talk of athletes finding a second wind. Even those of us who have played only amateur sports have found this second wind. For boxers, though, as the trainer tells the battered protagonist of Thom Jones's *The Pugilist At Rest*, 'there is a third wind. It is between here and death'. Ali found it in his fight with Foreman; Eubank found it in his second fight with Watson (like most fighters he will never dare to look for it again). Benn and McClellan both found it on Saturday. For 10 rounds McClellan wrung out of his destiny every last drop that it could concede. Wrung it dry. Even in his failure there was greatness. The rest of us languish, content to let destiny pass us by, to happen to other people. Now McClellan is on a life-support machine. For most of us life is little more than a life-support machine.

Boxing is terrible, tragic. It is awful. That is why it exerts such power over us. The job of our lives, perhaps of evolution itself, is to become gentler, more pacific. But the raw materials we are dealing with have scarcely changed in thousands of years. As a species human beings have hardly changed physically since antiquity. When we watch boxers we feel exactly the same awe, horror and respect expressed by Plutarch in a passage from his *Life Of Theseus*: 'At that time there were men who, for deftness of hands, speed of legs and strength of muscles, transcended normal human nature and were tireless. They never used their physical capacities to do good or to help others, but revelled in their own brutal arrogance and enjoyed exploiting their strength to commit savage, ferocious deeds, conquering, ill-treating, and murdering whosoever fell into their hands.'[52]

The debate concerning the legitimacy of boxing will no doubt continue, especially in the aftermath of periodic tragedies in the ring. Interestingly, in what has been seen as very much a preserve of men, women's boxing has dramatically increased in popularity although not without controversy; women are formally barred from official events organised by the British Boxing Board of Control.[53] Boxing as a sport has not only been criticised in terms of safety issues, it is one of those sports where cynicism of its commercialisation, spectacularisation and exploitation has grown. In the controversial WBO heavyweight contest between Mike Tyson and Evander Holyfield, the two fighters shared nearly £40 million.[54] Tyson biting off the top of his opponent's ear led to a revoking of his license and $3 million fine.[55] The plethora of world boxing championships is also a symptom of this; the WBO (World Boxing Organisation), WBC (World Boxing Council), WBA (World Boxing Association), IBF (International Boxing Federation) all compete to be seen as the leading world body.

Martial Arts: The Problem of Gaining Acceptance

These ancient 'arts' are based on stringent moral codes. They have their origins in the Far East with different countries having their own philosophies founded on the purity of spirit and notions of self-control and discipline. They are mainly based on self-defence[56] although some have more of an emphasis on attack including the use of weapons. Over the last few years a number of hybrid martial arts, often combined with boxing have emerged, predominantly westernised and particularly Americanised and having little or no underlying moral philosophy.[57]

There are a plethora of different types of martial art sports. Below is a selection of them.

---

52 Dyer, G, 'In the Noble Art, Even Failure Contains Greatness', *The Guardian*, 27 February 1995, p 18.

53 See 'Boxing Clever for the New Feminism', *The Observer*, 9 April 1995. In the USA, female amateur boxing has received official recognition since 1993 when a successful action for gender discrimination was brought against the National Amateur Boxing Organisation. Also see 'Gloves Coming off in Battle over Woman's Boxing', *Sunday Telegraph*, 28 March 1993 and 'Women boxers put men on ropes', *The Sunday Times*, 20 February 1994, p 7.

54 'Tyson Faces Fight for Future After Ear Biting', *Daily Telegraph*, 30 June 1997.

55 'Tyson's Exile Likely to be Short-lived', *The Times*, 10 July 1997, p 52.

56 See 'The Art of Pulling Punches', *The Times*, 2 October 1995.

57 Kick-boxing is an example as portrayed by exponents in films such as those starring Jean-Claude Van Dame.

Name	Explanation	Sports Council Recognition
Hapkido	Korean art of self-defence involving equal amounts of grappling and striking techniques	Yes
Karate	Japanese martial art involving striking with kicks and punches with very few throws	Yes
Tai Chi Chuan	Chinese school of Kung Fu emphasising relaxation an the development of internal strength	Yes
Escrima	Filipino weapons art where participants use short sticks or short swords and spar with each other or alone against the air	Yes
Aikido	Japanese martial art involving grappling between participants with strikes at the opponents arm or leg joints	Yes
Ju Jitsu	Japanese martial arts involving throws, locks and holds and ancillary strikes to weaken opponents	Yes
Taekwondo	Korean martial arts involving punches and kicking to unprotected body	Yes
Kendo	The Japanese sport of Kendo is an example where the proponents use a bamboo or oak sword and wear a head guard, a face grill, a breast plate and gauntlets	Yes
Muay Thai	Thai martial art where full force blows with feet, knees, elbows and fists against opponents	No
Semi- and full-contact Karate	American derived amalgam of a number of martial arts developed in the 1960s where full force blows are allowed to the body and heads and often held in a boxing ring	No
Knockdown Karate	Derivative Karate based on knocking the opponent down with bare fists and feet	No
Thai Boxing and Kick Boxing	Generic name for a number of martial arts derived from Thailand and developed in different cultures.	No
Knockdown Sport Budo	Japanese derived hybrid where players strike with kicks and punches to body and outer thigh	No

Martial arts can be divided into five categories: light or touch contact; semi-contact; knockdown and grappling with no full-contact strikes to the head; knockdown with full-contact strikes to the head; and full-contact.[58]

A number of British Martial Arts organisations have received recognition by the Sports Council. However a number of martial arts have not been recognised in terms of either the organising authority or the sport itself.[59] A problem to which the Sports Council has alluded to is the number of martial arts where there are a large number of different supervisory organisations. These disparate groups have been encouraged by the Sports Council to unify in attempting to attain recognition. However this has not occurred to any great extent, even though, a unifying British Thai Boxing and Kick Boxing Federation was formed in 1994 in an attempt to provide an effective submission towards a goal of achieving recognition.[60]

An examination of one of the varieties of Thai Boxing which has not been able to attain individual recognition is useful. Muay Thai, as the national sport of Thailand, is based on traditions that have been passed from generation to generation for over 2000 years. It has been part of military training for the last 500 years. As a sport, it reached prominence during the early 18th century with competition being on a local level. In 1930 a set of standardised rules were introduced including boxing gloves, groin guard and weight categories making it more humane and safer. The fighting is seen as only part of the philosophy of Muay Thai. Communal values and self-disciple are stressed in all the teachings. There is also a pre-fight ritual, Ram Muay, a slow motion ballet-like dance, which is a celebration of control and aesthetics. Muay Thai is recognised as a sport in Thailand and the International Amateur Muay Thai Federation is funded by the Thailand government. This organisation is concerned that its failure to attain recognition is because of the association that is made between Muay Thai and the Western bastardisation and obvious violence of kick boxing.

Conclusion: Boxing v Martial Arts

In the light of the proposals by the Law Commission discussed in the last chapter, there is a danger that a lack of recognition will make such 'sports' prone to criminal liability. The use of kicking of the feet seems to be a major area of concern.[61] The Law Commission cites evidence that Thai boxers run a

---

58 The Law Commission Consultation Paper No 139 (1995) *Criminal Law: Consent in the Criminal Law*, London: HMSO, para 12.45.

59 See 'Martial Arts and the Sports Council' (1992) *Sports Council,* SC/130/18/1B93 and 'Statement on Martial Arts' (1994) *Sports Council* SC/353/15M/10/94.

60 For further analysis see Farrell, R, 'Consent to Violence in Sport and the Law Commission, part 2' (1996) 4(1) *Sport and the Law Journal* p 5.

61 See, 'Call for Tighter Safety Checks as Kick-Boxer Dies After Fight', *The Times*, 27 May 1997, p 3.

considerable danger of becoming impotent due to blows to their groin.[62] However in light of the realisation of the extensive dangers to bodily injury through punching of the fists in boxing, the inconsistency of the approach of the authorities to legal classification becomes exposed.

It is the comparison that the Law Commission makes between boxing and what it calls 'martial art activities'[63] that is interesting. They view boxing as not having an ultimate aim of 'infliction of serious injury' or to 'knock [his] opponent out'.[64] This is a questionable conclusion and they seem to have been persuaded away from their earlier claim that 'the ultimate objective of every boxer is to knock his opponent out ... this conduct is inherently hostile'.[65] Martial arts, acknowledged as concerning both defence and attack, tends to be emphasised as 'for the purpose of attack'[66] and 'may be equally or more dangerous than (traditional) boxing'.[67] The Law Commission makes a distinction between what it sees as a 'a striking difference' between the levels of safety 'on an organised basis' in boxing, and the 'provision for safety in some of the equally dangerous full contact, unrecognised martial arts'.[68] Certain shades of cultural imperialism can be detected about cosy acceptance of boxing and suspicion of, and reification of the 'difference' of martial arts.

SPORT AND ANIMALS

As was discussed in Chapter 1, animals have been involved with human sport from the beginning of time. The more barbaric forms of animal sport, involving fighting often to the death, are for the main part unlawful in modern Britain. The modern involvement of animals in sporting activities can clearly be labelled sport: they share the characteristics of sport that have been identified earlier.

The use of animals in sporting activities is varied. Animal sports can be divided into three categories which we examine below.

The first category are sports in which humans use animals in the pursuit of athletic excellence. These are mainly horse related sports; horse racing, show jumping, and polo. The so called 'sport of kings', horse racing, has a long

---

62 *Ibid,* Law Commission (1995) p 169. However Farrell, *ibid,* n 63, does stress the need to formulate a view on the these associated dangers of kick boxing with reliable research rather than anecdotal evidence.

63 *Ibid,* para 12.45.

64 *Ibid,* para 12.35.

65 Law Commission, Consultation Paper No 134 (1994) 'Criminal Law: Consent and Offences Against the Person', London: HMSO, para 10.20.

66 *Ibid,* Law Commission 1995 para 12.39.

67 *Ibid,* Law Commission 1994 para 10.23.

68 *Ibid,* Law Commission 1995 para 12.38.

history and remains immensely popular. Indeed there is a substantial body of law surrounding the equine industry with issues such as riding accidents litigation, disciplinary issues concerning jockeys in horse racing and those concerned with protecting the pedigree of horses.

The second are sports where the animal is pitted against another animal either in competition of athletic prowess, eg greyhound racing and pigeon racing or fighting involving combat often to the death, eg dog, quail and cock fighting.

The history of governmental regulation of animal fighting has been chronicled. Regulation clearly still continues – prosecutions for cock fighting and dog fighting are not uncommon. The legal banning of these activities has often been based on the barbarity of the acts. It is a case of shades of Ellias's 'civilising process' or perhaps moralistic government control.

Cashmore, E, *Making Sense of Sports*

Hugh Cunningham, in his Leisure in the Industrial Revolution, relates a Sunday morning meeting in London in 1816 at which several hundred people were assembled in a field adjoining a church yard. In the field, 'they fight dogs, hunt ducks, gamble, enter into subscriptions to fee drovers for a bullock'. The Rector of the nearby church observed: 'I have seen them drive the animal through the most populous parts of the parish, force sticks pointed with iron, up the body, put peas into the ears, and infuriate the beast.'

Although condemned systematically from the eighteenth century, blood sports persist to this day, most famously in the Spanish bull rings and in the streets of Pamplona. England's bull ring in Birmingham reminds us that such events were not always confined to Spain; bull running ceased in England in 1825, a year after the founding of the Royal Society for the Prevention of Cruelty to Animals (RSPCA). The same organisation brought pressure against cock fighting, which was banned in 1835, only to go 'underground' as an illicit, predominantly working-class pursuit.

The decline of cock fighting, bull baiting and the like coincided with cultural changes that brought with them a range of alternative leisure pursuits. The whole spectrum of changes were part of what some writers have called the civilising process ... But, before we are tempted into assuming that barbaric tastes and activities have completely disappeared, we should stay mindful of Holt's caution: 'The tendency by members of all social classes to maltreat animals for excitement or gain is by no means dead even today.' Dog fighting in particular persists in the West to this day and dogs are bred for the specific purpose of fighting. In the early 1990s, amid a panic over the number of ferocious breeds proliferating, Britain banned the import of American pit bulls (such animals are required to be registered in Britain under the Dangerous Dogs Act 1991; there are about 5,000 unregistered pit bulls trained for fighting rather than as pets).[69]

---

69 Cashmore, E, *Making Sense of Sports*, 2nd edn (1996), London: Routledge, p 66.

Parker, C and Thorley, J, *Fair Game*

Cock fighting, like the baiting of dogs and badgers, is an illegal and secretive practice which legislation has failed to eliminate. It has an ancient history, probably originating in Greece about 500 BC. In Britain, it was the sport of all classes and its general acceptance made it difficult to ban. Edward III prohibited it as early as 1365, as did subsequently Henry VIII, Elizabeth I and Cromwell, but all with little success.

In England and Wales, a further attempt to stop cock fighting was made in the Cruelty to Animals Act 1835, which was followed with tougher penalties in 1849. However the sport continued quite openly throughout the country, most fights being too well-organised for the police and RSPCA to obtain evidence to sustain a conviction.

As late as 1930, a cock pit where the Chief Constable and magistrates were spectators was guarded by local police. Today, cock fighting does not have such powerful defenders, but the clandestine nature of the sport makes it difficult to enforce the law against it.[70]

Prosecutions for illegal cock fighting continue to be brought periodically:

Bowcott, O, '17 held in raid on cock fight by police and RSPCA'

RSPCA inspectors and police using a surveillance helicopter arrested 17 people yesterday when they raided a cock fight on a travellers' site in south-east London. Among those detained was a boy aged eight. Seven dead birds and several cock fighting spurs were seized from a shed on land between an industrial estate and the Thames marshes at Erith. The co-ordinated operation follows one last month when six people were arrested in a shed on allotments in Kelloe, Co Durham, and 14 dead cockerels, spurs, a weighing machine, a board listing birds' names and betting odds were found. The gathering was described as a well-organised event with seating around a fighting ring. The RSPCA yesterday condemned cock fighting as a barbaric blood sport. It had been outlawed since 1849, but still attracted a regular following.[71]

The final category includes sports where the animal becomes pitted against human in test of athletic excellence by use of a gun, other instrument or animal agency. These can be termed 'blood sports'. Examples include angling, one of the most popular sports in Britain with a myriad of regulatory legislation,[72] hunting including use of guns and although not carried out in Britain, bull fighting.

These are where philosophical argument arises: are blood sports morally justified? Hunting includes fox hunting, but connected activities are deer and

---

70 Parker, C and Thorley, J, *Fair Game* (1994), London: Pelham Books, p 271.

71 Bowcott, O, '17 held in raid on cock fight by police and RSPCA', *The Guardian*, 10 April 1995, p 2. For continued activity abroad see 'Deadly game for the birds of play', *The Guardian*, 20 December 1996, p 6.

72 See Gregory, M, *Angling and the Law* (1992), London: Charles Knight; 'Moves are launched to untangle legal lines', *The Times*, 10 July 1997, p 45, concerning a new regulatory framework for angling.

stag hunting, hare coursing and mink hunting. These are all lawful within the qualifications of legal safeguards.

Legal Regulation of Blood Sports

The historical regulation of blood sports was discussed earlier in Chapter 1. They can be divided into three types: baiting including bear, bull and badger baiting; fighting including with dogs and cocks; and hunting, including birds and foxes. Fox hunting continues to be lawful, and the debate about its continued existence will be evaluated shortly, but first a short summary of the legal position of hunting sports needs to be considered.

Activity	Lawful	Legal Prohibition or Qualification
Deer hunting	Yes	Deer Act 1991
Hare coursing	Yes	Hares Act 1848; Protection of Animals Act 1911
Mink hunting	Yes	Protection of Animals Act 1911
Bird shooting	Yes	Wildlife and Countryside Act 1981; Games Act 1831 and Games Act 1971
Cock fighting	No	Cock fighting Act 1952; Protection of Animals Act 1911
Dog fighting	No	Protection of Animals Act 1911; Protection of Animals (Amendment) Act 1911
Badger baiting	No	Protection of Badgers Act 1992
Angling	Yes	Salmon and Freshwater Fisheries Act 1975; Control of Pollution (Angler's Lead Weight) Regulations 1986
Fox hunting	Yes	Protection of Animals Act 1911

This provides a summary of the main statutory regulation of blood sports in Britain. Those activities that are lawful are in a qualified sense, either as to when it can occur as with shooting of game birds within certain seasons under the Game Acts, or regulated as with hunting, as to the type of prey. There are general Acts in this area, for example, the Protection of Animals Act 1911 which prohibits cruelty to domestic or captive animals and the Wildlife and Countryside Act 1981 which protects certain types of birds, such as the golden eagle and certain animals such as the otter from being hunted. There is additionally a large body of law surrounding poaching and rights over land used for blood sports both of a criminal and civil nature.

The regulatory framework has grown, often in a piecemeal and arbitrary way. Extensive campaigning has often been needed to improve legal prohibition and protection of the hunted animals. A good deal of the legislation has been initiated in the form of Private Members' Bills. One activity that has been controlled by a series of legislative controls is badger baiting. First controlled in 1835 at the same time as prohibition of baiting of other captive animals such as bears and bulls, badger baiting continued however to be widespread. Subsequently Parliament enacted the Badgers Act 1973 which made it a criminal offence for a person to 'wilfully kill, injure or take, or attempt to kill, injure or take, any badger'. Due to pressure from fox hunters, the legislation however had an exemption for landowners and their agents from persecuting badgers on their land. The subsequent Wildlife and Countryside Act 1981 strengthened the law to make it an offence to be in possession of a badger or part of one; however the increasing activity of attacking badger setts with dogs, remained specifically not prohibited, although the Wildlife and Countryside (Amendment) Act 1985 helped by reversing the burden of proof to that of the accused. Two Private Members' Bills have attempted to improve the regulatory framework The first failed[73] but the second became the Badger Bill 1991[74] and subsequently the Protection of Badgers Act 1992. It is now an offence to interfere with a badger sett without a government licence.

This also reflects the powerful interests groups present in this area, most notably those of landowners. The total expenditure on countryside sports has been estimated at £1.4 billion in 1991, with the government being paid £459 million through various forms of taxation, by The Standing Conference on Countryside Sports, a powerful umbrella group representing the continuing value of such activities.[75]

Fox Hunting

The legality of fox hunting has continually been questioned in recent years. The whole issue of its legitimacy and justification for fox hunting is one that is highly charged. The debate has two well-organised protagonists: the British Fields Sport Society[76] and the League Against Cruel Sport.[77] In addition, the Countryside Movement is a new umbrella coalition formed in 1995 to campaign against any prohibition on hunting and the general way of life in the country.[78] Underlying the debate are complex questions as to hunting's morality and a determination of what are the rights of animals and should they be protected from this 'exploitation'. There has been persistent controversy surrounding fox hunting. Many issues have surrounded the use

---

73 The Badger Sett Protection Bill 1989 introduced by Tony Banks MP.
74 Introduced by Roy Hughes MP.
75 *Countryside Sports: Their Economic and Conservation Significance* (1992), Reading: The Standing Conference on Countryside Sports.
76 *Hunting the Facts* (undated), British Field Sports Society, London BFSS.
77 *Wildlife Protection: The Case for the Abolition of Hunting and Snaring* (1992), London: The League Against Cruel Sport.
78 'Land Rights: Hunt, shoot, fish ... Kill', *The Guardian*, 15 November 1995, p 25.

of land for hunting, first the rights of those participating in the hunt and secondly protesters, who have been regulated by the Criminal Justice and Public Order Act 1994, which criminalised the normally civil law wrong of trespass with hunt saboteurs seen to be the major target.[79]

Although many blood sports including animals have been severely regulated or banned, the persistence of fox hunting indicates the deep seated role that these activities have played and continue to play in British society. Its continued existence and longevity needs to be explained:

Cashmore, E, *Making Sense of Sports*

Blood sports in general and fox hunting in particular are seen as having central importance by Norbert Elias and his collaborator Eric Dunning. The 'civilising' of society demanded greater personal self-control and a stricter constraint on violence, but the process of hunting or just observing allowed 'all the pleasures and the excitement of the chase, as it were, mimetically in the form of wild play' (1986). While the passion and exhilaration associated with hunting would be aroused, the actual risks would be absent in the imagined version (except for the animals, of course) and the effects of watching would be, according to Elias and Dunning, 'liberating, cathartic'. The comments could be applied without alteration to all of the activities considered so far. They are products of a human imagination ingenious enough to create artificial situations that human evolution has rendered irrelevant. But, once created, they have seemed to exert a control and power of their own, eliciting in both participants and audience a pleasurable excitement that encapsulates the thrill or 'rush' of a hunt, yet carries none of the attendant risks.[80]

Fox hunting is Elias's favourite example. Once synonymous with the word 'sport', fox hunting is now an anachronism and pressure against it would have no doubt prompted its demise were it not a pursuit practiced exclusively by England's landowning elite. Developing in the late 18th century, this peculiarly English sport was quite unlike the simpler, less regulated, and more spontaneous forms of hunting of other countries and earlier ages where people were the main hunters and foxes were one amongst many prey (boar, red deer, and wolves being others). Fox hunting (itself an example of a figuration) was bound by a strict code of etiquette and idiosyncratic rules, such as that which forbade killing other animals during the hunt. Hounds were trained to follow only the fox's scent, and only they could kill, while humans watched.

The fox itself had little utility apart from its pelt; its meat was not considered edible (not by its pursuers, anyway) and, while it was considered a pest, the fields and forests were full of others which threatened farmers' livestock and crops. The chances of anyone getting hurt in the hunt were minimised, but each course in the wall of security presented a problem of how to retain the immediacy and physical risk that were so important in early times. Elias

---

79 See Bailey, S, Harris, D and Jones, B, *Civil Liberties: Cases and Materials*, 4th edn (1995), London: Butterworths; *The Unacceptable Face of Protest* (1993), London: British Field Sports Society; 'Rivals stalk each other in rural battle of Britain', *The Observer*, 6 August 1995, p 24.

80 Cashmore, E, *Making Sense of Sports*, 2nd edn (1996), London: Routledge, pp 66–67.

believes that the elaboration of the rules of hunting were solutions. The rules served to postpone the outcome, or finale of the hunt and so artificially prolong the process of hunting. 'The excitement of the hunt itself had increasingly become the main source of enjoyment for the human participants.' What had once been foreplay to the act of killing became the main pleasure. So the fox hunt was a virtual 'pure type' of autotelic hunt: the thrill for participants came in the pace and exhilaration of the chasing and the pleasure of watching violence done without actually doing the killing.

But the influence of the civilising spurt is apparent in the restraint imposed and exercised by the participants. The overall trend was to make violence more repugnant to people, which effectively encouraged them to control or restrain themselves. Elias stresses that this should be seen not as a repression but as a product of greater sensitivity. The fox hunters did not secretly feel an urge to kill with their own hands; they genuinely found such an act disagreeable, but could still find pleasure in viewing it from their horses – what Elias calls 'killing by proxy'.

Despite all attempts to abolish them, hunts persist to this day, probably guided by appetites similar to those whetted by the sight of humans being masticated by sharks. Hundreds of millions of Jaws fans can attest to the enjoyable tension provided by the latter, albeit through the medium of film. While Elias does not cover the modern hunts, we should add that their longevity reveals something contradictory about the civilising trend and the impulse to condone or even promote wanton cruelty. To ensure a long and satisfying chase, and to be certain that foxes are found in the open, 'earth stoppers' are employed to close up earths (fox holes) and badger sets in which foxes may take refuge. Many hunts maintain earths to ensure a sufficient supply of foxes through the season (foxes used to be imported from the continent). The hunt does not start until after 11am to allow the fox time to digest its food and ensure that it is capable of a long run. During the course of a hunt, a fox may run to ground and will either survive or be dug out by the pursuant dogs, a virtual baiting from which even the dogs emerge with damage. New hounds are prepared by killing cubs before the new season, a practice observed and presumably enjoyed by members of the hunt and their guests.

In Elias's theory, fox hunting was a solution to the problems created by the accelerating trend toward civilisation and the internal controls on violence it implied. The closing up of areas of excitement, which in former ages had been sources of pleasurable gratification (as well as immense suffering), set humans on a search for substitute activities and one which did not carry the risks, dangers, or outright disorder that society as a whole would find unacceptable – what Elias, in the title of one of his books, calls the Quest for Excitement. The English form of fox hunting was only one example of a possible solution, but Elias feels it is an 'empirical model', containing all the original distinguishing characteristics of modern sport. Other forms of sport, such as boxing, soccer, cricket, and rugby showed how the problem was solved without the use and abuse of animals.[81]

---

81 *Ibid,* Cashmore (1996) pp 81–83.

The argument in favour of fox hunting tends to focus on the practical need to control the fox because of it being a great pest to the farmer. Philosophically the focus is on fox hunting being a part of the natural order of things:

Ortega Y Gasset, J, 'The Ethics of Hunting'

Every authentic refinement must leave intact the authenticity of the hunt, its essential structure, which is a matter of a confrontation between two unequal species. The real care that man must exercise is not in pretending to make the beast equal to him, because that is a stupid utopia, a beatific farce, but rather in avoiding more and more the excess of his superiority. Hunting is the free play of an inferior species in the face of a superior species. That is where one must make some refinement. Man must give the animal a 'handicap', in order to place him as close as possible to his own level, without pretending an illusory equivalence which, even if it were possible, would annihilate *ipso facto* the very reality of the hunt. Strictly speaking, the essence of sportive hunting is not raising the animal to the level of man, but something much more spiritual than that: a conscious and almost religious humbling of man which limits his superiority and lowers him toward the animal.

I have said 'religious' and the word does not seem excessive to me. As I have already pointed out, a fascinating mystery of nature is manifested in the universal fact of hunting: the inexorable hierarchy among living beings. Every animal is in a relationship of superiority or inferiority with regard to every other. Strict equality is exceedingly improbable and anomalous. Life is a terrible conflict, a grandiose and atrocious confluence. Hunting submerges man deliberately in that formidable mystery and therefore contains something of religious rite and emotion in which homage is paid to what is divine, transcendent, in the laws of nature.[82]

Arguments against fox hunting focus both on the falsity of the view that foxes are a major problem in the country and that hunting is the best way to counter it. They also focus on the rights that animals including foxes have, including the right not to be hunted:[83]

Regan, T, 'Why Hunting and Trappings are Wrong'

Since animals can pose innocent threats and because we are sometimes justified in overriding their rights when they do, one cannot assume that all hunting or trapping must be wrong. If rabid foxes have bitten some children and are known to be in the neighbouring woods, and if the circumstances of their lives assure future attacks if nothing is done, then the rights view sanctions nullifying the threat posed by these animals. When we turn from cases where we protect ourselves against the innocent threats wild animals pose, to the activities of hunting and trapping, whether for commercial profit or 'sport', the rights view takes a dim view indeed. Standard justifications of

---

82 Ortega, J and Gasset, Y, 'The Ethics of Hunting' in Morgan, W and Meier, K, *Philosophic Inquiry in Sport*, 2nd edn (1995), Champaign: Human Kenetics.

83 See Brooman, S and Legge, D, *Law Relating To Animals* (1997), London: Cavendish Publishing, for full discussion on arguments for and against fox hunting and also generally on issues concerning animals and sport.

the 'sport' of hunting – that those who engage in it get exercise, take pleasure in communion with nature, enjoy the camaraderie of their friends, or take satisfaction in a shot well aimed – are lame, given the rights view. All these pleasures are obtainable by engaging in activities that do not result in killing any animal (walking through the woods with friends and a camera substitutes nicely) and the aggregate of the pleasures hunters derive from hunting could only override the rights of these animals if we viewed them as mere receptacles, which, on the rights view, they are not.

The appeal to tradition – an appeal one finds, for example, in support of fox hunting in Great Britain – has no more force in the case of hunting than it does in the case of any other customary abuse of animals – or humans. All that appeals to tradition signal in this case, and all they signify in related contexts, is that it is traditional to view animals as mere receptacles or as renewable resources. These appeals to tradition, in other words, are themselves symptomatic of an impoverished view of the value animals have in their own right and thus can play no legitimate role in defending a practice that harms them. Such appeals are as deficient in Great Britain, when made in behalf of the 'sport' of fox hunting, as they are when made in Japan or Russia in defence of commercial whaling, or in Canada in defence of the annual slaughter of seals. To allow these practices to continue, if certain quotas are not exceeded, is wrong, given the rights view, for reasons that will become clearer as we proceed.

Of course, those who hunt and trap sometimes rest their case on other considerations. It is not their pleasure that justifies what they do; rather it is the humane service they perform for the animals that does. The situation, we are enjoined to believe, is this: if a certain number of animals are not hunted or trapped, there will be too many animals belonging to a given species for a given habitat to support. That being so, some of these animals will die of starvation because of their inability to compete successfully with the other animals in the habitat. To cull or harvest a certain number of these animals thus has the humane purpose and achieves the humane goal of sparing these animals the ordeal of death by starvation. How can the rights view, or any other view that is sensitive to the welfare of animals, find fault with that?

The rights view finds fault with this defence of hunting and trapping on several counts. First, the defence assumes that the death endured by hunted and trapped animals is always better (ie always involves less suffering) than the death these animals would endure as a result of starvation. This is far from credible. Not all hunters are expert shots, and not all trappers tend their traps responsibly or use traps that exhibit their 'humane' concern for animals, the infamous leg-hold trap being perhaps the most notorious example to the contrary. Is it obvious that animals who experience a slow, agonising death as a result of a hunter's poor shot or a poorly tended trap have a 'better death' than those who die from starvation? One looks for an argument here and finds none. Unless or until one does, the defence of hunting and trapping on the grounds that they kill 'more humanely' is specious.

Second, appeals to 'humane concern' are dramatically at odds with the philosophy of current hunting and trapping practices, as well as with wildlife management generally. This philosophy, or the creed of maximum sustainable yield, applies to hunting and trapping in the following way. Those who hunt and trap are legally permitted, within specified seasons, to 'harvest' or 'crop' a certain number of wildlife of various species, the quota for that season, both collectively and for each individual hunter, to be fixed by determining whether, together with the best estimates of natural mortality, those who hunt and trap will be able to 'harvest' the same number next season, and the next, and so on. In this way the maximum sustainable yield is established. If this philosophy is applied successfully, hunters and trappers will be legally licensed to do the same thing in future seasons as others were licensed to do in the past namely kill up to a certain number (a certain quota) of animals. If, that is, restraint is exercised in each season, the total number of animals that can be harvested over time will be larger or to put the point in its simplest, starkest terms, if fewer animals are killed now, future generations of hunters will be able to kill a larger (aggregate) number of animals in the future, which will be better. This implication of the creed of maximum sustainable yield unmasks the rhetoric about 'humane service' to animals. It must be a perverse distortion of the ideal of humane service to accept or engage in practices the explicit goal of which is to insure that there will be a larger, rather than a smaller, number of animals to kill! With 'humane friends' like that, wild animals certainly do not need any enemies.

Essentially the same point can be made regarding the aggregate amount of suffering animals will endure if the creed of maximum sustainable yield is successful. If successful, the total number of animals who will die an agonising death as a result of the poor shooting of hunters, plus those who die in similar agony as a result of poorly tended 'humane' traps, plus those who die by natural causes will be larger than if other options were adopted. It is a moral smoke screen, therefore, to defend sport hunting and trapping by appeal to their humane service. The actions allowed by the philosophy of maximum sustainable yield speak louder than the lofty words uttered in its defence. The success of this philosophy would guarantee that more, not fewer animals will be killed and that more, not fewer animals will die horrible deaths either at the hands of humans or in the course of nature.

But it is not only the inconsistency between what it proclaims and what it implies that marks the undoing of the creed of maximum sustainable yield. That approach to decision making regarding wildlife management policies profoundly fails to recognise or respect the rights of wild animals. No approach to wildlife can be morally acceptable if it assumes that policy decisions should be made on the basis of aggregating harms and benefits. In particular, these decisions should not be made by appeal to the minimise harm principle. That principle sets before us what seems to be a laudatory goal – namely, to minimise the total amount of harm in general and suffering in particular. But that principle lacks the moral wherewithal to place any limits on how this laudatory goal is to be achieved; it lacks the means to assess the means used to achieve this end. If the rights of individuals are violated, that simply does not compute morally, given the minimise harm principle, if violating these rights is instrumental in achieving the goal of minimising total harm. The rights view categorically denies the propriety of this approach to decision making. Policies that lessen the total amount of harm at the cost of violating the rights of individuals, whether these individuals are moral agents or patients and, if the latter, human or animal, are wrong. Even if it were true, which it is not, that the philosophy of maximum sustainable yield would lead to a reduction in the total amount of death and suffering for undomesticated animals, it still would not follow that we should accept that philosophy. As it systematically ignores the rights of wild animals, so does it systematically violate them.

The rights view categorically condemns sport hunting and trapping. Though those who participate in it need not be cruel or evil people, what they do is wrong. And what they do is wrong because they are parties to a practice that treats animals as if they were a naturally recurring renewable resource, the value of which is to be measured by, and managed by reference to, human recreational, gustatory aesthetic, social and other interests.[84]

Conclusion

The Labour party came into power in 1997, with a promise of a free vote on fox hunting. In June 1997, a Private Members' Bill had its first hearing, but was considered to have major problems in successfully progressing without some move away from a total ban.[85] Campaigners on both sides of the argument have been vociferous in stating their case. Public opinion seems to be evenly balanced on this issue.[86] Whether the State will prohibit fox hunting or perhaps increasingly regulate is a question for the future.

REGULATION OF ACTIVITY CENTRES

New legislation came into force in 1996 to regulate centres that run activity holidays and courses for young people. It was in response to the Lyme Bay canoeing tragedy which lead to the death of four Plymouth school children. A prosecution for manslaughter was brought successfully against the directors of the company, and the company itself, that ran the centre. This was an historic conviction, being the first successful prosecution for corporate manslaughter in English law. The company in question, OLL Ltd, was based at Lyme Bay and organised outdoor adventure activities including off-shore canoeing trips. If a conviction was ever going to be secured for corporate manslaughter, this perhaps was the most likely situation in that the company was small with only two directors. It was reasonably straightforward to align the managing director with the company itself.

---

84 Regan, T, 'Why Hunting and Trappings are Wrong' in William, J and Meier, K (eds), *Philosophical Inquiry in Sport*, 2nd edn (1995), Champaign: Human Kinetics, p 46.

85 'Foxhunters Scent Victory as Ban Recedes', *The Independent*, 30 July 1997, p 1.

86 A Gallup poll in August 1997 indicated 63% in favour of a ban, 35% against, 'Fox Hunting Opponent Fail to go in For the Kill', *Daily Telegraph*, 11 August 1997, p 4.

This prosecution has implications for organisations running similar activities and the supervision of the plethora of sporting and recreational activities in this country. This is not the first incident involving deaths of participants in similar organised activities. The events that lead to the death of the four teenagers can be seen as a catalogue of misjudgments and mistakes concerning the safety of the trip that were likely to result in such a tragic consequence.

The Lyme Bay Tragedy

The plan was to canoe across Lyme Regis Bay moving close to the shore to Charmouth leaving mid-morning and returning to Lyme Bay. It was estimated that the round trip would take about two hours. There were a number of safety checks that were ignored:

- no early morning check on the weather conditions;
- no provision of adequate clothing;
- no distress flares carried by the two instructors;
- coastguard not informed of trip;
- no spray covers on canoes;
- perhaps most crucially the two instructors had only been on a basic training course for three days.

Soon after the trip started the sixth-formers who beforehand only had one afternoon's practice of capsizing techniques in a swimming pool, had difficulty controlling their canoes. Two of the party soon capsized including the group's teacher. The whole group began to drift out to sea well out of their depth. The prevailing wind although blowing parallel to the shore was well known locally as being deflected off the land and back out to sea. The fact that this particular local condition was not considered by the organisers of the trip was stressed by the prosecution in the case.

An increasing number of the group began to capsize. They were instructed to hold their canoes together but in the increasingly rough sea, the group became separated with the teacher and one of the instructors left alone. The remaining instructor tried to summon help by blowing a whistle. She did not have any emergency flares. The lack of spray decks to keep water out of the canoes caused them to become increasingly waterlogged.

The failure of the group to return to Lyme Regis during the early afternoon led to searches along the shore using the centre's safety boat and a vehicle on land. The failure to trace the group was not reported to the coastguards until after 3 pm. There were allegations that they were not informed accurately about how long the group was overdue. The coastguards' response was criticised too. They failed to observe that the wind was not blowing on-shore and initially carried out a shore search; the first helicopter was not launched until nearly an hour later; a lifeboat a half hour later; a second and third helicopter followed an hour after the first.

By the time the group was detected several miles out to sea, they were all in the water except the teacher and the instructor who had got separated from the rest. The main group had been in the sea for nearly three and a half hours before they were detected and picked up. The instructor with them had failed to inform them to blow up their life jackets and they were therefore only partially inflated. Two of the group made to swim to the shore and they survived one of them being picked up eight miles away from Lyme Regis. The other four, after suffering from severe hypothermia, were not able to be revived.

The prosecution for manslaughter was against the company, OLL Ltd, the managing director Peter Kite, and the manager of the centre, Joseph Stoddart. The latter was acquitted but both the company and Kite were convicted with sentences of a fine for the company, and a custodial sentence for Kite.

There was concern about the limited regulatory requirements that only needed minimal compliance at that time under the Health and Safety at Work Act 1974. David Jamieson, the MP for the Plymouth area sponsored a Private Members' Bill which led to the Activity Centres (Young Persons' Safety) Act 1995 and the Adventure Activities Licensing Regulations 1996. The law came into place on 1 August 1996 and requires that the centre hold a licence under the existing regulatory authority.[87]

Scope of the Act

The Statutory scheme is aimed at anyone who sells adventure activities within the scope of the Act to young people under 18. Caving, climbing, trekking and water sports are within the scope of the Act. There are exclusions, however, which include the provision of such activities by voluntary associations, by educational establishments to their pupils and when the young person is accompanied by a parent or legal guardian.

What is an Activity Centre

A centre is defined as an establishment which at the time in question is primarily used as a base for the provision of instruction or leadership in sporting recreational or outdoor activities for at least 28 days a year. Where

---

87 See Jacobs, Y, 'Adventure Activities Licensing Regulations 1996' (1996) 8(4) *Education and the Law* 295 and (1996) 24(5) *Health and Safety Bulletin* for further analysis of the new legislation.

multiple centres exist, a separate licence is required for each activity centre operated at the same time by the same individual.

The only licensing authority appointed so far is the private company, Tourism Quality Services Ltd. If a licence is granted they may at anytime revoke or vary the license. Standard conditions which are attached include a duty to ensure that the requirements related to safety remain effective, a duty to cooperate with the licensing authority by allowing inspections and providing information and also a duty to make the licence available to inspection by the public.

Additional special conditions may be attached. If a licence is refused, the failed applicant may appeal to the Secretary of State. The licensing authority is expected to appoint an inspector to carry out an inspection and make a report evaluating the application.

Offence

It is an offence for a person to do anything for which a license is required by him under the regulations. It is also an offence to make a statement to the licensing authority either knowing it to be false in a material particular or being reckless as to its falsity.

Good safety management practice and risk assessment needs to be in place. The focus is primarily on assessment of risk to participants, the measures identified as necessary to reduce these risks and any arrangements to give continued effect to the measures.

The Health and Safety Commission's guide on this risk assessment is outlined below:

Health and Safety Commission, 'The Risk Assessment'

Before granting a license, the authority must be satisfied that the provider:

- has identified the hazards created by the activity;
- has decided who might be harmed, and how;
- has evaluated the risk and decided whether existing measures (safety precautions) are adequate or more should be done;
- reviews the assessment from time to time and revises it as necessary.

As part of their application, providers must set out the significant findings of their risk assessment, and the measures and arrangements relating to it. (A provider with more than five employees needs to record these matters to comply with other health and safety legislation.)

The scope of the risk assessment should be sufficient to identify the significant (non-trivial) risks arising from the activity. It should be suitable to enable the provider to identify and prioritise the measures that need to be taken to ensure, so far as is reasonably practicable, the safety of participants or others who may be affected by the activity. The licensing authority should include a non-standard condition which restricts the facilities for adventure activities covered by any licence so they are no wider than those set by the provider in the risk assessment.[88]

The Health and Safety Executive publication Five Steps to Risk Assessment[89] is stressed as an appropriate guide to establishing the risk of a particular activity as with any workplace. In establishing these criteria, the applicant needs to provide supporting documentary proof.

Conclusion

There are a number of issues that will need to be reconciled in the future as far as this Act is concerned. The courts may well need to provide definitive interpretation of the scope of the Act and surrounding regulations. Another major question is how effective the regulatory framework will be. This will be determined essentially by how well it is policed, both when the licence is awarded and then how well the conditions are observed. The Act is, however, a good example of how a regulatory framework with an emphasis on prevention and risk management can try to provide a safer environment for sport and recreation.

RACISM IN SPORT

Racism in sport as with racism generally in society is an endemic problem. The focus of this section will be on the regulation of spectator racism against those participating in sport, although there are other types of racism or racist issues found in sport. Growing concern has been voiced about the low levels of representation of sports administrators or coaches from ethnic minority backgrounds, especially for ex-sports men and women. Another is that sporting excellence by black athletes has become itself a racist issue; many racist myths and scientific half truths have been spun to provide psychological, physiological and genetical explanations between blacks and whites.[90] A third issue is the way that it seems black school children are channelled into sport due to lack of available alternative opportunities. This is often in deference to perceived stereotypes that blackness is synonymous with physical prowess and intellectual backwardness; the more blacks excel in

---

88 *Guidance to the Licensing Authority on The Adventure Activities Licensing Regulations 1996* (1996), London: Health and Safety Commission C65 4/96.

89 'Five Steps to Risk Assessment: A Step by Step Guide to a Safer and Healthier Workplace' (1996), London: Health and Safety Executive 7/96.

90 The recent assertion by Dr Roger Bannister that black athletes have better developed tendons due to climatical factors illustrates the multitudes of explaining racial differences, see *The Times*, 23 November 1995. Also see 'Racist Myths that refuse to go away', *The Times*, 2 May 1990.

sport, the more black youths are pushed into it and drawn into it and subsequently excel at it and so on. This section will provide a background and link to discussion on racism in sport in the context of employment and regulation of sports stadiums.

Sport and race have a complex and self-perpetuating symbiotic role in constructing social understanding of racial difference.[91] Sport is a useful measure of how far we have come and how far there is to go in terms of racial integration. In the USA, the exploits of 'Tiger' Woods and his US Masters triumph in 1997 along with the 50th anniversary of Jackie Robinson's breaking of the colour bar in professional baseball, and indeed in all major league sport, when he played for the Brooklyn Dodgers, has regenerated the race debate in US professional sport.[92] Although in many sports such as professional basketball and notably the National Basketball League, the representation of African Americans is very high, in others such as professional golf it is very low. However in the higher echelons of professional sport in positions such as team mangers, whites rule supreme.[93] In the UK, similarly, very few black ex-players have been able to progress into coaching and management positions.[94] Spectator racism has been a particular problem and will be discussed later but first the perpetuation of racial stereotypes will be discussed.

Greater participation of black athletes in sport is often used to illustrate the belief in greater tolerance in contemporary society to racial difference. In some sports such as athletics, they seem to have been at the cutting edge of equal opportunities. However in an array of other sports, swimming, snooker, golf, horse racing for example, there is virtually no black presence. Britain clearly has black stars: John Barnes, Denise Lewis, Devon Malcom, Martin Offiah, Linford Christie, Frank Bruno. The last two are interesting to contrast. Bruno is probably the most loved black athlete, an 'honourable white'. His blackness has never been very visible, partly due to his own lack of racial self-promotion and the conflation of blackness and boxing. In contrast, Christie, who is arguably the greatest British sportsman of the last decade, has never had his achievements appropriately acknowledged. He has never hidden his colour; some see him as an opinionated, arrogant, fast black man focused on winning. As Hill argues:

> Unlike the loveable loser Bruno, Christie does not play up to a recognisable British character role ... he is deemed at least in part an outsider in his own land.[95]

---

91 See Cashmore, E, *Black Sportsmen* (1982), London: Routledge, and Jarvie, G (ed), *Sport, Racism and Ethnicity* (1991), London: Falmers Press.

92 See 'A Race Apart', *The Guardian*, 16 April 1997.

93 See 'The Town Meeting', ESPN television February 1997 (copy available Anglia Sports Law Research Centre).

94 'Racism Bars Way to Top Jobs in Football', *The Guardian*, 19 February 1996.

95 'Unlevel fields', *The Guardian* (section 2), 21 March 1995, p 2.

Racism in social life can be brutally visible both in terms of physical attacks and clear denial of the fundamental freedoms accepted in contemporary liberal society. However it also exists in the hidden interstices of society in abundance. Verbal racism is more insidious, but as all black sportsmen will know in Britain, it is only too real. Racism has been a part of sport as long as sport has been played.

The aetiology of spectator racism in sport is as complex as it is of racism generally in society:

Hammond, D, *Foul Play: A Class Analysis of Sport*

The success of blacks in professional sports such as soccer has not, of course, eradicated racism either from the changing room or the terracing, but it has clearly made a difference. It is very difficult for racists to continually abuse blacks while supporting a team that is peppered with blacks, especially if the team is successful and the black players can be seen to be an integral part of that success.

Perhaps this effect should not be over estimated though. Terrace language still refers to 'our niggers' as opposed to 'theirs', and equally disturbing when a team reverts to an all white line-up the abuse heaped on blacks playing for the opposing team increases. Blacks are undoubtedly still racially abused albeit on a smaller scale, and they have still yet to make the breakthrough into senior positions on the coaching and management jobs are not available to blacks after their playing days are over must be a consideration before they take up serious sport in the first place. The effect of ignoring other opportunities to take up a sport that will eventually leave one uneducated and unemployed can be catastrophic.[96]

The controversy within cricket in 1995 as far as the doubted application by black players not born in England to the cause of the English team is a contemporary example. Perhaps it is not surprising that at times of national decline in sports such as cricket, the focus of blame falls on those who are different.[97]

Racism in Football

Within football, the participation of black players has dramatically increased over the last three decades. There are about 2,000 black professional players.[98] This tends to hide the particular battles that black players have had to fight to

---

96 Hammond, D, *Foul Play: A Class Analysis of Sport* (1993), London: Ubique, p 52.

97 See Marqusee, M, *Anyone But England: Cricket and the National Malaise* (1994); Greenfield, S and Osborn, G, 'Oh to be in England? Mythology and Identity in English Cricket' (1996) 1(2) *Social Identities* 89.

98 This is vastly over-representative in terms of Afro-Caribbeans as part of the general population. It is interesting to note that their are virtually no Asian professional footballers. See 'Asians Can't Play Barrier', *The Guardian*, 10 February 1996 and 'Ooh, aah ... Jaginder', *The Independent* magazine, 17 August 1996.

achieve prominence and that this has been despite the dominant values within football culture. The stereotyped but long held wisdom that 'coloured players', as they were called for many years, did not have suitable temperament and 'lacked heart' and 'would not be able to stand the cold' is still present in modified forms.[99]

The causes of spectator racism are complex.[100] This is a reflection of the whole academic debate concerning the study of football hooliganism as a social phenomenon, where there are many competing theories.[101] The composition of the professional football leagues is becoming increasingly cosmopolitan with the signing of more foreign players. English football has always had many players from the other home countries of the United Kingdom. It was not until the emergence of black players, both from the Caribbean and Africa, during the 1960s, that the first manifestation of any real identifiable spectator reaction became evident. Some of these early players seem to have been grudgingly tolerated.[102] Perhaps it was not until the late 1970s, when the number of black players began to increase significantly, that they became visible and began to represent a perceived threat. Sections of spectators, at some clubs more than others, began to react actively, through stereotyping racial comments and abuse, monkey chants, and the throwing of bananas onto the ground.

99 An example are the comments by the Crystal Palace chairman, Ron Noades, in *Cutting Edge*, Channel 4 in 1993 that black players could not be trusted in the 'heat of battle' and 'lacked heart', which drew considerable criticism.

100 See Greenfield, S and Osborn, G, 'When the Whites Come Marching In' (1996) 6(2) *Marquette Sports Law Journal* 315; Fleming, S and Tomlinson, A, 'Football, Racism and Xenophobia in England (I) Europe and the Old England' and Garland, J and Rowe, M, 'Football, Racism and Xenophobia in England (II) Challenging Racism and Xenophobia' in Merkel, U and Tokarski, W (eds), *Racism and Xenophobia in European Football Sports, Leisure and Physical Education Trends and Developments* (1996), Vol 3, Aachen: Meyer and Meyer Verlag.

101 See for example Armstrong, G and Harris, R, *Football Hooligans: Theory and Evidence* (1991) 39(3) *Sociological Review* 427; Williams, J, Dunning, E and Murphy, P, *Hooligans Abroad: The Behaviour of English fans at Continental Matches*, 2nd edn (1989), London: Routledge; Dunning, E, Murphy, P and Waddington, I, 'Anthropological versus Sociological Approaches to the Study of Soccer Hooliganism: Some Critical Notes' (1991) 39(3) *Sociological Review* 459; Taylor, I, 'On the Sports Violence Question: Soccer Hooliganism Revisited' in Hargreaves, J (ed), *Sport, Culture and Ideology* (1981), London: Routledge; Marsh, P, Rosser, E and Harre, R, *The Rules of Disorder* (1978), London: Routledge and Hobbs, D and Robins, D, 'The Boy Done Good: Football Violence, Changes and Continuities' (1991) 39(3) *Sociological Review* 551.

102 It is interesting to compare Albert Johanneson, a South African, who played for Leeds United from 1960–70 and Clyde Best, a Bermudian, who played for West Ham from 1967–77. Johanneson's career petered out and suffering from chronic alcoholism died in late 1995 in poverty in Yorkshire. In comparison, Best returned to the Caribbean at the end of his career and is a successful business man.

L'Affaire Cantona

There is evidence that the racial nature of football hooliganism has increasingly become politicised and co-ordinated throughout Europe with groups such as 'Combat 18'.[103] Legal and non-legal initiatives have had some positive impact upon manifestations of spectator racism within football.[104] The 'L'Affaire Cantona' incident in 1995 can be used to illustrate the speculation that racial abuse and indifference may spread beyond the black/white demarcation that has been constructed over the last 30 years.[105] As the four professional divisions become increasingly diverse in terms of ethnic origins and nationality, especially within the ambiguity and instability of the New Europe, the fear of difference may escalate.

The incident in question occurred on 25 January 1994, when Eric Cantona, playing for Manchester United at Selhurst Park against Crystal Palace was sent off after kicking out at an opposing player. He was walking along the touch line towards the exit to the dressing rooms when Matthew Simmons ran down to the front of the crowd and 'verbally and digitally'[106] abused Cantona. He was reported as saying the words 'fucking, cheating French cunt. Fuck off back to France, you mother fucker'.[107] Simmons's version of this outburst was rather different. He told the police after the event that he actually had walked 11 rows down to the front because he wanted to go to the toilet and said: 'Off, off off. Go on, Cantona, have an early shower.'[108] Cantona reacted by leaping over the advertising hoardings with a two-footed kick against Simmons's chest. He struck him a number of times before the two were parted by police, stewards and team officials. Cantona was charged and convicted under the law of assault and was originally sentenced to two weeks' imprisonment which was reduced on appeal to 120 hours of community service.

This incident highlighted the issue of control of racist 'hate speech'. Is legislation the answer to the xenophobia of the likes of Simmons? He was convicted under public order offences for racial hatred. He could not be charged under section 3 of the Football Offences Act 1991 for indecent and racist chanting because he fell outside the scope of this legislation due to his

---

103 The crowd disorder which caused the abandoning of the international game between the Republic of Ireland and England in Dublin in early 1995 was seen as involving organised hooligan groups such as 'Combat 18'. See 'Troublemakers caught police on the hop', *The Guardian*, 16 February 1995.

104 It is important not to see this as a problem only limited to football. A report compiled for The Rugby League Association showed levels of racial abuse by spectators. See below p 143.

105 For an analysis of the case see Gardiner, S, 'Eric Cantona: Sport, Racism and the Limits of the Law' in McDonald and Carrington, B, *Land of Hope and Glory? Racism and British Sport*, Leicester University Press (forthcoming 1998).

106 See Ridley, I, *Cantona: The Red and the Black* (1995), London: Victor Gollancz, for a full discussion of court hearing of Cantona's prosecution.

107 *Ibid.*

108 *Ibid.*

actions being solitary. Liability only occurs when in a designated football match, words or sounds are chanted in concert with one or more others which are threatening, abusive or threatening to a person by reason of his colour, race, nationality or ethnic or national origins. The Act has been the second dedicated piece of legislation for the regulation of football stadiums. The first Act was the Football Spectators Act 1989, which like the 1991 Act had its origins in the recommendations of the Taylor Report based on the Hillsborough disaster.[109] The Taylor Report considered that the provisions of the Public Order Act 1986 concerning 'threatening, abusive or insulting words or behaviour' did not adequately cover indecent or racist chanting. This was due to the need to have a clearly identifiable victim to establish liability, in that either another person believed 'unlawful violence will be used against him or another'[110] or the chanting was 'within the hearing or sight of a person likely to be caused harassment, alarm or distress'.[111] Under the 1991 Act, no recognisable individual is needed, although the racial abuse will generally be directed at a particular player.

The issue that the Simmons/Cantona incident highlighted was the limitation of the 1991 Act to 'chanting in concert with one or more others'.[112] During the Parliamentary progress of the legislation it was argued that to criminalise a single racist or indecent remark would have created 'too low' a threshold. After the Cantona incident, there have been calls for the legislation to be extended to include individual acts. However as Parpworth argues:

> There is a certain futility in creating statutory offences which are effectively moribund due to difficulties associated with detection.[113]

Section 3 of the Football Offences Act 1991 has been little used, suggesting that it has been used symbolically.[114] As Chambliss and Seidman[115] argue, the way to identify legal symbolism is to measure the levels of enforcement. If they are low, symbolism is likely. Up until early 1996, there were only about 50 convictions. One of the major problems is the issue of policing, even though closed circuit television cameras are used to aid identification of perpetrators during matches. The individualising of the offence would arguably be even harder to enforce with police and ground stewards finding difficult to identify

---

109 Mr Justice Taylor, *The Hillsborough Stadium Disaster* (Cm 962), London: HMSO, 1990.

110 Section 4 of the Public Order Act 1986, 'Fear or Provocation of Violence'.

111 Section 5 of the Public Order Act 1986, 'Harassment, Alarm or Distress'. An additional offence has recently been created with s 4A of the Public Order Act 1986, Intentional Harassment, Alarm or Distress, as substituted by s 154 of the Criminal Justice and Public Order Act 1994, again needing an identifiable victim.

112 See 'It takes two to chant, court decides', *The Times*, 23 January 1993 and Pendry, T, *A Law with a Flaw, Kick it Again: Uniting Football Against Racism* (1995), London: Commission of Racial Equality.

113 Neil Parpworth, 'Football and Racism: a Legislative Solution' (1993) *Solicitors Journal*, 15 October.

114 See *ibid*, Greenfield and Osborn (1996) for an analysis.

115 Chambliss, W and Seidman, R, *Law, Order and Power*, 2nd edn (1982), New York: John Wiley.

the cries of a lone racist. There have been calls for crowds to engage in greater peer policing. This may well put individuals who would want to report to the authorities the activities of a racist, who may well have a general propensity to violence, into an invidious position.[116]

This debate about extension and individualising of racist hate speech on the football field reflects the calls for creation of a discrete offence for racial attacks to penalise more stringently the recent spate of racially motivated assaults generally in society.[117] The creation of a new offences is premised on the argument that further legislation would 'encourage a welcome realism in the levels of reporting of racial attacks, and could act as a deterrent to possible attackers'.[118] There is a view that a major problem is the lack of implementation of existing provisions by the police and other enforcement agencies, suggesting a failure in practice of these agencies to take racial violence and abuse seriously:

Francis, P, 'Race Attacks: Do We Need New Legislation?'

What the evidence does highlight is the overall paucity of political discussion on tackling racial attacks and the absence of any realistic assessment of existing legal and extra-legal provision ... further legislation will suffer the same problem existing legislation has encountered, and may not even provide symbolic importance. Rather what is needed is a genuine commitment from government and existing agencies to an imaginative use of existing powers, coupled with the continuing development, monitoring and evaluation of extra-legal provision.[119]

Gardiner , S, 'Ooh Ah Cantona: Racism as Hate Speech'

The process of criminalisation of problems such as racist hate speech can often be used to deflect political responsibility for them, as failures of social policy. It is convenient if such incidents can be seen as a criminal issue based on individual responsibility and wickedness. Legislation has a role to play, but it should not be at the expense of other non-legal social practices.[120]

There is a strong argument that the use of legislation can be seen as diverting attention and resources from educational and social policy initiatives which might more successfully eliminate the causes of the problem. Football stadiums have become one of the most overtly regulated public spaces. There is an increasing danger that this regulatory approach to social problems by the

---

116 Simmons had previous convictions for assault.

117 See Bindman, G, 'Outlawing Hate Speech', *The Law Society Gazette*, 8 April 1992, p 17; Fidgett, P, 'Responding to Racial Violence' (1993) 89(14) *The Probation Journal* 88 and Loveland, I, 'Hate Crimes and the First amendment' (1994) *Public Law* 174.

118 Labour Party, *Racial Attacks: Time to Act* (1993), London: Labour Party. Also see Labour Party, *The Rising Tide* (1994).

119 Francis, P, 'Race Attacks: Do We Need New Legislation?' (1994) 16 *Criminal Justice Matters* Summer.

120 Gardiner, S 'Ooh Ah Cantona: Racism as Hate Speech' (1996) 23 *Criminal Justice Matters*, Spring, p 23.

use of the law will create increasingly anodyne environments where freedom of expression and movement is overtly suppressed through the law. Law is often made too hastily to deal with what is seen as a pressing problem. Panic law is invariably bad law. The alternative approach is the use of campaigns such as that conceived in 1993, when the Professional Footballers' Association and the Commission of Racial Equality launched the 'Let's Kick Racism out of Football' Campaign.[121] The campaign has been periodically re-launched. In addition many clubs have developed their own policies against racism with the 'football in the community' programme. Anti-racist fanzines have also developed as an informal method of campaigning.

The main objective of the 'Let's Kick Racism Out of Football' Campaign was to 'encourage all those associated with the game of football to improve standards of behaviour, especially with reference to racial abuse, harassment, and the discrimination in and around grounds. To therefore make grounds safe for spectators, and to motivate public opinion generally against all forms of racism associated with the game and other spheres of life'. An 'Action Plan for Football Clubs' was put forward:

- Adopt a policy statement outlining the club's opposition to racism, and the actions it will take on supporters who shout 'indecent or racial chanting' ... This should be included in match programmes and displayed permanently in a prominent part of the ground.
- If racist chanting occurs at matches, make a public announcement condemning such behaviour.
- Ensure that a condition for season-ticket holders prohibits them from throwing missiles onto the pitch, etc.
- Take action to prevent the sale or distribution of racist literature in and around the ground on match days.
- Take disciplinary action against players who racially abuse players during matches.
- Liaise with supporters' clubs to make the club's opposition to racism clear.
- Ensure that stewards and police have a strategy for working together to eject supporters who are contravening the Football Offences Act. If in the case of individuals who are behaving in a racist or otherwise antisocial way, it would seem dangerous or inappropriate to take action against them during the match, that those individuals be identified and barred from all other matches.
- Remove all racist graffiti from the grounds as a matter of urgency.
- Adopt an equal opportunities policy in the areas of employment and service provision.[122]

---

121 It has been seen as having been effective. As Brendon Batson of the PFA says: 'The CRE's campaign has helped and so has the emergence of high profile black players ... racial abuse is on the decline and its much easier for young black players. It is being tackled by the game, but it's still there and must be tackled', 'Anti-racist TV advert delayed in aftermath of Cantona case', *The Guardian*, 24 March 1995.

122 See Greenfield, S and Osborn, G, 'When the Whites Come Marching In?' (1996) 6(2) *Marquette Sports Law Journal* 330–31 for further details.

A multi-agency approach has been adopted in the fight against racism with the formation of an Advisory Group Against Racism and Intimidation (AGARI), comprising the Commission of Racial Equality, Football Association, Professional Footballers Association, Football Trust, Football League, FA Premier League, League Managers Association, Football Supporters Association, National Federation of Football Supporters' Clubs and the Association of Metropolitan Authorities.

The issue of racism has also been highlighted in rugby league and cricket:

Long, J, Tongue, N, Spracklen, K and Carrington, B, 'What's the Difference? A Study of the Nature and Extent of Racism in Rugby League'

Having accepted the challenge of trying to cast light on the nature and extent of racism in rugby league, we recognised that we were not going to get the answer but would unearth different shades of meaning. These we have tried to present here to represent the range of views expressed during the course of the research. At the same time we have tried to respect the confidences shared with us. We are most grateful to those who took part in the various surveys, ensuring through their cooperativeness high levels of response which lend credibility to the findings. The rugby league fans in particular were very tolerant of those crazy researchers. This, we believe, represents their desire to be involved in everything associated with the game, a commitment that can be used to good effect by the RFL and the individual clubs.

Discussing racism in the sport you love (which was how most of our respondents regarded rugby league) is uncomfortable, because for most of us it is one of those things that is 'not nice' and we would prefer it if it were not really there. That meant we felt we had to be especially careful with the questions we asked and the way they were presented in the surveys.

We cannot speculate on the views of those who did not respond, but the following quotes represent two of the most commonly held positions:

- I feel we could be highlighting a problem which by and large does not exist. Our supporters are not moronic flag-waving National Front supporters (Club Official 102).
- We need to stop racism before it spreads. It is there in the game and there is no point hiding it (Club Official 89).

Our research suggests that the first of these views is probably the more frequently held, and there is a third set of people who flatly deny that there is any racism in rugby league. However while our research confirmed that racism in professional rugby league is not on a par with what has been evidenced in professional soccer, there is a small but significant problem. Our evidence also suggests that although the intensity may vary, racism is evident throughout the game and should not be dismissed as simply being the preserve of a minority of rogue clubs. People on the inside refer to rugby league as the greatest game, which has been taken as the name of one of the fanzines. This kind of pride is obviously one of the game's great strengths, but can also encourage complacency, making it difficult to alert people to significant issues. It is important that people should be honest enough to recognise problems and seek to address them appropriately. It should be possible to appeal to the pride that fans have in the game to enlist their support in ridding the game of racism and setting an example for other sports to follow.

Among the supporters almost half had heard chanting against black players. While 87% feel that it is not acceptable for players to be abused because of the colour of their skin, that still leaves 13%; while 90% disagreed that black players are lazy, that still leaves 10%. There is still a message to be conveyed that while an individual player who happens to be black may be lazy (or have any number of other attributes, including positive ones), it is not because they are black that they are lazy.

Fewer club officials reported hearing chanting against black players, but a third were aware of it even at their own club and over half had witnessed racist behaviour at other clubs. Almost all clubs were named or included within a more general category so would be ill-advised to consider racism as just somebody else's problem. Many of the club officials (especially the chairmen) had stereotypical views of the attributes of ethnic minority players, most commonly relating to the athletic prowess of Afro-Caribbean players. Black players experiencing racism are rather ambivalent about that kind of stereotyping because some of it appears favourable to them. Other aspects about suitability only for certain positions may be very limiting.

Players were more aware of racism within the game than the coaches and other club officials. All the players interviewed acknowledged that there is racist chanting from the stands and terraces. They know that it is a small number but identified a significant problem. The players were also aware that racial abuse was not just confined to the stands and terraces. All the black players and some of the white players talked about the racial abuse they were aware of on the pitch. While this was considered to be a 'winding-up' tactic, the players felt there was no justification for it. Not surprisingly, players were reluctant to point the finger at their own team, but some of the dressing room jokes were not felt to be funny. Some coaches were also identified as adopting racist stereotypes.

It is important for it to be recognised that abuse because of the colour of a player's skin is racist and not just one of those things that can be laughed off. Clubs can and should do something. On balance the feeling of club officials was that the anti-chanting campaigns had had a beneficial effect, and the supporters also thought they had been a good idea. However, beyond that, club officials identified very little that had been done to date to counter racism and promote the game within ethnic minority communities. There have been some notable exceptions like the Keighley Classroom and the Batley free ticket scheme. But Asian and black people are still extremely rare among rugby league crowds. The players in particular saw the need for development initiatives to make sure that as many as possible be introduced to a great game and that talent be encouraged.

The black players we interviewed felt that when they encountered racism they just had to get on with the game, but did not see why they should have to accept it. Whether or not racist abuse was directed at them personally, they as black players were affected by it. There was also a feeling that many had been deterred along the way, deciding that if that was what the game was going to be about there were better directions they could go in. Of course, there are many reasons why people stop playing, but any sport should be concerned about an avoidable loss of talent. Moreover, experiencing racism like this may affect the form of black players, so it is in the interest of coaches and team mates to try to counter anything that has a detrimental effect on their players.

Not surprisingly, when confronted with racist chanting the majority of supporters ignored it. In the pressures of the crowd it is not easy for the individual to know what to do. Part of the 'Let's Kick Racism Out of Football' campaign was to suggest to fans what they could do if they came across racist behaviour in football.

While beginning to question that it is, people do still want to see rugby league as a family sport and an environment in which racism is evident is not conducive to that image. If racism were to spread it could hit clubs in their pockets through lower attendances.

For the white players it was clear that rugby league is indeed very much a family game. Their families and network of family friends and social contacts had been instrumental in introducing them to rugby league clubs. Lacking that kind of introduction, Asian and black players had had to find other routes into the game. To avoid missing out on talent in the various ethnic minority communities, rugby league needs to offer the kind of support that few youngsters will get from their networks of family and friends.

We have tried not to create a scare about 'a cancer sweeping through the game'. We are persuaded that such a conclusion would be unwarranted. However we also believe it would be wrong for those in rugby league to shirk their responsibility and hide behind the protestations that there is no issue to address. Although racism is a problem in society at large, that is no reason for inaction within the game, which should instead acknowledge its social responsibility. There is an opportunity for rugby league to take an initiative for the good of the game and the communities that support it.[123]

In cricket, the 'Hit Racism for Six' campaign was initiated in late 1995 in response to the article by Robert Henderson in the July 1995 edition of *Wisden Cricket Monthly*. Henderson had argued that foreign players were less committed to the success of the national team than those born in England. The flavour of Henderson's beliefs can be discovered from his statement that: 'an Asian or negro raised in England will, according to the liberal, feel exactly the same pride and identification with the place as a white man. The reality is somewhat different.' Permission was denied to reproduce Henderson's article. The following extract examines the problem of racism in cricket and attempts to counter it in the light of such views:

123 See Long, J, Tongue, N, Spracklen, K and Carrington, B, *What's the Difference? A Study of the Nature and Extent of Racism in Rugby League* (1995) School of Leisure and Sports Studies, Leeds Metropolitan University, pp 43–45.

McDonald, I, 'Why we must hit racism for six'

What is Hit Racism for Six?

We are a group of cricket fans who have formed an independent organisation committed to challenging racism wherever it is found in English cricket. The outcry against Robert Henderson's article, 'Is it in the blood', in the July 1995 edition of *Wisden Cricket Monthly* was the catalyst behind our creation. Henderson argued that black and foreign born players lacked commitment to England, and called for the Test XI to be made up of 'unequivocal Englishmen'. Disgusted that such racist nonsense should appear in the country's biggest selling cricket magazine, we held a meeting the following month to discuss how racism in cricket could be challenged. As a result of this meeting, Hit Racism for Six was born.

But Robert Henderson was universally condemned within cricket, so what's the problem?

The article was almost universally denounced, but why was it published in the first place? This was no aberration. It is the more extreme manifestation of a racism which plagues English cricket. It was the third time Henderson's racist views had appeared in print in *Wisden Cricket Monthly*, and racial stereotyping and racial insinuation have been commonplace in cricket writing and broadcasting for generations. The mere mention of 'racism' and 'cricket' in the same sentence is greeted by the cricket establishment with, at best, incredulity, but more frequently, hostile indignation. After all, racism is 'just not cricket'. Some fans also have difficulty in accepting that cricket has a problem with racism. But the 'don't mention racism' approach has to be challenged. What it really means in cricket today is 'let's accept racism'. Some people (including Robert Henderson) are trying disingenuously to exploit the unease felt when cricket is linked with racism, claiming that it is the anti-racists who are introducing racial conflict into the 'sacred game'. It has been suggested that Devon Malcolm only brought the subject up last year because some people with ulterior motives put ideas into his head! Racism is a reality in cricket as it is in other parts of our society, and it is people like Robert Henderson, and his apologists, who are creating conflict. Hit Racism for Six is for all cricket fans who have had enough of racism, which has for far too long been allowed to besmirch the game.

What other evidence do you have of racism in cricket to justify setting up a campaign?

If you are prepared to look at the record, and if you are prepared to listen to the experiences of black and Asian cricketers and supporters, there is plenty of evidence. There are examples of racist behaviour by a minority of supporters, by elements in the press and among the cricket authorities. Press racism towards black cricketers, whether from overseas or from Britain, has been well documented. Probably the worst example was the treatment of the Pakistanis team during the so called 'ball tampering' Test series in 1992. Reports indicate that Asian cricketers at all levels have suffered increased levels of racial verbal and physical abuse during and since the 1992 series. (Unlike Euro 96, there was no apologetic reaction from MPs and other prominent figures to this tabloid incitement of racial hatred).

Although supporter-racism has traditionally been seen as less of an issue in cricket than football, there have still been problems. For example, racism was a key feature of the crowd trouble at last season's Headingley NatWest tie between Yorkshire and Northants, when Indian spinner Anil Kumble was abused and pelted with fruit. No doubt the untold number of Yorkshire born and bred black and Asian cricketers who remain conspicuous by their absence from the Yorkshire CCC XI would not have been surprised by this outbreak of racism. Cricketers in club and league cricket also have reported incidents of racial abuse. Many in the cricket world dismiss these incidents as atypical. But why should they be allowed to happen at all?

For more than two decades the English cricket authorities and many of the top names in English cricket carried on a campaign against the isolation of apartheid South Africa. This sent out a less than welcoming message to black and Asian cricketers in England.

More recently we have also witnessed the treatment of Devon Malcolm by the England management team in South Africa. Illingworth and the bulk of the English cricket press have denied vehemently that this incident had anything to do with race. Malcolm raised a serious question: would he have been treated the same if he were white? Neither the cricket authorities nor the cricket press were prepared even to investigate that question. Yet the background to the Malcolm affair was explicitly racial: first, Malcolm won damages from *Wisden Cricket Monthly* for printing the Henderson article alleging, in effect, that he did not try hard enough because he was black.

Then Nelson Mandela singled him out in South Africa. Illingworth's unprecedented public put-down came within days. It is, at best, naive to pretend that this has nothing to do with race.

Racism is often subtle and indirect. The admissions and pricing policy for Test Matches has caused a dramatic decline in attendance by black spectators. The former Chief Executive of Surrey CCC explained that this was because we could not have 'no go' areas at Test matches. At the least, the TCCB should review its policy of banning flags, banners and musical instruments from international cricket grounds.

Why has race become an issue in cricket now?

Two related factors are important. First, the context of the Henderson furore is the long running, often anguished debate over what's wrong with English cricket. The country's decline as a cricket power provides an uncomfortable parallel to what is widely perceived as its economic and political decline. As the England test side has been outplayed by one former colony after another, the search for scapegoats has intensified. 'Foreigners' are easy targets. The *Caribbean Times* headline, 'England shamed, Malcolm blamed', neatly summed up the syndrome.

Secondly, outside of cricket, 'race' has risen up the political agenda. Hence, the inhumane legislative assault on asylum seekers, and the unsubstantiated claims by the Metropolitan Police Commissioner that most muggers in London are young black men. There has been an increase in racially motivated attacks and an increase in the police harassment of young black men. Equally disturbing has been the re-emergence of Nazi parties like the BNP as a minor but significant force to contend with in parts of the country. All this helps to set an agenda for a racially charged discussion of English/British identity – who belongs and who doesn't – based on colour and a narrow and largely mythical national culture. This is why racial and national stereotyping needs to be challenged. It provides fertile terrain in a climate of escalating racism and xenophobia, as those who fail to measure up to Robert Henderson's idea of an 'unequivocal Englishman' are made to pay the price for economic and social tensions.

But hasn't opposition to stereotyping got more to do with political correctness than challenging racism?

Stereotypes like 'aggressive' West Indian bowlers, 'wily' Indian spin bowlers, or 'volatile' Pakistanis carry more sinister connotations, especially given the colonial context of English cricket history ... In the current climate, they have a real and damaging impact on people's lives. The great West Indian cricket writer and scholar, CLR James, once asked: 'what do they know of cricket who only cricket know?'

The tabloid treatment of Germany in the run up to the Euro 96 semi-final with England demonstrates where the slippery slope of racial stereotyping leads. Shamelessly defended by one tabloid editor as harmless fun, on par with 'Allo Allo' and 'Dad's Army', the coverage fuelled riotous displays of aggressive nationalism following England's penalty shoot-out defeat. Foreign made cars were attacked in Trafalgar Square and a Russian student was stabbed in a park in Surrey on suspicion of being German.

How significant is it that black and Asian players should be playing for England?

Watching the partnership between Madras born Nasser Hussain (on route to his maiden test century, and eventually England's Man of the Series) and Bombay born Min Patel take the England score past India's first innings total during the summers' test match at Edgbaston was pleasing, especially as Robert Henderson was on the radio later that evening arguing that black players were responsible for England's dismal test record. But racism has never just been about test selection. There are literally thousands of cricketers, black, Asian and white, who feel excluded from the mainstream. The success of Hussain and others will hopefully encourage clubs to look beyond traditional structures for new talent, for example to the inner-cities and leagues such as the Quiad-i-Azam in Yorkshire and tournaments like the Inter-Island Amateur Cup in London.

So Henderson has got the argument the wrong way round. It is the absence of black and Asian cricketers, not their presence, that's to blame for the recent spate of poor England performances.

As Chris Searle argues ... it is the reluctance of the authorities to seek talent in the urban and inner-city areas, where most ethnic minority cricketers are found, which is the problem. The failure to tap into these wells of cricketing talent ... represents the triumph of prejudice and complacency over cricketing acumen. The attitude of the TCCB towards Sri Lanka, also illustrates this attitude. Despite being the current World Cup holders, Sri Lanka are only due to play one test match (not series) against England before the next World Cup in 1999. This is in sharp contrast to the 11 games planned against Australia, six against New Zealand, five each against the West Indies and South Africa, three each against Pakistan and India, and two against Zimbabwe. The solitary test with Sri Lanka comes at the start of the 1998 English season. This is not only disappointing for fans in England who would love to see the world champions here, but a missed opportunity for the national side to compete and improve by playing one of crickets most exciting teams ...

Nevertheless, isn't it the case that most cricket fans are not political or angry enough to demand change ?

This is wrong on two counts. First, progress has been made. Robert Henderson's argument failed to gain widespread acceptance in cricket. DeFreitas and Malcolm both received out-of-court settlements from *Wisden Cricket Monthly* over the article,[124] and the magazine's editor, David Frith, has taken early retirement. We believe that Hit Racism for Six was not irrelevant in this successful challenge to the racism of Henderson.

Secondly, there is an increasing gulf between ordinary grass roots cricket fans and the cricket authorities and establishment. It is among the ordinary genuine cricket fans, alongside sympathetic players and administrators, that the force for change will make itself felt.[125]

Henderson's views reflected the same sensibilities voiced by the politician Norman Tebbit in the mid-1980s when he claimed that ethnic minorities needed to pass the 'cricket test': that is, support England rather than the team of their ancestry, so as to be seen as properly assimilated in British society. The editor of *Wisden Cricket Monthly*, David Firth, was almost alone in justifying the publication of Henderson's article:

The aim was to launch a constructive debate ... reservations (about non-English players) have rumbled around the cricket grounds and in the sports columns of the newspapers for several years.[126]

The declared aims of the 'Hit Racism for Six' are:

- Racism has no place in cricket.
- We reject any suggestion that cricketers may lack commitment to their team because of their race or country or origin.
- We condemn slurs or insults aimed at cricketers or cricket fans because of their race or country of origin.
- We commit ourselves to opposing all forms of racism in cricket at all levels.[127]

---

124 'Malcolm and DeFreitas issue writs', *The Guardian*, 13 July 1995, p 20 and 'Cricketer to get High Court apology for "racist" article', *The Guardian*, 16 October 1995, p 4.

125 McDonald, I, 'Why we must hit racism for six', Centre for Sport Development Research, *Hit Racism for Six: Race and Cricket in England Today* (1995), London: Roehampton Institute.

126 Firth, D (1995) *Wisden Cricket Monthly* August; see this edition for a large number of letters in response to Henderson's article.

127 Centre for Sport Development Research, *Hit Racism for Six: Race and Cricket in England Today* (1995), London: Roehampton Institute.

The controversy caused by the ex-England cricket manager Ray Illingworth's comments concerning Devon Malcolm are another example of the racist undertones found in cricket.[128] Yorkshire cricket has been evidenced as a clear example of cricket's problem of racism:

Hubbard, A, 'Racism in sport: Malignant malady that lingers on'

Things do not seem to have changed that much in Leeds since the night some 30 years ago when a United director was overheard remarking to a colleague at the end of a home defeat: 'Trouble was, nigger were reet off t'neet.' The 'nigger' in question happened to be the late Albert Johanneson, a South African born winger who was among the first to run the gauntlet of what apparently still passes for humour in the banana-throwing republic of West Yorkshire. Racism is slowly being eradicated in sport, though there are still pockets of resistance, the deepest of which appears to be on Headingley's Western Terrace. It was there last weekend that reader Chris Searle experienced what he described to us as his worst moments in 40 years of watching cricket. He had vowed never to return to Headingley after witnessing a vicious, unprovoked attack on a West Indian supporter who was defending Viv Richards from abuse in 1990. 'I thought things might have changed,' he said. 'Obviously I was wrong. It is depressing.' Depressing is a sizeable understatement. It is sickening and shameful. And also very puzzling.

The incidents on the Western Terrace during the second Test went largely unpublicised, not least by BBC TV, who once again apparently decided that the nation's eyes should be averted from such unseemly goings-on. 'Dashed bad show and all that, chaps. But we wouldn't want to spoil a good day's cricket, would we?' Auntie is far too fond of doing her sniffily censorious bit these days. Turning a blind camera eye to streakers is one thing, but pretending that incidents like the Headingley fracas didn't happen really isn't cricket. It is poor news judgment, something of which the BBC's prissy sports department is increasingly guilty. The scenes at Headingley witnessed at first hand by Mr Searle cannot be dismissed as laddishness. It was lager loutishness at its most despicable and reflects badly on the ground, the city, the county and the game. If Headingley cannot clean up its act then it must be discarded as a Test venue.

Leeds has an unfortunate association with racism in sport. Until fairly recently, black footballers would tell you that Elland Road was the place they dreaded visiting most. Thankfully, under Howard Wilkinson, those awful images have largely disappeared, though not totally. But Wilkinson's efforts to establish a rapport with the local ethnic community is something the cricket club should aim to emulate. Headingley remains a running sore. In 1992 a pig's head was hurled into a group of Pakistan supporters, and another unsavoury racist incident led to a formal complaint being made to the club by a baronet's wife after members allegedly made lewd and offensive remarks about blacks and Jews.

---

128 See below p 356.

As the latest issue of the publication 'Hit Racism for Six' reports, it must be intimidating to have a section of the crowd chanting 'black bastard, black bastard' in time with the steps of a bowler's run-up, as Norman Cowans found in a NatWest semi-final. David 'Syd' Lawrence recalls that when he played at Headingley they called him 'nigger, black bastard, sambo, monkey, gorilla, and threw bananas'. He also received a letter with a Yorkshire postmark which read: 'Don't shout yer mouth off, nigger, you won't be welcome next time. Nig, nig.' Devon Malcolm and Philip DeFreitas were awarded substantial damages and an apology when *Wisden Cricket Monthly*, seen as part of the game's establishment, foolishly published the odious rantings of a National Front sympathiser, Robert Henderson, who had questioned the players' commitment to England. Then we had Malcolm asking whether he would have been treated so disdainfully by the England management had he been a white bowler; and recently allegations of racism were bandied about alongside the seam-picked balls in the High Court's *Imran Khan v Botham and Lamb* libel case.

Of course, Headingley is by no means the last bastion of racism, nor cricket the only sport where it remains a problem. Yet by and large it has ceased to be an obstacle in individual sports such as athletics and boxing, and there are ongoing campaigns to remove the final vestiges of bigotry from football and rugby league. But in cricket, unlovely cricket, the malady lingers on. Why?[129]

The problem may not be perceived as great as that in football. Certainly there have been no calls for the extension of legislation such as the Football Spectators Act to cricket. The Yorkshire Cricket Club has introduced new grounds rules for spectators, replanned the operations of the stewards and re-designed the seating on the Western Terraces with greater space and access.

The major question is how to regulate spectator racism most effectively. What role does the law have to play? A suggestion is that the law may have a role to play, but only along side other quasi-legal and non-legal methods, and certainly not in substitution of them.

---

129 Hubbard, A, 'Racism in sport: Malignant malady that lingers on', *The Observer*, 18 August 1996, p 12. Also see 'Cricket: Booze, jeers and jingoism', *The Observer*, 1 September 1996, p 12.

CHILD PROTECTION: SPORTS COACHES AND CHILD ATHLETES

The issue of the treatment of children in sport mirrors increasing awareness of the rights of children generally in society.[130] Although the focus is on participation in sport, there is evidence of considerable exploitation of children within the wider sports industry.[131] Sport provides many positive opportunities for young people to participate individually or more commonly in groups. This is generally at a recreational 'play' level, however increasingly young people are taking part in highly competitive and sometimes elite level sport. The image of parents shouting at their children and haranguing the officials has become a common image in school and Sunday morning football: even at this level winning is all.[132] In sports such as tennis, swimming and gymnastics the age of participants at elite level has become ever younger.

Awareness of the existence and extent of sexual and physical abuse of children has appeared fairly recently in sport as it has generally in society.[133] The need to provide more effective protection of exploitation of children in sport has grown in recent years. This exploitation ranges from clear acts of sexual and physical abuse at one extreme to oppressive encouragement at the other. Clear acts of abuse are almost inevitably going to be contrary to the criminal law. Oppressive encouragement is much more problematic to regulate. However detection of all forms of exploitation in sport is difficult.

The main area of concern has been with the relationship between coaches and child athletes. In Britain over the last few years, there have been a number of criminal trials of sports coaches. The most notable has been the conviction of the swimming coach Paul Hickson who was the British team coach at the 1988 Olympics in Seoul. He was sentenced for 17 years after he was found guilty of two rapes, 11 indecent assaults and two other serious sexual offences. He was cleared of two other indecent assaults. Hickson had denied all charges, saying he was the victim of teenage girls' fantasies.

One of his victims, who was 13 when he first molested her, was reported as saying 'he was evil, a monster':

> The woman, an undergraduate, was angry that the Amateur Swimming Association seems to have failed to investigate complaints by three senior swimmers in 1986 about Hickson's behaviour towards women. The Association said yesterday that there had been no allegations of criminality,

---

130 See the Children Act 1989.

131 'A Sporting Chance' (1997) *Christain Aid*, p 217, concerning exploitation of children in India some as young as 10 stitching footballs for about 10 pence a ball.

132 See 'Soccer Brawl Father is told to pay £750', *Daily Telegraph*, 15 February 1997.

133 See 'Report of the Inquiry into Child Abuse in Cleveland 1987', Cm 412 (1988), London: HMSO.

but it would re-examine the way it protects athletes. The woman said: 'Investigations should have been made because some people were aware that something was not quite right'. The woman cannot bring herself to utter the name of Hickson, who fondled her and forced her to perform oral sex. 'I was so young,' she said, 'and I just felt that what he was doing was something I had to endure, something that was necessary. I trusted in everything that he told me.'[134]

The case of Hickson came to light almost accidentally when an off-duty policeman at a party overheard some teenage girls recounting allegations against Hickson. He had been reprimanded in 1987 by his employer, the University of Wales at Swansea, for telling a woman to strip for a 'naked fitness' test, and then undressing himself. He subsequently moved to the public school, Millfield, as swimming coach. It has been reported that two separate legal actions were likely to lead on from the conviction: one by Millfield against the University of Wales for the impressive references given when he moved jobs and secondly by four women swimmers against the Amateur Swimming Association for failing to act on complaints in the mid-1980s.[135]

One real problem is that often allegations are viewed with disbelief from those associated with the individuals in question. Victims often believe that they are the only ones involved and only find out later that other fellow athletes were subject to similar treatment. The sports coach-child athlete relationship is one where the coach has immense power and influence over the child and it is difficult for the child to raise the alarm. Celia Breckenridge has produced a significant body of work concerning the causes of abuse in sport, particularly against women, and she shows how abusive coaches take care and time to 'groom' their athletes so that they will submit to their advances.[136] Child sport as with other activities involving working with children attracts those with a propensity to paedophilia. What has arisen is a rightful awareness of the reality of this problem, but also confusion and uncertainty: issues such as how to deal with false allegations, as with the suicide of Cliff Temple, the athletics correspondent of *The Sunday Times* after false allegations of sexual harassment,[137] and the problem of how to develop good practice for sports coaches when working with child athletes so that both parties are not inhibited from working effectively together. Hickson's

---

134 'Olympic coach jailed for rapes', *The Times*, 28 September 1995, p 1. See also 'Swimmer blew whistle on Hickson nine years ago', *The Times*, 28 September 1995, p 5; 'The great betrayal', *The Sunday Times*, 1 October 1995, p 14.

135 'Abuse of power', *The Guardian*, 4 October 1995, p 8.

136 See Brekenridge, C, 'He owned me basically ...': Women's Experience of Sexual Abuse in Sport' (1997) 32(2) *International Review for the Sociology of Sport* and 'Sexual Harassment and Sexual Abuse in Sport' in Clarke, G and Humberstone, B (eds), *Researching Women and Sport* (1997), London: Macmillan.

137 See Downes, S and Mackay, D, *Running Scared* (1996), Edinburgh: Mainsteam Publishing.

case is not the only one of recent years,[138] but hopefully more effective mechanisms are beginning to be put in place in sport to protect children.

Clear proven allegations of sexual and physical abuse can be subject to the general criminal and civil law. What is more problematic is how oppression short of abuse of child athletes should be defined and regulated.[139] Of course as has already been noted brutality is sanctioned in sports, whose 19th century origins lie in:

> ... militarism and muscular Christianity, the Chariots Of Fire ethos: a Bible under one arm and a ball under the other ... Sport promotes and protects bad behaviour, because it is not politically responsible. The coaches' word is law, they dominate players' every waking moment – it is not about empowerment or democracy. It is like a cult.[140]

A number of graphic accounts have been made of the treatment of children, to which girls especially are subject. In gymnastics, there has been growing concern of the pressures on girls, to conform to a certain body size and weight seen as most likely to lead to success. There is evidence that puberty is artificially delayed and its effects minimised.[141]

Joan Ryan's *Little Girls in Pretty Boxes*[142] provides a moving account of elite female gymnasts and ice skaters, who every four years, captivate millions by the seemingly effortless skill and grace at the Olympic Games. However she provides a very different image of the frail, tiny figures performing feats of co-ordination and power and exposes the suffering and sacrifice they have endured, and the hundreds who didn't make it, broken in their early teens by the demands of their sport. Unerringly, Ryan, one of America's leading sports journalists, presents a catalogue of what she describes as 'legal, even celebrated child abuse', in which girls starve themselves (her research shows that 60% of college gymnasts in the US suffer from eating disorders), risk osteoporosis, curvature of the spine, and untold psychological damage, at the behest of brutal, self-promoting coaches, and parents driven by misguided sentiment. As far as coaches' impropriety, Ryan focuses on the Romanian Bela Karolyi who spotted Nadia Comaneci as a six-year-old and groomed her to Olympic stardom. His coaching approach:

---

138 See cases of Cecil Mallon, a gym coach jailed for indecent assault; David Low athletics coach given 18 months probation for sending obscene questionnaires to young girls. Also see television programmes, 'Bad Sports', *On the Line*, BBC2 Television, 26 January 1994 (on sexual misconduct in US sport) and *On the Line*, BBC2 Television, 25 August 1993 (on sexual harassment and sexual abuse in UK sport) and *Diverse Reports*, Channel 4 Television, 23 January 1997 (on sexual abuse in English football).

139 See Nelson, M *The stronger Women get, the more Men love Football: Sexism and the Culture of Sport* (1996), New York: The Women's Press.

140 Breckenridge, C, quoted in Campbell, B, 'Why The Coast is Clear', *The Guardian*, 7 November 1996, p 4.

141 See 'Hungry For Success', *Fair Game*, Channel 4, 10 June 1996.

142 Ryan, J, *Little Girls in Pretty Boxes* (1995), New York: Warner Books.

Ryan, J, *Little Girls in Pretty Boxes*

... was based on militaristic control. His gymnasts lived in dormitories at the gym in Romania, trained seven to eight hours a day, fit in a few hours of school and ate only what the Karolyi fed them. There was no talk or fooling around inside the gym. The only proper response to Karolyi's instructions was a nod. He trained them like boxers, like little men, introducing rigorous conditioning and strengthening exercises to their workouts, transforming their bodies into muscled machinery. Karolyi insisted on small young girls for his team, not only for their pliability and resilience but for the little doll look he believed enchanted the spectators and swayed the judges.[143]

After his defection to the United States, Ryan produces evidence of continued physical and emotional exploitation by Karolyi:

He rushed the gymnasts back in the gym sooner than doctors recommended, rationalising that the doctors were simply concerned with (legal) liability ... Kristie Phillips, for instance, trained for three years with a fractured wrist because Karolyi did not feel it was serious enough to warrant full rest. Nearly ten years later the wrist barely bends ... Similarly before the 1991 World Championships a Karolyi doctor diagnosed Kim Zmeskal's wrist injury pain as a sprain, leading Karolyi to suggest on national television that the injury was more in Zmeskal's head than in her wrist. It turned out that Zmeskal's problem was a fracture of the distal radius, or growth plate – a common injury amongst elite gymnast but one with which Karolyi's doctor was apparently unfamiliar.[144]

Injuries had no place in Karolyi's carefully designed formula for producing a star every four years. He built his program around the girl with the most talent. 'Your top athlete is a very strange creature,' Karolyi explains. 'Of course, I never studied psychology, but through these years these little guys have taught me. We paid our dues on our mistakes, praising our little guys and cheering and clapping and showing our enthusiasm and baying them. And those are the ones who turn around and show disappreciation, ignorance and even arrogance. They take advantage of your sincere urge to show your appreciation. Give them everything in the world and ensure your getting a big, big, big, big slap. She is the first to turn her back.'

So Karolyi constructed a training environment that kept his star athlete questioning her worth. In selecting five other gymnasts to train with her, he carefully chose each to play a specific role. Perhaps the most tortuous position was that of the secondary star: like the understudy in a play, the girl was just talented enough to present a threat to the star's status. Nadia had Teodora Ungureaunu, Dianne Durham had Mary Lou Retton, Kristie Phillips had Phoebe Mills, and Kim Zmeskal had Betty Okino. The four remaining gymnasts were the 'crowd', as Karolyi called them, chosen as much for their personality traits as their talents. One girl from the 'crowd' was always chosen as his pet. She might be the least talented, but she possessed the qualities he wanted to reinforce in his star: hard work, discipline and stoicism. Karolyi

---

143 *Ibid*, pp 198–99.
144 *Ibid*, p 209.

would praise her lavishly and hold her up as an example, angering the more talented gymnasts who resented his favouritism. Anger, Karolyi knew, was a powerful motivator.[145]

Background to Abuse

In the United States, many strategies to expose and eradicate exploitation of child athletes have been developed including criminal and civil law remedies, organisation awareness and pro-active development of plans, specific codes of conduct, screening potential coaches etc.[146] In Britain the issue of developing greater awareness and recognition of child abuse and promotion of good practices for working with children has become a priority. Bodies such as the Sports Council[147] and the National Coaching Foundation have produced considerable literature on this area:[148]

National Coaching Foundation, *Protecting Children from Abuse*

What is child abuse?

Child abuse is a term used to describe ways in which children are harmed, usually by adults and often by people they know and trust. It refers to the damage done to a child's physical or mental health. Children can be abused within or outside their family, at school and even in the sports environment. Child abuse can take many forms:

– Physical abuse where adults:

  physically hurt or injure children (eg by hitting, shaking, squeezing, biting or burning);

  give children alcohol, inappropriate drugs or poison;

  attempt to suffocate or drown children.

In sport situations, physical abuse might also occur when the nature and intensity of training exceeds the capacity of the child's immature and growing body.

Neglect includes situations in which adults:

– fail to meet a child's basic physical needs (eg for food, warm clothing);

– consistently leave children alone and unsupervised;

---

145 *Ibid*, p 211.

146 Fried, GB, 'Unsportsmanlike Contact: Strategies for Reducing Sexual Assaults in Youth Sports' (1996) 6(3) *Journal of Legal aspects of Sport*, 155.

147 Breckenridge, C (ed), *Child Protection in Sport – Policies, Procedures and Systems: Report of a Sports Council Seminar for National Governing Bodies* (1996) Cheltenham and Gloucester College of Higher Education.

148 See *Codes of Ethics and Conduct for Sports Coaches* (1995); *Protecting Children from Abuse: a Guide for Everyone Involved in Children's Sport* (1996); *The Successful Coach: Guidelines for Coaching Practice* (1996); *Guidance for National Governing Bodies on Child Protection* (1996) all from Leeds: National Coaching Foundation. Also see Crouch, M, *Protecting Children: a Guide for Sportspeople* (1995) NCF/NSPCC.

- fail or refuse to give children love, affection or attention.

Neglect in a sports situation might also occur if a teacher or coach fails to ensure children are safe or exposes them to undue cold or risk of injury.

Sexual abuse. Boys and girls are sexually abused when adults (male or female) use them to meet their own sexual needs. This could include:

- full sexual intercourse, masturbation, oral sex, fondling;
- showing children pornographic books, photographs or videos, or taking pictures for pornographic purposes.

Sports situations which involve physical contact (eg supporting or guiding children) could potentially create situations where sexual abuse may go unnoticed. Abusive situations may also occur if adults misuse their power over young people.

Emotional abuse can occur in a number of ways. For example, where:

- there is persistent lack of love or affection;
- there is constant overprotection which prevents children from socialising;
- children are frequently being shouted at or taunted;
- there is neglect, physical or sexual abuse.

Emotional abuse in sport might also include situations where parents or coaches subject children to constant criticism, bullying or unrealistic pressure to perform to high expectations.

What can I do to protect my child or children in my sport from abuse?

If you are a parent or carer:

- check to see if the club has a policy which ensures children are protected and kept safe from harm;
- check that staff and volunteers are carefully recruited, trained and supervised;
- know how to voice your concerns or complain if there is anything you are not happy about;
- ensure your children know how to voice their concerns or complain if there is anything they are not happy about;
- encourage your child to talk to you about any worries.

If you are a coach/member of staff/volunteer you can reduce situations for abuse of children and help to protect staff and volunteers by promoting good practice. Everyone should be aware that, as a general rule, it does not make sense to:

- spend excessive amounts of time alone with children away from others;
- take children alone in a car on journeys, however short;
- take children to your home.

Where any of these are unavoidable, ensure they only occur with the full knowledge and consent of someone in charge in the organisation or the child's parents.

You should never:

– engage in rough, physical or sexually provocative games, including horseplay;

– allow or engage in inappropriate touching of any form;

– allow children to use inappropriate language unchallenged;

– make sexually suggestive comments to a child, even in fun;

– let allegations a child makes go unchallenged or unrecorded – always act;

– do things of a personal nature that children can do for themselves.

However it may be sometimes necessary for your staff or volunteers to do things of a personal nature for children, particularly if they are very young or disabled. These tasks should only be carried out with the full understanding and consent of parents. In an emergency situation which requires this type of help, parents should be fully informed.

In such situations, it is important to ensure all staff are sensitive to the child and undertake personal care tasks with the utmost discretion.[149]

Conclusion

There clearly is a problem of balance here. Young athletes need support and encouragement in their endeavours. All the emotions from elation to despair can be experienced. Coaches need to be able to show encouragement sometimes in a physical way, a hug of joy or a shoulder to cry on. In some sports, for example gymnastics, physical contact is needed between coach and child to assist in certain techniques.

Oppressive encouragement and abuse in all its forms needs to be exposed and effectively eradicated. More effective vetting and screening of applicants to coaching positions need to be implemented and perhaps a register of convicted paedophiles who have or attempt to get involved in sports coaches needs to be initiated.[150] What is of importance is that a safe working environment for child athletes needs to be guaranteed. The law has a role to play perhaps, but this will need to be alongside other regulatory mechanisms such as codes of practice. All parties need to be better informed of the distinction between acceptable and unacceptable behaviour.

---

149 *Protecting Children from Abuse: A Guide for Everyone Involved in Children's Sport* (1996), Leeds: National Coaching Foundation.

150 See the general proposals for regulation of convicted paedophiles in the Sex Offenders Act 1997.

FINAL THOUGHTS

The preceding examples show the State using the law in different ways to regulate areas of sporting activity. The legitimacy and scope of the law's intervention is not always obvious. The following chapter will focus on another area of legal intervention in sport: the role that the law should have in the regulation of the use of drugs in sport.

CHAPTER THREE

THE REGULATION OF DRUG USE IN SPORT

INTRODUCTION

There are few issues in sport that are more emotive than the taking of performance enhancing drugs and athletes at the centre of drug taking controversies such as Diane Modahl and Butch Reynolds have received extensive media coverage. This is in part because drug taking is viewed by many as being contrary to the very essence of sport. Top sporting performers are viewed as society's heroes and are often held up to our children as role models. Their demise therefore undermines not only the sport but the very values on which our society is based.

Drug abuse or doping encompasses a wide range of behaviour and applications. When one talks of doping it is necessary to consider not only the taking of substances but also other complex scientific processes such as blood doping where blood is taken from the athlete's body, re-oxygenated and then pumped back into the athlete.[1] Sport wages a continuing war against the scientist and the doctor with each scientific development which enables the athlete to evade detection being countered by more complex testing procedures and rules.[2]

Although doping in humans is used almost exclusively to enhance performance, the doping of racehorses, greyhounds and other animals is often a destructive technique aimed at adversely affecting performance.[3] This chapter concentrates on the doping of humans but most of the issues raised in this chapter are equally applicable to the doping of animals.

Positive drugs tests on athletes in the UK have risen in recent years[4] and this picture is mirrored in the USA.[5] Charlie Francis, Ben Johnson's coach, has insisted that most elite athletes take some form of performance enhancing drug.[6] Even if competitors are not exposed as drug takers, rumour and accusations serve to undermine sport in general and individual competitors in

---

1   Perry, C, 'Blood Doping and Athletic Competition' (1983) 1(3) *The International Journal of Applied Philosophy* 39.

2   'How "Biotech" Drugs May Win at Atlanta', *Daily Telegraph*, 24 July 1996.

3   However, it is not unknown for steroids to be used on animals, see *The Guardian*, 8 November 1996 and *Daily Telegraph*, 9 December 1996.

4   *The Guardian*, 31 January 1996.

5   *The Guardian*, 27 June 1992, *The Observer*, 28 August 1994 and 2 March 1997.

6   *The Guardian*, 6 February 1991.

particular.[7] After finishing fourth in the Barcelona Olympic 100m final for women, Gwen Torrence accused two of the medallists of being 'not clean'. Torrence later made a public apology under threat of suspension but the damage had been done.[8] In the same way, extraordinary feats of sporting brilliance are now questioned[9] and 'increasingly the myth and mystique that surrounds drug misuse in sport implies that if a competitor passes a drugs test then they must have used a masking agent'.[10] We have almost reached a situation where there is a presumption of guilt which athletes may feel the need to rebut. The outstanding swimming performances of Ireland's Michelle Smith at the 1996 Atlanta Olympics were questioned by the media and rival competitors despite the fact that she had undergone regular tests prior to the games.[11]

National governing bodies (NGBs) have developed regulations to deal with drug abuse in sport and many of those regulations deal more strictly with the problem than the corresponding criminal law provisions. The overwhelming majority of investigations, inquiries and hearings into drug usage in sport are carried out 'in house' by the relevant NGBs which conduct elaborate drug testing procedures and administer fines and bans.

It would be wrong to assume that the lawyer only takes an interest when the accused appeals to the courts from a fine or ban administered by the NGBs. Increasingly, lawyers are instructed to represent athletes at the NGBs tribunal level.[12] As the sport's drugs regulations become more complex to counter the regulatory inadequacies and legal loopholes exploited by lawyers, so the need for lawyers to interpret them and stand in judgment upon them becomes greater. Undoubtedly, this type of legal intervention in sport will continue to increase. At these tribunals, lawyers are applying the rules of the sport and not the law and it is when sporting rules and the law cannot be reconciled that recourse to the law becomes necessary.

This chapter is divided into two parts. The first part examines the arguments why NGBs ban certain types of drugs. The second examines the application of rules by NGBs and athlete appeals.

---

7   *The Observer*, 10 September 1995.

8   *Evening Standard*, 1 July 1996, p 66.

9   For example the case of the Chinese athlete Wang Junxia who took 6 seconds off the womens 10,000m world record only to take an amazing further 42 seconds off her own record 24 hours later.

10 *Sports Law Administration and Practice*, September/October 1996, p 10.

11 *The Observer*, 10 November 1996.

12 Notably by athletes Harry Butch Reynolds and Diane Modahl.

WHY BAN DRUGS?

Perhaps the most obvious answer to this question is, because they are banned by national law. Many drugs which would feature on an NGB's list of banned substances will also appear in Schedule 2 of the Misuse of Drugs Act 1971. The MDA 1971 is the principal legislation criminalising the consumption of drugs in Britain and contains a list of various drugs outlawed. However there are other drugs, the taking of which do not amount to criminal offences,[13] that are also banned by NGBs. There are two principal arguments proffered as to why the list of banned drugs is so extensive. First the NGBs wish to prevent the use of certain drugs which could damage the health of the athlete and secondly because drug taking is gaining an unfair advantage and therefore cheating.

Substance or technique	Benefits	Side effects
Anabolic agents, eg Stanozolol, testosterone	Increased strength and endurance	Aggression, impotence, baldness, kidney damage, breast development in men. Development of male features, facial and body hair, aggression in women
Beta-Blockers, eg Atenolol, Oxprenolol	Reduced heart rate and blood pressure	Low blood pressure, tiredness
Blood doping	Oxygenated blood, increased energy	Allergic reactions, blood clotting problems, kidney damage
Diuretics, eg Frusemide, triameterine	Weight loss, increased urination (preventing discovery of other drugs)	Nausia, cramps, dehydration
Narcotic analgesics, eg Methadone, Pethidine	Reduces pain caused by injuries	Addiction, respiratory problems
Peptide hormones, Analogues, eg Chorlonic gonadotrophin, EPO	Pain control, muscle growth	Abnormal growth of hands, feet, face and internal organs, increase risk of stroke, blood clots
Stimulants, eg Amphetamine, Cocaine	Increased mental and physical stimulation	Raised blood pressure, irregular heartbeat, addiction

---

13 Caffeine for example.

Drugs can Damage your Health

Listed above is a table of the main doping techniques illustrating their main advantages and disadvantages.

To most sporting participants the side effects of these drugs outweigh the advantages of taking them. At the highest level the competitive instincts of many participants may blind them to the dangers.

Goldman, Dr B and Klatz, Dr R, *Death in the Locker Room*

The desire to win is so great that people sometimes lose the concept of right and wrong due to being single-minded driven individuals. Sometimes it is very difficult to view life as a whole, as sports goals for the obsessed individual are the only true tangible goal. It can totally dominate your life and effectively shut out any vision of the world beyond. Mental perceptions of right and wrong may become misty and clouded and your attempts at experiencing the ethics and fun of sport are so nebulous, that it is hardly worth mentioning, let alone planning for in your mind. In some athletes' minds, the present is a set of stair steps of relatively minor competitions leading up to the moment when they have the opportunity to be the best in their designated sport.

There is great uncertainty in their minds about life-beyond-victory and that is one of your toughest challenges as an athlete. To be a good sports champion and leader you must not only compete successfully but also have an overview of your true life goals.

An example of this mindset was the results of a poll performed by Gabe Mirkin MD, author of *The Sports Medicine Book*. He is a devoted runner and in the early 1980s polled more than a hundred top runners and asked them this question, 'If I could give you a pill that would make you an Olympic champion – and also kill you in a year – would you take it?' Mirkin reported that more than half the athletes he asked responded that yes, they would take the pill. I was stunned by Mirkin's survey and wondered whether this indicated the willingness to die was universal among athletes; perhaps it was idiosyncratic to runners.

I performed a series of polls on athletes in the mid and late 1980s, those in combative and power sports such as weightlifting, track and field competitors – discuss throwers, shot putters, jumpers, football players, etc. I found these competitors were just as crazy as runners.

I asked 198 top world class athletes a question similar to Mirkin's, 'If I had a magic drug that was so fantastic that if you took it once you would win every competition you would enter, from the Olympic decathlon to the Mr Universe, for the next five years but it had one minor drawback – it would kill you five years after you took it – would you still take the drug?' Of those asked, 103 (52%) said yes, that winning was so attractive, they would not only be prepared to achieve it by taking a pill (in other words through an outlawed, unfair method – that is, in effect, cheating) but they would give their lives to do it.[14]

---

14 Goldman, B and Klatz, R, *Death in the Locker Room 2* (1992), Chicago: Elite Sports Medicine Publications Inc, p 23.

So how justified are NGBs in taking a paternalist approach and protecting the welfare of sporting participants?[15] Traditional paternalist jurisprudence would argue that this approach is only valid if the effect of the prohibition is to protect those unable to make an informed and rational judgment for themselves or to prevent harm to others. The obvious example of the former would be a ban on the taking of performance enhancing drugs by children and junior athletes but extending the ban beyond this point is difficult to justify on this basis.

Mill, JS, *On Liberty*

The object of this essay is to assert one very simple principle, as entitled to govern absolutely the dealings of society with the individual in the way of compulsion and control, whether the means used be physical force in the form of legal penalties or the moral coercion of public opinion. That principle is, that the sole end for which mankind are warranted, individually or collectively, in interfering in the liberty of action of any of their number, is self protection. That the only purpose for which power can be rightfully exercised over any member of a civilised community, against his will, is to prevent harm to others. His own good, either physical or moral, is not a sufficient warrant. He cannot rightfully be compelled to do or forbear because it will be better for him to do so, because it will make him happier, because, in the opinions of others, to do so would be wise or even right. These are good reasons for remonstrating with him or reasoning with him or persuading him or entreating him but not for compelling him or visiting him with any evil in case he do otherwise. To justify that, the conduct from which it is desired to deter him must be calculated to produce evil to someone else. The only part of the conduct of any one, for which he is amenable to society, is that which concerns others. In the part which merely concerns himself, his independence is, of right, absolute. Over himself, over his own body and mind, the individual is sovereign.[16]

It can be argued that drugs are not taken freely. Athletes are coerced into taking them by a belief that without them they would have little chance of sporting success.[17] This argument also forms the basis for another objection, that an athlete taking performance enhancing drugs is coercing others into taking them for the same reasons. There are many training regimes which athletes may and do reject on the basis that they may cause long term physiological damage, so it is difficult to understand why drug taking should

15 Simon, RL, 'Good Competition and Drug-enhanced Performance' (1984) XI *Journal of the Philosophy of Sport* 6, Brown, WM, 'Paternalism, Drugs and the Nature of Sports' (1984) XI *Journal of the Philosophy of Sport* 14, Lavin, M, 'Sports and Drugs: Are the Current Bans Justified?' (1987) XIV *Journal of the Philosophy of Sport* 34, Fairchild, D, 'Sport Abjection: Steroids and the Uglification of the Athlete' (1987) XIV *Journal of the Philosophy of Sport* 74.

16 Mill, JS, *On Liberty* (1962), London: Fontana. See also Dworkin, G, 'Paternalism' (1972) in *The Monist*, 56, 64–84, Dworkin, G, *Paternalism: Some Second Thoughts* (1983), Satorius, R (ed), *Paternalism*, Minneapolis: University of Minnesota Press; Feinberg, J (1971) *Legal Paternalism Canadian Journal of Philosophy* 1, 106–24.

17 Thomas, CE, *Sport in a Philosophic Context* (1983), Philidelphia: Lea & Febiger; Alan Wertheimer Coersion Princeton University Press (1989).

be treated differently. Further, many young sportsmen and women undertake training routines or compete when injured, to their later physical detriment.

On what basis then can society be justified in favouring the prohibition of performance enhancing drug when as Mill argued, intervention in an athlete's life can amount to a greater wrong than the risk of illness voluntarily accepted?

Brown, WM, 'Paternalism, Drugs and the Nature of Sport'

Often, too, we stress human factors such as determination, fortitude and co-operativeness over risk taking and technology. But in other cases – skiing, mountain climbing, hang gliding – risk and technology dominate. We believe in the capacity of sports to promote health and fitness but many originate in the practice of war and routinely involve stress and injury, sometimes death. We fashion rules and continually modify them to reduce hazards and minimise serious injury but few would seek to do so entirely. Perhaps we are tempted to require in athletes only what is natural. But our sports have evolved with our technology and our best athletes are often unnaturally, statistically, endowed with abilities and other characteristics far beyond the norm. It seems artificial indeed to draw the line at drugs when so much of today's training techniques, equipment, food, medical care, even the origin of the sport themselves, are the product of our technological culture.

Nevertheless, something more may be said for the claim that sports reflect a broader set of values. In discussing the justification of paternalism in coaching the young, I have stressed the formation of the values of honesty, fairness and autonomy, values central to my conception of personhood. But they are not the only ones that might be stressed. Obedience, regimentation, service to others or sacrifice might have been proposed. These, too, in the proper context, might also be developed together with the skills of athletics. The values, perhaps even a conception of what is good for human life, are associated with sports, not because of their nature but due to the way we choose to play them. We can indeed forbid the use of drugs in athletics in general, just as we do in the case of children. But ironically, in adopting such a paternalistic stance of insisting that we know better than the athletes themselves how to achieve some more general good which they myopically ignore, we must deny them the very attributes we claim to value: self-reliance, personal achievement and autonomy.[18]

If it is difficult to sustain an argument for the prohibition of performance enhancing drugs taken by adults, perhaps a stronger argument is to ban them on the basis that they undermine the sporting ethic by giving some participants an unfair advantage over others or over the sport itself.

---

18 Brown, WM, 'Paternalism, Drugs and the Nature of Sport' (1994) XI *Journal of the Philosophy of Sport* 14, 22.

Taking Drugs is Cheating

On a philosophical level it is argued that taking drugs will give the taker an advantage over a competitor who has not taken drugs and is therefore cheating.[19] Therefore there are two grounds on which the prohibition of performance enhancing drugs may be justified. First they give some athletes an unfair advantage over other athletes.[20] Secondly they give the athlete an unfair advantage over the sport. NGBs run the risk that the image of their sport would be undermined by a belief that their sport was being conducted on an uneven playing field. This knowledge would undermine the validity of the sport and lead to a loss in popularity.

Following the drugs revelations surrounding Ben Johnson, the Canadian sprinter, a governmental inquiry chaired by Mr Justice Charles Dubin concluded:

de Pencier, J, 'Law and Athlete Drug Testing in Canada'

The use of banned performance enhancing drugs is cheating, which is the antithesis of sport. The widespread use of such drugs has threatened the essential integrity of sport and is destructive of its very objectives. It also erodes the ethical and moral values of athletes who use them, endangering their mental and physical welfare while demoralising the entire sport community.[21]

Whilst we may concur with these sentiments, eradicating all the unfair advantages that one participant may have over another may not only be impossible to achieve but also undesirable. Competitive sport is all about one athlete being better than another and therefore it is desirable to have physiological and psychological differences between the participants.

There are many advantages inherent in, for example, the nationality of an athlete. The skier raised in Austria or Switzerland has an advantage over one raised in Belgium; the runner living at altitude over the runner at sea level; the height advantage of the average American basketball player over the average oriental player; or the technological, training and dietary advantages of the rich nation over the impoverished third world county.[22] All these are advantages and may be considered unfair in terms of sporting equality. The argument that the above examples are natural advantages compared to the artificial advantage of drug taking is countered in the following extract:

---

19 Simon, RL, *Fair Play: Sports, Values and Society* (1991), Boulder: Westview Press, Chapter 4.

20 Gardner, R, 'On Performance Enhancing Substances and the Unfair Advantage Argument (1989) XVI *Journal of the Philosophy of Sport* 59; Brown, WM, 'Drugs, Ethics and Sport' (1980) VII *Journal of the Philosophy of Sport* 15; Brown, WM, 'Fraleigh Performance enhancing Drugs in Sport' (1985) XI *Journal of the Philosophy of Sport* 23; Brown, WM, 'Comments on Simon and Fraleigh' (1984) XI *Journal of the Philosophy of Sport* 14.

21 de Pencier, J, 'Law and Athlete Drug Testing in Canada' (1992) 4(2) *Marquette Sports Law Journal* 259.

22 *The Guardian*, 5 April 1996 and 12 July 1996.

Gardner, R, 'On Performance Enhancing Substances and the Unfair Advantage Argument'

In the first case we do not object to differences in the endurance capabilities of athletes resulting from increased haemoglobin count, provided that increase is the result of high-altitude training. In the second case, we do not object to discrepancies in the size of skeletal muscles, providing that size results from genetic endowment or training (eg weight lifting). In each case, we are not objecting to the advantage but to the way in which the advantage is gained. So what is it about blood doping or human growth hormone that somehow distinguishes these methods of securing an advantage and seems to render their effects unacceptable? The obvious difference is the advantages gained by blood boosting and HGH are achieved through the use of a (supplemented) substance. However if the basis of our objection is to be that using a substance is an unacceptable means to gaining an advantage, then the inconsistencies are more than apparent.

There are many legal substances used by athletes in their attempt to gain an advantage over competitors – for example, amino acids, protein powders, vitamin and mineral supplements (sometimes injected), caffeine (legally limited to 12 micrograms per millilitre of urine, about seven cups of coffee), glucose polymer drinks and injections of ATP (a naturally produced chemical involved in muscle contraction). The list could go on and on. Clearly we do not object to gaining an advantage through the use of a substance; it is only particular substances to which we are opposed. This being the case, it seems that some form of definitive criteria would have to be established in order to differentiate between permissible and prohibited substances. Yet, such criteria do not seem to exist.[23]

An alternative argument is that rather than cheating fellow competitors, the drug taker is cheating the sport itself. Clearly the essence of a sport would be compromised by certain breaches of the rules. It would be totally unacceptable for Linford Christie to be beaten in an Olympic 100 metres final by a competitor on a motor cycle or for 'Tiger' Woods to lose the Masters to a player with a radio controlled golf ball. As Gardner has questioned 'would allowing unrestricted use of steroids in the 100 metres be somewhat like providing the participants with motorcycles?'[24]

There are two problems with an affirmative answer. First not all tactical or technical deviations from the norm are prohibited. Carbon fibre racquets have dramatically altered the game of tennis and Chris Boardman's radically different bicycle has revolutionised pursuit cycling, yet these developments were accepted by the respective sports. Secondly the question presumes that performance enhancing drugs are an extrinsic aid unrelated to the skills and physical condition of the athlete. However as their name would suggest these

---

23 Gardner, R, 'On Performance Enhancing Substances and the Unfair Advantage Argument' (1989) XVL *Journal of the Philosophy of Sport* 59, 66.

24 *Ibid*, p 68.

drugs enhance performance, ie they allow the athlete to reach their full potential and so parallels with motorcyclists are difficult to sustain.

However can a competitor truly claim victory if it is achieved with the assistance of drugs? Victory is inextricably linked to rules. It is questionable whether the drug taking athlete has competed in the first place. Successful athletes are afforded a unique place in society. Sporting heroes are society's heroes. By heralding the success of a drugs assisted athlete we are in danger of undermining society itself.[25]

Perhaps the most acceptable reason for prohibiting performance enhancing drugs is that otherwise sporting competition fails to be a test of persons and therefore, drug taking is ethically indefensible:

Simon, R, 'Good Competition and Drug Enhanced Performance'

Where athletic competition is concerned, if all we are interested in is better and better performance, we could design robots to 'run' the 100 yards in three seconds or hit a golf ball 500 yards when necessary. But it isn't just enhanced performance that we are after. In addition, we want athletic performance to be a test of persons. It is not only raw ability we are testing for; it is what people do with their ability that counts at least as much. In competition itself, each competitor is reacting to the choices, strategies and valued abilities of the other, which in turn are affected by past decisions and commitments. Arguably, athletic competition is a paradigm example of an area in which each individual competitor respects the other competitors as persons. That is, each reacts to the intelligent choices and valued characteristics of the other. These characteristics include motivation, courage, intelligence and what might be called the metachoice of which talents and capacities are to assume priority over others for a given stage of the individual's life.

However if outcomes are significantly affected not by such features but instead by the capacity of the body to benefit physiologically from drugs, athletes are no longer reacting to each other as persons but rather become more like competing bodies. It becomes more and more appropriate to see the opposition as things to be overcome – as mere means to be overcome in the name of victory – rather than persons posing valuable challenges. So, insofar as the requirement that we respect each other as persons is ethically fundamental, the prevailing paradigm does enjoy a privileged perspective from the moral point of view.[26]

---

25 Simon, RL, *Fair Play: Sports Values and Society* (1991); Coakley, J, *Sport in Society*, 5th edn.
26 Simon, RL, 'Good Competition and Drug Enhanced Performance' (1994) XI *Journal of the Philosophy of Sport* 6, 13.

THE RULES OF SPORTING GOVERNING BODIES

An inevitable consequence of the increased rewards available to athletes[27] is that banned athletes are far more likely to seek to overturn bans and fines of NGBs in appellate tribunals and courts of law.[28] Sandra Gasser, a Swiss athlete who tested positive and was banned for two years by the IAAF, was estimated to have lost over US$250,000 in endorsements and appearance fees. The cost to the IAAF of defending the legal action was more than £100,000. The American courts initially awarded Butch Reynolds US$27,000,000 in damages and American shot putter Randy Barnes commenced an action for US$55,000,000 after suspension for a positive drugs test.[29] If the constitution or procedures of the NGBs are defective then athletes are now in the financial position to commission highly paid lawyers to exploit those flaws.

The outcome of such challenges is that NGB rules have become increasingly complex. This is illustrated by the detailed extracts below which are taken from the IAAF Handbook 1996–97 and the IAAF Procedural Guidelines for Doping Control 1996. The first extract from the IAAF Handbook 1996–97 outlines, in general principles, the control of drug abuse:

IAAF Handbook 1996–97

Rule 55 – Doping

(1) Doping is strictly forbidden and is offence under IAAF Rules.

(2) The offence of doping takes place when either:

    (a) a prohibited substance is found to be present within an athlete's body tissue or fluids; or

    (b) an athlete uses or takes advantage of a prohibited technique; or

    (c) an athlete admits having used or taken advantage of a prohibited substance or a prohibited technique.

(3) Prohibited substances include those listed in Schedule I to the 'Procedural Guidelines for Doping Control'. This list shall be constantly reviewed by the Doping Commission and may added to or amended by them. Such addition or amendment must be approved by the Council and shall come into force three months from the date of such approval.

(4) It is an athlete's duty to ensure that no substance enters his body tissues or fluids which is prohibited under these Rules. Athletes are warned that they are responsible for all or any substance detected in samples given by them.

---

27 'Olympic winners of 10 years ago went home with gold medals, today they take with them a portfolio of contracts worth six figure sums.' Cashmore, E, *Making Sense of Sport* (1990), London: Routledge, p 122.

28 *The Guardian*, 9 September 1993.

29 Gay, M, 'Doping Control – The Scope for a Legal Challenge', *Seminar on Doping Control*, The Sports Council Doping Control Unit 1994.

(5) An athlete may request the Doping Commission to grant prior exemption allowing him to take a substance normally prohibited under IMF Rules. Such an exemption will only be granted in cases of clear and compelling clinical need. Details of the procedure for such an application are to be found in the 'Procedural Guidelines for Doping Control'.

(6) The expression 'prohibited substance' shall include a metabolite of a prohibited substance.

(7) The expression 'prohibited technique' shall include:

(a) blood doping;

(b) use of substances and methods which alter the integrity and validity of urine samples used in doping control.

However a fuller, non-exhaustive, list of such techniques is to be found in Schedule 2 of the 'Procedural Guidelines for Doping Control'. (See also Rule 60. 2 'Sanctions'.)

(11) A departure or departures from the procedures set out in the 'Procedural Guidelines for Doping Control' shall not invalidate the finding that a prohibited substance was present in a sample or that prohibited technique had been used, unless this departure, was such as to cast real doubt on the reliability of such a finding.

(12) The IAAF or its Members may delegate the collection of samples to any Member, governmental agency or any other third party that they deem suitable.

Rule 56 – Ancillary Offences

(1) An athlete who fails or refuses to submit to doping control after having been requested to do so by the responsible official will have committed a doping offence and will be subject to sanctions in accordance with Rule 60. This fact shall be reported to the IAAF and his national governing body.

(2) An athlete shall only be entitled to refuse to provide a blood sample in circumstances where the mandatory procedures and safeguards set out in the Procedural Guidelines for Doping Control are not observed.

(3) Any person assisting or inciting others or admitting having incited or assisted others, to use a prohibited substance or prohibited techniques, shall have committed a doping offence and shall be subject to sanctions in accordance with Rule 61. If that person is not an athlete, then the Council may, at its discretion, impose an appropriate sanction.

(4) Any person trading, trafficking, distributing or selling any prohibited substance otherwise than in the normal course of a recognised profession or trade shall also have committed a doping offence under these Rules and shall be subject to sanctions in accordance with Rule 60.

BANNED SUBSTANCES

The following extract is the list of banned substances taken from the IAAF Procedural Guidelines for Doping Control 1996. It will be noted that the use of the expression 'and chemically or pharmacologically related compounds' prevents the athlete's representatives, in most cases, distinguishing the drug or drugs discovered from those specified in the schedules:

IAAF Procedural Guidelines for Doping Control 1996

PROHIBITED SUBSTANCES

PART I

(a) Anabolic Agents

(I) Androgenic Anabolic Steroids

  eg bolasterone methyltestosterone

      boldenone nandrolone

      chlordehydromethyltestosterone norethandrolone

      clostebol oxandrolone

      dihydrotestosterone oxymesterone

      fluoxymesterone oxymetholone

      mesterolone stanozolol

      methandienone testosterone

      methenolone

      and chemically or pharmacologically related compounds

Dihydrotestosterone: a sample will be deemed to be positive for dihydrotestosterone where the concentrations of dihydrotestosterone and its metabolites and/or their ratios to non-salphas-steroids in urine so exceed the range of values normally found in humans as not to be consistent with normal endogenous production.

Testosterone: a sample will be deemed to be positive for testosterone where either the ratio in urine of testosterone to epitestosterone or the concentration of testosterone in urine, so exceeds the range of values normally found in humans as not to be consistent with normal endogenous production

A sample will not be regarded as positive for dihydrotestosterone or testosterone where an athlete proves by clear and convincing evidence that the abnormal ratio or concentration is attributable to a pathological or physiological condition.

(II) Other anabolic agents eg beta-2-agonists (eg clenbuterol)

Exceptionally, the administration of the beta-2-agonists salbutamol, salmeterol or terbutaline is permitted by inhalation where prescribed for therapeutic purposes by properly qualified medical personnel and where prior clearance has been given by the relevant National Federation or the IMF.

(b) Amphetamines

amineptine methoxyphenamine
amphetamine methylamphetamine
amphetaminil methylphenidate
benzphetamine morazone
dimethylamphetamine pemoline
ethylamphetamine phendimetrazine
fenethylline phenmetrazine
fenproporex pipradrol
furfenorex pyrovalerone
mesocarb

and chemically or pharmacologically related compounds.

(c) Corticosteroids

Corticosteroids by oral, intramuscular or intravenous application.

(d) Peptide Hormones and analogues

Chorionic Gonadotroohin (HCG – human chorionic gonadotrophin): it is well known that the administration to males of human chorionic gonadotrophin (HCG) and other compounds with related activity leads to an increased rate of production of endogenous androgenic steroids and is considered equivalent to the exogenous administration of testosterone.

A sample will be deemed to be positive for HCG where the concentration of HCG in urine so exceeds the range of values normally found in humans as not to be consistent with normal endogenous production.

A sample will not be regarded as positive for HCG where an athlete proves by clear and convincing evidence that the abnormal concentration is attributable to a pathological or physiological condition.

Corticotroohin (ACTH): corticotrophin has been misused to increase the blood levels of endogenous corticosteroids notably to obtain the euphoric effect of corticosteroids. The application of corticotrophin is considered to be equivalent to the oral, intramuscular or intravenous application of corticosteroids.

Growth Hormone (HGH, somatotrophin): the misuse of growth hormone in sport is deemed to be unethical and dangerous because of various adverse effects, for example. allergic reactions, diabetogenic effects and acromegaly when applied in high doses.

Ervthroooietin (EPO) is a glycoprotein produced principally in the kidney which stimulates the production of red blood corpuscles.

All the respective releasing factors of the above mentioned substances are also banned.

(e) Cocaine

(f) Prohibited Techniques ...

PART II

(a) Stimulants

amiphenazole fencamfamin

caffeine mefenorex

cathine methylephedrine

chlorphentermine nikethamide

clobenzorex pentetrazol

clorprenaline pentetrazol

cropropamide phentermine

crotethamide phenylpropanolamine

ephedrine prolintane

etafedrine propylhexedrine

ethamivan strychnine

and chemically or pharmacologically related compounds

For caffeine the definition of a positive finding is one in which the concentration in urine exceeds 12 micrograms per millilitre.

(b) Narcotic Analgesics

alphaprodine ethylmorphine

anileridine levorphanol

buprenorphine methadone

dextromoramide morphine

dextropropoxyphene nalbuphin

diamorphine pentazocine

dipipanone pethidine

ethoheptazine trimeperidine

and chemically or pharmacologically related compounds

Note – codeine, dextromethorphan, dihydrocodeine, diphenoxylate and pholcodine are permitted.

For morphine the definition of a positive finding is one in which the concentration in the urine exceeds 1 microgram per millilitre of free and conjugated morphine.

PART III

Substances and prohibited techniques to be detected during Out-Of-Competition Testing.

(a) Anabolic Agents (see PART I (a))

(b) Peptide Hormones and Analogues (see PART I (d))

(c) Prohibited Techniques (see SCHEDULE 2)

In addition to this comprehensive list of banned substances the IAAF procedural guidelines cover other techniques ranging from blood doping to the more extreme methods of detection avoidance such as the addition of uncorrupted urine into the body of the athlete by means of catheterisation.

SCHEDULE 2

PROHIBITED TECHNIQUES

The expression 'prohibited techniques' shall include:

(i)   Blood doping (including the use of erythropoietin (EPO). See SCHEDULE I PART I (d)).

(ii) Use or attempted use of substances and of methods eg diuretics, which alter the integrity and validity of urine samples used in doping controls. Examples of prohibited techniques are catheterisation, urine substitution and/or tampering, inhibition of renal excretion, eg by probenecid and related compounds.

(iii) Epitestosterone: a sample will be deemed to be positive for epitestoslerone where either the concentration of epitestosterone in urine or the ratio of epitestosterone to other endogenous steroids in urine, so exceeds the range of values normally found in humans as not to be consistent with normal endogenous production.

No matter how comprehensive the list of banned substances there is always the danger that the 'dirty chemist'[30] will be one step ahead, altering the chemical structure of compounds so as to distinguish the drug from those encompassed by the regulations. An alternative to the ever increasing list system would be to look generally for abnormalities in samples. This has been proposed by administrators in the sport of swimming.[31] It has been suggested that the world governing body assemble a panel of medical and legal experts who would examine samples for irregularities, decide whether they are performance-enhancers, irrespective of whether they appear on lists of banned substances and sanction the competitors accordingly. Such a system could face legal challenge under the rules of natural justice. Competitors could argue that the contract between themselves and the NGB contains an implied right to be treated fairly. An athlete could argue that it becomes impossible to act within the rules of the governing body if it is unclear exactly what those rules are until they are broken. Problems may arise over the definition of 'performance enhancing'. Whilst it is accepted that the introduction of such a system would enable NGBs to ensnare the 'cheats', it may be at the expense of many innocent athletes.

---

30 *The Independent*, 21 May 1997.

31 *Ibid*.

Sampling and Testing

IAAF Procedural Guidelines for Doping Control 1996

DOPING CONTROL DURING COMPETITION

Facilities and Materials

2.1 A Doping Control Station shall be provided. It should consist of a waiting room, working room and WCs (men and women. It should be equipped with all necessary IAAF approved materials including collecting vessels, bottles and sealing equipment. There should be a varied selection of sealed drinks for the athletes. The Doping Control Officials should ensure that the facilities are clean and adequate and that the materials are acceptable prior to the start of the competition.

2.2 The Doping Control Station should be clearly identified.

Selection of Athletes to be Tested

2.3 Selection of athletes shall be on a final position basis and/or random basis.

2.4 In addition, selection of further athletes may be ordered at the discretion of the IAAF, the Doping Control Official or the Doping Delegate by any method that it or he shall choose.

2.5 Doping control shall also be conducted or any athlete who is deemed to have broken or equalled an Area or World Record.

Collection of Urine Samples

2.6 Athletes selected for doping control must be handed a notice at the completion of their event stating that they are required to undergo doping control. For the assistance of meeting organisers a specimen notice is shown in Schedule 3. The handing over of the notice shall be carried out as discreetly as possible and the athlete shall acknowledge receipt on the relevant section of the notice.

2.7 If an athlete refuses to sign the doping notice, the steward shall immediately report this to the official in charge of the Doping Control Station who shall inform the relevant referee of the Meeting. The referee shall make every effort to contact the athlete to inform him of his obligation to undergo doping control. If the athlete fails or refuses to sign this notice and/or fails to report to doping control within one hour of acknowledging the notice he shall be deemed to have refused to submit to doping control for the purpose of Rule 56.

2.8 Once the athlete has been given a notice, he should report to the Doping Control Station as soon as possible but no later than one hour after receipt of the notice. During the period between notification and reporting a steward should accompany the athlete. Once the athlete has reported to the Doping Control Station, he shall be expected to remain until the procedure is completed. He may leave that Station only under unusual circumstances and only if accompanied by an official steward.

2.9 When attending the Doping Control Station, the athlete may be accompanied by a representative of his choice and/or an interpreter. A urine sample shall be collected under supervision. The competitor shall have fulfilled his duty to submit to doping control only after having delivered the necessary volume of urine, irrespective of the time required for this.

2.10 In addition to the above, only the following persons should be allowed in the working room of the Doping Control Station:

- IAAF Doping Delegate (if appointed) – Officials in charge of the Station
- Sampling Officers
- Doping Control Stewards
- Other persons as determined by the IAAF Doping Delegate (if appointed) or other Official in charge of the Station It is recommended that a security person be positioned outside the Doping Control Station to monitor the flow of people in and out and to keep unauthorised persons from entering the Station.

2.11 When an athlete feels he is ready to provide a sample, he shall select a sample collecting vessel from a number of clean, unused vessels and proceed to the WC.

2.12 To ensure authenticity of the sample, the Doping Control Officer may require such disrobing as is necessary to confirm the urine has been produced by the competitor. This means the exposure of the body from the middle of the back to below the knees.

2.13 No one other than the athlete and an official of the Doping Control Station should be present in the WC when the urine is collected.

2.14 An athlete shall be requested to provide a minimum of 70 ml of urine. The collection of urine shall be witnessed by an official of the Doping Control Station. The witness shall be of the same gender as the athlete. If the athlete is unable to provide the required amount of urine, his sample should be sealed and kept secure in the working room. The athlete should return to the waiting area until he feels he is able to provide a further sample. He should then add to or 'top up' the urine previously provided to the required amount.

2.15 Specific gravity and pH of the urine shall be measured using a residual volume of urine in the collecting vessel. A specific gravity of 1.010 or higher is required. If the first sample does not meet these specifications a second sample may be required. Samples which do not meet the required specific gravity should be processed. sealed and documented in accord with normal IAAF practice. Any subsequent sample collected from the athlete on this occasion shall also be processed in the normal manner and documented on the form.

2.16 An athlete shall be allowed the choice of two bottles from a selection of clean, unused bottles. One bottle shall be marked main sample 'A' and the other reserve sample 'B'.

2.17 The sample shall be divided in the presence of the athlete and the Doping Control Official into the two chosen bottles. It is recommended that the main sample 'A' be of at least 40 ml and the reserve sample 'B' 30 ml. However any shortfall in the amount of urine shall not invalidate a test, provided there is sufficient urine for the test to be adequately performed.

2.18 The two bottles or the individual outer container in which each bottle has been placed shall be sealed in the presence of the athlete who should ensure that the code on each bottle is the same as that entered by the official on the athlete's Doping Control Form. An example of a suitable form is shown in Schedule 3.

2.19 Signatures of the athlete, the accompanying person (if any) and an official of the Doping Control Station must appear on the Doping Control Form, confirming that the above procedures were carried out. If the athlete feels the procedures were not carried out satisfactorily, he should declare so on the Doping Control Form and state the reasons for dissatisfaction. In the absence of any such declaration the athlete shall be deemed to have waived any alleged procedural breach. The athlete shall also provide details of any medication recently used by him on the Doping Control Form.

2.20 The Doping Control Form should be so devised that duplicate copies are produced at the same time. These should be dealt with as follows: (a) a copy to be retained by the representative of the relevant authority (eg the IAAF, National Federation or Area Association); (b) a copy to be transmitted to the relevant authority (eg the IAAF, National Federation or Area Association); (c) a copy to be given to the athlete; (d) a special copy to be Sent to the laboratory which is to conduct the analysis. The copy which is sent to the laboratory should not contain any information which could identify the athlete who provided the sample.

2.21 If the Doping Control Official believes that the circumstances surrounding the giving of a sample are suspicious, he may request the athlete to provide a second sample. The first sample provided shall be retained by the Official for analysis. The second sample shall be collected in accordance with the procedures governing the collection of the first sample as set out above. Once the second sample has been taken, all samples (being the main 'A' and reserve 'B' portions of both samples) shall be despatched to the laboratory for analysis. The laboratory shall be informed (without disclosing the athlete's identity that the first and second samples were taken from the same athlete).

2.22 If the athlete refuses to provide a urine sample (or a second sample) the Doping Control Official should explain to the athlete that by refusing to provide a sample he shall be deemed to have refused to submit to doping control and may be subject to sanctions under IAAF Rule 60. If the athlete still refuses to provide a sample (or a second sample), the Doping Control Official should note this on the Doping Control Form, sign his name on the form and ask the athlete to sign the form. The Doping Control Official should also note any other irregularities in the doping control process.

Collection of Blood Samples

2.23 If an athlete is selected to provide a blood sample he shall be handed a notice at the completion of his event stating that he is required to undergo blood testing. The notice shall be given to the athlete as discreetly as possible and the athlete shall acknowledge receipt on the relevant section of the notice.

2.24 If an athlete refuses to sign the notice or in any other way indicates that he is refusing to provide a blood sample. the steward shall immediately report this to the official in charge of the Doping Control Station who shall inform the IAAF Doping Delegate or relevant referee of the meeting. The Doping Delegate or referee shall make every effort to contact the athlete to inform him of his obligation to provide a blood sample. If an athlete fails or refuses to sign this notice or fails or refuses to report for blood testing within one hour of being given the notice, he shall be deemed to have refused to submit for doping control for the purpose of IAAF Rule 56.

2.25 Once an athlete has been given a notice he must report to the Doping Control Station within one hour. In the time between receiving notification and attending for the purpose of providing the sample, the athlete should be accompanied by an official.

2.26 When attending the Doping Control Station the athlete may be accompanied by a representative of his choice and/or an interpreter.

2.27 Only those persons specified in paragraph 2.10 above shall be allowed to be present in the working room of the Doping Control Station at the time the sampling takes place.

2.28 Blood sampling shall only be conducted by medically qualified personnel. The official conducting blood sampling shall provide the athlete with evidence of medical qualification before blood sampling takes place.

2.29 No samples shall be taken unless an athlete has had the blood sampling procedures explained to him and has signed the form of consent to blood testing to be found in Schedule 3 to these Procedural Guidelines. If an athlete refuses to sign the form of consent a sample shall not be taken from him. Such a failure, other than in the circumstances set out in paragraph 2.33 below, will, however, be regarded as a refusal to submit to doping control and an athlete will be subject to sanctions under IMF Rule 56.

2.30 The equipment necessary to conduct blood sampling shall consist of the following items in sufficient quantity for each test. Items (I) to (vi) inclusive shall be of a quality suitable for blood sampling for medical purposes and items (i) to (v) inclusive shall be disposable and sterile where appropriate.

(i) venous canulae

(ii) vacuum tubes

(iii) plastic syringe-like holders for the vacuum sample tubes

(iv) shipping containers

(v) sterile disinfectant serviettes

(vi) tourniquet

The items specific to an individual test ((i) to (iv) inclusive) shall be contained within a module.

2.31 The athlete shall be given a choice of a blood sampling module from a selection of at least two modules.

2.32 The athlete shall select a blood sampling module and sampling shall begin. The official conducting blood sampling shall apply a tourniquet to the athlete's arm. No attempt shall be made to take blood from any other area of the athletes body. The official shall clean the skin with a supplied sterile disinfectant serviette and shall take the blood sample from a superficial vein, preferably in the antecubital region. The official shall attempt to do this as painlessly as possible. Four of the blood sample tubes to be found in the Blood Sampling Module shall be filled. No more than 25 ml of blood shall be withdrawn from an athlete during blood sampling.

2.33 An athlete shall be entitled to refuse to provide a blood sample if:

(i) the person purporting to conduct blood sampling is unable to provide evidence of medical qualification;

(ii) the items (i) and (iv) above, to be found in the blood sampling module, are not contained within clean sealed packaging or if such packaging is not intact;

(iii) if an official seeks to withdraw more than 25 ml of blood from the athlete.

2.34 The blood shall be withdrawn from the athlete into the four vacuum tubes. These tubes will be put directly into the transportation containers for the A and B Samples and these containers shall be immediately sealed.

2.35 Each sample tube shall be marked with a code number. This code number should be written by the relevant official on the athlete's Doping Control Form. The athlete should ensure that the code on the sample tubes corresponds to that entered by the official on the form.

2.36 Signatures of the athlete, the accompanying person (if any) and an official of the Doping Control Station must appear on the Doping Control Form, confirming that the above procedures were carried out. If an athlete thinks that the procedures were not carried out satisfactorily, he should declare so on the Doping Control Form and state his reasons for dissatisfaction. In the absence of any such declaration the athlete shall be deemed to have waived any alleged procedural breach.

2.37 The athlete shall also provide details on the Doping Control Form of any medication taken by him recently and of whether a blood transfusion has been received by him in the last six months.

2.38 The Doping Control Form shall be so devised that duplicate copies are produced at the same time. These should be dealt with as follows:

(a) a copy to be retained by the representative of the relevant authority (eg the IAAF, Area Association or National Federation);

(b) a copy to be transmitted to the relevant authority (eg the IAAF, Area Association or National Federation);

(c) a copy to be given to the athlete;

(d) a special copy to be sent to the laboratory which is to conduct the analysis. The copy which is sent to the laboratory should not contain any information which could identify the athlete who provided the sample.

Storage and Despatch of Samples

2.39 Before the bottles containing the urine and/or blood are packed, it should be confirmed that all samples taken are present and that the number is in accordance with the list of code numbers. All samples should be stored, if possible, in a refrigerator or freezer.

2.40 The main 'A' and reserve 'B' samples should be placed in a suitable outer container and should be despatched to the laboratory as soon as possible after doping control.

2.41 If at all possible, the outer container should not be opened during transit to the laboratory. The IAAF will provide identification labels, if required. for customs purposes. The opening of the outer container will not, of itself, invalidate doping control.

Analysis of Samples

2.42 Samples provided by athletes for the purpose of doping control immediately become the property of IAAF or relevant authority.

2.43 Only laboratories accredited or approved by the IAAF/IOC may be used to carry out analysis on samples taken in accordance with doping control.

2.44 The analysis of samples should be carried out as soon as is reasonably practicable after arrival at the laboratory.

2.45 Access to the laboratory during the analysis should be restricted to laboratory personnel, members of the IAAF Doping Commission and to authorised observers.

2.46 If at any stage, any question or issue arises on the testing or interpretation of results. the person responsible for testing at the laboratory may consult the IAAF for guidance.

2.47 If at any stage. any question or issue arises in relation to the sample, the laboratory may conduct any further or other tests necessary to clarify the fact or issue so raised and such tests may be relied upon by the IAAF when deciding whether a sample has tested positive for a prohibited substance.

2.48 The analysis of blood samples shall be conducted primarily to determine:

(a) whether the concentrations of growth hormone, corticotrophin or erythropoietin present in the sample are abnormal; and

(b) whether an athlete has utilised any prohibited technique, in particular blood doping.

2.49 Subject to the athletes consent if the analysis of a sample, whether of urine or blood, reveals the presence of any ailment, illness, disease or condition detrimental to the health of the athlete (other than the presence of a substance prohibited under IAAF Rules), this must be disclosed by the laboratory to the IAAF. The IAAF shall ensure that the athlete is advised of such condition as soon as possible and shall hold this information in the strictest confidence.

Communication of Results

2.50 If the analysis of the main 'A' sample indicates the presence of a prohibited substance, the laboratory shall inform the IAAF immediately. The IAAF shall then inform the athlete's National Federation and request that the National Federation seek an explanation from the athlete within a period set by the IAAF. The National Federation shall, in turn, inform the athlete of the results of the analysis as soon as is reasonably practicable and seek such an explanation. The explanation, if any, should be conveyed by the National Federation to the IAAF as soon as reasonably practicable but within the time limit set by the IAAF.

2.51 If no adequate explanation is received from the athlete or his National Federation within the time limit set by the IAAF, the test shall be regarded as positive and the athlete shall be suspended from this time, suspension being a provisional matter pending the resolution of the case. This fact shall be reported by the IAAF to the athlete's National Federation who shall immediately inform the athlete. The National Federation shall also be informed that the athlete should be subject to disciplinary proceedings in accordance with IAAF Rule 60.

2.52 The athlete may, at any time before the hearing (see 2.58 below) by the athlete's National Federation, raise any matter he feels relevant with the IAAF (whether by its Doping Commission or otherwise) via his National Federation. The IAAF is empowered to consider all such representations, to require further information from the relevant parties and, in exceptional circumstances, to request the athlete to appear before it. The IAAF may give any weight it chooses to representations made to it and is under no obligation to explain to any party what account it took of representations submitted to it in reaching any decisions it may take.

2.53 If the athlete raises matters which the IAAF thinks indicate that a doping offence has not been committed or if the results of the 'B' sample analysis requested by an athlete do not indicate the presence of the substance detected in the 'A' sample, the IMF may lift an athlete's suspension and declare that he will no longer be subject to disciplinary proceedings in accordance with IAAF Rule 60.

2.54 Every athlete shall have the right to request that the reserve 'B' sample be tested to ascertain whether that sample discloses the presence of the same prohibited substance detected in the main 'A' sample. Such request must be made within 28 days of the notification to the athlete that the main 'A' sample discloses the presence of a prohibited substance. A laboratory shall not be obliged to keep any reserve 'B' samples after this time, unless so requested by the IAAF. An athlete shall remain suspended, despite the fact that he has requested analysis of the 'B' sample.

2.55 Once an athlete has requested analysis of the reserve 'B' sample, a date shall be arranged within 21 days of the request for the conduct of the analysis. A date and time shall be arranged for the analysis which is convenient both for the athlete and for the IAAF. The athlete's National Federation shall be informed of the date and time of the analysis. Should he wish to do so, the athlete and/or his representative may be present at the analysis. A representative of the athlete's National Federation may also be present, as may a representative of the IAAF. Once testing on the reserve 'B' sample is complete, the laboratory report should be sent to the IAAF as well as, in due course, a copy of all relevant laboratory data.

2.56 The IAAF may at any time request analysis of the 'B' sample if it believes that this will be relevant to the consideration of an athlete's case.

2.57 Confidentiality shall be observed by all persons connected with doping control until such time as the athlete is suspended in accordance with 2.51.

2.58 Every athlete shall have the right to a hearing before the relevant tribunal of his National Federation before any decision on eligibility is reached. This hearing should take place as soon as possible and under normal circumstances not later than three months after the final laboratory analysis.

2.59 If the athlete is found at a hearing before his National Federation to have committed a doping offence or he waives his right to a hearing, he shall be declared ineligible. His ineligibility shall begin from the date on which the sample was provided.

OUT-OF-COMPETITION TESTING

International Sampling Officers (ISOs)

3.1 The IAAF Bureau may, on the advice of the Doping Commission, appoint International Sampling Officers (ISOs) to conduct Out-Of-Competition doping control.

3.2 The IAAF Bureau shall maintain a register of persons selected by the IAAF to act as ISOs. However the fact that an Officer's name has not yet been added to the register of ISOs will not affect his competence to carry out this function.

3.3 The appointment of a person as an ISO shall be evidenced by the issue of an ISO's licence or a letter of appointment. Before a sampling officer can validly conduct Out-Of-Competition Testing. he must also receive a letter of authorisation from IAAF specifying. in general terms, where and when he is to conduct Out-Of-Competition doping control.

Selecting the Athlete

3.4 The IAAF Bureau shall keep a register of athletes who may be required to undergo Out-Of-Competition doping control.

3.5 Individual athletes or groups of athletes may be tested at the discretion of the IAAF.

Contacting the Athlete

3.6 When an athlete has been selected for Out-Of-Competition doping control, the ISO or IAAF may either make an appointment to meet the athlete or he may arrive unannounced at the athlete's training camp accommodation or any other place where the athlete is likely to be found.

3.7 Where an arrangement has been made for the collection of a sample a time and a place for collection will be agreed. The sample should be collected as soon as possible thereafter.

3.8 Where such an arrangement has been made it is the athlete's responsibility to check prior to the arranged meeting that there is no possible confusion over the arranged date, time and precise location where the meeting will take place. The ISO will wait up to two hours beyond the time agreed but thereafter the athlete will be declared absent from testing. An appeal on the grounds that the athlete did not fully understand where to go or went at the wrong time will not normally be considered. An athlete who is absent from testing will be deemed to have refused to submit to doping control contrary to Rule 57 and may be subject to sanctions under IAAF Rule 60.

3.9 Where an ISO arrives unannounced he must give the athlete reasonable time to complete any activity in which he is engaged. Such activity must be within the ISO's clear and continuous view, notwithstanding this, testing should commence within one hour of his first contact.

Identification

3.10 When an athlete and an ISO meet, the ISO must show his: (a) proof of identity or ISO's licence; (b) letter of appointment as an International Sampling Officer from the IAAF including authorisation to collect the Sample.

3.11 The ISO may also require proof of identity of the athlete. Whenever possible this will involve photographic proof of identity (passport, ID Card, etc).

Collecting the Sample

3.12 The International Sampling Officer will make every effort to collect the urine sample as discreetly as possible and with maximum privacy but circumstances may impose difficulties on the ISO that cannot be overcome.

3.13 When the athlete feels he is ready to provide a sample, he shall select a sample collecting vessel from a number of clean, unused vessels.

3.14 An athlete shall be requested to provide a minimum of 70 ml of urine. The collection of urine shall be witnessed by an ISO or his appointee. The witness shall always be of the same gender as the athlete. If the athlete is unable to provide the required amount of urine, his sample should be sealed and kept secure. When the athlete feels he is able to provide a further sample, he should then add to or 'top up' the urine previously provided to the required amount.

3.15 Specific gravity and pH of the urine shall be measured using a residual volume of urine in the collecting vessel. A specific gravity of 1.010 or higher is required. If the first sample does not meet these specifications a second sample may be required. Samples which do not meet the required specific gravity should be processed, sealed and documented in accord with normal IAAF practice. Any subsequent sample collected from the athlete on this occasion shall also be processed in the normal manner and documented on the Form.

3.16 An athlete shall be allowed the choice of two bottles from a selection of clean, unused bottles. One bottle shall be marked main sample 'A' and the other reserve sample 'B'. The sample shall then be divided in the presence of the athlete into the two chosen bottles. It is recommended that the main sample 'A' be of at least 40 ml and the reserve sample 'B' at least 30 ml. However any shortfall in the amount of urine provided shall not invalidate a test, provided there is sufficient urine for the test to be adequately performed.

3.17 The two bottles or the individual outer container in which each bottle has been placed shall be sealed in the presence of the athlete who should ensure that the code on each bottle is the same as that entered by the ISO on the athlete's Doping Control Form.

(Examples of suitable forms are shown in Schedule 3).

3.18 Signatures of the athlete, the accompanying person (if any) and the ISO must appear on the Doping Control Form, confirming that the above procedures were carried out. If the athlete feels that the procedures were not carried out satisfactorily, he should declare so on the Doping Control Form and state the reasons for dissatisfaction. In the absence of any such declaration the athlete shall be deemed to have waived any alleged procedural breach The athlete shall also provide details of any medication recently used by him on the Doping Control Form.

3.19 The Doping Control Form should be so devised that duplicate copies are produced at the same time. These should be dealt with as follows:

(a) a copy to be retained by the ISO;

(b) a copy to be transmitted to IAAF;

(c) a copy to be given to the athlete;

(d) a special copy to be sent to the laboratory which is to conduct the analysis. The copy which is sent to the laboratory should not contain any information which could identify the athlete who provided the sample.

3.20 If the athlete refuses to provide a urine sample (or a second sample). the ISO should explain to the athlete that by refusing to provide a sample, he shall be deemed to have refused to submit to doping control and may be subject to sanctions under IAAF Rule 60. If the athlete still refuses to provide a sample (or a second sample), the ISO should note this on the Doping Control Form, sign his name and ask the athlete to sign the form. The ISO should also note any other irregularities in the doping control process.

Collection of Blood Samples

3.21 Blood samples may be collected in the course of an Out-Of-Competition control. Where blood Samples are taken, the procedures Set out in paragraphs 2.23 to 2.38 of the Guidelines covering In-Competition testing will apply to the collection of these samples. Additionally, any other provisions dealing with blood sampling which apply when samples are taken In-Competition shall also apply when blood samples are taken Out-Of-Competition.

Storage and Despatch of Samples

3.22 The main 'A' and reserve 'B' samples should be placed in a suitable outer container and should be despatched to the laboratory as instructed by the IAAF.

3.23 If at all possible, the outer container should not be opened during transit to the laboratory The IAAF will provide identification labels, if required. for customs purposes. The opening of the outer container will not, of itself, invalidate doping control

Analysis of Samples and Communication of Results

3.24 The same procedures as listed in the Procedural Guidelines for Doping Control During Competition should be followed.

Waiver

3.25 The nature of Out-Of-Competition doping control makes it inevitable that little or no prior warning is given to the athlete. Every effort will be made by the International Sampling Officer to collect the sample speedily and efficiently with the minimum of interruption to the athlete's training plans and/or social or work arrangements. If there is an interruption, however, no athlete may take action to gain compensation for any inconvenience caused.

The NGB or its agent is under considerable pressure to ensure that the regulations are adhered to scrupulously. Although a minor error in sampling or transportation may not prove fatal, an accumulation of a number of seemingly insignificant oversights may result in the overturning of a ban inasmuch as they cast doubt on the overall findings. This approach was successfully utilised by the lawyers representing Butch Reynolds before the USA Track and Fields Doping Control Review Board. The Board concluded that as the doping control room was not secured and guarded, the doping control officer had left the control station (even though by then the sample had been safely processed) and there was doubt as to whether unauthorised persons had been allowed into the station, that the validity of the procedures had been undermined.

In a similar vein lawyers for Katrin Krabbe argued unsuccessfully that a sample collected from the athlete in South Africa which was transported to Cologne and which had been left at Cologne airport for two days before collection was proof that the chain of custody had been breached making the results unreliable.[32]

The 'A' test of Diane Modahl showed significant levels of testosterone in her body. Testosterone makes an athlete stronger and more aggressive. It does little to aid endurance: one of the key characteristics of a successful middle distance runner. Modahl emphatically denied taking any drug. An alternative

---

32   Gay, M, *The Sports Council Doping Control Unit Seminars on Doping Control*, 1994 and 1996.

explanation, that she was producing the testosterone herself because of a medical condition, was eliminated.

Even before the 'B' test began there were grounds for questioning the validity of the 'A' test. First the chain of custody documents were missing. These are the documents that not only map the movements and storage of the samples[33] but also identify the person responsible for their security at any time. Secondly when the seal of the 'B' sample was broken a strong smell of ammonia was present. In many laboratories the test would not be undertaken with a sample so corrupted. The 'B' sample showed a pH reading of nine. As a normal sample should have a pH of five, the sample had obviously undergone enormous change. However the Portuguese laboratory insisted on going ahead with the test on the basis that the pH reading would not have a bearing on a test for testosterone. The result of the 'B' test confirmed the result of the 'A' test.[34]

Hearing and Sanctions

IAAF Handbook 1996–97 Rule 59

Disciplinary Procedures for Doping Offences

(1) Where a doping offence has taken place, disciplinary proceedings will take place in three stages: (i) suspension; (ii) hearing; (iii) ineligibility.

(2) The athlete shall be suspended from the time the IAAF or, as appropriate, an Area or a Member, reports that there is evidence that a doping offence has taken place.

(3) Every athlete shall have the right to a hearing before the relevant tribunal of his National Federation, before any decision on eligibility is reached. When the athlete is notified that it is believed that a doping offence has taken place, he shall also be served with a notice informing him of his right to a hearing, together with a notice of application. If an athlete does not return this notice of application within 28 days of receipt, he will be deemed to have waived his right to a hearing.

(4) If an athlete is found to have committed a doping offence and this is confirmed after a hearing or the athlete waives his right to a hearing, he shall be declared ineligible. In addition, where testing was conducted in a competition, the athlete shall be disqualified from that competition and the result amended accordingly. His ineligibility shall begin from the date on which the sample was provided.

(5) Where a hearing takes place, the IAAF or the member (as the case may be) shall have the burden of proving, beyond reasonable doubt, that a doping offence has been committed.

---

33 For an analysis of the evidential validity of the chains of custody documentation see Grayson, E, 'Drugs in Sport – Chains of Custody' (1995) *New Law Journal*, 20 January.
34 *The Guardian*, 28 March 1996.

(6) More detailed guidelines for the conduct of disciplinary procedures are to be found in the 'Procedural Guidelines for Doping Control'. See also Rules 21–23 and the IAAF 'Guidelines for the Conduct of Arbitrations', for procedures to be followed when conducting hearings.

Diane Modahl's hearing into the test results was heard before a panel under the auspices of the British Athletic Federation. Rather than adopting an inquisitorial style which may appear the most appropriate for such a tribunal hearing, the style was adversarial, with the BAF both judge and prosecutor. The defence attempted to establish reasonable doubt as to the credibility of the test procedure and result. By this time it had been established that the test had lain unrefrigerated for two days in the Lisbon heat. This would have accounted for the changes in pH. The defence also argued that taking testosterone would have produced a reaction in the liver causing the production of metabolites. No metabolites where discovered in the sample. To explain the high testosterone level the defence called an expert medical witness who explored the theoretical possibility that bacterial could have caused the corrupted sample to produce testosterone. The panel took two hours to reach a unanimous verdict that a doping offence had been committed. The panel were unconvinced that the theoretical arguments altered the balance of probability. A four year ban was imposed.

Diane Modahl's appeal against her ban was heard by the Independent Appeal Panel. The same evidence was put forward however by this time the defence could show that the bacterial transformation theory could be replicated under laboratory conditions. On this ground the panel held that the drug taking allegations could no longer be sustained on the balance of probabilities. The judgment was overturned and the ban quashed.[35]

Sanctions and Exceptional Circumstances

IAAF Handbook 1996–97 Rule 60

Sanctions

(1) For the purpose of these Rules, the following shall be regarded as 'doping offences' (see also Rule 55.2):

   (i)   the finding in an athlete's body tissues or fluids of a prohibited substance;

   (ii)   the use or taking advantage of forbidden techniques;

   (iii) admitting having taken advantage of or having used, a prohibited substance or a prohibited technique;

   (iv)   the failure or refusal of an athlete to submit to doping control (Rule 56.1);

---

35 (1996) *The Diane Modahl Story*, 3 February, BBC 2.

(v) the failure or refusal of an athlete to provide a blood sample;

(vi) assisting or inciting others to use a prohibited substance or prohibited technique or admitting having assisted or incited others (Rule 56.3);

(vii) trading, trafficking, distributing or selling any prohibited substance.

(2) If an athlete commits a doping offence, he will be ineligible for the following periods:

(a) for an offence under Rule 60.1(i) or 60.1(iii) above involving the substances listed in Part I of Schedule I of the 'Procedural Guidelines for Doping Control' or, for any of the other offences listed in Rule 60.1:

(i) first offence for a minimum of four years from the date of the provision of the sample or of the sanctionable offence and any additional period necessary to include a subsequent equivalent competition to that in which the athlete was disqualified;

(ii) second offence for life

(b) for an offence under Rule 60.1(i) or 60.1(iii) above, involving the substances in Part II of Schedule 1 of the 'Procedural Guidelines for Doping Control':

(i) first offence – for three months from the date of the provision of the sample;

(ii) second offence – for two years from the date of the provision of the sample;

(iii) third offence – for life.

(c) for an offence under Rule 60.1(vii) involving any of the substances listed in Schedule I of the Procedural Guidelines for Doping Control – for life.

(3) Where a substance is detected in an athlete's body tissues or fluids which falls within Part I and II of Schedule I of the Procedural Guidelines for Doping Control, it shall be regarded as falling primarily within Part I of Schedule I for the purpose of determining the appropriate period of eligibility.

(4) Where an athlete has been declared ineligible, he shall not be entitled to any award or addition to his trust fund to which he would have been entitled by virtue of his appearance and/or performance at the athletics meeting at which the doping offence took place or at any subsequent meetings. The IAAF or any Member organising a meeting shall ensure that a clause to this effect is contained in any contract with meeting organisers.

(5) Where an athlete has committed a doping offence under Rule 60.1(iii), then any result obtained or title gained subsequent to the admitted offence shall cease to be recognised by the IMF and by the athlete's Member Federation and this from the date the athlete admitted the doping offence.

(6) Once the period of an athlete's ineligibility has expired, provided;

(i) he has complied with Rule 57.4; and

(ii) the athlete has made a satisfactory report on the circumstances surrounding the doping offence to his National Federation; and

(iii) his National Federation has submitted its report on the ease to the IAAF;

he will then become automatically re-eligible No application by an athlete or by his National Federation will then be necessary.

(7) If the results of any testing carried out on an ineligible athlete (see Rule 57.5) prove positive, this will constitute a separate doping offence and the athlete will be subject to a further sanction as appropriate.

(8) In exceptional circumstances, an athlete may apply to the Council for re-instatement before the IAAF's period of ineligibility has expired. Where an athlete has provided substantial assistance to a Member in the course of an inquiry into doping carried out by that Member, this will normally be regarded by the Council as constituting exceptional circumstances. However it is emphasised that only truly exceptional circumstances will justify any reduction. Details of the procedure and the criteria for application are to be found in the 'Procedural Guidelines for Doping Control'.

Under IAAF regulations, an athlete who tests positive is suspended from competition pending a hearing. In the USA the national governing body has felt obliged to allow athletes to compete pending a hearing because of potential conflict with national law. Sandra Farmer-Patrick was allowed to compete in the 400 metres hurdles in the Atlanta Olympics although she had recently failed a doping test. The IAAF however insists that the regulations are followed strictly in some other countries where there is no incompatibility with national laws. With what is in effect a two tier system in operation, revision of the regulations is inevitable.

Although it is important to emphasise the importance of consistent and rigorous application of the rules, the rules themselves, ie the provisions of the NGB's constitution have also given rise to challenge. The principal ground for such a challenge has been the strict liability nature of the doping offence. It is not a defence under the IAAF rules or the rules of the Football Association to claim that there was no intention to take the drugs.[36] This appears to eliminate as an argument that the athlete's food or drink had been tampered with or that they were given drugs on the understanding that they were not banned under the NGB's doping provisions.

Whilst by no means all NGBs operate a system of strict liability for drug offences, an increasing number do. A rule that a positive test leads to an automatic ban is attractive in its clarity and simplicity but denies what many of us would view as the fundamental right of an opportunity to prove a lack of fault, knowledge or intent. In practice this would mean that even if an athlete could prove that the consumption of the drug was accidental or as a result of malice on the part of another, the athlete would still be found guilty.

---

36 However, see the attitude of the RFU and the rugby league towards the 'innocent' taking of drugs, *The Guardian*, 17 April 1991 and 20 October 1992.

This may appear to be a draconian provision. The reason for it is a fear that rules requiring proof of intent would be impossible to implement and it is likely that athletes would find little difficulty in producing a coach or doctor prepared to take responsibility and vouch for the athlete's innocence.

A challenge to, *inter alia*, strict liability regulations was made by Sandra Gasser, a Swiss athlete:

Gasser v Stenson and Another

Scott J: Mr Blackburne submitted with great force that a rule which did not permit an athlete even to try to establish his or her innocence, either in resisting conviction or in mitigation of sentence was unreasonable and unjustifiable. But the consequences if the absolute nature of the offence was removed or if the length of the sentence became discretionary and not mandatory must be considered.

Suppose an athlete gives evidence that he or she did not take the drug knowingly and that it must therefore be inferred that the drug was digested unknowingly. How is the IAAF to deal with such an explanation? How can credibility be tested? Suppose a third party, perhaps a member of the athlete's team of coaches, perhaps a medical adviser, perhaps a malicious prankster, gives evidence that he or she administered the drug to the athlete and that the athlete had no knowledge that this was being done. How is the credibility of the third party's evidence to be tested? The pressure for success in international athletics, as well as domestic athletics and the national pride and prestige which has become part of international athletics has to be borne in mind. Will the credibility of the athlete or the third party vary depending on the nation to which he or she belongs? If a competitor or third party from nation A is believed, what will be the position when similar evidence is given by a competitor or third party from nation B? The lengths to which some people will go in order to achieve the appearance of success for their nation's athletes in athletics competitions is in point. The long jump in last year's World Championship illustrates the point. Cynicism, sadly, abounds. Mr Holt in his evidence, said that in his view, if a defence of moral innocence were open, the floodgates would be opened and the IAAF's attempts to prevent drug-taking by athletes would be rendered futile. He had, in my opinion, reason for that fear

Mr Blackburne submits that it is not justifiable that the morally innocent may have to suffer in order to ensure that the guilty do not escape. But that is not a submission that is invariably acceptable. The criminal law in this country (and in, I would think, all others) has various absolute offences and various mandatory sentences.

For my part I am not persuaded that the IAAF's absolute offence and mandatory sentence applicable to an athlete who is found to have dope in his or her urine is unreasonable.[37]

---

37 (1988) unreported.

Scott J is correct when he states that there are a number of examples of English criminal sanctions that are strict in their liability. Such an example is s 58(2) of the Medicines Act 1968 which provides that no person shall sell by retail specified medicinal products except in accordance with a prescription given by a medical practitioner. The Misuse of Drugs Act 1971, which in s 5 'Restriction of possession of controlled drugs', most closely parallels the IAAF's provisions, does not impose strict liability:

Section 28 of the Misuse of Drugs Act 1971

(2) Subject to subsection (3) below, in any proceedings for an offence to which this section applies it shall be a defence for the accused to prove that he neither knew of nor suspected nor had reason to suspect the existence of some fact alleged by the prosecution which it is necessary for the prosecution to prove if he is to be convicted of the offence charged.

(3) Where in any proceedings for an offence to which this section applies it is necessary, if the accused is to be committed of the offence charged, for the prosecution to prove that some substance or product involved in the alleged offence was the controlled drug which the prosecution alleges it to have been and it is proved that the substance or product in question was that controlled drug, the accused:

    (a) shall not be acquitted of the offence charged by reason only of proving that he neither knew or suspected nor had any reason to suspect that the substance or product in question was the particular controlled drug alleged; but

    (b) shall be acquitted thereof:

        (i) if he proves that he neither believed nor suspected nor had reason to suspect that the substance or product in question was a controlled drug; or

        (ii) if he proves that he believed the substance or product in question to be a controlled drug or a controlled drug of a description, such that, if it had in fact been that controlled drug or a controlled drug of that description, he would not at the material time have been committing any offence to which this section applies.

However the IAAF regulations do provide for a power to reinstate athletes in exceptional cases:

IAAF Procedural Guidelines for Doping Control 1996

4. EXCEPTIONAL CIRCUMSTANCES

4.1 Under IAAF Rule 60, an athlete may apply to the Council for reinstatement before the IAAF's period of ineligibility has expired. It is not possible to state comprehensively the circumstances in which the discretion to reinstate will be exercised by the Council. However the Council will not regard as exceptional for the purposes of Rule 60 an allegation that the prohibited substance was given to an athlete by another person without his knowledge, an allegation that a prohibited substance was taken by mistake or a suggestion that medication was prescribed by a doctor in ignorance of the fact that it contained a prohibited substance. The Council may, however, consider that exceptional circumstances exist where an athlete has provided substantial evidence or assistance to a national federation or the IAAF in the course of disciplinary or legal proceedings brought against those dealing in prohibited substances or coaches or athletes representatives who are taking or inciting or assisting others to take such substances.

4.2 Where an athlete believes that exceptional circumstances exist, application should be made through the athlete's National Federation to the General Secretary of the IAAF. No applications can be accepted otherwise than through an athletes National Federation.

4.3 The General Secretary shall consider the circumstances put forward by the athlete through his National Federation and, if he feels there is some merit in the case put forward, shall include discussion of the case on the agenda of the next meeting of the Council.

4.4 If he feels there is no merit in the case he shall write to the athlete's National Federation in those terms. Despite this, the athlete's National Federation may, within 28 days of the General Secretary's letter, reply requesting that the matter be placed on the Council's agenda. The General Secretary shall then place the matter on the Council's agenda for its next meeting.

4.5 Where an athlete's application for early reinstatement has been added to the agenda of the Council meeting. the Council shall consider the question of reinstatement. It shall consider both the application by the athlete and the circumstances surrounding the athlete's ineligibility.

5. PROCEDURES FOR APPLICATION FOR EXEMPTION TO USE PROHIBITED SUBSTANCES

5.1 IAAF Rule 55.5 was introduced in order to make it possible for an athlete to participate in sport who, for a limited or prolonged period of time, needs a prohibited substance for medical reasons.

5.2 Exemption will not, therefore, normally be granted in cases of acute disease and never when sporting activity may be hazardous to the athlete.

Exemptions, consequently, will be granted only rarely and in very special cases.

5.3 Out-of-Competition doping control is used as a deterrent for the use of anabolic agents and peptide hormones. Application for exemption of drug use during training is, therefore, needed only for these substances.

It would appear that the rules of such NGBs as the IAAF impose sanctions on a stricter basis than those imposed by the criminal law.

The principle of no penalty without fault has been received more sympathetically in other jurisdictions. Sandra Gasser herself was more successful in her native court. In 1987 the Swiss court refused to uphold the strict liability standard of the IAAF on the basis that the NGB had failed to consider pleas by Gasser that she must have consumed the drugs innocently.

A similar approach was taken by the German courts towards Katrin Krabbe and her ban was upheld by the Munich Appeals Court on the basis only that she had taken the drugs deliberately.[38]

The fact that there appears to be a trend towards athletes pursuing legal rights in court suggests a dissatisfaction with the rules of NGBs. One criticism that can be levelled at NGBs is that they fail to distinguish between different types of drug taking situations. This results in decisions which are capricious and unfair and therefore athletes are dealt with inappropriately in terms of establishing guilt and punishments. An analysis of the approach of NGBs to drug taking athletes becomes more revealing when distinct drug taking situations are identified. Although to many people the deliberate use of performance enhancing steroids, the use of recreational drugs and the accidental taking of drugs are distinct situations, many NGBs seem unable or unwilling to make a clear distinction.

There appears to be a consistency of approach by sporting bodies towards positive tests for steroid or other long term performance enhancing drugs. For a first offence bans are nearly always imposed and normally range from between one and four years.[39] Diane Modahl was initially banned for four years when a random test showed a ratio of 42:1 epi-testosterone to testosterone. An allowable ratio would be up to 6:1. This sample showed levels four times that of Ben Johnson's positive sample. Butch Reynolds, the American athlete, was banned for two years following his positive steroid test.[40] At the IAAF congress in Athens in July 1997, the minimum period of suspension was reduced from four years to two, due largely to the problems on enforceability of four year bans in some countries.[41]

In rugby league, a positive drugs test will usually lead to the imposition of a two year ban. Both Jamie Bloom, the South African, and Englishman David Stevenson were banned for two years when tests revealed the steroid Nandrolone.[42] The cyclist Shawn Lynch was banned for one year only following a positive test for testosterone,[43] however this was the maximum ban permitted by the governing body, the BCF. In swimming the former world 400 metres freestyle champion, Yang Aihua, was banned for two years for excessive levels of testosterone.[44] The extent of the powers contained in

---

38 (1996) XIV *The Sports Lawyer*.

39 Some administrators have advocated harsher penalties, *The Guardian*, 31 October 1991, however the European Athletic Association are backing proposals to reduce bans from four years to two years because of the refusal of some national courts to uphold four year bans, *The Independent*, 23 June 1997.

40 *The Guardian*, 18 May 1994.

41 *Daily Telegraph*, 1 August 1997.

42 *The Guardian*, 13 October 1995.

43 *The Observer*, 6 August 1995.

44 *The Guardian*, 24 November 1994.

NGB rules are highlighted by the lifetime ban imposed on Ben Johnson following his second positive test.

Therefore it would seem that sports governing bodies perceive an athlete who has failed a drugs test for performance enhancing drugs as cheating and subject to a lengthy ban for a first offence. When an athlete fails a test for recreational drugs or where athletes themselves confess to having taken a recreational drug, then the response of the governing bodies becomes more difficult to comprehend. This is inevitable because while governing bodies would wish to eradicate all uses of banned substances by athletes within their jurisdiction, most athletes will not have gained a sporting benefit from using recreational drugs and so punishments cannot logically be imposed on the grounds of cheating.

Testing for steroid abuse can be undertaken at any time because of the long term impact of such drugs. Recreational drugs, such as cocaine, amphetamine or cannabis, even if they are stimulants, have a short term effect. Therefore unless tests prove conclusively that players were under the influence of the drug at the time of the performance then it cannot be 'cheating' in the sporting context. Roger Stanislaus, an English soccer player who tested positive for cocaine, was banned for one year by an FA disciplinary commission.[45] The ban was the longest given to a soccer player since three Sheffield Wednesday soccer players were given life bans for match fixing in 1965. Stanislaus's offence was not that he had taken the cocaine as much as tests proved that he had taken the drug within two hours of playing for his soccer club Leyton Orient and was therefore probably under the influence of the drug during the course of the match.

The logic of this ban was brought into question by comments made by the Commission that leniency had been shown toward Stanislaus because it had been accepted that he was not a habitual drug user. It is submitted that even if Stanislaus was a habitual drug user it would be hard to justify a ban if the drugs had never enhanced his sporting performance.

Paul Merson, the Arsenal soccer star who publicly confessed his addiction to alcohol and drugs, was treated with leniency by the FA. The FA ordered him to spend six weeks in a rehabilitation clinic and no other punishment was imposed.[46] This would suggest that recreational drug use is likely to be punished only if it falls into the same category as those athletes mentioned above, ie the drug use could have had an effect on performance and so therefore was cheating. If this is the case then it is difficult to reconcile the treatment of cricketer Ed Giddins who was banned for two years after traces of recreational drugs were found in his system following a routine drug test.[47] It was never proven that Giddens had been under the influence of drug whilst

---

45 *The Guardian*, 2 February 1996.
46 *The Guardian*, 8 September 1995.
47 *The Guardian*, 19 September 1996 and 1 November 1996.

participating in his sport and therefore the punishment seems excessively harsh if the objective of punishment is to prevent cheating.

Jonah Lomu, the New Zealand rugby union player, announced in 1997 that due to treatment for a kidney disorder he would be unable to play for six months. Part of the reason was that even if he was physically fit enough, his treatment would involve the use of steroids and as a result he would fail a drugs test. If Giddins can be banned for taking cocaine when he was not playing then why should Lomu not be likewise banned? It is clear that the FA is handing out bans for reasons other than cheating. If the answer is an issue of morality then this would also explain why Merson's 'public confession' received more sympathy than Giddins's 'discovery'.

This idea of absolution rather than a ban gains credence from the case of Danny Harris, an American athlete, who tested positive for cocaine. In accordance with IAAF rules he was banned for four years. Harris's problem was not that he wished to enhance his performance but rather that he was addicted to the drug. Following a course of treatment and rehabilitation the IAAF reinstated Harris.[48]

The third category of drug offenders are those that have taken drugs considered performance enhancing and therefore banned by the sport, but who had done so innocently. In these circumstances, the treatment of different sportsmen and women has differed markedly. In 1978 Scotland's soccer international Willie Johnston was sent home in disgrace from the World Cup finals following a positive drugs test. His own soccer club doctor had lawfully prescribed Reactivan pills for a nasal condition. Johnston had been warned about drugs by a Scottish FA doctor but had not realised that the Reactivan pills contained a banned substance, Fencamsamin.[49]

Following sprinter Linford Christie's fourth place in the Seoul Olympic 200 metres final in 1988, he tested positive for pseudoephedrine, a banned stimulant. A further examination of a sample taken following Christie's earlier second place in the 100m final showed traces of the drug there too. A hastily convened IOC medical commission heard evidence that Christie had mistakenly taken the drug in adulterated ginseng. Ginseng is a traditional oriental remedy for fatigue. Christie was cleared by one vote and allowed to compete in relays the following day.[50]

Rugby league's approach to accidental consumption perhaps falls between the two previous examples. Great Britain full back Graham Steadman was fined £1,000 in 1992 after failing a drug test. He escaped a ban because the drug had been taken accidentally in a cough medicine.[51]

---

48 See Woodhouse, C, 'Role of the Lawyer in Sport Today' (1993) 1(1) *Sport and the Law Journal* 1.
49 See Grayson, E, *Sport and the Law*, 2nd edn (1994), London: Butterworths, p 196.
50 *The Observer*, 16 June 1996.
51 *The Guardian*, 13 October 1995.

Sports governing bodies are able to achieve a level of consistency when the motive for drug consumption is deemed to be cheating. When wider issues are involved, such as the reputation of the sport but where the athlete has not been cheating, the diversity of responses has resulted in an undesirable lack of certainty.

CONCLUSION

The commercialised nature of modern professional sport is a recurring theme in this book. With greater prizes on offer the temptation for professional sporting competitors to use performance enhancing drugs is correspondingly greater. It can be argued that a higher level of positive doping tests brings a sport into disrepute and a consequent downturn in popularity and revenue. However, the rumour that a blind eye is being turned to the failed tests of top sporting performers is ultimately far more damaging. The courts, in their reluctance to interfere with the decisions of NGBs, have offered sports the opportunity to conduct their disciplinary procedures without the fear of continual legal intervention. Ultimately the law will always provide a remedy and so the onus weighs heavily on the shoulders of sports administrators to ensure that the rules of NGBs remain fair and reasonable and that they are applied equitably and consistently.

Lawyers can play an important role in ensuring that this absence of legal intervention continues. By drafting NGB regulations and interpreting them rigorously in internal hearings, NGBs will retain the discretion to deal with breaches of internal regulations. Sports regulations are complex. The IAAF rules deal with a wide range of situations from testing at competitions to testing in an athlete's own home out of season. They attempt to ensure an unimpeachable chain of custody, a fair hearing and reasonable sanctions. However, on rare occasions, an athlete, having exhausted the sport's internal regulations, may still consider himself unjustly treated. It is then that recourse may be made to the law of the land and this is the subject matter of the Chapter 5.

CHAPTER FOUR

LEGAL REGULATION OF GOVERNING BODIES

INTRODUCTION

In the 1996–97 season, Middlesbrough Football Club decided not to play a league game away at Blackburn because of sickness and the number of injuries being carried by the team. As a result, three points were deducted. The results at the end of the season showed that, had these points not been deducted, Middlesbrough would have survived in the Premier League. Instead it was relegated to the first division of the Football League thus potentially incurring massive losses. The Chairman immediately implied that legal action might be taken. In the event, the club decided not to pursue this course.

That clubs and players are turning to the law when they do not like a decision of a governing body is becoming more common. When Leicester City were put out of the 1997 FA Cup as a consequence of a goal being disallowed, many said at the time that such decisions could no longer go unchallenged when so much money was at stake. This is the crux of the matter. It should be recognised that sport is no longer a Corinthian ideal; it is big business with the participants in it standing to make or lose fortunes. As such, it is inevitable that legal challenges will be made.

Jones v Welsh Rugby Union

There are likely to be many people who take the view that the processes of the law have no place in sport and the bodies which run sport should be able to conduct their own affairs as they see fit ... However, sport today is big business. Many people earn their living from it one way or another. It would, I fear, be naive to pretend that the modern world of sport can be conducted as it used to be not very many years ago.[1]

The aim of this chapter is to examine the legal relationship between governing bodies and those who participate in sport, be it the sportsman or woman or the club. That is, whether such relationships are regulated by private or public law. The importance of this public/private distinction will be the procedure to be used in seeking any remedy. If the relationship is one of public law, then any action brought will have to be by way of an application for judicial review under Order 53 of the Rules of the Supreme Court (RSC) (1977) (which was given statutory effect by s 31 of the Supreme Court Act 1981). If the relationship is one of in private law, then any action brought will be a civil

---

1 Ebsworth, J, in *Jones v Welsh Rugby Union* (unreported). See Rose, N and Albertine, L, 'Jones v The Welsh Rugby Union: New Law for the New Era' (1997) 5(1) *Sport and the Law Journal* 20.

action begun by writ or originating summons. The appropriate causes of action will thus be examined. In addition, this chapter will consider alternative means of settling disputes between athletes and their governing bodies.

Governing bodies are essentially self-regulating bodies. Julia Black describes such bodies as being those 'which have no formal legal or institutional links with government',[2] that is that the source of the power is neither statutory nor prerogative.

Black, J, 'Constitutionalising Self-Regulation'

Defining self-regulation

In discussions of self-regulation three sources of confusion emerge: what is meant by 'self', what is meant by 'regulation' and what is the nature of the State's involvement. The term 'self' is used to mean two different things: self as in individual and self as in collective. Thus the term 'self-regulation' is used to describe the disciplining of one's own conduct by oneself, regulation tailored to the circumstances of particular firms and regulation by a collective group of the conduct of its members or others. The definition of regulation varies from the 'command and control' model of regulation, to regulation by the market, to voluntary decisions of each individual to control their own behaviour. Finally, the term can be used to imply no relationship with the State at all or to describe a particular, corporatist arrangement.

It is argued here that the essence of self-regulation is a process of collective government. The term 'self' is thus used to describe a collective. 'Self-regulation' describes the situation of a group of persons or bodies, acting together, performing a regulatory function in respect of themselves and others who accept their authority. As such it should be distinguished from what may be termed individualised regulation. The two may coexist but they are analytically distinct and raise significantly different public law issues.

No particular relationship with the State is implied by the term 'self-regulation'. This interpretation contrasts with some of the corporatist or neocorporatist approaches which see self-regulation as simply a species of the genus corporatism. Broadly, we can identify four types of possible relationship: mandated self-regulation, in which a collective group, an industry or profession for example, is required or designated by the government to formulate and enforce norms within a framework defined by the government, usually in broad terms; sanctioned self-regulation, in which the collective group itself formulates the regulation, which is then subjected to government approval; coerced self-regulation, in which the industry itself formulates and imposes regulation but in response to threats by the government that if it does not the government will impose statutory regulation; and voluntary self-regulation, where there is no active State involvement, direct or indirect, in promoting or mandating self-regulation. Further, self-regulation may vary not only in its relationship with the State but in the nature of its participants (which may be solely members of the collective or may be outsiders), its

---

2   Black, J, 'Constitutionalising Self-Regulation' (1996) 59 *Modern Law Review* 24.

structure (there may be a separate agency or it may be a cartel), its enforcement (it may enforce its own norms or it may rely on individuals to enforce) and its rule type (its rules may be of legislative, contractual or no legal status, be general or specific, vague or precise, simple or complex).

The role of self-regulatory associations

Self-regulatory associations (SRAs) combine the governmental function of regulation with the institutional and often legal structure and interests of a private body. They impose conditions of membership and expulsion, they formulate their own rules and impose their own discipline. In the regulation literature, self-regulation is advocated as a more effective technique of regulation, although as we have seen, the form of regulation that these writers envisage is not always self-regulation in the collective sense. In modern political and socio-legal theory SRAs play a more fundamental role, acting as intermediaries linking different parts of society. It is this role of SRAs as linkages which it is suggested should form the basis for developing principles for their regulation. In different strands of socio-legal theory SRAs act as vital institutional linkages between various sections of society. Their use to perform one particular intermediating role, that of developing and furthering public policy, is captured in the corporatist and neo-corporatist literature. Streeck and Schmitter use the term 'private interest government' to describe both SRAs and to refer to the arrangements under which an attempt is made to make the associative, self-interested, collective action of these bodies contribute to the achievement of public policy objectives. Their role is not simply to be consulted on issues but to implement public policy: essentially, it means sharing in the State's authority to make and enforce binding decisions. What concerns us here is the nature of the intermediation which SRAs provide, which in turn rests on a particular conception of society. In the socio-legal literature, as in Streeck and Schmitter's conception of neo-corporatism, the role of the SRAs is not to act as a go-between, mediating between the State and the individual within a hierarchical framework which has the State at the top and the individual at the base. SRAs do not sit in the middle of such a hierarchy, acting as the principal link between the State's interests and the individual's interests. In the fragmented society envisaged by modernism no such hierarchical relationship is possible: politics, like economics, law or religion, is decentered. In place of the hierarchy of 'State-individual' there is a hierarchy of different spheres of society. SRAs thus mediate in a horizontal manner between these different spheres, for example the State, the market and the community. It is suggested that this conception of the nature of society and the role of SRAs is crucial to developing an understanding of their publicness' and to developing principles for their regulation. In acting as horizontal linkages between different systems, SRAs link politics not with the individual but with other specialised sectors of society. They participate simultaneously within those different sectors; the legal rules governing their public status and those governing their internal democratic processes thus need to be reformulated in the light of the different claims of these sectors.[3]

---

3   *Ibid*, Black, J, pp 26–29.

If an individual wants to challenge the decision of governing body, how will the court respond? Will it require the individual to bring an action in private or public law? Private law regulates the relationship between private persons, whether natural or legal. Public law regulates the relationship between governmental bodies and individuals and reflects the principle that no one is above the law.[4] A fundamental question to be addressed is whether sports governing bodies are governmental and therefore subject to the court's public law jurisdiction of judicial review or whether they are like any ordinary legal person and therefore not public and not subject to judicial review. The importance of this is that in *O'Reilly v Mackman*[5] the House of Lords made it clear that where a matter is one of public law, any action brought in private law will be struck out as an abuse of the court process. Where a matter is one of public law, then anyone seeking to challenge must proceed by way of Order 53 (RSC) 1977.

WHAT IS JUDICIAL REVIEW?

Judicial review is essentially the legal means of controlling or holding to account the activities of government.[6] It is the inherent jurisdiction of the Court to supervise, on the basis of certain principles and procedures, the activities of public bodies. The court will intervene only if there is illegal exercise of power. Judicial review must be distinguished from an appeal. An appeal allows the court to determine the correctness of a decision and to substitute a fresh decision. The court examines the merits of a decision. Judicial review on the other hand, merely examines the legality of the decision making process. If the process is found to be unlawful, the decision cannot stand. The decision maker may go back and make the same decision but this time via a lawful process.

The Judicial Review Procedure

The procedure for judicial review is set out in Order 53 RSC as given statutory force by s 31 of the Supreme Court Act 1981.

> **Council of Civil Service Unions v Minister for Civil Service [1985] AC 375 - 1996 MLN**
>
> **Lord Diplock**: To qualify as a subject for judicial review a decision must have consequences which affect some person (or body of persons) other than the

---

4   See Dicey, A, *Introduction to the Study of the Law of the Constitution*, 10th edn (1959), London: Macmillan.

5   [1983] 2 AC 237.

6   This part of the chapter can only be a superficial analysis of judicial review and readers should refer to standard texts on judicial review for a more full analysis, eg Stott, D, and Felix, A, *Principles of Administrative Law* (1997), London: Cavendish Publishing; Cane, P, *An Introduction to Administrative Law*, 3rd edn (1996), Oxford: Clarendon Press.

decision maker, although it may affect him too. It must affect such other person either (a) by altering rights or obligation of that person which are enforceable by or against him in private law; or (b) by depriving him of some benefit or advantage which either (1) he had in the past been permitted by the decision maker to enjoy and which he can legitimately expect to be permitted to continue to do until there has been communicated to him some rational grounds for withdrawing it on which he has been given an opportunity to comment; or (2) he has received assurance from the decision maker will not be withdrawn without giving him first an opportunity of advancing reasons for contending that they should not be withdrawn. I prefer to continue to call the kind of expectation that qualifies a decision for inclusion in class (b) a 'legitimate expectation' rather than a 'reasonable expectation', in order thereby to indicate that it has consequences to which effect will be given in public law, whereas an expectation or hope that some benefit or advantage would continue to be enjoyed, although it might well be entertained by a 'reasonable' man, would not necessarily have such consequences ...

For a decision to be susceptible to judicial review the decision maker must be empowered by public law (and not merely, as in arbitration, by agreement between the private parties) to make decisions that, if validly made, will lead to administrative action or abstention from action by an authority endowed by law with executive powers, which have one or other of the consequences mentioned in the preceding paragraph. The ultimate source of the decision making power is nearly always nowadays a statute or subordinate legislation made under the statute; but in the absence of any statute regulating the subject matter of the decision the source of the decision making power may still be common law itself, ie that part of the common law that is given by lawyers the label of 'the prerogative'. Where this is the source of the decision making power, the power is confined to executive officers of central as distinct from local government and in constitutional practice is generally exercised by those holding ministerial rank.[7]

The procedure is two stage in that the applicant must obtain the leave of the court to seek a remedy. This application is made *ex parte*, ie the respondent is not present. Leave may be refused where the applicant has no reasonable case. In *IRC v National Federation of Self-Employed and Small Businesses (NFSESB)*[8] Lord Diplock said that it should be sufficient for the applicant to show that he has 'an arguable case'. This stage is usually carried out on paper but if the judge is uncertain, he should invite the respondent to attend and make argument as to the grant or refusal of leave. Although this stage has been criticised on the ground that it is an additional hurdle for the individual in an action against the State, it has been defended on the ground that it allows an applicant to know quickly whether he has an arguable case so that costs are not incurred unnecessarily. Sir Harry Woolf (as he then was) has argued that this is a useful filter to keep out frivolous and vexatious litigants and that it

---

7   *Per* Lord Diplock, 408–09.
8   [1982] AC 617.

'enables a litigant expeditiously and cheaply to obtain the view of a High Court judge on the merits of his application'.[9]

An application for judicial review must be brought within three months. This is another mechanism for protecting public bodies in that public authorities should be able to make decisions in the knowledge that they are not going to be challenged for an unlimited period of time. This is a requirement of good administration.

O'Reilly v Mackman [1983] AC 237[10]

The need, in the interests of good administration and of third parties who may be directly affected by the decision, for speedy certainty as to whether it has the effect of a decision that is valid in public law ... Unless such an action can be struck out summarily at the outset as an abuse of the process of the court the whole purpose of the public policy to which the change in Order 53 was directed would be defeated.[11]

An applicant must also have *locus standi* (standing). He must have 'a sufficient interest in the matter to which the application relates'.[12] In *IRC v NFSESB* Fleet Street casual workers had been giving false names so that it was impossible for the IRC to collect tax due from them. This resulted in large losses for the IRC. In a bid to end this practice, the IRC entered into an arrangement which would ensure the proper collection of tax in the future. If the terms of the arrangement were accepted the IRC agreed not to investigate tax lost in previous years. The NFSESB applied for judicial review claiming a declaration that the IRC acted unlawfully in entering into such an arrangement and an order of *mandamus* directing the IRC to collect income tax from the casual workers. It was held that the question of *locus standi* could not be considered in isolation from the legal and factual context of the case:

IRC v NFSESB [1982] AC 617

There may be simple cases in which it can be seen at the earliest stage that the person applying for judicial review has no interest at all or no sufficient interest to support the application: then it would be quite correct at the threshold to refuse him leave to apply ... But in other cases this will not be so. In these it will be necessary to consider the powers or duties in law of those against whom the relief is asked, the position of the applicant in relation to those powers or duties and to the breach of these said to have been committed. In other words, the question of sufficient interest cannot, in such cases, be considered in the abstract or as an isolated point: It must be taken together with the legal and factual context.[13]

---

9   Woolf, Sir H, *Protection of the Public – A New Challenge* (1997), London: Sirvens.
10   [1983] AC 237.
11   *Ibid, per* Lord Diplock, 284.
12   Order 53 RSC 1977.
13   *Ibid, per* Lord Wilberforce, 630.

Thus it is a matter of mixed fact and law to be decided on legal principles. It is not simply a matter of discretion and the decision that an applicant has sufficient interest does not prevent the matter being raised at the full hearing and the courts should not take an unduly restrictive approach to the question of standing. Thus the test established in *IRC v NFSESB* is a wide one permitting the issue of standing to be determined on a case by case basis. The width of the test is demonstrated in recent public interest cases. In *R v Inspectorate of Pollution ex parte Greenpeace Ltd (No 2)*,[14] Greenpeace was held to have *locus standi* to challenge the decision by the Inspectorate of Pollution to authorise BNFL to discharge radioactive waste from its premises. A relevant factor in establishing Greenpeace's standing was the extent of its interest in the matter. In *R v Secretary of State for Foreign Affairs ex parte World Development Movement*,[15] a challenge was made regarding the misuse of overseas aid money. The Secretary of State had entered into an agreement with the Malaysian government to provide aid and trade for the Pergau Dam Scheme. It was held that the WDM had standing given the importance of the issue raised, the necessity to safeguard the rule of law, that there was no other challenger and WDM's international role.

The grounds on which a decision making process can be challenged were usefully set out by Lord Diplock in *CCSU v Minister for the Civil Service*[16] as being illegality, irrationality and procedural impropriety. He did state a fourth ground of proportionality but that ground has not as yet been adopted in English administrative law.[17] By illegality he meant 'that the decision maker must understand correctly the law that regulated his decision making power and must give effect to it'.[18] This ground may be compared to Lord Greene MR's ground in *Associated Provincial Picture Houses v Wednesbury Corporation*[19] of what may be described as broad *Wednesbury* unreasonableness; 'taken into account matters which it ought not to take into account or, conversely, has refused to take into account or neglected to take into account matters which it ought to take into account'.[20] By irrationality Lord Diplock meant '*Wednesbury* unreasonableness'. That is 'It applies to a decision which is so outrageous in its defiance of logic or of accepted moral standards that no sensible person who had applied his mind to the question to be decided could have arrived at it'.[21] In *Wednesbury* Lord Greene defined this as being a decision 'which is so unreasonable that no reasonable authority could have come to it'.[22] This

---

14 [1994] 4 All ER 329.
15 [1995] 1 All ER 611.
16 [1985] AC 374.
17 See *R v Secretary of State for the Home Department ex parte Brind* [1991] AC 696.
18 *CCSU, per* Lord Diplock, 410.
19 [1947] 2 All ER 681.
20 *Ibid, per* Lord Greene, 685.
21 *CCSU, per* Lord Diplock, 410.
22 *Wednesbury, per* Lord Greene, 685.

ground has been criticised as going beyond the remit of the court's supervisory jurisdiction in that it inevitably requires the examination of the merits of a decision when this is clearly not the function of the court in judicial review. The third ground set out by Lord Diplock is procedural impropriety. Statutes conferring a power may set out a procedure to be followed, eg a consultation process. Where it does so then the decision maker should follow that procedure and failure to do so may give rise to challenge on the grounds of procedural impropriety. Even if no procedure is set out, then the common law principles of natural justice will apply. These principles have now been restated as being a duty to act fairly.[23] The requirements of fairness will vary from case to case and *may* include a hearing, notice of the allegations which must be adequate to prepare a defence, notice of the hearing in adequate time, legal representation, submission of evidence, calling of witnesses, examination and cross examination and the giving of reasons. In addition there must be no bias on the part of the decision maker. The test for bias was set out by Lord Goff in *R v Gough*[24] as being a 'real danger of bias'; that is a 'real possibility' of bias.

At one time it was thought that the principle of natural justice or the duty to act fairly were only applicable to judicial or quasi-judicial decision making bodies. In *Ridge v Baldwin*,[25] however, the House of Lords extended the application of the rules of natural justice. Lord Reid identified what he saw as a misunderstanding of a statement made by Lord Atkin in *R v Electricity Commissioners*.[26] Lord Atkin had there stated 'Wherever any body of person having legal authority to determine questions affecting the rights of subjects and having a duty to act judicially, act in excess of their legal authority, they are subject to the controlling jurisdiction of the King's Bench exercised in these writs'. Lord Reid asserted that the judicial element was to be inferred from the nature of the power. If a decision affected the rights of individuals, then it was judicial and subject to control. The decision making body need no longer be of judicial nature to be subject to challenge. It is the nature of the power exercised which is relevant. As such, the principles of natural justice may be applicable to sport governing bodies.

The remedies available in judicial review are the prerogative orders of *certiorari* (an order quashing a decision), prohibition (preventing a body from acting or continuing to act unlawfully) and *mandamus* (an order requiring decision maker to comply with his duty). In addition an applicant may seek a declaration (declares the law) or injunction. Also available are damages (compensation) but these are only available if the applicant can establish that

---

23 *Per* Lord Diplock *Council for Civil Service Unions v Minister for the Civil Service* [1985] AC 374.

24 [1993] AC 646.

25 [1961] AC 240.

26 [1924] 1 KB 171.

they would be available had the matter been pursued independently. It should be noted that the remedies are discretionary in that they are not available automatically and the court may choose not to grant the relief requested even if it is established that the action complained of is unlawful.

THE PUBLIC/PRIVATE LAW DIVIDE

The crucial question as regards governing bodies is whether challenges to their decisions arise in public or private law. If they arise in public law then the Order 53 procedure must be used (*O'Reilly v Mackman*). So how do the courts determine whether a matter arises in public or private law?

Traditionally, the test for determining whether a matter was one of public law and thus susceptible to judicial review was to examine the source of the decision making body's power. If the source of the power was statute or prerogative, then it would be subject to the court's supervisory jurisdiction in judicial review.[27] Where the source of the power is in contract (private law) then this will be a strong indication that judicial review is not available. In *R v BBC ex parte Lavelle*,[28] Lavelle was an employee of the BBC charged with theft. The BBC began disciplinary proceedings and subsequently dismissed her. She was only given one hour's notice of the disciplinary proceedings and as such she was not able to have any representation as permitted by the procedure. She applied for judicial review of the decision though she did have a right of appeal to the Director General of the BBC. Her application for *certiorari* was refused since there was a relationship of master and servant although the court exercised it power under Rule 9(5) to construe the action as if begun by writ.

The Court has recognised that if this traditional test of the source of the power determining the availability of judicial review is strictly applied, the result may be that extremely powerful bodies are made immune from legal supervision. The courts have developed a broader test based on the nature and impact of the actions of the body. The test was established in *R v Panel on Takeovers and Mergers ex parte Datafin Plc*:

R v Panel of Takeovers and Mergers ex parte Datafin Plc [1987] 1 All ER 564

Sir John Donaldson MR: The Panel on Takeovers and Mergers is a truly remarkable body ... it oversees and regulates a very important part of the United Kingdom financial market. Yet it performs this function without visible means of legal support. The panel is an unincorporated association without legal personality. It has no statutory, prerogative or common law powers and it is not in contractual relationship with the financial market or with those who deal in that market.

---

27   *R v Criminal Injuries Compensation Board ex parte Lain* [1967] 2 QB 864.
28   [1983] 1 WLR 23.

No one could have been in the least surprised if the panel had been instituted and operated under the direct authority of statute law, since it operates wholly in the public domain. Its jurisdiction extends throughout the United Kingdom. Its code and rulings apply equally to all who wish to make take-over bids or promote mergers, whether or not they are members of bodies represented on the panel. Its lack of a direct statutory base is a complete anomaly, judged by the experience of other comparable markets worldwide. The explanation is that it is an historical 'happenstance', to borrow a happy term from across the Atlantic.

... In all the reports it is possible to find enumerations of factors giving rise to the jurisdiction but it is a fatal error to regard the presence of all those factors as essential or as being exclusive of other factors. Possibly the only essential elements are what can be described as a public element, which can take many different forms and the exclusion from the jurisdiction of bodies whose sole source of power is a consensual submission to its jurisdiction

In fact, given its novelty, the panel fits surprisingly well into the format which this court had in mind in *R v Criminal Injuries Compensation Board*. It is without doubt performing a public duty and an important one. This is clear from the expressed willingness of the Secretary of State for Trade and industry to limit legislation in the field of takeovers and mergers and to use the panel as the centrepiece of his regulation of that market. The rights of citizens are indirectly affected by its decisions, some but by no means all of whom may in a technical sense be said to have assented to this situation, eg the members of the Stock Exchange. In its determination of whether there has been a breach of the code, it has a duty to act judicially and it asserts that its *raison d'être* is to do equity between one shareholder and another. Its source of power is only partly based on moral persuasion and the assent of institutions and their members, the bottom line being the statutory powers exercised by the Department of Trade and Industry and the Bank of England. In this context I should be very disappointed if the courts could not recognise the realities of executive power and allowed their vision to be clouded by the subtlety and sometimes complexity of the way in which it can be exerted.

In reaching my conclusion that the court has jurisdiction to entertain applications for the judicial review of decisions of the panel, I have said nothing about the substantial arguments put forward by counsel for the panel based on the practical problems which are involved. These, in my judgment, go not to the existence of the jurisdiction but to how it should be exercised and to that I now turn.[29]

Datafin has resulted in the court's supervisory jurisdiction in judicial review being extended to bodies which exercise a public law function (Lord Lloyd) or to one whose power has a public law element (Lord Donaldson). Black argues that the case poses two intractable problems:

---

29 [1987] All ER 564, 566–79.

Black, J, 'Constitutionalising Self-Regulation'

First the notion of public law function or public law element used in the case is explanatory, not 'dispositive'. Secondly whereas source and function together are the test for whether the body is public, source is the sole test for establishing that it is private. In the Court of Appeal, both Lloyd LJ and Sir John Donaldson MR agreed that if the body's sole source of power is consensual submission to its jurisdiction or is contractual, then it is not subject to review. Thus there is a long observed tension in the case between the recognition of institutional power as a reason for subjecting a body to review and the exclusion of bodies with a contractual source of power.[30]

As noted by Black 'a body with no statutory, prerogative or contractual power exercising a regulatory function is perhaps now one of the clearest cases for the availability of judicial review'.[31]

This test in *Datafin* appears to have been restated in subsequent cases. *R v Chief Rabbi ex parte Wachman*[32] concerned an orthodox rabbi appointed in 1972 to a synagogue by a congregation which belonged to the United Hebrew Congregations of Great Britain and the Commonwealth. The spiritual leader was the Chief Rabbi. Allegations of adultery were made against the applicant. The Chief Rabbi notified the applicant that he had appointed a commission to inquire into the allegations and that in the meantime, he was suspended from his duties. The Commission found the applicant guilty of serious misconduct unbecoming of a rabbi and that he was no longer morally and religiously fit to hold his office. As a consequence, the congregation terminated his employment with three months' notice. The rabbi then applied for judicial review of the Chief Rabbi's decision. The question was whether the Chief Rabbi was subject to judicial review. The Chief Rabbi argued that his decisions were not subject to judicial review since the applicant had consented to his jurisdiction, there was no public law element in his decision and it would be against public policy for a secular court to regulate his functions:

R v Chief Rabbi ex parte Wachman [1993] 2 All ER 249

For a decision of a body to be a public law decision with public law consequences which attracts the court's supervisory jurisdiction, the effect of the decision had to be more then merely of great interest or concern to the public or to have consequences for the public. Instead, there has to not merely, a public but potentially a governmental interest in the decision making power in question. The Chief Rabbi's functions were essentially intimate, spiritual and religious functions which the government could not and would not seek to discharge in his place were he to abdicate his regulatory responsibility and parliament would never contemplate legislating to regulate the discharge of his functions.[33]

---

30 Black, J, 'Constitutionalising Self-Regulation' (1996) 59 *Modern Law Review* 24, 32.
31 *Ibid*, 35.
32 [1993] 2 All ER 249.
33 *Ibid, per* Simon-Brown J, 255–56.

It followed that the Chief Rabbi's decision contained no public law element. David Pannick argues that this approach adopted by the court is restrictive. He argues that the crucial question should be whether the body concerned is operating a monopolistic power. Where it is, then judicial review should not be ruled out on the basis that there is agreement since the 'individual has no effective choice but to comply with their rules, regulations and decisions in order to operate in that area'.[34] Further, he argues that the test of asking whether there would be governmental interest should the body in question abdicate its powers required the courts to almost second guess what parliament would or would not do. Black argues that this is almost 'a pantomime-like game with judges replying to the hypothetical question 'but for this body would the government regulate?' with cries of 'oh yes they would' or 'oh no they wouldn't'.[35]

THE REGULATION OF GOVERNING BODIES

How have the courts dealt with the issue of governing bodies in sport?[36] The first issue to be addressed is whether governing bodies are subject to control by the courts. One of the earliest cases in which the courts indicated a willingness to subject sport governing bodies to their control was *Russell v Duke of Norfolk.*[37] The courts have also shown a willingness to consider the validity of the rules of sport governing bodies.

In the case of *Enderby Town Football Club v FA*[38] Enderby Town FC wanted to be legally represented at an appeal to the FA following a finding of gross negligence in the administration of the club by the Leicestershire County Association which was affiliated to the FA. The request to be so represented before the FA was refused. The club issued a writ seeking an injunction to restrain the FA from hearing the appeal unless the club was permitted legal representation. The FA based its refusal on Rule 38(b) which it argued excluded legal representation:

---

34 Pannick, D, 'Comment: Who is subject to judicial review and in respect of public law' (1992) *Public Law* 1.

35 Black, J (1996) 59 *Modern Law Review* 24.

36 Beloff, M, and Kerr, T, 'Judicial Control of Sporting bodies: The Commonwealth Jurisprudence' (1995) 3(1) *Sport and the Law Journal* 5; Parker, R, 'Disciplinary Proceedings from the Governing Body Point of View' (1995) 3(3) *Sport and the Law Journal* 3; Bitel, N, 'Disciplinary Procedures from the Point of View of the Individual' (1995) 3(3) *Sport and the Law Journal* 7; Parpworth, N, 'Sports Governing Bodies and the Principle of Natural Justice: An Australian Perspective' (1995) 3(3) *Sport and the Law Journal* 7; Grayson, E, 'Reviewing Sporting Bodies' (1991) *New Law Journal*, 9 August.

37 [1949] 1 All ER 109.

38 [1971] 1 Ch 591

Enderby Town Football Club v FA [1971] 1 Ch 591

Lord Denning MR: A preliminary point arises here: Has the court any power to go behind the wording of the rule and consider its validity? On this point Sir Elwyn Jones made an important concession. He agreed that if the rule was contrary to natural justice, it would be invalid. I think this concession was rightly made and I desire to emphasise it. The rules of a body like this are often said to be a contract. So they are in legal theory. But it is a fiction – a fiction created by the lawyers so as to give the courts jurisdiction ... Putting the fiction aside, the truth is that the rules are nothing more nor less than a legislative code – a set of regulations laid down by the governing body to be observed by all who are or become, members of the association. Such regulations, though said to be a contract, are subject to the control of the courts. If they are in unreasonable restraint of trade they are invalid: see *Dickson v Pharmaceutical Society of Great Britain* [1967] Ch 708; [1970] AC 403. If they seek to oust the jurisdiction of the court, they are invalid: see *Scott v Avery* (1856) 5 HLC at 811. If they unreasonably shut out a man from his right to work, they are invalid: see *Nagle v Feilden* [1966] 2 QB 633; *Edwards v Society of Graphical and Allied Trades* [1971] Ch 354. If they lay down a procedure which is contrary to the principles of natural justice, they are invalid: see *Faramus v Film Artistes' Association* [1964] AC 925, 947, *per* Lord Pearce. All these are cases where the judges have decided, avowedly or not, according to what is best for the public good. I know that over 300 years ago Hobart CJ said that 'Public policy is an unruly horse'. It has often been repeated since. So unruly is the horse, it is said [*per* Burrough J, *Richardson v Mellish* (1824) 2 Bing 229, 252] that no judge should ever try to mount it lest it run away with a good man with him. I disagree. With a good man in the saddle, the unruly horse can be kept in control. It can jump over obstacles. It can leap the fences put up by fictions and come down on the side of justice, as indeed was done in *Nagel v Feilden* [1966] 2 QB 633. It can hold a rule to be invalid even though it is contained in a contract. Take an instance from this present case. The FA have a rule 40(b) which says 'The rules of the association are sufficient to enable the council as the governing authority to deal with all cases of dispute and legal proceedings shall only be taken as a last resort and then only with the consent of the council'. If that rule were valid, it would prevent the club from bringing any action in the courts without the consent of the council. But the rule is plainly invalid. Foster J said that 'it is against public policy to make provisions ousting the jurisdiction of the court'. Lord Kilbrandon in Scotland said simply that it is 'contrary to public policy', *St Johnstone Football Club Ltd v Scottish Football Association Ltd*, 1965 SLT 171.[39]

He also indicated the court's willingness to leave sports to regulate themselves providing that the body's discretion is properly exercised:

Justice can often be done in them better by a good layman than by a bad lawyer. This is especially so in activities like football and other sports where no points of law are likely to arise and it is all part of the proper regulation of the game. It is not at liberty to lay down an absolute rules: 'We will never allow anyone to have a lawyer to appear for him' ... The long and short of it is that if

---

39 *Per* Lord Denning, 606–07.

a court sees that a domestic tribunal is proposing to proceed in a manner contrary to natural justice, it can intervene to stop it. The court is not bound to wait until it has happened.[40]

Lord Denning made it clear that although it is for a domestic tribunal to determine its procedures, the courts will intervene where they breach the principles of natural justice.

The question that now needs to be addressed is whether this control is exercised in public or private law. The issue of whether governing bodies are subject to judicial review has revolved around the distinction between public and private law. Judicial review would not have been available to Duncan Ferguson in England.[41] Sport is regulated on a national basis often by powerful governing bodies. They have no statutory basis or authority and as such the traditional test set out above of source determining susceptibility to review is not relevant. They do however have monopolistic powers in that anyone wishing to participate in their chosen sport must accept their control and submit to their disciplinary procedures which may have serious repercussions, such as total exclusion from the sport. That the courts have refused to extend their jurisdiction to sport governing bodies and bring them within public law can be seen in a number of cases that will now be examined.

The case which has formed the basis of all subsequent decisions, is *Law v National Greyhound Racing Club Ltd*.[42] The National Greyhound Racing Club (NGRC) appealed against a decision refusing to strike out the plaintiff trainer's claim for want of jurisdiction. Under the NGRC rules, penalties including suspension of licence could be imposed against a trainer whose dog was found to have in 'its tissues or body fluids or excreta any quantities of any substance which by its nature could affect the performance of a greyhound'. An inquiry was held, which the plaintiff attended, and it was decided that he had a dog which showed the presence of substances which would affect its performance. His licence was suspended for six months. The plaintiff sought a declaration that the suspension was void and *ultra vires* in that the action amounted to a breach of the implied term that all action which would deprive the plaintiff of his licence would be reasonable and fair and made on reasonable grounds. Further he claimed that the club's action was an unreasonable restraint of trade and contrary to public policy. The defendants argued that any complaint should have been made by an application for judicial review. They tried to persuade the court that s 31 of the Supreme Court Act 1981 meant that when a domestic tribunal is alleged to have made, in abuse of its powers, a decision which affects a member of the public or the public generally, the complainant must apply for judicial review and cannot proceed by way of an action or originating summons for either a declaration or injunction:

---

40 *Ibid, per* Lord Denning, 605.
41 See below, pp 230–31.
42 [1983] 3 All ER 300.

Law v National Greyhound Racing Club Ltd **[1983] 3 All ER 300**

Lawton LJ: In my judgment, such powers as the stewards had to suspend the plaintiff's licence were derived from a contract between him and the defendants. ... Stewards' inquiry under the defendants' rules of racing concerned only those who voluntarily submitted themselves to the stewards jurisdiction. There was no public element in the jurisdiction itself. Its exercise, however, could have consequences from which the public benefited as for example, the stamping out of malpractices and from which individuals might have their rights restricted by, for example being prevented from employing a trainer whose licence had been suspended. Consequences affecting the public generally can flow from the decisions of many domestic tribunals.

Before the passing of the Supreme Court Act 1981, as I think counsel for the defendants accepted, anyone aggrieved by a decision of a domestic tribunal could only proceed by way of a claim for damages or for relief by way of a declaration or an injunction ...

Counsel for the defendants, however, submitted that s 31 of the Supreme Court Act 1981 has given the court jurisdiction to entertain judicial review of the proceedings of a domestic tribunal if, as in this case, those proceedings were likely to have consequences affecting the public generally. It was desirable, he said, that the quick remedy of judicial review should be available ...

I cannot accept this submission. The purpose of s 31 is to regulate procedure in relation to judicial reviews, not to extend the jurisdiction of the court ... It did not purport to enlarge the jurisdiction of the court so as to enable it to review the decisions of domestic tribunals ...[43]

Slade LJ: ... this is a claim against a body of persons whose status is essentially that of a domestic, as opposed to a public, tribunal, albeit one whose decisions may be of public concern. Counsel for the defendants has not been able to refer us to any case in which relief, by way of any of the prerogative orders, has ever been granted against any such domestic tribunal ...

Accordingly, in my opinion, it is plain that, apart from any changes in law or procedure which may have been affected by s 31 of the Supreme Court Act 1981, the present is not a case where the process of judicial review would have been open to the plaintiff.

... The wording of this subsection, in my opinion, shows that the Act was not intended to extend the jurisdiction of the court to make orders of *mandamus*, prohibition and certiorari and I did not understand counsel for the defendants to contend otherwise. I therefore think it clear that the court would not have jurisdiction to make orders of this nature at the suit of the plaintiff in the present case ...

... Accordingly, in the present case there is, in my opinion, nothing in RSC Order 53 or in s 31 to oblige or entitle the plaintiff to proceed against the NGRC by way of application for judicial review. Correspondingly, there is no procedural objection to his seeking the declaration which he seeks under RSC

---

43 *Ibid, per* Lawton LJ, 303–04.

Order 15 or 16 in the ordinary way. I therefore think that Walton J was right to refuse to strike out his proceedings and I too would dismiss this appeal.[44]

Argument in the case was dominated by the correct application of Order 53 with the court holding that the Order 53 procedure could not be used to seek a declaration that the decision in question was void. Declarations were only available where prerogative orders could previously have been given and prerogative orders had never been given to a body such as the NGRC whose powers derived purely from contract. Order 53 the court found was simply a procedure which did not purport to enlarge the court's jurisdiction. The clear finding of the court in law was that the relationship between governing bodies (NGRC) and its members arises purely in contract. This is not a matter of public law which must be pursued under Order 53.

The question of whether the Jockey Club was a body whose decision could be challenged by judicial review was considered in *R v Jockey Club ex parte Massingberd-Mundy*.[45] The application by Massingberd-Mundy was for the judicial review of a decision of the disciplinary committee of the Jockey Club. This was communicated to him by a letter from the chairman of the disciplinary committee informing him that the committee had decided not to approve him as a person to act as a chairman at meetings of local stewards at Doncaster Racecourse. Massingberd-Mundy argued that, since the power of the Jockey Club derived from royal charter, its decisions were susceptible to judicial review. Alternatively, consideration of the nature of the powers of the Jockey Club would show that that disciplinary committee was not merely a domestic tribunal. It exercised control over a large and important industry and over the livelihoods of those who work in the industry. As such, it was subject to the court's jurisdiction in judicial review. The Jockey Club, on the other hand, argued that its proper jurisdiction was derived from contract and thus the proper procedure was by way of writ. It accepted that the disciplinary committee was under a duty to act fairly but argued that this arose out of an implied term of the contract between the Jockey Club and those who agreed to be subject to its jurisdiction in accordance with the Rules of Racing. They argued further that the fact that the Jockey Club was incorporated by royal charter did not mean its powers were derived from prerogative any more than a public company's powers are derived from statute because the company is incorporated under the Companies Act. In addition, they contended that the remedy of judicial review was unsuitable since, if it was available, it would mean that any person interested in the result of a steward's inquiry, eg members of the public who had placed bets, could seek a judicial review:

---

44 *Ibid, per* Slade LJ, 308–10.
45 [1993] 2 All ER 207.

R v Jockey Club ex parte Massingberd-Munday [1993] 2 All ER 207

Neill LJ: In other cases, however, it may be necessary to examine the nature of the duties which the body is called upon to perform to determine whether these duties are in the public domain. Indeed it seems to me to be probable that it is the public element in the relevant body's decision rather than the source from which its powers are derived which is likely to provide the surest answer to the question whether the decisions of that body can be reviewed by the process of judicial review ...

In the present case I am not persuaded that the source of the powers of the Jockey Club can properly be regarded as derived from the prerogative even though it has been set up under a royal charter. On the other hand an examination of the charter and of the powers conferred on the Jockey Club strongly suggest that in some aspects of its work it operates in the public domain and that its functions are at least in part public or quasi-public functions. Accordingly, if the matter were free from authority I might have been disposed to conclude that some decisions at any rate of the Jockey Club were capable of being reviewed by the process of judicial review... The matter is not, however, free from authority. In *Law v National Greyhound Racing Club Ltd* [1983] 3 All ER 300, [1983] 1 WLR 1302 the Court of Appeal held that the authority of the stewards of the National Greyhound Racing Club to suspend a trainer's licence was derived wholly from a contract between him and the club and that the status of the stewards was that of a domestic tribunal. The court recognised that the decisions of the stewards might affect the public but concluded that the decisions were not decisions in the sphere of public law. For my part I am unable to find any satisfactory distinction between the status of the stewards of the National Greyhound Racing Club and the stewards of the Jockey Club for the purpose of deciding this present appeal.

Furthermore, the decision of the Privy Council in *Calvin v Carr* [1979] 2 All ER 440, [1980] AC 573 is of some limited assistance to the Jockey Club in this case. In *Calvin*'s case the Privy Council was concerned with an appeal from the Supreme Court of New South Wales. The claim in the action was for a declaration that the plaintiff's disqualification by the stewards of the Australian Jockey Club and the dismissal of this appeal were void and of no effect. The issue of judicial review was not raised. Nevertheless it seems clear from the opinion of the Privy Council that it was there considered that the Australian Jockey Club was not a body within the domain of public law and that the proceedings before the stewards of that club were domestic proceedings where the source of power was a consensual submission to the jurisdiction. I would therefore decide the first issue in favour of the Jockey Club.[46]

Roch J: The first issue is whether the applicant's claim to relief can be brought by way of judicial review. The answer to that question turns on whether the applicant is seeking to enforce some public right or the performance or proper performance by some public or other similar authority of a public duty. Thus the general test seems to be the question: was the person or body performing a

---

46 *Ibid, per* Neill LJ, 219–20.

public duty when carrying out the act or reaching the decision in respect of which the applicant seeks judicial review?

If the matter were free of authority, I would have reached the conclusion that the Jockey Club was a body susceptible to judicial review ...

... the Jockey Club holds a position of major national importance. Further, it has near monopolistic powers in an area in which the public generally have an interest and many persons earn their livelihoods.

The Jockey Club has just over 100 members. Mr Milmo QC has demonstrated that horse owners, horse trainers and jockeys as well as the executives of various race courses have a contractual relationship with the Jockey Club in that they agree to be bound by the Rules of Racing produced by the stewards of the Jockey Club. Rule 231 of the Rules of Racing provides 'All persons who have agreed to be bound by the Rules of Racing and the overseas owners, riders, trainers and their employees of horses trained outside Great Britain and which are entered to run under these Rules are subject to these Rules and are deemed to have knowledge of them howsoever amended'.

However those persons would have no vote or voice in the amendment of those rules any more than they had any vote or voice in the promulgation of those rules. The alternative to their accepting the Rules of Racing is to be excluded from all the recognised racecourses and race meetings in the United Kingdom, be they on the flat or over jumps.

Thus in the absence of authority I would have concluded in this case that the Jockey Club was a public or similar authority whose actions under the power-conferred on them by royal charter should be subject to the supervisory jurisdiction which the courts exercise under s 31 of the Supreme Court Act 1981 and RSC Order 53.

Such a conclusion would not in my judgment lead to the Jockey Club or its disciplinary committee or local stewards appointed by the Jockey Club being subjected to a flood of cases, because in each case it would be for the applicant to show that he had a sufficient interest in the decision before leave could be granted, as well as having to show a *prima facie* case that there existed grounds on which the court could exercise its supervisory jurisdiction. Against that there would appear to be cases where a person with a legitimate interest in the decision or act of the Jockey Club does not at the present time have any or any effective remedy because such a person would be unable to demonstrate a contractual relationship with the Jockey Club. However, there are decisions which relate directly to this matter ...

It is true that certain distinctions exist between the facts in that case (*Law*) and the facts in the present case. First and Mr Beloff suggests most important, is the fact that the National Greyhound Racing Club is a company limited by guarantee whereas the Jockey Club is a body established by royal charter. Secondly the National Greyhound Racing Club controlled dog racing in an area which represented approximately half of the United Kingdom, whereas the Jockey Club operates its Rules of Racing throughout the whole of the United Kingdom. But apart from these two matters, the organisation, the objectives, the rules and the functions of the National Greyhound Racing Club and the Jockey Club are strikingly similar; so similar that I do not feel able to draw a distinction between that case and the present for either of those reasons and I agree with the conclusion reached by Neill LJ on the first issue. In *Law's* case the authority of the stewards to suspend the plaintiff's licence was derived wholly from contract. There may be cases where the authority of the stewards of the Jockey Club will not be derived from a contract between them and the person aggrieved by their act or decision or alternatively may not be derived wholly from a contract. It seems to me that, if such a case were to arise, then the question is such an act or decision of the Jockey Club susceptible to judicial review? We may receive an answer different from that given by the court in *Law's* case.[47]

Although the court felt bound by the previous decision it seemed that the way had been left open; that is where there is no contractual basis for the authority of a governing body, then it may be that in the absence of any effective alternative remedy the court may extend its supervisory jurisdiction.

The same issue of jurisdiction arose again in *R v Jockey Club ex parte RAM Racecourses*.[48] In 1988 the Jockey Club had carried out a review on the need to allocate additional fixtures in the future to accommodate the needs of existing racecourses and possible new courses. The resulting report stated that an additional 60 fixtures ought to be allocated in 1990 and 1991 and that an unspecified number of fixtures should be made available to any newly licensed racecourses. The report was adopted by the Jockey Club and sent to existing racecourse owners but not new racecourse owners such as the applicant. The Jockey Club then made it known that it had an additional 30 fixtures to allocate in 1990 and a further 30 in 1991. The applicant purchased a site with a view to establishing a racecourse and having indirectly obtained a copy of the report spent £100,000 on it in the belief that the new racecourse would be allocated 15 fixtures in 1991. He subsequently sent the Jockey Club a copy of his development proposals for the new racecourse. The Jockey Club wrote to the applicant stating that notwithstanding the report, the Jockey Club made no commitment as to the number of fixtures which would be allocated to new racecourses. It was later made clear that the applicant would not be allocated any fixtures and it was not indicated when any such an allocation might be made. The applicant sought a judicial review of the Jockey Club's decision arguing that the report had raised a legitimate expectation in the applicant that the Jockey Club would grant him a minimum of 15 fixtures for the new racecourse for 1991. The Jockey Club argued that its decisions were not susceptible to judicial review, that the applicant could not rely on the document for the legitimate expectation and if the court did have jurisdiction to hear the application, it ought to exercise its discretion by refusing relief to the applicant.

---

47   *Ibid, per* Roch J, 220–24.
48   [1993] 2 All ER 225.

Stuart-Smith LJ did not find it necessary, since no legitimate expectation arose, to consider the question of jurisdiction but did give his opinion. He began by noting that Roch J in *Massingberd-Mundy* must had in mind the issue raised in the case when he had considered the possibility that a case may arise where there was no contract:

R v Jockey Club ex parte RAM Race Courses [1993] 2 All ER 225

Stuart-Smith LJ: It seems possible that the learned judge had in mind such a case as the present which is plainly unconnected with contract.

But I have had difficulty in reconciling this with the equally undoubted fact that there was no contractual relationship between Mr Massingberd-Mundy and the Jockey Club. It is of course trite law that, in respect of a body some of whose decisions are amenable to judicial review, that remedy is not available to every decision ... But I do not see how it is possible to distinguish *Massingberd-Mundy* on this basis. Mr Beloff has submitted that the Divisional Court's decision was wrong and that we are at liberty not to follow it ...

Mr Beloff argues that, since both judges in *Massingberd-Mundy* said that if the matter was free from authority they would have decided the matter in favour of the applicant, the question is whether they were so bound or whether they a were in error in so concluding. I think it is certainly clear that if any decisions of the Jockey Club are amenable to judicial review the decisions in the present case fall within the category of those that are reviewable. He argues with great force that *Law*'s case is distinguishable because the source of power in that case was wholly consensual ...

Furthermore, Mr Beloff points out that in *Law*'s case counsel for the applicant argued that it was in effect axiomatic that, if the respondent's powers derived from charter, judicial review would lie: see [1983] 3 All ER 300 at 306, 309, [1983] 1 WLR 1302 at 1311, 1315 *per* Fox and Slade LJJ, where this argument is rehearsed. But it is not in terms adopted by either judge. I have been much impressed by Mr Beloff's argument.

Mr Milmo sought to counter it with four submissions. First, that powers of the Jockey Club to issue licences and control fixtures do not derive from the royal prerogative itself; the charter is granted under the prerogative but the Jockey Club powers are no different than would be the case if it had been incorporated under the provisions of the Companies Act or as in the case of the National Greyhound Racing Club it was a company limited by guarantee. He points out rightly as it seems to me, that so far as its functions of issuing licences an controlling fixtures is concerned the Jockey Club is in no different position from a practical point of view after the charter than before. The ultimate sanction which it enforces its monopoly is not one granted by the charter but depend upon its power to exclude disqualified persons or horses, which is a contractual basis ...

Thirdly Mr Milmo accepted that in an appropriate case where a body enjoys monopoly position such that it can prevent a person from earning his living, not admitting him or from conducting a legitimate business in restraint of trade it will be amenable to a declaratory judgment in an action begun by writ, if it had acted in an arbitrary and capricious way in refusing to permit the applicant's activities: see *Eastham v Newcastle United Football Club Ltd* [1963] 3 All ER 139 at 157, [1964] Ch 413 at 446 *per* Wilberforce J, *Greig v Insole, World Series Cricket Pty Ltd v Insole* [1978] 3 All ER 449 at 495, [1978] 1 WLR 302 at 345 *per* Slade J and *Nagle v Feilden* [1966] 1 All ER 689, [1966] 2 QB 633. Thus, in my opinion, if the Jockey Club, enjoying the monopoly power that it does, had given a clear an unambiguous statement to anyone seeking to open a new racecourse that he would be allotted a certain number of fixtures, that being in accordance with their declared policy, it would be *prima facie* unlawful and in restraint of trade to refuse such an application. And equally, if a licence to operate a racecourse depends, as it appears to do, on the allocation of fixtures (all other necessary conditions being satisfied), it would *prima facie* be in restraint of trade and unlawful if the Jockey Club refused a licence on the grounds that they had not allocated the necessary fixtures to the applicant, contrary to their declared policy and clear representation. The significance of the declared policy and representation in these circumstances would be that it would be virtually impossible for the Jockey Club to contend that the restraint of trade was reasonable. For these reasons it appears to me that in an appropriate case, very similar relief could be obtained by a writ action, to that which is sought by the applicant in this case. And indeed there is no doubt that such procedure is more appropriate when the courts are required to consider matters of restraint of trade: see *Dairy Crest Ltd v Pigott* [1989] ICR 92. Nevertheless, like Simon Brown J, I suspect that if these cases had first arisen for determination after *R v Panel on Takeovers and Mergers ex parte Datafin Plc (Norton Opax Plc intervening)* [1987] 1 All ER 564, [1987] QB 815, relief might well have been sought and granted along the public law rather than the private law route.

Finally, Mr Milmo submitted that there have been no successful applications for judicial review against sporting bodies, such as the Football Association, British Board of Boxing Control or the MCC. This may be so; but it is of limited value: each case will depend on the source of powers and nature of functions of the body and whether there is a sufficient public element involved. Quite clearly the majority of cases, involving disciplinary disputes or adjudications between participants in the sport, will be of an entirely domestic character and based upon the contractual relationship between the parties. Such disputes have never been amenable to judicial review.

Nevertheless, at the end of the day I am unable to say that I am convinced that the decision of this court in *R v Disciplinary Committee of the Jockey Club ex parte Massingberd-Mundy* (1989) [1993] 2 All ER 207 was wrong. It is quite clear that it was not in any way *per incuriam*, the court having given careful consideration to *Law's* case and, we are told, other extensive citations of authority. But for this authority I should have held that the decisions of the Jockey Club in this case were amenable to judicial review ...[49]

Simon-Brown J: The two central issues raised upon this challenge are: (1) the jurisdictional issue as to whether the Jockey Club are in any circumstances amenable to judicial review ...

---

49 *Ibid, per* Stuart-Smith LJ, 241–44.

... But I do desire to express certain thoughts of my own upon the jurisdictional question ...

Given that this identical issue has recently been determined by another division of this court in *R v Disciplinary Committee of the Jockey Club, ex parte Massingberd-Mundy* (1989) [1993] 2 All ER 207 it necessarily follows that I must expressly consider the correctness of that decision. Let me say at once that, like Stuart-Smith LJ, I fall far short of being 'convinced' that it was wrong. Accordingly, were the jurisdictional issue decisive of the present application, I would not decide it in the applicant's favour ... Mine, let me immediately indicate with both diffidence and respect, is one of limited dissent ...

Before endeavouring to state why I disagree with the conclusions of the court in *Massingberd-Mundy*, let me first indicate the limited extent of my disagreement. The substantive decision there subject to challenge was that of the disciplinary committee to remove the applicant's name from the list of those eligible to sit as chairmen of local panels of stewards. All that the applicant had therefore enjoyed was a non-renewable privilege. I have no difficulty in regarding that particular decision as one taken within an essentially domestic context lacking any significant public dimension and as non-reviewable on that ground. It is only in so far as the court's decision rested upon the wider ground that the Jockey Club can *never*[50] be reviewable in regard to any of their decision making functions that I would respectfully question its correctness.

My reasons are essentially these. First I accept Mr Beloff QC's argument that *Law v National Greyhound Racing Club* [1983] 3 All ER 300, [1983] WLR 1302 was distinguishable from *Massingberd-Mundy* – as to my mind it is, yet more plainly, from the present case ...

Even, therefore, without considering the impact of the developing jurisprudence over the last seven years, I myself would feel able to distinguish, rather than driven to follow, *Law's* case ...

Even, however, had I concluded that the Court of Appeal's decision in *Law's* case on its face governed also the position in *Massingberd-Mundy* and this case, I would still have concluded that the issue-remained open in the light of *R v Panel on Takeovers and Mergers ex parte Datafin Plc (Norton Opax Plc intervening)* [1987] 1 All ER 564, [1987] QB 815. This clearly was a landmark decision in respect of the true scope and extent of this court's supervisory jurisdiction: all earlier cases need now to be re-examined in its light. Stuart-Smith LJ has cited the critical passage from Donaldson MR's judgment which sets out what may be regarded as the parameters of the debate. At one end of the spectrum are reviewable decisions with a sufficient 'public element'; at the other, non-reviewable decisions of a body 'whose sole source of power is a consensual submission to its jurisdiction' ...

I find myself, I confess, much attracted by Mr Beloff's submissions that the nature of the power being exercised by the Jockey Club in discharging its functions of regulating racecourses and allocating fixtures is strikingly akin to the exercise of a statutory licensing power. I have no difficulty in regarding

---

50 Emphasis added.

this function as one of a public law body, giving rise to public law consequences. On any view it seems to have strikingly close affinities with those sorts of decision making that commonly are accepted as reviewable by the courts ...

... I agree that the incorporation of the Jockey Club under charter with effect from 1970 cannot of itself be a decisive consideration in attracting the review jurisdiction. On the other hand, I do not regard it as an irrelevance. Rather it seems to me to indicate a governmental (in the widest sense) recognition of the national importance of the Jockey Club's position in this important field of public life. It is a position which could as well have been enshrined in legislation.

... Mr Milmo's third submission is found in the *Nagle v Feilden* [1966] 1 All ER 689, [1966] 2 QB 633 line of authority and, as I understand it, amounts essentially to this. Given the development of a free standing right to declaratory judgments in private law 'restraint of trade' cases, there is no need to stretch the bounds of the court's supervisory jurisdiction to encompass the licensing-like functions of bodies such as the Jockey Club. The force of the submission is readily apparent. But the answer to it is, in my judgment, this. Cases like *Eastham v Newcastle United Football Club Ltd* [1963] 3 All ER 139, [1964] Ch 413, *Nagle v Feilden* [1966] 1 All ER 689, [1966] 2 QB 633, *Breen v Amalgamated Engineering Union* [1971] 1 All ER 1148, [1971] 2 QB 175 and *McInnes v Onslow-Fane* [1978] 3 All ER 211, [1978] 1 WLR 1520, had they arisen today and not some years ago, would have found a natural home in judicial review proceedings. As it was, considerations of public policy forced the courts to devise a new private law creature: a right in certain circumstances to declaratory judgments without any underlying cause of action.

But clear recognition of the true, essentially public law, nature of these to be found in the judgment of Lord Denning MR in *Breen v Amalgamated Engineering Union* itself and I for my part would judge it preferable to develop these principles in future in a public law context than by further distorting private law principles. *Nagle v Feilden* was never in my judgment a restraint of trade case properly so called; rather it brought into play clear considerations of public law.

Mr Milmo's final argument can be shortly stated and quickly seen inconclusive. It is that never hitherto has any sporting body been found to review. So be it, although, as I have suggested, that is really only because courts have in the past sought to meet the needs of public policy by developing private law principles instead. But put that thought aside. We are in a dynamic area of law, well able to embrace new situations as justice requires ...

Plainly the Jockey Club for the most part take decisions which have an affect on at least essentially those voluntarily and willingly subscribing to their rules and procedures. The wider public have no interest in all this, certainly not sufficient to make such decisions reviewable. But just occasionally, as when exercising quasi-licensing power here under challenge, I for my part would regard the Jockey Club as subject to review.[51]

---

51 *Ibid, per* Simon-Brown J, 244–48.

The court was clearly here of the view that the Jockey Club would be subject to the court's supervisory jurisdiction under judicial review were it not for authority. What is also important is the court's recognition that private law had been manipulated to provide a cause of action when in actual fact these were issues of public law which should have been addressed in this way.

In *R v Football Association of Wales ex parte Flint Town United Football Club* (1991) COD 44 the applicant football club was a member of the Football Association of Wales and played in the Welsh amateur league. When the club tried to change football leagues, permission was refused because of a proposed reorganisation of the football league in Wales. The decision was upheld on appeal. The applicant subsequently sought a judicial review of the decision. The court noted that the law had developed since *Law v NGRC* but nevertheless felt bound by precedent. It found that a contractual relationship existed between the applicant and respondent and it was not able to distinguish *Law* in the way suggested by Simon-Brown J in *Ram Racecourses*.

The view that governing bodies are purely domestic was again considered in *R v Football Association ex parte Football League Ltd.*[52] The case arose out of the FA's decision to form a Premier League consisting of the top first division clubs to be run by the FA and not by the League. Under the rules of the League any club wishing to resign from it was required to give notice to that effect of three seasons or indemnify the League if it terminated membership earlier. To facilitate the teams leaving the League to form the Premier League, the FA amended its sanction regulations to provide that any rule by which the League purported to require a club to give longer notice than that required by the FA's regulations was void. The League had entered into a contractual agreement with the FA since it applied annually for the FA's sanction to run the four divisions which made up the League. The League brought judicial review proceedings of the decision of the FA to set up the Premier League and the decision to amend their rules. It argued that the FA was subject to the court's jurisdiction because it had monopoly control over the way the game was played, its rules were in effect a legislative code for the game and it regulated an important aspect of national life in circumstances that, if it did not do so, that state would have to create a public body to perform its functions:

R v Football Assoication ex parte Football League Ltd [1993] 2 All ER 833

Rose J: ... the first question is whether the FA is a body which is susceptible to judicial review ...

Its importance in national life has been expressly recognised by the Chester Report in 1968 (Report of the Committee on Football (chairman DN Chester), Lord Justice Taylor's Report in 1989 (The Hillsborough Stadium Disaster, 15 April 1989 (Cm 765, 962)) and by the Minister of Sport in 1991 and it has

---

52 [1993] 2 All ER 833.

achieved a limited degree of statutory recognition in that, by s 4 of the Football Supporters Act 1989, which has not yet been brought into force, it has to be consulted in relation to a national membership scheme.

... judicial review might lie because the FA rules, though in contractual form, are effectively a legislative code (see *per* Lord Denning MR in the *Enderby Town* case [1971] 1 All ER 215 at 219, [1971] Ch 591 at 606). The FA's monopolistic control, Mr Oliver submitted, is greater than that of the Greyhound Club. On this basis and on the basis that the decision was merely a domestic one on the rules, he distinguished *Law v National Greyhound Racing Club* [1983] 3 All ER 300, [1983] 1 WLR 1302.

The FA's powers extend beyond contract to affect the lives of many hundreds of thousands who are not in any contractual relationship, though Mr Oliver accepted that much the same could be said about large public companies. He submitted that, by reason of *Datafin*, judicial review may now go to a non-statutory body which exists otherwise than as a result of the exercise of the prerogative and the courts in recent years have shown a clear desire to apply judicial review to sporting bodies.

Mr Oliver submitted that the FA fulfils the *Datafin* test, namely it is a body which regulates an important aspect of national life and does so with the support of the State in that but for its existence, the State would create a public body to perform its functions. Accordingly, he said, it is amenable to judicial review in certain respects at least ...

It is clearly of great importance whether the League is in a contractual relationship with the FA. This goes to the source of the FA's powers and the nature of their duties ...

On any view, it seems to me that the FA and League were contractually bound both at the time the challenged decisions were made and at the time proceedings were started.

For the FA, Mr Dyson QC submitted that the FA is a private body deriving its authority to make binding decisions from contract and the consent of its members. The source of its power is in its memorandum, articles, rules and regulations. It has no authority, save by contract. Its position is indistinguishable from the other sporting bodies whom the courts have held not to be susceptible to judicial review, save that the Jockey Club seeks to exercise power directly over the public by warning off. Accordingly this court is bound to hold that judicial review is not available ...

... In my judgment, *Enderby* and *Breen* are no more than examples of the courts injecting principles of natural justice into the decision making processes of domestic bodies which could not be controlled by prerogative writ (see *Breen* [1971] 1 All ER 1148 at 1154, [1971] 2 QB 175 at 190 *per* Lord Denning MR). In both cases it appears that the plaintiff was contractually bound in accordance with the defendant's rules.

In *McInnes v Onslow-Fane* [1978] 3 All ER 211 at 218, [1978] 1 WLR 1520 at 1528 there was no contract or statute but Megarry VC approved counsel's concession that the court was entitled to intervene to enforce natural justice and fairness. I do not regard these authorities as lending any support to the view that the FA, trade unions or the British Boxing Board of Control should be regarded as public bodies carrying out public law functions susceptible to judicial review.

In my judgment, public bodies must comply with the requirements of natural justice but so, in many cases, must private bodies. A requirement so to comply does not of itself characterise a body as public or private ...

In my judgment, the authorities before *Datafin* provide no support for the League's argument that the FA is or should be subject to judicial review ...

I accept Mr Oliver's submission that *Datafin* extends judicial review to a non statutory body which exists otherwise than as the result of the exercise of the prerogative and that the ratio of the decision is that a body may be subject to judicial review if it regulates an important aspect of national life and does so with the support of the State in that but for its existence, the State would create a public body to perform its functions. But *Datafin* does not, in my judgment, impinge on the decision in *Law* which I earlier sought to summarise. It is common ground that both *Law* and *Datafin* are binding on me.

I turn to the seven Divisional Court decisions since *Datafin* to which I have been referred ...

Mr Oliver, in an ingenious reply on the recent authorities, invited me to conclude that none stands in the way of judicial review of the FA or its decisions which are the subject of challenge. His argument was that, whereas in *Law* the question was whether the particular decision had a public law impact, in *Datafin* the question was whether the particular body was open to judicial review. Successive Divisional Courts have, he said, confused these two separate questions. In particular, Neill LJ in *Massingberd-Mundy* [1993] 2 All ER 207 at 218–220 posed in the first issue a *Datafin* question but gave a *Law* answer. Roch J (at 220–24) posed and answered a *Law* question.

In *RAM Racecourses* [1993] 2 All ER 225 at 240–44 Stuart-Smith LJ posed an ambiguous question which was either *Law*, *Datafin* or both, misled himself by failing to appreciate that Neill LJ in *Massingberd-Mundy* had not given a *Datafin* answer and wrongly treated *Massingberd-Mundy* as a case where there was no contractual relationship between the applicant and the Jockey Club. Simon Brown J (at 244–48) posed and answered a *Law* question, as did Farquharson LJ in *Flint*, which, said Mr Oliver, is a straightforward application of *Law*'s case. Accordingly, submitted Mr Oliver, provided I give a *Datafin* answer to a *Datafin* question or a *Law* answer to a *Law* question, no authority stands in my way in quashing the FA's decision.

I accept that the authorities sometimes refer to the decision and sometimes to the body making the decision and it is trite law that not every decision of a reviewable body will be reviewable. But I do not accept that a decision stands in a vacuum separately from the body which makes it. Accordingly, I reject Mr Oliver's premise. In my judgment, the ratio of *Law* was that the decision could not be struck down by judicial review because the decision making body was a domestic body. 1 am strengthened in this conclusion because in *ex parte Aga Khan* Woolf LJ, who analysed Neill LJ's judgment in *Massingberd-Mundy*, does not appear to have found the answer given by Neill LJ on the first issue either inappropriate or confusing. I see no basis for distinguishing the Jockey Club cases, still less the *Flint United* case. It follows that I am bound not only by *Law* and *Datafin* but by these cases as well.

I have crossed a great deal of ground in order to reach what, on the authorities, is the clear and inescapable conclusion for me that the FA is not a body susceptible to judicial review either in general or, more particularly, at the instigation of the League, with whom it is contractually bound. Despite its virtually monopolistic powers and the importance of its decisions to many members of the public who are not contractually bound to it, it is, in my judgment, a domestic body whose owners arise from and duties exist in private law only. I find no sign of underpinning directly or indirectly by any organ or agency of the State or any potential government interest, as Simon Brown J put it in *Wachmann*, nor is there any evidence to suggest that if the FA did not exist the State would intervene to create a public body to perform its functions. On the contrary, the evidence of commercial interest in the professional game is such as to suggest that a far more likely intervener to run football would be a television or similar company rooted in the entertainment business or a commercial company seeking advertising benefits such as presently provides sponsorship in one form or another.

I do not find this conclusion unwelcome. Although thousands play and millions watch football, although it excites passions and divides families and although millions of pounds are spent by spectators, sponsors, television companies and also clubs on salaries, wages, transfer fees and the maintenance of grounds, much the same can also be said in relation to cricket, golf, tennis, racing and other sports. But they are all essentially forms of popular recreation and entertainment and they are all susceptible to control by the courts in a variety of ways. This does not, of itself, exempt their governing bodies from control by judicial review. Each case will turn on the particular circumstances.

But, for my part, to apply to the governing body of football, on the basis that it is a public body, principles honed for the control of the abuse of power by government and its creatures would involve what, in today's fashionable parlance, would be called a quantum leap. it would also, in my view, for what it is worth, be a misapplication of increasingly scarce judicial resources. It will become impossible to provide a swift remedy, which is one of the conspicuous hallmarks of judicial review, if the courts become even more swamped with such applications then they are already. This is not, of course, a jurisprudential reason for refusing judicial review but it will be cold comfort to the seven or eight other substantive applicants and the many more *ex parte* applicants who have had to be displaced from the court's lists in order to accommodate the present litigation to learn that, though they may have a remedy for their complaints about the arbitrary abuse of executive power, it cannot be granted to them yet.[53]

Thus the court again refused to extend is jurisdiction finding that the relationship arose in private law despite the monopolistic powers of the FA and the importance of its decision to many members of the public. There was, Rose J said, no evidence that the State would intervene to create a public body

---

53 *Ibid, per* Rose J, 840–49.

to perform its functions. This view now no longer seems to be correct given the Labour government's football charter.[54] The then shadow National Heritage Secretary, Jack Cunningham, said Labour would set up a football task force made up of football organisations, government officials and representatives of fans and players to report within a year of Labour taking office. The group would restructure the FA to speed up decision making, investigate the role of television and examine claims that fans were being priced out of the game. Mr Cunningham also said that Labour's football charter would address key issues in football including hooliganism, match fixing, drug taking and the financial position of small clubs. He said that legislation would be introduced. A task force has now been set up under David Mellor to report on the position.[55] If the present government does indeed intervene to this extent, it would seem difficult for Rose J's view to be supported and it may be that the courts would extend their supervisory jurisdiction to the FA.

The issue of jurisdiction was raised again in *R v Disciplinary Committee of the Jockey Club ex parte HH The Aga Khan*.[56] The applicant's filly was routinely tested after she had won the Oaks at Epsom in 1989. A sample of her urine was said to contain a substance prohibited by the rules and she was disqualified and her trainer fined. The applicant sought leave to apply for an order of *certiorari* to quash the committee's decision. The Court of Appeal held that, although the Jockey Club exercised dominant control over racing activities in Great Britain, its powers and duties were in no sense governmental but derived from the contractual relationship between the club and those agreeing to be bound by the Rules of Racing. The powers gave rise to private rights enforceable by private action in which effective relief by way of declaration, injunction and damages was available. Therefore the Jockey Club's decision was not amenable to judicial review. The court did however appear to leave some hope in that where there was no contractual relationship and no other effective private law remedy, then the court might extend its jurisdiction:

> **R v Disciplinary Committee of the Jockey Club ex parte HH The Aga Khan [1993] 1 WLR 909**
>
> **Sir Thomas Bingham MR:** No case directly raising the issue whether a sporting regulatory body is susceptible to judicial review and if so in what circumstances, has yet reached the House of Lords ...
>
> ... I have little hesitation in accepting the applicant's contention that the Jockey Club effectively regulates a significant national activity, exercising powers which affect the public and are exercised in the interest of the public. I am

---

54 See 'Labour aims to kick hooliganism out of football', *The Times*, 8 December 1995, p 9.
55 See 'True Blue Mellor is happy to wear Labour's football kit', *Daily Telegraph*, 29 July 1997.
56 [1993] 1 WLR 909.

willing to accept that if the Jockey Club did not regulate this activity the government would probably be driven to create a public body to do so.

But the Jockey Club is not in its origins, its history, its constitution or (least of all) its membership a public body. While the grant of a royal charter was no doubt a mark of official approval, this did not in anyway alter its essential nature, functions or standing. Statute provides for its representation on the Horse Race Betting Levy Board, no doubt as a body with an obvious interest in racing but it has otherwise escaped mention in the statue book. It has not been woven into any system of governmental control of horse racing, perhaps because it has itself controlled horse racing so successfully that there has been no need for any such governmental system and such does not therefore exist. This has the result that while the Jockey Club's powers may be described as, in many ways, public they are in no sense governmental.

I would accept that those who agree to be bound by the Rules of Racing have no effective alternative to doing so if they want to take part in racing in this country. It also seems likely to me that if, instead of Rules of Racing administered by the Jockey Club, there were a statutory code administered by a public body, the rights and obligations conferred and imposed by the code would probably approximate to those conferred and imposed by the Rules of Racing. But this does not, as it seems to me, alter the fact, however anomalous it may be, that the powers which the Jockey Club exercises over those who (like the applicant) agree to be bound by the rules of Racing derive from the agreement of the parties and give rise to private rights on which effective action for a declaration, an injunction and damages can be based without resort to judicial review. It would in my opinion be contrary to sound and long-standing principle to extend the remedy of judicial review to such a case.

It is unnecessary for purposes of this appeal to decide whether decisions of the Jockey Club may ever in any circumstances be challenged by judicial review and I do not do so. Cases where the applicant or plaintiff has no contract on which to rely may raise different considerations and the existence or non-existence of alternative remedies may then be material. I think it better that this court should defer detailed consideration of such a case until it arises. I am, however, satisfied that on the facts of this case the appeal should be dismissed.[57]

Farquharson LJ: ... The question remains whether the Jockey Club or this particular decision of it, can properly be described as a domestic body acting by consent.

In principle it is difficult to see any distinction between the National Greyhound Racing Club (or its corporate equivalent) and the Jockey Club. The only apparent factual difference lies in the extent of its jurisdiction. For that matter the other governing bodies of the major sports come in the same category unless some distinction can be found in the rules. Neither do I find any public element in the Jockey Club's position and powers within the meaning of that term as explained in *ex parte Datafin Plc* [1987] QB 815. No doubt, as Lawton LJ observed in *Law*'s case [1983] 1 WLR 1302, 1307, many of

---

57 *Ibid, per* Sir Thomas Bingham MR, 923–24.

the decisions of the Jockey Club through its committees will affect members of the public who have no connection with it but there is a difference between what may affect the public and what amounts to a public duty. It is difficult to see that the disqualification of this particular filly important though the race was – could transform the role of the Jockey Club from a domestic to a public one. The courts have always been reluctant to interfere with the control of sporting bodies over their own sports and I do not detect in the material available to us any grounds for supposing that, if the Jockey Club were dissolved, any governmental body would assume control of racing. Neither in its framework nor its rules nor its function does the Jockey Club fulfil a governmental role.

I understand the criticism made by Mr Kentridge of the reality of the consent to the authority of the Jockey Club. The invitation to consent is very much on a take it or leave it basis. But I do not consider that this undermines the reality of the consent. Nearly all sports are subject to a body of rules to which an entrant must subscribe. These are necessary, as already observed, for the control and integrity of the sport concerned. In such a large industry as racing has become, I would suspect that all those actively and honestly engaged in it welcome the control of licensing Jockey Club.

For these reasons I would hold that the decision of the Disciplinary Committee of the Jockey Club to disqualify Aliysa from the 1989 Oaks is not susceptible to judicial review.

As to Mr Milmo's assertion that the question of the Jockey Club's susceptibility to judicial review must be answered or, an all or nothing basis, I can only say as at present advised that I do not agree. In *R v Jockey Club ex parte RAM Racecourses Ltd* [1993] 2 All ER 225 Simon Brown J had similar reservations. In both that case and *R v Disciplinary Committee of the Jockey Club ex parte Massingberd-Mundy* [1993] 1 All ER 207, the applicants had no contractual relationship with the Jockey Club. While I do not say that particular circumstances would give a right to judicial review I do not discount the possibility that in some circumstances the remedy might lie. If for example the Jockey Club failed to fulfil its obligations under the charter by making discriminatory rules, it may be that those affected would have a remedy in public law.[58]

If an individual wishes to challenge a decision of a governing body, he must establish a private law cause of action. Where membership is contractual there may be express or implied terms which might be enforced in private law. What if there is no contract? The courts have indicated that there may still be some protection in *Nagle v Feilden*.[59] The plaintiff, a woman, had been refused a licence as a trainer. She alleged that it was the practice of the stewards of the Jockey Club to refuse a licence to train racehorses to any female applicant and that this was evidenced by the fact that her head lad had been awarded one:

---

58 *Ibid, per* Farquharson LJ, 929–30.
59 [1966] 2 QB 633.

Lord Denning MR: ... Now, I quite agree that if we were here considering a social club, it would be necessary for the plaintiff to show a contract. If a man applies to join a social club and is blackballed, he has no cause of action: because the members have made no contract with him. They can do as they like. They can admit or refuse him, as they please; but we are not considering a social club. We are considering an association which exercises a virtual monopoly in an important field of human activity. By refusing or withdrawing a licence, the stewards can put a man out of business. This is a great power. If it is abused, can the courts give redress? That is the question.

It was urged before us that the members of a trading or professional association were like a social club. They had, it was said, an unrestricted power to admit or refuse to admit, any person whom they choose ...

The common law of England has for centuries recognised that a man has a right to work at his trade or profession without being unjustly excluded from it. He is not to be shut out from it at the whim of those having the governance of it. If they make, a rule which enables them to reject his application arbitrarily or capriciously, not reasonably, that rule is bad. It is against public policy. The courts will not give effect to it ...

When a man is wrongly rejected or ousted by one of these associations, has he no remedy? I think that he may well have, even though he can show no contract. The courts have power to grant him a declaration that his rejection and ouster was invalid and an injunction requiring the association to rectify their error. He may not be able to get damages unless he can show a contract or a tort; but he may get a declaration and injunction ... The true ground of jurisdiction in all these cases is a man's right to work. I have said before and I repeat it now, that a man's right to work at his trade or profession is just as important to him as, perhaps more important than, his rights of property. Just as the courts will intervene to protect his rights of property, so they will also intervene to protect his right to work.

In the present case Mrs Nagle does not seek admission as a member of the Jockey Club. She only applies for a trainer's licence; but this makes no difference. If she is to carry on her trade without stooping to subterfuge, she has to have a licence. When an association, who have the governance of a trade, take it on themselves to license persons to take part in it, then it is at least arguable that they are not at liberty to withdraw a man's licence and thus put him out of business-without hearing him. Nor can they refuse a man a licence and thus prevent him from carrying on his business-in their uncontrolled discretion. If they reject him arbitrarily or capriciously, there is ground for thinking that the courts can intervene ... The right to work has become far better recognised since that time. So has the jurisdiction of the courts to control licensing authorities. When those authorities exercise a predominant power over the exercise of a trade or profession, the courts may have jurisdiction to see that this power is not abused.

In this case Mrs Nagle alleges that the stewards of the Jockey Club make a practice of refusing any woman trainer who applies for a licence. She is refused because she is a woman and for no other reason. The practice is so uniform that it amounts to an unwritten rule. The only way she can get round it is to get her head lad to apply. The licence is granted to him, not to her. It seems to me that this unwritten rule may well be said to be arbitrary and capricious. It is not, as if the training of horses could be regarded as an unsuitable occupation for a woman, like that of a jockey or speedway-rider ... If this practice, this unwritten rule, is invalid as being contrary to public policy, there is ground for thinking that the court has jurisdiction to say so. It can make a declaration of right whenever the interest of the plaintiffs is sufficient to justify it.[60]

It should be noted that this case concerned an action to strike out the statement of claim. Nevertheless, it is of value in that it demonstrates the court's willingness to recognise the cause of action.

The approach adopted by the courts in England has not been one taken by courts throughout the UK.[61] In Scotland, the distinction between public and private law is rejected and the supervisory jurisdiction of the Court of Session is available wherever a decision making power is conferred on some body be it statute, contract or some other instrument. The court may intervene if any body violates its own constitution or rules or errs in law or infringes natural justice even if it is the governing body of a private association. Judicial review in Scotland may be extended to governing bodies of sports.[62] A recent example is the case of Duncan Ferguson in which the opinion was delivered in February 1996.[63] The proceedings, both in judicial review and criminal law, arose out of an incident on the football pitch in a match between Rangers and Raith Rovers. Ferguson head butted his opposing player John McStay. Although no action was taken at the time by the match official, the referee supervisor's report criticised the referee for taking no action. This report then gave rise to disciplinary proceedings by the Scottish Football Association (SFA). The SFA wrote to Ferguson stating that in view of the supervisor's report, the matter was to be referred to the Committee. A further letter then required him to attend the meeting and stated that given the serious nature of the alleged action, the committee might treat the matter as an exceptional case of players misconduct in accordance with paragraphs 3(1) and 4 of the SFA Disciplinary Procedures.

At the disciplinary committee hearing and the appeals tribunal, Ferguson's representative submitted that the proceedings were *ultra vires* but this was rejected. At the judicial review, Ferguson's counsel argued that the matter fell to be decided on the basis of paragraphs 3(1) and 4. He noted that

---

60 *Ibid, per* Lord Denning, 644–47.

61 For approach taken in other jurisdictions see Stewart, W, 'Judicial Control of Sporting Bodies: Scotland' (1995) 3(3) *Sport and the Law Journal* 45; McCutcheon, P, 'Judicial Control of Sporting Bodies: Recent Irish Experiences' (1995) 3(2) *Sport and the Law Journal* 20; Beloff, M and Kerr, T, 'Judicial Control of Sporting Bodies: The Commonwealth Jurisprudence' (1995) 3(1) *Sport and the Law Journal* 5.

62 See *St Johnston Football Club v Scottish Football Association* [1996] SLT 353; *West v Secretary of State for Scotland* [1992] SLT 636.

63 See Duff, A, 'Own Goal' (1993) 4(1) *Sport and the Law Journal* 12.

paragraph 3(1) related to '*additional* penalties' and so there needed to be penalty already in force. This, he argued, was not the case since there had been no caution or sending off during the game. He further argued that paragraph four, which relates to the procedure to be followed when players are called to appear before the committee, required 'the reports submitted' in connection with the case be sent to the player. These reports, he said, were those referred to in paragraph one; that is, those of the referee and linesman and these had not been submitted. He argued, that on this basis, the committees had acted *ultra vires*. Counsel for the SFA argued that 'additional' in this context meant 'other' and thus a previous penalty was not a necessity. In addition, he argued that, if Ferguson's argument that there must be a match report was correct, then there would be a gap in the SFA's disciplinary procedure in that they would not be able to discipline any player whose action had not formed part of a match official's report. Lord Macfayden agreed with the arguments put forward by Ferguson's counsel. With regard to there being a gap in the procedure, he said 'if there is a *lacuna* in that the disciplinary procedures do not provide a mechanism for dealing with incidents which escape the attention of the referee and other match officials (and as I have indicated it is not necessary for me to decide whether there is) I see no difficulty for the respondents in making as appropriate amendment to their constitutional arrangements, so as to cure the matter for the future'. He went to find that the committee had acted *ultra vires* and 'that the severe censure and 12 match suspension which they imposed were invalid and of no effect'. Having laid down their procedures, the SFA were then required to follow them.

CAUSES OF ACTION AVAILABLE TO CHALLENGE A GOVERNING BODY

Restraint of Trade

The rules or decisions of a governing body cannot operate as an unreasonable restraint of trade. Given the level of income that athletes and clubs as businesses achieve these days, this is an important means of challenging a governing body. The basis of the doctrine of restraint of trade is that the imposition of restraints on an 'individual's' ability to carry on a trade is contrary to public policy. The position is clearly stated by Lord MacNaughten in *Nordenfelt v Maxim Nordenfelt Guns and Ammunition Co* when he says 'all interference with individual liberty of action in trading and all restraints of trade themselves, if there is nothing more are contrary to public policy and therefore void'. Such restraints are subject to exceptions in that they:

... may be justified by special circumstances in a particular case. It is a sufficient justification and indeed it is the only justification, if the restriction is reasonable – reasonable that is, in reference to the interests of the parties concerned and reasonable in reference to the interests of the public – protection to the party in whose favour it is imposed while at the same time it is in no way injurious to the public.[64]

For the doctrine of restraint of trade to be applicable in the context of sport then, it must be established that sport amounts to trade. This was clearly established in *Eastham v Newcastle United FC*,[65] which also made clear that there need not be a contractual relationship which between the parties concerned to sustain such an action. Wilberforce J said:

If I am right so far, then the court has jurisdiction to grant a declaratory judgment, not only against an employer who is in a contractual relationship with the employee but also against the association of employers whose rules and regulations place an unjustifiable restraint on his liberty of employment.

That the action was available in the sporting arena was confirmed in *Greig v Insole*.[66] Kerry Packer as manager of World Series Cricket Pty Ltd contracted a number of leading cricketers to play in a series of 'test matches' in Australia and elsewhere. The ICC disapproved and passed a resolution excluding players who participated from playing 'official' test matches. The TCCB also amended its rules to exclude such players from County cricket. Greig and others issued proceedings seeking a declaration that the ICC and TCCB had acted *ultra vires* and in restraint of trade. Slade J confirmed that, although the plaintiffs were not in any contractual relationship with the ICC and TCCB, following *Eastham* they were entitled to seek a declaration as to whether the rules, as applied, were a justifiable restraint of trade. Governing bodies had a legitimate interest to protect the organisation of their sport but the position adopted by the ICC and TCCB went beyond that which was necessary to protect that interest. The retrospective ban could not be justified. A prospective ban might however be permissible. In response to the argument that such groups may prove a threat to the cricket bodies, Slade J said 'these threats however could have been adequately met by merely imposing a prospective disqualification from test cricket on all players who should thereafter contract with or play for WSC or other unapproved private promoters'. He did not say that such a clause would in fact be valid but said that this would be more arguable.

It is clear then that individual athletes may challenge the rules of governing bodies as being an unreasonable restraint of trade even where there is no contractual relationship. The fact that clubs may challenge on this

---

64 [1894] AC 535.
65 [1963] 3 All ER 139. See below pp 357–63 for a detailed analysis of restraint of trade doctrine.
66 [1978] 1 WLR 302.

ground was recently made clear in *Stevenage Borough Football Club v Football League Ltd.*[67] Stevenage finished at the top of the Vauxhall Conference League but were refused admission to the Football League because they did not meet the criteria relating to grounds and finances. They argued that the criteria were in restraint of trade. Carnworth J found that the criteria were an unreasonable restraint of trade but refused to grant the club relief since their challenge was too late. The Court of Appeal held that if the finding on the criteria was correct Stevenage could not challenge since it would be unfair to Torquay United who would go out of the Football League if Stevenage came in. Everyone knew what the criteria were during the 1995–96 season and Stevenage should not have waited until the end of the season before challenging. Stewart argues that the test in Stevenage is misleading:

Stewart, N, 'Stevenage Borough FC v The Football League – A Misleading Test'

Carnwath J found this test, as formulated in *Greig v Insole* and adopted by Blackburne J in the Welsh football case, potentially misleading in that it gave insufficient weight to the distinction between the private and the public aspect. According to Carnwath J the distinction had been more significant in cases where (as in the Stevenage case before him) the plaintiff had no direct contractual or other legal relationship with the body against which complaint was made. Here he appears to have overlooked the fact that, as Blackburne J made clear in his judgment the Welsh clubs' complaint was not that the FA of Wales was restricting their freedom as members of the FAW but as clubs affiliated to English county associations.

The absence of a direct contractual or other legal relationship was therefore a feature of both cases and there was therefore no obvious reason for applying a different test in the Stevenage case.

However, in Carnwath J's view, where the restraint was part of a system of control imposed by a body exercising regulatory powers in the public interest, different considerations arose. Where the system of control itself could be seen to be in the public interest, the onus lay on those seeking to challenge particular rules of establishing that those rules were unreasonable in the narrow sense – broadly equivalent to 'arbitrary and capricious' or to the well-known test of *Wednesbury* unreasonableness applied on judicial review.

One objection to this part of the judgment is that Carnwath J had lost sight of the fact that the Football League was a regulatory body only in a rather heavily qualified sense. Its principal activity, as expressed in its last annual report, is the organisation of League Football and the protection and promotion of League Football and Football League Clubs. It is the 72 existing members of the Football League which together make its rules, including Rule 29. Where the plaintiff's whole complaint was that the door was being unreasonably shut with those 72 clubs on the other side in the warm and the plaintiff outside in the cold, it was arguably ingenuous to treat the Football League as a regulatory body.

---

67   *The Times*, 1 August 1996.

But that specific objection, however significant to the judge's thinking in the particular case, can be put on one side for the sake of argument. It is perfectly possible to suppose a situation in which exactly the same restrictions on promotion from the Conference to the Football League had been imposed by the true regulatory body, the Football Association. The FA, unlike the Football League, could fairly be regarded as having no interest beyond what it saw (rightly or wrongly) as the best interests of football in this country.

The problem raised by the judgment of Carnwath J but which he did not claim to be fully answering, was the reconciliation of different strands of authority:

(1) Restraint of trade cases, as discussed above: The restrictions are void unless they go no further than reasonable and it is the court which decides on the evidence whether they do so.

(2) Cases involving membership or expulsion from organisations of applications and refusals of licences: *Nagle v Feilden* [1966] 2 QB 633; *McInnes v Onslow-Fane* [1978] 1 WLR 1520; *Breen v Amalgamated Engineering Union* [1971] 2 QB 175: An apparently more demanding threshold of 'arbitrary or capricious' may be applied before the relevant rule or decision will be held void (though in *Nagle v Feilden* none of the three judges in the Court of Appeal drew a clear distinction between 'capricious' and 'unreasonable' and on the facts it is plain that they would have regarded the plaintiff's objection as meeting any test of unreasonableness, wide or narrow).

(3) Judicial review of decisions of regulatory bodies, extended by *R v Takeover Panel ex parte Datafin Plc* [1987] QB 815 beyond bodies deriving their powers from statute.

The court can strike down a decision which it finds that no reasonable body could have reached on a proper consideration of the matter but cannot substitute its own view and cannot interfere simply because it would have reached a different conclusion. Accordingly the onus is very firmly on the applicant to show grounds for interfering with the decision.

It was not being suggested in the judgment that the judicial review test was in terms the applicable yardstick, as it is clearly established that decisions of sporting authorities are not susceptible to that public law procedure: *R v Jockey Club ex parte RAM Racecourses* [1993] 2 All ER 225; *R v Football Association Ltd ex parte Football League Ltd* (1991) *The Times*, 22 August 1991 (the latter case presumably brought by the Football League before it had fully developed its recently expressed concern at the courts' involvement in sporting matters). The relevance of the judicial review test was its similarity to the 'arbitrary and capricious' test, particularly given the judge's implicit view that a rather fine line had developed between bodies susceptible to judicial review and those which were not.

The view of Carnwath J that the earlier cases has failed to give sufficient weight to the distinction between the private and the public aspect is difficult to reconcile with those decisions or what the judges actually said in deciding them. Wilberforce J in the *Eastham* case, Slade J in *Greig v Insole* and Blackburn J in *Newport v FAW* all very clearly recognised and took account of the wider responsibilities of the football and cricket authorities, including them in the concept of the 'legitimate interests' to be protected and taking them into consideration as part of the overall assessment of reasonableness.

There was no distinguishing element of the *Stevenage* case which justified some extra recognition of the public element – if anything the public element was less, precisely because of the private interests of the League and its member clubs.

In all those other cases the system of control was in the public interest. Outside the sporting context the same could be said of the Pharmaceutical Society in the *Dickson* case. Yet the courts found no difficulty about adopting the established restraint trade test and the established principles on onus of proof. That should have been the test unequivocally applied in the *Stevenage* case.

The judge's findings on the evidence meant that on both ground and financial criteria the League would have failed the established restraint of trade test, though he doubted whether they could be termed 'arbitrary or capricious' – a questionable view given his express finding that the financial criteria were 'unfairly discriminatory'.

However, in the end he did not actually decide which test was applicable or attempt an overall reconciliation of the authorities from different branches of law. The question was posed but left unanswered.[68]

In *Newport Association Football Club v Football Association of Wales*[69] restraint of trade was raised again. The Welsh FA passed a resolution preventing Welsh clubs playing in the league organised by the English FA, with the aim of promoting the Welsh competition. The plaintiffs resigned from the FAW and joined the English Association. The FAW then imposed sanctions on the resigning clubs objecting to their home matches being played in Wales. The English FA honoured these objections and required all home matches to be played in England. As a result, the home gate receipts fell dramatically as did sponsorship. The plaintiffs then brought an action for unreasonable restraint of trade and seeking an injunction. The importance of the case lies in the finding of Jacob J that a declaration for an unreasonable restraint of trade is a cause of action so that an interlocutory injunction is available and there is no need to wait for final trial.

There is no need for a sportsman or woman to be a professional in order to bring an action in restraint of trade. This can be seen in *Gasser v Stinson and another*.[70] Sandra Gasser challenged an IAAF ban imposed after she tested positive for anabolic steroids. She argued that the IAAF rules, which allowed the banning of athletes who tested positive regardless of guilt or intent, were in restraint of trade and void. Scott J refused to accept that Gasser's status as an amateur within the IAAF rules meant that she could not seek such a challenge. This was because amateur under the IAAF rules did not mean that

---

68   Stewart, N (1996) 4(3) *Sport and the Law Journal* 110.
69   [1995] 2 All ER 87.
70   Transcript of 15 June 1988, unreported case, High Court.

athletes could not earn a living at all since sponsorship was permissible. He said that ' ... in a sport which allows competitors to exploit their ability in the sport for financial gain and which allows that gain to be a direct consequence or participation in competition, a ban on competition is, in my judgment, a restraint of trade'. The critical question which he then identified was whether this restraint was in fact unreasonable. He noted that the rules were those which the IAAF used to discourage and prevent the practice of doping as an aid to performance and the public interest in doing so. He referred also to the evidence of the General Secretary of the IAAF, who had stated that the use of drugs was cheating and that if it became known that a sport is infiltrated by drugs the sport is likely 'to suffer substantially in its public image and reputation'. He stated that it was against this background that the reasonableness or otherwise of the rules had to be judged. He went on, 'For my part I am not persuaded that the IAAF's absolute offence and mandatory sentence is unreasonable to an athlete who is found to have dope in his or her urine. On the contrary I think that in the circumstances the restraints are reasonable'.

Restraint of trade has been the means used to challenge drug testing procedures and was recently seen in *Wilander v Tobin*.[71] Tennis players Wilander and Novacek sought an order to stay any proceedings against them on the basis of Rule 53 of the International Federation Rules which concern the misuse of drugs. They argued that Rule 53 of the Tennis Federation Rules was an unreasonable restraint of trade and as such void. This was the case on four grounds. First, absolute offences were created; secondly rule 53 laid down mandatory penalties; thirdly the burden of proof was on the player to prove his innocence; and fourthly if the medical procedure of the IOC did not apply to the procedures to be followed by the ITF then the ITF procedures were defective and unfair because they did not provide a proper protection for players. Neill J found the shifting of the burden of proof 'troublesome' in that the presumption of innocence was the cornerstone of English criminal law. After considering the whole procedure, he concluded that the safeguards provided in the procedure were sufficient to ensure that the testing was carried out in a proper manner and according to the proper rules of a competent laboratory. He therefore rejected the argument that Rule 53 was arguably void as being a restraint of trade.

Breach of the Implied Term to Act Fairly

That the principles of natural justice are applicable to the decision making process of bodies other than those of a judicial or quasi-judicial nature was stated in *Ridge v Baldwin*.[72] The first steps in arguing the application of the

---

71   Transcript of 26 March 1996, unreported case, High Court.
72   See above, p 206.

principles in the sporting context had been taken in *Russell v Duke of Norfolk*.[73] The case concerned the disqualification of a trainer's licence by the Jockey Club on the grounds of misconduct pursuant to the Rules of Racing. The plaintiff alleged, amongst other things, that the decision to withdraw his licence was contrary to the principles of natural justice. The majority in the Court of Appeal held that the stewards had an unfettered power to withdraw the licence arising from contract. It was impossible, therefore, to imply a term in the contract that any inquiry, if held, should be in accordance with the principles of natural justice. Denning LJ however found that the rules did not require a hearing if withdrawal was without a penalty but, when the withdrawal was on the grounds of misconduct, then the trainer must be given the opportunity to defend himself. He indicated when the principles of natural justice would be applicable:

> **Russell v Duke of York [1949] 1 All ER 104**
>
> This penalty of disqualification is the most severe penalty that stewards can inflict ... It disqualifies the trainer from taking part in racing and this takes away his livelihood. Common justice requires that before any man is found guilty of an offence carrying such consequences, there should be an enquiry at which he has the opportunity of being heard ... The Jockey Club has a monopoly in an important field of human activity. It has great powers with corresponding responsibilities.[74]

The finding of the majority, Tucker and Asquith LJJ, would be decided differently post *Ridge v Baldwin*.

In *McInnes v Onlow-Fane and Others*[75] the plaintiff held a licence for boxing matches issued by the British Boxing Board of Control (BBBC) in the 1950s. He was granted a trainer's licence in 1971 and in 1973 a master of ceremonies licence. In 1973, after an incident at a match, all his licences were withdrawn. Following this, an application for a manager's licence was rejected. He sought a declaration that the BBBC had acted contrary to the rules of natural justice or unfairly by failing to inform him of the case against him and by not granting him an oral hearing prior to rejecting his application for a manager's licence. Sir Robert Megarry VC accepted that 'the point is of considerable general importance. There are many bodies which, though not established or operating under the authority of statute, exercise control, often on a national scale, over many activities which are important to many people both as providing a means of livelihood and for other reasons'.[76] Sir Robert distinguished between three cases: 'forfeiture cases', 'application cases' and 'expectation cases'. He noted that there was a substantial distinction between

---

73 [1949] 1 All ER 109.

74 *Ibid, per* Lord Denning, 119.

75 [1978] 3 All ER 211; [1978] 1 WLR 1520.

76 *Ibid*, 216.

the forfeiture and application cases since in the forfeiture cases there is a threat to take something away whereas in the application cases, nothing is taken away. He was of the view that in forfeiture cases, 'the right to an unbiased tribunal, the right to notice of the charges and the right to be heard in answer to the charges (which in *Ridge v Baldwin* [1964] AC 40, 132 Lord Hodson said were three features of natural justice which stood out) are plainly apt'. This was not the case in application cases. He said 'the distinction is well recognised, for in general it is clear that the courts will require natural justice to be observed for expulsion from a social club but not on an application for admission to it'. According to Sir Robert, the expectation cases were more akin to the forfeiture cases for 'although in form there is no forfeiture but merely an attempt at acquisition that fails, the legitimate expectation of a renewal of the licence or confirmation of the membership is one which raises the question of what it is that has happened to make the applicant unsuitable for the membership or licence for which he was previously considered suitable'.

A recent application of these principles can be seen in *Jones v Welsh Rugby Union*.[77] Mark Jones was sent off following a fight in a match between Ebbw Vale and Swansea in November 1996. The Disciplinary Committee of the Welsh Rugby Union (WRU) wrote to the club with a copy of the referee's report setting out Jones's options. Jones wanted to appear before the Committee to explain his actions and to make representations. He wanted legal representation to do so but was refused permission. However, since Jones had a speech impediment, the WRU agreed to allow Patrick Harrington QC, who was treasurer of the club, to attend but only as a 'shoulder' and not as an advocate. Harrington wanted to comment on the video to show that Jones had been provoked and that his action was defensive. He also wanted to question the referee. Both requests were refused and the video was watched in private by the Committee. The Committee found that the sending off was correct and Jones was suspended for four weeks. This suspension had potentially serious repercussions for Jones and his club. As such, they thought that they should at least have had a fair hearing. They brought an action alleging breach of contract in that the WRU had breached the implied term that the conduct of the disciplinary proceedings would be fair and in accordance with the principles of natural justice. Ebsworth J held that she was 'satisfied that the procedural defects ... in relation to the refusal to watch the video during the course of the public part of the hearing and the lack of power to challenge evidence by way of questioning and to adduce evidence, taken in the context of a now professionalised sport, amount to an arguable case that the plaintiffs' right to defend themselves properly and effectively was denied them. I accept on the basis of *Ridge v Baldwin* that to act with such fairness is required of the defendants'. Since these were only interlocutory proceedings,

---

77 *The Times*, 28 February 1997. See also Rose, N, and Albertini, L, '*Jones v Welsh Rugby Union*: New Law for the New Era' (1997) 5(1) *Sport and the Law Journal* 20.

the finding was not that the proceedings were unfair but only that the plaintiffs had an arguable case.[78]

The case left open the question of whether the duty to act fairly required legal representation and the provision of an appeals procedure. In *Enderby Town Football Club*[79] it was stated that players do not have a right to legal representation but Lord Denning MR however made clear that a tribunal should have a discretion to allow legal representation in an appropriate case and should exercise such a discretion. There is no right to legal representation; only the right to have the tribunal exercise its discretion. It would seem, however, that where a tribunal refuses representation then reasons will have to be given since the court may infer that if no reasons are given then there were no good reasons.[80] With regard to the necessity for an appeals procedure, in *Wilander v Tobin* it was held that it was 'respectably arguable' that the lack of an appeals procedure might render a decision objectionable on the grounds that it would constitute an unreasonable restraint of trade and be a breach of Article 59 of the Treaty of Rome.

What Lord Denning says with regard to good laymen[81] may be true but as Grayson says, 'In today's changing sport scene even the 'good laymen' would be wise to be assisted by the services of a good lawyer if natural and indeed, any justice is to be guaranteed for sport and its proper administration according to law'.[82] Grayson usefully sets out a checklist for governing bodies to ensure that their disciplinary procedures conform with a duty to act fairly:

Grayson, E, *Sport and the Law*

(1) avoid any risk of pre-judgment or prejudice or bias or likelihood of it;

(2) formulate and notify clearly, preferably in writing, any assertions needing reply;

(3) notify clearly and preferably in writing, any date for investigation or hearing;

(4) act *intra vires*, within any rules and not *ultra vires*, outside them;

(5) remember the right to be heard in defence of any allegation;

(6) in cases of difficulty or complexity, consider carefully any request for legal representation.[83]

---

78 *Ibid*, Rose, N and Albertini, L (1997).

79 [1971] 1 Ch 591, see above p 210.

80 *Padfield and Others v MAFF and Others* [1968] AC 997.

81 *Nagle v Feilden* [1966] 2 QB 633.

82 Grayson, E, *Sport and the Law*, 2nd edn (1994), London: Butterworths, p 305.

83 *Ibid*, p 306. See also Wearmouth, H, '"No Winners on the Greasy Pole?" Ethical and Legal Frameworks of Evaluating Disciplinary processes in Sport' (1995) 3(3) *Sport and the Law Journal* 29.

ARGUMENTS FOR AND AGAINST THE EXTENSION OF JURISDICTION

'The court's reluctance to extend judicial review to bodies such as sporting associations seems to be rooted in largely technical and pragmatic concerns.'[84] This pragmatic view was also stated by Beloff.[85] He wrote that 'It is, I suspect, the floodgates argument that is the unspoken premise of the Vice Chancellarial observation, the fear that limited court time will be absorbed by a new and elastic category of case with much scope for abusive and captious litigation'. In the *FA* case, Rose J made no secret that this was one reason he would not extend jurisdiction. He said:

> ### *R v Football Association ex parte Football League Ltd* [1993] 2 All ER 823
>
> But, for my part, to apply to the governing body of football, on the basis that it is a public body, principles honed for the control of the abuse of power by government ands its creatures would involve what, in today's fashionable parlance, would be called a quantum leap. It would also, in my view, for what it is worth, be a misapplication of increasingly scarce judicial resources. It will become impossible to provide a swift remedy, which is one of the conspicuous hallmarks of judicial review, if the courts become even more swamped with such applications then they are already.[86]

He recognised that such an argument is not a jurisprudential argument for refusing to extend jurisdiction but nevertheless argued:

> it will be cold comfort to the seven or eight other substantive applicants and the many more *ex parte* applicants who have had to be displaced from the court's list in order to accommodate the present litigation to learn that, though they may have a remedy for their complaints about the arbitrary abuse of executive power, it cannot be granted to them yet.[87]

Beloff is of the view that such a floodgates argument 'intellectually has little to commend it and pragmatically is usually shown to be ill-founded. For it is often the case, that once the courts have shown the willingness to intervene, the standard of bodies at risk of their intervention tend to improve. The threat of litigation averts its actuality'.[88]

The courts have rejected the exercise of monopolistic power as providing justification for extending its judicial review jurisdiction. But those who wish to participate in a sport have no option but to submit to the rules of a governing body. There can be no clearer situation of an unequal bargaining

---

84   Black, J, 'Constitutionalising Self-Regulation' (1996) 59 *Modern Law Review* 37.
85   Beloff, M, 'Pitch, Pool, Rink ... Court? Judicial Review in the Sporting World' (1989) *Public Law* 95.
86   *Ibid, per* Rose J, 849.
87   *Ibid, per* Rose J, 849.
88   *Ibid*, Beloff (1989), p 95.

position. Such monopolistic powers can be open to abuse and it seems appropriate that in such situations judicial review should be available. Further the courts seem obsessed by a concern about the legitimate role of public law rather than a concern for community values. They have adopted, as Black argues, 'a narrow approach to the question and have conceived the role of judicial review in the traditional terms of the judicial regulation of executive power ... They have not adequately addressed the power, autonomy or legal dominion arguments'.

In addition, opening up challenge by means of judicial review may give standing to those who may not have standing in a private law action. The floodgates argument against such an extension is not sustainable in that the Order 53 hurdle of sufficient interest would have to be met. A private law action may not quantify the loss suffered to the plaintiff's satisfaction. This could be seen in the *Ebbw Vale* case where although Jones's loss of income was quantifiable, there were other matters which were not – such as whether Jones would have made the difference between winning or losing a game or, indeed, whether he would have been selected for a game. In any event, athletes want to participate in their sport and the award of damages does not in fact achieve this end. Any private action may go on for a considerable period of time and keeps the athlete out of the sport during this time. In contrast an application for judicial review would be quickly resolved making it possible for the athlete to return to his sport.

There are arguments against the extension of judicial review as a means of challenging decisions of governing bodies. The nature of Order 53 is that it is protective of the bodies being challenged.[89] Rather than making a challenge easier, it would in fact result in greater difficulty for anyone seeking to challenge a governing body. This would seem attractive to governing bodies themselves as the protections currently available to bodies recognised in public law would similarly be available to them even though there would appear to be no reason why sport governing bodies should be entitled to the privileged position given to governmental (in the narrow sense) bodies. The benefits of a civil law action would be lost; there is no need for leave to bring a civil law action and the limitation period is longer. The danger of an extension of the judicial review jurisdiction is that the individual may end up with no cause of action at all whereas at the moment, though the available cause of action would appear to be a lesser one, at least there is some means to challenge a sport governing body.

89   See Lord Diplock in *O'Reilly v Mackman* [1983] 2 AC 237.

ALTERNATIVE DISPUTE RESOLUTION (ADR) AS A MEANS OF SETTLING DISPUTES

It seems that any action challenging the decisions of sport governing bodies must be brought in private law. As with all private law actions, the danger is that the action will be protracted and expensive. The ultimate aim of any athlete must be to secure the right to compete and what is really required is the quickest and cheapest means of settling any dispute. An alternative means of dealing with disputes may then be arbitration or mediation:

Doyle, B, *The Anzsla[90] Dispute Resolution Service*

The most important aspect of our service is that of providing a mediation service. It was the catalyst for the service to be inaugurated.

It is the most important factor service we can provide to reduce costs, avoid delays and reduce the breakdown in friendships in sport.

The concept of mediation is probably not all that well known in the community. Mediation is but one aspect of alternative resolution but it is the most common.

It is, of course, a system of resolving a dispute by getting the parties together with an independent, trained facilitator who will assist the parties to reach their own agreement by isolating the issues in dispute and developing options. The aim is to avoid the problems of Court where one party wins and one loses (but probably both at great expenses). A successful mediation is said to be a Win-Win situation. The mediator will be a trained person who may, depending upon the circumstances and the attitude of the parties, take either a passive or an active role. He will invariably be looking at alternative solutions to place before the parties. In the end a mediator, contrary to what some people see as his role, does not impose any decisions on the parties but enable them to come to their own agreement. Of course, once that agreement is reached, it is committed to writing.

The parties, of course, must be agreeable to the mediation and their agreement may be either:

(a) expressed in the contract which originally gave rise to the dispute; or

(b) decided by them after the dispute arises;

The great advantages of mediation are:

(1) informality;

(2) by having the parties agree, it gives a better opportunity for the relationship between the parties to be preserved;

(3) a saving on legal costs and time.

I have expressed some of these advantages several times in the paper because they, compared to the problems that confront people when they go court, should be emphasised.

---

90 The Australian and New Zealand Sports Law Association.

At the same time, if agreement cannot be reached by the parties to resolve their dispute, access to the courts is still open to them.

In fact, though some disputes might be referred to a mediator at an early stage, others might only go to mediation after court proceedings have been commenced.[91]

Arbitration as a viable alternative has been recognised by the Arbitration Acts, the most recent of which was the Arbitration Act 1996. The object of arbitration according to s 1(1) of the Act is 'to obtain the fair resolution of disputes by an impartial tribunal without unnecessary delay or expense'. According to s 1(b) 'the parties should be free to agree how their disputes are resolved, subject only to such safeguards as are necessary in the public interest'. Under s 5(1), for the Arbitration Act to apply the arbitration agreement must be in writing. Although the courts will only intervene in an arbitration agreement as provided for in Part 1 of the Arbitration Act 1996,[92] access to the courts is not denied in that under s 69(1), unless otherwise agreed, a party to an arbitration agreement may appeal to the courts on a point of law. The implication here must be that the jurisdiction of the court may be excluded by agreement. Questions of fact are never subject to appeal since these are issues to be settled by the arbitration tribunal.

Where there is an arbitration clause and legal proceedings are commenced, a party to the arbitration agreement may apply to the court to stay the proceedings under s 9(1) of the Arbitration Act 1996. That is, arbitration must be sought where there is an agreement to do so. The issue was recently addressed in *Notts Incorporated FC Ltd v The Football League Ltd and Southend United FC Ltd*.[93] The case concerned a complaint from Southend United that Notts County had illegally approached their manager in June 1995 to take up the post of assistant manager with Notts County. The Football League appointed a commission, as required by its regulations, to enquire into the complaint. The commission found in favour of Notts County but indicated that Southend United had a right of appeal under the regulations. Southend subsequently brought an appeal to which Notts County argued that the regulations did not provide for an appeal on their true construction. Notts County then issued proceedings in the High Court to determine whether Southend had the right of appeal as claimed. The Football League then sought a stay in the proceedings under s 4 of the Arbitration Act 1950[94] on the grounds that all differences between members should be referred to arbitration under Article 58 of the FIFA rules which provides that all clubs should refrain from litigating in court 'until all the possibilities of sports jurisdiction within or under the responsibility of their national association

---

91 Doyle, B, 'The Anzsla Dispute Resolution Service' (1995) 3(3) *Sport and the Law Journal* 38.
92 Section 1(c) of the Arbitration Act 1996.
93 Unreported. See *Sports Law Administration and Practice* (1997) March/April, p 9.
94 Now s 9 of the Arbitration Act 1996.

have been exhausted'. Neuberger J noted that different considerations may apply to cases involving club rules as opposed to commercial contracts. He stated that courts should in principle give effect to arbitration clauses and noted that it was unseemly that disputes covered by arbitration provisions should be aired in the courts and the view of the Football League that if the court was willing to decide the point then the effect would be more cases in the courts. However, he found that it would not, in the circumstances, be appropriate to grant a stay. The level of costs awarded had been less than £20,000 and since both parties were ready to argue the point, referring the matter back to arbitration may have increased the costs. He was also influenced by the fact the issue was one of construction and not a dispute as to facts. In addition, he noted that one party (Notts County) wanted the court to determine the matter and the other (Southend) was equivocal as to whether the matter should be dealt with by the court or arbitration. Neuberger J stated that this was a decision based on the particular facts of the case and the balance between granting and not granting a stay was only just outweighed by factors against.

Arbitration awards will have the same effect as judgments of ordinary courts.[95] In addition to settling disputes quickly an inexpensively, another advantage of arbitration may be that it ensures that common rules are applied in all disputes as opposed to the differing laws of countries which may produce different results in similar matters depending on the jurisdiction in which a decision is challenged. This is particularly so given that sport is now very much more of an international nature. Arbitration and voluntary self-regulation is considered to have the advantage of, as Samuel and Gearhart argue, 'lower costs, privacy, the presence of expertise on the tribunal and rapidity'.[96] However, Inglesby stresses caution in suggesting that compulsory alternative dispute resolution mechanisms may not always be the most desirable way of solving a particular kind of dispute.[97]

The Court of Arbitration for Sport (CAS)[98] was the first attempt to set up an arbitration procedure for disputes arising in sport. It was set up by the IOC in 1983. It is chartered under Swiss law and has its headquarters in Lausanne, Switzerland. Arbitration is defined in the Court of Arbitration for Sport Guide to Arbitration as 'a private, independent and impartial legal institution authorised by the state legal system, which enables dispute under private law

---

95   Section 66(1) of the Arbitration Act 1996.

96   Gearhart, S, 'Sporting Arbitration and the International Olympic Committee's Court of Arbitration of Sport' (1989) 6 *Journal of International Arbitration* 39.

97   Ingelsey, R, 'Court sponsored mediation: The case against mandatory participation' (1993) 56 *Modern Law Review* 441. Also see Gardiner, S, and Felix, A, 'Juridification of the Football Field: Strategies for Giving Law the Elbow' (1995) 5(2) *Marquette Sports Law Journal* 214.

98   See Polvino, A, 'Arbitration as preventative medicine for olympic ailments: the International Olympic Committee's Court of Arbitration for Sport and the Future of the Settlement of International Sporting Disputes' (1994) 8 *Emory International Law Review* 347.

to be settled'. The Court arbitrates 'disputes of a private nature arising out of the practice or development of sport and in a general way, all activities pertaining to sport and whose settlement is not otherwise provided for in the Olympic Charter. Such disputes may bear on questions of principle relating to sport or on pecuniary or other interests'.[99] The function of the court is to address issues which in its absence, would be dealt with by the courts. 'These include eligibility and suspension of athletes, the adequacy of breaches of contract between an athlete and sports clubs, the validity of contracts for sale of sports equipment and the nationality of an athlete for the purposes of competition.'[100] Under Article 5 CAS Statute, all international and national sports organisations have standing to seek an award from the court, as does 'in a general way, any natural person or corporation body having the capacity or power to compromise'. Parties in a dispute must submit it to the arbitrators by virtue of an express agreement, which may arise out of a contract to do so.

The Court as a forum for resolving sporting disputes has developed rapidly. On 22 June 1994, 31 international sports federations signed an agreement in Paris to set up the International Council of Arbitration for Sport (ICAS) and in so doing recognised the jurisdiction of CAS. The 20 member International Council of Arbitration for Sport (ICAS) detaches the CAS from the IOC. Members of ICAS are appointed by the International Sports Federation, the Association of National Olympic Committees and the IOC. ICAS oversees the CAS and in this way enhances its legitimacy. It also divides into an arbitration section and appeals section. Ordinary arbitration proceedings are applied to resolve disputes arising from contracts which include arbitration clauses or from parties agreeing after the dispute has arisen to submit to the CAS. The dispute is decided according to the rules of law chosen by the parties or that contained in the contract and in the absence of agreement according to Swiss law. The appeals process is applied to disputes arising from decisions taken by internal tribunals where the regulations of the body provide for arbitration by the CAS. It presupposes that all internal remedies have been exhausted. The CAS will decide according to the regulations of the body involved and if it needs to, it will apply the laws from the country in which the body is domiciled. Under ICAS nearly all international federations have accepted arbitration clauses in their licensing contracts. This has the result of the CAS being the exclusive forum for resolving disputes between athletes and their governing bodies. It means that an individual seeking to challenge a governing body which has come within the jurisdiction of the CAS, must bring the dispute before the court.

The agreements provide a basis for enforcing the court's decisions against individual athletes. This is by reason of the fact that the eligibility of athletes

---

99 Article 4, CAS Statute.

100 Nafziger, J, 'International Sports Law as a Process for Resolving Disputes' (1996) 45(130) *International Comparative Law Quarterly* 143.

normally depends on membership of an international federation at a national level and the acceptance of their rules. To participate, athletes enter into contracts with their national federation and in the contract is a mandatory clause which helps ensure that CAS awards will generally be binding on an individual athlete. There would seem to be no clearer unequal bargaining position; for an athlete to compete he must be a member of the appropriate national federation and to enter into an agreement with that body, the athlete must agree to the arbitration clause. As a result the athlete has no choice but to agree to the arbitration clause. It seems that the courts will not interfere in such agreements unless permitted to do so by the Arbitration Act 1996.

The effect of CAS awards would seem to be settled by the Arbitration Act 1996. Section 101(1) provides for the awards made by arbitration tribunals in countries party to the New York Convention[101] to be binding on the parties to the agreement in that they may be relied upon in defence or be set off in legal proceedings. Since Switzerland is party to the convention, CAS awards are enforceable in English law. In *Gasser v Stinson*, Scott J implied that the courts would be reluctant to interfere with decisions of governing bodies. Although he did not comment specifically on the enforceability of decisions of the CAS, he did comment generally on challenging of sport governing bodies. He quoted from:

MacInnes v Onslow-Fane [1978] 3 All ER 211

I think that the courts must be slow to allow an implied obligation to be fair to be used as a means of bringing before the courts for review honest decision of bodies exercising jurisdiction over sporting and other activities which those bodies are far better fitted to judge than the courts. This is even so where those bodies are concerned with the means of livelihood of those who take part in those activities. The concepts of natural justice and the duty to be fair must not be allowed to discredit themselves by making unreasonable requirements and imposing undue burdens.[102]

Perhaps this may be interpreted as indicating that the courts will be as loathe to interfere with decisions of the CAS as they are with interfering with decisions of governing bodies. This does not mean however that the courts will never interfere; only that they are reluctant to do so.

There are a number of advantages to arbitration before CAS. These are identified in the CAS Guide to Arbitration as being: suitable for international disputes in that a sole jurisdiction is applied and therefore avoids choices of jurisdiction. It is specially designed for settlement of sport related disputes; it is simple and flexible; it is quick; it provides for a single instance finding; it is confidential and it is not expensive. The benefits of the CAS can be seen in a

---

101 Convention on the Recognition and Enforcement of Foreign Arbitral Awards 1958.
102 Megarry VC in *MacInnes v Onslow-Fane* [1978] 1 WLR 1520, 1535.

number of cases. In *Gundel v FEI/CAS*[103] Eric Navet, a world show jumping champion, was suspended by the International Equestrian Federation for four months after an excessive quantity of a stimulant was found in his horse's urine in a doping test at the European Championships in 1992. Navet successfully argued before the CAS that his horse must have produced abnormally high quantities of the stimulant and the decision was quashed. By contrast, the Butch Reynolds saga is an illustration of the protracted course that a challenge before courts can take and indeed the costs that can be incurred.[104] Reynolds had tested positive for a banned substance in 1990 and was suspended for two years by the IAAF. Reynolds protested his innocence and appealed to the American Arbitration Association and the federal arbitrator ordered the governing body of US track and field (the Athletics Congress) to allow Reynolds to run in the championships in New York. The arbitrator had found Reynolds' suspension improper. The IAAF threatened to put its contamination rule into effect which enabled the IAAF to suspend any athlete competing in the same meet as a suspended athlete. Instead it reprimanded the Athletics Congress. The Athletics Congress doping review panel then overturned the IAAF suspension on the grounds of procedural errors but this decision only cleared Reynolds for domestic competition. The IAAF submitted the case to its own arbitration panel, which upheld the suspension and announced that the contamination rule would be enforced. In May 1992 Reynolds filed an action in the courts seeking $12.5 million in damages against the IAAF and the Athletics Congress. This began the long haul of litigation in the US courts. Had the matter been dealt with by the CAS, time, trouble and money would have been saved by all those concerned.

The 1996 Atlanta Olympic Games saw the CAS provide an *ad hoc* division to sit during the Games.[105] It was not greeted with enthusiasm in that the entry form for the Games required participating athletes to accept the binding arbitration by the CAS. The entry form contained the undertaking 'I shall not constitute any claim, arbitration or litigation or seek any other form of relief in any other court or tribunal'. The clause was not challenged but Beloff argues that since both Swiss and US law 'respect sports arbitral process, there is no reason to believe that had any challenge been made, it would have succeeded'.[106] Beloff is also of the view that the *ad hoc* division was a success in that despite the reticence of athletes, they did in fact reach 'athlete friendly' decisions. He says 'In my view, the panel served the purposes for which it was established well; and those purposes were proper ones. I would hope that the experience of the AHD in Atlanta will persuade the powers that be not

---

103 I Civil Court, Swiss Fed Trib 15 March 1993. See also 'No End to the Dream For a Pair of Old War-horses', *The Times*, 26 July 1992.

104 See above, Chapter 3.

105 See Beloff, M, 'The Court of Arbitration for Sport at the Olympics' (1996) 4(3) *Sport and the Law Journal* 5.

106 See n 33.

merely to repeat the procedure in Sydney but to use it for other major international competitions'. The involvement of lawyers is of course another issue. 'It has been argued that there is a risk that their association adversely affects the efficacious qualities of such mechanisms.'[107] But Beloff states that 'it was the consensus view of those who served upon the Panel that disputes in which they were assisted by lawyers from either side tended to be disposed of more efficiently than those from which lawyers were absent'.[108]

The benefits of having a arbitration procedure has been identified by the Australia and New Zealand Sports Law Association (Anzsla) and has resulted in them setting up such a system[109] providing a mediation service, training for the judiciary, expert investigations and arbitration. In addition the CCPR has identified the need for such a service and it too is in the process of setting up a system.[110]

THE INTERNATIONAL NATURE OF GOVERNING BODIES

The tendency of sport to be of an international nature means that many governing bodies now have an international jurisdiction. The question then arises as to what this means for challenging decisions of such bodies. In *Gasser v Stinson*, the IAAF argued 'that the restraint of trade rules of English law should not be applied to the IAAF rules which are concerned to regulate the eligibility of athletes of many different nationalities to appear in athletic competitions in many different parts of the world'. It was submitted by counsel for the IAAF that as a matter of policy, the English courts should not impose a rule of English public policy founded on English views of freedom of economic competition to regulate international athletics. This argument was rejected by Scott J on the grounds that authority was against it (see *Greig v Insole*) and because as a matter of principle, he 'did not see why English courts should hold their hands in a case such as the present ... Is it to be said that the IAAF is beyond the reach of the courts and the law? ... To the extent, therefore, that there is a policy decision to be made, I am of the opinion that the English restraint of trade rules should be applied to the validity of the IAAF's rules'. In addition, the laws of different countries produce different results in the application of the rules which arguably means that governing bodies have double standards. For example the IAAF rules require that where an athlete tests positive in a doping test, then the national body should ban the athlete

---

107 Gardiner, S, and Felix, A, 'Juridification of the Football Field: Strategies for Giving Law the Elbow' (1995) 5(2) *Marquette Sports Law Journal* 189, 214.

108 *Ibid*, Beloff (1996).

109 See Doyle, B, 'The Anzsla Dispute Resolution Service' (1995) 3 *Sport and the Law Journal* 38.

110 See 'Letter to the Editor' (1996) *Sports Law Administration and Practice* September/October, p 6.

for a period of four years. This period has however been found to be unreasonable on a number of countries. The consequence of this is that athletes are treated differently depending on their nationality.

The problem is clearly demonstrated in the case of the British shop putter Paul Edwards who was sent home from the 1994 Commonwealth Games. His application to be reinstated after three years was thrown out although two German athletes were reinstated after a two year ban since German law deems the four year ban unreasonable. Britain has no such law of proportionality which leaves Edwards banned whilst fellow athletes guilty of the same offence continue competing. Dr Arne Ljungqvist, chairman of the IAAF medical commission, recognises that the position is unfair but has stated that the position is such that either the IAAF expels the national member federation which is responsible for enforcing rules (and which cannot act contrary to the laws of its countries) or it reinstates the athletes from countries which have deemed the ban unreasonable under the exceptional circumstances rule.[111] The IAAF has as a result of this double standard recommended to the congress that the ban be reduced to two years since the rule cannot be enforced worldwide. The congress, having met on 4 July 1997, voted 112–56 in favour of reducing the period of the ban to two years. The decision has not met with total support[112] with those against arguing that the decision is degrading and undermining the position of drug testers.

---

111 See 'Edwards singled out by IAAF's double standards', *The Times*, 22 March 1997.
112 See *Daily Telegraph*, 1 August 1997.

CHAPTER FIVE

SPORT, MONEY AND THE LAW

INTRODUCTION

Barnes, S, 'Zero Rated'

Here are some more fascinating facts about the most important subject in sport; all sums, naturally, in American dollars. Michael Jordan is still the highest-paid sportsman, even though the sum he receives for playing basketball is a mere $3.9 million. He gets a further $40 million in endorsements. Compare and contrast with Mike Tyson, second in the list, who got $40 million for boxing and $0 for endorsements. The biggest gap for non-rapists concerns Jack Nicklaus, who made $0.6 million for playing golf and $14.5 million from endorsements.[1]

The argument has already been made that the commercial orientation of contemporary sport is not a new phenomenon. However the vast amounts of money currently found in sport make it one of the most commercially powerful forms of business. It may have been generally accepted in the past that although sport was a form of business, sporting success should traditionally outweigh financial profit as the main aim. However, increasingly money has come to represent the destiny of much sport. Massive amounts of income have been generated from the selling of television rights. The four year deal for Premiership football starting in the 1997–98 season is worth £670 million.[2] The European rights for the Olympic Games until 2008 have cost nearly £1 billion.[3] Astronomical sponsorship deals have become common.

Michael Jordan is estimated as being the highest paid sportsman in the world.[4] His earnings from personal endorsements far exceed his salary for playing. Jack Nicklaus, who has not been a top golf player for many years, is still one of the highest paid sportsmen due to his endorsements. Sport is now clearly big business.

---

1   Barnes, S, 'Zero-rated', *The Times*, 9 December 1995, p 46.

2   'BSkyB football deal faces new OFT probe', *The Observer*, 23 June 1996, p 1.

3   The European Broadcasting Union have secured European television rights from the International Olympic Committee for the summer and winter games until 2008 for £961.3 million ($1.442 billion). This was in opposition to a bid of £13 million by Rupert Murdoch which would have seen the Olympics primarily on satellite TV, see Culf, A, '£961m bid wins Olympics for BBC', *The Guardian*, 31 January 1996, p 20. The American television rights alone for the Atlanta Games were sold for $456 million. The same rights for the USA for the Sydney Games of 2000 have already been sold for $705 million, an increase in revenue of just over 50%.

4   'Rivers of dollars flow with Jordan', *The Observer*, 9 April 1995, p 15.

This chapter will provide an account of how the vast majority of elite professional sport is increasingly dominated by commercial interests. The changes in British football will be used to illustrate this process. The competing economic models of sport will be briefly examined and the financial regulatory framework will be evaluated. One major source of money in sport is gambling, and as with all its forms, there are opportunities for corruption. Football more than any other British sport has been subject to financial scandals, some of those connected to gambling, others generally concerning ineffective regulatory accountability of financial transactions. The amount of money being received by football has increased many times during the 1990s. There is an obvious clash between two cultures, that of normal financial probity, and that of football, perhaps other sports too, where idiosyncratic and often illegal financial dealings has been understood as normal.

The process of commodification will be explained. This is the process whereby social activities such as sport become increasingly commercialised and seen primarily as a product, a commodity to be consumed. This process is seen as having negative consequences and leads to the question of whether sport is inherently different to other forms of entertainment and should be safeguarded from just being another commodity. This process will be illustrated by two sports, cricket and rugby, both of which have gone through considerable changes in recent times. The move from amateurism to professionalism and the pretence of the former in the guise of 'shamateurism' will be discussed in the context of rugby and athletics. Finally, the role of television and sport in the above issues will be briefly discussed.

The underlying theme is that for good or bad, modern sport is big business.

COMMERCIALISATION OF SPORT

Hofmann, D and Greenberg, M, *Sport$biz*

Sports has become a modern merchandising monster. And it eats money. Incredible amounts of money. Mind-boggling mounds of money. *Sports Inc* magazine conducted a study in 1987 to try to find out just how much money, and the results were right out of a Pentagon budget session. The magazine pegged the gross national sports product at $50.2 billion.

That is more than we spend in this country on oil and coal and even automobiles. It is about 1% of the gross national product. In other words, for every hundred dollars that changes hands in the United States, a buck finds its way to one kind of game or another.

Not only that, but the creature gets bigger every year. Most of us play or watch something. If we do not, we buy products or services from companies with big investments in athletes or athletics. Even little old ladies in tennis shoes get the shoes with Boris Becker's autograph on them.[5]

Sport has become an ideal medium for sponsorship and advertising, mainly due to the vast exposure on television. This has led to a debate concerning the extent to which sport is in control of sponsors and television companies. Additionally a specific issue concerns whether there should be prohibitions on alcohol and tobacco advertising, and this will be discussed later.[6] As has been noted earlier, much of the law's involvement in sport concerns the regulation of these commercial dealings.

It is interesting to see how some sports in Britain became commercialised in the early years of being in an organised form, and others did not. Wray Vamplew notes how at the end of the 19th century, some sports such as football became fully commercialised and others, such as cricket, decided not to go down that path and indeed he shows how the cricket establishment positively resisted commercial opportunities.[7] However, although football has been run as a business since the birth of the professional game, it has rarely been seen as a serious way to make money. The investors have often been local business people uninterested in a return on their money.

FOOTBALL: AN EXAMPLE

For the most successful football clubs today, a return on investment is considered vital.[8] Although we have seen the recent emergence of multi-millionaire benefactors such as Jack Hayward at Blackburn Rovers and Jack Warner at Wolverhampton Wanderers, who are portrayed as indulging their philanthropy in childhood allegiances, Britain has also seen the rise of entrepreneurs such as Sir John Hall at Newcastle, who sees a football club as he would any other business. They provide an opportunity to make money and must be run as such. Since the early 1990s there has been a trickle of clubs including Manchester United and Tottenham Hotspurs becoming Public Limited Companies listed on the Stock Exchange. In 1996 and 1997 this

---

5   Hofmann, D and Greenberg, MJ, *Sport$biz* (1989), Champaign Illinois: Leisure Press, p xi.
6   See Chapter 6.
7   Vamplew, W, *Pay up and Play the Game* (1989), Cambridge University Press.
8   See Corry, D, Williamson, P and Moore, S, *A Game Without Vision: The Crisis in English Football* (1993), London: Institute for Public Policy Research; Boon, G, 'Is Football a Going Concern' (1994) 3(3) *Sport and the Law Journal* 24; Fynn, A and Guest, L, *Out of Time* (1994), London: Pocket Books and Boon, G and Thorpe, D, 'Going Concern Considerations in Relation to Football Clubs' (1995) 3 *Sport and the Law Journal* 44, for an analysis of the financial state of football.

development has increased,[9] and football is being promoted as a worthwhile investment for individual and institutional investors.[10] However the financial picture for some football clubs is not so rosy.[11] In Italy, many clubs are owned and controlled by multinational companies and magnates,[12] although it is interesting to see the Italian club, AC Milan moving to be listed on the London Stock Exchange.[13] Other sports such as cricket, rugby league and rugby union have much greater incomes than ever before. The position of rugby union and league will be discussed in detail later. However many sports are in financial straits; increasingly survival is reliant upon attracting sponsorship and television interest.

The decision by the European Court of Justice in *Bosman*[14] is one that has already caused many changes in the financial dynamics of football and other sports. Its impact is such that the case will probably cause many more changes in the future.[15] The facts of *Bosman* will be discussed at length later in the context of employment and the freedom to move to a new employer without the requirement for the payment of a transfer fee.[16] The importance of *Bosman* has principally been the questioning of the legality of the transfer system. The likelihood of a successful challenge under European law was one that had been noted for quite a period of time – it was perhaps only a question of when someone would bring a discrimination case to court.[17] The *Bosman* decision ruled Article 48 of the Treaty of Rome and freedom of movement provisions, but largely ignored the position as far as Articles 85–86 concerning controls on anti-competitive practices. This last issue may well be revisited by the European Court of Justice in a future sporting case.

A major issue in British Football is that the gap between the rich elite clubs and the smallest clubs in the lower professional leagues has widened. *Bosman*

---

9   Leeds United have been brought by the Caspian Leisure Group and are part of their Stock Market listing; Newcastle, Queen's Park Rangers and Sunderland are amongst other clubs. See, 'Football Fever sees City United', *The Guardian*, 18 January 1997, p 13; 'Soccer in the City: Top Clubs, High Finance and Fickle Fashions', *The Guardian*, 7 February 1997, p 2; 'Float values football club at more than £150m', *The Guardian*, 17 January 1997, p 22.

10   'Football Fund Attracting Big Crowds', *Daily Telegraph*, 11 May 1997, p 3.

11   'Millwall ask players for pay cut', *The Guardian*, 11 February 1997, p 22.

12   For example in Italy, AC Milan is owned by the Italian media mogul and ex-president, Silvio Berlusconi.

13   'AC Milan plan pounds 500m London stock market float', *The Guardian*, 25 February 1997, p 3.

14   *Union Royale Belge des Societés de Football Association ASBL and Jean-Marc Bosman* Case C-415/93, 15 December 1995

15   See Miller, F, 'Beyond *Bosman*' (1996) 4(3) *Sport and the Law Journal* 45.

16   See Chapter 7 and Farrell, R, 'Transfer Fees and Restraint of Trade' (1996) 4(3) *Sport and the Law Journal* 54.

17   See Weatherill, S, 'Discrimination on Grounds of Nationality in Sport', in *Yearbook of European Law 1989* (1990), Oxford: Clarendon Press, p 55 and Miller, F, and Redhead, S, 'Do Markets make Footballers Free' in Bale, J and Maguire, J (eds), *The Global Sports Arena: Athletic Talent Migration in an Interdependent World* (1994), London: Frank Cass.

is likely to increase this division. The long-term implications of this decision are not easy to foresee. The potential problematic consequences of the decision are seen as including the fatal threat to the lower division professional or semi-professional clubs. It is argued that the transfer system has acted in the past as 'a powerful mechanism for redistributing wealth'.[18]

Boon, G, '1996 Football Survey'

The financing of clubs in the lower divisions is clearly a cause for concern. With escalating wage bills and less money filtering down from the top clubs, some difficult decisions will have to be taken if professional football in England is to remain in its present form. The transfer market has historically been the saviour of many clubs, not only the smaller ones, and if this source of funding diminishes then an alternative mechanism of distributing monies to the lower divisions' clubs, perhaps through a re-distribution of TV income, will have to be found to save clubs from either going part-time or out of business completely.[19]

The accountants Deloitte & Touche in their 1997 survey of English Football Clubs Accounts[20] found that £25.2 million of the £139.6 million spent on players' transfers in the season 1995/1996 between the 92 English professional clubs (excluding players purchased from Scottish and overseas clubs) moved from the Premier League to the other three Football League divisions. This was up from £9.5 million the previous season. The vast majority of this went to Division One clubs with the amount of money received by Divisions Two and Three, falling dramatically. The view that the saviour of poorer clubs is often the transfer market where 'home grown' players are sold to the more profitable clubs for substantial sums may becoming less persuasive.

The 1997 report clearly indicates that the rich clubs are getting richer and the poor clubs are getting poorer.

Deloitte & Touche, 'Annual Review of Football Finance'

The Premier League continues to dominate football finance. It generates two-thirds of total football revenues, and nearly £52 million of operating profits. All this is before any impact of the new BSkyB deal or pay per view television is felt.

Success breeds success and in the Premier League operating profitability and League position are highly correlated. Seven of those clubs in the top 10 League positions were in the top 10 ranked Premier League clubs at operating level. The correlation is not as strong in the lower divisions, where wages are a much larger drain. While the top three wage payers in the Premier League were the top three finishers in the League, they had sufficient income for them to still be profitable. In Division Two the top four wage payers finished in the

---

18 Lee, M, 'A Game of Two Halves: Putting the Boot in' (1995) *New Statesman and Society* 27.

19 Boon, G, 'Football Survey' (1996) 4(2) *Sport and the Law Journal* 46.

20 *Ibid,* Boon (1996); also see Boon, G, 'Soccer Scores in the Business League' (1994) 2 *Sport and the Law Journal* 23; '1995 Football Survey' (1995) 3 *Sport and the Law Journal* 36.

top four positions, but represented four of the five biggest operating loss makers in the Division.

The 'average' club in the Premier League is now better off to the tune of £3.8 million at the operating profit level when compared to an 'average' Division One club which is now spending even more heavily than in previous years in the hope of attaining Premier League status. Division One clubs spent £26 million more than they earned in 1995/96, making a total deficit of £50 million in the last three years.

The promise of riches from television has coaxed clubs to part with millions on overseas transfers – a net £126 million having flowed out of England in the 1994/95 and 1995/96 seasons! But it is not all a bed of financial roses in the Premier League. After transfers and interest charges, the Premier League lost a staggering £62.4 million in 1995/96. Indeed, take out Manchester United and pre-tax losses of the Premier League would be nearly £80 million – or £4 million per club! When the losses of £35.9 million in The Football League are taken into account, the English game as a whole lost £98 million in 1995/96 – a figure dramatically distorted by treating transfer costs as a write-off, rather than as an asset.

Football finance will become even more distinctly polarised between the big clubs at the top of the Premier League, and the small clubs in The Football League. To put it all in perspective there won't be a big difference between what Premier League clubs generate from TV next season, and what the whole of The Football League was able to turnover for the 1995/96 season. In financial terms the trapdoor has nearly closed!

The amount of money in football dramatically increases each season – but football knows how to spend it! Perhaps the requirements of a relatively new, recently much increased, audience – the stock market investor – will prove a tempering influence on football's propensity to spend? Longer-term we believe this will be right, but in the short-term the scramble to position clubs amongst the longer-term winners in the game (a number less than twenty, or even eighteen) is actually discouraging thrift.[21]

Despite Bosman, transfer activity is greater than ever. Something like £250 million was spent by English clubs in 1995/96 – over three quarters of it by the Premier League. An English transfer provided the world record and Division One clubs almost doubled their spending. Given clubs' propensity to write off the cost of players as an expense, this activity blew a massive hole in football's financial results, contributing to an overall pre-tax loss of almost £100 million. But at least transfers between English clubs kept the money in the domestic game. A huge amount – £93 million – left the game entirely to go to foreign clubs. It raises an interesting question: who, after television, is the highest financier of continental football? The answer could well be the English Premier League![22]

Total wages – in particular players' wages – continue to grow faster than turnover. Only the Premier League has the revenue base to support the wages

---

21 Boon, G (ed), *Annual Review of Football Finance*, Deloitte & Touche, August 1997, p 23.

22 *Ibid*, p 28.

it pays. Even so, the rate of increase there (surely in anticipation of the much heralded TV deal) cannot be sustained for many more years in any other than a few financially sound clubs.

Some Football League Clubs are gambling on paying high wages in an attempt to join the Premier League. Examples such as Millwall highlight the risks of this strategy, and the profound financial damage that results and worsens with each passing year. Most Football League clubs are running wage bills which exceed two-thirds of turnover excluding transfer fees. Fourteen clubs have wage bills which exceed their turnovers. If Football League turnovers and wages continue to grow at current rates then wage bills will exceed turnovers for The Football League as a whole within six years. The alarm bells are ringing!

Premiership wages will continue to rise due to changes in the transfer system and increasing television and commercial revenue streams. Competition to achieve Premiership status will ncrease and more clubs will take higher risks to achieve it – even though the numbers don't stack up. And the safety net of being able to sell a player to balance the books will be partially removed as a result of *Bosman*. Ultimately, those clubs that miss out on the Premier League will only achieve a long-term viable future by maximising commercial income and controlling player wages. Many painful decisions have yet to be taken – they cannot be avoided for much longer.[23]

The English game suffered a massive loss during 1995/96, wiping out more than 40% of its net assets. We should, perhaps, rationalise this as a conscious and premeditated strategy followed with open eyes through a substantial increase in transfer spending on overseas players. It's a moot point whether the English Premier League is now a major financier of Italian football. If annual losses continue at this level, the game will have serious financial problems. And those will be much more widespread than is presently recognised.

The principal reason that the game has been able to continue is the amount of money now coming into football from BSkyB. This review is based on the accounts of clubs for 1995/96, the year before the effects of the current TV deal began to impact. The full effect of the new deal will not be fully felt for a while, but it is clear that the banks were prepared to lend to clubs in 1996 in anticipation of the funds coming through in later years. And the clubs were prepared to spend it. The Stock Exchange has undoubtedly provided significant further funds in the 1996/97 season.

The change seen in the financing of the game during 1995/96 is not good news for the clubs in Division Two and Division Three. Whilst banks have been happy to support the game as a whole, this has been concentrated into a smaller number of larger clubs, leaving the smallest clubs reliant upon loans from other sources – 'financial supporters'. As we said in our last review – making no comment on the validity of any particular view – with the changing state of the transfer market, it is inevitable that either the structure of the game changes or that the smaller clubs receive bigger support payments. The consequence of inaction is either an ever increasing need for 'financial supporter' involvement or a number of clubs going to the wall for good. One

---

23   *Ibid*, p 33.

thing is clear; as limited companies, the responsibility rests firmly with each individual club's Board of Directors.[24]

If there is some redistribution of money from the Premier League clubs to the Football League it is minimal. As Sir John Hall, Chairman of Newcastle United, argues, 'the trickle down effect is a bit of a myth ... the really big money has circulated in the last five years ... in the Premier League or the top of the First Division'.[25] He believes that to rely on this money circulating around the system is to rely on 'old money rotating between the same clubs'.[26] From this perspective, the future of football lies in the new opportunities that exist in making money from sponsorship and marketing and the great increase in the revenue from television rights. The deal worth £125 million negotiated in 1996 for coverage of the Football League can be used as illustration and will help compensate the lower clubs who will lose out from transfer fee revenue.

The relationship between the powerful top clubs and the lower divisions will change. One possible development is that the lower division clubs will become training and farming clubs for the elite. Such a system exists in professional sports in the United States such as baseball and in football in countries such as Spain. The elite clubs own the 'farm club' or 'nursery club' and the promising player learns his trade playing at the lower level and then hopefully will progress. In English football, such relationships cannot operate due to prohibitions on multiple ownership. However informal relationships can develop such as the one that exists between Liverpool and Crewe Alexandra.[27]

One of the problems with a formal structure is that this hierarchical relationship also provides a break on the normal dynamics of relegation and promotion. Farm teams cannot compete with their parent and could not be promoted to a higher league if the parent is there already. In all the four American team sports, there is no promotion to or relegation from the top league. The farm team will always be the poor relation and the inability of these smaller clubs to break through into the big time increases the centralisation and oligopoly of a small number of elite clubs. Even without the development of such a formal system, it is viewed by many that the emergence and rise of clubs such as Barnsley, Watford and Wimbledon will no longer be possible in the post-Bosman era.[28] Connected with this argument

---

24   *Ibid*, p 44.

25   'Bosman the Man for Hall Seasons', *Independent on Sunday*, 10 December 1995.

26   *Ibid*.

27   'Small Clubs have to accept Hand that Feeds them', *The Times*, 3 March 1997, p 37.

28   Note the reported plans for Wimbledon to move from South London to alternative locations in Dublin or Cardiff, 19 December 1995. This perhaps reflects a money driven weakening of the ties between club and locality with television being able to substitute for the loss of the loyalty of local supporters. We are not yet though seeing the 'franchise' system that operates in the USA.

is the view that the elite clubs need to invest more money in finding and nurturing home grown talent. However, there is evidence that this can lead to very sharp practices by clubs desperate to sign promising youngsters with many questionable inducements, as has been recognised with clubs such as Manchester United, who came under investigation by the FA.[29]

THE ECONOMICS OF SPORT

It is clear that the early corporatism of professional clubs in England, in the sense of each club being mutually reliant on each other, is a thing of the past. There may be alliances between groups of clubs but these are shifting ones and tend to be around particular single issues. But as generally with sport, and unlike most other businesses, football clubs have a mutual interest in each other's business health. Each club plays each other. In team sport the product to be marketed is the game itself. Therefore no single team can sell the product itself. A team needs to play another in a league or cup. There is a need for competition and although this may be keen on the field, the clubs are dependent on each other to a much greater extent than in other businesses.

A major issue is how sports are to be structured and financed in the professional world of team sports. There are various economic models that can be applied to the structure of sport. Two possibilities are a structure that emphasises 'win maximisation' with profits being reasonably unimportant, and one of 'profit maximisation' where generating of profits is the main aim. The former model reflects the traditional view of team sports in Europe where even in football most professional clubs make a loss in the long run. The latter model characterises American team sport.

In American sport, a number of systems work to provide a financial structure particularly in terms of regulation of the labour market. In the early days of all the main American sports, a player reservation system of 'reserve clauses' gave clubs exclusive rights over the services of each player registered to them. The player was only free if the rights were traded to another club. This process was similar to the transfer system in a number of European sports. As a distribution of player talent evenly between teams, it seems that the reserve clause or transfer system is not a very effective mechanism.[30] In terms of wealth distribution, the transfer system has worked to some degree and has facilitated in Britain the perpetuation of 92 professional clubs.

---

29   See 'Coaching and Poaching', *Fair Game*, Channel 4, 3 June 1996.
30   See Cooke, A, *The Economics of Leisure and Sport* (1994), London: Routledge; El-Hodri, M and Quirck, J, 'An Economic Model of a Professional Sport League' (1971) *Journal of Political Economy*; Cairns, J, Njennet, S and Sloane, P, 'The Economics of Professional Team Sports: A Survey of Theory and Evidence' (1986) 8(2) *Journal of Economic Studies*.

Some professional team sports in the US, such as football and baseball, have accepted a system of revenue sharing between clubs in order to help guarantee a reasonable degree of competition and uncertainty of outcome. In American football, the gate receipts are split 60/40 between home and away team and broadcasting rights are almost equally divided.

Another attempt to improve the competitive balance in US sports leagues is the so-called salary cap. This is a league-wide maximum on team payrolls, but not on individual salaries. It has been suggested that a salary cap is the most effective way to do bring about competitive balance in a league.[31] With the same overall money spent by each team on their players, all teams have roughly the same strength. Enforcement problems exist though: the large teams have to stay below the cap, the small teams have a problem affording it and may need subsidising. The National Basketball Association (NBA) has perhaps been the most successful professional league and has seen enormous growth over the last 10 years. The salary cap that has operated reflects the growth in the revenue capacity of the NBA: it was set at $3.6 million in the 1984–85 season and rose to $23 million in 1995–96 season. League revenues have increased from $135 million in 1982 to $925 million in 1994. The NBA is moving to expand into a global market.[32]

Kesenne, S, 'What Player Market Regulation, if any, is Needed in Professional Team Sports'

If European sports clubs are indeed non-profit organisations as distinct from the American clubs, the results of economic research shows that there is a case for some regulation of the sector by the league authorities in order to guarantee a more balanced competition. However the transfer system turns out to be totally ineffective in that respect. If the salary cap seems to be effective in the profit maximising US world of professional sports, it raises some doubts in the non-profit European sports sector. If one conclusion from our research can be drawn for European professional team sports, this conclusion will be that revenue sharing between teams in a league is the best way to guarantee a more balanced competition without running into the ethical and legal problems of the transfer market.[33]

---

31 Quirk, J and Fort, RD, *Pay Dirt: The Business of Professional Team Sports* (1992), Ewing, New Jersey: Princeton University Press. Also see Farrell, R, 'Salary Caps and Restraint of Trade' (1997) 5(1) *Sport and the Law Journal* 53.

32 See Greenberg, MJ, 'The NBA – A Model for Success' (1995) 3 *Sport and the Law Journal* 9.

33 Kesenne, S, 'What Player's Market Regulation, if any, is Needed in Professional Team Sports?', *Conference Paper University of Neuchatel*, February 1995.

Gambling and Sport

Gambling and sport have almost been inseparable and gambling has been subject to considerable regulation by the State. Gambling has close links with the general commercialisation of sport and with corruption in sport. An extended extract on gambling follows, again looking at its historical context, with an aim to understanding its vast significance within modern sport:

Mason, T, *Sport in Britain*

Gambling has always been a part of the modern sporting world, although the public response to it has varied from one period to another. Gambling was endemic in 18th century Britain, but before 1850 a puritanical reaction had begun, aimed particularly at working class betting. The greatest achievement of the anti-gambling lobby was probably the Street Betting Act 1906, but it remained a powerful and influential opponent certainly up until the second Royal Commission on the subject in 1949. Since then gambling on sport has been increasingly raided by governments to provide income for the State and has also played a crucial role in the financing of the major sports of football and horse racing.

Betting had always been a part of rural sports, both those involving animals, such as cock fighting and bear baiting, and those involving contests between men. Pedestrianism, for example, probably began in the 17th and 18th centuries, when aristocrats and gentry promoted races between their footmen. These men had been used as message carriers between town house and country residence, although this function lapsed as roads improved and coaches became speedier and more reliable. Their masters often gambled heavily on the results of such races. Sometimes the young master ran himself. Pedestrianism, like prize-fighting, seems to have enjoyed a fashionable period from about 1790–1810. It could almost be characterised as the jogging of the early 19th century. Its most famous gentlemanly practitioner was Captain Barclay, a Scottish landowner whose real name was Robert Barclay Allardice. He was prepared to bet 1,000 guineas in 1801 that he would walk 90 miles in 21 and a half hours. He failed twice and lost his money each time. But on 10 November 1801 he did it, for a stake of 5,000 guineas.

Betting on horses was also commonplace, often taking the form of individual challenges between members of the landed classes. In the 18th century it was the usual practice to ride your own horse, but the employment of a professional jockey became increasingly common. Betting added another dimension of excitement to the uncertainty of sport itself and it was excitement which the leisured rural classes were especially seeking, particularly in a countryside whose range of more conventional pursuits soon began to pall in the eyes of the young, married, leisured, pleasure seeking males.

Cricket was another rural pastime that the landed bucks found attractive. By the beginning of the 18th century newspaper advertisements told of forthcoming matches 'between 11 gentlemen of a west part of the county of Kent, against as many of Chatham, for 11 guineas a man'. With money at stake it was important to reduce the chances of disagreement by drawing up a body of rules and regulations by which both sides would abide. In this way gambling made its contribution to the development of the laws of cricket. In fact, in the code of 1774 it was specifically mentioned:

> If the Notches of one player are laid against another, the Bet depends on both Innings, unless otherwise specified. If one Party beats the other in one Innings, the Notches in the first Innings shall determine the Bet. But if the other Party goes in a Second Time then the Bet must be determined by the numbers on the score.

Football was, of course a very attractive proposition both to bookmakers and punters. Before 1900 some newspapers had offered prizes for forecasting the correct scores as well as the results of a small number of matches and early in the 20th century a system of betting on football coupons at fixed odds had developed in the north of England. It has been suggested that the early pools might have been partly emulating the pigeon pools by which a prize fund was collected for a particular pigeon race, with each competitor subscribing. The owner of the winning bird collected.

Newspapers began publishing their own pools coupons (until the Courts declared the practice illegal in 1928) and individual bookmakers offered a variety of betting opportunities. By the end of the 1920s, the football pools, and particularly Littlewoods, under the entrepreneurial guidance of the Moores brothers, had begun to thrive. The pool for one week in 1929–30 reached £19,000. By the mid-1930s the firm was sponsoring programmes on Radio Luxembourg which broadcast the results of matches on Saturdays and Sundays. The football coupon asked backers to forecast the results of a given number of matches from a long list or a selected short list. The latter was given attractive names like 'family four' and 'easy six', 'three draws' or 'four aways'. In January 1935 the penny points was introduced and soon became the favourite pool with the largest dividends, consisting of fourteen matches chosen for their special degree of difficulty. The eight draw treble chance replaced it as the most popular pool after 1945. By 1935 estimates put the number of punters at between five and seven million and it was 10 million by the time war broke out. In 1934 those companies founding the Pools Promoters' Association had a turnover of about £8 million which had increased by 1938 to £22 million of which the promoters retained a little over 20%. This is not the place to animadvert on the place of the pools in British society.

By the mid-19th century, therefore, betting and sport were firmly established as the closest of associates. But the middle class evangelicalism of the new urban industrial Britain was already beginning to take steps against what was increasingly characterised as a social evil. Gambling was typical of a corrupt aristocracy and it served them right if it led to the sale of their estates and the impoverishment of ancient families. But when the poor were led to emulate those who should have set a better example then something had to be done. By 1850 the State was being pressurised into doing it. The arguments used by the opponents of working class betting remained more or less unchanged for the next 100 years. Betting by the poor led to debt which led to crime. Even where crime was avoided, deterioration of character was not, especially among the young and women. Spending sums on betting which could not be afforded weakened the material basis of family life thereby making a major contribution to poverty. Finally gambling undermined proper attitudes to work. As *The Times* so succinctly put it in the 1890s, it 'eats the heart out of honest labour. It produces an impression that life is governed by chance and not by laws'. These arguments carried most days until the Royal Commission of 1949–51.

The anti-gamblers first legislative success was an Act of 1853 to suppress betting houses and betting shops which had been springing up in many places, very often inside public houses. In future, bookmakers operating from such places, exhibiting lists or in any way informing the public that they were prepared to take bets were liable to a fine of £100 and a six month prison sentence. The Bill went through both Houses without a debate. Betting shops may have found difficulty in surviving: betting itself moved outside to the streets and places of employment. The expansion of horse racing in particular, with after 1870, the electric telegraph and a cheap press providing tips and results, provoked the opposition to organise itself, which eventually resulted in the formation of the National Anti-Gambling League. It was in its heyday in the two decades or so before 1914. Sociologists such as BS Rowntree, the economist JA Hobson and radical politicians like J Ramsay MacDonald contributed to its publications. They saw the working class gambler exploited by the bookmaker and those upper class sportsmen who supported him. After failing with the law the League turned to Parliament with the clear aim of eradicating street betting. It was this off-course variety which was responsible for the bulk of working class gambling. A House of Lords Select Committee first examined the matter in 1901–02. In 1906 came the legislation.

The Street Betting Act of 1906 has gained some notoriety as an example of class biased legislation. It was not aimed at all off-course betting. A person who could afford an account with a bookmaker who knew his financial circumstances well enough to allow him to bet on credit did not have a problem. This ruled out many working men and women. It was ready money betting of the sort they went in for that was to be prosecuted. In future it was to be an offence for any person to frequent or loiter in a street or public place on behalf of himself or any other person for the purpose of bookmaking or betting or wagering or agreeing to bet or wager or paying or receiving or settling bets.

It is unlikely that the Act did much to diminish the amount of betting. It did of course enhance the excitement of it all, especially at those times and in those places where local magistrates decided that the full rigour of the law must be enforced. Moreover it placed the police in an increasingly difficult position trying to enforce a law for which there was little popular support. Allegations that they frequently looked the other way or had an agreement with local bookmakers to prosecute a runner from each of them in turn were commonplace. By 1929 the police were very critical of both the law and their role in enforcing it and said so before the Royal Commission which was examining the police service in that year. It took the liberalising impact of the Second World War and the relatively buoyant economic circumstances which eventually succeeded it to bring about a more relaxed attitude to gambling. This was also facilitated by the Royal Commission of 1949–51 having relatively sophisticated economic and statistical apparatus which enabled it to show that personal expenditure on gambling was only about 1% of total personal expenditure, that gambling was then absorbing only about 0.5% of the total resources of the country and that it was by then rare for it to be a cause of poverty in individual households. They still regarded gambling as a fairly low level activity and were not impressed by the amount of intellectual effort some enthusiasts brought to it. But they were in favour of the provision of legal facilities for betting off the course and the licensed betting shop reappeared in 1960, 107 years after it had first been made illegal. Six years later the government's betting duty reappeared too.

Gambling's relationship with sport has been significant in two other respects: as a motive for malpractice and corruption and as a source of finance for sporting activities. The latter is closely connected to the growth of football pools of which more in a moment. Not all sports lend themselves to result fixing with equal facility. The team games should, in theory, prove the most difficult, because there are so many more players who would have to be 'squared' if an agreed result was to be secured. In the early 19th century the relatively small number of professionals could exert a disproportionate influence on some cricket matches and they were occasionally bribed or removed from the game by false reports of sickness in the family. One professional was banned from Lord's in 1817 for allegedly 'selling' the match between England and Nottingham. The gradual assumption of authority by the MCC and the county clubs, the improvement in the material rewards of the average professional cricketer and the increasing opportunities to bet on other sports – notably horse racing and, after 1926, greyhound racing – probably killed off gambling on cricket by cricketers. Today the Test and County Cricket Board (TCCB) has a regulation forbidding players to gamble on matches in which they take part. It was thought to be overly cynical even by late 20th century standards when Dennis Lillee and Rodney Marsh won £5,000 and £2,500 respectively by betting against their own team, Australia, in the Leeds Test of 1981. By then, of course, betting by spectators could be encouraged because it brought in revenue. Ladbrokes had been allowed to pitch their tent at Lord's since 1973.

Football has occasionally been shaken by allegations that matches have been thrown, usually in the context of championship, promotion or relegation struggles. Attempts to fix the results of matches in order to bring off betting coups appear to have been very rare but in 1964, 10 players received prison sentences for their part in a so-called betting ring. Three of the players were prominent English internationals and they were banned from football playing and management for life. Two, Peter Swan and David Layne, were later re-instated on appeal but by then were too old to take up where they had left off. Certainly the FA and the Football League were anxious to keep betting and football apart. When coupon betting first appeared in the North of England, before 1914, the FA Council threatened to suspend permanently any player or official who could be proved to have taken part in it. In 1913 they failed, but in 1920 succeeded in getting Parliament to push through a Bill forbidding ready money betting on football matches.

Football itself had not profited from the growth of pools. But it seems clear that early in 1935 discussions were taking place between the League's Management

Committee and representatives of the Pools Promoters' Association about the possibility of the pools making a payment to the League for the use of their fixtures. But the public attitude of many of the leaders of League football was that the pools constituted a menace to the game and should be suppressed either by the action of the football authorities or by State intervention via an Act of Parliament. The negotiations broke down, perhaps because the pools promoters did not wish to pay what was being asked so long as there was some doubt about whether the fixtures were copyright. All out war was declared and an attempt made to damage the pools by secretly changing the fixtures on two consecutive Saturdays at the end of February and the beginning of March 1936. Unfortunately for the Football League, dissension in the ranks led to the plans being leaked and the scheme sank. They had no better luck with a Private Members' Bill to abolish the pools which was easily defeated in the Commons in the same year. Moreover, the League felt it did not need tainted money from the pools, whose promoters therefore kept their hands in their pockets. They did not take them out again until 1959 (although they offered to, briefly, at the end of the war).

It is hard to escape the feeling that not only football but sport in Britain missed a real financial opportunity, although it is clear that it would have required government help to have realised it. In the 1930s the private firms running British football pools set up offices and agencies in several European countries. In Sweden, for example, where betting on pools was illegal, around 200,000 people were completing coupons every week, the stake money swelling the profits of Littlewoods and Vernons among others. The Swedish government acted to stop it in 1934 by establishing the Swedish Betting Corporation to run a State owned pool. Switzerland and Finland soon followed and by 1950 similar State run pools had begun in Norway, Spain, Italy, West Germany, Denmark and Austria. Later Poland, Czechoslovakia, Belgium and Holland adopted similar schemes. After administration and prize money had been found, much of what remained was channelled into the support not merely of football but of sport and physical recreation in general. For example £8 million had been so raised by the Swedish government over a three year period at the end of the 1930s. There were three moments when a similar scheme might have been set up in this country.

The first was early in the Second World War when it was clear that some rationalisation of existing commercial institutions in a range of fields would have to take place. The Secretary of the Football Association, Stanley Rous, together with Sir Arthur Elvin, who ran Wembley Stadium, proposed the creation of an independent pools company, half of whose profits would go to football. Nothing came of it. Instead the government agreed to an amalgamation of the existing companies for the duration. It was known as Unity Pools.

Rous returned to the problem with even more radical proposals in 1943. Reconstruction was in the air and he had been finding out about Sweden in particular. Rous proposed that appropriate government departments should be approached with the suggestion that part of the proceeds from the pools should go into a centrally administered fund, out of which would come money for sports grounds, gymnasia, recreation rooms and sports centres. Again nothing came of it.

The subject was raised for a third time during the sitting of the Royal Commission on Betting Lotteries and Gaming 1949–51. The English, Scottish and Welsh Football Associations all supported the idea of a non-profit-making football pool under government control. But the Commission disagreed, partly because they felt a considerable body of public opinion would not like it, partly because of practical difficulties and partly because of the loss of revenue to the government. If there had been a moment for such radical change, it must have been during those reforming years of the third Labour government. By 1951, its legs were very shaky indeed. Moreover it had been the Labour government that had instituted a 10% tax on the pools in 1947 and increased it to 30% in 1949. Football, of course, could always do its own deal with the pools and in the summer of 1959 it did. In the previous October the Football League had issued a writ against Littlewoods claiming that the League fixtures for the following season were its copyright. In May 1959 a judge agreed. By July an agreement had been signed, to last for 10 years, by which the Pools Promoters' Association was to pay the Football League and the Scottish League a royalty of 0.5% on total stake money, which would not be less than £245,000 a year. There have been several subsequent agreements, the latest a 12 year one signed in December 1984 which ensures the Football League £5 million per year. This, though, is but a small proportion of the income of the pools companies, three of whom – Littlewoods, Vernons and Zetters – paid the government £220 million in tax in 1984–95 but still made a profit of £17 million.

The treatment of football was different to that of horse racing. The government did not introduce a tax on gambling on horse racing until 1966. In 1985 it was still being levied at only 8%. As we saw above, the tax on pools betting came much earlier and was much higher: 42% in 1985. When betting shops were legalised the government established a Horserace Betting Levy Board, allegedly to compensate racecourses for the fall in attendance that would ensue. Its role was to assess and collect a levy from bookmakers and the tote and use the money for the benefit of racing. According to the leading authority on the subject, the Levy Board saved racing in this country. Perhaps there should be a Football Betting Levy Board. It is not clear why there has not been. British sport has had to get on terms with gambling in the 20th century; it seems that the terms could have been better.[34]

Betting on sport is growing in popularity, with many new forms such as spread betting.[35] Specialist companies now operate to give advice and odds.[36] The regulatory framework of the British betting industry has been liberalised during the first half of the 1990s.

---

34 Mason, T, *Sport in Britain* (1988), London: Faber and Faber, pp 59–68.

35 'Bookies bet on a football bonanza', *The Observer*, 7 January 1996, p 6.

36 See Hunter, W, *Football Fortunes: Results, Forecasting, Gambling and Computing* (1996), Harpenden: Oldcastle Books; 'A Good Bet', *Fair Game*, Channel 4, 22 May 1995.

SPORT BABYLON: FRAUD AND CORRUPTION

What seems certain, is that increased money in sport leads to more opportunities for fraudulent and corrupt activities. Although certainly not the first,[37] the most recent corruption scandal in football has concerned the allegations of match fixing against Bruce Grobbelaar, Hans Segers and John Fashanu.[38] At their first trial, the prosecution allegations were that Grobbelaar whilst playing for Liverpool and Segers for Wimbledon, let in goals to try to achieve certain results and thereby fix matches in Premier League games during the 1993–94 season. In addition it was alleged that there was a conspiracy involving Fashanu acting as a middle-man in the payment of sums to the two goalkeepers for a Malaysian businessman, Heng Suam Lim. At their first trial, lasting 34 days, the jury could not reach a verdict.[39] At their second trial, with the prosecution only relying on the conspiracy to defraud charges, the four were acquitted. It has been estimated that the two trials have cost more than £10 million.[40]

The allegation were first made by Grobbelaar's ex-business partner Chris Vincent in *The Sun* newspaper. Mr Vincent, who became the chief prosecution witness, told the jury that Grobbelaar had spoken of earning 'big bucks' to 'chuck' games. He claimed the goalkeeper received £40,000 from Lim via Fashanu, for his help in fixing one result and expected to earn at least £250,000 more from rigging other results, which he failed to deliver. He was also seen on video, covertly recorded by *The Sun* newspaper, discussing match fixing and accepting £2,000 from a bogus syndicate devised by the paper to establish if he was prepared to throw games. In court Grobbelaar claimed he was stringing Vincent along, trying to discover more about who he was working with before going to the authorities. The allegations were that Grobbelaar let in goals in a number of matches including one against Newcastle when Andy Cole scored a first half hat-trick.

In the two trials, the prosecution alleged that after police enquired into Fashanu, Lim and Segers after the initial newspaper allegations, they uncovered telephone links and large sums of money being paid into bank accounts which proved they were also involved in a conspiracy. But the defence argued that Vincent was exaggerating a forecasting service which Grobbelaar and Segers were providing for Lim and his paymasters, a Far East gambling syndicate. They also had other legitimate sources which accounted

---

37 See Tongue, S, 'Bribery and Corruption: English Football's Biggest Ever Match Fixing Scandal', *Total Sport*, March 1997, p 52.

38 Also note conviction of the former president of Olympic de Mareille, Bernard Tapie for match fixing, 'Tapie just a Scapegoat for Paris', *The Guardian*, 16 May 1995, p 22.

39 'Footballers face new trial', *The Guardian*, 5 March 1997, p 3; and 'Footballers to face £750,000 retrial in match fixing case', *The Guardian*, 7 March 1997, p 3.

40 'Soccer Stars cleared of Match Fixing', *Daily Telegraph*, 7 August 1997, p 1.

for the money, in Segers's case a tie-making business and in Fashanu's, various business interests, including property speculation and investments in Africa. The decision by the prosecution to only rely on a conspiracy and not to allege specific match fixing at the second trial, was largely due to the inconclusive nature of the video evidence. Expert witness from retired goalkeepers Gordon Banks and Bob Wilson supported the view that there was no evidence that the two goalkeepers aimed to 'throw a game'. After the acquittals, the FA announced that an inquiry into the internal footballing rules on betting and forecasting would be carried out by the former Deputy Commissioner of the Metropolitan Police, Sir John Smith, now a consultant to the FA.[41] The dynamics of gambling in the Far East need to be understood to explain the significance of this trial. Gambling is generally illegal in countries such as Malaysia. This does not stop large sections of the population gambling widely, and virtually any contest will attract betting. Largely because gambling is underground, prohibited rather than regulated, the opportunities for irregularities and inducements to fix matches are clear:

Raja, N, 'Sports Gambling in Malaysia'

V Thanasegar was on the brink of a brilliant career in soccer. In the 1994–95 season, he was a regular for Kedah which played in the Dunhill Cup professional league. He was only 18 then and his performance on the field prompted a call-up to train with the national youth team in Kuala Lumpur. Three days into training, a telephone call from his hometown of Alor Star changed his life. He was put on the next available flight and on arrival at the airport, he was arrested and spent the night in the cells of a police station ...

Thanasegar was one of the approximately 115 soccer players arrested on a crackdown on soccer bribery in Malaysia in 1995. Like all others, he was arrested on 'suspicion of committing an offence' and detained for 24 hours to 'facilitate' investigations under s 28 of the Criminal Procedure Code.

As expected, the police were unable to complete their 'investigations' and under s 117 of the same Code the players were produced before a magistrate who ordered them remanded into custody to enable the 'investigations' to be completed. Detention periods ranged from four days to two weeks. Lumped together with robbers, rapists and murderers in the police cells, most of the athletes broke – Thanasegar included.

He had only accepted RM500 once and claimed that he was 'forced to accept' the money from a team mate. He was released a week later, but this spelled a premature end to a promising career in the fledging professional league. He is now banned from the league for life.

Gambling is frowned upon in Malaysia. Half the population is Muslim, a religion which strictly forbids placing wagers and getting returns. There is only one licensed casino in the country of 18 million and Muslims are forbidden by law to enter. Gambling licenses have also been issued to the three turf clubs in Kuala Lumpur, Penang and Ipoh which host races on weekends on rotation.

---

41 *Ibid*, n 34.

Three companies also have licenses to operate a thrice weekly four digit lottery draw. Against this backdrop, the pressure was on the soccer administrators and the police to confirm or deny rumours that all the Dunhill Cup matches were 'fixed'. Each time a favourite lost to a bottom rung team, it was inevitable that the accusing finger was pointed to bookies who, it was alleged, paid money to key players to determine the outcome of the game.

When the nationwide arrests took place in July 1995, it came as no surprise. What astonished society was the extent to which it had existed. After all, the league matches drew crowds of up to 50,000 each and spectators had forked out up to RM20 to watch each game. The final toll was that more than a quarter of the league players had been 'implicated'.

Long after the month-long crackdown ended and after the players were unconditionally released, no charges were proffered. Most of the players made 'statements' (read confessions) in which they implicated themselves and fellow footballers. Instead of using provisions in the Anti-Corruption Act and the Penal Code to prosecute those suspected of taking bribes, the police used an antiquated statute – the Restricted Residence Act – to handle the problem.

48 players were hauled up before the Disciplinary Board of the Football Association of Malaysia. All of the players pleaded guilty to charges of 'bringing the game into disrepute'. Apparently the police had given the Association a list of those who had 'owned up' and thus the charge. All were banned from the game for periods ranging from one to five years – some were banned for life.

The word 'disrepute' appears to be wide and all encompassing. When Ian Botham admitted smoking marijuana while on a tour of Australia, the Test Cricket and Control Board charged him with bringing the game into disrepute. Each time sports administrators cannot find a clause to handle a particular problem, the 'disrepute' clause is invoked.

Through hindsight, it would be interesting to discuss how the authorities would have handled the issue if one or all 48 players had pleaded not guilty to the charge. Having inherited the British system of judiciary, in Malaysia a man is innocent until proven guilty. Therefore, what kind of evidence would the Football Association of Malaysia have used to prove their case?

Initially, the confessions made to the police would have been inadmissible because they can only be used in court proceedings and not hearings by sports bodies. Secondly, even if they had been used, the player would have claimed that he had made the confession under duress. Why then did they confess? According to one player, what was utmost on his mind was to 'admit and get out of the mess ... You do not know what it is like in detention. The cells are filthy, the food is terrible and all I wanted to do was to get home to the comforts of my bed as soon as possible. If I had challenged the confession I made, I could have been re-arrested and would have been forced to go through it all over again'.

However 12 others were not so lucky. Based on the statements, the police described them as 'hardcore' and 'ringleaders' and banished them to small towns in the country away from their usual place of residence. They could not be outdoors between dusk and dawn, they had to report to the police station once a week and they could not leave the area without the consent of the police officer in charge.

One player who was from the north was banished to the outskirts of the capital city Kuala Lumpur and openly defied the conditions. When newspapers reported frequently sighting him in nightspots, he was sent away to a remote town away from the bright lights of the city. S Raveychandran from the Borneo state of Sabah, who was banished, challenged the validity of applying the Act to footballers like him. The court held that powers vested in the Minister of Home Affairs cannot be challenged as long as 'he had complied with all the provisions of the Act'.

The question then becomes: are such arbitrary powers the answer to solving all the woes that plague sports? Is it fair to use powers of the State to handle the problems of sports associations? While the ethical and moral issue from the human rights perspective may have somewhat tainted the efforts of the police, it seems to have had a positive effect on Malaysian sports, especially soccer. Although the occasional suspicion is cast when a favourite team loses, this could only be described as pure 'conjecture' and 'coincidence'.

For sports to be clean, there must be a commitment from all those involved – players, officials, referees, administrators and governing bodies – to play the game on and off the field according to rules and laws. When there is a slight wavering from set principles and goals, then the rot starts to set in.[42]

Football is not the only game to have allegations raised as far as match fixing is concerned. Sports as diverse as boxing,[43] and horse and greyhound racing periodically are subject to such scandals. Cricket was subject to allegations made by a number of the Australian Test side against approaches by the Pakistani player Salim Malik in 1994 to throw matches.[44] Even snooker has seen allegations in 1995 concerning a match between Jimmy White and Peter Francisco, prompted by what were officiously described as 'irregular betting patterns'.[45] The official investigation found no evidence of corruption. The common theme is sports where gambling and betting are common.

---

42   Raja, N, 'Sports Gambling in Malaysia' (1997) 8(2) *For the Record* – The Official Newletter of the National Sports Law Institute 3 and 5.

43   See 'ABA concerned about referee cash allegation', *Daily Telegraph*, 3 December 1996.

44   See Fraser, D, 'Balls, Bribes and Bails: the Jurisprudence of Salim Malik', *Law and Popular Culture Research Group Working Papers* (1995) Manchester Metropolitan University. 'Pakistan's captain denies his role as the "Mr Fixit" in Bribery Scandal', *The Guardian*, 16 February 1995.

45   'Scan: Bunged out', *The Guardian*, 28 April 1995, p 4.

Bungs and Brown Paper Bags

Burrell, I and Palmer, R, 'Taxman Blows Whistle on Football's Fiddles'

Some call it a bung, others know it as brown paper bagging. It has become as much a part of football as FA Cup final day or supporters' hats and scarves. The tax-free under-the-counter payment is part of the culture of corruption which has become endemic in English football. It is widespread yet the game's ruling bodies have proved powerless to stop it. This week football's dirty linen will be hung out in public when the High Court hears evidence of alleged irregular payments to players, agents and managers as part of a power struggle at one of the Premier League's top clubs, Tottenham Hotspurs.

The evidence submitted by Alan Sugar, the computer businessman, in his case against Terry Venables, who denies any impropriety, will concentrate on one transfer deal between two of the wealthiest clubs. However documents obtained by *The Sunday Times* show that clubs at all levels of English soccer are implicated in corruption. Statements given to a special Inland Revenue team investigating tax fiddles in football have confirmed long-held suspicions that financial irregularities are widespread at clubs all over the country. The revenue team, based at Solihull in the West Midlands, is examining transfer fees, money channelled through third parties such as agents, and other secret cash payments to players and officials, including undeclared top-ups of pensions.

The most common fiddle being investigated by the revenue is the ex gratia payment which is not declared. In a statement given to inspectors, Dave Bassett, the manager of Sheffield United, has described how he helped to arrange such a payment for one player when he was manager of the Premier League club, Wimbledon. Bassett said: 'The player indicated he wanted an immediate lump sum signing-on fee and it was suggested that if the agreed transfer fee of £100,000 was increased to accommodate this sum then it could be given to the player in the form of an *ex-gratia* payment, tax-free.'

Revenue officials have visited other clubs, including Sheffield Wednesday, Arsenal and Blackburn Rovers, to determine whether similar payments were given to their players. Officials have produced no evidence to suggest that anything illegal has been done. Other clubs, including West Ham and Aston Villa, have had to pay extra tax because of underpayment. Investigators have also examined transfer deals during a seven year period at Aston Villa when the club had four managers, including Graham Taylor, the present England manager, but uncovered no evidence of impropriety. Another Premier League club, whose players have given statements to revenue officials, is estimated to have paid out as much as £1m in back-handed or under-the-counter deals to staff, including large signing-on fees. Lou Macari, the manager of Stoke City, was himself acquitted last year of conspiring to cheat the Inland Revenue while at Swindon. He said many clubs had colluded in providing tax-free payments. 'One player at another club was given £80,000 just for signing on,' he said. 'The payment was made to him by that club's chairman and should have been written into his contract. Instead it was paid up front and tax-free, which is a blatant breach of football league regulations,' he said. 'When I left Manchester United in 1984 I was given an *ex-gratia* payment of £20,000. The club was forced to pay tax on similar payments to at least 20 other players after an Inland Revenue inquiry,' he said.

The scam was described in court last year when Macari's former chairman at Swindon Town, Brian Hillier, was jailed for six months for conspiracy to defraud the Inland Revenue. Statements given at that time by 10 players and 13 officials to the inquiry implicated several other clubs, including Oxford United, Wimbledon, Brentford, Bristol Rovers and non-league Hyde United, in undeclared cash transactions. A senior revenue investigator who has spent two years investigating corruption in football described last week how other football clubs conspired with Swindon in the payment of sweeteners to smooth the way for transfers. The other clubs agreed that as part of the transfer Swindon would pay thousands of pounds direct to the player. To disguise the payment, the selling club agreed to act as a conduit for the money by describing it as a signing-off fee which they were paying their player. 'What they used to do was dress it up as a lump sum payment terminating the services of the player. To do that they had to route the funds (from Swindon) through the club that was selling the player'. The revenue inspector said bigger clubs use more sophisticated methods to avoid paying tax. 'The clubs in the lower divisions use more crude means. The more sophisticated clubs use the offshore type of arrangement,' he said.

In their latest investigations into transfer dealings, the inspectors have examined the role of agents representing players or managers. Deals involving foreign clubs have been closely monitored because of the involvement of agents, and suspicions that some clubs have sent money offshore which should have been liable to tax in this country. Last week Newcastle United officials said they had been questioned about the signing of the Brazilian international, Mirandina. Other deals involving the transfers of British players to Italian clubs have also come under scrutiny. Other fiddles which have been investigated include win bonuses known as 'boot money' because they were sometimes left in the boot, and other payments given to players from petty cash. Jimmy Quinn, a Northern Ireland international, has described how man of the match payments at Swindon were pooled together and given to the squad tax-free. 'At no time when the additional bonuses were paid did anyone at the club mention tax,' he said. Players at some clubs have also received tax-free bonuses from club sponsors, or shared the proceeds of foreign tours. Hillier, who was released from Ford open prison in December, is bitter about his experience at Swindon and blames footballers for demanding such tax-free allowances. 'Players feel they have a right to tax-free earnings from football and that is rather sad,' he said. According to Hillier, much of the illicit money is now channelled through third parties, usually agents or their companies. Even managers are now represented by middle men. 'There are now a number of managers with agents and when they are selling a player their agent immediately introduces himself to the buying club to negotiate a fee for the manager,' he said. 'The agent operates under the disguise of a company which then distributes the money to whoever it has got to go to. On the invoice they would just use their imagination they could put it down as many things'.[46]

---

46 Burrell, I and Palmer, R, 'Taxman Blows Whistle on Football's Fiddles', *The Sunday Times*, 6 June 1993, p 7.

The position of taxation in sport has always been problematic. This is first in terms of arguments that sport should not be subject to the formal application of taxation, especially VAT, in the same way as other businesses.[47] The following extract indicates the tax burden of sport:

Baldwin, R, 'Taxation of Sport'

Tax law is the area of the law which probably has the most serious adverse impact on the finances of sport. Despite expressing vigorous support for sport and exhorting us all to participate in what is good for us, successive governments for the last 25 years have done little to alleviate the significant tax burden that the tax regime places on sport. The Sports Council estimates that for every £1 contributed by Central government to sport, it returns £5 in tax to the Exchequer – not a bad return! Examples of the harshness of the burden exist at all levels:

The British Olympic Association is the only national Olympic body anywhere in the world that pays corporation tax. Despite the Association spending thousands of pounds fighting a successful case before the Special Commissioners last year and winning, the Inland Revenue have still not accepted that the Commissioners' decision applies in the future. Questions are asked why we do not win more medals when at the same time the Exchequer has been in the habit of taking over £2m from the Association in tax during every four year run up to the Summer Games.

The recent European football championship Euro '96, which was probably one of the most successful international sports events held in this country for many years, contributed an estimated £64m in taxes with very little direct government financial support. How can we expect to continue to attract international sports events to this country when we tax them so heavily. Other countries grant tax exemptions, for example Australia has for many years exempted non-profit distributing sports bodies from income tax.

Value added tax is charged at the full 17.5% rate on all admissions to major spectator sports events unlike some of our European counterparts. For example during the next European Championships Holland will charge only 6% on admission receipts compared with 17.5% here. How many people appreciate that of the £20 ticket price to watch a major sports event, £3 goes in VAT and only £17 is received by the organisers?

The average sports club which is non-profit-making is still potentially subject to all the taxes. Indeed recently the press has contained reports that in golf alone there is almost £19m which the Inland Revenue is seeking to collect from members' golf clubs. We also know that rugby union has been pursued by the taxman.

---

47 See Grayson, E, *Sport and the Law*, 2nd edn (1994), London: Butterworths, Chapter 14; Collins, V, *Recreation and the Law*, 2nd edn (1993), London: E&FN Spon, Chapter 6; Grayson, E, 'Guilding the Lily: Guild v IRC' (1993) 1(1) *Sport and the Law Journal* 4; 'Sports Charaties: Taxation Implications of Guild v IRC' (1993) 1(1) *Sport and the Law Journal* 5; Farrell, R, 'VAT and Amateur Sport' (1993) 1(1) *Sport and the Law Journal* 22; Virgo, E, 'Sports Clubs and VAT: The Log-Standing Errors' (1994) 2(2) *Sport and the Law Journal* 17.

Possibly the worst example is National Lottery Grants. In the Inland Revenue's view, capital grants made towards projects organised by sports organisations carrying on taxable trades will reduce the amount of tax relief in the form of capital allowances which those organisations can claim on their capital expenditure. To my mind this amounts not to double but triple taxation, the three levels being first the tax which you and I as individuals pay on our income before we buy our National Lottery ticket, secondly the 12% Lottery duty which the gross ticket proceeds attract and thirdly the reduction in tax relief which sports organisations would otherwise have been able to claim. This particular tax problem is unlikely to apply to the other good causes which by and large qualify as charities and therefore can organise themselves so that they pay no tax.

It is not only the tax cost which is of concern but also the significant effort that has to be put in by sports organisations to collect tax on behalf of the tax authorities. Over 150,000 sports organisations from the smallest club to the largest governing body potentially face PAYE, value added tax and corporation tax. In many cases volunteers have to deal with complex tax matters which are unfamiliar to them. They can often be tripped up by the myriad of forms and numerous deadlines and often officers can be personally liable to substantial tax liabilities, interest and penalties. With the advent of self assessment for both companies and individuals the burden on the sporting taxpayer is ever increasing.[48]

Secondly as with other areas in the entertainment business, financial transaction have been at best unorthodox and at worst illegal:

Downes, S and Mackay, D, *Running Scared: How Athletics Lost its Innocence*

But for the majority of athletes, the sense of perspective was always maintained: it was just a sport. These athletes might train at the track every Tuesday and Thursday, come rain or shine, hail or snow, and compete each weekend. After their time as competitors, some of them might have stayed with their club as a coach, or become an official judge or timekeeper, perhaps helped to organise the club's affairs. Like most sports at a grass roots level, no one did these sort of things with any reward in mind. They did it because they enjoyed doing it. But through the 1980s and 1990s, athletics at the elite level steadily became part of the entertainment industry, just like any other professional sport. International athletes became highly paid performers, some of them becoming millionaires. Yet this new professional sport continued to exist within an amateur structure. By 1995, it was this dichotomy which was threatening to tear British athletics apart.

Whatever way you look at it, 15p per mile travel allowance is not in the Linford Christie league for earnings from athletics. Yet that was all Gordon Dixon, one of Christie's predecessors as a sprinter for Thames Valley Harriers, got for his hours of effort as an official at the London Grand Prix extravaganza at Crystal Palace one hot night in July 1995.

48　Baldwin, R, 'Taxation of Sport' (1996) 4(3) *Sport and the Law Journal* 95.

It was in 1985 that international athletics introduced a set of new eligibility rules which at last permitted athletes to be paid openly for competing, although only a handful of international 'star' athletes would benefit. At first, there was not much money available, and even among the top performers many kept their 'proper' jobs, and continued to train and compete in their spare time. Only a very few were able to become what was euphemistically called 'full time athletes'. The sport still shied away from the word 'professional'. But sure enough, athletics during the 1980s finally went pro.

Not only could athletes legitimately earn money from 'endorsements' by lending their name to a product for advertising without fear of the ultimate sanction of being banned from the next Olympic Games, but they could even be paid a fee for competing at certain top invitation meetings. With television and sponsors eager to invest in track and field athletics during the 1980s, meetings such as Zurich, Oslo and Cologne were soon openly offering tens of thousands of dollars to the big name draw cards such as Steve Cram, Carl Lewis and Edwin Moses. So much so that, by the summer of 1995, the organisers of the top 15 meetings on the international Grand Prix circuit paid a total of £10 million in appearance fees for athletes. The London Grand Prix, staged at Crystal Palace that July, had one of the smaller overall budgets that year, about £650,000 in total. Of that sum, the majority was spent on the athletes. Although there could be no meeting without the officials, timekeepers and track judges, it meant that there was little left over to be paid to the likes of Gordon Dixon. Dixon is typical of the legion of unsung heroes in athletics who just for the love of the sport give up their time and energy to organise track and field meetings. At the very highest levels of the sport, such officials do at least get their out-of-pocket expenses reimbursed plus a small food allowance or a cardboard box of sandwiches, and sometimes if they are very lucky, perhaps a waterproof nylon jacket in the garish colour-scheme of the event sponsors.

Then, from the in-field at these elite events, officials like Dixon can watch as top stars race past them on the track, sometimes earning five figure sums by the second. The division between the haves and have nots in athletics has yet to be reconciled. In the main the sport is still administered by enthusiastic amateurs in their spare time. Every day they confront mundane, seemingly trivial problems in the running of their area association, their county, or their club, and rarely do they command the means with which to deal with them.

While the Linford Christies of this world may demand £50,000 per meeting, much of the rest of the sport is struggling just to make ends meet. In 1995 the British Athletic Federation – BAF, the governing body for the whole sport in Britain – decided to make a stand against the ever rising fees demanded by a few star athletes. The result was a summer-long feud between the BAF and the Olympic sprint champion Christie and his business partner, Colin Jackson, the sprint hurdles world record holder. By the end of the summer, Christie and Jackson had raced in only two of BAF's programme of televised meetings, their 'strike' at British events splitting the sport right down the middle, with Jackson vowing never again to race at BAF meeting as long as Peter Radford remained executive chairman of the Federation.

But it was not only in Britain that meeting promoters, feeling the pinch between the spiralling demands of athletes and a decline in television an sponsor revenues, had begun to cut back in their spending. In Oslo since the early 1970s, the climax of the Bislett Games had always been the Dream Mile. Coe, Ovett, Cram, Elliott, Walker, Wessinghage had all taken part in the Dream Mile, the world record always seeming to be in danger of revision in Oslo. In many years, that one race had been the highlight of the entire season. Yet in 1995 there was no Dream Mile at Oslo.

By 1995 the greatest middle distance runner of the moment, Noureddine Morceli, held six world records, including the mile, and was so far ahead of all of his rivals that it seemed that no one else could threaten the Algerian's world marks. Morceli, though, does not come cheap demanding up to £50,000, plus bonuses for records, to race. Sven Hansen, the Oslo meeting promoter, was unable to afford such an amount for just one athlete. He decided that no Dream Mile would be better than a Dream Mile without Morceli.[49]

The activities of the athletics promoter, Andy Norman, has led to a good deal of controversy:

Downes, S and Mackay, D, *Running Scared: How Athletics Lost its Innocence*

If by a balanced view, Radford meant consulting some of the athletes who had worked closest to Norman for longest, then Steve Ovett seemed to have a clear view of Norman's contribution. After Curtis Robb, the country's leading 800 metres runner (who is managed by Norman), had expressed his view that Norman and only Norman could run British athletics, Ovett said, 'I suppose even Hitler had his good points. What Norman did for the sport was good but I do not think it was exceptional,' Ovett said. 'I think he sold what people wanted, and he had talented athletes available to him that everybody wanted to see. He came in and saw that there was material there to be used – and abused to a certain extent – and he saw that he could get a lot of money back, and it was fairly obvious how to do it. I do not even think Andy Norman is a great promoter. When you have been given a vast purse, as Andy was given, it is not difficult to produce good meetings. The difficult thing would be to be to do it with hardly any money and without the reservoir of talent to call on. Andy is a good administrator, that is his strong point, but he is a man of limited vision.'

Ovett had cause to complain of treatment he felt he had received at Norman's hands. In August 1989, Ovett had broken down in tears in front of millions of television viewers at that year's AAA Championships in Birmingham. The championships, being used to select the England team for the following year's Commonwealth Games, had as its highlight a 1,500 metres final including both Ovett and Sebastian Coe. This was the race the whole world had wanted to see, but it came to fruition perhaps five, even 10 years too late. By 1989 both great champions were in the twilight of their careers. It was the only time in their senior careers that Coe and Ovett met in a race outside major

---

49 Downes, S and Mackay, D, *Running Scared: How Athletics Lost its Innocence* (1996), Edinburgh: Mainstream Publishing, pp 16–17.

championships: despite all the power and influence he exercised as a promoter, Andy Norman had never managed to get this race organised. How he finally achieved this coup was to be the subject of some close scrutiny.

The AAA Championships, the world's oldest organised annual athletics meeting, had always tried to remain robustly amateur, even after payments had been allowed in athletics, and professionals had been allowed in the Olympics. Some top competitors had been paid subventions in the past but generally the administrators would get the athletes to compete for nothing at the AAAs. The reasoning was simple: often, as in 1989, the AAAs were also team selection trials for the next major international event, so if an athlete wanted to be chosen he or she had to compete at the AAAs.

Ovett alleged that in the week before the 1989 Championships, he was telephoned and offered a share of £40,000 to compete in the 1,500 metres against Coe. It was only after they had both qualified from heats on the Saturday afternoon that Ovett approached Coe and told him that he was being paid. Coe told him that he was not receiving any payment.

What no one could understand was why anyone would complain about being paid. As the 1,500 metres final was staged, won by Coe with Ovett down the field in ninth place, the reason became apparent. Ovett really was not in the sort of shape to challenge for another AAA title. He might have chosen not to race at all, so the money may have been persuasive. But once he discovered he was the only person being paid at a non-paying trials event, Ovett's alarm bells sounded: he feared that the reason he was offered cash was that he might have been set up.

The night before the final, it took a great deal of persuasion to get Ovett to race at all. After the race, Ovett jogged over to his kit, and then gave an emotional interview to his ITV commentary colleague, Jim Rosenthal. Frustrated and angry, Ovett told millions of television viewers, 'There are people in this sport who are trying to use it for their own ends. They have got to be stopped'.

Only when AAA officials said that they would not investigate his allegations did Ovett name Norman as the person who had made the telephoned offer. Norman of course denied that any offer had ever been made. Mike Farrell, then secretary of the AAA, hardly helped to clarify the position when the day after the championships he said, 'Andy did it without permission if he did it, and he is denying it'.

By the time an inquiry was set up, further financial problems had also come to light: $39,000 in cash had been stolen from Norman's room at the Queen's Hotel, Crystal Palace, a month before the AAAs. There was nothing untoward about Norman having the cash, which he said he had been given to pay athletes following another meeting in Nice. It was suggested that the money was in fact to pay Linford Christie, Colin Jackson, John Regis and Yvonne Murray, but Norman said, 'You cannot pay people like Africans with cheques, it has to be cash,' adding with a surprising degree of calmness for someone who had just lost £25,000, 'The money is insured, so no one loses'.

Eventually, the AAA set up an inquiry into Ovett's allegations, conducted by Robert Reid QC and David Pickup, a senior Sports Council official. It was the second investigation into allegations against Norman in the space of just two years. In 1987, Peter Coni QC had chaired an investigation into allegations by international hammer thrower Martin Girvan that Norman had colluded in the evasion of a drug test. 'We found this all very unhappy,' Coni was to say later, 'but we were quite unable to say that it was true. Nor did we feel able to go as far as to say that we were absolutely satisfied it was untrue'. Despite clearing Norman, Coni – who described Norman's behaviour as 'extraordinary' and 'consistent with somebody who does not think and who just bulldozes in a singularly inappropriate way' – was unconvinced by the official's testimony. 'He made one or two comments which were entirely inappropriate. One of the comments was: 'I would not put myself in jeopardy for an athlete of Girvan's standard', which you or I could turn around and say, 'Well, what standard of athlete would you put yourself in jeopardy for?'.

The Reid-Pickup Report ended up being largely inconclusive. 'A 0–0 draw,' was the way one official described it. Its release was delayed by nearly three weeks, apparently to allow Norman's legal advisers to scrutinise it first. Eventually, the report was published in late January 1990, nearly six months after the AAA Championships and also just after most of the athletics journalists who had been following the case had left the country to cover the following month's Commonwealth Games in Auckland.

Norman, according to the report, was 'the most probable candidate for the maker of the call'. But they could not prove that he had made the cash offer to Ovett. In seeking to offer an explanation, the 60 page report even made the unlikely suggestion that Ovett might have been victim of a hoax caller who was impersonating Norman, the official who had been his business partner and best man at his wedding. The findings did not shake Ovett's opinion: 'I am pleased the inquiry admits I was telling the truth when I said I had been offered money. I know who phoned me – it was Andy Norman.'

The report did point out, though, that because Norman's methods of operation were condoned by the governing body, the promotions officer believed 'his powers of discretion could be stretched'. Reid and Pickup offered a series of recommendations for future business practices, including the introduction of confirmations of all Norman's deals with athletes, to be written by another association officer. The Reid-Pickup Report also said that Norman should be barred from acting as an agent for athletes.

If Reid and Pickup felt that Norman's actions had been condoned by the sport's governing body before their report, then the governing body's decision, just months after the report's publication, to register Norman as an accredited agent with the International Amateur Athletic Federation, could only be interpreted as yet another pat on the back for the former policeman.[50]

It is football, the most commercialised of British sports, that has the most infamous history as far as questionable financial payments are concerned. There are historical examples that date back to the early days of the professional game. Call them what you will, bungs, sweeteners or plainly illegal payments, they have been made to ensure deals are concluded. The

---

50 *Ibid*, pp 74–77.

illegality derives from the fact that they are secretive and not disclosed for tax purposes. A major question is whether they are illegal just as far as the internal rules of football or whether they are also illegal as far as the law.

The development of the professional game was in fact first initiated by 'illegal payments' to players as far as their services were concerned by Preston North End in 1884. The payments were contrary to the rules of the Football Association at the time, but as the scale of payments by other clubs in the north of England increased, this led to the professional football primarily developing in the north of England. In 1919, Leeds City was expelled from Division Two for illegal payments to players. Leeds United were formed to replace them. Until the 1960s and the introduction of a minimum wage for professional footballers, largely achieved by the campaign of Jimmy Hill of the Professional Footballers Association, the wages were reasonable in terms of average wages, but in no way comparable with wages of footballers today. In the context of the insecurity, risk of injury and short-term nature of the job, the scope for additional back-hand payments was obvious.

The one modern incident that has led to financial dealing coming under the gaze of the law is that involving Tottenham Hotspurs.

Williams, R, *Football Babylon*

June 1992 saw a routine check of Tottenham Hotspurs' PAYE files by the Inland Revenue which revealed serious financial irregularities – a can of worms had been opened. As the taxmen probed deeper into the club's affairs, more and more irregularities were uncovered and a full scale Inland Revenue investigation began. Spurs commissioned city accountants Touche Ross to do a thorough review of the club's affairs. The irregularities under Irving Scholar's regime were numerous and scandalous. Amongst the revelations uncovered were ex-gratia payments to players that would result in considerable back tax liabilities for Spurs. Belgian Nico Claesen had been given a secret payment of £42,000 when he joined Spurs in 1986 which had not included the statutory PAYE deductions. Icelandic international Gudni Bergsson also benefited from a payment which was, like Claesen's, made via his former club. Irving Scholar authorised both payments.

Paul Gascoigne's and Chris Waddle's pension papers were backdated by two years and loans to both players used to buy houses around London were illegal. Scholar also gave a secret undertaking to both players, guaranteeing them *ex-gratia* payments of up to £120,000 after they had left Spurs. A letter from Scholar to Gascoigne's agent Mel Stein promised to pay the player '£70,000 net of all UK taxes, up to a maximum of £120,000 gross'. The implications of such payments were, in the words of Touche Ross, 'like having a gun held to the club's head'. The special inquiry at Tottenham began on 17 July 1992. A few months later, in November, the Inland Revenue demanded a payment of £500,000, with the promise of more to come.

The transfers of Chris Waddle to Marseille and Paul Gascoigne to Lazio both involved payments to the football agent Dennis Roach who, as *The Sunday People* reported, was being paid by both sides in the deals which was in total breach of FIFA, UEFA and FA regulations. Scholar brought Roach into the equation and, even after Italian fixer Gino Santin was detailed to finalise Gascoigne's Lazio transfer, he received a pay-off payment of £27,500. However this was not the end of the line for Roach who continued to receive money. A Spurs document stated: 'It would appear that Mr Roach has been on the payroll of the club, unknown to Mr Solomon and Mr Berry, having been paid £64,400 in the year ending 31 May 1991. It would also appear that Lazio may also be paying Mr Roach in connection with the Gascoigne sale. This is forbidden both under Football League and FIFA regulations.'

Most damaging of all were the irregular payments made over three transfers: the £250,000 transfer of Mitchell Thomas from Luton to Spurs in 1986; the £425,000 signing of Paul Allen from West Ham in 1985 and the £387,500 transfer of Chris Fairclough from Nottingham Forest in 1987. Thomas had been given a £25,000 loan when he joined Spurs but papers forwarded to the Football League Tribunal at the time of transfer omitted to mention it. Thomas also received a letter stating that, in effect, the money was never going to have to be repaid. The loan was made three weeks before he actually became a Spurs player. Allen and Fairclough also received loans before joining Spurs – £55,000 and £25,000 respectively – and neither payment was disclosed to the Transfer Tribunal.

When Irving Scholar left Spurs the club was in big trouble. Terry Venables desperately searched for a business partner to save the club from financial ruin and certain closure. His knight in shining armour (or so he thought) was Amstrad boss Alan Sugar, a man with a bruising business reputation. It was not long before Sugar became concerned about the goings on at Spurs; the result of a combination of rumours and Inland Revenue facts. The relationship between Venables and Sugar became increasingly uneasy. Venables was dismissed by Sugar in a blaze of publicity and in 1993 the two men slugged it out in the High Court as Venables took legal action against his former partner. The legal proceedings were the usual claim and counterclaim, including evidence suggesting that some managers accept cash bungs as part and parcel of transfer deals. Alan Sugar knew that Tottenham's troubles with the Inland Revenue were to be laid directly at Scholar's door, yet Venables felt that Sugar consistently tried to portray him as the bad guy. As manager of the team under Scholar, Venables was employed by Tottenham Hotspurs FC, a subsidiary of Tottenham Hotspurs PLC and each organisation had its own independent board of directors. The FA examined the evidence and cleared Venables of any wrong doing. They must have been satisfied because, two years later, they appointed him England coach.[51]

An FA Commission of Inquiry ruled Tottenham Hotspur were guilty of 'avoidance and evasion of fees' concerning transfers. They were fined £600,000, had 12 points deducted from the next season's FA Carling Premiership total and were barred from the 1994–95 FA Cup. The subsequent three man FA Appeals Board cut the 12 point deduction to six. The ban on the

51   Williams, R, *Football Babylon* (1996), London: Virgin Books, p 139.

club's participation in the 1994–95 FA Cup remained and the fine was increased from £600,000 to £1.5 million.[52] Tottenham then considered taking the FA to the High Court but agreed to go to arbitration in keeping with the guidelines of FIFA, the sport's world governing body. The independent arbiters made a confidential decision but decreed that the FA acted outside its jurisdiction.[53] Subsequently the FA ruled that Tottenham still had to pay the £1.5 million fine imposed for financial irregularities but it was confirmed that the FA Cup ban and six point deduction from their FA Carling Premiership total had been annulled.[54] That was the end of this particular saga.

Certainly 'the bung' has become part of football parlance. The allegations were made in the High Court in the case between Terry Venables and Alan Sugar and surrounded the transfer of Teddy Sheringham from Nottingham Forest to Tottenham Hotspurs, concerning allegations of illegal payments made to Venables and the Nottingham Forest manager, Brian Clough. This court action was the culmination of a drawn out feud between Venables and Sugar and on-going allegations as to the fitness of Venables acting in financial dealings.[55] Some bemoaned this as another example of the malaise of football and sport in general. Questions were raised in Parliament, primarily by the Labour MP Kate Hoey.[56] A number of people in football said that this was all part of the culture and tradition. In another court case involving Terry Venables, the former Scottish international Frank McLintock whose First Wave Agency acted in the Sheringham transfer and who was paid £50,000 in cash on an invoice that did not mention his help in transfers. Justifying the payment, he said at the trial that 'This is used by a number of clubs to get out of what they consider to be the antiquated laws of the Football Association. Some agents call it merchandising and have done no work of that kind whatsoever, but we have at least done some genuine work, which we can prove'.[57]

The bung allegation led to an FA investigation carried out by an inquiry team consisting of the Premier League chief executive Rick Parry, Robert Reid QC and Steve Coppell. There had been many false hopes raised in the past that publication was imminent.[58]

---

52 'Tottenham save six points but pay £1.5m', *The Times*, 7 July 1994, p 44.
53 'Arbiters give Tottenham new Hope of Cup Reprieve', *The Times*, 26 November 1994, p 48.
54 'FA upholds Spurs' £1.5m fine', *The Times*, 14 December 1994, p 42.
55 See Harris, H and Curry, S, *Venables: The Inside Story* (1994), London: Headline, for further details; and *Panorama*, BBC 1, 16 September 1993.
56 'Why I'm so angry: Bungs are tainting the game I love', *The Observer*, 5 November 1995, p 10.
57 'Soccer: Clubs often dodge FA rules – McLintock', *The Guardian*, 13 December 1995, p 22.
58 'League Prepares new "Bung" Report', *The Independent*, 3 August 1995.

After more than three and a half years of investigation, the report was published in September 1997.[59] At the time of writing only one successful prosecution has been made under FA rules against the then Arsenal manager, George Graham, largely due to disclosures in *The Mail on Sunday* and an investigation by the Inland Revenue was convened to look into the whereabouts of £50,000 which had allegedly gone missing from the £2.1 million transfer of Teddy Sheringham from Clough's Nottingham Forest to Tottenham in 1992. But here the inquiry immediately met the problem that would plague it again and again: an allegation followed by a denial – and few powers to get to the truth. Over the following months, more and more allegations were referred to the inquiry. Three years, 60 witnesses, tens of thousands of pages of evidence and over £1 million later, the villains would appear to be still on the loose. So has the inquiry been, as some would suggest, merely a cosmetic exercise? The report is over 1,000 pages in length. As far as the alleged £50,000 bung in the Sheringham transfer, the report concludes, 'We are satisfied that cash payments were made from the £50,000 to members of staff at (Nottingham) Forest.'[60] A cash culture is exposed as existing at Forest, with members of the management and coaching team regularly receiving money-filled brown envelopes after transfers.

The Report also looks at the transfers of all foreigners to England between 1992 and 1994, around 35 cases. It seems likely that charges under FA rules will be brought against those individuals still working in football. Whether criminal charges may be brought is open to speculation. What seems to be clear is that many of the dealings investigated cannot really be characterised as any form of villainy. It does seem to be a part of football culture, albeit, a part that needs to be challenged and exposed. The investigation by Sir John Smith into the football match fixing allegations has been widened to consider the bung allegations too.

The one convicted individual George Graham, received a national and international ban lasting for one year.[61] The police and the Serious Fraud Office (SFO) have continued to be interested in some of the events investigated and raised from his case.[62] The Premier League has acted in a multi-agency approach with the police, the SFO, the Inland revenue and overseas fraud police.[63] Graham is now actively back in the world of football.[64]

---

59 The FA Premier League Inquiry into Transfers, 'The Bung Report' (1997).

60 See 'Bung-busters prepare to act on "cult of dishonesty"', *Daily Telegraph*, 20 September, p 28.

61 'FA hands Graham one-year ban', *The Times*, 14 July 1995, p 40; 'Ban Graham for Life, says UEFA Chief', *The Guardian*, 4 March 1995.

62 'Sheringham Deal could face new Probe by Police', *Daily Telegraph*, 19 April 1997.

63 See 'Souness in new "bung" inquiry', *The Guardian*, 6 March 1995.

64 'The resurrection of brother George', *The Observer*, 7 April 1996 and 'Soccer: Leeds forget past and pin faith on Graham', *The Guardian*, 11 September 1996, p 20.

SPORTS AGENTS

The bung saga has been influential in a move to a greater regulatory framework for football agents. FIFA first introduced regulations in 1994, revising them in 1996. To register, an agent has to be approved by FIFA and deposit a £110,000 bond in a Swiss bank account. FIFA's agent regulations give it the power to punish clubs with a ban on all national and or international footballing activity.[65] That would mean clubs being suspended from the Premier League and banned from Europe. FIFA says it will also suspend all or part of the management bodies. This may lead to world bans like that meted out to George Graham for any manager or chairman dealing with an unlicensed agent. The regulations also speak of 'an interdiction to carry out national or international transfers' and a fine of up to 100,000 Swiss francs.[66] Rune Hauge, the agent at the centre of the Graham case has been outlawed from acting as an agent and has been subject to police investigation.[67]

Players' agents have been active in sport for a significant period of time. They are able to provide advice on contracts commercial endorsements etc. There are a number of large agencies such as the International Management Group under the control of Mark McCormack. Other agents work in smaller companies such as Jon Holmes of Park Associates agent to ex-footballer Gary Lineker and rugby player Will Carling, and Eric Hall of Hall Management.[68] In football they have been active for a large number of years. However some, particularly managers, have increasingly seen them as an irritant and a barrier between them and their players.[69] Other sports where player representation has a reasonably long history are tennis, rugby league, golf and athletics. The top cricket players are increasingly seeking representation.[70] The professionalistion of rugby union has meant the game has become colonised with agents offering their services.[71]

There are a number of lawyers who act as agents: one of the most high-profile is Mel Stein who acts for Paul Gascoigne.[72] There are issues of conflict

---

65 See Miller, F, 'Not Every Agent is a Bad Guy' (1996) 4 *Sport and the Law Journal* 36, for details of regulations and how they have been incorporated within English national footballing regulations.

66 'Soccer: FIFA threatens bans for using unlicensed agents', *The Guardian*, 23 December 1995, p 16.

67 'Bung Scandal Gets High Court Hearing', *The Guardian*, 28 March 1997, p 26.

68 'Fact: "There are no bungs in football. I deal with most clubs and have never been offered one"', *The Independent on Sunday*, 19 March 1995.

69 'Football Review: Furious Smith slams the "pimp" agents', *The Observer*, 22 January 1995, p 24.

70 'Cricket: Gough turned by US agent', *The Guardian*, 15 April 1995, p 15.

71 'Agent cracks the oval-ball code', *The Guardian*, 4 March 1995.

72 'Stein convicted', *Daily Telegraph*, 15 July 1997.

of interest that can arise, but lawyers have the professional code of ethics as guidance. As with FIFA above, the whole question of whether there should be a general regulatory framework for sports agents has arisen. In America many states have regulatory legislation concerning sports agents.[73] Incidents such as the 'bung scandal' in football increase the call for such measures in Britain.

Players' associations as forms of trade unions increasingly have an active role in representing players as their agents. The Professional Footballers Association, formed at the end of the 19th century, represents the vast majority of professional footballers in England. Newer bodies have been recently been formed in boxing, rugby and athletics. A new international Association of Professional Footballers has been formed with Eric Cantona and Diego Maradona as prime movers to give players more say in developments in world football.[74] A greater form of collective representation of professional sportsmen and women, often representing the interests on an individual as well as collective level, is developing, perhaps in response to the greater commercialisation of modern sport.

COMMODIFICATION

This creeping commercialisation has brought incremental changes to sport. The financial base of sport has become increasingly dependent on sponsorship and marketing activities. Sports clubs have become a brand image and have a corporate identity as distinctive as Disney or McDonalds. For example Manchester United Plc are valued at £429.85 million.[75] In 1994 £23.5 million came from their merchandising operations such as the sales of replica shirts. Sport is developing as an integral part of the leisure industry as a product that can be consumed in recognisable and discrete entities. As with other sectors of the entertainment business, sport is in the 'hits' business. Much time is spent in trying to make the big hit – to come top of the league or win a medal or cup. This can often lead to gambling for the 'big hit' in ways which would be seen as irrational in conventional enterprises.

---

73 See *Focus* special section on 'Sports Agents and Agency' in 16(2) *Journal of Sport and Social Issues*, especially Roberts, G, 'Agents and Agency: A Sport's Lawyer's View'; Cohen, G, 'Ethics and Representation of Professional Athletes' (1993) 4(1) *Marquette Sports Law Journal*; Arkell, T, 'Agent Interference with College Athletics: What Agents can and cannot do and what Institutions should do in Response', and Shulman, J, 'The NHL Joins in: An Update on Sports Agents Regulation in Professional Team Sports' (1997) 4(1) *The Sports Lawyers' Journal*; Champion, Jr, W, 'Attorneys *qua* Sports Agents: An Ethical Conundrum', and Stiglitz, J, 'A Modest Proposal: Agent Deregulation', both in (1997) 7(2) *Marquette Sports Law Journal*. Also note film, *Jerry Maguire*, starring Tom Cruise, about the US sports agent of same name.

74 'Cantona helps set up Union', *The Guardian*, 19 September 1995.

75 See 'Football Clubs slip down the Shares League', *The Observer*, 27 July 1997, p 9.

The process of commodification as an extension of the process of commercialisation is vital to explain. The theory has developed within the discipline of cultural studies and can be seen originating in the work of the Italian political writer, Antonio Gramsci.[76] He developed the concept of hegemony, that is the achievement of consent or agreement to dominant ideology (values and ideas) in society. These ideas are created by those groups who have most social, economic and political power in any particular society. The argument is that the masses largely agree to and accept these ideas and values even though they are not in their best interests, because they are transmitted and reinforced by the many different institutions in society, such as the education process and the media.

This process of hegemony has been identified with the commodification of culture, commodity fetishism and the creation of 'false needs'. Writers such as Marcuse,[77] Horkheimer and Adorno,[78] aligned with the Frankfurt School of political thought, indicate how individuals are seduced into compliance in capitalist society by the attraction of superficial commodities, especially entertainment. This is a process of globalisation where the ruling class inculcates its own values throughout society. Sport falls neatly into this theoretical analysis. Modern sport is used to make money through attracting spectators, selling satellite subscriptions and increasingly by selling sports merchandise. We as sports fans seem to accept it.

Through this process of commodification of increasing areas of social life such as sport, the argument is that the masses increasingly become compliant and in agreement with capitalism. However it has been acknowledged that an absolute notion of hegemony is never attained, with cultural resistance or counter-hegemonic strategies coming from sub-cultures expressing antipathy towards these dominant views. Perhaps some of the football fans' pressure groups and activities such as fanzines are good examples of this:

Strinati, D, *An Introduction to Theories of Popular Culture*

The cultivation of false needs is bound up with the role of the culture industry. The Frankfurt School sees the culture industry ensuring the creation and satisfaction of false needs, and the suppression of true needs. It is so effective in doing this that the working class is no longer likely to pose a threat to the stability and continuity of capitalism.[79]

The Frankfurt School have developed a neo-Marxist analysis seeing culture and in this context, sport, promoted as a 'product'; to be consumed to help pacify the populous and achieve consent to the existing social order. This of

76 See Gramsci, A, *The Prison Notebooks* (1971), London: Lawrence and Wisehart.

77 Marcuse, H, *One-Dimensional Man* (1968), London: Abacus.

78 Horkheimer, M, and Adorno, T, *The Dialectic of Enlightenment* (1973), London: Allen Lane.

79 Strinati, D, *An Introduction to Theories of Popular Culture* (1993), London: Routledge, p 63.

course is in opposition to theoretical perspectives that see sport as a natural human activity. It is clearly true that the modern form of elite sport is increasingly mediated and packaged. This has led to complaints that the nature of modern sport has changed for the worse. The argument is that no longer is sport something to admire in terms of its virtue; sport is sullied by commercial priorities, gamesmanship and a 'winner takes all' mentality. There may be some revisionism in terms of the way that sport in the past is viewed, a false nostalgia of a perfect past where 'playing the game' was the sole aim. In fact the historical evidence suggests that sport has been subject to these characteristics throughout its history.

PROFESSIONALISATION AND GLOBALISATION OF SPORT

A good deal of elite sport is played on the world stage. The four-yearly Olympic Games and football World Cup are clear examples. The two processes of globalisation, where social activities and processes are increasingly ceasing to be explained purely in national terms, and professionalisation of sport can be seen as advancing hand in hand. Changes in cricket at the end of the 1970s and in both codes of rugby will be discussed to illustrate these developments.

CRICKET WARS: THE PACKER LEGACY

The development of World Series Cricket sponsored by Kerry Packer as a challenge to established Test Cricket in Australia had major implications and consequences for world cricket. The mid-1970s cricket world was ideally placed for commercial exploitation. Although there was a semi-professional game in Australia and professional game in England, wages were very low compared with other similar sports and television rights were cheap. In Australia the top players who played Test cricket were continually in dispute over pay. Kerry Packer, who owned a series of commercial TV stations in Australia, was under pressure to increase audiences and televised sport was seen as a cheap way to achieve this. He had successfully obtained exclusive rights to golf; he saw cricket as even more appropriate in terms of the ability to fit in commercial breaks. Television rights had been presented to the non-commercial channel Australian Broadcasting Corporation (ABC) since the 1950s ritually on a non-exclusive basis with local commercial TV bids then being made. This process had kept down the price paid for rights. Packer wanted to buy exclusive rights to Test cricket. Even though in 1976 he was prepared to pay over six times the price that ABC had agreed with the Australian Cricket Board, he failed in his bid. Effectively closed out of established cricket he decided to develop a rival international cricket competition and began to sign up established Australian test cricketers such as Ian Chappell and to approach established international starts from England, the West Indies, Pakistan, India and talented South African players excluded from international cricket because of sporting bans induced by apartheid. Instrumental in the recruitment of a number of these players was Tony Greig, then the England Test captain. One legal issue that needed to be reconciled was first what name could be used: the term 'Supertest' was viewed as sufficiently distinct. Also:

Haigh, G, *Cricket War: the Inside Story of Packer's World Series Cricket*

Benaud worried, though, that the Laws of Cricket themselves might have a legal character. The MCC did hold their copyright. It would be important to play a form of stand alone rules 'based on' the Laws to avoid further legal troubles.[80]

The vast majority of the world's best players were signed up and 'Packers Circus', as the press described it, was publicised in May 1977. The plan met a lot of resistance from the cricket establishment and although there was a possibility of compromise between the Packer organisation and the cricket establishment, notably the International Cricket Conference, the international governing body, the issue of exclusive rights to Tests in Australia proved insurmountable. This led over two months later to:

Reports ... of an International Cricket Conference ultimatum issued the previous evening at Lord's: WSC players should be barred from all first class and Test Cricket if they did not shred their contracts before 1 October 1977. Though the Test and County Cricket Board's Doug Insole and Donald Carr had received Queen's Counsel advice that enforcement would be legally difficult, the counties were passionate. Glamorgan's Ossie Wheatley went into the TCCB minute book expressing the view: 'Our duty is to drive this wedge of uncertainty into the player's mind.' Insole echoed: 'War situation. We must make sure this thing does not get off the ground.'[81]

The World Series Cricket (WSC) matches that were to be played during the Winter of 1977–78 in Australia were scheduled to be played at the same time as the test series between Australia and the West Indies. The contracted players would not be available for test selection whatever the moves of the ICC. The view was that:

The ICC's self-appointing as cricket's sole promoter could not go unchallenged and barring signatories from first class cricket appeared an unenforceable restraint of trade ... CPH (Packer's Consolidated Press Holdings), it was decided, would back Greig, Snow and Proctor in a High Court challenge to the ICC.[82]

---

80 Haigh, G, *Cricket War: The Inside Story of Packer's World Series Cricket* (1993), Melbourne: Text Publishing Company, p 82.

81 *Ibid*, p 114.

82 *Ibid*, p 85.

The High Court in London became the focus of attention that October:

> WSC, Greig, Proctor and Snow were litigants; the defendants were the Test and County Cricket Board and chairman Doug Insole – the ICC had no legal personality. A barrage of lawyers and twenty one star witnesses were gathered to impress Justice Sir Christopher Slade.
>
> The sole absentee was Sir Donald Bradman. Ray Steele arrived in his stead. 'He was such a shrewd little bugger of course,' Steele chuckles. Nobody relished the fiery court wicket with hostile Queen's Counsels from both ends: WSC's Robert Alexander downwind, the ICC's Michael Kempster coming uphill but making Greig flinch as testimony began. Ross Edwards was struck at how detested Greig had become. 'Jeez, he was like Lord Haw-Haw,' says Edwards. 'He was very bad meat.'
>
> 'For some reason, I felt like a criminal,' Greig recalled. 'Especially when I was first attacked by the opposition counsel. My initial impulse was to tell all our opposition to go jump in the lake ... It became like a battle, with the opposition trying to pull me apart and Alexander protecting me.'[83]
>
> The judge handed out a greater hammering even than Clive Lloyd. The ICC's only gratification came in Justice Slade's observations that cricket administrators were a thoroughly decent breed who 'believed that they acted in the best interests of cricket'. The judge could also understand sense of betrayal at Greig's recruiting role, but retaliation had 'strained the bounds of loyalty'. In fact, they should have foreseen events: 'The very size of profits made from cricket matches involving star players must for some years have carried the risk that a private promoter would appear on the scene and seek to make money by promoting cricket matches involving world class cricketers.'[84]

Greig v Insole [1978] 1 WLR 302

The question for decision has been whether the particular steps which the ICC and TCCB took to combat what they regarded as the threat from World series Cricket were legally justified. The long investigation has satisfied me that the positive demonstrable benefits that might be achieved by introducing the ICC and TCCB bans and applying them to players who had already committed themselves to contracts with World Series of Contracts were at best somewhat speculative. On the other hand there were, as has been mentioned, a number of demonstrable disadvantages if the bans were to be applied in this way. They would preclude the players concerned from entry into the important fields of professional livelihood. This would subject them to the hardships and injustice of essentially retrospective legislation. They would deprive the public of any opportunity of seeing the players concerned playing in conventional cricket, either at test or at English county level, for at least a number of years. By so depriving the public, they would carry with them an appreciable risk of diminishing both public enthusiasm for conventional cricket and the receipts to be derived from it. Furthermore the defendants by imposing the bans, in the form which they took and with the intentions which prompted them, acted

---

83 *Ibid*, p 101.
84 *Ibid*, p 120.

without adequate regard to the fact that World Series Cricket had contractual rights with the players concerned, which were entitled to the protection of the law. The defendants acted in good faith and in what they considered to be the best interests of cricket. That, however, is not enough to justify in law the course which they have taken. In the result, I find for the plaintiffs in both actions.[85]

The legal costs of the ICC amounted to nearly £200,000. World Series Cricket was played over a period of about 18 months mainly in Australia but also in the West Indies. A mixture of 'Supertests' and one-day internationals led to many innovations such as improved televising and night-day games, that have become a norm of the modern game. Detractors point to the increased gamesmanship in the form of 'sledging' and intimidatory fast bowling stimulated by WSC. What is not in doubt is that this period of history led to the financial contours of the game changing at the elite levels of cricket. It is also an example of how change in sport can be seen as occurring on the world stage: the globalisation of sport.

RUGBY WARS

Rugby perhaps more than any other world game has gone through enormous change since the early months of 1995. This has happened in both the codes of the game- union and league. Rugby, whose exact historical origins are open to some contention,[86] developed in the first half of the 1800s when one game of football divided into two, rugby and association, primarily due to the emergence of carrying of the ball as a legitimate practice. Rugby has continued to be identified primarily with the higher strata of the social hierarchy, although there was a split at the end of the nineteenth century between rugby union as the mainly middle class and amateur game in the South of England and rugby league as the working class and professional game in the North. An exception to this is in South Wales where the working class were absorbed into rugby union, largely as Hargreaves[87] suggests, due to the game's representation and articulation of Welshness against the English outweighing any class antagonism.

The two games are international ones with union's main powerhouse in Australasia, South Africa, Britain and France. League has its presence similarly in Australia and England. However in England, compared to union, it has the vast majority of its presence in the Northern counties of Yorkshire

---

85 *Greig v Insole* [1978] 1 WLR 302, Slade LJ, 364–65.

86 See Holt, R, *Sport and the British* (1989), Oxford: Clarendon Press; Farrell, R, 'The Beginning (and the End?) of the Bifurcation of Rugby' (1995) 3(2) *Sport and the Law Journal* 8.

87 Hargreaves, J, *Sport, Power and Culture* (1984), London: Polity Press.

and Lancashire. After over one hundred years of bifurcation between the two rugby codes, there is a view that the two codes might well be united in the not too distant future. How has this come about?

The catalyst for this change has been the battle between the media tycoons Rupert Murdoch and Kerry Packer. Interestingly Packer was on the side of the establishment resisting changes to the status quo. The story starts in March 1995 when it was announced by New Limited (the Australian division of Murdoch owned New Corporation International) that a new rugby league competition was to be launched in competition to that operated under the auspices of the Australian Rugby League (ARL), by signing up clubs and players that were contractually bound to the ARL. Contracts were being offered that were three to four times the value of those that were in existence. As Peter Fitzsimons in his book, *The Rugby War*, states:

> 'Super League' – a naked attempt by the corporate forces of Rupert Murdoch to take over Australian domestic rugby league competition – had been launched.[88]

In similar circumstances to the Packer affair, the catalyst of this move was the battle emerging in 1995 between rival pay television consortiums, Opus Vision aligned with Packer, and Foxtel aligned with Murdoch. The two were due to go on air at the end of 1995 and were looking for material to sell subscriptions. As with BskyB television in Britain, sport was seen as a very attractive product. Rugby league was seen as the prime target. The problem for Murdoch and Foxtel was that Packer held both free-to-air and pay television rights to broadcast the ARL's competition right up until the start of the next millennium. Murdoch's response was to start his own competition and in essence try to buy up the game of rugby league. New Limited started litigation challenging the ARL's right to restrict competitors entry into the game in Australia. Court proceedings were initiated by News Corporation, which claimed that loyalty agreements signed between the ARL and the New South Wales Rugby League and its 20 clubs in November 1994 and February 1995 were invalid.[89]

The ARL counter sued giving 29 reasons why Super League should not start a rival competition before 31 December 1999 – when Packer's TV rights were due to end. After a 51 day hearing before Justice James Burchett's ruling in Sydney he found in favour of the ARL on all major points of contention and ordered the eight breakaway Super League clubs to return to the ARL.[90] It seemed impossible that its competition in Australia for 10 clubs would not start as planned. This lead to mixed views. Mark O'Brien, lawyer for the ARL, said:

---

88 Fitzsimons, P, *The Rugby War* (1996), Sydney: HarperSports.
89 See Garnsey, D, 'A League of Their Own' (1995) 5(2) *Anzsla Newsletter*.
90 See Doyle, B, 'News from Down Under Super League Case' (1996) 4(1) *Sport and the Law Journal* 17.

There is no way Super League will get under way. Murdoch has tried to hijack the game and failed.

But Maurice Lindsay, the English game's chief executive, insisted:

The judgment will not affect the European Super League. Our contract with BSkyB is also unaffected.

Lindsay said he had been assured by Ken Cowley, chairman and chief executive of News Corporation, that its commitment to the rest of the world was 'unshakeable'. With considerable understatement Cowley admitted that the judge's ruling was 'a setback' but he said News Corporation's 'commitment to our players, clubs and followers is unchanged'.[91] The case was appealed to the Full Federal Court:

'Anzsla News Ltd's Super League Appeal Success'

On 15 November 1996, the High Court of Australia refused the application of the Australian Rugby League (ARL) for special leave to appeal from the decision of the Full Federal Court given on 4 October 1996 in the 'Super League' case. Thus ended the most significant and publicised case involving sports interests in Australia's history, a case which plunged the sport of rugby league into chaos and a very uncertain future. In a dramatic reversal, the Full Federal Court had unanimously overturned the judgment of his Honour Mr Justice Burchett and consequently freed News Limited and its associated companies to organise and participate in the Super League rugby league competition in opposition to the competition conducted by the ARL. The three members of the Full Court drew many different conclusions from the primary facts and deemed unnecessary for their consideration the issue which dominated Burchett J's analysis of the case, namely the definition of the market within which to view the alleged anti-competitive behaviour of News Limited. Perhaps the most significant finding of Lockhart, Von Doussa and Sackville JJ was their decision that the so-called Commitment Agreements and Loyalty Agreements contained 'exclusionary provisions' as defined in the Trade Practices Act 1974 (Cth), and were therefore void. According to the Full Court, the agreements contained exclusionary provisions because:

- the ARL clubs were in competition with each other for the services of News Limited as a rival competition organised when the agreements were entered into.
- the clubs and the ARL had entered into a 'contract, arrangement or understanding' within the meaning of the Act.
- a substantial purpose for them entering into the Commitment and Loyalty Agreements was to restrict the supply of rugby league teams and players available to the rival competition, this being a prohibited purpose under the Act.

---

91 See 'Court Casts Doubt on Super League', *The Guardian*, 24 February 1996 .

They said 'It is plain that the League and ARL brought the clubs together, in circumstances that were redolent of great urgency, for the purpose of arresting the nascence of News as a real competition organiser'.

Also contrary to Burchett J, the Full Court held that the relationship between the ARL and the 20 clubs admitted to the national competition in 1995 was not such as to create reciprocal fiduciary obligations among those parties. In particular, on their reading of the evidence, the members of the Full Court did not believe that there was the degree of 'mutual trust and confidence' that is to be found among partners in a commercial venture. They found that the ARL and each of the clubs had conflicting commercial interests in relation to sponsorship and marketing opportunities and that the ARL exercised considerable control over the clubs, notably through the annual admission process (no club was entitled to enter as of right and any club could be excluded). Finally, a club's right of withdrawal was inconsistent with the existence of fiduciary duties, as that right left a club free to act in its own interests. The Full Court also disagreed with Burchett J's analysis concerning the alleged breaches of contract by News Limited. According to the Full Court, the only breaches by the so-called 'rebel' clubs were of the term implied in the 1995 competition contract requiring the clubs to do everything reasonably necessary to enable the 1995 competition to be carried on in a manner which allowed the ARL to receive the benefit of that competition. The Full Court found breaches of that term by the rebel clubs in:

– making public their proposed alignment with Super League;

– participating in the promotion of Super League;

– encouraging players to sign secretly with Super League.

The Full Court upheld the trial Judge's findings that News Limited and the Super League companies had induced the rebel clubs to breach the implied term, however the remedies available to the ARL were to be confined to an award of damages, as the ARL had the benefit of an injunction for the 1996 season.

The Full Court also considered the following matters:

in making orders directly affecting the rights and obligations of Super League players and coaches when those players and coaches were not parties to the litigation, there had been a breach of the principle that persons should be joined as parties if orders are to be made which affect them. Those orders were consequently set aside.

Burchett J erred in as much as he indicated that he would have refused relief on discretionary grounds, even if News Limited had established contravention of the Trade Practices Act, because he had found News Limited had induced breaches of contract and procured the 'corruption of fiduciaries'. A breach of the Trade Practices Act makes an agreement void and the Full Court stressed that was not an area for the exercise of discretion.

Burchett J must still determine the following matters: claims by the ARL that News Limited and the Super League companies have engaged in misleading or deceptive conduct, passing off and infringement of trade marks; claims for unjust enrichment; claims against News Limited for unlawful interference with the activities of the ARL; claims for damages under the Corporations Law for Clubs acting in a manner inconsistent with their objects; damages and costs.

In short, leaving aside the differences of opinion relating to the trade practices matters, the Full Federal Court strongly disagreed with Burchett J's conception of the co-operative nature of ARL style rugby league, which gave rise to fiduciary duties and constructive trusts, and his view that the alleged impropriety of News Limited's corporate tactics made it undeserving of a remedy from the Court. However it is probably also fair to say that the Full Court's judgment is not particularly remarkable in terms of the legal principles to be found in it; what is more significant are the consequences which are likely to flow from it, namely:

–   the existence of two separate rugby league competitions in Australia for the foreseeable future;

–   the fact that representatives teams selected from players in the 'rebel' league will play representative teams consisting of the best players from other rugby league countries;

–   continuing spectator bitterness and disinterest.[92]

The Super League has therefore been able to move ahead in Australia. In the European league (with all the clubs being English except for Paris St Germain) the move to Super League has been free from any major legal resistance although there was a good deal of vociferous opposition. Murdoch and BskyB have been able to literally buy the game. Some may see this as an example of 'sports hijacking'. Whether it will be in the long-term interests of rugby league is open to speculation.

At the same time as the birth of Super League, the world of rugby union was about to enter a period of monument change. Packer, with the threat of the ARL losing all of its best players to Murdoch and left with a very second class competition, was persuaded:

... to switch their attention to rugby union. Maybe it was a time to set the genuinely worldwide up on a truly professional basis and then return to choke the living daylights out of Murdoch's rugby league, which, by comparison, was quite simply a piss-ant parish pump game.[93]

This led to a small band of executives, a business advisor, a consultant accountant and a lawyer acting on behalf of Packer trying to interest potential backers in the sports and television world to the potential of this plan. This plan would become the embryonic World Rugby Corporation. In competition, a rival vision was beginning to take shape originating in the fear of the southern hemisphere rugby unions that Super League was going to rob them of all their best players. Rugby union had to be able to meet the financial

---

92 'News Limited's Super League Appeal Success', *Anzsla Newsletter Update*, January 1997. Also see Farrell, R, 'Super League Success for Murdoch' (1996) 4(3) *Sport and the Law Journal* 134.

93 *Ibid*, Fitzsimons (1996), p 4.

rewards that Super League could offer. They saw Murdoch as possibly being interested in a complementary rugby union world competition. Clearly the spirit of amateurism was in its death throes:

Fitzsimons, P, *The Rugby War*

Since rugby league's very beginnings it had fought a long-running guerilla war against the amateurs of rugby union. For the last century or so, the monied war lords of league had made an art form out of periodically tearing down from the hill tops on hit and run raids, where they lured away whichever union player took their fancy with promises of enormous amounts of moolah.

For just as long, the war had been more or less manageable, with rugby union able to hold most of its favoured players with the persuasive argument that rugby was the truly international game which offered the best benefits overall. If it was money you were after, no other game anywhere offered even half the contacts with the rugby-mad business community, and let us not forget the honour and glory, the glory and honour, the honour and glory.

This Super League thing, Richie Guy concluded, was something else again. Even run of the mill rugby league players were being offered up to four times more than they had been earning previously, and it simply did not bear thinking about what some of his star All Black players might now be offered to defect.

Actually, they were already getting paid to a certain extent. The best of the All Blacks that year could expect around NZ$130,000 through endorsements and promotions – raised largely through the marketing of the All Black name – but that was clearly not going to be enough any more. 'I think we realised immediately,' Guy says, 'that we had to give the All Blacks vastly larger incomes. The first provisional figure we talked about was another five million dollars to protect the All Blacks and obviously the protection needed to be much wider than just the national team, so we started thinking we would need to initially target 150 players, to have them getting a good income too. The question I was thinking a lot about then was where would we get the money from?'[94]

All of the broadsheets and tabloids alike were still chock-a-block with the enormous brouhaha that had been created by a comment the English rugby captain Will Carling had made on a British television program the week before. 'What gets me and a lot of players now is the hypocrisy of the situation,' Carling had said as the cameras rolled. 'Why are we not just honest and say there is a lot of money in the game? If the game is run properly, as a professional game, you do not need 57 old farts running rugby.'

Well they never! Carling was immediately dropped from the captaincy for his troubles, causing the controversy to enormously escalate. But other of Carling's comments, and the response to them, also give a feel for the temper of the times: 'There seems to be an awful lot of things the Union now does to make money out of the sport,' Carling said, 'but there is still this feeling that the

---

94 *Ibid*, pp 9–10.

players should not make any money out of it. Everyone seems to do very well out of rugby union except the players. It has become more than a fun game. You do not have a World Cup for fun and recreation'.

The English Rugby Football Union Secretary Dudley Wood had said in reply: 'We believe we are running a sport as a recreation for players to play in their spare time. I think money is a corrosive influence.'

This enormous gap between the attitudes of the players and those of the officials, Turnbull says, was absolutely typical of what he discovered around the world. 'It was just extraordinary,' he says now, 'how everybody I talked to agreed that the players really disliked the officials, and that the officials simply did not understand what the players were on about'.[95]

So the lines were drawn:

... the fights between the World Rugby Corporation and the national rugby unions was a clash of generations, of footballing ideologies, of one set of business interests against another. Most of all it was about a violent difference of opinion between revolutionaries, as to what form the revolution should take.[96]

As with Packer's World Series Cricket, WRC began to in clandestine fashion, sign up the top Rugby Union talent.[97] That this should largely take place during the 1995 Rugby Union World Cup adds to the drama.[98] However the rival group representing the power base of the world national rugby unions were in no mood to capitulate. Different national unions brought pressure upon their players to give up their WRC contracts.[99] In South Africa this led to a court case where the WRC claimed the South African Rugby Football Union induced South African players to break their contracts with them. Clearly the Unions were determined to fight back on a global scale and in addition to this specific legal defeat:

... the Australians were wavering, England still had only 10 players of their World Cup Squad signed, legal advice had been received that indicated that the Federation Francaise de Rugby had the overwhelming weight of French law on its side – in that any such 'rebel' organisation as WRC was outright illegal in that country ... all up, it was plainly not going to be possible to do this thing without there being an enormous split in the ranks of world rugby.[100]

Every sport has its own culture and, of course, the two – sport and culture – feed off the other. While the World Rugby Corporation to this point had been

---

95   *Ibid*, pp 43–44.

96   *Ibid*, p 53.

97   'Rugby Union: Rebels weigh up options', *The Guardian*, 18 July 1995, p 18.

98   'Rugby Union: World Cup players warn that Packer is serious', *The Guardian*, 20 July 1995, p 20.

99   'Rugby Union: Home unions hit back at Packer', *The Guardian*, 25 July 1995, p 22; and 'Rugby Union: Packer seeks to strike deal with the unions', *The Guardian*, 28 July 1995, p 19.

100 *Ibid*, Fitzsimons (1996), pp 293–94.

amazingly successful in getting the top players around the world to sign contracts – the culture as a whole simply refused to be so lassoed. And it was not just that the rugby union public remained clearly against it ...

From the beginning, Levy and Turnbull's plan required the Rugby Union administrators around the world to see sweet reason – to see either that the WRC scheme was truly visionary and should be embraced or alternatively to see that they were so heavily outgunned in terms of player manpower that they simply must wave the white flag so as to salvage what they could.

This did not transpire. Why? In part, because the WRC were uniformly dealing with rugby men, and it is a point of honour among rugby men, never to give in to intimidation. The ethos runs strongly through rugby veins that you should never back down and at the very least it is taken as given that if you cannot actually beat an intimidatory opponent you must at least try and take a piece of him home with you.

Thus with the possible exception of some slight wavering among individuals in New Zealand, at no point in any of the WRC manoeuvres did it ever seem even remotely possible that the national unions around the world would give in to them.[101]

No world Rugby Union competition transpired. However the move to professional status in Britain has not occurred without a good deal of bloodshed and a turf war between different factions, notably the English Rugby Football Union (RFU) and the English Professional Rugby Union Clubs Ltd (EPRUC), the representative body of the professional clubs, as to the right to govern the sport.[102]

This media-initiated challenge to the existing order was not the first time that the issue of the distinction between professional and amateur rugby had been aired. In mid-1994, The Sports (Discrimination) Bill was presented as a Private Members' Bill by the Wakefield MP David Hinchliffe, aiming to end the power of the Rugby Football Union to ban for life any player who defected to play rugby league.[103] In the spring of 1995 the National Heritage Parliamentary Select Committee, chaired by the Labour MP Gerald Kaufman, looked at relations between rugby union and rugby league, particularly the issue of amateurism and distinctions in the way players from each sport are treated.[104] The media-determined wars in both rugby codes have brought about change that was probably only a question of time.

---

101 *Ibid*, p 298.

102 This was almost a daily news event from Summer 1996 until Summer 1997; see eg 'RFU tempts Clubs to £18m Deal', *The Guardian*, 24 October 1996, p 22.

103 'Rugby Union: Union cuts life ban on league players', *The Guardian*, 15 March 1995, p 21.

104 'Amateur status "not accurate"', *The Guardian*, 17 March 1995, p 21 and 'Commentary: Time to tackle the thorny question of "shamateurs"', *The Guardian*, 17 March 1995, p 24.

THE END OF AMATEURISM

Will Carling's famous statement perhaps crystallises the legacy of the past:

'Shamateurism's End: Taking the Money and Running'

The timing could not have been more ironic: on the very weekend rugby league was celebrating its centenary, Rugby Union announced it too was now a professional game. Rugby league was launched 100 years ago tomorrow by 21 union clubs, which wanted to pay their players for taking time off from work to play, but failed to persuade other union clubs to go along. It led to the two separate rugby codes – one openly professional and the other where payments were not supposed to be made. Slowly but inexorably, union's amateur status has become a sham. First came expenses, then came lucrative PR jobs with big companies, and then full blown product endorsement (so long as there was no direct mention of the individual player's links with rugby). Other countries went much further than the home nations. France began paying some of its top players in the thirties. But it was television – and the large audiences generated by the 1987 and 1991 World Cups – that tolled the final amateur bell. Rugby has become a multimillion pound business. Just before the start of this year's world cup, Murdoch's News Corporation struck a £360 million deal with the rugby unions of Australia, New Zealand and South Africa.

It was the fear of Murdoch – or his rival Kerry Packer – grabbing control of the sport that finally forced the International Rugby Union Board to move this weekend. Some rugby union officials were expressing regret yesterday. They should not have been. The new system will end the hypocrisy of the old. It will allow a few – and it will only be a few – top players to a share in the game's growing riches. They deserve that. The main core of the sport – just as in tennis, golf, even soccer – will remain amateur. Remember, even within rugby league, the vast majority of players have another job as well as playing rugby. Our own sports reporters put the number of union players who are likely to receive direct payments at between 60 and 100. Even within this group, few are likely to be full-time rugby players. The risks are too great – both from injury and loss of form. Big policemen and massive army officers are still likely to be found in the pack. Although payments can be made at any level, few clubs are likely to be in a position to offer them. Even the most successful club, Bath, holds fewer than 10,000. Compare that to United's 40,000 plus.[105]

This change in status of the game[106] has brought obvious changes: sports agents,[107] professional players union;[108] television revenues. However there have been those who lament the end of the amateur ethos.[109]

---

105 'Shamateurism's End: Taking the Money and Running', *The Guardian*, 28 August 1995.

106 'Small change for most Rugby Union players', *The Guardian*, 28 August 1995, p 3; 'The Rugby Revolution: Amateurism ditched in pay go-ahead', *The Guardian*, 28 August 1995, p 16.

107 'The future starts here: Rugby sports agents', *The Observer*, 31 December 1995, p 26.

108 'Moon is the man as sun sets on amateurism', *The Guardian*, 20 December 1995, p 21.

109 'Rugby Union: Top club official quits over "ethos"', *The Guardian*, 1 September 1995, p 23.

Similar changes have occurred in athletics:

Downes, S and Mackay, D, *Running Scared: How Athletics Lost its Innocence*

Athens was also the venue in 1982 for the greatest revolution in a century of modern athletics. There were no races run, no jumps leaped nor implements thrown: the revolution took place in a conference hall, where the IAAF took the first tentative steps towards allowing athletics to go professional.

The process had begun at the IAAF's conference in Moscow prior to the 1980 Olympics. There, the Federation established a nine man working group on 'eligibility' – in other words, to examine the amateur status of athletes.

During the 1960s and 1970s amateurism, although increasingly regarded as an anachronism in the modern sporting world – cricket had abandoned its 'Gentlemen and Players' distinction, and the Wimbledon tennis championships had gone open – it had still been strictly applied by the International Olympic Committee, first under the autocratic leadership of the American, Avery Brundage, and then under the Irish peer, Lord Killanin. The Games were still the most important event in any amateur sportsman's career, so no athlete could risk being banned for receiving money. But with Michael Killanin set to retire as IOC president in July 1980, the ground was laid for a moderniser to succeed him. The Spaniard Juan Antonio Samaranch duly became the IOC's first full-time president. Fittingly, he was to preside over a period which made it increasingly possible for Olympic competitors to become full-time, professional athletes.

The mood at the IAAF's congress in Moscow had reflected this turning point in world sport. When the IAAF working party on eligibility delivered its report to the governing council when it met in Cairo the following March, its findings were hardly a surprise. The tone of the report was categorical: the very future of the IAAF was in the balance. The shamateur game was up, according to the working party. 'The year 1980 has brought to a head the fact that the future of the IAAF and its members is at stake,' the report began. 'It is felt that at international level, athletics is a semi-professional (in the widest sense) sport already, with many leading athletes in top countries training for at least 30 hours per week. The Group aims, however, to make a clear distinction between a professional sport and athletics, which, by its very nature, can never become this. It is recognised that there is dissatisfaction among the elite athletes and meeting organisers with the present rules on eligibility, and in different countries, violations of the rules occur, which causes accusations of hypocrisy to be levelled against the whole sport of athletics.'

Conscious of the need to prevent an amateur-professional schism in the sport, but also subjected to political pressures from the eastern bloc nations – who wanted the status quo maintained, so that their State-funded athletes would maintain their apparent advantage over part-time western athletes the working party proposed a set of rule changes which would openly allow payments to athletes, through a system of prize-money and trust funds. The recommendations, though, were only a majority view of the working party.

The proposed new eligibility rules were debated heatedly when put before the IAAF Conference held just before the European Championships in Athens in September 1982. The reactionaries on the working party, who wanted to avoid change, seemed to have swung opinion among the IAAF Congress – the sport's 'parliamentary' body, made up of representatives of every national member federation, with the authority to make or change the sport's rules.

Compromise was offered. Although the working party had favoured prize-money over appearance fees ('an athlete receiving money merely because he is a champion is felt to be an unfair and unworthy system for the sport. Appearance money inevitably takes the stimulus away from competition, just as it may be argued that prize money gives added stimulus'), it was the latter, appearance money scheme which had attracted more support. Yet even moves towards this new system of appearance payments seemed to have stalled until a rousing address by a member of the British delegation. The man who turned the day in favour of appearance fees was Andy Norman.

Before breakfast, sensing that the mood of the Congress might reject all proposals for athletes' payments at that afternoon's debate, Norman had banged on the door of the hotel bedroom of The Guardian reporter, John Rodda. After a typically journalistic late night, Rodda was feeling a little fragile when he was awoken by the knock on the door from the policeman, but he was persuaded nonetheless to help Norman by writing what Rodda later described as 'a blatantly provocative speech' in favour of change.

Standing in front of all the IAAF's power brokers at the Athens conference, and with Rodda's speech to guide him, Norman warned that if the national governing bodies continued to pretend that under-the-counter payments were not happening, then what they all feared most – a breakaway, professional circuit – might happen. Norman 'knew what the athletes wanted,' Rodda recalled, 'and how it was obtainable'.

'Rule 17 – Athlete's Funds', the new payment rule, went through by 367 votes to 16, though not without hitch. The IAAF very quickly rushed out a two page, 10 point 'Explanatory Statement', it said 'to make the Athens decisions completely clear'.

The first point of the explanatory statement read: 'The IAAF is against the introduction of commercialism and professionalism in our sport, and the IAAF Council will always actively struggle against any such introduction'. Not only did that seem to contradict the entire argument in Athens, but the evidence of the next 14 years showed the IAAF to be the prime movers in the commercialisation of international athletics. The explanatory statement was just shouting at the gale. While the IAAF tried to give the appearance of shoring up the position of its members by ruling that all deals and payments for athletes must be routed through the national federations, any qualifications top the new rules proved to be unenforceable. The tide had turned professionalism's way.[110]

---

110 Downes, S and Mackay, D, *Running Scared: How Athletics Lost its Innocence* (1996), Edinburgh: Mainstream Publishing, pp 100–02.

Although the enormous areas of amateur sporting activity often in the form of recreational activity must never be forgotten in these discussions, virtually all of elite modern sport is clearly professional.[111] The general commercialisation and commodification of sport has been shown to be influential in this process. The law is never far behind in these circumstances, and the commercial origins of much legal intervention in sport are clear to see.

TELEVISION

Television has also had a pivotal role to play in this change. An extract from Garry Whannel suggests the importance that television has on contemporary sport. Written before the enormous impact of satellite television on sport in Britain in the context of the vast amounts of money that BSkyB have paid for television rights, Whannel's argument is that increasingly our view of sport is mediated through television. This is unlikely to decrease in the future:

Whannel, G, Fields in Vision: Television Sport and Cultural Transformation

What is so important about television sport that it warrants a whole book? There is a lot of it, over 2,000 hours a year, not including the satellite channels; and while it is not all wildly popular it is watched by significant numbers and on major occasions like the Cup Final or the Olympic Games, by as much as half the population. Television sport is by any standards a component of popular culture and to understand it better is to understand more about the culture in which we live.

In that it chooses particular sports and gives us a particular view of them, television must inevitably affect the ways in which we see and understand sports. Moreover the coverage is not simply concerned with sport; it inevitably also continually makes implicit and explicit statements, in words and pictures, about our sense of nation, of class, of the place of men and women, our relation to other nations and so on. Think how many stock stereotypes of foreigners (temperamental Latins, happy-go-lucky West Indians, dull but efficient Germans, faceless factory-bred East Europeans) have unfolded partly around images of sport.

Second, television, in association with sponsorship, has been responsible for changing the face of sport in the last 25 years. You only need to think of the rise of snooker, one day cricket, shirt advertising in football or the decision to stage the next World Cup in the USA. These changes are evident not only at the elite levels. Organisers of the smallest local competition or league now seem convinced that nothing can be accomplished without sponsorship. In a very real sense sport has become a branch of the advertising and public relations industries.

111 See Strenk, A, 'Amateurism: The Myth and the Reality', in Segrave, JP and Chu, D, *The Olympic Games in Transition* (1988), Champaign: Human Kenetics, pp 307–21; Holt, R, 'Amateurism and its Interpretation: The Social Origins of British Sport' (1992) 5(4) *Innovation* 19.

I like sport and it has given me some treasured memories – seeing golfer Harold Henning get a hole in one in 1963, Fulham beat Liverpool 2–0 at Craven Cottage in 1966, Crystal Palace clinch the Second Division Championship in 1979, Dave Moorcroft beat Sydney Maree over 3,000 m in 1982, and Ian Botham get his 355th and 356th Test wickets at the Oval to become the greatest taker of Test wickets of all time in 1986. I also like television sport and have many more golden memories as a result, but they are probably similar to yours. One interesting effect of the vivid full colour realism of television is that after a while you begin to be unsure about which events you saw in the flesh. Sport has also, increasingly, made me angry – sitting in crowds of people wearing cheap cardboard hats to advertise a building society, watching interminable award ceremonies staged for the benefit of sponsors, or watching cricket amongst sales executives so saturated with corporate hospitality they have difficulty focusing on the game. As this is a fairly dispassionate and analytic book, neither pleasure nor anger are given full rein – I am saving that indulgence for a subsequent project. I began studying television sport in 1978 as an embryonic PhD thesis, which I eventually finished in 1987. During this time both my children were born, both my parents died, Mrs Thatcher came to the throne, Fulham went down to the Third Division and Seb Coe, Alex Higgins, Martina Navratilova and Ian Botham all had their golden days.

While it is possible to debate whether the changes wrought by television and sponsorship are good or bad, it is more relevant to try to understand the conventions of television, how they emerged, and how television, as an economic reality and a set of aesthetic conventions, has intervened in and transformed the cultural practices of sports.[112]

CONCLUSION

The next chapter will look at, amongst other things, the specific legal issues concerning the regulation of the televising of sport within the general context of the commercial reality of modern sport. What this chapter has shown is that elite sport is subject to immense commercial and financial pressures. The spirit of sport as an activity in its own terms, and not merely as a form of entertainment, is in some danger in the face of these pressures. The law's involvement in regulating sports commercial structure is seen by some as adding to those pressures, by others as necessary and as a mechanism to bring order.

---

112 Whannel, G, *Fields in Vision: Television Sport and Cultural Transformation* (1992), London: Routledge, pp 1–2.

CHAPTER SIX

COMMERCIAL ASPECTS

INTRODUCTION

A theme throughout this book, particularly in Chapter 5, is the increasing levels of money involved in sport and the business nature of sport today. Sports can be said to have a commercial value. But it cannot be said that sport can be 'owned'. The question that needs to be addressed is how can the commercial value arising from sport be used and protected. One can 'only own and control the vehicle through which sports are played (eg sports entertainment events, sports facilities, sports equipment, player contracts, trade marks, telecast, publications and other copyright material including advertising and promotional literature'.[1]

This chapter will examine what the commercial values in sport are, who can own them and how they can be exploited, how they can be abused and how they can be protected.

The relevant legal rights that can be claimed and protected in this area are intellectual property rights. Cornish described intellectual property as the 'application of ideas and information that are of commercial value'.[2] Bainbridge states 'Intellectual property law is that area of the law which concerns legal rights associated with creative effect or commercial reputation and goodwill'.[3] Intellectual property may be described as being a product of the mind. It is of economic value in that it may be bought, sold, licensed or assigned; it may be transferred just as any other form of property. Intellectual property is essentially about legal rights; the exclusive rights of the owner to control them which is recognised by the law. Relevant intellectual property rights for our purposes are:

Copyright

Section 1 of the Copyrights Designs and Patents Act 1988

(1) (a) Original literary, dramatic , musical and artistic works;

    (b) sound recordings, films, broadcasts or cable programmes; and

    (c) the typographical arrangements of published editions.

---

1   Wall, A, 'Sports Marketing and The Law' (1996) 7(1) *Marquette Sports Law Journal* 77.
2   Cornish, WR, *Intellectual Property*, 3rd edn (1996), London: Sweet & Maxwell.
3   Bainbridge, D, *Intellectual Property*, 3rd edn (1996), London: Pitman.

Trade marks

Section 1 of the Trade Marks Act 1994

(1) any sign capable of being represented graphically which is capable of distinguishing goods or services of one undertaking from those of other undertakings. A trade mark may in particular, consist of words (including personal names), designs, letters, numerals or the shape of goods or their packaging

Passing Off

The common law protects goodwill pertaining to business and this is what distinguishes passing off from trade mark protection. Goodwill has been defined as 'the attractive force that brings in custom'.[4] It is a property right even though intangible. It is a product of the business relationships a trader has with his customers. The nature of the right was described by Buckley LJ when he said:

A man who engages in commercial activities may acquire a valuable reputation in respect of the goods in which he deals, or of the services which he performs, or of his business as an entity. The law regards such a reputation as an incorporeal piece of property, the integrity of which the owner is entitled to protect.[5]

The rights arise in different ways. Copyright arises automatically.[6] The moment the work is created it attracts copyright. There are no formal registration procedures. A trade mark is 'any sign which is capable of being represented graphically and which is capable of distinguishing goods or services or one undertaking from those of another'.[7] This in turn is subject to the absolute[8] and relative[9] grounds of refusal. The rights arise upon registration of the mark. The rights against passing off seek to protect the goodwill of a business. The goodwill may be attached to, for example, a name or 'get up' of a product. Goodwill may be established by use but the period of use necessary to establish the goodwill is a question of fact to be determined in the circumstances of the case. The rights are dealt with by means of contract and infringements of the rights are tortuous. Intellectual property rights are also available under the Patents Act 1977 for inventions but the requirements of novelty, non-obviousness and industrial application together with exclusions means that its application in the sporting context is unlikely.

---

4   *Per* Lord Macnaghten, *IRC v Muller* [1901] AC 217.

5   *Bulmer Ltd v Bollinger SA* [1978] RPC 79.

6   For copyright to subsist in literary, dramatic or musical works, they must be original (s 1(1)(a) (*University of London Press Ltd v University Tutorial Press Ltd* [1916] 2 Ch 601)) and the works must be fixed (s 3(2)). Artistic works must meet the requirement of originality (s 1(1)(a)).

7   Section 1(1) of the Trade Marks Act 1994.

8   Sections 3 and 4.

9   Section 5.

The application of intellectual property rights in sport is demonstrated in the following extracts:

Letts, Q, 'Sports Stars Coached on Patent Law'

Dick Fosbury, the high jumper who invented the 'Fosbury flop', would be a millionaire today under a proposal from a US lawyer that sportsmen patent their best known moves.

Robert Kunstadt, a senior Manhattan lawyer, urged athletes taking part in next month's Atlanta Olympics to legally protect their sporting innovations. It is a proposal that could bring chaos to the playing field but earn fortunes for sports stars.

Mr Kunstadt, who publishes his proposal next week in the National Law Journal, said yesterday that he has already received inquiries from leading sportsmen and sportswomen curious as to how to capitalise on innovations. Sports such as gymnastics, baseball and basketball are rich in opportunities, he said, and protection could be sought under existing laws.

A basketball player such as Michael Jordan of the Chicago Bulls who has a distinctive way of approaching the hoop, would stand to benefit, as would Kareem Abdul Jabbar, formerly of the Los Angeles Lakers, who invented the 'sky hook' scoring shot. Bob Cousy, formerly of the Boston Celtics, could have made a great deal of money from his much copied behind-the-back basketball pass.

'At least three forms of intellectual property protection might be used to secure rights in sports moves – copyright, patent and trade mark,' Mr Kunstadt said. 'Sports stars are not properly protecting their interests at present.'

'Gymnasts could easily cite the widespread use of copyright law in protecting dance and choreography steps,' he said. Protection could also be demanded by, for instance, the skier who comes up with a particular stance or the wrestler who invents an effective hold.

'Sportsmen deserve more security and coaches and trainers are often unrewarded,' he said. It would be up to umpires and referees to stop a player using an unlicensed move.

Dick Fosbury himself replied that he was not interested in making money out of sport. For other sports innovators of the past, such as Mark Spitz with his double jointed butterfly swimming stroke, it is probably already too late to capitalise.

For patent law to apply, real inventiveness had to be proved, said Mr Kunstadt, but trade mark and copyright laws might be used to safeguard characteristic moves.

Mr Kunstadt, who has in the past represented the US Olympic Committee, added that patent protection could relieve the pressure for State funding of sports as it would generate large sums.[10]

---

10   Letts, Q, 'Sports Stars Coached on Patent Law', *The Times*, 14 May 1996, p 12.

Ford, A 'Whose Move is This?'

Could Dick Fosbury and others patent their sports ideas?

Now, though, a New York lawyer has proposed radical reforms that would strengthen still further the law's grip on sport. Robert Kunstadt has published an article in the *National Law Journal* which throws open a whole new area for potential exploitation – 'sports moves'. These are the distinguishable ways in which an athlete goes about his business – Langer's inverted putting grip, rugby player Rob Andrews's crouched kick, or Australian cricketer Shane Warne's 'flipper'. He suggests that athletes can, and should, use current laws to protect innovative and creative moves through patent and/or trade mark registration and via copyright. But would this apply only in America?

Mr Kunstadt's firm counts the NBA, the US Tennis Association and the US Olympic Committee among its clients. He argues that patents will apply only to new ideas which, in the fullness of time, will benefit sport. He assumes that athletes will want to issue non-exclusive licences to competitors (at a nominal price) and teach others how to perform the move. If an athlete can patent a revolutionary football boot (eg the Adidas Predator, invented about two years ago by Craig Johnson, the former Australian footballer), why can he not patent a revolutionary way to jump over a bar – such as Fosbury's flop, the backwards leap made famous by the American high jumper?

For an innovation to be legally protected, it must be new, inventive and capable of industrial application. In most cases, sports moves are simply a variation on a theme and will fail on the first two counts. But what about the third – for is sport not an industry? The UK Patent Office will probably maintain that any sports move falls within the excluded category of schemes, rules or methods for playing a game.

Copyright exists in any original literary, dramatic, musical and artistic work. The Copyright Designs and Patents Act 1988 provides that dramatic work includes 'dance'. Sports such as ice skating, gymnastics and, some say, wrestling are barely more than dancing. Such choreographic work could arguably be protected by copyright. So perhaps choreographed passages of play are capable of protection: could we see *Spurs v Arsenal* in court, should the Gunners wish to copy the now famous 'Tottenham Corner' deployed regularly throughout Euro 96? And what if Cher were to release an aerobic video which materially reproduced the 'moves' contained in a Jane Fonda tape?

Sports moves may also be reduced to writing, becoming original literary works capable of protection. Formula One teams compile data and details to help them to set up their cars' suspension, aero dynamics and engine management systems for each circuit. If these were to fall into the hands of a competitor by dishonest means, the team might bring an action for breach of confidence, and might seek to enforce its copyright in written details. The same could apply to caddies' notebooks.

Mr Kunstadt's final suggestion relates to trade mark protection. Nike products, for example, are identified by an image of the leaping Michael Jordan. Technology may present us with a situation where a product bears a moving mark. Following the Trade Marks Act 1994, marks no longer have to be static, merely capable of graphic representation. So while a moving image of, say,

Jordan as a screen saver on computers can be an IBM trade mark, this would not stop any player producing the same move on court. But Mr Kunstadt extends the principle beyond the scope of UK legislation. If Colombian goalkeeper Rene Haguita could register as a trade mark his 'scorpion kick' on goods sold commercially, Mr Kunstadt contends that Haguita could make a claim against, say, David Seaman should he copy the kick.

Many of the above examples, while ridiculous to sports fans, are technically arguable. But sporting bodies would undoubtedly prohibit the monopolising of a move and Mr Kunstadt recognises this. It is unlikely that the UK Patent Office would allow the registration of sports moves. Nevertheless, copyright protection of a sequence of choreographed moves and those reduced to writing is possible though they are not dance or literary.

Every intellectual property lawyer's Holy Trinity is to 'identify, protect and exploit'. It may be that Mr Kunstadt has identified a new area of work. Come the Sydney 2000 Olympics, lawyers may be doing more than just troubleshooting.

Keep lawyers out of sport? It is already too late.[11]

THE COMMERCIAL VALUE IN SPORT

Contemporary elite sport is a form of entertainment and as such there is commercial value in it. People will pay to see it. It therefore has a clear economic value. The media recognition of its entertainment value has resulted in sport becoming an integral part of television programming. Its appeal to viewers enable viewing ratings to improve and as a consequence, increase advertising revenues. This in turn impacts on sports itself transforming it into a multimillion pound industry. Sport then is an investment opportunity. It is big business.

The value is not only in the sport itself but also attaches to the off-field activity. In the financial year ending July 1995, Manchester United Plc's turnover from merchandising was £23.5 million, conference and catering £3.36 million, sponsorship and royalties £7.36 million and television revenue £6.35 million. The gate receipts in comparison were £19.6 million.[12] Arguably then, the greatest commercial value is not in the game so much as in the other commercial activities of those who participate in sport. Sport itself is used to create the brand image which is then commercially taken advantage of through such activities as merchandising. This of course will put pressure on the playing of the sport; the success of the merchandising products will depend on the success of the team. It should be noted then that it is not the

---

11 Ford, A, 'Whose Move is This', *The Times,* 30 July 1996, p 33.
12 Watkins, M, 'Asset Exploitation – Manchester United's Experience', Unpublished Conference Paper, Sports Forum '96 Chelsea Football Ground, 26 November 1996.

sport itself that is being exploited but the name (for example of the club) that is associated with the sport, the sport being used only to provide the brand image.

OWNERSHIP OF COMMERCIAL RIGHTS

Individual Athletes

Individual athletes are not only assets of their clubs, although to this extent they will be protected. For example, the Molson beer advertisement featuring a look-alike Cantona kicking at a crowd with the words 'A Molson moment in a sea of madness' resulted in a complaint to the Advertising Standards Authority being upheld. But the individual athletes themselves have a value which they will want to protect to ensure that no one other than themselves can take commercial advantage of such value. As a result recent times have seen the registration of trade marks: Paul Gascoigne registering 'Gazza'; Eric Cantona 'Cantona 7' and 'Ooh aah Cantona' and Damon Hill the image of his eyes in his racing helmet.

One obvious way for athletes taking advantage of their own value is to endorse products so that the athlete's personality and playing attributes are associated with the product. Robert Downing, editor of *Sports Marketing News* has said 'The really successful endorsees can make three times as much money off the field as they can on the field, and most of then will turn down more offers than they can accept, either because they do not believe in the product or they do not want to be over exposed'.[13] What is really involved here is sponsorship and this will be discussed later.

As regards individual athletes, one issue that needs addressing is whether they have rights in their personalities which can be protected. That is, where there is no authorised endorsement by a sportsman or woman, will the use of their name or nickname be actionable? The issue involved is that of character merchandising. Copyright will not protect a name only in that it will meet the requirements of originality needed to amount to a literary work. That only leaves an action in passing off if the name is not a registered trade mark. Crucial to a passing off action is a common field of activity. That is, there must be some common ground between the plaintiff and defendant in their business activities. The requirement is demonstrated in *McCullogh v May*.[14] The plaintiff was an well known children's broadcaster known as Uncle Mac. The defendant sold cereal under the name Uncle Mac with indirect reference

---

13 Quoted in Hoffman and Greenberg, *Sport$biz* (1989), Champaign, Illinois: Leisure Press.
14 [1946] 65 RPC 58.

to the plaintiff without his permission. It was held that there was no passing off since there was no common field of activity between the plaintiff's business of being a broadcaster and the defendant's business of making cereals. Applying this to our situation the argument would be that there would be no common field of activity between a sportsman and the product. A good example is the Britvic 'Red Card' high energy drink advertising campaign. Together with posters featuring Chelmsford City Football Club as the 'New Force in British Football', a series of advertisements were run connecting the drink with a number of high profile players such as Cantona and Shearer. No passing off action was possible since there was no common field of activity; one being sports and the other being drinks. Bitel has criticised this approach arguing 'reputation is a valuable property be it the reputation of an individual or an event and shame on the law if it fails to protect his property right'.[15]

Some hope can be taken from the case of *Mirage Studios v Counter Feat Clothing Co Ltd*[16] which concerned the Teenage Mutant Hero Ninja Turtle characters. The defendant had made drawings of the characters similar to those of the plaintiff and licensed them to be produced on merchandise such as T-shirts. Browne-Wilkinson VC found an arguable case of copyright breach and passing off. The misrepresentation as regards the passing off was that the public would believe that the reproductions were authorised by the plaintiff and their goodwill would be damages because of the defendants inferior quality drawings. The case shows the courts recognising character merchandising but its limits should be noted in that there was a drawing here to which copyright attached and the case did not simply concern a name. It seems then that where names of sports personalities are concerned, then the requirement of a common field of activity still stands but the position may be different if control over the quality of the goods to which the name is applied can be demonstrated.

Australian law seems to be more developed in respect of character merchandising and this is reflected in the case of *Pacific Dunlop v Hogan*[17] which concerned an advertisement based on the 'knife scene' in the film Crocodile Dundee. The misrepresentation was established by the court on the basis that the film's star, Paul Hogan, had been selective about the products that he had chosen to endorse and the advertisement tended to damage his reputation in that it suggested that he was endorsing yet another product and it would reduce the impact of Hogan's advertising which he might choose to engage in using the film as the basis.

The public clearly recognise character merchandising and make a connection of quality where products are endorsed and it is to be hoped that

15 Bitel, N, 'Ambush Marketing' (1997) 5(1) *Sport and the Law Journal* 12.
16 [1991] FSR 145.
17 (1989) 14 IPR 398.

the courts will recognise this and offer the appropriate protection as seems to have occurred in Australia. Solutions have been achieved in other countries too:

Bitel, N, 'Ambush Marketing'

There are models for the solution which events need. In Switzerland a person's picture, name, voice and reputation are protected as part of his or her personality (Articles 27 and 28 of the Swiss Civil Code). Germany and Switzerland both have unfair competition laws (Unlauteren Weltbewerb 16.12.1986 (Switzerland) and 7.6.1909 (RGBL s 499) (Germany). But perhaps the most directly applicable law is the Lanham Act (15 USC 1125(a)) in America.

Under that statute the law prohibits ' ... any false designation of origin, false or misleading description of fact or false or misleading representation of facts which ... is likely to cause confusion, or to cause mistake, or to deceive as to the affiliation, connection or association of such person' with a particular product.

Using this the basketball player Kareem Abdul-Jabbar was even able to stop General Motors from using without his consent his former name, Lew Alcinder, in an advert (*Abdul-Jabbar v General Motors Corporation* (9th Circ 2/8/96)) and another basketballer, Dennis Rodman could even protect his body tattoos and injunct a manufacturer from reproducing them on a T-shirt (*Rodman v Fanatix Apparel Inc* (DNJ 5/28/96)).

How Cantona would have liked this particular piece of legislation when faced with the unauthorised 'Cantona Fine Wines'.

Perhaps the answer is to sue in America; after all the tabloids in which the Red Card adverts appear were all distributed in the United States, and the American Courts seem to grab jurisdiction at every opportunity. Certainly the IOC's successes against Amex have come in jurisdictions such as France where the protection is far better than in the UK.[18]

In the United States the right of publicity is recognised:

Wall, A, 'Sports Marketing and the Law'

The right of publicity is the property right a person has in his or her own identity. This right includes the exclusive right to control the asset value in commercial exploitation of the individual's name, likeness and personality. It is a right that is not recognised by all States, nor is it recognised in all countries. For example, passing off and defamation actions are still used to protect celebrities' images and reputations in courts around the Pacific Rim. Where recognised, the law protects the individual's proprietary interest in his or her own performance. The right of publicity in one State protects a resident celebrity in all others. Not surprisingly, California law offers resident celebrities broader right of publicity protection than most other States.

Like the right of privacy, publicity rights preclude commercial use without consent. The rationale parallels the tenets underlying copyright and trade mark laws which prevent unjust enrichment by theft of goodwill. The guiding

---

18   Bitel, N, 'Ambush Marketing' (1997) 5(1) *Sport and the Law Journal* 12.

principle behind the court's ruling is the belief that the defendant should be made to pay fair market value for the privilege of benefiting from commercial use of the plaintiff's name, image, reputation or persona.[19]

There are some protections available in English law. Section 1(1) of the Trade Marks Act 1994 now permits the registration of 'any mark capable of being graphically represented' and specifically gives 'names' as an example. If a name meets these requirements and is 'capable of distinguishing the goods or services of one undertaking form those of another undertaking' then it would be *prima facie* registrable. Sport is within the definition of activities in which trade marks can be used (s 103(1) – any profession or business). Unlike the United States where individual athletes may use privacy rights to protect themselves, in the UK there is no such right.

In the absence of UK privacy law, the only cause of action would lie in defamation. An example of this is *Tolley v Fry*.[20] The plaintiff was a well known amateur golf player. The defendants, who were manufacturers of chocolates, published a caricature of the plaintiff which showed him in golfing clothing having just completed a golfing drive with a packet of defendant's chocolates in his back pocket. It also showed the plaintiff's caddie holding the defendant's chocolates. Underneath was a verse comparing the defendant's chocolates to the plaintiff's drive. The plaintiff alleged that the advertisement meant, and was understood to mean, that the plaintiff had agreed/allowed the use of his picture for the advertisement and therefore had prostituted his reputation and that he had been guilty of conduct unworthy of his status as an amateur golfer. It was held that the advertisement was defamatory; it implied that the plaintiff agreed to the advertisement for reward and at time this would have meant being thrown out of any respectable golf club. In *Williams v Reason*[21] allegations of 'shamateurism' were made against an amateur Welsh international rugby player and this was held to be defamatory. Damages of £20,000 were awarded.

Given the growth of advertising and endorsements it is highly unlikely that such an action would be sustained today. An example of such a defamation action failing, in Australia, is *Ettinghausen v Consolidated Press Ltd*.[22] Consolidated Press published an unauthorised photograph of Ettinghausen, an Australian rugby player, in the shower. The photograph showed his genitalia and Ettinghausen argued that it was defamatory. The court held that the photograph was not capable of being defamatory.

The problems for individual athletes and clubs as regards the unauthorised use of their names is demonstrated in the case *Cantona v Cantona*

---

19   Wall, A, 'Sports Marketing and the Law' (1996) 7(1) *Marquette Sports Law Journal* 77, pp 150–51.

20   [1931] All ER 131.

21   [1988] 1 All ER 262.

22   (1991) 23 NSWLR 443.

French Wines.[23] Entrepreneurs registered the company names Cantona French Wines Ltd, Cantona French Brandy Ltd and Cantona Pour Homme Ltd to sell wine, brandy and aftershave. The advertisements contained the phrases 'Ooh aah' and 'Celebrate Manchester United's Incredible Double in Style'. The wine label also carried the number seven (worn by Cantona on his shirt). Cantona and Manchester United had no connection in that they had not licensed, permitted or endorsed the products. A consent order was made to end the situation. The position of individual athletes in relation to their clubs is demonstrated by the claims made by Eric Cantona against Manchester United in respect of merchandise carrying his name, sold after he left the club.

Clubs

The real commercial value lies not so much in the actual playing of the game but in all the off-field activity. As a result clubs will concern themselves with using the sport to promote their name/brand. As such they will register as trade marks their club badges, their name and anything else that can be identified with themselves to ensure no one else can take an unfair advantage. As the figures for Manchester United stated earlier show, clubs make the biggest proportion of the profits from merchandise such as replica kits, scarves, hats etc. In addition, they have begun to venture into other non-traditional areas, for example Manchester United's 'Red Cafe'. Although Manchester United may at present be an exception to the rule, they are probably market leaders in that recent times have seen other football clubs and other sports move into generating income in these ways.

Event Organisers

Do the organisers of sports have any rights in an event itself? An event organiser can be a club, a federation, a league or anyone who organises an event. There is no specific case in English law rejecting the notion of a 'property' right in an event. Given, however, that any allegations will usually arise out of the defendant's activity competing and the lack of a tort of unfair competition in English law, it is difficult to see how the courts would recognise such a right. The Australian case of *Victoria Park Racing v Taylor* is however worth considering in this context.

Victoria Park Racing v Taylor (1937) 58 CLR 479

The plaintiff organised racing events at Victoria Park. The defendant owned land near the race course and set up a platform on his land from which he could see the races and read information on boards as regards starting times and winners etc. From the platform the second defendant commentated and

---

23 Unreported, see Gannon, P, 'Sporting Glory' (1996) 146 *New Law Journal* 1160.

announced the winners. The third defendant was the Commonwealth Broadcasting Corporation which broadcast the commentaries. The plaintiff wanted the broadcasting stopped arguing that it stopped people going to the races. He argued that the money spent on creating the spectacle gave rise to a quasi-property in it which the law protects. The argument was rejected:

> I find difficulty in attaching any precise meaning to the phrase 'property in a spectacle'. A spectacle cannot be owned in any ordinary sense of that word. Even if there were any legal principle which prevented one person from gaining an advantage for himself or causing damage to another by describing a spectacle produced by that other person, the rights of the latter person could be described as property only in a metaphorical sense. Any appropriateness in the metaphor would depend upon the existence of the legal principle. The principle cannot itself be based upon such a metaphor.[24]

The position in the United States is in direct contrast. Under New York law, misappropriation of property interests are recognised as a branch of unfair competition.

Wise, A, 'Property Right in a Sports Event: Views of Different Jurisdictions'

The concept of a property right in a sports event or its factual elements is intricately tied to the doctrine of commercial misappropriation: that no one should be permitted to 'rip off' or 'free ride' on the labour and expense of the creator thereof.

The misappropriation branch of the tort of unfair competition harks back to the US Supreme Court's decision in *International News Service v Associated Press* (248 US 215, 63 L Ed 211, 39 SCt 68 (1918)), to which we hereafter refer as INS. INS involved two wire services, Associated Press (AP) and International News Service (INS), that transmitted news stories by wire to member newspapers. INS would lift factual stories from AP bulletins and send them by wire to INS papers. INS would also take factual stories from east coast AP papers and wire them to INS papers on the west coast that had yet to publish because of time differentials. AP had assembled the data at considerable expense and effort. The Supreme Court upheld a decision enjoining INS action and held that INS conduct was a misappropriation of AP's property under federal common law ... (at 242) Over time, the misappropriation doctrine became widely accepted. Both as to unfair competition generally, and misappropriation in particular, courts have over the years granted relief in a vast variety of situations. Both the larger doctrine and the narrower subdivision can be described as broad and flexible. They encompass misappropriation of another's skill, expenditures and labors and/or of a benefit or property right belonging to another.

American case law, and in particularly, New York decisions post-INS but prior to the Second Circuit's SportsTrax ruling, are consistent on the point that the sports event organiser has a property right in its event and in the event's factual components to prevent unfair competition, specifically, commercial

---

24 *Per* Latham CJ, (1937) 58 CLR 479.

misappropriation. The bulk of these decisions, particularly New York ones, were decided prior to 1976, the date on which Congress enacted significant amendments to the Federal Copyright Act. One such 1976 amendment was specifically to ensure that simultaneous recorded transmissions of live performances and sporting events – as opposed to the sporting events themselves – are entitled to copyright protection. Prior to 1976, there was arguably some doubt as to whether recorded broadcasts of such events were entitled to copyright protection.

Some of the post-INS, pre-SportsTrax New York cases, particularly radio cases, applied a broad misappropriation theory based largely on ethical and moral considerations. Essentially, where an event organiser or valuable information generator or assembler expended significant money and effort in organising, generating or assembling same, and treated it as a valuable asset, it was found to have a protectible property right in the event or information (for some undefined time period). If someone else, without authorisation, infringed, misappropriated or interfered with that property right in a manner or with a result that appeared commercially unfair or unethical, the organiser, generator or assembler prevailed. Some, like the Second Circuit in SportsTrax, believe that those cases adopted a misappropriation theory considerably broader than that of INS. Others, like this writer, believe those post-INS, pre-SportsTrax decisions are consistent with INS.[25]

When the US Court of Appeals, Second Circuit heard the appeal in *National Basketball Association and NBA Properties Inc v Sports Team Analysis* and *Tracking Systems Inc and Motorola Inc v Sportstra*,[26] it found that the defendants engaged in no unlawful misappropriation in electronically transmitting NBA game information on a real time basis.

In Canada in *NHL v Pepsi Cola Canada*[27] the National Hockey League (NHL) argued that it had an exclusive quasi-property right in the schedules, scores and popularity in the Stanley Cup playoffs. The case arose out of Pepsi's ambush marketing tactic.[28] The court rejected the NHL's contention with Carrothers JA stating, 'I have not been shown that such a right exists'.

If there are no property rights in events themselves that can be claimed and protected, the question arises as to what commercial interests there are in events. Sports events clearly have a commercial value in that the public want to watch them. So what commodities do event organisers have which have a commercial value and which can be exploited?

---

25 Wise, A, 'Property Right in a Sports Event: Views of Different Jurisdictions' (1997) 5(1) *Sport and the Law Journal* 36.

26 *Ibid*, p 63, n 23.

27 (1995) 122 *Dominion Law Reports* 4th 412.

28 For 'Ambush Marketing' see below, p 329.

Broadcast Rights

Sport is good for television in increasing levels of revenue from advertising. As such, broadcasters will want the right to broadcast an event. But who owns the television rights in an event? Bitel has argued that the rights belong to the participants in an event. In contrast Abramson has argued that the rights belong to the owner of the premises in which the event is taking place by reason of the fact that only he/she has the right to control who enters the premises. On that basis he argues that television rights are essentially contractual rights which are sold to the organiser who in turn can sell them to the broadcaster. 'Strictly speaking the right to televise [this] year's Olympics belonged in the first instance to the proprietor of the stadium in Atlanta. Any prospective bidder to stage the Olympics that sought to reserve the television rights to himself would, however, have received very short shrift indeed from the IOC. Instead, it was a prerequisite of bidding to stage the Olympics that all television rights were ceded to the IOC for onward exploitation.'[29]

Having contractually obtained the television rights in the event, these may then be sold by the event organiser. The organiser's aim will be to obtain the widest possible coverage of the event. But this has to be balanced against the need to obtain the highest fee. For example, the IOC has sold the right to broadcast the Sydney 2000 Games in Europe to the European Broadcasting Union even though the highest bid came from *News Corporation*.[30] In the context of clubs, who arguably could seek to sell the rights of their own matches, what has tended to happen is that television broadcasting contracts have been negotiated on a league basis. For example, the Premier League negotiates the contract for all Premier League matches. The arguments for doing so are that they are in a stronger position to negotiate and more importantly it ensures that the smaller, not so fashionable clubs, also gain some income. The Premier League agreements to sell to the highest bidder have been referred to the restricted practices court by the Office Of Fair Trading.[31] The Director General has been reported as saying that any business acting in this way would be subject to competition law and he saw no reason why sport should be treated differently. The argument of the OFT is that in negotiating as a league, the clubs are acting as a cartel. The court will have to decide whether the agreements operate in the public interest.

In the context of European Law, the matter would fall to be judged by reference to Articles 85 and 86 of the EU Treaty. Article 85 prohibits 'all agreements between undertakings, decisions by associations of undertakings

---

29 Abramson, L, 'Whose Rights are they Anyway?' (1996) 4(3) *Sport and the Law Journal* 100.

30 Stupp, H, 'Television and Sponsorship, Maximising your Events Potential: The Olympic Experience', unpublished Conference Paper, Sports Forum '96 Chelsea Football Ground, 26 November 1996.

31 'Club TV Football Deal Referred to Court', *The Guardian*, 7 February 1996, p 2.

and concerted practises' and Article 86 prohibits 'any abuse by one or more undertakings of dominant position within the common market on a substantial part of it'. In either case, there must be an effect on the intra-community trade. The question of whether football clubs and national associations are undertakings has been clearly addressed. In *Bosman*[32] Advocate General Lenz held that both engaged in economic activities to constitute undertakings. Bell sets out a persuasive argument as to why sports entities should be treated as other economic entities and why the handling of television rights should not be treated as anti-competitive:

Bell, A, 'Dispatch from Brussels'

The application of competition law (both national and EU competition law) to structures and practices in professional sport is becoming increasingly significant. At the EU level, the main rule in this domain is Article 85 of the EU Treaty. This Article outlaws restrictive business agreements between undertakings or 'associations of undertakings' which distort competition and which affect cross-border trade in the EU.

Today there is no serious argument that Article 85 cannot apply, in principle, to the activities of football clubs, associations or leagues. The key question is rather how Article 85 can, and should, be applied to the world of sport in particular over the unique, collective, nature of organised sport leagues.

Competition or co-operation

The general philosophy underlying Article 85 is that competition between undertakings is itself the best guarantor of economic efficiency. Thus the normal approach of the EU Commission is to require parties to an agreement to demonstrate why it is better for them to co-operate than it is for them to compete. This basic approach is however fundamentally inappropriate in the case of sports leagues.

A sport can only function on the basis of competition between clubs. Of course clubs compete very hard against each other on the field of play, but they clearly have no incentive to drive each other out of business altogether. This is a crucial difference between football clubs and conventional business entities, and it has clear implications for the way in which competition law should be applied to football and other sporting structures. These structures are designed to maintain at least a minimum degree of competitive balance so that matches are reasonably close and interesting to spectators. With this objective in mind, rules are also designed to help redistribute wealth throughout a league, to help preserve that balance.

Television rights

Against this background it is entirely logical that a national league or association should market the television rights to the tournaments which they organise and which member clubs play in on behalf of all those clubs. The participating clubs are not engaged in some kind of individual business

---

32 *Union Royalle Belge des Societes de Football Assocation (ASBL) v Jean-Marc Bosman* (Case C-415/93) [1996] All ER (EC) 97.

venture: rather they are engaged in a collective (league) venture. It is therefore understandable that leagues should dispose of television rights in 'global' packages with all the clubs pooling their individual television rights. This is not anti-competitive; it is in fact pro-competitive, since monies redistributed from the league contract should enhance competition within the league structure itself.

The US position

In America, this question is dealt with under the Sports Broadcasting Act of 1961. Basically, the 1961 Act creates an anti-trust exemption allowing a sports league to restrict individual clubs from selling television rights to games which are covered by the league contract. The purpose of the legislation is to allow clubs to 'pool' their television rights and permit the league to sell the resulting package of pooled rights to a television network, without violating the antitrust rules. From a policy perspective, pooling is necessary to assure the weaker clubs of continuing television income and television coverage on a substantially equal basis with the stronger clubs. Thus at the time the legislation was passed the US Congress noted that 'should these weaker teams be allowed to flounder, there is a danger that the structure of the league would become impaired and its continued operation imperilled'.

The same concerns are equally valid with respect to football in Europe today. At a time when the rich are getting richer and the poor are getting poorer, the pooling and collective sale of television rights is surely desirable in Europe as well. It would be ironic to say the least if the 'socialist vision' was permissible in the 'free market' United States but not in Europe.

The way ahead!

An encouraging sign was the approach taken by a Dutch court on this issue when Feyenoord recently brought a case challenging the competence of the Dutch league (KNVB) to enter into a global contract with a broadcaster.

Basically Feyenoord argued that league rules prohibiting it from exploiting TV rights to its own matches was a violation of Article 85. The Court was not too impressed with that argument, noting that the rights in question related to matches which took place in the framework of a competition organised by the national association. In such a case, possible restrictions of competition had to be seen against the background of their aim, which included the smooth functioning of the association and the competitions organised under it.

Preserving competitive balance

Whilst this is a preliminary decision (which Feyenoord will appeal) the attitude of the Court is to be welcomed: collective marketing of television rights should not be regarded as an infringement of Article 85 when at least part of the income is redistributed and employed to preserve competitive balance within the league structure. Commissioner Van Mert (responsible for competition policy) has indicated that the EC Commission supports this approach. It is to be hoped that the OFT will take a similar view, when examining the English Premier League's new and old television contracts.[33]

---

33 Bell, A, 'Dispatch from Brussels', *Sports Law Administration and Practice*, July/August 1996, p 7.

The issue of broadcasters jointly bidding for broadcasting rights has also been addressed at the European level. The Commission's decision exempting the European Broadcasting Union from the Article 85 prohibitions has been annulled by the European Court of First Instance.[34]

The broadcasting of sports events has not been uncontroversial particularly when BSkyB secured the rights to broadcast Premier League matches. The argument centred around the rights of the public to see major sporting events without having to pay for the right to do so. Lord Howell in the debate over the Broadcasting Act 1996 said that 'to deny millions of elderly who supported sport in better days the opportunity to do so now, in old age or difficult circumstances, is not acceptable. It is anti-social'.[35] The result has been:

Section 97 of the Broadcasting Act 1996:

For the purposes of this Part, a listed event is a sporting or other event of national interest which is for the time being included in a list drawn up by the Secretary of State for the purposes of this Part.

The Secretary of State shall not at any time draw up, revise or cease to maintain such a list as is mentioned in subsection (1) unless he has first consulted:

the BBC;

the Welsh Authority;

the Independent Television Commission; and

in relation to a relevant event, the person from whom the rights to televise that event may be acquired;

and for the purposes of this subsection a relevant event is a sporting or other event of national interest which the Secretary of State proposes to include in, or omit from, the list.

As soon as he has drawn up or revised such a list as is mentioned in subsection (1), the Secretary of State shall publish the list in such manner as he considers appropriate for bringing it to the attention of:

the persons mentioned in subsection (2); and

every person who is the holder of a licence granted by the Commission under Part I of the 1990 Act or a digital programme licence granted by them under Part I of this Act.

In this section 'national interest' includes interest within England, Scotland, Wales or Northern Ireland.

The addition of any relevant event to such a list as is mentioned in subsection (1) shall not affect:

the validity of any contract entered into before the date on which the Secretary of State consulted the persons mentioned in subsection (2) in relation to the proposed addition; or

---

34 Bell, A, 'Dispatch From Brussels', *Sports Law Administration and Practice*, November/December 1996, p 6.

35 Hansard Lords 16/1/96 Col 528.

the exercise of any rights acquired under such a contract.

The list drawn up by the Secretary of State for the purposes of s 182 of the 1990 Act, as that list is in force immediately before the commencement of this section, shall be taken to have been drawn up for the purposes of this Part.

There is no formal list available; the sporting bodies concerned are informed if their sport is on the list. The list is under review but currently includes:

Home Cricket Test Matches including England

The Derby

Federation Internationale de Football Association (FIFA) World Cup Finals

Football Association (FA) Cup

Scottish Football Association (SFA) Cup

Grand National

The Derby

Olympic Games

Finals weekend of Wimbledon Championship.[36]

The position of these 'crown jewels' of sport have been the subject of much debate fuelled by the Secretary of State for Culture, Media and Sport's announcement that cricket, football and rugby would not have a place at the National Sports Academy. This has resulted in cricket administrators arguing that if they are to finance their own 'grassroots' development programme, then they must have greater rights to sell broadcast rights in their matches to the highest bidder. The statute only applies to contracts entered into after the statute is enacted:

Section 99: Contract for exclusive right to televise listed event to be void

Any contract entered into after the commencement of this section under which a television programme provider acquires rights to televise the whole or any part of a listed event live for reception in the United Kingdom, or in any area of the United Kingdom, shall be void so far as it purports, in relation to the whole or any part of the event or in relation to reception in the United Kingdom or any area of the United Kingdom, to grant those rights exclusively to any one television programme provider.

In this Part 'television programme provider' means the BBC, the Welsh authority or any person who is the holder of any licence under Part I of the 1990 Act or a digital programme licence under Part I of this Act.

For the purposes of this section rights to televise the whole or any part of an event live for reception in any area granted to a television programme provider are granted exclusively if the person granting them:

–   has not granted any such right to any other television programme provider; and

–   is precluded by the terms of the contract from doing so.

---

36   Source: Department of Culture, Media and Sport, 1997.

As a result, the minister may not list an event which was subject to a contract prior to the statute taking effect. Section 101 is also of importance:

Section 101: Restriction on televising of listed event

A person providing a service falling within either of the categories set out in subsection (1) of s 98 ('the first service') for reception in the United Kingdom or in any area of the United Kingdom shall not, without the previous consent of the Commission, include in that service live coverage of the whole or any part of a listed event unless:

– another person, who is providing a service falling within the other category set out in that subsection ('the second service'), has acquired the right to include in the second service live coverage of the whole of the event or of that part of the event; and

– the area for which the second service is provided consists of or includes he whole, or substantially the whole, of the area for which the first services provided.

The Commission may revoke any consent given by them under subsection (1).

Failure to comply with subsection (1) shall not affect the validity of any contract.

Subsection (1) shall not have effect where the television programme provider providing the first service is exercising rights acquired before the commencement of this section.

The result is that if a broadcaster from one category buys the right to broadcast the listed event it cannot do so unless a broadcaster from the other category does so also. The categories are set out in s 98; one category containing regional and national Channel 3 services, Channel 4 and the BBC with all other services falling into the second category. The broadcaster may have purchased the rights but may not be able to broadcast. Scholes and Woods suggest 'conditional contracts or tripartite arrangements involving a broadcaster from each category may be the answer here'.[37] The Independent Television Commission does have the power to grant permission to broadcast where a broadcaster from only one category has rights (s 101(1)) but the statute does not make clear under what circumstance such permission will be granted. Scholes and Woods suggest 'it would be inappropriate to do so where the broadcasters in question were substantially responsible for such a situation'.[38]

Broadcasters have agreed to a voluntary code of conduct relating to the televising of all sporting events, not just those that are listed.[39] The stated aim is 'to provide for the availability at a fair market price of either live, recorded or highlights coverage of the event on a terrestrial channel on the one hand and on any subscription channel on the other'. Scholes and Woods report that

---

37 Scholes, J and Woods, L, 'The Broadcasting Act 1996', 7 *Entertainment Law Review* 298, 305.

38 *Ibid*, p 305.

39 Major Spectator Sports Voluntary Code of Conduct 1996.

doubts have been expressed about the effectiveness of the code given that it is voluntary and that under the code any party is free to withdraw and publish a written notice to the monitoring committee of their reasons.

The listing of events was not met with absolute enthusiasm by event organisers. Woodhouse has reported that governing bodies had jointly sought legal advice as regards the listing of events and had been advised by counsel 'that changes in legislation to regulate sports bodies powers and sole rights could breach the UK's obligations under the European Convention on Human Rights'.[40] Sports governing bodies themselves however have agreed a voluntary code of conduct:

CCPR and Sports Council, 'Broadcasting Rights – A Voluntary Code of Conduct for Sports Events'

The signatories acknowledge that the duties of sports bodies to maximise, income from rights sales for the benefit of their sports and the desirability of the widest possible broadcasting exposure may not always coincide. They undertake to make every reasonable effort to strike a balance for doing these objectives that is in the best interests of sports development and the wider sporting public alike. The central principle of this code is to ensure that coverage of major sporting events will be available to the general public in five recorded and/or highlights programmes. Therefore a principal objective in any negotiation that a signatory may undertake will be assuming interest on the part of the broadcasters to provide for the availability, at a fair market price, of either live, recorded or highlights coverage of the event on a terrestrial channel, on one hand, and on any subscription channel on the other.[41]

The main aim is to ensure that major sporting events, not just those listed, are available either live, recorded or as highlights and '... reflected the social responsibility of sport for the widest possible audience terrestrial satellite and cable. It was a compromise which came close to the just and fair balance between the legitimate interests of sport, broadcasters and the public. It recognised the role of sports governing bodies in negotiating with all broadcasters to obtain the best market rate. It acknowledges the governing bodies rights to maximise income from sales – a balance between the best interests of sports development and the wider sporting public alike'.[42]

Broadcasters also retain rights under the Copyrights, Designs and Patents Act 1988 in that a copyright is vested in a broadcast.[43] The right to show excerpts of events as part of a news programme is provided for under section 30 of the Copyrights, Designs and Patents Act 1988 – fair dealing for the

---

40 Woodhouse, C, 'Sport and Law in Conflict: Role of Sports Governing Bodies', unpublished Conference Paper, Sports Forum '96 Chelsea Football Ground, 26 November 1996.

41 CCPR and Sports Council, 'Broadcasting Rights – A Voluntary Code of Conduct for Sports Events'.

42 'Sport and Law in Conflict: Role of Sports Governing Bodies', Sports Forum '96, 25 November.

43 Section 1(1)(b) of the Copyrights Designs and Patents Act 1988.

purpose of reporting current events. This section was litigated in *British Broadcasting Corporation v British Satellite Broadcasting*.[44] The case arose out of the 1990 FIFA World Cup, the live broadcast rights of which belonged to the BBC. BSB used short excerpts from the live broadcasts in a sports news programme, each excerpt lasting between 14 and 37 seconds and being shown up to four times in the 24 hours following a match. The BBC brought an action for breach of copyright. BSB argued that their use came within the fair dealing exception of reporting current events in s 30(2) of the CDPA 1988. It was held that the use came within s 30(2) because the matches were current events and the exception was not limited to general news programmes but included sports news bulletins. Having regard to the quantity and quality of the material used and its relevance to the news reporting character of the programme, the material was used in a genuine way.

One fear surrounding the involvement of broadcasters in sport is that they impact on sport itself. Wall gives excellent examples of the 1995 Americas Cup and the 1980 New York Marathon:

Wall, A, 'Sports Marketing and the Law'

The force of the media and commercial sponsorships was evident in the Citizen Cup Finals of the 1995 America's Cup. After completing the semi-finals, all but one team should have been eliminated from the Defender and the Challenger selections. The final uncontested Challenger was Team New Zealand, a team that won all but one match race against Australia One in the Louis Vuitton Cup. But when it came to the final Defender selection, all three American teams continued to compete. It was no coincidence that ESPN's television coverage of the match races did not begin until the final round of competition. In a press conference, Dennis Conner told reporters, 'Pardon me if I sound commercial, but if Bill [Koch] or ourselves were eliminated here, there would have been a lot of sponsors that would have been disappointed'. So all three American teams competed in the finals: Young America, America and Stars & Stripes.

Another demonstration of the chilling power of the media's impact on sports entertainment events is the author's own experience with the New York Marathon during the 1980s. It was a cold, wet, bone chilling day. The marathon was scheduled to begin and over 25,000 competitors were standing ready at the starting line, but the starting gun did not go off for nearly an hour and a half after the scheduled start time. While the racers waited nervously in the cold rain, the licensed broadcaster interrupted its television coverage of the marathon to cover breaking news about the Beirut massacre. A bomb had exploded at the American Embassy in Beirut killing dozens of people. Once the network resumed its coverage of the marathon, the runners were able to start. By that time, their muscles were cold and clothes were soaking wet from standing in the rain. Thousands of spectators lined the streets of New York

---

44   [1991] 3 All ER 833.

City and hundreds of thousands of television viewers waited anxiously for the start of the race while everyone mourned the deaths of their fellow citizens in Beirut.[45]

Another example is the 1994 FIFA World Cup in the USA. It was rumoured at one time that matches would have to be played in four quarters to meet the demands of television advertising. The sale of broadcasting rights in Premier League matches to BSkyB has also seen matches being moved to Sunday and Monday to suit televisions schedules. This has resulted in complaints of unfairness by teams who have had to play on Saturday and then again on Monday.

The power of broadcasters can also be seen in the classic example of the 'Superleague' saga, discussed earlier.[46]

Event Emblems

Many major sporting events are associated with a particular insignia or emblem. These can be protected by trade mark registration and their use thus controlled. The use of the emblem can be licensed for use on all kinds of merchandise related to the event from which a substantial royalty can be taken. The emblems relating to the Olympics have special statutory protection:

Olympic Symbol etc (Protection) Act 1995

Section 2 Rights Conferred

The Olympics association right shall confer exclusive rights in relation to the use of the Olympic symbol, the Olympic motto and the protected words.

Subject to ss 4 and 5 below, the rights conferred by subsection (1) above shall be infringed by any act done in the United Kingdom which:

– constitutes infringement under section 3 below; and

– is done without the consent of the person for the time being appointed under s 1(2) above (in this Act referred to as 'the proprietor').

The proprietor may exploit the rights conferred by subsection (1) above or gain, but may not make any disposition of or of any interest in or over them.

This section shall not have effect to permit the doing of anything which would otherwise be liable to be prevented by virtue of a right:

– subsisting immediately before the day on which this Act comes into force;

created by:

– the registration of a design under the Registered Designs Act 1949 on or after the day on which this Act comes into force; or

---

45 Wall, A, 'Sports Marketing and The Law' (1996) 7(1) *Marquette Sports Law Journal* 77, 140.
46 'Murdoch's global game takes rugby into new league', *The Guardian*, 7 April 1995, p 26.

–   the registration of a trade mark under the Trade Marks Act 1994 on or after that day.

Consent given for the purposes of subsection (2)(b) above by a person pointed under s 1(2) above shall, subject to its terms, be binding on any person subsequently appointed under that provision; and references in this Act to doing anything with or without, the consent of the proprietor shall be construed accordingly.

Section 3 Infringement

A person infringes the Olympics association right if in the course of trade he uses:

–   a representation of the Olympic symbol, the Olympic motto or a protected word; or

–   a representation of something so similar to the Olympic symbol or the Olympic motto as to be likely to create in the public mind an association with it, (in this Act referred to as 'a controlled representation').

For the purposes of this section, a person uses a controlled representation if, in particular, he:

–   affixes it to goods or the packaging thereof;

–   incorporates it in a flag or banner;

–   offers or exposes for sale, puts on the market or stocks for those purposes goods which bear it or whose packaging bears it;

–   imports or exports goods which bear it or whose packaging bears it;

–   offers or supplies services under a sign which consists of or contains it; or

–   uses it on business papers or in advertising.[47]

Sponsorship

Sponsorship allows sports events and individual athletes and clubs to be used as a means of advertising and for promoting the sponsor's products. Sport is of course popular and this makes sponsorship of sport an ideal way for companies to market their products. It allows companies to associate their products, be they sports related or otherwise, with the clean healthy image of sport. It allows companies to suggest it is a winner if it associates itself with the successful individual or club. If it sponsors a national team it allows itself to be seen as patriotic. 'Sponsors seek out sport as it purports to promote a healthy and clean lifestyle for their products.'[48] Both the sponsor and the sporting organisation (sponsee) benefit from a sponsorship agreement. There are of course dangers in sponsorship if the sponsee fails to meet expectations. For example it is reported that Tetley have withdrawn their sponsorship from

---

47   Mellstrom, B, 'Statutory Protection For Olympic Merchandise' (1996) 4(3) *Sport and the Law Journal* 93.

48   Grayson, E, *Sport and the Law*, 2nd edn (1994), London: Butterworths, p 335.

the England cricket team as a result of its poor performances. In addition the private life of an individual athlete may reflect badly on the sponsor and at such times sponsors will seek to distance themselves.[49]

Nettleton, J, 'Legal Aspects of Sports Sponsorship'

From a sponsor's perspective, the objectives of sports sponsorship are to take advantage of a unique marketing opportunity, target a particular market and maximise exposure to that market in a non-threatening manner.

From a sporting organisation's perspective, the purpose in obtaining sponsorship will be motivated by various factors including, for example, the desire to obtain funds for your sport, to enable a particular competition to be held, to offer prize money and attract overseas competitors, to fund the sport at its grass roots, to improve facilities in which the sport is played and to fund the day to day operation of the sport.[50]

Sponsorship has no legal definition or status in English law. Townley and Grayson define it as 'a mutually acceptable commercial relationship between two or more parties in which one party (called the sponsor) acting in the course of business, trade, profession or calling seeks to promote or enhance an image product or service in association with an individual event happening, property or object (called the sponsee)'.[51] Townley states 'sponsorship represents an opportunity. Analysed legally it is a contractual relationship. The contractual relationship embodies a number of elements, depending upon the point of entry of the sponsor to the opportunity'.[52]

Nettleton, J, 'Legal Aspects of Sports Sponsorship'

In summary, the principal objectives of a sponsor are as follows:

Increase brand or company awareness to the sport's audience (eg Budweiser had a very successful sponsorship of grid iron on Channel 4 in England a few years ago. At that time grid iron was relatively unknown in Britain, as was Budweiser, and it proved a mutually successful arrangement). A similar example can be seen in Australia through Hyundai's 'cherry picking' leading teams in rugby league (Canterbury) and AFL (Carlton) for sponsorship.

Improve, change or reinforce brand image. One of the primary examples of this objective of sponsorship is Mobil's sponsorship of netball. In an article which appeared in The Financial Review in November 1993, the promotions manager of Mobil indicated that the rationale for doubling its sponsorship of netball to $1,000,000.00 over three years was that netball is a huge participation sport with more than 750,000 players, it obtains television coverage and is an ideal medium in which to market to women.

---

49 See Bailey, D, 'Altered images' *Sports Law Administration & Practice*, November/December 1996, p 11.
50 Nettleton, J, 'Legal Aspects of Sports Sponsorship' (1995) 3(3) *Sports Law and Finance* 28.
51 'Sponsorship of Sport', *Arts and Leisure*.
52 Townley, S, 'Sponsorship and Major Events' (1995) 2(6) *Sports Law and Finance* 68.

Obtain exposure. One example of this category can be seen through the sponsorship by tobacco companies of motor racing. This is of particular relevance for any sport which may be broadcast on pay television due to the prohibition on advertising on pay television before 1997. Sponsorship of sports covered on pay television is the only effective way to advertise on this medium.

The hospitality/entertainment of clients. Apart from the plethora of entertainment boxes which are now an essential part of the facilities constructed at any new stadium around the country, one can see at any official outdoor sporting events what a huge business this is. However whilst one may not like this industry, it has certainly brought significant funds into many sports.

Promotion for internal morale or training. Examples of this may be to enable a sporting association's facilities to be used, together with personnel of the relevant sporting association for an internal training activity for companies.

Product association. This may include the right to use assets of the relevant sporting association as endorsement of the sponsor's products or otherwise in the sponsor's advertising. One example of this will be a future promotion of Mitre 10's products by Mark Larkham as part of a naming rights sponsorship recently signed up by Mitre 10 with Mark Larkham's touring car racing team.

But, most importantly, the objective is to get money's worth out of the sponsorship. This is a mutual objective and in order to achieve this the sponsor and the sporting organisation must work in partnership.[53]

Sponsorship has clearly grown with the growth of involvement of television in that it gives the sponsor greater coverage. One result of this has been to allow event organisers to sell sponsorship rights for greater amounts. One of the most important developments was the exclusive sponsorship agreement. This in turn has been developed into exclusive sponsorship agreements in particular categories. For example an event may have an exclusive sponsorship agreement for restaurants, credit cards, airlines, etc. This has allowed event organisers to generate much greater income from sponsorship. In 1981 the CCPR recognised the importance of sponsorship and set up the committee of enquiry into sports sponsorship under the chairmanship of ex-Minister for Sport, Dennis Howell. The committee reported in 1983 and some of the conclusions are worthy of note:

CCPR: 'The Howell Report'

CONCLUSION 1

The sponsorship of sport provides a service to the whole of sport and to the community which sport serves; in this respect therefore it also serves the public interest.

---

53   Nettleton, J, 'Legal Aspects of Sports Sponsorship' 3(3) *Sports Law and Finance* 28, 31.

RECOMMENDATION 2

The Sports Council should be responsible for establishing and supervising the principles and practice of sports sponsorship: for the application of proper ethical standards and for the protection of sports people from improper exploitation. The Sports Council should report annually and publicly upon its stewardship in these areas.

RECOMMENDATION 3

Governing bodies must at all times accept responsibility for the application, provision, practice and control of sponsorship within their own sports. They should establish machinery which ensures that these matters are dealt with efficiently and effectively, if necessary by obtaining appropriate professional advice. Above all governing bodies need to protect the integrity of their sports.

CONCLUSION 6

The sponsorship of sport is fully accepted by the British public, provided there is no attempt by sponsors to influence unduly the essential nature or the government of sport. Public attitudes also reflect a desire that sponsorship income should, in part, be used to improve facilities and ensure that clubs make a contribution to the life of the community in which they are situated.

CONCLUSION 7

There is little public support for any prohibition by government of sports sponsorship which would deprive sport of income from any legitimate sources.

RECOMMENDATION 14

Each governing body of sport should establish a 'sponsorship committee' to obtain and regulate sponsorship for the benefit of its sport and, where appropriate, to assist in finding sponsorship for its competitors of outstanding potential. Such committees should include competitor representatives.

RECOMMENDATION 17

The CCPR should play an educative role in encouraging its member organisations to become more proficient in marketing their products and learning the associated skills of sponsorship either by arranging seminars or providing an advisory service. In addition the CCPR should play an active role in assisting governing bodies where necessary to assess their administrative structures with a view to the institution of beneficial changes.

RECOMMENDATION 18

Governing bodies should guard against an over reliance upon sponsorship income and should maintain as wide a portfolio of sponsorship as is practical in order to minimise the dangers when sponsors end their involvement. They also should endeavour to avoid an over dependence upon any one product.

RECOMMENDATION 19

Governing bodies should maintain a sympathetic and realistic attitude towards the financial interests of their leading competitors yet also take account of the fundamental interests of sport as a whole.

CONCLUSION 21

Without interfering with the independence of sport, sponsoring companies should provide as much professional assistance as is practical to ensure that events in which they are involved are efficiently marketed and presented as this is to the benefit of both partners.

CONCLUSION AND RECOMMENDATION 43

It is eminently reasonable for sports events to be staged at times convenient to television, provided that the needs of sport and the competitors are prime considerations. Sports bodies should ensure that consultative machinery exists to allow these interests to be taken into account.

CONCLUSION 71

The Voluntary Agreement concluded between the government and the tobacco industry is the right way to regulate sponsorship of sport by tobacco interests. Government, sport and the industry should ensure that the Agreement is properly observed at all times.

CONCLUSION 72

It is the responsibility of all concerned with the sponsorship of sport, governing bodies, promoters, organisers, sponsors and agents to protect their collective interests by taking firm action against abuse and exploitation of advertising and other publicity rights. The need to protect is particularly relevant to television, the prime target of those who seek to obtain publicity to which they are not entitled.[54]

Of particular interest is Conclusion 7, which says that '... there is little public support for any prohibition by government of sport sponsorship which would deprive sport of income from legitimate sources'. This is particularly so given the government's decision regarding the banning of tobacco advertising. This will clearly impact on the many sports sponsored by tobacco manufacturers – the Silk Cut Challenge Cup in rugby league, the Benson and Hedges Cup in cricket. Tobacco advertising on television was banned in 1965 and this was the impetus for tobacco to sponsor sport as the alternative to advertising. The tobacco industry provides £8 million of the £350 million sponsorship in British sport.[55] The Health Secretary, Frank Dobson, has said that the ban will extend to logos of tobacco companies appearing on cars in international motor racing events.

---

54 Central Council for Physical Recreation, Committee of Enquiry into Sports Sponsorship, 'The Howell Report' (1983).

55 See 'Deals put brand names before armchair audience of millions', *The Times*, 20 May 1997. See also 'Sports organisers fear £8m hole in their finances', *The Times*, 20 May 1997, p 12; 'Tobacco loophole for motor racing', *The Guardian*, 20 May 1997, p 3.

Ambush Marketing

The commercial nature of sport together with the increased levels of competition to secure a sponsorship agreement has meant that the loss of sponsorship opportunity by a company has come to be regarded as a great loss of a valuable marketing opportunity. Rather than risk losing out altogether, companies have developed other means of associating themselves indirectly. They are particularly attractive in that more often than not they will cost a fraction of the price of being an official sponsor. The means used by companies to do this have come to be described as ambush or parasitic marketing.

Gray defines ambush advertising as 'activities by companies who are not official sponsors of a particular event yet they attempt to take advantage of the popularity of that particular athletic event'.[56] Townley defines it as 'the unauthorised association by business of their names, brands, products or services with a sports event or competition through any one or more of a wide range of marketing activities; unauthorised in the sense that the controller of the commercial rights in such events, usually the relevant governing body, has neither sanctioned nor licensed the association itself or its commercial agents'.[57] A good example is the way American Express responded to Visa being selected as the official sponsor of the 1992 Barcelona Olympics. It negotiated an agreement with the Spanish government to be the official sponsor of tourism in Spain. It thereby associated itself with the Games without having to pay for the opportunity. The price was $3.3 million.[58]

The central aim of an ambusher is associate itself with an event by confusing the public; to make the consumer believe that their product is associated with the event in question. The consequence of doing so is to achieve cheap advertising. Indeed, statistics and surveys show that they are successful at doing so. Gray reports statistics from the 1992 Winter Olympic Games. The table shows what percentages of those surveyed believed that either the official sponsor or its rival was, in fact, the official sponsor.

---

56 Gray, J, 'The Legality of Ambush Advertising on Corporate Sponsorship of Athletic Events' (1993), Working Paper, Milwaukee: Genesis Sports International.

57 Townleys Solicitors, 'Ambush/Parasitic Marketing and Sport, An Intelligence Report' (1992), London: Professional Direction Ltd.

58 *Ibid*, Gray, J (1993).

Official	%	Rival	%
Nuprin	15	Tyleno	41
US Postal Services	13	Federal Express	61
		UPS	20
United	24	American	28
		Delta	22
Reebok	44	Nike	41
Chrysler/Jeep	25	Buick	29
		Subaru	18
McDonalds	76	Burger King[59]	8

Bitel reports 'after the last winter Olympics most Americans, in fact 66%, when questioned thought American Express was the official credit card of the Lillehammer Games and therefore did not realise American Express were an ambusher to think the worse of'.[60] The way American Express achieved this was through the advertising slogan 'If you are travelling to Norway this winter you will need a passport but you do not need a visa'.

So ambush advertising seems to work. Another reason to engage in it is that it is often cheaper. The official sponsor of Euro '96 football championships was Umbro and for this it paid £3.5 million. Nike on the other hand, spent £2 million on their highly memorable poster campaign carrying players already associated with them. No mention was made of Euro '96 but was the campaign based on placing the posters close to the venues. This kind of ambush marketing can be described as 'direct ambushing' but there are many different means used:

Broadcast sponsorship. This is the method used by Wendy's Hamburgers at the 1988 winter games in Calgary. McDonalds was an official sponsor of the games; Wendy's responded by sponsoring the ABC Broadcast of them.

Promotional advertising at the event and give aways. An example of this was PepsiCo at the 1995 Notting Hill Carnival. The carnival was sponsored by Lilt. PepsiCo gave away 50,000 cans of Lipton Ice. At the 1994 World Cup, ambushers gave away free footballs.

Sponsoring individual athletes or teams. Bitel describes this as 'ambush by conflict'. The conflicts that can arise are between the event and team, event and individual and team and individual. An example of this was Green Flag's sponsorship of the England Football team. Although not an official sponsor of the event, they appeared in the media everyday during Euro '96. Another example was Ravinelli's undershirt with the Nike logo which was revealed by the player when he scored. Middlesborough was sponsored by Cellnet while

---

59 *Ibid.*

60 Bitel, N, 'Ambush Marketing' (1997) 5(1) *Sport and the Law Journal* 12.

the event was the Carling Premier League. Other cases of such ambushes were Michael Johnson's gold Nike trainers and Linford Christie's Puma Contact Lenses at the Atlanta Olympic Games. Another example was the US basketball 'Dream Team' at the 1992 Olympic Games, some of whose members had a contract with Nike whilst the official sponsors of the team were Reebok. The relevant team members threatened to boycott the medal ceremony if they were forced to wear the official team strip. A compromise was reached in that they draped the US flag over their uniform to hide all Reebok emblems.

Governing bodies have been seen to take action in this country against players who seek to wear equipment other than that of their sponsor. Leigh Davies, the Cardiff rugby player, was fined £2,000 by his governing body for wearing a tracksuit manufactured by a rival of the Welsh rugby union's sponsor, Reebok.[61] Although in fact the actions were dismissed, the following extract from a Canadian case is a good example of all these issues:

NHL v Pepsi Cola Canada, 92 DLR (4th) 349

The action arose primarily out of an advertising campaign put on by the defendant in the spring of 1990 called the 'Diet Pepsi $4,000,000 Pro Hockey Play off Pool' and the promotional material related to that campaign (hereafter collectively referred to as the 'Contest'). A second contest called 'Pepsi's Shoot & Score Hockey Draft' (the 'Draft Contest'), that was publicised in the 6 September 1990 edition of the *Ottawa Sun*, was also pleaded. The great majority of the trial was however devoted to the Contest. I presume that was because of the vastly wider sector of the Canadian public it was designed to reach. In addition to the National Hockey League (NHL) and that association's affiliated company, National Hockey League Services Ltd (NHLS), all 21 hockey clubs that were members of the NHL when the action was commenced are parties to the action.

The NHL was established in 1917. Its membership consists of teams of professional hockey players. Most of the teams that are parties to the action are based in various cities in Canada and the United States. Three of the teams call the States of Minnesota, New Jersey and New York 'home'. All the team names incorporate the name of their home city or State.

NHL teams are recognised as being made up of the pre-eminent hockey players from both countries with the addition, in relatively recent years, of players imported from different European countries. There can be little doubt but that in North America the NHL is at the pinnacle of professional hockey.

The plaintiffs allege in their statement of claim (and it was not disputed) that over the past several decades the NHL has grown into an operation generating hundreds of millions of dollars in revenue. Thus it has become a major business enterprise. Because of the league's success in attracting large numbers of paying spectators and sizeable radio and television audiences, particularly in Canada, commercial sponsors are willing to pay substantial fees or other

---

61   'Howley to Face Fine for Breach of Contract', *The Times*, 6 February 1997.

consideration for the right to align themselves with the NHL for promotional purposes.

Each year after the conclusion of the regular season a series of play off games are played between the four top teams in each of the four divisions into which the NHL is divided. That series is followed by a further series of games in which the four winners of the division finals play off to determine the winner in each of the league's two conferences, popularly known as the Campbell Conference and the Wales Conference. The culmination of the season comes when the winning team from the Campbell Conference plays a best of seven series against the Wales Conference winner. The winner of this final series is awarded the much coveted Stanley Cup. The entire play off series, from the divisional play offs to the final Stanley Cup event, has come to be known as the Stanley Cup play offs.

Apart from ticket sales and the sale of broadcast rights, an important source of revenue for the plaintiffs comes from the sale by NHLS of licences to the producers of a variety of products to display the league's registered trade marks on or in conjunction with their products and to claim affiliation in one way or another with the NHL and collectively its member teams. The NHL's registered marks include its name, a logo emblazoned with its initials, the names and logos (when used collectively) of its member teams, and the words 'Stanley Cup'. The names and logos of the member teams of the NHL are also registered.

In the spring of 1989, NHLS entered into a licensing agreement with the defendant's arch rival Coca-Cola Ltd (Coke). By the terms of that agreement, Coke was designated as an official sponsor of the NHL and with that attained the right, *inter alia*, to describe its product Diet Coke as 'the official soft drink of the NHL'. With those rights Coke also received the right to use NHL symbols and, collectively, team symbols for its promotional programs in Canada and the United States. In consideration of the rights it attained under the agreement, Coke agreed to pay NHLS approximately $2.6 million.

What Coke did not obtain by its agreement with NHLS was any right to advertise during the broadcast in Canada of any televised NHL games. Such rights were not vested in NHLS but rather in the NHL. In 1988 that organisation sold them to Molson Breweries of Canada Ltd for a five year period.

By arrangement with Molson, the Canadian Broadcasting Corporation broadcasts at least one NHL game nationwide in Canada every Saturday night during the regular playing season. It also broadcasts many of the post season play off games, as well as all the final Stanley Cup play off games. These broadcasts have become known as 'Hockey Night in Canada' (HNIC).

As licensee of all the broadcast rights in Canada, Molson granted the defendant the right to be the exclusive advertiser of soft drinks during the broadcast of all HNIC games. Thus although Coke was the 'official soft drink of the NHL', it had no right to advertise its products during HNIC broadcasts.

As part of its HNIC advertising, the defendant sponsored an inter-period program called 'Coach's Corner'. This program featured Mr Don Cherry being interviewed by a CBC sports commentator. Occasionally, Mr Cherry's English bull terrier, 'Blue', would be seen with him during these programs.

Mr Cherry, who for some years was the coach of the Boston Bruins, may fairly be described as having a very distinctive public character. He dresses in a manner calculated to catch attention and excite comment. His manner of speech is turgid. He projects a 'tough guy' image and appears to favour a violent brand of hockey that includes on-ice fights between players.

The Stanley Cup play off games are the most watched television sporting event in Canada. Many people who during the regular season would not count themselves as hockey fans tune in for the Stanley Cup finals. Thus the television broadcasts of these games provide a prime opportunity for advertisers to expose their wares to a large segment of the Canadian public. Those who have this opportunity naturally want to make the most of it by means of the most attention-getting advertisements they can devise. If the on-air advertising can be reinforced or supplemented by a collateral promotional campaign, so much the better.

In order to participate in the Contest, the public was invited to collect bottle cap liners or specially marked cups used to dispense any of the defendant's soft drink products during the Contest period. Anyone not wishing to purchase a soft drink could obtain, without charge, a Contest scratch card. On the Contest bottle cap liners or beneath an opaque film that could be scratched off the Contest cups and Contest scratch cards, there appeared. the statement 'If [followed by the name of a city or State that was home to one of the plaintiff teams] wins in [followed by one of the numbers four, five, six or seven] games you win'. There followed a description of the prizes that could be won which ranged from a free supply of one of the defendant's products to the sum of $10,000. Thus for example if a contestant obtained a Contest bottle cap liner, Contest cup or Contest scratch card with the words 'If Quebec wins in four games you win $10,000' and in the (unlikely) event that the Quebec Nordiques won a place in the Stanley Cup finals and went on to sweep that series in four straight games, the lucky contestant would be eligible for a $10,000 prize. To collect the prize, the consumer was required to fill out a Contest entry form and send it together with the winning game piece to the defendant. The entry form included a skill-testing question in arithmetic. One counsel assured me that the question was so simple it could hardly be classified as a skill-testing question. However the solution to the question he suggested was incorrect.

The Contest was widely publicised. Bottles of the defendant's products had hang tags, approximately three and a half inches by nine and a half, placed over their necks. The front of the hang tags displayed prominently the words 'Diet Pepsi $4,000,000 Pro Hockey Play off Pool'. Beneath those words was a picture of a goal tender making a glove save. The goal tender was wearing a shirt on which appeared the Diet Pepsi logo. The reverse side of the hang tag contained the contest rules. Both the front and back of the hang tag displayed a disclaimer stating 'Diet Pepsi's $4,000,000 Pro Hockey Play off Pool is neither associated with nor sponsored by the National Hockey League or any of its member teams or other affiliates'. The same disclaimer was reproduced on all the other printed promotional material.

In addition to the Contest bottle cap liners, Contest cups, Contest scratch cards and hang tags, the defendant also caused the Contest to be publicised by means of various other point of sale printed material including posters, counter cards, shelf talkers, cooler stickers and table tents in retail outlets where the defendant's products were sold. Many of the delivery trucks used by the defendant's licensees also bore back signs measuring six feet by four feet' advertising the Contest.

To promote the Contest and thereby the sale of its products beyond that which was possible by point of sale advertising the defendant also advertised the Contest on television during the broadcast of the Stanley Cup play off series. The television advertisements appeared in four forms, two of which were in the English language and two in French. The latter appeared on the French language network of the CBC shown in Quebec. I was not provided with a translation of these versions of the advertisement and I do not know if they followed the same format as the English language versions. The speaking part in the French version was not played by the same person that appeared in the advertisements that were in English.

The English language advertisements were shown nationwide on the CBC's English language network. Both of these versions of the advertisement featured Mr Cherry dressed in his own inimitable style. The setting was a hockey dressing room and in one of them Mr Cherry was accompanied by the faithful 'Blue'. In both, Mr Cherry was seen and heard explaining the Contest to three men dressed as hockey players and exhorting them to participate.

In one of the English language versions of the television advertisements, the audio portion consisted of a monologue by Mr Cherry in which he stated:

> Just cool it! Just cool it! There are $4 million to be won in Diet Pepsi's Play off Pool.
>
> Now look here! Check under the caps of Pepsi and 7 Up products. If for instance it says 'Calgary in 6' and they win the Play off finals in six, you could win $10,000, $10, or free Diet Pepsi. Now, hit the ice you guys! Play Diet Pepsi's $4 million Play off Pool.
>
> Can you believe these guys?

In the other English language version Mr Cherry was heard to say:

> All right, this is a big game. Diet Pepsi's $4 million Play off Pool.
>
> And you could win.
>
> You look under the caps of any Pepsi or 7 Up products. If it says 'Boston in 6' and they actually win the Play off final in six, you are a winner. You could win ten thousand bucks, ten bucks or free Diet Pepsi.
>
> And you wonder why I got out of coaching?

During the first seven seconds of both the English language television advertisements the same disclaimer as was on the printed advertising material was displayed at the bottom of the television screen.[62]

---

62 2 DLR (4th) 349.

Since there are no rights in events as such, the traditional rights must be relied on. So trade marks can be used to prevent unauthorised companies using the emblems belonging to an event. To this extent, the Olympic insignia are in the strongest position given their specific statutory protection. But even trade mark registration has its limits. In *Trebor Bassett Ltd v FA Ltd*,[63] Trebor produced football cards showing photographs of England players wearing their England strip carrying the three lions logo. The FA's action for trade mark infringement was struck out. Rattee J stated 'it cannot be seriously argued that by publishing and marketing on the cards concerned photographs of players wearing the England team football strip, Trebor Bassett is in any sense using the logo in respect of the cars on which the photograph appears ... by such reproduction, in my judgment, Trebor Bassett is not even arguably using the logo, as such, in any real sense of the word "uses"...'.[64]

The other cause of action is an action in passing off which seeks to protect the goodwill in a mark. But the limits of this action have been identified earlier.[65]

The danger of ambush marketing is that if those who award sponsorship agreements fail to control the ambushers, then sponsors will leave the market or join the ranks of the ambushers themselves. The sufferer will obviously be the sport itself ultimately. Gaspar identifies dangers not only to Sports Events Organisers (SEO) in the following extract:

Gaspar, T, 'Protecting Events: Catching Ambush Marketing Offside'

It is not just sport that is affected. Attracting major international sporting events to a country is considered by many governments to be a legitimate means of stimulating the economy. It will have direct and indirect benefits for tourism, jobs creation and encouraging investment in local business in a range of industries.

Staging events such as the Olympics provides a country with the opportunity to enhance its international reputation not just as a venue for other international sporting events but as a reliable trading partner. It is an advertisement for its economic strength.

The ability of governments and SEOs to attract such events will be greatly affected by their ability to maximise the commercial revenues associated with the event. SEOs and governments will be unable to achieve this unless they are able to devise an effective anti-ambush strategy and eliminate the loopholes and weaknesses in the legal regime available to deal with ambush activities.[66]

---

63   [1997] FSR 211.

64   *Ibid, per* Ratter J, 212.

65   See 'Individual Athletes', above p 308.

66   Gaspar, T, 'Protecting Events: Catching Ambush Marketing Offside' (1994), Working Paper, University of Melbourne, p 10.

If the legal mechanisms are limited then organisers should seek self-help remedies:

Bitel, N, 'Ambush Marketing'

It may seem surprising but some of the most effective controls are in the hands of the event organisers but are not used. They have the ability to control and regulate their own event but do not use it. Just consider some examples:

The sky above the finish of this year's New York City Marathon featured an unofficial air display planes writing the legend 'Greenwich Mercedes Benz'. It will come as no surprise that Toyota were the official sponsor. Indeed as if to illustrate a point I made earlier, Mercedes had been the official car in 1995 but got fed up with the antics of unofficial operators. The result was this spectacular stunt. But it could have been avoided. At the London Marathon we have an air exclusion zone over the course partly because of police and television helicopters and partly at our request. I suppose in truth it also helps that any unauthorised low flying aircraft over our finish area, including Buckingham Palace and Parliament, are more likely to be shot down than sued. I was reminded of some clients of mine for whom we won a case against Gulf Oil. They then hired a plane and towed a sign saying 'Gulf exposed in fundamental breach' over the hospitality tent at the Cheltenham Gold Cup where Gulf were entertaining their most important clients. Unfortunately Lord Justice Parker found this to be a conspiracy to injure and immediately injuncted the miscreants (*Gulf Oil (UK) Ltd v Page and Others* [1987] 3 AER 14). Well if it could work for Gulf, who had broken their contract, why not the event. After all, Mercedes are doing just the same; they are conspiring to injure the event by pretending they are authorised. Of course it is far better to prevent the infraction by control of the skies.

I have mentioned Nike's billboard campaign – well how did we react? First we ensured that the host broadcaster shot their pictures from angles which did not show the offending posters wherever possible. In the one case where this could not be achieved we placed some large mobile advertising boards and lots of balloons in front of their poster. The result of this self help was that not one billboard was seen by the television viewers. Nike's efforts at ambushing the London Marathon cost about £450,000. In this case their ambushing actually cost them more than the official rights and because of our efforts they certainly did not get value for money.

(1) The problem of the athlete as an advertising site is probably the area where most can be done. The winner of last year's Mercedes Championship was Mark O'Meara who is sponsored by Toyota. Thus for four days the television coverage concentrated on O'Meara who wore a sun visor emblazoned with the name of Toyota. We do not see this sort of ambush on the European Tour because there are rules which prevent players from wearing clothing which endorse competing marks. If you can do it in Europe why not America. In theory a football team could have an official boot and make the player wear those. I remember the 1975 FA Cup Final when Fulham did just that and found themselves in conflict with their Captain Bobby Moore who had a contract with a competing manufacturer.

There followed an unedifying farce with the mark of one manufacturer being painted on the boots of another. But this only arose because this was a one off deal by Fulham especially for the final. If this was a condition in Moore's contract from the start then there should have been no problems. Why not try it – because players now believe this to be their right? How far does it extend? Ravinelli's goal celebrations involve him putting his shirt over his head. Ever quick to spot an opportunity, Nike got him to wear an undershirt with a massive Nike logo when playing for Italy – far larger than would be allowed under FIFA rules. Yet he got away with it because of official inaction. It would be so simple to stop this and other ambushes like it. Just introduce a rule modification making it ungentlemanly conduct to have any sponsor's name or mark anywhere on a player except the Club's own kit. Enforce breaches by bookings and sendings off and the message would soon get home.

(2) At the London Marathon, we have to contend with the BAF and IAAF rules which we do not make and we cannot therefore control what the athlete wears in the race. But we can and do control all other appearances. In our contracts we insist that athletes either wear official branded clothing or clothing with no brands at all at press conferences, interviews and photo calls. Old cat eyes would not have appeared at our press conference with his contact lenses! The manufacturers still try to get around this, dressing their athletes in logo festooned hats, pins and even sunglasses as soon as their athlete is about to mount the podium or join the press conference. We have to be vigilant and check the athlete closely before each such appearance. It can be done and for the sake of official sponsors it should.

(3) When selling television rights, event owners can probably insist on the right to prevent ambushers sponsoring the coverage. If we do not take control of this sector we are in danger of alienating the sponsors on whom the events depend. Watching the American coverage of the 1996 New York City Marathon I got a glimpse of what life could be like here if we are not careful. The broadcaster had sold sponsorship rights not only to the overall coverage but only separately to the Men's results, Women's results, the start lists and so on. Thus Toyota were faced not only by Mercedes in the sky but also Jeep on the screen. How can we expect them to renew if we offer no protection.

(4) Taking this protection of television even further, the Australian rugby league has signed a deal with Channel 9 giving their sponsor, Quantas, first option to all break advertising during games. I said that organisers can only probably protect themselves from television ambush because I recognise that if, say, Sky are paying £670 million for the rights to Premier League Football they are going to want to be able to recoup a lot of that from, say, Ford, for the broadcast sponsorship rights and many sports are just grateful to have their sports shown on television without being able to insist on anything. But one word of warning, there is one other problem and that is UK and European competition legislation. I have to say that the Australian example I think could be challenged here. It is one thing to control the advertising during the programme but to deny rivals

advertising slots in between programmes might well be said to be a restrictive trade practice or anti-competitive.

(5) One other simple measure that can be taken to prevent ambushing is in relation to granting of rights to official merchandisers. I have seen in America examples where, say, one soft drink company was offering as part of a promotion free official merchandise, key rings, base ball hats and the like, where they were not the official soft drink. They had not produced pirate merchandise but had merely acquired from the official merchandisers the products. Subject to the same caveat about anti-competitive and restrictive trade practices this sort of pirate operation could be avoided by ensuring that in the contract with the official merchandisers provides they cannot supply rivals to official sponsors and suppliers.

(6) We should remember that many sponsors are not buying awareness. McDonalds are now the world's most recognised brand. When they sponsor an event surely their central aim is to sell more products. Therefore one of the most effective things that event organisers can do is to build a package of rights to help the sponsor achieve its aim. Only 2.8% of people may recognise Beefeater as the sponsor of the Boat Race but they are happy. Their package of rights has allowed them to reach their most important customers – the trade – and sell more product. Access to good hospitality and personal appearances by the athletes can be more important than awareness in securing contracts. Coming back to the London Marathon, the reason why our official shoe and clothing company, Asics, are not that upset by Nike's efforts is that Asics make a substantial sum from the official clothing, shoes and merchandise which they sell. This type of direct benefit is difficult for the ambusher to acquire and is therefore exactly the type of benefit that the event organiser has to incorporate in the rights packages which they make available to sponsors.[67]

But prevention is better than cure and so effective strategies need to be developed to prevent the ambush occurring at all. The first thing to note is that all rights can only be contractual and as such this must be the starting point:

Gaspar, T, 'Protecting Events: Catching Ambush Marketing Offside'

To support the anti-ambush strategy SEOs are well advised to implement some of the following plans:

Establish a close working relationship with all sponsors. The co-operation of sponsors is important if the anti-ambush strategy is to be effective and many of the plans below are to be implemented. Close cooperation also helps build a relationship that will lead to continuing sponsorships in future years. Ongoing relationships are important for ensuring the success of an event and lead to maximum benefits from the sponsors perspective.

---

67 Bitel, N, 'Ambush Marketing' (1997) 5(1) *Sport and the Law Journal* 2.

A market activity watch program co-ordinated with all sponsors to identify and respond quickly to any ambush activity. Sponsors are likely to learn of such activities before the SEO because they are active in the market and therefore their co-operation is crucial to the success of this aspect of the strategy.

Advertise and promote along with the sponsors, the event, its logo, the sponsors (and their products) and official merchandise to the public. If done effectively this will discourage ambush activity and reduce the likelihood that ambush marketers can 'fool' the public into believing that they are associated with the event.

Publicising successes in the fight against ambush activity will also help to deter others from engaging in similar activities.

Brief all the participants in the event and its commercial program about what the program is and how it works so that they can tailor their conduct to support the program. If this is not achieved the SEO runs the risk that the participants may pursue deals that will conflict with existing arrangements and are undesirable. Involving the participants in this way will foster co-operation and build goodwill between them and the SEOs.

Promote the program to the general public and ensure that they understand that support of the official sponsors benefits sport by rewarding the commercial partners for their contribution/investment and encouraging new or continued investment. Promoting the event's commercial program in this way builds the value of program and is a good public relations exercise to strengthen the relationship with the event's commercial supporters.[68]

CONCLUSION

This chapter has sought to examine the commercial values in sport and how they may be exploited. Major sporting events are valuable commodities that can boost the economy. The lack of legal protections for event organisers and those who participate in sport, however, makes it a risky investment in this country. If we want to attract major events then we must put the legal framework in place to attract them. Sport is now part of the entertainment industry and there seems no reason why these rights should not extend as they do to other aspects of the entertainment industry.

---

68   *Ibid*, Gaspar (1994).

CHAPTER SEVEN

SPORT AND CONTRACTS OF EMPLOYMENT

INTRODUCTION

Participants in sport fall into three main categories. They are amateurs, self-employed professionals or employed professionals. It is this last category that this and the following two chapters concentrate on as professional sportsmen and women, who are regarded in law as employees, will find themselves subject to and protected by the ordinary law of employment in both its common law and statutory forms. The major source of statutory employment rights used to be the Employment Protection (Consolidation) Act (EPCA) 1978. The EPCA has been repealed and incorporated into a new piece of consolidating legislation – the Employment Rights Act (ERA) 1996. This chapter will examine the formation and performance of the contract of employment, and will analyse the interaction between the core legal principles and the interests of employers and employees in the world of sport.

WHO IS AN EMPLOYEE?

In order to ascertain which sports participants are covered by the law of employment it is necessary to understand the legal tests for defining an employee. This question is essential in the contexts of termination of employment, taxation, health and safety and vicarious liability. Surprisingly perhaps there is no useful statutory definition of an employee; s 230 of the ERA 1996 merely defines an employee as a person who has entered into or works under a contract of employment. Thus it is case law arising out of disputes concerning these practical issues that provides us with the tests to help resolve specific problems.

The control test was the traditional common law means for ascertaining whether a person engaged in work was an employee. A person was controlled by an employer if that person was told not only what to do but also how to do it. Arguments that skills possessed by individual sportsmen took them beyond the control of clubs who paid them were quickly discounted.

Walker v Crystal Palace Football Club [1910] 1 KB 87 (CA)

Cozens-Hardy MR: It has been argued before us ... that there is a certain difference between an ordinary workman and a man who contracts to exhibit and employ his skill where the employer would have no right to dictate to him in the exercise of that skill, eg the club in this case would have no right to dictate to him how he should play football. I am unable to follow that. He is bound according to the express terms of his contract to obey all general directions of the club, and I think in any particular game in which he was engaged he would also be bound to obey the particular instructions of the captain or whoever it might be who was the delegate of the authority of the club for the purpose of giving those instructions. In my judgment it cannot be that a man is taken out of the operation of the Act simply because in doing a particular kind of work which he is employed to do, and in doing which he obeys general instructions, he also exercises his own judgment uncontrolled by anybody.[1]

It is interesting to note the emphasis given to the authority of the team captain as the 'delegate of the authority of the club'. Is the notion of captain as foreman consistent with the status and attitudes of the modern professional footballer? On the other hand, there is no doubt that the footballer who exercises too much individual initiative, contrary to instructions during training, is likely to find himself dropped from the first team.

Compare the contemporary footballer with his cricketing counterpart. Clause 5(a) of the Contract For Professional Cricketers requires the cricketer to '... obey all the lawful and reasonable directions of the captain or deputy captain'.[2]

Any problems for modern professional sport which might have been posed by relying on decisions at the start of the century have been pre-empted as the control test in itself has long been regarded as inadequate. The modern emphasis is much more on whether an individual who provides a service is or is not working on his or her own account. This is determined not by a single test but by taking into account and weighing up a number of different factors.[3] It is clear from the decision in this case that whilst control may be a significant factor in a given situation, an individual will still not be an employee if she or he bears the risk of loss. Compare professional footballers or cricketers with sports participants who are not considered in law to be employees – such as professional boxers or snooker or tennis players. These individuals, albeit under the guidance or even control of an agent or manager and subject to the rules of the sport, negotiate their own entry into matches and the consequent payment they receive.[4]

---

1   At p 92.

2   This standard contract of employment for professional cricketers was originally negotiated between the Test and County Cricket Board (TCCB), acting on behalf of County Cricket clubs, and the Cricketers' Association, acting on behalf of professional cricketers.

3   This 'multiple' approach is exemplified by the judgment of Mackenna J in *Ready Mixed Concrete (South East) Ltd v Minister of Pensions and National Insurance* [1968] 2 QB 497 (QBD).

4   However, this position might not be so clear cut if a more flexible approach is taken to determining who is an employee. By way of comparison see Engelbrecht, G and Schinke, M, 'The Social Status of the Sporting Profession' (1996) 4(2) *Sport and the Law Journal* 16–19. In particular, consider the argument that in German law a competition organiser or a sponsor could be considered an employer.

The method by which tax is paid is a relevant but by no means decisive factor. It is clear from case law that club managers will generally be considered employees even if they were to be treated as self-employed for tax purposes. On the other hand, the decision in *Massey*[5] might be applied to those who occupy special positions such as Director of Football, as exemplified in recent years by Kenny Dalglish at Blackburn FC or Terry Venables at Portsmouth FC. Both of these clearly possessed the bargaining power to enter into genuine agreements concerning their employment status and indeed what precisely their roles at the clubs involved. This was especially true with Terry Venables who did not regard himself as under contract to Portsmouth and went on to buy the club for one pound. Kenny Dalglish, of course, returned to the world of management with Newcastle FC.

The above tests are illustrated by an Employment Appeals Tribunal decision[6] that a bar manager whose contract described him as self-employed was nevertheless an employee as the terms of his contract revealed that he could not be considered 'his own boss'. This case also serves as a reminder that generally sports employers will employ 'ordinary' employees as well as sportsmen and women.

AGENTS AND MANAGERS

Of major importance in today's world of sport is the role and position of agents and managers engaged by individual sportsmen and women. A professional boxer in formal terms employs a manager despite in general being the subordinate party. The manager will enter into a contract of agency which will normally permit him to enter into similar contracts of his choice, and in reality will control the boxers who employ him. The boxer is in an analogous contractual position to professional musicians who to secure fame are dependent on securing a recording contract, but technically are in the position of principal in the agency relationship. Such professionals are excluded from employment protection rights, but receive some protection from the common law doctrine of restraint of trade.

Similarly the professional footballer who has an agent is the principal in that relationship. The essential difference between the boxer and footballer is that the latter is an employee of his club, and is more genuinely employing an agent's services to assist in negotiations with the employer. The boxer, on the other hand, like the aspiring rock band, is dependent on the agent for work and thus remuneration. Compare the boxer with, as examples, professional golfers, tennis players and snooker players, who generally more clearly

---

5   *Cf Massey v Crown Life Insurance Co* [1978] ICR 509 CA with *Young and Woods Ltd v West* [1980] IRLR 201 CA.

6   *Withers v Flackwell Health Football Supporters Club* [1981] IRLR 307.

possess the economic independence to be regarded as self-employed professionals. In so far as they employ agents they may be genuinely regarded as principals in what are essentially commercial relationships.

Individual sports participants who employ agents are bound by any contract entered into by the agent deemed to be within the scope of the latter's express and usual authority. The concept of usual authority covers any contract which it is reasonable for the third party to assume the agent to possess the authority to make in light of the norms of the commercial situation and other relevant factors. Usual authority may thus be wider than express authority. Therefore, for example, a boxer would generally not be able to object to a contract made by his manager to fight a particular boxer or to fight at a particular venue.

The Football League Contract

Clause 14(b)

The club and the player shall arrange all contracts of service and transfers of registration to any other football club between themselves and shall make no payment to any other person or agent in this respect.

This contractual provision is in accordance with the rules of the Football Association (FA) and the Premier and Football Leagues. Given the role currently played by agents in professional football, it would appear that clause 14(b) is more honoured in its breach than observance.[7] However the clause should act to restrict the scope of an agent's usual authority. For example, a footballer would not be bound by a transfer agreed to by an agent in the player's absence.

FORMATION AND TERMS OF A CONTRACT OF EMPLOYMENT

In accordance with common law principle a contract of employment may, but need not, be in writing. In practice contracts entered into by sportsmen and women, irrespective of their employment status, will be in writing. Therefore it can be noted in passing that sports participants, in so far as they are considered employees, are entitled to specified information in writing – ss 1–3 of the ERA 1996. This includes all the major contractual terms, the identity of any relevant collective agreements and copies of disciplinary rules and procedures.

---

7   Strictly speaking, agents are only permitted to offer professional advice to players that employ them. In all probability, football agents do negotiate on behalf of their clients. Nevertheless, the agent has no authority to enter into a contract on a player's behalf.

Trainees and Apprentices

Minors do not normally possess contractual capacity. This is however not a problem in sport as a contract of employment or analogous contract for services is deemed to be for the minor's benefit.[8] It matters not that the contract contains particular terms which the minor regards as detrimental, provided that the contract taken as a whole is to the minor's benefit.[9]

Contracts of apprenticeship are important in, for example, professional football. Apprentices are in a special position. The contract must be in writing and the contract cannot be terminated during its currency other than by reason of grave misconduct on the part of the apprentice. The apprentice may accrue statutory employment rights including the right not to be unfairly dismissed. However, ironically but nevertheless the norm in employment law, a dismissal may be fair even although it constitutes a breach of contract.[10] On the other hand, contrary to the normal principles of contract law, apprentices dismissed in breach of contract can receive damages for loss of future prospects as well as immediate financial loss.[11] Thus clubs are ill-advised to prematurely terminate an apprentice's contract.

Unless the contract of apprenticeship expressly permits dismissal for reason of redundancy such a dismissal will be in breach of contract. This will not be so if an employer can establish a complete closure of the workplace or a fundamental change in the nature of the business.[12] Short of, for example a football club going into liquidation, it is hard to conceive how these exceptions could apply in sport. However it is clear that on expiry of the contract the apprentice cannot argue that he has been made redundant.[13]

Youth trainees engaged by a club under a statutory training scheme will not have the status of either employees or apprentices, and are thus generally excluded from the protection conferred by statutory employment rights. However they are covered by health and safety legislation and the Sex and Race Discrimination Acts.

---

8 For example, *Roberts v Grey* [1913] 1 KB 520, in which damages were awarded against a minor who broke a contract to accompany a professional snooker player on a world tour in order to receive training and develop experience.
9 See *Doyle v White City Stadium Ltd* [1935] 1 KB 520, in which a minor boxer was bound by rules permitting suspension and a fine for hitting his opponent below the belt. Indeed, the court held that the rules were just as much for his protection as for the protection of his opponents. *Cf De Francesco v Barnum* [1890] 45 Ch 430, in which a minor was released from her contract as a professional dancer, where she was contracted to work only for the defendant, whilst he was under no duty to find her engagements and her remuneration was deemed inadequate.
10 See *Finch v Betabake (Anglia) Ltd* [1977] IRLR 470.
11 *Dunk v George Waller & Son Ltd* [1970] 2 All ER 630.
12 *Wallace v CA Roofing Services Ltd* [1996] IRLR 435.
13 *North East Coast Shiprepairers v Secretary of State for Employment* [1978] IRLR 149.

The FA and the Premier and Football Leagues, in conjunction with the Professional Footballers Association, provide written guidance to trainee players with respect to their contractual rights and duties:

'The Code of Practice and Notes on Contract for FA Premier League and Football League Contract Players and Trainees'[14]

Trainees

When a boy leaves school he may be registered by the club as a trainee player. Sixteen year old school leavers will be registered for 104 weeks, or up to their 18th birthday whichever is the longer: 17 year old school leavers for 104 weeks, or up to their 19th birthday whichever is the longer and for players who sign for a club after leaving school and taking up employment elsewhere the period of registration shall represent the balance of 104 weeks or up to their 19th birthday whichever is the longer.

The player will participate in youth training. This aims to provide training and coaching in the skills and abilities necessary to follow a career in professional football and to provide opportunities for acquisition of skills and knowledge in other occupations.

The managing agent for youth training in the FA Premier League and the Football League is The Footballers' Further Education and Vocational Training Society.

The payment to trainees is geared to the training allowance laid down. Subject to a club meeting the YT criteria and being granted placements the club will receive reimbursement for all or part of the trainees' allowance. Under certain conditions travelling and lodging expenses may also be reclaimed. Clubs which fill all the placements granted may sign additional players as trainees and pay the wages themselves.

The trainees will be expected to perform certain menial tasks, eg cleaning boots and equipment, sweeping dressing rooms, preparing strip, and general dressing room duties. These duties should not take up more than 10 hours per week, and should not include general stadium maintenance, groundsmanship or other ground work with the exception of the two day work experience in these areas.

The trainee may be signed as a full contract player at any time on or after his seventeenth birthday.

Not less than two months before the end of the player's traineeship the club must inform him in writing by recorded delivery whether or not it wishes to offer him terms as a contract player specifying (where applicable) such terms. It is important to note that players who are released on the expiry of their traineeship are entitled to receive two months' notice. The player is under an obligation to let the club know within 21 days of receiving the offer whether or not it is acceptable. If the player rejects the offer he may sign for the club of his choice after his traineeship has finished but such club will be liable to pay a

---

14   Hereafter referred to as FA Code of Practice and Notes on Footballers' Contracts. A copy of the Code must be given to all players and trainees at the time they sign for a club.

compensation fee to the club with which he was registered as a trainee. Either club may appeal to the Football League Appeals Committee to determine the compensation fee.

A club which grants a trainee player's request for the cancellation of his registration may also demand compensation from any other club signing the player as a trainee or under a written contract within a two-year period.

Trainees are governed by the same disciplinary rules as contract players. The sections headed 'Inducements' and 'Grievance Procedure' also apply equally to trainees.

Where appropriate, these provisions will apply equally to young players who have been offered a contract of apprenticeship.

Collective Bargaining

Trade unions and the world of industrial relations are not immediately associated in peoples' minds with the world of sport (at least this is so in Britain. In the USA, by way of contrast, professional sport is a heavily unionised sector of the economy). However the Professional Footballers Association (PFA) is affiliated to the British Trade Union Congress (the major national trade union confederation) and cricketers also have their own trade union, the Professional Cricketers Association. The role of both of these organisations, as is the case with any trade union, is to represent the individual and collective interests of their members.

Trade unions are most significant in the workplace when they are recognised by employers for the purposes of collective bargaining. The objective of collective bargaining is for trade unions to reach collective agreements with employers. In Britain such agreements are presumed, both at common law and under statute law, not to be legally binding on the respective parties, and thus normally do not have the status of contracts.[15] However part or all of the content of a collective agreement can be incorporated into the individual contracts of employment of the employees on whose behalf the union was negotiating. This will normally be all relevant employees, not just those who happen to belong to the union. A collective agreement so incorporated is of course legally enforceable between the individual employee and the employer.

The standard contract for professional cricketers is a major example of this process. The contract is derived from a collective agreement which was originally negotiated between the Professional Cricketers Association and the Test and County Cricket Board. This contract is not legally binding on either of the organisations which negotiated it but it is binding as an individual

---

15   See *Ford v AUEW* [1969] 2 QB 303, and s 179 of the Trade Union and Labour Relations (Consolidation) Act 1992.

contract on any club which adopts it with respect to its individual players. Both collective agreements and individual contracts derived from them can survive even if one of the parties, in formal terms, ceases to exist. Thus cricketers' contracts are not substantially affected by the fact that in 1997 the TCCB was replaced by the England and Wales Cricket Board.

Another major role of trade unions is to represent individual members who have a grievance with or are being disciplined by the employer. Both professional footballers and professional cricketers have the right to union representation at individual hearings. Footballers may also be represented by the PFA before a transfer tribunal.

The PFA has a higher public profile than the Professional Cricketers Association, and like many trade unions also engages in active campaigning on behalf of its members. One of its most important and relatively successful campaigns in recent years has been 'Let's Kick Racism Out of Football'.

If collective bargaining is not associated with the world of sport then this is even more the case with strikes. In 1996, however, the PFA balloted its members employed by clubs in the Nationwide League on strike action. This would have involved the collective withdrawal of labour with respect to games to be broadcast live on television. The cause of the dispute was the decision by the Football League to terminate a 30-year agreement under which the PFA receives 10% of the income from television. This money is used by the PFA for the welfare of its members – particularly those who are forced by injury to end their careers prematurely. Strike action was ultimately averted as the dispute was resolved by agreement between the League and the PFA.

Ironically perhaps, it may have been the case that any strike would have run foul of current legal controls aimed at more 'traditional' trade unions. Industrial action is only lawful if it is in furtherance of a trade dispute between employees and their employer. This dispute may have been perceived by a court to be between the PFA and the Football League. If this was so, then the PFA would have lost statutory immunity (conferred by s 219 of the Trade Union and Labour Relations (Consolidation) Act 1992) for the tort committed by any trade union in the course of organising any strike, that is inducing employees to act in breach of their contracts of employment.[16]

---

16 See *The Guardian*, 15 October 1996 for a report on the possible legal implications of the proposed strike.

PERFORMANCE OF THE CONTRACT

Express Terms

The interplay between the standard terms in a sports professional's contract and general employment law is of central importance. This is particularly the case with the rights and duties of the contracting parties. As is generally the case with written employment contracts, many of the respective rights and duties of the parties derive from express contractual terms. For example on the club's part there are normally express obligations to provide medical treatment and to continue to pay a player's basic wages during periods that he is injured or otherwise incapacitated. For employees in general such rights may not be in their contracts, and there are no equivalent statutory duties imposed on employers.

On the player's part there are duties to behave in a professional manner and to abide by the rules of the game. Consider the practical implications and consequences of the following:

The Football League Contract

Clause 2. The player agrees to play to the best of his ability in all football matches in which he is selected to play for the club and to attend at any reasonable place for the purpose of training.

Clause 5. The player agrees to observe the rules of the club at all times. The club and the player shall observe and be subject to the rules and regulations of the Football Association and the Football League. In the case of conflict such rules and regulations shall take precedence over this agreement and the rules of the club.

Clause 7. The player shall at all times have due regard for the necessity of his maintaining a high standard of physical fitness and agrees not to indulge in any sport, activity or practice that might endanger such fitness.

Clause 13. The player may, save as otherwise mutually agreed and subject to the overriding obligation not to bring the game of Association Football into disrepute, contribute to the public media in a responsible manner. The player, whenever circumstances permit, must give to the club reasonable notice of his intention to make such contributions to the public media in order to allow representations to be made to him on behalf of the club if it so desires.

Clause 14(a). The player shall not induce or attempt to induce any other player employed or registered by the club, or by any other Football League club, to leave that employment to cease to be so registered for any reason whatsoever.

Similar provisions to the above can be found in the standard Contract For Professional Cricketers and the England and Wales Cricket Board's (formerly the TCCB's) Rules and Regulations. Of particular interest, in both football and cricket, is the catch all offence of 'bringing the sport into disrepute'.

The above terms are particularly interesting when related to the following much publicised incidents. The ban on Ian Botham after being convicted for the possession of cannabis; the alcoholism of Tony Adams and Paul Merson and the latter's addiction to cocaine and gambling; the short ban imposed on Chris Armstrong for smoking cannabis; the dismissal of Craig Whittington for the same offence; the dismissal of Roger Stanislaus for using cocaine; the termination of cricketer Ed Giddins' contract for the same offence; the decisions by Chelsea FC and Manchester United FC not to impose club penalties on Dennis Wise and Eric Cantona after their respective convictions for assault; the fine imposed by the TCCB (and its subsequent lifting) on Ray Illingworth for publicising his version of the dispute with Devon Malcolm after the latter was dropped from the England test team during the 1995 tour of South Africa.[17]

Clubs appear to have extremely wide discretion in these matters either towards lenience or towards harshness. This can be related to the range of reasonable responses test in unfair dismissal law. Providing a player is not cheating, should not his private behaviour be his own affair? With respect to 'whistle blowing' are we as the paying public (not to mention loyal and often long suffering supporters) not entitled to be told what is happening behind the scenes? There certainly seems to be a different attitude taken towards drugs as against alcohol. The former may involve commission of a criminal offence, but is it as damaging, let alone more damaging, to a player's fitness than the 'refuelling' for which some professional footballers are renowned? Taking drugs would also appear to be viewed more seriously than acts of violence on or off the field of play.

With respect to clause 14(a) in the Football League Contract, it is a tort for any individual to induce another to act in breach of contract. A cynic might observe that in football the major culprits are the clubs themselves with respect both to players and managers. This is however a context where

---

17 The ongoing ramifications of the latter are evidenced by the criticisms of staff and students at Leeds Metropolitan University of the decision to award an honorary degree to Ray Illingworth. See *The Guardian*, 13 May 1997 and the *Higher Education Guardian*, 27 May 1997. With respect to dismissals for the use of drugs see below Chapter 8, pp 391–92, and the *Guardian Sport 96*, 1 November 1996; *The Express*, 27 November 1996. In an article entitled 'Cocaine, the lurking danger', *The Guardian*, 26 November 1994, Christopher Elliott analyses the relationship between drug taking and the demands imposed on, and lifestyles expected of, the modern professional footballer.

See *The Guardian*, 31 January 1996 (positive drug tests up by 15%) for an analysis of the extent of drug taking in sport.

mutual accommodation plays a rather more important role in practice than litigation, given that private out of court settlements are the norm.[18]

Judicially Implied Terms

Judges are more prepared to imply terms in contracts of employment than is the case with contracts in general. The orthodox business efficacy and officious bystander tests are not without relevance, but judges recognise that certain rights and duties arise naturally from the relationship between employers and their employees, and will identify and imply contractual terms accordingly.

Judicially Implied Duties of the Employer

The duty to provide work

Traditionally this duty applied only to those who were paid on a commission or piecework basis or an exceptional category of employee who needed to work in order to establish and enhance a professional reputation, for example, an actor or a singer. For other employees, irrespective of their status, the following dictum applied:

> It is true that the contract of employment does not necessarily, or perhaps normally, oblige the master to provide the servant with work. Provided I pay my cook her wages regularly, she cannot complain if I choose to take any or all of my meals out.[19]

---

18 One of the most controversial examples of alleged 'poaching' was when Mike Walker left Norwich to become the manager at Everton. For further controversy surrounding Mike Walker (after his return to Norwich), and an analysis of the legal issues concerning 'poaching', players' contracts and the transfer system, see Nash, M, 'The Legality of Poaching: Footballers' Contracts Revisited' (1997) 5(1) *Sport and the Law Journal* 49–52. Also see Nash, M, 'Playing Offside: Footballers' Contracts (1992) *New Law Journal*, 1 July and 'Players and their Promises: Footballers' Contracts' (1993) *Solicitors' Gazette*, 15 October.

Also see, *The Times*, 6 November 1993 for a report of threatened legal action by West Bromwich Albion after the club's manager, Ossie Ardiles, was appointed by Tottenham Hotspur to replace Terry Venables; and *The Guardian*, 4 July 1995 for an article by Lawrence Donegan, 'New kicks on the block', on the poaching of young players and a dispute between Arsenal and Manchester United over an England schoolboy international, Matthew Wicks.

For an analysis of the availability of equitable relief to prevent a player from acting in breach of contract through moving to another club, and a comparison with North American law, see McCutcheon, P, 'Negative Enforcement of Employment Contracts in the Sports Industries' (1997) 17(1) *Legal Studies* 65–100.

19 *Per* Asquith J in *Collier v Sunday Referee Publishing Co Ltd* [1940] 2 KB 647, 650.

An alternative view was put forward by Lord Denning:

> In these days an employer, when employing a skilled man, is bound to provide him with work. By which I mean that the man should be given the opportunity of doing his work when it is available and he is ready and willing to do it. A skilled man takes a pride in his work. He does not do it merely to earn money. He does it so as to make his contribution to the well-being of all. He does it so as to keep himself busy, and not idle. To use his skill, and to improve it.[20]

Sports professionals might well be included in the traditional exceptional category of employees who need to work in order to develop a reputation. Lord Denning's reasoning may be of limited value as it was used to grant an injunction restraining a dismissal in the politically controversial context of the closed shop. Nevertheless it seems more compatible with modern perspectives on the employment relationship than in the days where all employees were considered servants.[21] For example, the 'servant', in the first of the above quotes, was employed as a subeditor of a newspaper. If Lord Denning's view is to be followed it must surely cover professional footballers and the like. If this is the case to what extent is there a right to be selected for a competitive game, if only for a reserve team? Arguably, a club might be fulfilling its duty if it merely requires a player to attend training sessions.

Does this concept of the right to work as well as receive a salary or wage have implications for football clubs in the wake of the *Bosman* ruling? A possible consequence of this ruling is that professional clubs in the Premier and Nationwide Leagues will not be able to demand a transfer fee for a player who is out of contract. Such a player will be free to negotiate a new contract with his current club or a new club in accordance with that individual's preferences.

To minimise the impact of *Bosman*, players could be employed under indefinite contracts containing a long notice provision before a player's resignation may take effect. There is nothing at common law or under statute that prevents the requisite notice of dismissal being for a shorter period than notice of resignation. Whilst the contract subsists, a transfer fee could still be demanded by the employing club. This could be important with respect to a player who is out of favour with the club management and as a result wishes to leave the club but is denied a free transfer. If he were required to work a long notice period a club ready and willing to purchase him would have to pay a transfer fee. If however such a player is not being selected for the first or reserve teams, and he is not purchased by another club, is he being denied the

---

20 *Langston v AUEW* [1974] ICR 180, 190.

21 Lord Denning's view has received subsequent approval by way of *obiter dicta* in subsequent cases. See *Breach v Epsylon Industries Ltd* [1976] IRLR 180 (EAT); *Provident Financial Group Plc v Hayward* [1989] ICR 160 (CA). The latter case was concerned with the issue of employees being subjected to long notice periods before being able to resign in order to restrict the potential for 'head-hunting'.

right to work as suggested in the *Provident Financial* case?[22] If so, he could argue that he has been discharged from the contract and is thus free to move to another club on terms that he negotiates.

Equally, the requirement of long notice could be used as a device to inhibit a player from simply working out his current contract with a view, upon its termination, to negotiating a new contract with another club. A player might be deterred from giving notice of resignation if he feared this would result in him being dropped from the first team. Alternatively, might clubs behaving in this way be guilty of acting in breach of the duty of respect or in restraint of trade?[23]

Another possibility in the wake of *Bosman* is that up and coming players will be employed on a long fixed term contract. Again, if a player is not picked but is required to stay at the club without being able to further his career there might be a breach of one or both of these implied duties or a restraint of trade.

The duty to take reasonable care with respect to the health, safety and welfare of the employee

All employers are subject to this common law duty as well as various statutory duties imposed by legislation and the requirements of EU law. Such duties will normally be more than met by professional clubs, given that their employees will be perceived as valuable investments. There is nothing more infuriating to the club – and the supporters – than learning that a valued player has received a serious injury during training. Contrary to the norm in employment law, it is the player's corresponding duty to the employer which potentially is of more practical significance.

The duty to treat the employee with respect

This duty is an example of the dynamism of judicial creativity in implying new terms into employment contracts. The duty was identified during the 1970s – particularly in order to expand the circumstances where a resignation by an employee could be construed as a dismissal.

The classic statement of the duty is provided by Browne-Wilkinson J:

Woods v W/M Car Services [1981] ICR 666 (EAT)

... it is clearly established that there is implied in a contract of employment a term that the employers will not, without reasonable and proper cause, conduct themselves in a manner calculated or likely to destroy or seriously damage the relationship of confidence and trust between employer and employee ... To constitute a breach of this implied term it is not necessary to

---

22 *Ibid, Provident Financial Group* (1989).
23 See above, p 345 and below, pp 357–63.

show the employer intended any repudiation of the contract: the tribunal's function is to look at the employer's conduct as a whole and determine whether it is such that its effect, judged reasonably and sensibly, is such that the employee cannot be expected to put up with it.[24]

Many of the decided cases in which employers have been found to be in breach of this duty have revolved around the issues of verbal and physical abuse and harassment. Given the often quoted statement that professional football is a man's game, to what extent can the individual player be expected to tolerate swearing, barracking, public criticism, humiliation and practical jokes from manager, team captain and team mates? Generally this could be considered part of the necessary locker room culture to build and maintain team solidarity and spirit. However in law, established workplace culture can still be found unlawful – particularly in the context of behaviour which constitutes racial or sexual harassment. In football, being required to accept a verbal 'bashing' may be one thing. It would be altogether different if, for example, a public dressing down was tainted with racist language or innuendo.

Could a refusal to select a player for the first team ever constitute a breach of this duty? As suggested above this could assume importance in the context of Bosman, where a player is not being picked in order to pressurise him into staying with a club. Such a practice would be counter-productive if it would enable a player to claim he had been constructively dismissed and thus was now a free agent.

Judicially Implied Duties of the Employee

The duty of obedience

An employee must obey all lawful and reasonable instructions of the employer. An instruction is reasonable if it is compatible with the job the employee is employed to do and is not excessive in terms of the demands imposed on the individual. It is clear that the duty can extend to personal factors such as appearance and dress and to behaviour in the employee's own time.

In light of the clauses in the Football League Contract quoted above, it is worth considering what types of instructions can be issued to professional footballers beyond attending training sessions and reporting on match days. For example with respect to diet, family life and standards of personal behaviour.

---

24 At pp 670–71.

The duty to take reasonable care

Given the financial consequences to a club if a player injures himself, a team mate or in certain circumstances an opponent, and the high salaries that some sports professionals may command, it is at least conceivable that a club (or its insurance company) could require a player to indemnify it for such loss where it is the consequence of reckless conduct or negligence on the player's part. This might be especially so if the player concerned is no longer with the club, and therefore the effect on the player's morale would not be an issue for the plaintiff.

The employer's right to an indemnity was upheld by the House of Lords in *Lister v Romford Ice and Cold Storage Co Ltd*.[25] The decision has attracted much criticism because of the implications for good employee relations and has been subjected to some judicial restriction.[26] In a non-industrial context such as sport, contemporary judges might feel more inclined to apply the reasoning in *Lister* that an employee who breaks a contractual obligation of care, and thereby causes damage to the employer, is accordingly liable to compensate the employer or perhaps more likely the club's insurance company.[27] The potential importance of *Lister* is now particularly significant in the light of high profile cases of litigation arising from fouls committed on the field of play.[28]

The duty of fidelity – exclusivity

Employees are under an obligation not to use or disclose confidential information obtained in the course of employment without the employer's consent. In other circumstances, however there is no general obligation not to engage in 'moonlighting'. Employers who wish to secure the exclusive services of their employees will need to incorporate appropriate clauses into contracts of employment.

Clause 7 of the Football League Contract (above) prevents players from participating in their sport, or any other form of sporting activity, without the club's previous consent. Professional cricketers are subject to a wider restriction:

---

25 [1957] All ER 125.

26 See, for example, the Court of Appeal's decision in *Morris v Ford Motor Co* [1973] QB 792 which restricts the possibility of subrogation, ie an insurance company substituting itself as the plaintiff to recover the money that it has paid to the insured.

27 Note that in *Morris* the majority of the Court of Appeal refused to accept Lord Denning's argument that an insurer should never be able to benefit from subrogation in an employment context.

28 See further Chapters 10 and 11.

The Contract for Professional Cricketers

Clause 5(c)

... the cricketer will ... not without the prior consent in writing of the club accept other employment or on his own account carry on any business calling or profession. Such consent will not be withheld where in the reasonable opinion of the club the proper performance by the cricketer of his obligations under this agreement is not affected and where the interests of the club are not harmed.[29]

The duty of fidelity – maintaining confidentiality

Duties relating to confidential information are important in the context of 'whistle blowing'. The scope of the implied duty of fidelity can be amplified by express terms in the contract, as in clause 13 of the Football League Contract (above).

Cricketers owe a similar duty not to bring the game into disrepute and owe an express duty not to 'engage in any activity or pursuit which is or may be prejudicial to the club' – clause 6(e).

The concept of public interest may be invoked to justify a disclosure which would be otherwise a breach of contract:

Initial Services Ltd v Putterill [1968] 1 QB 396 CA

Lord Denning: ... disclosure must, I should think, be to one who has a proper interest to receive the information. Thus it would be proper to disclose a crime to the police; or a breach of the Restrictive Trade Practices Act to the Registrar. There may be cases where the misdeed is of such a character that the public interest may demand, or at least excuse, publication on a broader field, even to the press.[30]

Should the much publicised row between Devon Malcom and Ray Illingworth be seen as a matter of public interest? Does (or should) the public have right to know why a player has been selected or dropped from a national team? When should disclosure be to the proper authorities rather than the media? What would be the position if a player or an agent or a manager discovered and publicised financial irregularities within a club? Should such publication be limited to bodies such as the Football Association or the Football League or the England and Wales Cricket Board?

---

29 On the other hand, cricketers have the contractual right to play international cricket if selected – clause 5(d). *Cf* the position of footballers where a club may decide not to release a player who the England manager has indicated he would like to select.

30 At pp 406–06.

RESTRAINT OF TRADE

The duty of fidelity applies whilst the contract subsists but ceases to apply on its termination except to information which comes within the category of a trade secret. Nevertheless contract law permits express terms which affect an individual's freedom to work for whom he pleases once an employment contract has come to an end. Such clauses are *prima facie* in restraint of trade and thus void. However a restraint is permitted if an employer has a legitimate interest to protect and the clause is reasonable in that it is no wider than necessary so to protect the employer.

Sports professionals often begin their careers whilst young. They are thus in a similar position to entertainers such as rock musicians in that in order to get a foot on the rung of the ladder of success they may sign a contract without fully understanding the practical implications of what they are agreeing to. Indeed even if they do fully understand what the contract provides they may feel they have no option but to sign if their careers are to progress.[31]

The doctrine of restraint of trade is of particular significance in professional football in light of the transfer rules laid down by the Premier and Football Leagues. When a player's contract comes to end he is not unconditionally free to negotiate a contract with a different club unless he is given a free transfer. In this case he is literally a free agent who can move to a new club on whatever terms he or his agent can negotiate. Alternatively, and almost certainly if the player is not towards the end of his career, the club can retain him as a registered player by offering a new contract on terms no less advantageous than the expired contract. The player is free to negotiate a move to another club but this is subject to the clubs agreeing a transfer fee. If a fee cannot be agreed between the two clubs the issue may be referred to the Football League Appeals Committee whose decision on the value of the transfer fee is final. In practice, a player's desire to move may be frustrated if other clubs are not prepared to pay the required or prescribed transfer fee. Moreover, a player may submit to pressure to sign a new contract with a club to regain some security of employment:

---

31 For an analysis of the operation of the implications of the doctrine of restraint of trade for boxers' contracts, see Greenfield, S and Osborn, G, 'A Gauntlet for the Glove: The Challenge to English Boxing Contracts' (1995) 6(1) *Marquette Sports Law Journal* 153–71. Of particular concern is the situation where a young boxer signs a contract under which the same person is 'employed' by the boxer to manage him and promote his fights.

FA Code of Practice and Notes on Contract[32]

Retain and Transfer Rules

The player's contract will run for a stated period. During that time the club and player have binding obligations to each other. These can be ended by agreement, so it is possible for the club to suggest to the player that he might like to consider joining another club, and the player can indicate to the club that he would like to leave. Agreement of both sides is essential. No one is entitled in law to induce either a club or player to break a contract; such action is tortuous and could lead to an action for damages.

The aim of the current rules is to enable a player to leave a club freely at the end of his contract, but to recognise that the club is entitled to compensation from the club he joins, provided that this does not seriously hamper the player's moving. It is implicit in the rules that the happy club and player should be able to continue their relationship smoothly. Contracts of any length are possible and a contract can be renegotiated so that it runs for a further or a longer period.

If however player and club decide to part at the end of a contract then the player is free to look for another club. He may do this even though his club has made him a fresh offer. In three instances there will be no compensation payable:

(a) the club has announced that he is free to move without fee.

(b) the club has made no offer to him.

(c) the club's offer is less favourable than his previous terms.

To calculate the position under (c) it is necessary to look at the most favourable year of the contract that has expired and to calculate the financial value and the bonus structure (the actual amount of bonus paid will of course depend upon appearances and results and is variable). If the previous contract contains a signing-on fee, paid in annual parts, the last part will be added unless the contract made clear that it was paid on a once only basis. players wishing to claim a free transfer on the basis that their offer of re-engagement is less favourable must make written application to The FA Premier League or the Football League (dependant on which league the club is in membership) with a copy to their club, by 30 June otherwise the club's compensation rights will be retained. If there is a dispute over whether or not the terms are as favourable, the matter will be determined by the board of the appropriate league and, on appeal, by the Football League Appeals Committee. A player granted a free transfer is entitled to receive from his club as severance payment his basic wage for a period of one month from the expiry date of his contract or until he signs for another club, whichever period is the shorter, provided that where a player signs for a club within the month at a reduced basic wage then his old club shall make up the shortfall in basic wage for the remainder of the month.

---

32 Pages 7–10 of the Notes provide guidance to footballers on the operation of the transfer system.

There is a timetable for the various stages that must be followed:

Third Saturday in May – This will usually be immediately after the end of the season. The club must have made its offer by that date. Practice varies but it should be noted that some clubs make a starting offer at the old rates and negotiate, others decide what they regard as the contract they wish to make at the outset. It is important that during the period set aside for negotiation the club officials (usually manager and secretary but often a director) and the player are available. In special cases, eg where clubs have outstanding fixtures affecting promotion or relegation, the notification may be delayed until no later than four days after the club's last such fixture.

Period for consideration – The player has at least a month (the offer may be sent early) to decide whether to accept the contract, to discuss it with the club and to let the club know his decision. Rules and regulations provide that the player must at the end of the period give the club his decision. A list of these players refusing offers (or free to move without compensation) will be circulated by the league concerned. It is in the interests of a player who receives an offer of re-engagement with which he is dissatisfied to inform the club in writing and in person in order to give the club the opportunity to make a revised offer.

Offer refused – If the player turns down the offer he can approach other clubs and they can talk to him. His club too can ask other clubs if they are interested in signing the player.

As a matter of courtesy, clubs intending to negotiate with players who have not accepted offers of re-engagement, should give notice of approach to the player's existing club. It is essential that both club and player keep each other informed where serious enquiries are made or interest shown. It is not only courteous, it is essential for the proper working of the scheme. Copies of all firm offers made for a player should be notified to The FA Premier League and/or the Football League as appropriate. A player who has refused his club's offer of re-engagement may notify the FA. Premier League or the Football League and the Professional Footballers Association of his refusal and his name will be circulated to all clubs.

The club may leave its offer open so that the player may, after talking to other clubs, decide to stay. On the other hand it is entitled to withdraw that offer (without losing the right to compensation) if it feels it must do so to finalise its squad of players for the new season.

A player is free to train with another club during this period, even though his transfer has not been fully agreed or the compensation fee settled and paid.

Compensation Fee – The compensation fee is a matter between the clubs and only affects the player if it makes his transfer difficult or unlikely. The clubs themselves will discuss and settle the fee. If no fee has been settled, then after 30 June the clubs, or the player to whom terms have been conditionally offered may appeal to the Football League Appeals Committee to determine the fee. The player must have either signed for his new club, or agreed terms subject to the fee being satisfactory.

30 June – All contracts apart from monthly contracts are dated to run out on this date. If the player has not been transferred by this date the club holding his registration may propose various action:

(a) the club may enter into a conditional contract with the player. A conditional contract allows a player to continue playing for a club until such time as another club wishes to sign him in which case he must be released even if the two clubs cannot agree on a compensation fee. A conditional contract should take the form of a normal contract with the player's remuneration and incentives being subject to mutual agreement. The following clause should also be included to safeguard the player's rights: 'This agreement is signed with the proviso that, should another club wish to acquire the player's registration, the registration will be transferred for a fee determined in accordance with the provisions of the FA Premier League Rules and the Football League Regulations.'

(b) the club may continue to pay the player the basic wage payable under the contract which shall have expired in which case the player is not eligible to play for the club nor is he subject to the regulations or discipline of the club. A club taking up this option is, by continuing to pay the player, retaining its rights to a compensation fee. This need not go on indefinitely and on or after the first day of the season, the club may apply to the Football League Appeals Committee to cease paying the basic wage, at the same time retaining its right to a compensation fee if it feels that circumstances warrant such action, for example, if the player has, without good reason, refused offers of employment with another club.

(c) where a club is desirous of playing a player who is in dispute yet does not wish to enter into a conditional contract, it may agree in writing with the player that he should continue to play for the club on a week to week basis under the financial terms of his last contract until such time as either the weekly agreement is terminated by either party or another club is prepared to sign the player. Copies of all weekly agreements must be forwarded to the league in which the club is a member and the Football Association and it is recommended that they take the following form: 'The player agrees to continue playing for the club on a week to week basis under the financial terms of his last contract unless the club incentive schedule paid in accordance with that contract has been changed in which case the player will receive the revised incentives, and to be subject to club regulations and discipline and to the rules and regulations of the Football Association and the FA Premier League or the Football League. The player agrees to give the club at least seven days' notice of his intention to terminate this agreement. It is understood that the notice need not apply where a player chooses to join another club in which case the agreement will terminate forthwith.' It would seem to be in the interests of all parties for the player to continue playing for a club as it gives other clubs who may be interested in signing him a chance to assess him in a match situation.

(d) the club may cease paying the player in which case he becomes a free agent.

A player who is paid under either option (b) or option (c) is entitled to 14 days' notice of the cancellation of his registration.

So that the player is able to understand the options open to him he is advised, if in any difficulty, to contact his PFA representative or the PFA Office.

Nelson, N, *Left Foot Forward*

... transfer tribunals were the logical and inevitable consequence of the PFA gaining freedom of contract rights for players. Their coming into being arose from the need for an independent body to reconcile the legal rights of the parties – existing employer club, employee player, would-be employer club – involved in negotiations or a dispute as an existing contract comes to its end. A player's current club have two options. They can dispense with a player – give him a 'free' – or retain him. Crucially to retain him they must offer him a new contract that is at least as favourable as the one just ending. This does create problems for boards. With players who are doing the business well enough to justify the original outlay on them and justify their first team selection, the club will not want the contract to expire. Every attempt will usually be made to offer a new one that is sufficiently attractive for the player to want to sign. But he (and certainly where applicable his agent) will appreciate that he is negotiating from a position of strength. What he now considers attractive may be a considerable escalation on his previous terms.

But the player may not be such an obvious asset. He may be getting long in the tooth, no longer performing at his former level. This may not weaken his bargaining position as much as might appear at first glance. Initially he may have been signed for a large transfer fee plus a huge signing-on fee and very substantial wages. The common sense move now may be to sell him. But in order to be able to command a transfer fee (as opposed to giving him the free and writing off all their past investment), the club must have him on their books. That is to say, they must renew his contract on at least the same terms. Knowing a good thing when he sees it, the player is almost certain to resign at once. The club is now paying the same high level of monies as before to a player they do not really want but whom, if they want to balance their books at all, they need to sell at the same top end of the market they bought him in.

Freedom of contract has made it possible for players to let their contracts expire and yet put themselves in an enhanced bargaining position. Consistently good form should clearly earn appropriate reward – no problem, you would think. But in many cases clubs offer even on-song players the legal limit they are obliged to – the same terms the players are already on. The Board's hope in such instances is that, not attracting any interest from other clubs, the player will be forced to resign on the old terms. But if there is outside interest and the player has more than one option, the club's gamble is more than likely to misfire. The player has leverage. He can wait to see what is the best offer on the table; even play both ends against the middle.

If, finally, a player refuses to resign with his existing club and signs for another, a transfer fee still has to be agreed between the two clubs. If they do not agree – and usually they do not – by now there is likely to be a lot of acrimony flying about and the transfer tribunal enters the equation. It will arbitrate and decide the fee.[33]

Eastham v Newcastle United FC [1963] 3 ALL ER 139 Ch D[34]

The transfer and retain system as it operated at the time was challenged by the footballer George Eastham as constituting an unlawful restraint of trade. Under the system on termination of a contract a club could decide to put a player on the retain list. As a consequence the player so retained could not play for any club in any country which was a member of FIFA. If the club refused to place him on the transfer list he had no choice but to accept the offer of a new contract from the club if he wished to work as a professional footballer. These regulations were declared in restraint of trade. However the rules enabling a club to require a transfer fee were upheld.

Wilberforce J: The transfer system has been stigmatised by the plaintiff's counsel as a relic from the Middle Ages, involving the buying and selling of human beings as chattels; and indeed to anyone not hardened to acceptance of the practice it would seem incongruous to the spirit of a national sport. One must not forget that the consent of a player to the transfer is necessary but on the other hand the player has little security since he cannot get a long term contract and while he is on the transfer list awaiting an offer, his feelings and anxieties as to who his next employer is to be may not be very pleasant.[35]

Despite this, Wilberforce J was prepared to uphold the transfer system taken alone as although there was an element of restraint a player could apply to have a transfer fee reduced or eliminated and could play professional football for a non-league club. The transfer system was protecting a legitimate interest as:

... within the league it provides a means by which the poorer clubs can on occasions obtain money enabling them to stay in existence and improve their facilities; and rather more generally ... it provides a means by which clubs can part with a good player in a manner which will enable them to secure a replacement. One player cannot easily be exchanged for another; the transferee club may not – indeed by the nature of things probably will not – have a player to offer in exchange: by giving cash, the transferor club is able to look all around the league for a replacement. Given the need to circulate players, money is necessarily a more efficient medium of exchange than barter and the system helps both money and players to circulate. Looked at in this way the system might be said to be in the interests of players themselves.[36]

---

33 This extract, from Nelson, G, *Left Foot Forward* (1995), London: Headline, pp 261–63, provides an useful insight into the view the professional footballer takes of the transfer system.

34 Although it was decided that it was unlawful for clubs to retain players who were out of contract, it was this landmark case that decided that the transfer system, on its own, did not constitute a restraint of trade and was thus legal.

35 [1963] 3 All ER 139, ChD 145.

36 *Ibid*, p 149.

Is the position adopted by Wilberforce J still acceptable or should we view the transfer system as 'the buying or selling of human beings as chattels' and thus an unlawful restraint of trade? The star player, particularly with the help of an agent, has the negotiating power to renegotiate a new contract with the current club or make himself available on the open market in the knowledge that a rival club can and will afford the huge transfer fee demanded and will in addition pay a signing on fee to the player himself. But does the commodification of football, exemplified by the revenue generated by and within the Premier League since its inception, justify maintaining the transfer system for players in the Nationwide League – particularly those employed by clubs in its lower reaches? Should the transfer fee system be restricted to a transfer negotiated whilst a player is still under contract?

Alternatively, is it the case that as the gap between the richer and poorer clubs grows ever and ever wider without the transfer system many of the latter will simply cease to exist? In which case from the perspective of clubs, players and supporters should the transfer system be seen as the lesser evil?[37]

Since the decision in the *Eastham* case the courts have shown themselves to be prepared to strike out clauses in restraint of trade where the terms in question have been imposed by one party on the other as a result of the former's stronger bargaining power. This has been particularly important in the music industry where in the words of Lord Diplock, 'one party uses his superior bargaining power so as to exact promises ... that were unfairly onerous or to drive an unconscionable bargain'.[38] At issue here is what the musician has to accept to secure a contract – often at a relatively young age. Is not the young footballer in a similar position? He signs for a club on terms it imposes – including acceptance of the transfer fee system.

What may prove to be the death knell for the transfer system is not so much the contractual doctrine of restraint of trade but freedom of movement of workers as required by EU law.

---

37 See Boon, G (1996) 4(2) *Sport and the Law Journal* 46-80, for a survey and in-depth analysis of football finance, the cost of players and the influence of transfer fees.

38 *Schroeder Music Publishing Co Ltd v Macaulay* [1974] 3 All ER 616, 623–24.

Applying this principle in *Clifford Davis Management v WEA Records and CBS Records Ltd* [1975] 1 All ER 237 the Court of Appeal released the group Fleetwood Mac from a contract to compose at least one song a month over a period of five to ten years with the copyright belonging to the company at the price of one shilling (5p) per song. Lord Denning declared that the publishing agreement was 'manifestly unfair' because: the composers were tied for 10 years without a retaining fee; the copyright fees were 'grossly inadequate'; they were in a weak bargaining position with the manager; and he brought undue influences or pressures to bear on them.

With respect to Fleetwood Mac the rest, as they say, is history. But that the problem continues to beset the music industry is shown by the long-running saga between George Michael and Sony and the self-description of the singer Prince as Slave (to his recording company). For further discussion see, Greenfield, S and Osborn, G, 'Sympathy for the Devil? Contractual Constraint and Artistic Autonomy in the Entertainment Industry' (1994) 15(1) *Journal of Media Law and Practice* 117–27.

THE BOSMAN CASE

The European Court's ruling in this case is based on its interpretation of Article 48 of the Treaty of Rome which provides for the right of EU nationals to work and reside in any Member State on equal terms with the nationals of that State. This article is directly applicable and thus enforceable by national courts and tribunals. The Article takes precedence over any conflicting national laws. Under Article 177 of the Treaty of Rome, at the request of either party, or at its own discretion, a national court may decide to request a preliminary ruling from the European Court of Justice on the meaning of Article 48 (or any other EU law). The European Court is not deciding the case on appeal but is answering the questions put to it by the national court. This court will then decide the case by applying the interpretation of the Article contained in the European Court's ruling, and any relevant national law which does not conflict with it, to the facts of the case. The opinion of an Advocate General to the European Court is highly influential, but not binding, on any ruling (or decision) that the Court gives.

This case came about because Bosman, a Belgium national, was placed on the transfer list by his club, RC Liege, once he refused to accept a new contract at a lower wage. Bosman wished to move to a French club, US Dunkerque, but RC Liege ultimately refused to process the transfer as it doubted US Dunkerque's ability to pay the agreed fee. Subsequently, the Belgian Football Association and UEFA became parties to the case as both bodies argued that their respective rules requiring transfer fees were lawful. The Cour d'Appel in Liege requested a preliminary ruling from the European Court:

ASBL *Union Royale Belge des Societes de Football Association and others v Jean-Marc Bosman* [1996] 1 CMLR 645 (Case C-415/93)

One question put to the European Court was whether Article 48 is to be interpreted as:

> ... prohibiting a football club from requiring and receiving payment of a sum of money upon the engagement of one of its players who has come to the end of his contract by a new employing club.

The Opinion of Advocate General Lenz was in the affirmative on the basis that:

> ... the transfer rules directly restrict access to the employment market in other Member States ... under the applicable rules a player can transfer abroad only if the new club (or the player himself) is in a position to pay the transfer fee

demanded. If that is not the case, the player cannot move abroad. That is a direct restriction on access to the employment market.[39]

In reaching his conclusion the Advocate General considered, and rejected, the following possible grounds of justification for the retention of the transfer system:

> A number of points have been put forward as justification of the transfer rules. The most significant of them is in my opinion the assertion that the rules on transfers are necessary in order to preserve a certain financial and sporting balance between clubs. It is argued that the purpose of those rules is to ensure the survival of smaller clubs. At the hearing before the Court of Justice URBSFA expressly submitted in this connection that the transfer fees paid guaranteed the survival of the amateur clubs.

> That argument amounts to an assertion that the system of transfer rules is necessary to ensure the organisation of football as such. If no transfer fees were payable when players moved, the wealthy clubs would easily secure themselves the best players, while the smaller clubs and amateur clubs would get into financial difficulties and possibly even have to cease their activities. There would thus be a danger of the rich clubs always becoming even richer and the less well off even poorer.

> If that assertion was correct, then in my opinion it could indeed be assumed that the transfer rules were compatible with Article 48. Football is of great importance in the Community, both from an economic and from a sentimental point of view. As I have already mentioned, many people in the Community are interested in football the number of spectators in stadiums and in front of television screens emphatically confirms that. In some towns the local football team is one of the big attractions which contribute decisively to the fame of the place. Thus in Germany there are probably only a few interested contemporaries who do not associate the town of Mönchengladbach with football. The big clubs have in addition long since become an important economic factor. It would thus be possible, in my opinion, to regard even the maintenance of a viable professional league as a reason in the general interest which might justify restrictions on freedom of movement. In this connection it should be observed that I share the opinion – as moreover do the other parties to the proceedings – that a professional league can flourish only if there is no too glaring imbalance between the clubs taking part. If the league is clearly dominated by one team the necessary tension is absent and the interest of the spectators will thus probably lapse within a foreseeable period.

> Even more important is the field of amateur sport. There are currently a great many amateur clubs in which young people and adults are given an

---

39 Paragraph 210 of the Opinion of Advocate General Lenz. This reasoning was adopted by the European Court in its preliminary ruling. The Advocate General also argued that the transfer system was contrary to Article 85, which prohibits anti-competitive practices within the EU. However, this position did not form part of the European Court's ruling.

For an analysis of this dimension of *Bosman*, and further discussion of restraint of trade, see Morris, PE, Morrow, S and Spink, PM, 'EU Law and Professional Football: *Bosman* and its Implications' (1996) 59 *Modern Law Review* 893–902.

opportunity for sporting activity. The importance for society as such of the availability of a sensible leisure occupation needs no further explanation. If the transfer rules were necessary to guarantee the survival of those amateur clubs, that would without doubt be an imperative reason in the general interest, relevant in the context of Article 48.

It must therefore be examined whether the rules on transfers in fact have the significance attributed to them by URBSFA, UEFA and others. A distinction must be drawn between the effects on amateur clubs on the one hand and professional clubs on the other hand.

As regards the amateur clubs, no specific arguments, let alone figures, have been submitted to support the assertion that the abolition of the transfer rules would have life-threatening consequences for those clubs or at least for some of them. But the question need not be considered further in any case. The corresponding question submitted by the Liege Cour d'Appel for a preliminary ruling relates to the situation under the transfer rules of a player whose contract expires. What is concerned is thus the transfer of a professional player to another club. As I have stated above, there is thus no need to clarify in the present proceedings whether it is compatible with Community law that a transfer fee is payable on the transfer of an amateur player to a professional club. The present question is thus confined to professional football. It cannot be seen what effect the answer to the question of the lawfulness of the rules on transfers in that field could have on amateur clubs.

As regards the professional clubs too the interested associations have produced little convincing, specific material to support their argument. In my estimation the report on English football by Touche Ross, submitted by UEFA and already mentioned above, has the greatest significance for the examination required here. In England there is of course a four-level professional league divided up into – from top to bottom – the Premier League and the First, Second and Third Divisions. From the figures given in that report it can be seen that in the period used as a basis the clubs in the Premier League spent a total of about £18.5 million net (that is, after deducting income from transfer fees received by them) on new players. After deducting that sum from total receipts, the clubs were still left with a total profit of £11.5 million. The clubs in the First Division, by contrast, made a surplus on transfer deals of a good £9.3 million, those in the Second Division a surplus of just £2.4 million and those in the Third Division a surplus of around £1.6 million. It is noteworthy in addition that for the latter three divisions there was in each case a loss on ordinary trading which was more than covered by the income from transfers.

Those figures are an impressive demonstration of what an important role the lower divisions play as a reservoir of talent for the top division. They also show that income from transfers represents an important item in the balance sheets of the lower division clubs. If the transfer rules were to be regarded as unlawful and those payments thus ceased, one would expect those clubs to encounter serious difficulties.

I thus entirely agree with the view, once more put forward clearly by URBSFA and UEFA at the hearing before the Court, that it is of fundamental importance to share income out between the clubs in a reasonable manner. However I am nevertheless of the opinion that the transfer rules in their current form cannot be justified by that consideration. It is doubtful even whether the transfer rules are capable of fulfilling the objective stated by the associations. In any event, however there are other means of attaining that objective which have less effect, or even no effect at all, on freedom of movement.

With reference to the question of the suitability of those rules for achieving the desired objective, it must first be observed that the rules currently in force probably very often force the smaller professional clubs to sell players in order to ensure their survival by means of the transfer income thereby obtained. Since the players transferred to the bigger clubs are as a rule the best players of the smaller professional clubs, those clubs are thereby weakened from a sporting point of view. It is admittedly true that as a result of the income from transfers those clubs are placed in a position themselves to engage new players, in so far as their general financial situation permits. As has been seen, however the transfer fees are generally calculated on the basis of the players' earnings. Since the bigger clubs usually pay higher wages, the smaller clubs will probably hardly ever be in a position themselves to acquire good players from those clubs. In that respect the rules on transfers thus strengthen even further the imbalance which exists in any class between wealthy and less wealthy clubs. The Commission and Mr Bosman correctly drew attention to that consequence.

Mr Bosman has also submitted with some justification that the rules on transfers do not prevent the rich clubs from engaging the best players, so that they are only suitable to a limited extent for preserving the sporting equilibrium. The obligation to expend a sometimes substantial sum of money for a new player is indeed no great obstacle for a wealthy club or a club with a wealthy patron. That is emphatically shown by the examples of AC Milan and Blackburn Rovers.

The financial balance between the clubs is moreover also not necessarily strengthened by the rules on transfers. If a club engages players from clubs in other Member States or non-member countries, the funds required for the purchases flow abroad without the other clubs in the same league as the club in question benefiting therefrom.

Above all, however it is plain that there are alternatives to the transfer rules with which the objectives pursued by those rules can be attained. Basically there are two different possibilities, both of which have also been mentioned by Mr Bosman. First, it would be possible to determine by a collective wage agreement specified limits for the salaries to be paid to the players by the clubs. That possibility was described in more detail by Mr Bosman in his observations. He observed, however that that possibility is not as effective as the alternative, which I am about to discuss. In view of what I am about to say, it is thus not necessary for me to say any more on this possibility. Secondly, it would be conceivable to distribute the clubs' receipts among the clubs. Specifically, that means that part of the income obtained by a club from the sale of tickets for its home matches is distributed to the other clubs. Similarly, the income received for awarding the rights to transmit matches on television, for instance, could be divided up between all the clubs.

To avoid any misunderstanding, I would like to state clearly in this connection that I do not include financial support by means of State subsidies among the alternatives discussed here. The reason for that is that such subsidies would go beyond what is possible for the football associations, on the basis of their autonomy, using their own resources. Professional football would thereby be placed on a basis quite different from that at issue in the present proceedings.

It can scarcely be doubted that such a redistribution of income appears sensible and legitimate from an economic point of view. UEFA itself has rightly observed that football is characterised by the mutual economic dependence of the clubs. Football is played by two teams meeting each other and testing their strength against each other. Each club thus needs the other one in order to be successful. For that reason each club has an interest in the health of the other clubs. The clubs in a professional league thus do not have the aim of excluding their competitors from the market. Therein lies – as both UEFA and Mr Bosman have rightly stated – a significant difference from the competitive relationship between undertakings in other markets. It is likewise correct that the economic success of a league depends not least on the existence of a certain balance between its clubs. If the league is dominated by one over mighty club, experience shows that lack of interest will spread.

If every club had to rely on financing its playing operations exclusively by the income it received from the sale of tickets, radio and television contracts and other sources (such as advertising, members' subscriptions or donations from private sponsors), the balance between the clubs would very soon be endangered. Big clubs like FC Bayern Munchen or FC Barcelona have a particular power of attraction which finds expression in high attendance figures. Those clubs thereby also become of great interest for television broadcasters and the advertising sector. The large income resulting from that permits those clubs to engage the best players and thereby reinforce their (sporting and economic) success even more. For the smaller clubs precisely the converse would happen. The lack of attractiveness of a team leads to correspondingly lower income, which in turn reduces the possibilities of strengthening the team.

Mr Bosman has admittedly pointed out that there are those who consider that the necessary balance results as it were automatically, since by reason of the facts described above no club can be interested in achieving an overwhelming superiority in its league. Experience shows, however that club management do not always calculate in that way, but may at times allow themselves to be led by considerations other than purely sporting or economic ones. It therefore is indeed necessary, in my opinion, to ensure by means of specific measures that a certain balance is preserved between the clubs. One possibility is the system of transfer payments currently in force. Another possibility is the redistribution of a proportion of income.

Mr Bosman submitted a number of economic studies which show that distribution of income represents a suitable means of promoting the desired balance. The concrete form given to such a system will of course depend on the circumstances of the league in question and on other considerations. In particular it is surely clear that such a redistribution can be sensible and appropriate only if it is restricted to a fairly small part of income: if half the receipts, for instance, or even more was distributed to other clubs, the incentive for the clubs in question to perform well would probably be reduced too much.

Neither URBSFA no UEFA disputed that that solution is a realistic possibility which makes it possible to promote a sporting and financial balance between clubs. If I am not very much mistaken, they did not even attempt to rebut the arguments put forward by Mr Bosman in this connection.

It seems to me that that is not a matter of chance. The associations too can scarcely dispute that that possibility is an appropriate and reasonable alternative. The best evidence for that is the circumstance that corresponding models are already in use in professional football today. In the German cup competition, for example, the two clubs involved each to my knowledge receive half of the receipts remaining after deduction of the share due to the DFB. The income from awarding the rights of television and radio broadcasts of matches is distributed by the DFB among the clubs according to a specified formula. The position is presumably much the same in the associations of the other Member States.

A redistribution of income also takes place at UEFA level. Under Article 18 of the UEFA statutes (1990 edition), UEFA is entitled to a share of the receipts from the competitions it organises and from certain international matches. A good example is the UEFA Cup rules for the 1992–93 season, which have been produced to the Court by URBSFA. Under those rules UEFA receives for each match a share of 4% of gross receipts from the sale of tickets and 10% of receipts from the sale of the radio and television rights. For the two legs of the final UEFA's share is increased to as much as 10% and 25% respectively.

While that system serves to cover the expenditure of UEFA and thus only indirectly – by means of corresponding grants by UEFA to certain associations or clubs leads to a redistribution of income, the case is different with the UEFA Champions League. That competition, which took the place of the earlier European Champions' Cup, was introduced by UEFA in 1992. A UEFA document produced to the Court by Mr Bosman provides information on the purpose and organisation of that competition. The objective is stated to be the promotion of the interests of football. It is specifically noted that the profit is not only to be for the benefit of the clubs taking part, but all the associations are to receive a share of it.

A balance of the 1992–93 season makes that clear. According to that, the eight clubs which took part in the competition each kept the receipts from the sale of tickets for their home matches. In addition to that, the competition produced an income of 70 million Swiss francs from the marketing of television and advertising rights. That amount was divided up as follows. The participating clubs received SFR 38 million (54%). A further SFR 12 million (18%) was distributed to all the clubs which had been eliminated in the first two rounds of the three UEFA competitions for club teams. SFR 5.8 million (8%) was distributed between the 42 member associations of UEFA. The remaining SFR 14 million (20%) went to UEFA, to be invested for the benefit of football, in particular for the promotion of youth and women's football.

The example of the Champions League in particular clearly demonstrates, in my opinion, that the clubs and associations concerned have acknowledged and accepted in principle the possibility of promoting their own interests and those of football in general by redistributing a proportion of income. I therefore see no unsurmountable obstacles to prevent that method also being introduced at national level or at the level of the relevant association. By designing the system in an appropriate way it would be possible to avoid the incentive to perform well being reduced excessively and the smaller clubs becoming the rich clubs' boarders. I cannot see any negative effects on the individual clubs' self-esteem. Even if there were such effects, they would be purely of a psychological nature and thus not such as to justify a continued restriction on freedom of movement resulting from the transfer system.

Finally, it must be observed that a redistribution of a part of income appears substantially more suitable for attaining the desired purpose than the current system of transfer fees. It permits the clubs concerned to budget on a considerably more reliable basis. If a club can reckon with a certain basic amount which it will receive in any case, then solidarity between clubs is better served than by the possibility of receiving a large sum of money for one of the club's own players. As Mr Bosman has rightly submitted, the discovery of a gifted player who can be transferred to a big club for good money is very often largely a matter of chance. Yet the prosperity of football depends not only on the welfare of such a club, but also on all the other small clubs being able to survive. That, however is not guaranteed by the present rules on transfers.

In so far as the rules on transfers pursue the objective of ensuring the economic and sporting equilibrium of the clubs, there is thus at least one alternative by means of which that objective can be pursued just as well and which does not adversely affect players' freedom of movement. The transfer rules are thus not indispensable for attaining that objective, and thus do not comply with the principle of proportionality.

The second important argument on which the associations concerned base their opinion that the transfer system is lawful consists in the assertion that the transfer fees are merely compensation for the costs incurred in the training and development of a player. The Italian and French Governments have also adopted that argument. It is of course closely connected with the first argument, which I have just discussed.

However often that view has been repeated in the course of these proceedings, it still remains unconvincing.

The transfer fees cannot be regarded as compensation for possible costs of training, if only for the simple reason that their amount is linked not to those costs but to the player's earnings. Nor can it seriously be argued that a player, for example, who is transferred for a fee of one million EUU caused his previous club to incur training costs amounting to that vast sum. A good demonstration that the argument put forward by the associations is untenable can be found in the DFB transfer rule, described above, for the transfer of an amateur player to a professional club. As we have seen, under that rule a first division club had to pay a transfer fee of DM 100,000, whereas a second division club had to pay only DM45,000 for the same player. That shows that the amount of the transfer fee quite evidently is not orientated to the costs of training.

A second argument against regarding transfer fees as a reimbursement of the training costs which have been incurred is the fact that such fees – and in many cases extraordinarily large sums – are demanded even when experienced professional players change clubs. Here there can no longer be any question of 'training' and reimbursement of the expense of such training. Nor does it make any difference that in such cases it is often 'compensation for development' (not compensation for training) which is spoken of. Any reasonable club will certainly provide its players with all the development necessary. But that is expenditure which is in the club's own interest and which the player recompenses with his performance. It is not evident why such a club should be entitled to claim a transfer fee on that basis. The regulations of the French and Spanish associations have, quite rightly in my opinion, drawn the conclusion that – at least after a specified moment in time – no transfer fees can be demanded any more.

Finally, it is self-evident that the training of any player involves expense. Reimbursement of that expenditure would thus depend on whether or not that player was transferred to another club. That too shows that the reasoning advanced by the interested parties does not hang together.

That does not mean, however that a demand for a transfer fee for a player would, following the view I have put forward, have to be regarded as unlawful in every case. the argument that a club should be compensated for the training work it has done, and that the big, rich clubs should not be enabled to enjoy the fruits of that work without making any contribution of their own, does indeed in my opinion have some weight. For that reason it might be considered whether appropriate transfer rules for professional footballers might not be acceptable. Mr Bosman himself concedes that such transfer rules might be reasonable as regards transfers of amateur players to professional clubs. That question need not be discussed further in the present proceedings, which concern only changes of clubs by professional players. The Commission, however suggested quite generally that a reasonable transfer fee may be justified.

Such rules would in my opinion have to comply with two requirements. First, the transfer fee would actually have to be limited to the amount expended by the previous club (or previous clubs) for the player's training. Second, a transfer fee would come into question only in the case of a first change of clubs where the previous club had trained the player. Analogous to the transfer rules in force in France, that transfer fee would in addition have to be reduced proportionately for every year the player had spent with that club after being trained, since during that period the training club will have had an opportunity to benefit from its investment in the player.

The transfer rules at issue in the present case do not meet those requirements, or at best meet them in part. Moreover, it is not certain that even such a system of transfer rules could not also be countered by Mr Bosman's argument that the objectives pursued by it could also be attained by a system of redistribution of a proportion of income, without the players' right to freedom of movement having to be restricted for that purpose. The associations have not submitted anything which refute that objection. It should be noted, moreover, that the above-mentioned DFB rules on the transfer of amateur players to professional clubs, for instance, appear to follow basically similar considerations with their differing standard amounts.

In addition to the above arguments a number of other considerations have also been put forward as justification for the rules on transfers; they must now be considered.

UEFA has submitted that the payment of transfer fees enables and even encourages the clubs to search for talented players, an activity which is vital for football. Even if that is the case, I do not see why it should be necessary for that purpose to make the transfer of players depend on the payment of a transfer fee. The possibility already referred to several times, of redistributing a share of income would also give clubs the financial means for the discovery and training of talented young players. Such a system of redistribution can also very well be designed in such a way as to allow incentives to be maintained for seeking out talent and providing a good training.

The argument, also advanced by UEFA, that transfer fees make it possible for the clubs to take on staff – which probably did not only mean players – I do not find convincing. As I have already shown, there are other possible methods of financing open to the clubs which do not affect the freedom of movement of players.

The argument that the payment of transfer fees must be permitted in order to compensate clubs for the amounts they themselves have had to spend on transfer fees when engaging players requires no further discussion: that argument contains a *petitio principii*. So does the argument that the purpose of the transfer fee is to compensate the loss which the club incurs because of the player's departure: that presupposes precisely that a player can be regarded as a sort of merchandise for the replacement of which a price is to be paid. Such an attitude may correspond to today's reality, as characterised by the transfer rules, in which the 'buying' and 'selling' of players is indeed spoken of. That reality must not blind us to the fact that that is an attitude which has no legal basis and is not compatible with the right to freedom of movement.

Mr Bosman has expressed the supposition that the transfer rules are intended to serve the purpose of reserving the sums in question for the clubs: according to the view he has put forward, the abolition of the transfer rules would lead to a general increase in players' wages. There is something to be said for that view. If the transfer rules really were – *inter alia* – based on that (economic) purpose, it would in any event not be such as to justify the consequent restriction on freedom of movement, since no interest of the clubs deserving of legal protection can be discerned in their paying lower salaries than would be payable in normal circumstances in the absence of the transfer rules and thereby benefiting at the expense of the players.

URBSFA has submitted that the present rules on transfers pursue the aim of guaranteeing the quality of football and promoting sporting activity and the sporting ethos. That argument appears to me to be directed essentially to the amateur sphere, which – to repeat it once again – is not concerned by the present proceedings. Moreover, it is not evident in any case how the transfer rules are supposed to help attain those very generally stated objectives. I also have considerable doubts as to whether a system which ultimately amounts to treating players as merchandise is liable to promote the sporting ethos.

A more important objection is that the continued existence of those rules is necessary to guarantee the maintenance of the worldwide organisation of football. The question of the compatibility of those rules with Community law is of significance for world football only in so far as the associations in the Community are affected. It is thus clear that the decision in the present case will apply to those associations only. If the Court follows the opinion I am advancing, it will no longer be possible within the Community to make the transfer of a professional footballer whose contract has expired and who is a national of a Member State to a club in another Member State depend on the payment of a transfer fee. It will, on the other hand, be open to associations in non-member countries to maintain those rules. That would have the result that a club in the Community wishing to engage a player who previously played for a club in a non-member country would still have to pay a transfer fee – even if that player was a national of one of the Member States of the Community. That could well create difficulties.

Those difficulties must not be exaggerated, however. The example of France (and to a certain degree Spain) shows that even now the system of transfer fees can be largely dispensed with within a Member State while continuing to be applicable to relations with other countries. There is thus nothing to prevent the Community being treated as a unit within which transfer fees are to be dispensed with, while being maintained for transfers to or from non-member countries. Moreover, that altogether corresponds in my opinion to the logic of the internal market.

Finally, I must mention the fear that the abolition of the existing rules on transfers would lead to dramatic changes in football or even to an expropriation. The view I have put forward would certainly mean that considerable changes would have to be made to the organisation of professional football in the Community. In the medium and long term, however, no insuperable difficulties should arise. As the introduction by UEFA of the Champions League shows, for instance, the associations are perfectly capable of taking the measures necessary for the good of football. In the short term the abolition of transfer fees will certainly entail some hardships, especially for those clubs which have only recently invested money in such transfer fees. There can be no question of an expropriation, however. If someone regards players as merchandise with a monetary value, whose value may in some cases even be included in the balance sheet, he does so at his own risk. Moreover, it must be observed that the abolition of transfer fees will at the same time bring a club benefits, by giving it the possibility of taking on new players without having to pay a transfer fee. As to the clubs which have only just 'bought' new players, it must be noted that the contracts concluded with the players run for a specified term, during which those players can leave the club only with the club's agreement. The ending of transfer fees will thus become noticeable for those clubs only when that period has expired.[40]

The European Court emphasised that Article 48 was violated as the transfer rules prevented EU nationals from playing for clubs in other Member States if a transfer fee was not agreed. Can it be argued that the transfer system operating within and between the Premier and the Football Leagues is beyond the scope of the ruling if requirements to pay transfer fees are restricted to British nationals seeking to play for another British club?

At an FA Premier League Seminar,[41] organised in the wake of the European Court's ruling, the overall view of the speakers was that the *Bosman* case could not have arisen in Britain as it would not have been permissible to retain a player on a lower wage. The ruling does not explicitly cover the situation where a player wishes to move to another club within the same country. Thus the Premier and Football Leagues should not be panicked into making changes to the current transfer fee system:

Reid, R, 'Report of the FA Premier League Seminar'

Where does that leave English clubs today? First the ruling of the European court does not affect transfers during the currency of a player's contract. It is concerned with the transfer of players who are out of contract. I think last year it was only about 10% in value of the transfers that took place. Although obviously a considerable number more in numerical terms, but 10% in value of transfers related to players who were out of contract.

Second it does not affect the movement of a player from one club within the State of which he is a national to another club within the same State. I quote, 'the provisions of the Treaty concerning the free movement of workers, and particularly Article 48 cannot be applied to situations which are wholly internal to a Member State; in other words where there is no factor connecting them to any of the situations envisaged by Community law'. That is paragraph 89 of the judgment.

It is reported that another Belgian player has begun proceedings in Liege for, in effect, the declaration that he is entitled to move from one Belgian club to another at the end of his contract without transfer fees being paid. His case itself was based on the *Bosman* judgment; in my view his claim. whatever chance it may have of success on other grounds – and it may very well have good chances of success on other grounds given the oddities of the Belgian transfer system – will not succeed on the basis of Article 48.

---

40   The ECJ's ruling was delivered on 15 December 1995. For an immediate reaction to the ruling see press reports of 16 and 17 December 1995. On the personal fate of Jean-Marc Bosman and a survey of a responses across the EU to the ruling, see the *Independent On Sunday*, 18 February 1996.

   For the definitive academic analysis of *Bosman*, see Blanpain, R, and Inston, R, 'The Bosman Case The End of the Transfer System?' (1996), London: Sweet & Maxwell, Leuven: Peeters.

41   See 'Report of the FA Premier League Seminar' on the *Bosman* case, 8 January 1996, organised in conjunction with the British Association for Sport and Law.

Third the *Bosman* judgment does not in my view make unlawful the requirement of a transfer fee on a move by an out-of-contract EU national from one club in another EU State to another club in that same State.

The provisions of Article 48 are generally concerned with access to a market rather than with behaviour within the market once access has been obtained. Once an EU footballer has obtained access to the English – or for that matter Scottish – market by joining an English or Scottish club and being registered with the FA or the Scottish FA he is in, and he is bound by the rules of the market that he is in. The wording of the answer may be ambiguous but the situation is then 'wholly internal to a Member State, in other words where there is no factor connecting them to any of the situations envisaged by Community law', to use the words of paragraph 89 again.

Fourth the judgment does not affect out-of-contract transfers of non-EU nationals from one EU country to another. Article 48 is concerned with EU nationals. Bear in mind that in this context, EU includes the members of the EEA, such as the Icelanders.

Fifth there is scope for ingenuity in obtaining a player free at the end of his contract. I suspect nearly all of you have seen in the press what might be described as the three club trick – from club A in England to club – in France for an overnight stop, and back again to club C in England. In its most brazen form this will be regarded as a sham and it will not work. However there may be more difficulties if you have an out-of-contract transfer from an English club to a Swedish club for the summer season, and the player then comes back to England for the following English season. The Premier League has a rule, F29.11, which prevents it, and at the moment you need special permission if you intend to bring back a player within 12 months. There is a rather differently framed Football League rule as well.

Sixth there is plenty of scope for attaining the ability to receive a payment on transfer by ensuring that valuable players are given lengthy contracts. Some clubs – Wimbledon for one – have already stated that they have adopted a policy of giving valuable players longer contracts. Do others have the confidence or finance to follow suit with that. particularly where young players are concerned? Is there the possibility of including in players' contracts a term entitling the seller club to demand a fee for the transfer of the player's registration after the contract is over or will that be void as being a restraint of trade?

Seventh the scope for entering into contracts which contain an option on the part of a club for prolongation. In the *Eastham* case, going back to 1963, Mr Justice Wilberforce accepted that an option was not in restraint of trade. He then went on to hold that the arrangements that then existed did not amount to an option or a series of options. Clubs which take this route will have to be careful, particularly in the case of younger players, that there is no suggestion of undue influence: if you are trying to sign up a player who is under 18 it can cause particular problems, but if you induce a young player, say a 19 year old, a theoretical adult, without the benefit of one of our more egregious agents to help him to sign up a contract which gives the club a right to endless one year options, you may well find yourself in the same sort of litigation as a number of recording companies who gave young pop stars lengthy contracts.

Eighth the *Bosman* case does nothing to clear up the question whether the internal rules of each national association can be in breach of Article 85. Lenz's opinion deals with Article 85; the judgment steers entirely clear of it. The court specifically declined to deal with the point. Advocate General Lenz opined that the regulations were in breach of Article 85 so far as they affected transfers to a club in another Member State.

Ray Farrell – and since most of you will be members of the Association of Sport and Law, you will have read his article in the most recent edition of the magazine – expressed the view that Article 85 would not affect domestic transfers. I think this may be a bold view. Could not the rules affect trade between Member States even when applied only to internal transfers?

Take an English international at the height of his powers and at the end of his contract. He is with an English club: if he goes to an Italian club under Article 48 and Bosman, his English club will get no fee. If he goes to another English club he will command a very large fee. An English club with £8 million to spend on the player over three years would have to pay £7 million, say, in transfer fees and then have £1 million to pay for the player. The Italian club with £8 million to spend would have £8 million to keep the player happy. It might well tempt a large number of agents to think that some part of that might rub off on them along the way – one does not know.

But is that not something which is 'capable of constituting a threat to freedom of movement between Member States in a manner which might harm the attainment of the objective of a single market between the Member States'?

Ninth will the English law of restraint of trade be invoked again in the wake of the *Bosman* case? The last case in which restraint of trade was argued under English law in relation to footballers was in the *Eastham* case and since then, as you all no doubt know, cricketers have fallen foul of the rules in the Kerry Packer litigation, and I have certainly heard one High Court judge expressing unsympathetic views as to the transfer rules so far as they affect contract players.

It would be unwise to assume, just because Mr Justice Wilberforce in the *Eastham* case did not appear to find much wrong with them 30 years ago, that the transfer rules would necessarily prevail today. They have been brought up-to-date, of course; since then: they have been modified with a view to taking off their rough edges, but my impression is that there is a hardening of attitude against restraint of trade, not just in relation to sport but in relation to many other areas where attempts are made to keep people out of the market or to retain them. There have been, for example, a number of cases recently about gardening leave-type clauses in cases relating to persons employed on the money market and things of that sort, and there the courts have by and large been pretty unsympathetic to restraints of trade of any sort.

It may well be that judges now will be less sympathetic to restraints of trade and to arguments based on the overall good of the game – and indeed the overall benefit of the players in the lower divisions, which is one of the points which the PFA in particular keep making – than their more paternalistic forebears were 30 years ago.

The message for the clubs is that they cannot regard the position as finally settled by the decision. The decision itself is fine and dandy; it is clear, but the clubs must expect some form of challenge to their rights to demand transfer fees for the transfer of registration of players who are out of contract, even if they are UK nationals moving from one UK club to another. That is not because of anything in *Bosman:* that will either be because some bright spark thinks they can get an argument off the ground under Article 85 or because somebody wants to revisit *Eastham.*

My guess – and it is only a guess – is that given the amount of money currently at stake, and given that people's interest – and no doubt professional advisors' intellectual talents – have been awakened by the *Bosman* decision, you may well find some maverick – whether or not supported by the PFA, whether or not supported by some rival organisation, whether or not an EU national – deciding that he can afford with the help of his backers to run his case all the way and see what happens. So although for my part I would be reasonably happy and would say to any club chairman, 'whatever you do, do not start scrapping youth policies and the probabilities are that the *Bosman* case will not cause any great mayhem'. I would have to add 'you have to be made aware that attempts to challenge the system will be in the air'.

I myself believe that such changes as are necessary will come more gradually and will be effected in a comparatively civilised manner, but there may well be something of a storm before the calm.[42]

If the British system is outside the scope of the *Bosman* ruling, what weight should be given to a counter argument that a player's freedom of movement is being restricted by being forced to play for a club in another Member State, when the player's preference is to seek a contract with another British club. In other words a player might be forced to play abroad in order to avoid the transfer rules. Alternatively, in the light of *Bosman*, should the transfer system now be viewed as an unreasonable restraint of trade. The arguments accepted by the court in *Eastham* for the retention of the transfer system were similar to the purported justifications rejected by the Advocate General.

UEFA rules now permit a player to move to another club even if the transfer fee has not been agreed to. In such cases UEFA itself determines the transfer to be paid. However the Advocate General regarded even this relaxation as restricting freedom of movement on the basis that a player's ability to move is conditional on the club being ready and able to meet the set fee.[43]

Current proposals under discussion to amend the transfer system in Britain include providing for freedom of contract after a footballer has reached the age of 24. On termination of a given contract such players will be free to

---

42   *Ibid*, pp 6–8.
43   Paragraph 150 of the Opinion.

negotiate their own contracts with the same or a new club.[44] If the transfer system within Britain is so amended what if players with potential – in particular younger ones – are engaged on long contracts which could be perceived as tying players to clubs; and what if players, of any age, are employed under contracts which may be determined by notice but the resignation period is, for example, a whole season? The promising young footballer can be compared to, for example, the aspiring rock musician, in which case, the doctrine of restraint of trade may well act to restrict the lawful extent of such practices. Independently of this doctrine, the enforcement of a long notice period could constitute a breach of the implied duty to provide work if, for example, it was let known to a player that he would not be picked unless and until his notice of resignation was withdrawn.[45]

The Bosman ruling does not apply to players recruited from outside of the EU as players from, for example, Eastern Europe, the Americas, Africa or Australia are not protected by Article 48. The only protection for such players is to be found in contract law and the doctrine of restraint of trade. Such players might now be seen as better financial investments than players of equivalent reputation who are EU nationals. FIFA decided with effect from 1 April 1997 to change its rules to permit any player to move to other clubs within the EU on free transfers once their contracts expire.[46] Thus a British club would still have to pay a transfer fee to import a player from, for example, a Brazilian club. If it retained that player until his contract expired a transfer fee could not be claimed unless that player negotiated a move to a club outside of the EU. At the very least the FIFA decision will increase the bargaining power of the individual player concerned; although it may reduce the attractiveness of such players to British clubs given the initial cost

---

44 Agreement on this compromise has been reached in principle between the Premier League and the PFA. At the time of writing, negotiations with the Football League were still underway. See *The Sports Guardian*, 28 July 1997.

It is not intended to introduce any change to the transfer system until the end of the 1997/98 season at the earliest. A challenge to the current system may be brought by two Premier League players, Vinnie Jones and Des Walker, see *The Guardian*, 27 March and 8 April 1997. As their contracts expire at the end of the 1996/97 season, the players want change with immediate effect. Their argument is that they are disadvantaged as against foreign players who are more likely to be prepared to move to another country on expiry of their contracts, and thus can benefit directly from the *Bosman* ruling. Also see *The Guardian*, 3 June 1997 for a report of legal challenge to the Scottish League's transfer system which is being mounted by a former Airdrie player, Chris Honor.

Note, as explained in the extract by R Reid (see above, pp 374–77), these players could, *inter alia*, base their actions on Article 85 of the Treaty of Rome.

Cf the support for the proposed changes, through negotiation, given by G Taylor, Chief Executive of the PFA, in a letter to *Sports Law Administration and Practice*, May/June 1997.

45 See above, pp 352–53. See also the reference by R Reid, to 'gardening leave-type clauses', above, p 376.

46 See *The Guardian*, 27 March 1997.

involved in their purchase. Another relevant factor in this context is that rules are still permitted which restrict the number of non-EU nationals who may be picked for European competitions.[47] This will be of even greater practical significance if the much talked about European Super League ever becomes a reality.

Overall the FIFA ruling in voluntarily extending freedom of movement within the EU to non-EU nationals must cast further doubt of the validity of a transfer fee system operating within the territory of a single EU Member State.

In a poll of football supporters, players and managers conducted by the magazine *Four Four Two*, 93% of all players in the Premier and Nationwide Leagues approved of the *Bosman* ruling. Additionally, 34% of the supporters also approved of it, whereas 89% of managers regarded it as bad for football in general. There was particular concern on the part of managers for the adverse impact of the ruling on club youth policies.[48]

Although the *Bosman* ruling has obvious particular significance for professional football, it applies to any professional sport played within the EU where transfer fees are required before a player can move on termination of his contract. This is likely to be of particular potential importance to rugby union in light of the professionalisation of the sport. Decisions made on the future of the transfer system in football will almost certainly influence the formulation of employment contracts and transfer rules by rugby union clubs.[49]

---

47 The *Bosman* ruling also prohibits the imposition of quotas for the number of EU nationals who may be included in a club side. However, quotas are still permitted for non-EU nationals.

48 See *Four Four Two*, December 1996.

49 Also see *The European*, 8 May 1996 for a report of the impact of *Bosman* on ice hockey.

CHAPTER EIGHT

TERMINATION OF CONTRACTS OF EMPLOYMENT IN SPORT

COMMON LAW

Any employment contract can be terminated without cause if due notice is given. This can be the case with fixed term contracts although the normal expectation is that such contracts will end on the date of their expiry. Non-renewal would not constitute a dismissal.

Summary dismissal is *prima facie* a breach of contract and thus a wrongful dismissal by the employer unless the employee is guilty of gross misconduct. For this to be the case the employee must be in breach of a term – express or implied – which is at the root of the contract or have repudiated the contract in its entirety. Disobedience of a lawful and reasonable instruction by the employer may constitute gross misconduct:

Laws v London Chronicle Ltd [1959] 2 All ER 285 CA

The plaintiff accompanied her immediate superior to a meeting called by the managing director. A quarrel broke out between her superior and the managing director. The former left the meeting and instructed the plaintiff to leave with him. The managing director instructed her to stay. She left the meeting and was dismissed summarily for wilful disobedience.

The Court of Appeal upheld her complaint of wrongful dismissal on the basis that she had been posed with a dilemma resulting from conflicting loyalties. Although she was guilty of disobedience, in the circumstances this did not amount to gross misconduct.

Lord Evershed MR: To my mind, the proper conclusion to be drawn ... is that since a contract of service is but an example of contracts in general so that the general law of contract will be applicable, it follows the question must be – if summary dismissal is claimed to be justifiable – whether the conduct complained of is such to show the servant to have disregarded the essential conditions of the contract of service. It is no doubt generally true that wilful disobedience of an order will justify summary dismissal since wilful disobedience of an order shows a disregard – a complete disregard – of a condition essential to the contract of service, namely the condition that the servant must obey the proper orders of the master and that unless he does so the relationship is, so to speak, struck at fundamentally ... one act of disobedience or misconduct can justify dismissal only if it is of a nature which goes to show (in effect) that the servant is repudiating the contract or one of its essential conditions.[1]

---

1   [1959] 2 All ER 285 CA, 287.

There is no standard test for ascertaining whether misconduct is gross. The circumstances of the case must be taken into account in determining whether or not the employee has committed a repudiatory breach of contract. Only if this is the case is the employer justified in treating the contract as at an end. From a contractual perspective the dismissal is simply the employer communicating to the employee that the latter's breach has discharged the employer from his obligations under the contract and the employer has consequently elected to regard the contract as terminated.

The Court of Appeal had some sympathy with the position in which Ms Laws found herself. Subsequent cases reveal sympathy for an employee in circumstances where one would normally predict that a judge would perceive an employee as having committed gross misconduct:

Wilson v Racher [1974] IRLR 114 CA

In this case Wilson, a gardener, was unjustly and without foundation accused by his employer of shirking his work. The gardener was provoked into using swearwords, and ended the ensuing argument by telling his employer to 'get stuffed'. The court, in the circumstances, refused to accept that Wilson was guilty of gross misconduct and introduced a new perspective on the employment relationship which in the years since has been of fundamental significance.

Edmund Davies LJ: Many of the decisions which are customarily cited in these cases date from the last century and may be wholly out of accord with current social conditions. What would today be regarded as almost an attitude of Czar-serf, which is to be found in some of the older cases where a dismissed employee failed to recover damages, would I venture to think be decided differently today. We have by now come to realise that a contract of service imposes upon the parties a duty of mutual respect.[2]

In the years since this dictum was formulated the implied duty of respect has become increasingly and equally important to both actions for wrongful dismissal and statutory claims of unfair dismissal.[3]

For footballers' and cricketers' contracts,[4] in what circumstances could sports professionals be regarded as repudiating their employment contracts?

---

2   At p 115. Another case concerned with a swearing gardener – *Pepper v Webb* [1969] 2 All ER 216 – illustrates that gross misconduct may take the form of a series of incidents which culminate in a single event which can be regarded by the employer as the 'final straw'. In this case the gardener swore at his employer's wife and refused to put plants into a greenhouse as instructed by her. The court accepted the employer's evidence that there was a history of unsatisfactory behaviour.

Interestingly, the court took no note at all of the fact that had the gardener complied with the instruction he would have extended his working week by at least half an hour by way of what almost certainly would have been unpaid overtime. Indeed, each of the three cases cited illustrate just how difficult it is to predict in advance whether a court will perceive an employee's conduct as constituting a repudiatory breach of contract.

3   See above, Chapter 7, pp 353–54.

4   See above, Chapter 7, p 349.

Roger Stanislaus was clearly regarded by Leyton Orient as being guilty of gross misconduct once he had been found guilty by the FA of having been tested positive for cocaine. A similar view was taken by Sussex County Cricket Club with respect to Ed Giddins. Sussex claimed that it had not dismissed Giddins. His contract was deemed to have terminated automatically as a result of the cancellation of his registration by the TCCB. Does this frustrate the contract? If so, how? A term of imprisonment can frustrate a contract of employment. Should a ban for a lengthy period be considered analogous on the basis that it is qualitatively different to a ban for several matches? A short ban would be considered a normal occupational hazard.

For the manager of a professional football club instant dismissal is certainly par for the course. It is rarely based on allegations of gross misconduct. Indeed it is often the result of pressure from fans who sometimes rightly and no doubt sometimes wrongly hold the manager to blame if their team's performances are below expectations. The function of contract law here is essentially to provide a legal framework within which an out of court settlement can be negotiated; an action for wrongful dismissal is thereby precluded.[5]

REMEDIES FOR WRONGFUL DISMISSAL

The normal remedy for a wrongful dismissal, ie a dismissal in breach of contract, is damages for actual financial loss suffered. In the case of fixed term contracts, which are the norm in professional sport, this will, subject to the normal duty of mitigation, be loss of earnings for the period of time that the contract had left to run. In professional sport there is an obvious potential for awarding of high levels of damages. However for the reasons given above, in the circumstances where actions for wrongful dismissal would be most likely to occur clubs effectively co-operate to ensure the issue is dealt with by agreement.

Now that behaviour by professional sports participants – both on and off the field of play – has become an issue of national interest or concern it is perhaps only a matter of time before a player who has been dismissed summarily brings an action for wrongful dismissal. However as was the case with Ed Giddins (who has signed to play for Warwickshire once he has served his ban), the issue might be effectively resolved by a rival club employing the player who has been dismissed. If nothing else this shows that clubs who may

---

5   See *The Guardian,* 12 November 1994 for an article by Lacey, D, on the rash of dismissals of managers – as highlighted by the dismissal of Mike Walker by Everton a mere 10 months after he had left Norwich to join the club.

regard themselves as occupying the moral high ground are upholding their own standards rather than standards observed within the sport as a whole.[6]

Injunctions

It is a fundamental legal principle that courts will not compel performance of a contract of employment or any contract which involves the provision of personal services. Ever since the actress Bette Davies sought to break her contract with her film studio,[7] it has been clear that this principle applies to the entertainment industry. However this case revealed the potential for injunctions to be granted to restrain a breach of contract. In more recent times this has become an issue where injunctions have been sought to restrain dismissals in breach of disciplinary procedures contained in the employment contract.

In orthodox contract law the victim of a repudiatory breach of contract is not obliged to treat the contract as at an end. The injured party has a choice and thus can elect to treat the contract as continuing to exist. If an employee is dismissed in breach of procedures contained in the employment contract, it has been accepted in a number of cases that the employee can seek an injunction to prevent the dismissal from taking effect until and if contract-based procedures are observed.

In *Dietman v Brent LBC*[8] the High Court confirmed that an injunction could be so granted if the plaintiff acts quickly (as otherwise the employee will be deemed to have accepted the termination of the contract), if mutual trust and confidence have not been destroyed and if damages are inadequate. This might be the case if the dismissed employee could show that were he allowed to plead his case at a hearing the employer might decide against dismissal.

Both professional footballers and cricketers have contractual rights of appeal against dismissal to the appropriate authorities. A player could seek an injunction where these procedures are not followed, but it might be in sport that the necessary mutual trust and confidence will have been destroyed. If this were the case, an injunction would be refused.

---

6   See *The Guardian*, 1 November 1996 for a discussion of the Ed Giddins' affair and the fact that, once Sussex terminated his contract, he was approached by 10 of the 17 other first-class counties. The report also suggests that it was the general view of his fellow professionals that, in sporting terms, he had done nothing wrong.

7   *Warner Brothers Pictures Incorporated v Nelson* [1937] KB 209.

8   [1987] IRLR 259. In *Boyo v Lambeth LBC* [1995] IRLR 50 the Court of Appeal indicated support for the more restrictive view that a dismissal, even in breach of contract-based procedures, automatically terminates the contract of employment. Were this position to be endorsed by the House of Lords, then even as a theoretical possibility injunctions would cease to be available and the only remedy would be damages for wrongful dismissal.

     However in the case of cricketers' and footballers' contracts this might include the length of time the player would still have been employed if the dismissal had not occurred until

UNFAIR DISMISSAL

The right not to be unfairly dismissed is a statutory right which has been in existence since 1971. The right was contained in the Employment Protection (Consolidation) Act (EPCA) 1978. This has now been replaced with the Employment Rights Act (ERA) 1996 which came into force in August 1996.[9]

Employees' rights are based on statutory principles which operate independently and often in contradiction to the principles of contract law – although it is more than possible that a summary dismissal will be both wrongful and unfair. Claims for unfair dismissal must be presented to industrial tribunals no later than three months from the effective date of termination of the contract of employment – normally the date on which the dismissal took effect.

Industrial tribunals have jurisdiction over a number of areas of employment law which are governed by statute law – particularly the rights contained in the ERA and in the area of discrimination law (below). Tribunals have a distinctive composition. The chair of the tribunal must be legally qualified and will often be a practising solicitor or barrister. The other two members will be selected from panels drawn up by employers' associations and employees' bodies – in particular the British Trades Union Congress (TUC). Any individual has the right of audience before an industrial tribunal and therefore employees are often represented by officials of trade unions or appropriate professional associations. Although costs can be awarded against the losing party it is normal for the parties to bear their own costs. As is the case with most types of tribunals, legal aid is not available.

An appeal from a tribunal is permitted on points of law only. The appeal will be heard by the Employment Appeals Tribunal (EAT). The composition of the EAT is similar to that of an industrial tribunal although the chair will be a High Court judge. Legal aid is available in proceedings before the EAT. Further appeals lie to the Court of Appeal and the House of Lords. Decisions of the EAT (and relevant decisions of the Court of Appeal and the House of Lords) are often reported in the specialist Industrial Cases Reports (ICR) and the Industrial Relations Law Reports (IRLR).

---

after contractual procedures had been followed. In this case even if a player was guilty of gross misconduct he would be entitled to some compensation on the basis that his dismissal was procedurally wrongful.

9   Thus at the time of writing most cases are based on provisions of the EPCA. However as the ERA merely further consolidates the law, the cases remain authoritative interpretations of the statutory rights.

Continuity of Employment

Only employees with two years continuous employment can claim unfair dismissal. Such continuity can be acquired by a series of fixed term contracts. However under s 197 of the ERA 1996, if a fixed-term contract is for one year or more the right to claim unfair dismissal is lost if the employee has agreed in writing to waive this right in the event of the contract not being renewed. In practice waiver clauses are often to be found in written fixed term contracts. An example is clause 12 of the Cricketers Contract, which states that 'the cricketer shall not where his employment is terminated by reason of the expiration of this Agreement without its being renewed be entitled to be paid any redundancy payment or any payment or redress for unfair dismissal under the Employment Protection (Consolidation) Act or any statutory modification or re-enactment thereof'.

As can be seen from this clause, statutory redundancy rights may also be lost as a result of a waiver clause. It must be understood that waiver clauses only operate to exclude statutory rights in the event of the contract not being renewed. Unfair dismissal may still be claimed if an employer terminates the contract during its period of operation providing the employee has the necessary continuity of employment.

A cricketer may be employed on season by season basis. Does such a break in employment break continuity so that a player is never able to secure statutory rights? Under s 212 of the ERA 1996, weeks during which the employee has no contract of employment still count if the employee's absence from work is because of a temporary cessation of work. Should the out of season period be considered a temporary cessation so that a cricketer employed on a seasonal basis can in the due course of time establish continuity through a succession of fixed term contracts:

Ford v Warwickshire CC [1983] ICR 273 HL

A part time college lecturer was made redundant after 10 years employment. She was not employed during the summer period between academic years. The Law Lords held that this period constituted a temporary cessation and thus she secured statutory rights.

Lord Diplock: ... the length of successive fixed term contracts on which part-time lecturers are employed and the intervals between them vary considerably with the particular course that the part time lecturer is engaged to teach; so it by no means follows that a similar concession would be made or would be appropriate in each of their cases. It also follows from what I have said that successive periods of seasonal employment of other kinds under fixed term contracts, such as employment in agriculture during harvest time or in hotel work during the summer season, will only qualify as continuous employment if the length of the period between two successive seasonal contracts is so short in comparison with the length of the season during which the employee is employed as properly to be regarded by the industrial tribunal as no more than a temporary cessation of work in the sense that I have indicated.[10]

This mathematical approach might operate against a cricketer given the length of the out of season period. However the Law Lords have also espoused what has been described as the 'broad brush' approach where the whole history of the employment has to be taken into account.[11] Through applying the latter, it could be argued that a cricketer who has been with a county for a number of years has established continuity despite the lengthy breaks between seasons. Certainly, it would seem unjust if a player who had stayed loyal to a particular club was to discover that in the event of dismissal during a season and thus during the currency of his contract he had no statutory rights through a lack of continuous employment.

The problem of continuity does not arise where, as is the norm for professional footballers, a cricketer is employed for a period of years. Here the contract continues during the out of season period and thus there is no break in the continuity of employment.

Claiming Unfair Dismissal

Section 95(1) of the Employment Rights Act 1996

For the purposes of this Part an employee is dismissed by his employer if ...

(a) the contract under which he is employed is terminated by the employer (whether with or without notice);

(b) he is employed under a contract for a fixed-term and that term expires without being renewed under the same contract; or

(c) the employee terminates the contract under which he is employed (with or without notice) in circumstances in which he is entitled to terminate it without notice by reason of the employer's conduct.

A dismissal with notice and thus in accordance with the contract may still be unfair. Similarly non-renewal of a fixed-term contract, which is of no legal consequence at common law, may constitute an unfair dismissal. Resignation may constitute a constructive dismissal only where it is the employee's response to a repudiatory breach by the employer. Unreasonable conduct by the employer will not in itself convert a resignation into a constructive dismissal:

Western Excavating Ltd v Sharp [1978] ICR 221 CA

Sharp was suspended for five days without pay for taking an afternoon off without permission in order to play cards for his team. As he had no money he requested that either be given a loan form the company's welfare fund or be

---

10   [1983] ICR 273 HL, 286.

11   *Fitzgerald v Hall, Russell & Co Ltd* [1970] AC 984.

given an advance of his accrued holiday pay. This request was rejected and Sharp resigned as in so doing he became contractually entitled to pay owed in lieu of accrued holiday entitlement. His claim of unfair dismissal was rejected by the Court of Appeal on the basis that in law he had resigned. Whether or not the company had acted unreasonably it had not acted in breach of contract.

Lord Denning rejected the existence of a new test of 'unreasonable conduct' on the basis, *inter alia*, that it was 'too indefinite by far' and had resulted in 'findings of "constructive dismissal" on the most whimsical grounds'.

His explanation of the 'contract test' is still accepted as the authoritative statement of the law:

> If the employer is guilty of conduct which is a significant breach going to the root of the contract of employment or which shows that the employer no longer intends to be bound by one or more of the essential terms of the contract, then the employee is entitled to treat himself as discharged from any further performance. If he does so, then he terminates the contract by reason of the employer's conduct. He is constructively dismissed. The employee is entitled in these circumstances to leave at the instant without giving any notice at all or alternatively he may give notice and say he is leaving at the end of the notice. But the conduct must in either case be sufficiently serious to entitle him to leave at once. Moreover, he must make up his mind soon after the conduct of which he complains: for, if he continues for any length of time without leaving, he will lose his right to treat himself as discharged. He will be regarded as having elected to affirm the contract.[12]

Contracts of employment can be terminated by means other than dismissal or resignation. For example, by mutual agreement or frustration. Note the position of Ed Giddins and the argument by Sussex CCC that the cancellation of his registration automatically terminated his contract. Case law has established that the courts will not permit a dismissal to be disguised as termination of the contract through mutual agreement.[13]

Clause 2(c) of the Cricketers Contract states that '... this agreement will terminate immediately if the board cancels or terminates the registration of the cricketer by the club'. Do these decisions render this clause unenforceable? If so then surely Ed Giddins was dismissed by Sussex CCC as in reality the decision not to continue to employ him was taken unilaterally by the club and thus in law constituted a dismissal.

Although professional footballers are employed under fixed term contracts, non-renewal is unlikely to present a problem of a legal nature to the employing club. This is because under the Premier and Football League's rules a player out of contract will normally either be given a free transfer or

---

12 [1978] ICR 221 CA, 226.

13 See *Tracey v Zest Equipment Co* [1982] IRLR 268; and, in particular, the Court of Appeal decision in *Igbo v Johnson Matthey* [1986] IRLR 215.

retained on the club's books so that a transfer fee can be secured when he signs for a new club.[14]

Although unreasonable behaviour by an employer cannot turn a resignation into a constructive dismissal, it must be remembered that a breach of the duty of respect will constitute a repudiatory breach of contract by the employer. This clearly includes any form of discrimination on grounds of race or sex – including harassment or abuse. Does it include 'locker-room' behaviour which gets out of hand if the culprits are not disciplined by a club or indeed abuse of a player by a team captain, coach or manager? Does it include a refusal to select a player where this is motivated by reasons other than merit; for example to pressurise a player to agree to go onto or leave the transfer list?

The Meaning of Unfair Dismissal

Section 98 of the Employment Rights Act 1996

(1) In determining for the purposes of this Part whether the dismissal of an employee is fair or unfair, it is for the employer to show:

(a) the reason (or, if more than one, the principal reason) for the dismissal; and

(b) that it is either a reason falling within subsection (2) or some other substantial reason of a kind such as to justify the dismissal of an employee holding the position which the employee held.

(2) A reason falls within this subsection if it:

(a) relates to the capability or qualifications of the employee for performing work of the kind which he was employed by the employer to do;

(b) relates to the conduct of the employee;

(c) is that the employee was redundant; or

(d) is that the employee could not continue to work in the position which he held without contravention (either on his part or on that of his employer) of a duty or restriction imposed by or under an enactment.

(3) In subsection (2)(a):

(a) 'capability', in relation to an employee, means his capability assessed by reference to skill, aptitude, health or any other physical or mental quality; and

(b) 'qualifications', in relation to an employee, means any degree, diploma or other academic, technical or professional qualification relevant to the position which he held.

(4) Where the employer has fulfilled the requirements of subsection (1), the determination of the question whether the dismissal is fair or unfair (having regard to the reason shown by the employer):

14   See above, Chapter 7, pp 357–62.

(a) depends on whether in the circumstances (including the size and administrative resources of the employer's undertaking) the employer acted reasonably or unreasonably in treating it as a sufficient reason for dismissing the employee; and

(b) shall be determined in accordance with equity and the substantial merits of the case.

Under s 98(1) the burden of proof is on the employer to show the reason, or the principal reason, for the dismissal. If the employer cannot satisfy the tribunal that the reason was one or more of the above then the dismissal must be unfair. The only other possibility, in accordance with s 98(1)(b), is that the employee was dismissed for 'some other substantial reason of a kind such as to justify the dismissal of an employee holding the position which the employee held'.

Most of the case law which has been developed under this miscellaneous heading has been concerned with employees who refuse to accept commercial re-organisations by the employer which constitute a breach of contract. Of more potential relevance to sport is the situation where behaviour by an employee, whilst not strictly misconduct, is disruptive to working relationships.[15]

A particularly controversial decision was given by the Scottish Court of Session in upholding the dismissal of an employee who worked as a handyman at a children's camp once the employer discovered that he was gay. The dismissal was deemed fair on the basis that the parents of children attending the camp might object to his continued employment.[16] Given the homophobic culture apparently prevalent in sport, as evidenced by the reaction to Justin Fashanu when he 'came-out', would a club in any or all of the professional sports be able to justify as fair the dismissal of a player on the basis of his or her sexual orientation?

In the main it is the categories of incapability and misconduct which are clearly the most important in sport. Such dismissals will still be unfair if an industrial tribunal does not consider that the employer acted reasonably in deciding to dismiss. The decision as to the fairness of the dismissal is for the tribunal to make. The burden of proof is neutral. However as a point of law it is of primary importance that a tribunal does not substitute its views for that of the reasonable employer. Employers may operate within a range of reasonable responses. Only if a dismissal is outside of this range will it be unfair:

---

15 For example, in *Treganowan v Knee* [1975] IRLR 247 a secretary upset other office staff by boasting about her sexual exploits. Her dismissal was accepted as being for 'some other substantial reason' and was considered by the tribunal to be fair.

16 *Saunders v Scottish National Camps Association* [1981] IRLR 174. See Cranna, I, 'Not giving the game away', *The Guardian*, 12 August 1994, for a discussion of homophobia and its causes and effects in professional sport.

British Leyland (UK) Ltd v Swift [1981] IRLR 91 CA

Lord Denning MR: The correct test is: was it reasonable for the employer to dismiss him? If no reasonable employer would have dismissed him then the dismissal was unfair. But if a reasonable employer might reasonably have dismissed him, then the dismissal was fair. It must be remembered that in all these cases there is a band of reasonableness within which one employer might reasonably take one view; another quite reasonably take a different view ... if it was quite reasonable to dismiss him, then the dismissal must be upheld as fair: even though some other employers may not have dismissed him.[17]

Iceland Frozen Foods Ltd v Jones [1982] IRLR 439 EAT

Browne-Wilkinson J ... (1) the starting point must be the words [of the section] themselves; (2) in applying the section an Industrial Tribunal must consider the reasonableness of the employer's conduct, not simply whether they (the members of the Industrial Tribunal) consider the dismissal to be fair; (3) in judging the reasonableness of the employer's conduct an Industrial Tribunal must not substitute its decision as to what was the right course to adopt for that of the employer; (4) in many (though not all) cases there is a band of reasonable responses to the employee's conduct within which one employer might reasonably take one view' another quite reasonably take another; (5) the function of the Industrial Tribunal, as an industrial jury, is to determine whether in the particular circumstances of each case the decision to dismiss the employee fell within the band of reasonable responses which a reasonable employer might have adopted. If the dismissal falls within the band the dismissal is fair, if the dismissal falls outside the band it is unfair.[18]

It is clear that a dismissal may be reasonable even if a particular tribunal regards it as harsh, if it can be shown that other employers, particularly those in the same line of business, would regard dismissal as an appropriate penalty. Thus Saunders' dismissal[19] was within the range of reasonable response even although a significant number of us, including some employers, regard a dismissal for such a reason as a capitulation to bigotry.

The essential questions are who constitutes the reasonable employer and what stance will this elusive person take in response to misconduct etc on the part of an employee? The answers are no clearer in sport than in any other field of employment. In recent times the quite different reactions of football clubs to the use of drugs by their players – particularly those deemed recreational in nature and consumed in a social not sporting context – is a good example of the problem.[20] An alternative basis to misconduct for dismissing a player who has become addicted to drugs, be they legal or illegal, is incapacity. Of particular importance in this respect are clauses in

---

17   [1981] IRLR 91 CA, 93.
18   [1982] IRLR 439 EAT, 442.
19   *Saunders v Scottish National Camps Association* [1981] IRLR 174.
20   See above, Chapter 7, p 350.

players' contracts requiring them to maintain appropriate standards of fitness, form and health.

To date clubs have shown what could be viewed as remarkable tolerance of players convicted for violent offences on, off or adjacent to the field of play. Does this mean that the dismissal of a player in the future for such an offence should be regarded as beyond the range of reasonable responses and thus unfair? It is perhaps significant that all the names which immediately spring to mind are 'star' footballers from leading sides in the Premier League. Could a player employed by a Brighton or a Crewe Alexandra anticipate such a lenient response in similar circumstances – particularly if his absence through suspension or imprisonment had significant repercussions for the fortunes or finances of the club concerned? Would the reasonable club adopt a policy of the greater the 'star' the greater the latitude that will be given? Is violent conduct by a player more or less acceptable in other professional sports such as rugby or cricket?

Professional sports participants are obviously particularly prone to absence through physical injury, which may be long-term in nature. Again there are clauses in their contracts dealing with the rights of clubs and players respectively in this situation. The Cricketer's Contract expressly permits a club to dismiss a player who, having been injured in the previous season, is still unfit for play at the start of the new season – clause 8. Given the presence of such a contractual term it is likely, although by no means in all circumstances definite, that such a dismissal would be considered within the range of reasonable responses and thus fair.

A long term and certainly a permanent injury can terminate the contract through frustration in which case, as there is no dismissal, the player has no statutory rights which can be pursued. The Football League Contract, however, gives the player contractual rights to termination through notice in the event of permanent injury – clause 10.

PROCEDURAL FAIRNESS

A reasonable employer will develop and comply with proper disciplinary procedures. Model procedures are provided by the Advisory Conciliation and Arbitration Service (ACAS):

ACAS Code of Practice 1: Disciplinary Practice and Procedures in Employment (1977)

Introduction

This document gives practical guidance on how to draw up disciplinary rules and procedures and how to operate them effectively. Its aim is to help employers and trade unions as well as individual employees – both men and women – wherever they are employed regardless of the size of the organisation in which they work. In the smaller establishments it may not be practicable to adopt all the detailed provisions but most of the features listed in paragraph 10 could be adopted and incorporated into a simple procedure.

Why have disciplinary rules and procedures?

Disciplinary rules and procedures are necessary for promoting fairness and order in the treatment of individuals and in the conduct of industrial relations. They also assist an organisation to operate effectively. Rules set standards of conduct at work; procedure helps to ensure that the standards are adhered to and also provides a fair method of dealing with alleged failures to observe them.

It is important that employees know what standards of conduct are expected of them and the Contracts of Employment Act 1972 (as amended by the Employment Protection Act 1975) requires employers to provide written Information for their employees about certain aspects of their disciplinary rules and procedures.[21]

The importance of disciplinary rules and procedures has also been recognised by the law relating to dismissals, since the grounds for dismissal and the way in which the dismissal has been handled can be challenged before an industrial tribunal.

Where either of these is found by a tribunal to have been unfair the employer may be ordered to reinstate or re-engage the employees concerned and may be liable to pay compensation to them.

Formulating policy

Management is responsible for maintaining discipline within the organisation and for ensuring that there are adequate disciplinary rules and procedures. The initiative for establishing these will normally lie with management. However if they are to be fully effective the rules and procedures need to be accepted as reasonable both by those who are to be covered by them and by those who operate them. Management should therefore aim to secure the involvement of employees and all levels of management when formulating new or revising existing rules and procedures. In the light of particular circumstances in different companies and industries trade union officials may or may not wish to participate in the formulation of the rules but they should participate fully with management in agreeing the procedural arrangements which will apply to their members and in seeing that these arrangements are used consistently and fairly.

Rules

It is unlikely that any set of disciplinary rules can cover all circumstances that may arise: moreover the rules required will vary according to particular circumstance such as the type of work, working conditions and size of establishment. When drawing up rules the aim should be to specify clearly and concisely those necessary for the efficient and safe performance of work and

---

21   Sections 1–7 of the ERA 1996.

for the maintenance of satisfactory relations within the workforce and between employees and management. Rules should not be so general as to be meaningless.

Rules should be readily available and management should make every effort, to ensure that employees know and understand them. This may be best achieved by giving every employee a copy of the rules and by explaining them orally. In the case of new employees this should form part of an induction programme.

Employees should be made aware of the likely consequences of breaking and in particular they should be given a clear indication of the type of conduct which may warrant summary dismissal.

Essential features of disciplinary procedures

Disciplinary procedures should not be viewed primarily as a means of sanctions. They should also be designed to emphasise and encourage improvements in individual conduct.

Disciplinary procedures should:

- Be in writing.
- Specify to whom they apply.
- Provide for matters to be dealt with quickly.
- Indicate the disciplinary actions which may be taken.
- Specify the levels of management which have the authority to take the various forms of disciplinary action, ensuring that immediate superiors do not normally have the power to dismiss without reference to senior management.
- Provide for individuals to be informed of the complaints against them and to be given an opportunity to state their case before decisions are reached.
- Give individuals the right to be accompanied by a trade union representative or by a fellow employee of their choice.
- Ensure that, except for gross misconduct, no employees are dismissed for a first breach of discipline.
- Ensure that disciplinary action is not taken until the case has been carefully investigated.
- Ensure that individuals are given an explanation for any penalty imposed.
- Provide a right of appeal and specify the procedure to be followed.

The procedure in operation

When a disciplinary matter arises, the supervisor or manager should first establish the facts promptly before recollections fade, taking into account the statements of any available witnesses. In serious cases consideration should be given to a brief period of suspension while the case is investigated and this suspension should be with pay. Before a decision is made or penalty imposed the individual should be interviewed and given the opportunity to state his or her case and should be advised or any rights under the procedure, including the right to be accompanied.

Often supervisors will give informal oral warnings for the purpose of improving conduct when employees commit minor infringements of the established standards of conduct. However where the facts of a case appear to call for disciplinary action, other than summary dismissal, the following procedure should normally be observed:

> In the case of minor offences the individual should be given a formal oral warning or if the issue is more serious, there should be a written warning setting out the nature of the offence and the likely consequences of further offences. In either case the individual should be advised that the warning constitutes the first formal stage of the procedure.

> Further misconduct might warrant a final written warning which should contain a statement that any recurrence would lead to suspension or dismissal or some other penalty, as the case may be.

> The final step might be disciplinary transfer or disciplinary suspension without pay (but only if these are allowed for by an express or implied condition of the contract of employment) or dismissal, according to the nature of the misconduct. Special consideration should be given before imposing disciplinary suspension without pay and it should not normally be for a prolonged period.

> Except in the event of an oral warning, details of any disciplinary action should be given in writing to the employee and if desired, to his or her representative. At the same time the employee should be told of any right of appeal, how to make it and to whom.

When determining the disciplinary action to be taken the supervisor or manager should bear in mind the need to satisfy the test of reasonableness in all the circumstances. So far as possible, account should be taken of the employee's record and any other relevant factors.

Special consideration should be given to the way in which disciplinary procedures are to operate in exceptional case. For example:

> Employees to whom the full procedure is not immediately available. Special provisions may have to be made for the handling of disciplinary matters among nightshift workers, workers in isolated locations or depots or others who may pose particular problems for example because no one is present with the necessary authority to take disciplinary action or no trade union representative is immediately available.

> Trade union officials. Disciplinary action against a trade union official can lead to a serious dispute if it is seen as an attack on the union's functions. Although normal disciplinary standards should apply to their conduct as employees, no disciplinary action beyond an oral warning should be taken until the circumstances of the case have been discussed with a senior trade union representative or full-time official.

> Criminal offences outside employment. These should not be treated as automatic reasons for dismissal regardless of whether the offence has any relevance to the duties of the individual as an employee. The main considerations should be whether the offence is one that makes the

individual unsuitable for his or her type of work or unacceptable to other employees. Employees should not be dismissed solely because a charge against them is pending or because they are absent through having been remanded in custody.

Appeals

Grievance procedures are sometimes used for dealing with disciplinary appeals through it is normally more appropriate to keep the two kinds of procedure separate since the disciplinary issues are in general best resolved within the organisation and need to be dealt with more speedily than others. The external stages of a grievance procedure may however, be the appropriate machinery for dealing with appeals against disciplinary action where a final decision within the organisation is contested or where the matter becomes a collective issue between management and a trade union.

Independent arbitration is sometimes an appropriate means of resolving disciplinary issues. Where the parties concerned agree, it may constitute the final stage of procedure.

Records

Records should be kept, detailing the nature of any breach of disciplinary rules, the action taken and the reasons for it, whether an appeal was lodged, its outcome and any subsequent developments. These records should be carefully safeguarded and kept confidential.

Except in agreed special circumstances breaches of disciplinary rules should be disregarded after a specific period of satisfactory conduct.

Further action

Rules and procedures should be reviewed periodically in the light of any developments in employment legislation necessary, revised in order to ensure their continuing relevance and effectiveness. Any amendments and additional rules imposing new obligations should be introduced only after reasonable notice has been given to all employees and where appropriate, their representatives have been informed.

One of the central aspects of the Code is that a reasonable employer will form an appropriate view of the facts before reaching a decision to dismiss. The conducting of a reasonable investigation by the employer should therefore be a prerequisite to both the convening of a formal hearing and the reaching of a decision by the employer:

British Home Stores v Burchell [1980] ICR 303 EAT

Arnold J: First of all there must be established by the employer the fact of that belief; that the employer did believe it. Secondly that the employer had in his mind reasonable grounds upon which to sustain that belief. And thirdly, we think, that the employer, at the stage at which he formed that belief on those grounds, at any rate at the final stage at which he formed that belief on those grounds, had carried out as much investigation into the matter as was reasonable in all the circumstances of the case. It is the employer who manages to discharge the onus of demonstrating those three matters, we think, who must not be examined further. It is not relevant, as we think, that the tribunal would themselves have shared that view in those circumstances.[22]

It is clear from *Burchell* that if an employer satisfies this three stage approach his view of the facts must be accepted by an industrial tribunal. A tribunal cannot substitute its view of the facts for that of the reasonable employer. It does not follow however that an employer who fails to conduct an investigation must have acted unreasonably and therefore that a dismissal not preceded by an investigation must be unfair. The ultimate test is whether the employer has acted within the range of reasonable responses. Thus a dismissal may still be fair if the reasonable employer could have discounted the need for a full or even any investigation in the specific circumstances of the case.

For example if an employee is caught removing the employer's property from the workplace, all that needs to be established to view him as guilty of dishonesty is that permission had not be given by a superior for the employee to act in this way. It may even be the case that an employee could then be dismissed summarily. The failure to follow the normal procedures could be regarded as within the range of reasonable responses once the employee's guilt is established.

If an appropriate investigation does establish that it is reasonable to view an employee as guilty of dishonesty a dismissal will stand as fair even if by the time of the tribunal hearing the employee's innocence has been established. For example, a drugs test proves positive. By the time of the hearing new medical evidence not available to an employer at the time of dismissal reveals that the test was in some way flawed.

In professional sport it will often be the sport's regulatory bodies who carry out investigations and hold hearings prior to imposing a penalty on a participant. This is very much the case with respect to a positive drugs test or to a player who has committed a serious offence on the field of play. These procedures are exemplified by the Discipline Committee Regulations which operate in cricket:

Discipline Committee Regulations

JURISDICTION

1.1   The Discipline Committee (the 'Committee') shall have jurisdiction in disciplinary matters over:

    1.1.1   all registered cricketers;

    1.1.2   any other cricketers involved in any cricket match controlled by or conducted under the auspices of the Board (a 'Match') (other than cricketers involved in any cricket match as a member of an official touring team representing a member of the International Cricket Council) including but not limited to all matches in which one of

---

22   [1980] ICR 303 EAT, 304.

the participants is a team (whether a First or Second XI or a representative team under a particular age or at any other level) representing England or one of the Members of the Board or Scotland or Ireland or Holland or Oxford or Cambridge or British Universities or any official touring team representing a member of the International Cricket Council or, in a first class match, the MCC;

1.1.3 all Members of the Board who shall be responsible not only for their own decisions. acts or omissions and those of their governing bodies. but also for any decisions. acts or omissions of any committees or sub-committees, any member of their governing body or of any committees or sub-committees, any officers. employees or agents and any other such person over whom a Member exercises control;

1.1.4 all persons who serve as members of the committees of the Board including selectors and observers;

1.1.5 all umpires contracted to the Board and any other umpire who officiates in a Match (an Umpire);

1.1.6 any other person who has agreed in writing to be bound by all or any of the Board's Rules, Regulations, Directives and Resolutions for the time being in force.

For the avoidance of doubt, such jurisdiction shall extend to any person who has ceased to be within any of the foregoing categories but was subject to the jurisdiction at the time when the matter occurred in respect of which such jurisdiction is to be exercised.

1.2 For the purposes of these Regulations the terms 'Cricketer' and 'Cricketers' shall mean a cricketer or cricketers falling within the ambit of Regulations 1.1.1 and 1.1.2 hereof and, in the case of the Minor Counties Cricket Association, the term 'Member of the Board' shall be deemed to include each and every member of the Minor Counties Cricket Association.

INITIAL PROCEDURE

2.1 Any disciplinary matter may be referred to the Committee by any member of the Committee or by the Chairman or Chief Executive of the Board either of his own volition or upon request of any member of the Board.

2.2 The Chairman or a Deputy Chairman of the Committee shall decide whether the matter shall be referred to:

2.2.1 a Summary Panel, in which case the procedure set out in Regulation 3 shall apply; or

2.2.2 the Committee, in which case the procedure set out in Regulation 4 shall apply.

2.3 The disciplinary matters which may be referred in accordance with the procedure set out in Regulations 2.1 and 2.2 above include:

2.3.1 matters the subject of the Board's Directive on Conduct; (paragraph 2 of Appendix D) or the Board's Directive on public statements (paragraph 3 of Appendix D);

2.3.2   matters contained in a formal report to the Board pursuant to Law 42.13 in respect of a Cricketer's conduct in a Match;

2.3.3   a positive doping control test within Regulation 17 of the Anti-Doping Regulation (Appendix L); and

2.3.4   any other alleged breach of any of the Board's Rules, Regulations, Directives and Resolutions for the time being in force.

SUMMARY PANEL PROCEDURE

3.1   If any disciplinary matter shall be referred to a Summary Panel pursuant to Regulation 2.2, the Chairman or a Deputy Chairman of the Committee shall appoint three persons (who, subject as mentioned below, shall be members of the Committee) to constitute the Summary Panel. If a Cricketer is involved and it is reasonably practicable in all the circumstances, a person whose name appears on the list furnished to the Board from time to time by the Cricketers Association for this purpose shall be included as one of the three persons on the Summary Panel.

3.2   The Summary Panel shall take all necessary steps to investigate the matter as quickly as possible in all the circumstances. The Summary Panel shall determine its own procedure and may require any person subject to the jurisdiction of the Committee:

3.2.1   to attend upon it or any of its members;

3.2.2   to produce any books, letters, contracts, papers or other documents within his possession or power relating to the subject matter of the proceedings;

and any person so required shall take all necessary steps to secure such attendance and production.

A person required to attend before a Summary Panel to answer a disciplinary matter may request, either that he be allowed to be accompanied by a legal or other representative of his choice or that the matter be referred immediately to the Committee without any hearing by the Summary Panel. Any such request must be made promptly to the Chief Executive of the Board and shall be referred to the chairman of the Summary Panel whose decision thereon shall be conclusive and final. No person required to amend before a Summary Panel shall be entitled to be accompanied by a legal or other representative unless the chairman of the Summary Panel in his sole and unfettered discretion allows. If any person against whom any proceedings are brought pursuant to these Regulations remains silent during any such proceedings or, without good reason, fails to amend before the Summary Panel or to produce documents within that person's possession or power, the Summary Panel may construe such silence and/or failure in such manner as it thinks fit.

3.3   After such investigation as the Summary Panel shall think necessary, the Summary Panel shall decide that either:

3.3.1   the matter does not require any further action; or

3.3.2   a disciplinary offence has been committed with which the Summary Panel will deal; or

3.3.3   disciplinary charges should be laid before the Committee.

3.4   Any decision of the Summary Panel will be by a majority of its members. The Summary Panel shall communicate forthwith to the Chief Executive of the Board the Committee and to all other persons concerted any decision taken pursuant to Regulation 3.3.

3.5   In the event that the Summary Panel determines that a disciplinary offence has been committed the Summary Panel shall determine and shall be entitled to impose upon the person or persons concerned such penalty or penalties by way of official reprimand caution, as to future conduct, fine or suspension or any combination thereof as it thinks fit PROVIDED ALWAYS that no fine shall exceed £1,000 and in the case of a Cricketer or Umpire the period of suspension shall not exceed four playing days. Any fine imposed shall be paid by the person or persons concerned within 28 days of that person or persons being notified of the fine. The Summary Panel shall be entitled to suspend any penalty imposed pursuant to these Regulations for such period and upon and subject to such other terms and conditions as it shall think fit.

3.6   Any person upon whom any penalty has been imposed by the Summary Panel as aforesaid shall be entitled, by giving written notice to the Chief Executive of the Board within 14 days of being notified of the decision of the Summary Panel, to appeal to the Committee, in which case the matter shall be referred to and reheard by the Committee in accordance with the procedure laid down in Regulation 1 and any penalty imposed shall be suspended pending the rehearing of the matter or withdrawal or disposal of the appeal.

3.7   In the event of any such appeal or if the Summary Panel shall decide under Regulation 3.3.3 that disciplinary charges should be laid before the Committee, the Summary Panel shall make available to the Chief Executive of the Board its notes of the hearing and all other documents relevant to the manner and shall advise the Chief Executive as to the disciplinary charges which in its opinion should be laid before the Committee. The Chief Executive shall act as prosecutor and shall be responsible (with full power to delegate) for the formulation of the charges and the conduct of the proceedings before the Committee on behalf of the Board. Notwithstanding the provisions of Regulation 4.3 on any appeal to it from the Summary Panel the Committee shall not be entitled to impose any penalty or penalties in excess of the penalty or penalties which the Summary Panel is entitled to impose.

COMMITTEE PROCEDURE

4.1   The Committee shall determine its own procedure for any hearing. Unless otherwise determined by the Board or by the Committee, the quorum for any hearing shall be five members of the Committee one of which shall be appointed Chairman PROVIDED ALWAYS that any person who shall have been a member of a Summary Panel which dealt with a particular disciplinary manner in respect of which a chance has been laid before the Committee shall not sit as a member of the Committee at any hearing at which that matter is considered. If a

Cricketer is involved and it is reasonably practicable in all the circumstances, a person whose name appears on the list furnished to the Board from time to time by the Cricketers Association for this purpose shall be appointed as one of the members of the Committee.

4.2 The Committee may, in connection with any disciplinary manner falling within its jurisdiction, require any person subject to the jurisdiction of the Committee:

4.2.1 to attend at a hearing or hearings of the Committee; and

4.2.2 to produce books, letters, contracts, papers or other documents within his possession or power relating to the subject manner of the proceedings;

and any person so required shall take all necessary steps to ensure such attendance and production.

Any party to the proceedings attending a hearing of the Committee may call witnesses and may be accompanied by a legal or other suitable representative of his choice. If any person against whom any proceedings are brought pursuant to these Regulations remains silent during any such proceedings or fails, without good reason, to attend before the Committee or to produce documents within that person's possession or power, the Committee may construe such silence and or failure in such manner as it thinks fit.

4.3 Any decision of the Committee will be by a majority of its members. In the event that the Committee is unable to reach a majority the Chairman shall have a second and casting vote. The Committee, at the conclusion of any hearing by it of any matter falling within its jurisdiction, may impose such penalty or penalties or any combination thereof as it thinks appropriate in the circumstances including:

4.3.1 in the case of a Cricketer, a reprimand suspension from playing in any Match or Matches, suspension or termination of registration, suspension of eligibility for selection for England or fine;

4.3.2 in the case of a Member of the Board, a fine, suspension of the Member from any competition for which the Board is responsible or variation of results of the Member's matches in any such competition or of points awarded to the Member in relation to any such competition;

4.3.3 in the case of a person who serves as a member of a committee of the Board (including selectors), a reprimand, fine or suspension or removal from the committee on which he serves;

4.3.4 in the case of an Umpire, a reprimand, suspension, fine or dismissal by the Board;

4.3.5 in any case, an order that any party to any such hearing shall make such contribution as the Committee shall determine to each of the Board's or any other party's costs and expenses (including legal costs) of or in connection with the hearing.

Any fine, costs and expenses imposed shall be paid by the person or persons concerned within 28 days of that person being notified of the amounts thereof. In addition, the Committee shall be entitled to suspend any penalty imposed pursuant to these Regulations for such period and upon and subject to such other terms and conditions as it shall think fit.[23]

It should be noted that a further right of appeal lies to an Appeals Sub-Committee. Given the detailed nature of these procedures, surely an employing club will be acting reasonably if it does not conduct an investigation of its own, that is it reaches a decision based on the investigation conducted by the disciplinary committees. Arguably however the reasonable employer would still convene a hearing before reaching any decision to terminate the employee's contract. Compare this with the view taken by Sussex CCC that the finding of the TCCB that Ed Giddins had taken cocaine automatically terminated his contract of employment and thus further procedures by the club were superfluous.[24]

In the absence of proceedings by a sport's relevant regulatory body, it is important that an employing club complies with the Burchell test and overall with the requirements of the ACAS Code. It is clear from the Code that in many circumstances penalties short of dismissal should be imposed in the event of first time offences or offences short of gross misconduct. By virtue of contract law and s 13(1) of the ERA 1996[25] an employee should not be suspended without pay or fined unless this is permitted by an express term in the contract of employment. Clause 18 of the Football League Contract and clause 13(a) of the Cricketers Contract incorporate the necessary provisions. Indeed the use of such penalties is much more common in professional sport than in many other fields of employment.

Procedures contained in the ACAS Code need not be followed where an employer decides on a penalty short of dismissal. However a dismissal based on a series of offences by an employee will be unsafe if in the earlier stages proper procedures were not followed. Thus there should be an investigation and the holding of a formal hearing each and every time an employee is disciplined. In the cases of cricket and football, player's have contractual rights of appeal against the imposition of suspensions and fines. Note further that under the ACAS Code a disciplinary decision should not stay permanently on an employee's record. The norm is that it should removed if the employee 'keeps a clean sheet' for one year.

---

23 These regulations were adopted by the TCCB but it is unlikely that the new England and Wales Cricket Board will change any of the essential details.

24 For further discussion of the Giddins affair, drug testing and appeal procedures, see O'Gorman, T, 'Ed Giddins vs TCCB' (1997) 5(1) *Sport and the Law Journal* 23–25.

25 Formerly s 1(1) of the Wages Act 1986.

THE LEGAL STATUS OF THE ACAS CODE

This continues to be one of the trickiest problems of the law on unfair dismissal. It is clear that the Code is not law and therefore a failure to follow its provisions does not in itself render a dismissal unfair. However in the 1970s a procedural irregularity would normally be viewed as rendering a dismissal unfair as this was taken to mean that an employer must have acted unreasonably. As a reaction to this approach and as a result of the Court of Appeal's decision in *British Labour Pump v Byrne*,[26] the 'no difference' principle developed during the 1980s. Tribunals would no longer determine whether a procedural failure rendered a dismissal unreasonable but rather would pose the question: would the dismissal have been reasonable had proper procedure been followed? If the answer to this was in the affirmative then the dismissal had to be regarded as fair. This case-law clearly reduced the significance of the ACAS Code and *British Labour Pump* and all the cases decided on the basis of it, have been overruled by the House of Lords:

Polkey v AE Dayton Services Ltd [1988] ICR 142 HL

P was employed as one of four van drivers. In the summer of 1982 the employer found it necessary to reduce his overhead and decided that the four van drivers should be replaced by three van salesmen. P was considered unsuitable for the job of van salesman and was accordingly made redundant. The first he knew about this was when he was summoned to the branch manager's office, told of his redundancy, handed a letter setting out the payments due to him and dismissed.

A tribunal hearing his unfair dismissal complaint found that the employer behaved badly in failing to consult or warn P of impending redundancy but that even if a proper procedure had been adopted the result would have been the same, so the dismissal was not unfair. P's appeals to EAT and the Court of Appeal were dismissed.

Lord Mackay: This appeal raises an important question in the law of unfair dismissal. Where an industrial tribunal has found that the reason for an applicant's dismissal was a reason of a kind such as could justify the dismissal and has found that there has been a failure to consult or warn the applicant in accordance with the code of practice, should the tribunal consider whether, if the employee had been consulted or warned before dismissal was decided upon, he would nevertheless have been dismissed? The answer depends upon the application to this situation of s 57(3) of the Employment Protection (Consolidation) Act 1978 as amended ...

Where there is no issue raised by ss 58 to 62 the subject matter for the tribunal's consideration is the employer's action in treating the reason as a sufficient reason for dismissing the employee. It is that action and that action only that the tribunal is required to characterise as reasonable or unreasonable. That

---

26 [1979] ICR 347 CA.

leaves no scope for the tribunal considering whether, if the employer had acted differently, he might have dismissed the employee. It is what the employer did that is to be judged, not what he might have done. On the other hand, in judging whether what the employer did was reasonable it is right to consider what a reasonable employer would have had in mind at the time he decided to dismiss as the consequence of not consulting or not warning.

If the employer could reasonably have concluded in the light of the circumstances known to him at the time of dismissal that consultation or warning would be utterly useless he might well act reasonably even if he did not observe the provisions of the code. Failure to observe the requirement of the code relating to consultation or warning will not necessarily render a dismissal unfair. Whether in any particular case it did so is a matter for the industrial tribunal to consider in the light of the circumstances known to the employer at the time he dismissed the employee.

... the tribunal in the present case were bound by a stream of authority applying the so-called *British Labour Pump* principle [*British Labour Pump Co Ltd v Byrne* [1979] ICR 347]. Browne-Wilkinson J in *Sillifant v Powell Duffryn Timber Ltd* [1983] IRLR 91 thus described the principle, at p 92, 'even if, judged in the light of the circumstances known at the time of dismissal, the employer's decision was not reasonable because of some failure to follow a fair procedure yet the dismissal can be held fair if, on the facts proved before the industrial tribunal, the industrial tribunal comes to the conclusion that the employer could reasonably have decided to dismiss if he had followed a fair procedure'.

It is because one of its statements is contained in *British Labour Pump Co Ltd v Byrne* that it has been called the British Labour Pump principle although it did not originate in that decision. In *Sillifant's* case, EAT were urged to hold that the principle was unsound and not to give effect to it. After referring to the cases which introduced this principle, namely *Charles Letts & Co Ltd v Howard* [1976] IRLR 248, a decision relating only to compensation, *Lowndes v Specialist Heavy Engineering Ltd* [1977] ICR 1, *British United Shoe Machinery Co Ltd v Clarke* [1978] ICR 70 and the *British Labour Pump* case itself, Browne-Wilkinson J continued at p 97:

> Apart therefore from recent Court of Appeal authority and the Lowndes case, the *British Labour Pump* principle appears to have become established in practice without it being appreciated that it represented a fundamental departure from both basic principle and the earlier decisions. If we felt able to do so we would hold that it is wrong in principle and undesirable in its practical effect. It introduces just that confusion which *Devis v Atkins* was concerned to avoid between the fairness of the dismissal (which depends solely upon the reasonableness of the employer's conduct) and the compensation payable to the employee (which takes into account the conduct of the employee whether known to the employer or not).

In our judgment, apart from the authority to which we are about to refer, the correct approach to such a case would be as follows. The only test of the fairness of a dismissal is the reasonableness of the employer's decision to dismiss judged at the time at which the dismissal takes effect. An industrial tribunal is not bound to hold that any procedural failure by the employer renders the dismissal unfair: it is one of the factors to be weighed by the industrial tribunal in deciding whether or not the dismissal was reasonable within s 57(3). The weight to be attached to such procedural failure should depend upon the circumstances known to the employer at the time of dismissal, not on the actual consequence of such failure. Thus in the case of a failure to give an opportunity to explain, except in the rare case where a reasonable employer could properly take the view on the facts known to him at the time of dismissal that no explanation or mitigation could alter his decision to dismiss, an industrial tribunal would be likely to hold that the lack of 'equity' inherent in the failure would render the dismissal unfair. But there may be cases where the offence is so heinous and the facts so manifestly clear that a reasonable employer could, on the facts known to him at the time of dismissal, take the view that whatever explanation the employee advanced it would make no difference: see the example referred to by Lawton LJ in *Bailey v BP Oil (Kent Refinery) Ltd* [1980] ICR 642. Where, in the circumstances known at the time of dismissal, it was not reasonable for the employer to dismiss without giving an opportunity to explain but facts subsequently discovered or proved before the industrial tribunal show that the dismissal was in fact merited, compensation would be reduced to nil. Such an approach ensures that an employee who could have been fairly dismissed does not get compensation but would prevent the suggestion of 'double standards' inherent in the *British Labour Pump* principle. An employee dismissed for suspected dishonesty who is in fact innocent has no redress: if the employer acted fairly in dismissing him on the facts and in the circumstances known to him at the time of dismissal the employee's innocence is irrelevant. Why should an employer be entitled to a finding that he acted fairly when, on the facts known and in the circumstances existing at the time of dismissal, his actions were unfair but which facts subsequently coming to light show did not cause any injustice? The choice in dealing with s 57(3) is between looking at the reasonableness of the employer or justice to the employee. *Devis v Atkins* shows that the correct test is the reasonableness of the employer; the *British Labour Pump* principle confuses the two approaches.

I gratefully adopt that analysis ...[27]

Lord Bridge: Employers contesting a claim of unfair dismissal will commonly advance as their reason for dismissal one of the reasons specifically recognised as valid by s 57(2)(a), (b) and (c) Employment Protection (Consolidation) Act 1978. These put shortly are: (a) that the employee could not do his job properly; (b) that he had been guilty of misconduct; (c) that he was redundant. But an employer having prima facie grounds to dismiss for one of these reasons will in the great majority of cases not act reasonably in treating the reason as a sufficient reason for dismissal unless and until he has taken the steps, conveniently classified in most of the authorities as 'procedural', which are necessary in the circumstances of the case to justify that course of action ... If an employer has failed to take the appropriate procedural steps in any particular case, the one question the industrial tribunal is not permitted to ask in

---

27 [1988] ICR 142 HL, 153–57.

applying the test of reasonableness posed by s 57(3) is the hypothetical question whether it would have made any difference to the outcome if the appropriate procedural steps had been taken. On the true construction of s 57(3) this question is simply irrelevant. It is quite a different matter if the tribunal is able to conclude that the employer himself at the time of dismissal acted reasonably in taking the view that in the exceptional circumstances of the particular case the procedural steps normally appropriate would have been futile, could not have altered the decision to dismiss and therefore could be dispensed with. In such a case the test of reasonableness under s 57(3) may be satisfied.

My Lords, I think these conclusions are fully justified by the cogent reasoning of Browne-Wilkinson J in *Sillifant v Powell Duffryn Timber Ltd* [1983] IRLR 91 to which my noble and learned friend the Lord Chancellor has already drawn attention.

If it is held that taking the appropriate steps which the employer failed to take before dismissing the employee would not have affected the outcome, this will often lead to the result that the employee, though unfairly dismissed, will recover no compensation or, in the case of redundancy, no compensation in excess of his redundancy payment. Thus in *Earl v Slater & Wheeler (Airlyne) Ltd* [1973] 1 WLR 51 the employee was held to have been unfairly dismissed but nevertheless lost his appeal to the Industrial Relations Court because his misconduct disentitled him to any award of compensation, which was at that time the only effective remedy. But in spite of this the application of the so-called *British Labour Pump* principle [*British Labour Pump Co Ltd v Byrne* [1979] ICR 347] tends to distort the operation of the employment protection legislation in two important ways. First, as was pointed out by Browne-Wilkinson J in *Sillifant's* case, if the industrial tribunal, in considering whether the employer who has omitted to take the appropriate procedural steps acted reasonably or unreasonably in treating his reason as a sufficient reason for dismissal, poses for itself the hypothetical question whether the result would have been any different if the appropriate procedural steps had been taken, it can only answer that question on a balance of probabilities. Accordingly, applying the *British Labour Pump* principle, if the answer is that it probably would have made no difference, the employee's unfair dismissal claim fails. But if the likely effect of taking the appropriate procedural steps is only considered, as it should be, at the stage of assessing compensation, the position is quite different. In that situation, as Browne-Wilkinson J puts it in *Sillifant's* case, at p 96, 'There is no need for an "all or nothing" decision. If the industrial tribunal thinks there is a doubt whether or not the employee would have been dismissed, this element can be reflected by reducing the normal amount of compensation by a percentage representing the chance that the employee would still have lost his employment'.

... For these reasons and for those given by my noble and learned friend the Lord Chancellor I would allow the appeal and remit the case to be heard by another industrial tribunal.[28]

---

28 *Ibid*, 162–64.

One problem in the aftermath of *Polkey* was whether Lord Bridge was signalling a return to the 1970s in stating that procedural defects would render a dismissal unfair, unless the following of proper procedure could be regarded as futile. Lord Mackay's judgment emphasised the question was whether, in failing to follow the Code, an employer could still be regarded as acting reasonably, that is, within the range of reasonable responses. If so, then despite procedural deficiencies, in such circumstances a dismissal could still be fair. If there was a difference between the judgments of Lords Bridge and Mackay then it seems clear from cases decided since *Polkey* that the issue of procedure is to be considered within the overall context of the range of reasonable responses test.

For example in *Mathewson v Wilson Dental Laboratory*,[29] a dental laboratory assistant confessed to his employer that his late return to work after lunch was due to his arrest by the police for the possession of cannabis. He was dismissed 'on the spot'. The confession meant that there were no further facts to be investigated. The purposes of a formal hearing include the challenging of evidence through the employee giving his version of the facts and the cross-examination of witnesses; and any pleas of mitigation that the employee should be given the opportunity to present. As the employee was clearly guilty of being a user of cannabis and there were not (in the employer's view, there could not be) any mitigating circumstances, it was reasonable to view the following of the Code as futile. The only question to be determined was whether the substantive reason for the dismissal was within the range of reasonable responses. If so then, as the EAT indeed decided, the dismissal was fair.

This case has clear repercussions for sports participants who use prohibited or illegal drugs. Once a regulatory body has conducted its own investigation and hearing it might well be case that the employing club need not initiate further procedures prior to reaching a decision to dismiss. The sole question would then be whether the substantive basis of the dismissal is within the range of reasonable responses. Alternatively, it could be argued that a player should still be permitted to plead his side of the case. This is because factors such as past loyalty to the club or personal problems may not be the concern of the regulatory body but should be the concern of the reasonable employer.

Consistency of treatment is another relevant factor to be considered within the context of the range of reasonable responses. Thus clubs which in the past have taken a lenient or liberal view of the use of drugs by their players (such as Arsenal in the case of recreational drugs) might find it harder to justify, as fair, decisions to dismiss other players – at least for first-time offences.

---

29 [1988] IRLR 512.

Another major aspect of the Code is providing rights of internal appeal to an employee against a dismissal. Professional footballers and cricketers have contractual rights of appeal – ultimately to panels established by the relevant regulatory bodies. The FA Notes on Footballers' Contracts detail rights of appeal and disciplinary procedures which are compatible with the ACAS Code:

FA Code of Practice and Notes on Footballers' Contracts

A player is governed by four principal sets of rules, which will be found to overlap to a large extent – the Football Association and the FA Premier League rules or the Football League regulations, the club rules and the provisions of the contract (clause 5). Obviously whilst playing, a player is subject to the laws of the game (clause 4). The club will provide the player with an up-to-date copy of all the rules and regulations, the club rules and the provisions of the contract (clause 5). The player must also be given a copy of any insurance policy conditions affecting him that he needs to be aware of.

These rules are underpinned by a system of discipline. Each club may operate its own system, although the FA Premier League, the Football League and Professional Footballers Association have drawn up a disciplinary schedule containing recommended guidelines for clubs to follow It is essential that the method adopted is both consistent and fair If rules are laid down they must be followed. The player must always be made clear as to what is being alleged and he must be given a proper opportunity to state his case. Some clubs have found that discipline on minor matters can be enforced with the help of a club committee including players and officials. Representations on behalf of a player by his PFA representative should always be considered. Rarely will matters need to go further than the dressing room level. It is important to keep records.

The contract, however, lays down a formal system of discipline and punishment, with a system of appeals. Offences are divided into two categories:

- Serious (clause 16) or persistent misconduct: serious or persistent breach of the rules of the club or terms of the contract (which incorporates Football Association and FA Premier league Rules and the Football League Regulations). If the player is found to be guilty then his contract may be terminated by 14 days' notice being given. The club must set out its reasons in writing and notify the player.

- Less serious (clause 18) misconduct: breach of training or disciplinary rules or lawful instructions, breach of the provisions of the contract (which incorporates Football Association and FA Premier League Rules and the Football League Regulations). The player may be suspended, with or without pay, for up to 14 days or fined up to 14 days' basic wages. The club must set out its reasons in writing and notify the player.

A club may, if it so wishes, treat conduct that might be classed as serious under clause 16 as a lesser transgression under clause 18 so as to impose a lesser penalty. Each action by a club under clauses 16 and 18 carries with it the right of appeal and the penalties are suspended until the appeal procedure is exhausted. A fine may be paid directly by the player or may be stopped from his wages. If this procedure is used then the sum deducted in any week should not be greater than half the player's basic wage (clause 18). Under this procedure, for example, a two week fine (the maximum) would be deducted over four weeks.

The appeals procedure has two stages once the matter progresses beyond the level of the club (clause 16):

– To the FA Premier League or the Football League Board.

– By either club or player, depending of course on the outcome of the first appeal, to the Football League Appeals Committee.

In each case the appeal must be lodged within seven days of the formal notification of the previous decision. The Football League Appeals Committee has to hear a case within 14 days of its receipt.

The Football League Appeals Committee consists of an independent chairman and one member nominated by each of the Professional Footballers Association and the Institute of Football Management and Administration together with a Football League and/or a FA Premier League representative for cases involving their member clubs. It meets usually in London and Manchester or elsewhere convenient to the club and player.

In all appeals the player will be able to obtain advice and representation from the PFA (clause 20) if he so desires.[30]

Normally a refusal to permit a contractual right of appeal will be considered unreasonable and therefore the dismissal must be unfair. However again this is not automatic as the issue of whether an appeal should be permitted remains within the range of reasonable responses.[31] Could the refusal to permit a player to exercise contractual rights of appeal be regarded as reasonable where a regulatory body has already found the player guilty of a drug offence? Alternatively could this be a context where a player could obtain an injunction to prevent the dismissal from taking effect until he has been allowed to exercise his contractual right of appeal?[32]

---

30 FA Notes on Contract, pp 4–5.

31 Cf the Court of Appeal decisions in *Stoker v Lancashire County Council* [1992] IRLR 75 and *Westminster City Council v Cabaj* [1996] IRLR 399.

32 See above, p 384.

REMEDIES FOR UNFAIR DISMISSAL

Re-instatement and Re-engagement

Sections 114 and 115 of the ERA 1996 provide for the tribunal orders of reinstatement and re-engagement. The difference between the two is that a reinstated employee returns to the job he or she was doing prior to dismissal, whereas re-engagement requires the complainant to be engaged in comparable employment. This could be with an associated employer. A reinstated employee must receive arrears of pay and the full restoration of rights, including seniority and pension rights. The tribunal sets out the terms on which an employee must be re-engaged.

In practice it is relatively rare for either remedy to be awarded. Orders may be refused on the basis that it is not just and equitable to require an employer to take back an employee who has contributed to the dismissal through misconduct or incapability; or on the basis that it would not be reasonably practicable for the employer to comply.

The latter ground might be less significant in professional sport than in other areas of employment given that the norm is for there to be a squad of players and reinstatement would simply require a player to be returned to the squad. As always he would have no 'right' to be selected for the first team, or possibly even the reserves.

However employers are not obliged to comply with either of these orders. Failure to do so will entitle the employee to basic and compensatory awards plus an additional statutory award of between 13 and 26 weeks' pay. A tribunal order notwithstanding, in most cases a club would be able to afford to compensate a player that it did not wish to take back.

Basic Award

Under s 119 of the ERA this is calculated by reference to age, actual completed years of employment and a statutory week's pay. The latter reflects gross pay but is subject to a statutory maximum. In 1996–97 this was £210 – well below the actual weekly wage of many salary earners, let alone professional sportsmen. Only the last 20 years of employment can be credited, although such a length of employment will be uncommon in professional sport. Alan Knight, the Portsmouth goalkeeper known as 'The Legend' to the Portsmouth faithful, is one of the few players currently playing professional football who comes anywhere near this period of service with a single club.

Three scales apply: half a week's pay for every year completed aged under 22; one week's pay for every year completed aged 22 to 40; one and a half week's pay for every year completed aged 41 or more. With some obvious exceptions, such as Graham Gooch at Essex CCC, the highest scale will be rarely of relevance in sport.

A statutory redundancy payment is calculated in the same way as the basic award, although years worked under the age of 18 are not taken into account. Thus with the necessary two year period of continuous employment, an employee must be at least 20 to qualify for a statutory payment. Redundancy is not normally an issue in sport. However in recent years a number of football clubs have come perilously close to insolvency. Were a club ever so to fold all its employees would be redundant. Their entitlements to payments would be calculated on the above basis.

Compensatory Award

Section 123(1) of the ERA 1996 specifies 'the amount of the compensatory award shall be such amount as the tribunal considers just and equitable in all the circumstances having regard to the loss sustained by the complainant in consequence of the dismissal in so far as that loss is attributable to action taken by the employer'.

Section 123(4) applies the common law rule of mitigation. The function of the compensatory award is thus to compensate the dismissed employee for the actual financial loss suffered and has the equivalent purpose to damages for breach of contract. However unlike damages, loss of future earnings and pension rights can be taken into account, that is to cover the period after due notice or a fixed term contract has expired. However there is a statutory ceiling. In 1996–97 the maximum compensatory award which could be awarded was £11,300. Again this is well below the financial loss a professional sportsman is likely to suffer.

Both basic and compensatory awards can be reduced as the tribunal considers just and equitable by reference to the contributory conduct of the dismissed employee. Such deduction from the compensatory award should be made from the actual loss the individual incurs. Only after such deduction should the reduction to the statutory maximum figure take place. It is permissible to reduce both awards to nil. A tribunal might decide to do this, in line with the decision in *Polkey*, where misconduct is discovered after the dismissal retrospectively justifies it. Such a dismissal may be technically unfair but the employee may not receive any compensation whatsoever.

Overall, where possible, suing for wrongful dismissal rather than claiming unfair dismissal may be more advantageous to the sports professional. This is because, in accordance with contractual principles, damages are not subject to any pre-determined limit, but must reflect the actual financial loss suffered. Moreover, contributory conduct will not deprive an employee of the right to damages, if wrongful dismissal is still established.

CHAPTER NINE

SPORTS PARTICIPANTS
AND THE LAW OF DISCRIMINATION

INTRODUCTION

The world of sport remains a highly segregated one – particularly between men and women and the fully abled and disabled. With respect to the latter, events such as the Paralympics and the London Marathon notwithstanding, professional sport is predominantly and inevitably restricted to the fully abled – indeed generally to the super fit. Therefore the Disability Discrimination Act 1995 will not be discussed as part of this chapter, although its provisions do of course apply to those employed by clubs in a variety of positions not concerned with sports participation.[1]

Inroads have been made in the context of race as more and more professional sportsmen (but not women) come from the Afro-Caribbean and Asian communities. However there is more than a nagging suspicion that racism remains a major problem for sport, albeit for different sports in different ways – the lack of professional footballers of Asian origin being a clear example:

Chaudhary, V, 'Asians can play Football, too'

Why is there no Indian or Pakistani John Barnes playing the professional game? When the Premier League season kicks off on Saturday, there will not be a single professional footballer of Asian origin on the field around the country. While Afro-Caribbean players continue to make their mark in the highest echelons of the game, both at a domestic and international level, Asian players have remained largely invisible. Black players make up almost 20% of the 2,000 professionals currently playing in the Premier and Football Leagues. But the prospect of an Asian John Barnes remains as distant as England winning the World Cup.

---

1   Note in general terms the Disability Discrimination Act operates on similar principles to the Sex Discrimination and Race Relations Acts. For possible potential implications of the Act for sports participants with specific disabilities, such as heart complaints or diabetes, see Bitel, N and Bloohn, J, 'Fair Play for Disabled People in Sport' (1997) 5(1) *Sport and the Law Journal* 8–11.

The Disabilities Discrimination Act does not cover persons with non-symptomatic HIV. Employers are therefore not acting unlawfully in refusing employment to a person who has been diagnosed as HIV positive. A sports club which refused to sign or dismissed, a player who had been tested HIV positive would not be committing an unlawful act of discrimination. Morever, a dismissal would be fair if the club was deemed to have acted within the range of reasonable responses, see above Chapter 8, pp 390–92.

In the USA, the Americans with Disabilities Act 1990 does protect athletes who are HIV positive. See, Wolohan, JT, 'An Ethical and Legal Dilemma: Participation in Sport by HIV Infected Athletes' (1997) 7(2) *Marquette Sports Law Journal* 373–97.

There are currently around 60 Asian footballers playing in semi-professional high level amateur teams and six professional apprentices of Asian origin. But that is about it. Just why there is a dearth of Asian professionals is an enigma. If racism is endemic within football, why do black players do so well?

A project due to begin at the end of August will examine how and why Asians are being overlooked by the football industry. The project is backed by the Sports Council and the Commission for Racial Equality. Raj Patel, aged 35 and Jas Bains, aged 31, the project directors, were both keen amateur footballers in the Midlands and gained first hand experience of how Asian footballers are marginalised. Bains says that 'scouts never watch the Asian teams play and Asian players are hardly ever asked for trials. When I was playing, old stereotypes like Asians are not big enough and cannot physically compete, were always mentioned. It is just nonsense'.

... Both men believe it is not simply a matter of racism. The problem, they claim, lies between stereotyping of Asian players at all levels of the game and a reticence towards professional sport by older members of the Asian community. Unlike the black communities in Britain and America, sport has never been seen as a path to improving social status. Asian parents have traditionally coaxed their children towards commerce or professions like law or medicine.

... However they maintain that the crux of the problem lies in the attitude of coaches, managers and scouts. One young Asian footballer, who had trials at Chelsea, says 'from the moment I got on the pitch I did not stand a chance. I got abused by other players and was played out of position by the coach. Maybe I did not have the talent to make it but how do I know when I was never given fair treatment?'

Sally Westwood, a senior lecturer at Leicester University and a member of the research advisory group for the project, spent several weeks studying a mixed Asian-Afro-Caribbean football team in 1991. She says 'the stereotyping of Asian players is linked with the way South Asians are seen as culturally more different. White society sees them as "not like us", whereas Afro-Caribbeans are seen as conforming more to North European values'. She found that while some black players in the team were offered trials with Leicester City, Asian players of similar ability were overlooked.

Patel and Bains are confident that the football industry will eventually recognise the wealth of talent in the Asian community. After all, they maintain, it is less than 10 years since 12 English first division managers said – in an article by *The Sunday Times*'s Rob Hughes – they would not sign a black player because 'they lack bottle, are no good in the mud and have no stamina'. Back in 1975 not a single black player represented England at any level and there were fewer than 20 black professionals.

'We are not asking for special treatment, just for our youngsters to be given a fair chance,' says Bains.[2]

---

2   Chaudhary, V, 'Asians can play Football, too', *The Guardian*, 17 August 1994, p 34.

The problem of racism is partly, but only partly, derived from the attitudes of sections of the paying public. That issue is beyond the scope of this chapter.[3] The concern here is for the more covert forms of racism and other forms of discrimination that may exist at the level of the sports club as an employer. Moreover the institutions and structures of sport are such that the law as it stands can play only a limited role in regulating and eroding discriminatory attitudes and practices. This section is thus as much about the limits of the law as the protection it provides. This is particularly the case with the huge gulf in status which exists between men and women participants in sports such as football, rugby and cricket and indeed, albeit to a lesser extent, in tennis and golf:

Williams, J, 'Support For All?'

According to FIFA, 20 million women play organised football worldwide. In Scandinavia, where views about women as athletes and almost anything else are at least post-Jurassic, football is the most popular sport for females. Most local clubs cater for both male and female teams and foreign stars such as the USA's Michelle Akers are brought over to join semi-professional ranks. No surprise then that Norway won the recent women's World Cup in Sweden and that they and Denmark are as tough as they come in international competition. England? Well, you reap what you sow; in Sweden we were simply outclassed by, no avoiding it now, the Germans.

... And what generally of the women's game today? Well, things looked ready for major take off as far back as 1989. Then, Channel 4, looking for cheap and 'exotic' alternatives to mainstream sport, showed the Women's FA Cup Final. This was pre-Sky, of course and fans, 2.5 million of them, a record for sport on Channel 4, gobbled it up. Now? Well, serious television coverage has pretty much disappeared. Series A arrived on Channel 4. The BBC, desperate for soccer action, disgracefully provided the barest highlights of the recent women's World Cup and always around midnight. On Sky you can watch Northern Ireland v Scotland schoolboys live to your heart's content but no female coverage. Why is at least some female coverage not part of the new television deal? Without media coverage, serious sponsorship for the women's game is pretty much out of the question ...

Whilst some clubs, like Southampton, have taken female teams on board, here again progress is slow and uneven. Only Arsenal offer female players a full time paid coach/manager and a real level of integration into the male club. Not surprisingly the Arsenal women have produced recent successes and media coverage to match this commitment. A few others – Wimbledon, Millwall, Wolves – have shown a real interest in the women's game and cash and staff support to match ...

---

3   The 'Let's Kick Racism Out of Football Campaign', established by the Commission for Racial Equality in conjunction with the PFA, is primarily concerned with combatting racism amongst football supporters. For an account of the campaign, see 'Kicking Racism Out of Football' (1995) 84(4) *Labour Research*.

See also, above, pp 135–51 and below, pp 567–71.

But at best even large professional clubs still tend to offer a kit, use of some gym space and the occasional mention in the matchday magazine in the hope that some women will keep out of their hair and provide the club with some good PR. And off the WFCs troop to the park or local leisure complex to perform in front of 60–100 die hard fans and family members who can manage to track down the kickoff time. The 'blue riband' women's FA Cup Final still struggles for a prestige venue (recently, Crewe, Watford, Oxford, Tranmere, Millwall) while recently the German women's final took place immediately before the men's equivalent in the Olympic Stadium, Berlin.

This all provides for real equivocation about the development of the top level of the women's game here. Is the FA devoting enough resources to the women's game? Are we really improving and what, exactly, is the plan? ...

The PFA's Community programme has done some great work in promoting football for girls over the past few years and in starting up female teams in connection with professional clubs. We have female players who could inspire the next generation. Kerry Davies and Hope Powell of Croydon and their former team mates Brenda Sempare, Doncaster captain Gillian Coulthard and the charismatic Marianne Spacey of Arsenal have all served the women's game here with verve and distinction. We need them and others working in English football as coaches. Is anybody listening? You do want to beat the Germans, don't you?[4]

THE SEX AND RACE DISCRIMINATION ACTS

The Sex Discrimination Act (SDA) 1975 prohibits discrimination on the basis of gender under s 1 and on the basis that a person is married, under s 3. Discrimination against a married mother or father will contravene the latter as married persons will find it considerably harder to meet a requirement to be childless.[5] There is nothing in the Act that expressly gives similar protection to single parents. However refusing job opportunities to a mother on the basis that she is a lone parent probably constitutes indirect discrimination against women.[6] If this is so an employer would then be obliged to treat single fathers in the same way as single mothers.

The Race Relations Act (RRA) 1976 prohibits discrimination on racial grounds or by virtue of a person's membership of a racial group. 'Racial' covers colour, race, nationality or ethnic or national origins – s 3(1):

---

4   Williams, J, 'Support For All?', 121 *When Saturday Comes*, March 1997, pp 32–33.
5   *Hurley v Mustoe* [1981] IRLR 208.
6   See below, pp 419–22.

Mandla v Dowell Lee [1983] ICR 385 HL

Lord Fraser: ... It is not suggested that Sikhs are a group defined by reference to colour, race, nationality or national origins. In none of these respects are they distinguishable from many other groups, especially those living, like most Sikhs, in the Punjab. The argument turns entirely upon whether they are a group defined by 'ethnic origins' ...

For a group to constitute an ethnic group in the sense of the Act of 1976, it must, in my opinion, regard itself and be regarded by others, as a distinct community by virtue of certain characteristics. Some of these characteristics are essential; others are not essential but one or more of them will commonly be found and will help to distinguish the group from the surrounding community. The conditions which appear to me to be essential are these: (1) a long shared history, of which the group is conscious as distinguishing it from other groups and the memory of which it keeps alive; (2) a cultural tradition of its own, including family and social customs and manners, often but not necessarily associated with religious observance. In addition to those two essential characteristics the following characteristics are, in my opinion, relevant; (3) either a common geographical origin or descent from a small number of common ancestors; (4) a common language, not necessarily peculiar to the group; (5) a common literature peculiar to the group; (6) a common religion different from that of neighbouring groups or from the general community surrounding it; (7) being a minority or being an oppressed or a dominant group within a larger community, for example a conquered people (say, the inhabitants of England shortly after the Norman conquest) and their conquerors might both be ethnic groups.[7]

The scope of unlawful discrimination in employment covers arrangements for recruiting employees; refusal of employment; the terms on which employment is offered; opportunities for promotion or training; access to benefits, facilities or services; dismissal; subjection to any detriment. Unlike the Employment Rights Act, protection is not restricted to employees but covers employment under a contract 'personally to execute any work or labour' – s 82(1) of the SDA 1975; s 78(1) of the RRA 1976. This extension of the meaning of employment is of obvious importance in sport, as it covers any competition or sponsorship deal which involves a sportsman or sportswoman entering into a contract to perform – be it in a match or a marketing activity.

---

7   At 390. Applying the above test the Law Lords decided that Sikhs were an ethnic as against simply a religious group. Similarly: Jews (*Seide v Gillette Industries* [1980] IRLR 427); Gypsies (*CRE v Dutton* [1989] QB 783); and the Welsh (*Gwynedd CC v Jones* [1986] ICR 833) have been held to be ethnic groups. Conversely, Rastafarians have been held not to have an ethnic status different to that of the wider Afro-Caribbean community (*Dawkins v Department of the Environment* [1993] IRLR 284).

The Sex Discrimination Act 1975 and the Race Relations Act 1976 operate on similar principles with respect to defining direct and indirect discrimination:

Section 1 of the Sex Discrimination Act 1975

A person discriminates against a woman in any circumstances relevant for the purposes of any provision of this Act if:

> on the ground of her sex he treats her less favourably than he treats or would treat a man ...

Section 1 of the Race Relations Act 1976

A person discriminates against another in any circumstances relevant for the purposes of any provision of this Act if:

> on racial grounds he treats that other less favourably than he treats or would treat other persons ...

In *James v Eastleigh Borough Council*[8] the House of Lords decided that Mr James was directly discriminated against when he was charged a higher price than his wife for admission to a swimming pool. The sole reason for the differential treatment was that the concessionary cheaper price was for pensioners only. Although Mr and Mrs James were both aged 61 she was a pensioner and he was not. Clearly, there was no discriminatory intent and motive on the part of the Council. Nevertheless but for the fact that Mr James was a man he would have been treated the same as his wife.

Direct discrimination is in theory easier to establish as the 'but for' test means it is not necessary to establish an intention to discriminate and direct discrimination cannot be justified. The practical difficulty is with proof. Applicants may satisfy this burden of proof if they can convince the tribunal that it should draw inferences of discrimination and the employer is unable to justify a decision or practice by reference to non-discriminatory factors. For example discrimination might be proved if a person selected for a job was less experienced or less well qualified than the applicant. On the other hand, the employer might be able to show that the decision not to appoint the applicant was taken for grounds which are not discriminatory such as the applicant's perceived personality. Indeed it is because of the fact that subjective value judgments are so inherently connected to employer's decisions over matters such as recruitment and promotion that a direct discrimination claim is so hard to win. Even where there is evidence of discrimination, as a result of what the employer writes or says, a claim is not guaranteed of success.

In *Saunders v Richmond Borough Council*[9] the applicant, a former woman golf champion, was rejected for the post of professional golf coach. Despite questions such as: 'So you would be blazing a trail, would you? Do you think men respond as well to a woman golf professional as to a man? If all this is

8   [1990] ICR 554.
9   [1977] IRLR 362.

true, you are obviously a lady of great experience but do you not think this type of job is rather unglamorous?', she was not able to prove sex discrimination. Possibly the tribunal was influenced by the fact that the interviewer was a woman. Nevertheless, the reasoning is that there are cases when it is appropriate or least permissible to enquire into whether a person's gender or race/ethnic grouping may affect their suitability for a particular job.

The Sex Discrimination Act also tackles the issue of indirect discrimination:

Section 1 of the Sex Discrimination Act 1975

A person discriminates against a woman in any circumstances relevant for the purposes of any provision of this Act if:

> ... he applies to her a requirement or condition which he applies or would apply equally to a man but:
>
> which is such that the proportion of women who can comply with it is considerably smaller than the proportion of men who can comply with it and
>
> which he cannot show to be justifiable irrespective of the sex of the person to whom it is applied and
>
> which is to her detriment because she cannot comply with it.

Section 1 of the Race Relations Act 1976

A person discriminates against another in any circumstances relevant for the purposes of any provision of this Act if:

> ... he applies to that other a requirement or condition which he applies or would apply equally to persons not of the same racial group as that other but:
>
> which is such that the proportion of persons of the same racial group as that other who can comply with it is considerably smaller than the proportion of persons not of that racial group who can comply with it and
>
> which he cannot show to be justifiable irrespective of the colour, race, nationality or ethnic or national origins of the person to whom it is applied and
>
> which is to the detriment of that other because he cannot comply with it.

The case of *Price v Civil Service Commission*[10] provides a good illustration of indirect discrimination. The Civil Service advertised a vacancy. Applications were restricted to persons with one A level, aged 28 or less. The EAT accepted statistics which showed 'the economic activity of women with at least one A level falls off markedly about the age of 23, reaching a bottom at about the age of 33, when it climbs gradually to a plateau at about 45'. The reason for this was 'that a considerable number of women between the mid-20s and the mid-30s are engaged in bearing children and in minding children'.[11]

---

10 [1978] ICR 27.
11 *Ibid, per* Phillips J, 31.

Price was discriminated against not only reference to her age but as a woman. The Civil Service was unable to justify the age requirement and Price won her claim of unlawful indirect sex discrimination.

The statutory concept of indirect discrimination has been clarified and arguably narrowed by case law. The meaning of 'requirement or condition' was considered by the Court of Appeal in *Perera v Civil Service Commission.*[12] *Perera* was Sri Lankan by birth and well qualified. He had applied unsuccessfully on numerous occasions to progress in his career in the Civil Service. He discovered that the interview board took into account, *inter alia,* experience in the UK and whether the candidate had British nationality. The court rejected his claim as these factors were not 'musts'. They may have been taken into account by the employer but they were not an absolute bar to his selection.

Much difficulty has surrounded the 'pool of comparison' a tribunal should use in determining whether a requirement or condition does in fact give rise to indirect discrimination. The approach to be followed in sex discrimination cases was set out by the Court of Appeal in *Jones v University of Manchester.*[13]

First the relevant totals are all women (WT) and all men (MT) who would qualify were it not for the requirement or condition under complained. It is then necessary to calculate in percentage terms what proportion of women in their group (WY) do comply in comparison to the number of men in their group who do so (MY). This is achieved by dividing WT into WY and MT into MY and converting the figures into percentages. For example:

WT = 50; WY = 25; MT = 50, MY = 45.

WY is 50% of WT and MY is 90% of MT.

This reveals that as a percentage the proportion of the former (WY) is considerably smaller then the proportion of the latter (MY). On this basis there is indirect discrimination. There is no doubt that a similar method is to be used in cases of alleged indirect race discrimination.

Whilst this approach conforms with the words of the section, it does permit the possibility of allowing requirements to be imposed which may have a discriminatory impact against women. For example, Jones argued that an age requirement discriminated against women, as women mature students tend to graduate at an older age than their male counterparts. The court took the view that the pool of comparison was all graduates with relevant experience. Mature students were merely a subgroup within this pool, not a pool of comparison in their own right.

---

12 [1983] ICR 428.
13 [1993] IRLR 218.

Even where indirect discrimination is so established the employer may be able to justify it. The test for justification is today derived from EU law but is used in both sex and race discrimination cases.[14]

As propounded by the European Court of Justice in *Bilka-Kaufhaus Gmbh v Weber von Hartz*[15] the employer must establish that there is an objective economic or operational need for the discriminatory practice and that the discriminatory effects are no greater than necessary to secure the employer's objectives.

The requirement of proportionality means that even where an employer can establish genuine commercial objectives the discrimination will not be justified if it produces merely marginal advantages.

Indirect discrimination in employment occurs typically with respect to issues such as job sharing, part time working and forms of dress and appearance. These sorts of issues are not likely to occur in the context of sport – at least as far as participants are concerned. On the other hand, age restrictions, were they ever to be challenged, would almost certainly be justifiable given that most sports professionals retire in their late 30s. Moreover clubs need to maintain a pool of younger players and trainees. Age is not a significant factor in being employed as a manager or indeed match official.

The potential relevance of the reasoning in *Perera* and *Jones* can be illustrated by this hypothetical situation. A sports club decided that it would prefer to select its players from those born or who have lived in the locality for most of their lives. The club announces that 'outsiders', however, will be considered. X is a member of a particular ethnic group and has only lived in the locality for six months. Probably the issues of birth and residence are factors rather than 'conditions' or 'requirements' and therefore X would not succeed in establishing this element of indirect discrimination.

Even if on the basis of evidence they were seen as absolute bars to selection, X might not in all circumstances be able to show indirect discrimination. For example, different ethnic groupings, including his own, live in the area in similar numbers. Thus it would not be possible for X to show statistically that the residence requirement indirectly discriminated against the ethnic group to which he belonged. Nevertheless, the majority actually selected by the club come from one particular ethnic group. Members of the group to which X belongs are eligible for selection but choose not to apply.

The hidden, even unconscious, reason, why X is not selected is his membership of a particular ethnic group, as there is a perception that members of that group are not interested in or lack ability or the perceived

---

14 *Hampson v Department of Education and Science* [1989] ICR 179.
15 [1987] ICR 110.

necessary temperament for that particular sport. In reality X is being discriminated against as a result of belonging to that group whilst having a minority interest in the sport concerned. The over formalistic approach confirmed in *Jones* precludes this form of cultural racism from being exposed.

Even if X could establish indirect discrimination there would still be the possibility of justification. For example, what if the club says we are part of the local community and we want to contribute to tackling local unemployment; or it can show that local people are less likely to move and therefore will be potentially more loyal to the club?

Could not the above add up to a policy which in crude terms is actually saying members of this ethnic group need not apply? X could argue that he has been the victim of direct discrimination but how can this be proved if he is no more but no less talented than those actually selected? If X does establish direct discrimination there is a further statutory 'sting in the tail':

Section 39 of the Race Relations Act 1976

Nothing in Parts II to IV shall render unlawful any act whereby a person discriminates against another on the basis of that other's nationality or place of birth or the length of time for which he has been resident in a particular area or place, if the act is done:

in selecting one or more persons to represent a country, place or area or any related association, in any sport or game or

in pursuance of the rules of any competition so far as they relate to eligibility to compete in any sport or game.[16]

If X is a woman it is necessary to consider the situation where a club might impose factors based on physical strength and stamina, rather than on or in addition to, nationality or residence. Whilst it might be easier to establish indirect discrimination in this context, it could be predicted that justification would be similarly easier for clubs to plead; given the perceptions that still exist that most men are stronger than most women. Scope for re-evaluating these arguably bigoted perceptions are unlikely given the sports exemption contained in the Sex Discrimination Act:

Section 44 of the Sex Discrimination Act 1975

Nothing in Parts II to IV shall, in relation to any sport, game or other activity of a competitive nature where the physical strength, stamina or physique of the average woman puts her at a disadvantage to the average man, render unlawful any act related to the participation of a person as a competitor in events involving that activity which are confined to competitors of one sex.

16 This section has not generated any case law and its scope could be restricted by the interpretation of 'represent'. As noted by Osborn and Greenfield: 'Clubs and leagues do not represent, as opposed to cover, geographical areas.' They nevertheless conclude: 'Overall s 39 permits a very wide measure of discrimination that appears difficult to rationalise.' Osborn, G and Greenfield, S, 'Gentlemen, Players and the 6'9" West Indian Fast Bowler', 2(3) *Working Papers in Law and Popular Culture*, Manchester Metropolitan University, p 28.

This overt manifestation of sexist prejudice, of course, ignores the fact that professional sports participants are by definition not average men and women. With specialist weight training and coaching, women in sport can match the strength and stamina with that of many, albeit not all, men. Moreover all of us can think of, for example, top class professional footballers whose brilliant ball skills may not be matched with a 'Charles Atlas' (or even Vinnie Jones) physique. Should an Act intended to eliminate sex discrimination legitimise the sexist assumptions long ago questioned in popular culture by the likes of the film *Gregory's Girl* and the British television series *The Manageress*.

For the time being sport remains segregated on a gender basis – particularly where it is played as a professional game. Moreover media interest and thus national and international prestige and the 'big' money remains focused on the game as played by men. Desegregation might not be appropriate in all sports, that is those where physical strength is at the core of the sport but should not women at least be given the option to compete on equal terms where skill with hands or feet is the essence of the game concerned.

If traditional attitudes persist as far as players and thus managers are concerned, inroads have at least been made when it comes to referees and officials:

Petty v British Judo Association [1981] ICR 660 EAT

Petty argued unlawful discrimination when the British Judo Association refused to permit her to referee an All England men's contest. The association pleaded s 44 on the basis that a woman would not have the strength to separate two male combatants.

Browne-Wilkinson J stated: 'It is common ground that judo is a sport in which men and women ought not to compete one with the other. Section 44 saves from being unlawful 'any act related to the participation of a person as a competitor in that activity', eg judo ... we cannot see how provisions as to referees relate to the 'participation' of the competitors in the contest ... We think the words should be given their obvious meaning and not extended so as to cover any discrimination other than provisions designed to regulate who is to take part in the contest as a competitor. Any other construction would lead to great uncertainty: for example, would the section be extended to discrimination against the lady in the box office at a football ground?'[17]

Today in football the 'lady' may be found not only in the box office but on the pitch as a match official. We still await the day when the 'lady' will also be present as a member of a mixed sex professional club side.

The other defence to direct discrimination in the Sex Discrimination Act relates to gender as 'a genuine occupational qualification'. Section 7 makes an

---

17   [1981] ICR 660 EAT, 665–66.

exception 'where the job needs to be held by a man to preserve decency or privacy because ... the holder of the job is likely to do his work in circumstances where men might reasonably object to the presence of a woman because they are in a state of undress or are using sanitary facilities'. Without doubt, dressing room team talks and locker room culture are integral aspects of professional sport but one hopes, indeed assumes, that if the barriers erected by s 44 are ever overcome this provision will not be permitted to act as the final bastion of a male preserve. It should not be beyond the wit or resources of professional clubs to provide the separate facilities to be found in any municipal swimming pool whilst allowing players of both genders to mix once appropriately enrobed in the team kit.

Both the SDA and RRA inherently prohibit positive discrimination. It would be unlawful for example for a professional club deliberately to seek to increase the number of players it employs from ethnic groups under-represented in the sport or club concerned.

The main remedies available under the Acts are declarations and compensation. The latter covers actual financial loss and is not subject to any statutory maximum figure.[18] Compensation can include an element of aggravated damages where injury to feelings is caused by a deliberate intention to discriminate.

RACIAL AND SEXUAL HARASSMENT

The gender segregated nature of professional sport means that the problem of racist rather than sexist behaviour is of greater significance. This may not always be the case and harassment of women employees who are not sports participants also needs to be considered as a possibility. Cases decided under the RRA are strong persuasive precedents for cases brought under the SDA and vice versa.

The most likely context in professional sport in which black players will subject to racist abuse is on the field of play and this will be by members of the opposing team rather than by team mates. As is the case with racism on the part of fans, such conduct is not an issue for an employee and the employer and is thus beyond the scope of this chapter. Were racial harassment ever to give rise to liability in tort, then the case law on vicarious liability[19] might become of some relevance.

The display of racist attitudes by white players to black team mates, at least in football, is thankfully becoming a thing of the past but it would be wrong to conclude that racism within all clubs in all sports has disappeared.

---

18 Cf the ERA 1996 and remedies for unfair dismissal, see Chapter 8.

19 See below, pp 427–28.

Case law on the problem of racial and sexual harassment in employment must be considered:

De Souza v Automobile Association [1986] IRLR 103 CA

May LJ: ... In his submission on behalf of the employee, Mr Sedley suggested that the real question for determination was whether an ethnic minority employee who is upset when she hears herself spoken of or referred to as 'the wog' by a members of her employer's staff thereby suffers or is capable of suffering a 'detriment' within the meaning of s 4(2)(c) of the Race Relations Act 1976.

... [After reviewing three cases the judgment concludes] In each of these cases the detriment or disadvantage to the employee was in connection with what Mr Sedley described as the employment context. In the first it was having to do dirty work: in the second, it was losing more congenial work at the counter and having to work as a filing clerk in the rear office: in the third, it was being thoroughly checked when coming in to work, substantially more thoroughly than were white fellow employees. Apart from the actual decisions in these cases, I think that this necessarily follows upon a proper construction of s 4 and in particular s 4(2)(c) of the Act. Racially to insult a coloured employee is not enough by itself, even if that insult caused him or her distress; before the employee can be said to have been subjected to some 'other detriment' the court or tribunal must find that by reason of the act or acts complained of a reasonable worker would or might take the view that he had thereby been disadvantaged in the circumstances in which he had thereafter to work.[20]

Porcelli v Strathclyde Regional Council [1986] IRLR 134 Court of Session

Lord President (Lord Emslie): ... Although in some cases it will be obvious that there is a sex-related purpose in the mind of a person who indulges in unwanted and objectionable sexual overtures to a woman or exposes her to offensive sexual jokes or observations that is not this case. But it does not follow that because the campaign pursued against the applicant as a whole had no sex related motive or objective, the treatment of the applicant by Coles, which was of the nature of 'sexual harassment' is not to be regarded as having been 'on the ground of her sex' within the meaning of s 1(1)(a). In my opinion this particular part of the campaign was plainly adopted against the applicant because she was a woman. It was a particular kind of weapon, based upon the sex of the victim, which, as the industrial tribunal recognised, would not have been used against an equally disliked man ...

From their reasons it is to be understood that they were satisfied that this form of treatment – sexual harassment in any form – would not have figured in a campaign by Coles and Read directed against a man. In this situation the treatment of the applicant fell to be seen as very different in a material respect from that which would have been inflicted on a male colleague, regardless of equality of overall unpleasantness.[21]

---

20 [1986] IRLR 103 CA, 106–07.
21 [1986] IRLR 134, 137.

The reasoning in *De Souza* has to date not been overruled. The court was saying that an act of racist, and thus also sexist, abuse is not in itself a detriment unless the 'reasonable employee' would perceive it as disadvantageous to continue working in that environment. A disadvantage in addition to the words of abuse is required. The reasoning in *Porcelli* places the emphasis on the fact that an employee as a woman has been subjected to treatment to which a man would not and could not be subjected. In *Porcelli* the applicant did suffer a further disadvantage in that she, not the men guilty of the harassment, was required to move to another workplace.

The reasoning in *De Souza* has been further undermined by acceptance that a single act of sexual harassment can constitute a detriment;[22] and that the subjective perceptions of the employee should be taken into account.[23] The latter decision is double edged in that it permits a woman's style of dress and sexual attitudes to be examined as evidence as to whether or not in fact a detriment has been suffered. Nevertheless these cases do suggest that a single act of racist abuse could now constitute a 'detriment' within the meaning of the RRA.

If *De Souza* is still good law it facilitates the not uncommon argument in sport that insulting a player by referring to his skin colour is no more significant than referring to his size, weight or hair colour. It also suggests that players should not be overly sensitive to comments allegedly made in jest or in the heat of competition. It is contended that the realities of racism in Britain are such that it is qualitatively different to be called, for example, 'a black bastard' as against being called one from a region of the country such as Yorkshire or even a different country such as Denmark. In the latter context it is true that the player's different nationality is referred to but Danes in Britain do not have the collective memory and ongoing legacy of centuries of oppression, rooted in the slave trade and the spread of Empire, that remains the experience of the Afro-Caribbean and Asian communities. Racism in sport is as much derived from this history as it is in any other area of society.[24]

It is clear from De Souza, let alone Porcelli and the subsequent cases, that a sustained campaign of verbal and physical harassment designed to force a player to leave a club will constitute an unlawful detriment under the RRA or SDA. If such behaviour were to occur in a club it is more likely to come from team mates than the club management. A club is potentially liable in such a situation by virtue of the imposition of statutory vicarious liability:

---

22 *Bracebridge Engineering v Darby* [1990] IRLR 3.

23 *Wileman v Minilec Engineering* [1988] IRLR 144.

24 For an analysis of racism in football see Greenfield, S and Osborn, G, 'When the Whites go Marching in? Racism and Resistance in English Football' (1996) 6(2) *Marquette Sports Law Journal* 315–35. For comparative analysis and an examination of the experiences of black athletes in the USA, see Williams, P, 'Performing in a racially hostile Environment' (1996) 6(2) *Marquette Sports Law Journal* 287–314.

Section 32 of the Race Relations Act 1976

Anything done by a person in the course of his employment shall be treated for the purposes of this Act as done by his employer as well as by him, whether or not it was done with the employer's knowledge or approval ...

... In proceedings brought under this Act against any person in respect of an act alleged to have been done by an employee of his it shall be a defence for that person to prove that he took such steps as were reasonably practicable to prevent the employee from doing that act or from doing in the course of his employment acts of that description.[25]

Vicarious liability will be avoided by an employer if disciplinary codes prohibit acts of racial and sexual harassment, the rules are properly communicated to employees and complaints of harassment are investigated and otherwise properly acted upon.[26] It is clear that clubs which recognise the importance of tackling racism, were it to occur within the club, and display a practical commitment to doing so are likely to receive the protection of sub-section (3).[27]

The effectiveness of these provisions was potentially and seriously undermined by the heavily criticised decision of the EAT in the case of *Jones v Tower Boot Co.* In this case the applicant was subjected at the workplace to a series of brutal acts. It was clear that the employees responsible were motivated by racism. It was decided that the company could not be vicariously liable on the basis that the employees could not be regarded as acting within the course of their employment.

This reasoning required the conclusion that the more extreme the acts of racism or sexism the easier it becomes for an employer who takes no action nevertheless to evade liability. Emphasis on acts being within the course of employment also potentially excludes behaviour when employees are socialising with one another. This is more important in sport than many other forms of employment, where the club culture may require or at least put pressure on players to participate in post-training or post-match social activities.

These criticisms were taken on board by the Court of Appeal in reversing the EAT decision.[28] Waite LJ clarified it was wrong to apply the common law concept of vicarious liability to the Race Relations and Sex Discrimination Acts, as the purpose of the Acts is to make employers vicariously liable where in a work context they fail to protect employees from racist or sexist behaviour. It is now clear that only the proactive employer who takes

---

25   Section 41 of the SDA 1975 contains equivalent provisions.

26   *Balgobin v Tower Hamlets LBC* [1987] IRLR 401.

27   The FA Code of Practice and Notes on Contract specifies that racial harassment is a disciplinary offence. This is defined as including 'physical abuse, offensive language or jokes, offensive graffiti or posters and enforced isolation on the grounds of an individual's colour, race, ethnic or national origin or nationality', see p 12.

28   See [1997] IRLR 168. The EAT decision is reported in [1995] IRLR 529.

reasonable steps to stamp out racism and sexism will escape vicarious liability.

Welcome as the above decision is, it can be concluded overall that the law is not a completely effective instrument for protecting employees from racial and sexual harassment. On the other hand overt racism within football clubs at least appears to be on the wane. The reasons for this are probably the emergence of black icons such as Ian Wright and Les Ferdinand and the relative success of the 'Let's Kick Racism Out Of Football' campaign. If there are problems within clubs in other professional sports then it is perhaps what has happened in football, rather than relying on the law, which shows the way forward.

Football itself still has a long way to go in eliminating racist behaviour by sections of fans, currently a small minority, and by opponents on the field of play and in eradicating the insidious attitudes on which more overt racism is actually based. At the time of writing, there were allegations that Ian Wright and the Portsmouth striker Paul Hall had been the victims of racist abuse on the field of play. This was followed by the decision of Nathan Blake to refuse to play for Wales after the manager, Bobby Gould, had made racist statements about opponents in the dressing room. This last incident is especially revealing as initially Gould was not even capable of understanding that he had voiced racist sentiments.[29]

SEXUALITY AND TRANSSEXUALS

Discrimination against gays and lesbians in sport is not prohibited. In appropriate circumstances it is clearly permitted. As established in *Saunders*[30] it may be within the range of reasonable responses for clubs to dismiss gay players. This could be regarded as reasonable and thus fair if the presence of an openly gay player was causing tensions within the team or hostility from the paying public. This is particularly the case when it is remembered that in Saunders emphasis was placed on the attitudes of parents. By analogy gay professional players coaching young children or simply existing as role models could be perceived by parents as a potential source of corruption. That this confusion between gay sexuality and paedophilia is based on a misconception, which can best be described as superstitious bigotry, is not for a tribunal to find once it is clear that the reasonable employing club may act to preserve its reputation and paying support.

---

29 As reported in *The Guardian*, 2 April 1997. Also see Mitchell, K, 'Gould has the Gift of the Gaffe', *The Observer*, 6 April 1997.

30 See above, Chapter 8, p 390.

By the same token, harassment of a player on the basis of his or her sexuality is not considered unlawful under the SDA 1975.[31] If a club encourages or condones such harassment it would be acting in breach of the duty of respect.[32] This is relevant to a player with at least two years' continuous employment who resigns in response to such maltreatment. He might consequently succeed in a claim for constructive and unfair dismissal. It is permissible to refuse employment to an individual on the basis of that person's sexual identity.[33] In these cases the EAT and Court of Appeal were of the view that neither the SDA 1975 nor the Equal Treatment Directive offered any protection where discrimination was based on sexual orientation as against gender.

That the stigma attached to homosexuality is also attached to transsexuality is shown by the problems encountered by the professional tennis player Dr Renee Richards who prior to a sex change operation had been Dr Richard Rasskind.[34] In *P v S and Cornwall County Council*,[35] the European Court ruled that dismissal of an employee was contrary to the Equal Treatment Directive where the reason for the dismissal was that the employee proposed to undergo gender-reassignment surgery. The EAT's view had been that such discrimination is not by reason of gender providing male and female transsexuals are treated in the same way. The ECJ's view was that sex discrimination arises from 'comparison with persons of the sex to which he or she was deemed to belong before undergoing gender reassignment'. Alternatively such discrimination constitutes: 'failure to respect the dignity and freedom to which he or she is entitled and which the Court has a duty to safeguard'.

Assuming such discrimination cannot be justified in the context of professional sport and the ultimate position taken with respect to Renee Richards would suggest there can be no such justification, this ruling is as important in sport as it is for employment law in general. The general tenor of the ECJ's reasoning could open the way to finding that discrimination on grounds of sexual orientation is contrary to the Equal Treatment Directive.[36]

---

31   *Smith v Gardner Merchant Ltd* [1996] IRLR 342.

32   See above, Chapter 7, pp 353–54.

33   *R v Ministry of Defence ex parte Smith; R v Admiralty of the Defence Council ex parte Lustig-Pream* [1996] ICR 740.

34   See Grayson, E, *Sport and the Law* (1994), London: Butterworths, pp 240–41.

35   [1996] ICR 795.

36   For an argument to this effect, see Skidmore, P, 'Sex, Gender and Comparators in Employment Discrimination' (1997) 26(1) *Industrial Law Journal* 51–61.

DISCRIMINATION AND EU LAW

Other than in the context of freedom of movement, EU law prohibits sex but not race discrimination in employment. Article 2 of the Equal Treatment Directive[37] provides 'the principle of equal treatment shall mean that there shall be no discrimination whatsoever on grounds of sex either directly or indirectly by reference in particular to marital or family status'.

In accordance with the norms of EU law the Directive is only directly enforceable within the UK by State employees. Nevertheless, through the preliminary ruling process the ECJ has delivered a number of significant rulings which have conferred protection on women employees which may not have been provided for by national legislation. In the UK this has been particularly significant in the context of maternity rights. These rights should be appreciated by professional clubs who employ women either as players or in a variety of managerial or administrative capacities. Such rights are also relevant to women employed as match officials.

In the landmark rulings of *Dekker v VJV Centrum*[38] and *Hertz v Aldi Marked*[39] the ECJ ruled that refusal of employment to or dismissal of a women on grounds of pregnancy is contrary to the Directive. These rulings were subsequently accepted as appropriate interpretations of the SDA by the House of Lords:

Webb v EMO Air Cargo (UK) Ltd [1993] ICR 175 HL

The company had 16 employees, including four import operations clerks. One employee, S, discovered that she was pregnant in June 1987; her baby was due in February 1988 and she wanted to return to work after maternity leave. The company therefore employed W from 1 July 1987 to be trained by S and to take over from S during her maternity leave. It was envisaged that W would probably be kept on after S's return. Two weeks after starting work, W discovered that she, too, was pregnant. Since this meant that she was unlikely to be able to cover the very period for which she was needed, the employer dismissed her. She claimed that it was sex discrimination.

Lord Keith: ... The applicant's case alleges direct discrimination contrary to s 1(1)(a) or alternatively indirect discrimination contrary to s 1(1)(b). It is the case on direct discrimination which poses the really difficult problem. Section 1(1)(a) requires a comparison to be made between the treatment accorded to a woman and the treatment accorded or that would be accorded to a man. Here there is no treatment actually accorded to a man which can be the subject of comparison. So it is necessary to consider what treatment would be accorded to a man and under s 5(3) it is necessary to assume that the relevant circumstances in the case of the hypothetical man are the same as or not

---

37 Council Directive No 76/207.

38 [1991] IRLR 27.

39 [1991] IRLR 31.

materially different from the circumstances in which the treatment complained of was accorded to the woman. What in this case are the relevant circumstances which are to be assumed to be present in the case of the hypothetical man? Obviously they cannot include the circumstance that the man is pregnant, for that is impossible. This led a majority of the Employment Appeal Tribunal in *Turley v Allders Department Stores Ltd* to hold that dismissal of a woman on the pure ground of pregnancy could not constitute unlawful discrimination, comparison with a man who was in like position being impossible. Ms P Smith dissented, taking the view that the proper course was to compare the position of a pregnant woman with that of a man who by reason of some medical condition required a period off work equivalent to what a woman would require for her confinement. In *Hayes v Malleable Working Men's Club and Institute* an Employment Appeal Tribunal differently constituted upheld the dissenting opinion of Ms Smith in *Turley's* case. The Court of Appeal followed the same line in the present case. Glidewell LJ said, 'To postulate a pregnant man is an absurdity but I see no difficulty in comparing a pregnant woman with a man who has a medical condition which will require him to be absent for the same period of time and at the same time as does the woman's pregnancy'.

There can be no doubt that in general to dismiss a woman because she is pregnant or to refuse to employ a woman of child-bearing age because she may become pregnant is unlawful direct discrimination. Child-bearing are characteristics of the female sex. So to apply these characteristics as the criterion for dismissal or refusal to employ is to apply a gender-based criterion, which the majority of this House in *James v Eastleigh Borough Council* held to constitute unlawful direct discrimination. In that case the council had adopted the attainment of pensionable age, 65 for men and 60 for women, as the condition for being eligible for free use of their swimming pool. In the present case, however, there was not any direct application of a gender based criterion. If the applicant's expected date of confinement had not been so very close to that of Valerie Stewart she would not have been dismissed. It was her expected non-availability during the period when she was needed to cover for Valerie Stewart which was the critical factor. The question is whether it is legitimate to make a comparison between the non-availability of a woman by reason of expected confinement and the non-availability of a man, which may or may not be for medical reasons, for the purpose of postulating relevant circumstances under s 5(3) of the Act. If it is not legitimate, then cases can be envisaged where somewhat surprising results would follow. *For example, an employer might require to engage extra staff for an event due to take place over a particular period, such as the Wimbledon fortnight or the Olympic Games and for which a period of training is required. He advertises some months in advance and 10 candidates apply – five men and five women, all better qualified than the men, one of whom is pregnant, her confinement being expected to be on the first day of the event. The employer requires only four extra staff and he engages the four women who are not pregnant. Has there been direct discrimination against the pregnant woman?* [our emphasis] Mr Sedley, for the applicant here, would answer that question afffirmatively, saying that the pregnant woman has been deprived, on grounds of her sex, of one-fifth of a chance of being selected and should be compensated accordingly. He relies on the 'but for their sex' test adumbrated by Lord Goff of Chieveley in *R v Birmingham County Council ex parte Equal Opportunities Commission*. That was a case where the council operated single sex grammar schools for boys and for girls. There were fewer places in the girls' schools than there were in the boys' and as a result the girls had to gain higher marks in the entrance examination than did the boys in order to obtain a place. It was held in the Court of Appeal and this House that the council was in breach of the Act of 1975. Lord Goff of Chieveley, in the course of a speech concurred in by the other members of the Appellate Committee, said 'There is discrimination under the statute if there is less favourable treatment on the ground of sex, in other words if the relevant girl or girls would have received the same treatment as the boys but for their sex'.

This test was approved and applied by Lord Bridge of *Harwich in James v Eastleigh Borough Council*. In my opinion, however, the test so formulated is not capable of application to the circumstances of this case. The applicant was not dismissed simply because she was pregnant but because her pregnancy had the consequence that she would not be available for work at the critical period ...

Up to this point I have proceeded upon the basis of the relevant provisions of the Act of 1975 considered in isolation. It is, however, necessary to take into account certain recent decisions of the European Court of Justice. The decisions are concerned with the interpretation of Council Directive (76/207/EEC) of the Council of the European Communities, Article 2(1) of which states that 'For the purposes of the following provisions, the principle of equal treatment shall mean that there shall be no discrimination whatsoever on grounds of sex either directly or indirectly by reference in particular to marital or family status'.

The first decision is *Dekker v Stichting Vormingscentnum voor Jong Volwassenen* (VJV-Centrum) Plus. The facts were that Mrs Dekker applied for a job with VJV and informed the selection committee that she was three months pregnant. The committee recommended her to the board of VJV as being the most suitable candidate for the job but the board decided not to employ her. The reason was that under the applicable law of the Netherlands VJV would have been required to pay Mrs Dekker 100% of her salary while she was absent owing to her confinement but would not have been in a position to recover the amount so paid from its insurers because her pregnancy was a condition known about at the time her employment would have commenced. In that situation VJV would not have been able to afford to pay a replacement for Mrs Dekker and this might have led to a staff shortage. The Dutch courts held that the domestic equal treatment legislation had been breached but that VJV had a justifiable ground for the breach. The Supreme Court of the Netherlands, considering that the true interpretation of the Community Directive had a bearing on the meaning to be attributed to the domestic legislation, referred a number of questions to the European Court of Justice, the first of which asked:

> Is an employer directly or indirectly in breach of the principle of equal treatment laid down in Articles 2(1) and 3(1) of the Council Directive on the implementation of the principle of equal treatment for men and women as regards access to employment ... if he refuses to enter into a

contract of employment with a candidate, found by him to be suitable, because of the adverse consequences for him which are to be anticipated owing to the fact that the candidate was pregnant when she applied for the post ...?

In relation to this question the relevant passages in the judgment of the court were these:

> Consideration must be given to the question whether a refusal of employment in the circumstances to which the national court has referred may be regarded as direct discrimination on the grounds of sex for the purposes of the Directive. The answer depends on whether the fundamental reason for the refusal of employment is one which applies without distinction to workers of either sex or, conversely, whether it applies exclusively to one sex.

> The reason given by the employer for refusing to appoint Mrs Dekker is basically that it could not have obtained reimbursement from the Risicofonds of the daily benefits which it would have had to pay her for the duration of her absence due to pregnancy and yet at the same time it would have been obliged to employ a replacement. That situation arises because, on the one hand, the national scheme in question assimilates pregnancy to sickness and, on the other, the *Ziekengeldreglement* contains no provision excluding pregnancy from the cases in which the *Risicofonds* is entitled to refuse reimbursement of the daily benefits.

> In that regard it should be observed that only women can be refused employment on the ground of pregnancy and such a refusal therefore constitutes direct discrimination on the ground of sex. A refusal of employment on account of the financial consequences of absence due to pregnancy must be regarded as based, essentially, on the fact of pregnancy. Such discrimination cannot be justified on grounds relating to the financial loss which an employer who appointed a pregnant woman would suffer for the duration of her maternity leave.

> In any event, the fact that pregnancy is assimilated to sickness and that the respective provisions of the *Ziektewet* and the *Ziekengeldreglement* governing reimbursement of the daily benefits payable in connection with pregnancy are not the same cannot be regarded as evidence of discrimination on the ground of sex within the meaning of the Directive. Lastly, in so far as an employer's refusal of employment based on the financial consequences of absence due to pregnancy constitutes direct discrimination, it is not necessary to consider whether national provisions such as those mentioned above exert such pressure on the employer that they prompt him to refuse to appoint a pregnant woman, thereby leading to discrimination within the meaning of the Directive.

> It follows from the foregoing that the answer to be given to the first question is that an employer is in direct contravention of the principle of equal treatment embodied in Articles 2(1) and 3(1) of Council Directive on the implementation of the principle of equal treatment for men and women as regards access to employment, vocational training and promotion and working conditions if he refuses to enter into a contract of

employment with a female candidate whom he considers to be suitable for the job where such refusal is based on the possible adverse consequences for him of employing a pregnant woman, owing to rules on unfitness for work adopted by the public authorities which assimilate inability to work on account of pregnancy and confinement to inability to work on account of illness.

The second decision is that in *Hertz v Aldi Marked* given on the same day as the decision in the *Dekker* case. A Mrs Hertz gave birth to a child after a complicated pregnancy during which she was on sick leave with the consent of her employer. She was given maternity leave but later took frequent periods of sick leave due to complications arising from her confinement. After these had amounted to 100 days in one year her employer gave her notice of dismissal. Mrs Hertz complained that the dismissal contravened the Danish equal treatment law and the Danish Supreme Court referred to the European Court of Justice the question whether dismissal on account of absence due to illness attributable to pregnancy or confinement was in breach of the Directive, the answer to that question being considered relevant to the true interpretation of the Danish equal treatment law. The court answered the question in the negative. After citing various provisions of the Directive the judgment continues:

> It follows from the provisions of the Directive quoted above that the dismissal of a female worker on account of pregnancy constitutes direct discrimination on grounds of sex, as is a refusal to appoint a pregnant woman: see *Dekker v Stichting Vormingscentrum voor Jong Volwassenen (VJV-Centrum) Plus*.

> On the other hand, the dismissal of a female worker on account of repeated periods of sick leave which are not attributable to pregnancy or confinement does not constitute direct discrimination on grounds of sex, in as much as such periods of sick leave would lead to the dismissal of a male worker in the same circumstances.

> The Directive does not envisage the case of an illness attributable to pregnancy or confinement. It does, however, admit of national provisions guaranteeing women specific rights on account of pregnancy and maternity, such as maternity leave. During the maternity leave accorded to her pursuant to national law, a woman is accordingly protected against dismissal due to absence. It is for every Member State to fix periods of maternity leave in such a way as to enable female workers to absent themselves during the period in which the disorders inherent in pregnancy and confinement occur.

> In the case of an illness manifesting itself after the maternity leave, there is no reason to distinguish an illness attributable to pregnancy or confinement from any other illness. Such a pathological condition is therefore covered by the general rules applicable in the event of illness.

> Male and female workers are equally exposed to illness. Although certain disorders are, it is true, specific to one sex, the only question is whether a woman is dismissed on account of absence due to illness in the same

circumstances as a man; if that is the case, then there is no direct discrimination on grounds of sex.

It will be seen that the court made a distinction between the normal incidents of pregnancy and confinement and uncommon complications arising from those conditions. It equated the latter to illnesses of any kind, including those which could affect only men and did not regard such complications as being in a special category, notwithstanding that they could affect only women. It refused, however, to make a similar equation between normal pregnancy and confinement and illness. In the *Dekker* case the European Court of Justice held that the fundamental reason for the refusal of employment was pregnancy, a reason which did not apply to workers of either sex without distinction but which applied exclusively to the female sex and that this constituted direct discrimination on grounds of sex. That the refusal of employment was not on grounds of pregnancy as such but was on account of the adverse financial consequences to the employer of absence of the worker due to pregnancy was regarded as not material because, in the court's view, the refusal was essentially based on the fact of pregnancy ...

The European Court of Justice did not, in the *Dekker* and *Hertz* cases, have to consider the situation where a woman, on account of her pregnancy, will not be able to carry out, at the time when her services are required, the particular job for which she is applying or for which she has been engaged. The two decisions do not give any clear indication whether in such a situation the court would regard the fundamental reason for the refusal to engage the woman or for dismissing her as being her unavailability for the job and not her pregnancy. In the event of the court arriving at a decision that the latter and not the former is the correct view for the purposes of the Directive it would be necessary for this House to consider whether it is possible to construe the relevant provisions of the Act of 1975 in such a way as to accord with such decision. Further, it is not impossible to envisage that the sort of situation which existed in the present case might arise in circumstances where the Directive has direct application, namely where the employer is the State or an emanation of the State. So I think it appropriate that before final judgment is given on this appeal there should be referred to the European Court of Justice the following question:

> Is it discrimination on grounds of sex contrary to Directive (76/207/EC) for an employer to dismiss a female employee ('the applicant') (a) whom he engaged for the specific purpose of replacing (after training) another female employee during the latter's forthcoming maternity leave, (b) when, very shortly after appointment, the employer discovers that the applicant herself will be absent on maternity leave during the maternity leave of the other employee and the employer dismisses her because he needs the job-holder to be at work during that period, (c) had the employer known of the pregnancy of the applicant at the date of appointment, she would not have been appointed and (d) the employer would similarly have dismissed a male employee engaged for this purpose who required leave of absence at the relevant time for medical or other reasons?

I understand that all your Lordships agree that there should be a reference accordingly and that final disposal of the appeal should be postponed until the decision of the European Court of Justice has been made available.[40]

This decision brought to an end a long line of reasoning which required comparison between a pregnant woman and a man suffering from an illness. The Law Lords have accepted the subsequent ruling by the ECJ, in the response to their above questions, that it is indeed contrary to the Directive to dismiss (or refuse employment to) a woman on the grounds that her pregnancy will restrict her capacity to cover for another employee who has leave of absence, when her employment is required for that particular purpose.[41]

This ruling is apparently restricted to the situation where the substitute employee is employed under an indefinite contract. It remains unclear whether a woman can be refused employment on a temporary contract if the employer discovers she is pregnant before a formal job offer is made. This could be relevant in sport where a woman is refused employment, on the basis of her pregnancy, under a contract which is to last, for example, for one season or, in accordance with the examples provided by Lord Keith, for the Wimbledon fortnight or the Olympic Games.

As a result of s 99 of the ERA 1996, which implements the EU Pregnancy Directive,[42] dismissal of a woman is automatically unfair if it is by reason of her pregnancy. This protection lasts during pregnancy and during the period of maternity leave to which she is entitled. Under s 73 all women are entitled to 14 weeks' maternity leave. For women with at least two years' continuous employment this is increased to 40 weeks' leave – 11 before the expected date of birth and 29 weeks after the baby is born – s 79.[43]

The above provisions protect all professional sportswomen who have entered into a contract of employment. Sportswomen who are not employees are still protected by the SDA 1975 and the Equal Treatment Directive. Ironically a woman who has rights under both Acts might prefer to bring a claim under the SDA 1975. This is because compensation is not subject to any statutory maximum limit. For highly paid professionals a claim under the SDA will incorporate compensation for loss of any career opportunities. In all likelihood this will be far greater than the basic and compensatory awards available under the ERA 1996.[44]

---

40 At pp 179–88.

41 [1995] IRLR 645.

42 Council Directive No 92/85.

43 Note, if a woman wishes to exercise these statutory rights she must notify the employer that she is pregnant, identify the expected week of confinement and give, if reasonably practicable, 21 days' notice of her intention to begin leave (ss 74 and 75). Women with the 40 weeks' entitlement must also inform the employer of the wish to exercise the right to return to work (s 80) and at least 21 days' notice of the day on which she proposes to return.

44 See above, Chapter 8, pp 410–11.

EQUAL PAY

Article 119 of the Treaty of Rome, as amplified by the Equal Pay Directive,[45] provides for the right of equal pay for work of equal value. In the UK this right is implemented by the Equal Pay Act 1970. As is the case with the SDA and the RRA an applicant need not be an employee but may be any individual who has entered into contract to perform work. As a directly applicable treaty provision, Article 119 can be relied upon as the basis of a claim in an industrial tribunal. Claims can thus be brought under EU law or the Equal Pay Act or both. In recent years this area of law has been driven by rulings of the ECJ.

One of the problems with the law as a mechanism of achieving equal pay for women is that both Article 119 and the Equal Pay Act require the applicant to identify a male comparator. In the segregated context of professional sport with different competitions and different teams for men and women this is generally impossible. This has long been an issue in for example professional tennis, where women players generally earn less than their male counterparts.[46]

Performance related pay and salary structures determined by market forces are legitimate grounds for pay differentials even where the equal pay laws are applicable. In sport these factors often render pay differentials the norm between members of the same team. For example the pay that an individual footballer earns will be very much linked to the transfer or signing-on fee that a club is prepared to pay to secure his services. This is similarly the case where a club wishes to persuade a player to resign for it on expiry of his contract. In the event of a mixed sex team ever being fielded, these factors would make it extremely difficult for a female member of the team to compare successfully, in terms of a legal challenge, the pay she received with that of a male team mate earning a higher salary.

The equal pay laws do protect women employed by clubs as administrators, public relations officers and the like. They also apply to paid match officials. For the sports participant with whom this chapter is primarily concerned, equal pay law will generally remain of abstract relevance until and if mixed sport in terms of gender becomes a reality.[47]

---

45 Council Directive No 75/117.

46 For a comparison in levels of prize money, see, for example, Barrett, J (ed), *World of Tennis* (1992), London: Collins Willow, pp 205–17. The figures show that the total prize money earned by women professionals was generally lower than that earned by male professionals. Equal prize money is awarded at the Australian and US Open Championships but not at the French Open Championship or Wimbledon.

47 Equal pay laws do not cover pay differentials which can be attributed to racial discrimination unless this constitutes a violation of Article 48. The limitations of the law in this respect may be revealed by a study, carried out by Dr Stefan Szymanski at Imperial College London University, which suggests black football players are paid less than their white team-mates. See the business section of *The Observer*, 6 April 1997.

ARTICLE 48 OF THE TREATY OF ROME

The main impact of EU law on professional sport has clearly been the ECJ's ruling in *Bosman*. One of Bosman's complaints was that UEFA's '3+2' rule violated Article 48. This rule restricted the number of foreign players whose names could be included on a team-sheet in a UEFA competition to three. An additional two players could be included if they had played in a country for five years uninterruptedly, including three years in junior teams.

Bosman's argument was this restricts the freedom of movement of players who are EU nationals as clubs with their full quota of foreign players are likely to restrict new contracts to indigenous players. The ECJ agreed with the Opinion of Advocate General Lenz that this offends the rule that all EU nationals must be treated on an equal basis.

As seen above, EU law, in terms of general principle, permits discrimination to be justified. Arguments on this basis were considered and rejected by Advocate-General Lenz:

URBSFA v Jean-Marc Bosman [1996] 1 CMLR (Case C415/93)

A number of further considerations have been advanced as justification for the rules on foreign players and these must now be examined. Three groups of arguments can essentially be distinguished. First, it is emphasised that the national aspect plays an important part in football; the identification of the spectators with the various teams is guaranteed only if those teams consist, at least as regards a majority of the players, of nationals of the relevant Member State; moreover, the teams which are successful in the national leagues represent their country in international competitions. Second, it is argued that the rules are necessary to ensure that enough players are available to the relevant national team; without the rules on foreigners, the development of young players would be affected. Third and finally, it is asserted that the rules on foreigners serve the purpose of ensuring a certain balance between the clubs, since otherwise the big clubs would be able to attract the best players.

The arguments in the first group would appear to latch on to the Court's observation in Dona that matches from which foreign players can be excluded must have a special character and context. In this connection the representative of the German government spoke with particular emphasis at the hearing before the Court. He asserted that the 'national character of the performance' characterised first division professional football. A glance at the reality of football today shows that that does not correspond to the fact. The vast majority of clubs in the top divisions in the Member States play foreign players. In the German Bundesliga, for example, I am not aware of any club which does without foreign players altogether. If one considers the most successful European clubs of recent years, it becomes clear that nearly all of them have several foreign players in their ranks. In many cases it is precisely the foreign players who have characterised the team in question – one need only recall the AC Milan team in the early 1990s, whose pillars included the Dutch players Gullit, Rijkaard and Van Basten. There may indeed be certain differences from country to country with respect to the playing style or the mentality of players. That has, however, by no means prevented foreign players playing in the national leagues.

Even if the 'national aspect' had the significance which many people attribute to it, however, it could not justify the rules on foreign players. The right to freedom of movement and the prohibition of discrimination against nationals of other Member States are among the fundamental principles of the Community order. The rules on foreign players breach those principles in such a blatant and serious manner that any reference to national interests which cannot be based on Article 48(3) must be regarded as inadmissible as against those principles.

As to the identification of spectators with the teams, there is also no need for extensive discussion to show the weakness of that argument. As the Commission and Mr Bosman have rightly stated, the great majority of a club's supporters are much more interested in the success of their club than in the composition of the team. Nor does the participation of foreign players prevent a team's supporters from identifying with the team. Quite on the contrary, it is not uncommon for those players to attract the admiration and affection of football fans to a special degree. One of the most popular players ever to play for TSV 1860 Munchen was undoubtedly Petar Radenkovic from what was then Yugoslavia. The English international Kevin Keegan was for many years a favourite of the fans at Hamburger SV. The popularity of Eric Cantona at Manchester United and of Jurgen Klinsmann at his former club Tottenham Hotspurs is well known.

The inconsistency of those who put forward that view is moreover apparent if one considers an argument advanced by URBSFA in this context. It is argued that since the clubs often bear the name of a town, the spectators should be able to see players of the same nationality in the team in question. However, if a club adopts a name which contains the name of a place, it could at most be expected or demanded that that club's players should come from the place in question. Yet it is a well known act that in the case of Bayern Munchen, for instance, only a few of the players come from Bavaria (let alone Munich). If nationals who come from other parts of the relevant State are accepted without question, one cannot see why that should not also be the case for nationals of other Member States.

Finally, it should be observed that the success and playing style of a team are largely determined by the manager. The Court has already held, however, that football trainers enjoy the right to freedom of movement under Article 48. It did not even consider that those persons might perhaps be subject to restrictions other than those expressly permitted by Article 48. In practice frequent use is in fact made of that right. The best known example is probably FC Barcelona, which has had a Dutch manager for a long time. Hamburger SV achieved its greatest success with an Austrian manager and Bayern Munchen has had a whole series of foreign managers in recent decades. A country's national team is not always managed by a national of that country either. Thus the manager of the Irish national team, for example, is an Englishman. That emphasises that a 'national' characterisation of football, in the sense that players and managers must be nationals of the country in which the club in question is based, hardly comes into question.

It is further argued that the clubs which are successful in the national leagues represent the Member State in question in the European competitions and must therefore consist of at least a majority of nationals of that State; and that the 'German champions', for example, can thus emerge only from a competition between club teams for which 'at least a minimum number of German players play'. That argument too fails to convince. Firstly, the proponents of that view are unable to explain why precisely the rules currently applied are necessary to ensure that. If what mattered was that a team should consist predominantly of nationals of the State concerned, with eleven players in a team it would suffice generally to allow up to five foreign players. And if only a 'minimum number' of players had to possess the nationality of the State concerned, even more foreign players would have to be allowed. Moreover, it should be observed that the concept of 'German champion' can be interpreted without difficulty in a different way from that sought by the proponents of that view. There is no reason why that term cannot be taken as designating the club which has finished in first place following the matches played in Germany.

The argument fails to convince, however, for another reason too. In Germany, for example, the rules on foreign players do not apply to amateur teams. Some of those teams take part in the cup competition organised by the DFB. It is thus theoretically possible for an amateur team consisting of 11 foreign players to win the DFB cup and thus qualify to enter the European Cup Winners' Cup. That this is not a purely hypothetical case is shown by the example of the Hertha BSC Berlin amateurs who reached the German cup final in 1993. The weakness of the argument becomes even more apparent if one considers that an association such as Scotland has no rules on foreign players and the other British associations have special rules for their mutual relations. It can thus perfectly well happen that clubs from those associations use a large number of players from other Member States in the leagues and competitions organised by their associations but are forced to limit the number of such players when they take part in UEFA competitions. I cannot see how in such a case the above mentioned argument could be used to justify professional footballers from the European Community being forbidden to take part in the European Cup competitions.

The arguments in the second group are not convincing either. Nothing has demonstrated that the development of young players in a Member State would be adversely affected in the rule on foreign players were dropped. Only a few top teams set store on promoting their own young players as, for instance, Ajax Amsterdam do. Most talented players, by contrast, make their way upwards via small clubs to which those rules do not apply. Moreover, there is much to support the opinion that the participation of top foreign players promotes the development of football. Early contact with foreign stars 'can only be of advantage to a young player'.

It is admittedly correct that the number of jobs available to native players decreases, the more foreign players are engaged by and play for the clubs. That is, however, a consequence which the right to freedom of movement necessarily entails. Moreover, there is little to suggest that abolition of the rules on foreign players might lead to players possessing the nationality of the relevant State becoming a small minority in a league. The removal of the rules on foreign players would not oblige clubs to engage (more) foreigners but would give them the possibility of doing so if they thought that promised success.

The argument that the rules on foreign players are needed to ensure that enough players develop for the national team is also unconvincing. Even if that consideration were to be regarded as legitimate in the light of the Court's judgments in Walmve and Dona, it could not justify the rules on foreigners. As I have already mentioned, it is unlikely that the influx of foreign players would be so great that native players would no longer get a chance. It is also significant here that the success or failure of the national team also has an effect on the interest in the club matches of the country in question. Winning the World Cup, for instance, generally brings about increased interest of spectators in national league matches as well. It is therefore in a country's clubs' very own interests to contribute to the success of the national team by developing suitable players and making them available. The prestige which those players acquire in the national team also benefits the clubs as such. Moreover, the example of Scotland may be noted, where the lack of rules on foreign players has plainly not led to a shortage of players for the national team.

Moreover, the national teams of the Member States of the Community nowadays very often include players who carry on their profession abroad, without that causing particular disadvantages. It suffices that the players have to be released for the national team's matches, as is also provided for in the current rules of the associations. The best example is perhaps the Danish national team which won the European Championship in 1992. In the German national team which became world champions in 1990 there were several players who played in foreign leagues. It is therefore not evident that the rules on foreigners are necessary in order to ensure the strength of the national team.

Third and finally, it is argued that the rules on foreign players serve to preserve the balance between clubs. In the opinion of URBSFA, the big clubs would otherwise be able to secure the services of the best players from the entire Community and thereby increase further the economic and sporting distance between them and the other clubs. The interest thus given expression is – as I shall explain later – a legitimate one. Like Mr Bosman however, I am of the opinion that there are other means of attaining that objective without affecting the right of freedom of movement. Moreover, the rules are in any case only to a very limited extent appropriate to ensure a balance between the clubs. The richest clubs are still in a position to afford the best – and thus as a rule the most expensive – foreign stars. At the same time, such clubs have the opportunity to engage the best native players, without any comparable rule setting them limits.

In Britain the response of the FA to this dimension of the *Bosman* ruling has been simply to put players with EU nationality on an equal footing with players of British nationality. Thus the '3+2' rule will still apply to European players who are not nationals of EU Member States and players from outside of Europe. Such players will also remain subject to immigration laws which require them to be in possession of a work permit if they are to play for a club in the Premier or Nationwide League. A British club could field a team for a domestic competition which did not contain a single British player. Such a team would have to include at least six players with EU nationality.

The scope of s 39 of the RRA 1976[48] which permits exclusion of a player on basis of nationality is now subject to the Bosman ruling. By the same token there is now much more scope for British players to seek employment with a club in another EU Member State. This intersects with the issue of transfer fees as a British player at the end of his contract could leave a British club for, say, a French one. At the end of that contract he could negotiate a return to a British club. Freedom of contract as required by Bosman would override even any new provisions for transfer fees adopted by the Premier and Football Leagues.

The player will still have to apply with FA regulations as explained in the FA Notes on Premier League and Football League Contracts.[49] A player cannot move abroad, or having done so return, without the clearance of the FA Whilst these rules are now subject to Article 48, they will in all probability be permitted to prevent fake moves designed to circumvent the transfer system. For example a player at the end of his contract will not be able to negotiate a move to a French club with a view the following week to moving from that club back to another club in the Premier or Football Leagues.

If UEFA retains the '3+2' rule for non-EU nationals playing in European competitions then clubs from EU Member States would arguably have an advantage. They could recruit from the whole of the EU and still play up to five 'foreign' players. A team from say Estonia or Turkey would still have to play at least six players who were nationals of the country concerned. FIFA has extended freedom of contract to non-EU nationals who play for clubs within EU Member States.[50] The logical, if not legally required, outcome of this must be the abandonment of the '3+2' rule in any shape or form.[51]

---

48 See above, p 422.

49 See FA Notes on Footballers' Contracts, p 12.

50 See above, Chapter 7, p 378.

51 For a comparative analysis of quota systems in sport, with particular reference to United States sports leagues, see Greenberg, J and Gray, JT, 'Citizenship Based Quota Systems In Athletics' (1996) 6(2) *Marquette Sports Law Journal* 337–55.

CHAPTER TEN

LEGAL AND NON-LEGAL CONTROLS OF SPORTSFIELD VIOLENCE

INTRODUCTION

In recent years there has been a growing trend for participants who have been injured whilst playing sport to turn to the law for a remedy. Some participants are seeking compensation for a career breaking or ending injury[1] whilst others find themselves the subject of criminal prosecutions for their wayward challenges.[2] It is now no longer the case that all participants injured by their fellow players will willingly accept that injury as an integral part of the game. If they are injured due to somebody else's fault, they want a remedy, either from their sport's governing body or the law.

This chapter will explore the different regulatory methods used for controlling injury causing acts committed by participants, during a game, on the field of play. It will analyse the aims and effectiveness of the different methods of control and their interaction with each other. It will highlight the discrepancies and injustices of the current systems, as well as showing potential remedies for the future.

There are three mechanisms by which violence on the field is currently controlled: the criminal law, the law of tort and the disciplinary tribunals of the various sport governing bodies. Each of these will be examined in turn to show how, when and why they have a role to play in trying to control participator violence on the field.

---

1   See, for example, the cases of *Elliott v Saunders and Liverpool FC* unreported decision of the High Court, 1994 and *O'Neill v Fashanu and Wimbledon FC* unreported decision of the High Court, 1994, where the plaintiffs were seeking to establish that as a result of the negligent challenges of the defendants, their careers as professional footballers were prematurely ended.

2   See *R v Billinghurst* [1978] Crim LR 553; *R v Devereux* (1996) *The Times*, 26 February; *Ferguson v Normand* [1995] SCCR 770.

THE RATIONALE BEHIND CONTROLLING SPORTS VIOLENCE

Before any discussion can take place regarding the merits of each the mechanisms, the subject of sportsfield violence and the need for it to be controlled must be explored.

Definition of Violence

Violence is a difficult concept to define, especially as it has no legal definition. In criminal and civil cases, assault, battery and harm are used to describe and define attacks on others. Violence is used here to include all forms of behaviour which can cause harm to a fellow participator.

Sportsfield violence is a particularly difficult concept to define, not least because many sports have as part of their very nature a degree of interpersonal contact far in excess of that which would be acceptable in any other walk of life. It is probably better to give a description of what will be considered to be violent or perhaps more accurately injurious conduct, worthy of control by some mechanism or another.

Coakley draws a distinction between aggression, violence and intimidation.[3] Aggression is any behaviour intended to destroy another's property or harm their person. Violence is the physical manifestation of aggression, whilst intimidation is the verbal or physical threat of violence. Smith prefers a narrower interpretation, defining violence as physically assaultive behaviour that is designed to and does, injure another person or persons.[4]

This chapter will concentrate on violence as physical aggression but in a wider sense than defined by both Coakley and Smith. It will include not only intentionally caused injuries but will also examine those inflicted through reckless and negligent behaviour. Although this definition is extremely wide, it has the advantage of covering all aspects of the problem of sportsfield violence.

Is there a Problem of Sports Related Violence?

It is often suggested[5] that today's sports are more violent than those of the past and that for this reason there is a more urgent need for legal control than at any previous time. Statistics are pointed to, showing the increased number

3   Coakley, J, *Sport and Society*, 5th edn (1994), St Louis: Mosby, Chapter 7.

4   Smith, M, *Violence and Sport* (1983), Toronto: Butterworths, p 7.

5   Grayson, E, *Sport and the Law*, 2nd edn (1994), London: Butterworths, p 403 *et seq*.

of appearances before disciplinary tribunals, the high incidence of career ending injuries or even the increase in litigation between sports participants.

These statistics can also be used to show that the game is better regulated and safer to play than in the past. The increase in disciplinary tribunal activity can be ascribed to changes in the playing and safety rules of sports and stricter interpretations and applications of existing laws by the referees and other officials. Players are being penalised more frequently for technical offences, whilst all forms of violence are punished more severely. For example, in football, tackles from behind have been more seriously punished since the 1994 World Cup, as injury is more likely to occur with this kind of challenge. In rugby union the deliberate collapsing of scrums will now result in an award of either a penalty or a penalty try.[6] These rule changes and their stricter enforcement have made the games safer but have increased the likelihood of disciplinary action for players who transgress them.

The increase in the number of career ending injuries can also have a more innocent explanation. Modern players are bigger, faster, better trained and play more frequently than in the past. By the very nature of some contact sports, incidental injuries will be more serious than in earlier times. Although the statistics may lead to the inference that there is more foul play, it is possibly closer to the truth to say that dangerous play is being more harshly treated by referees and governing bodies, even if their motives are not always simply to protect those who play their sports.

The increase in litigation can be explained by the concept of juridification and the greater knowledge and use of legal rights amongst the general public. Juridification occurs when a sphere of private conduct which was previously ignored by the law becomes highly legally regulated. This phenomenon is not sport specific but is observable in many fields of life previously untouched by the law.[7] In relation to sport there is much debate over whether legal regulation should be increased. The arguments can be summarised by reference to the writings of Edward Grayson[8] and Simon Gardiner.[9] Grayson advocates the use of the law as a mechanism to punish and compensate acts of on-field violence that are in breach of the playing rules. To this end he has proposed a draft Safety of Sports Persons Act, specifically to outlaw all forms of violence in sports.[10] Gardiner is in favour of less legal regulation but increased powers for internal disciplinary tribunals, thus keeping the matter

---

6   Rule 26(3)(h).

7   See, for example, Flood, J and Caiger, A, 'Lawyers and Arbitration: The Juridification of Construction Disputes' [1993] *MLR* 412.

8   See for example, 'On the Field of Play' [1971] *New Law Journal* 413; *Sport and the Law*, 2nd edn (1994) and Bond, C, 'Making Foul Play a Crime' [1993] *Solicitors Journal* 693.

9   See for example, 'The Law and the Sportsfield' *Criminal Law Review* 513, 'Not Playing the Game: Is it a Crime?' [1993] *Solicitors Journal* 628 and with Felix, A, 'Juridification of the Football Field' (1995) 5(2) *Marquette Sports Law Journal* 189.

10   *Sport and the Law* (1994), Appendix 14.

'within the family'. Whichever view is subscribed to, it cannot be denied that the law is being used more frequently to punish and compensate incidents of sportsfield violence.

This does not mean that there is no violence in British sport but it demonstrates that looking backwards can often be of little practical assistance. The only way that sportsfield violence can be put into perspective, is to look at a particular sport in the context of contemporary society and decide whether what occurs during the course of a game is an acceptable way of playing it. If it is, from both a player's and society's point of view, then there is no problem. On the other hand, if either the participants or society believe that the level of violence in a sport is becoming unacceptable, then some form of regulation is necessary.

Obeying the Rules and the Relevance of the Rules

Obeying the rules is an important part of playing any sport. Without adherence to the rules you cannot truly be said to be playing the game: '[As] cheaters make moves not recognised by the constitutive rules of the sport, not only do they fail to prove themselves better players than their fellow competitors but they have not even succeeded in playing the game in the first place.'[11]

The role the rules have in the wider context of sport and the law must be examined in more detail:

R v Bradshaw (1878) 14 Cox CC 83

The question for you to decide is whether the death of the deceased was caused by the unlawful act of the prisoner. There is no doubt that the prisoner's act caused the death and the question is whether the act was unlawful. No rules or practice of any game whatever can make that lawful which is unlawful by the law of the land; and the law of the land says that you shall not do that which is likely to cause the death of another. For instance, no persons can by agreement go out and fight with deadly weapons, doing by agreement what the law says shall not be done and thus shelter themselves from the consequences of their acts. Therefore in one way you need not concern yourselves with the rules of football. But on the other hand if a man is playing according to the rules and practice of the game and not going beyond it, it may be reasonable to infer that he is not actuated by any malicious motive or intention and that he is not acting in a manner which he knows will be likely to be productive of death or injury. But independent of the rules, if the prisoner intended to cause serious hurt to the deceased or if he knew that, in charging as he did, he might produce serious injury and was indifferent and reckless as to whether he would produce serious injury or not, then the act would be unlawful. In either case he would be guilty of a criminal act and you must find him guilty; if you are of the contrary opinion, you will acquit him.

---

11 Simon, RL, *Fair Play: Sports Values and Society* (1991), Colorado: Westview Press, p 15.

His Lordship carefully reviewed the evidence, stating that no doubt the game was in any circumstances a rough one; but he was unwilling to decry the manly sports of this country, all of which were no doubt attended with more or less danger. The verdict was not guilty.[12]

The rules of the game are not conclusive when considering whether or not an action was illegal. Although they clearly cannot affect the legality of an act, they can be used as a gauge for assessing the mental state or *mens rea*, of a perpetrator of sports violence. It can be more easily inferred by a jury that a player playing within the rules was not deliberately trying to inflict injury on an opponent but was in fact trying to play the game (eg when making or attempting a tackle). On the other hand, if an incident was clearly a breach of the rules of the game then it is easier for the finder of fact to infer that there was some degree of culpability on the part of the perpetrator (eg where a player is attacked off the ball). The court is not supposed to treat incidents of sportsfield violence any differently from violent acts committed in any other setting.

Two examples highlight the point that sports rules and the law sit awkwardly with each other. The first was an act within the rules which *prima facie* could have attracted legal liability. The second was an act contrary to the rules of the game but permissible under the law of the land. Jack Tatum was a linebacker for the New England Patriots American football team. During one game his brief was to 'sack' the opposing quarterback, Darryl Stingley, using as much force as was possible. Tatum did this with a legitimate tackle, one that was so hard that it broke Stingley's neck, paralysing him. Later in his autobiography, Tatum admitted that his intention was to hurt his opponents so that they could not, or were too intimidated to, continue in the game.[13] Can this confession turn a tackle which was made within the rules into a violent criminal assault?

The second involves an English rugby union player, William Hardy. During a ruck, Hardy was hit from behind on the back of his neck. To defend himself he lashed out at his alleged assailant, Stefan Marty, knocking him out. Marty fell, cracking his head on the hard ground, and died later of a brain haemorrhage. In rugby union any punch is against the rules even if thrown in self-defence. However despite self-defence being successfully run by Hardy at his trial for manslaughter,[14] he was still banned retrospectively by the Rugby Football Union for the punch.[15]

The former case shows that until the later confession it would have been assumed that Stingley was playing the game hard but fair. The latter shows

---

12 *Per* Bramwell LJ, 84.

13 Tatum, J, and Kushner, B, *They Call Me Assassin* (1979), New York: Everest House.

14 *R v Hardy*, *The Guardian*, 27 July 1994.

15 *Daily Telegraph*, 19 September 1994.

that sport and the law do not consider the same act to be within the same category of behaviour.

Why should Sportsfield Violence be Controlled?

There are many reasons why participator violence should be controlled within sport, so far as is reasonably practicable. The following are some of the more compelling reasons.

Player protection

Violence is controlled to prevent unnecessary injury being caused to the participants. The object of non-fighting sports is not to cause injury but to play the game according to its rules. Violence is controlled to allow participants to continue to play the game with as little risk of injury as possible from acts likely to cause physical injury.

Fair play and discipline

One of the most often quoted reasons for the continued acceptance of sport as an integral part of society is that it instils a number of virtues which society holds to be important. Over 200 years ago, Sir Michael Foster explained that lawful sports should have a special legal status in relation to the law of offences against the person because they were 'manly diversions' that were supposed to 'give strength, skill and activity and may fit people for defence, public as well as personal, in times of need'.[16] The virtues attributable to sport are fair play and discipline. If sportsfield violence is allowed to flourish then these two basic ideals of sport are being ignored. If a player does not play by the rules of the game and play fairly, can he be said to be taking part at all? Violent conduct which goes beyond how the game should be played cannot be described as fair but is more closely associated with cheating.

The instillation of discipline is also often used to explain why sport, and especially boxing, should be encouraged amongst young people. The training regime and ethos of sport encourage a healthy and disciplined approach to life, not just sport.[17] When violent and injurious conduct becomes commonplace in sport, discipline breaks down and one of the reasons for sport's special legal status is removed. Without this the justification for sport's continued immunity from legal sanctions is thrown into doubt.

---

16 Foster, M, *Crown Law*, 3rd edn (1792), p 260.

17 For a longer discussion of this reasoning see Gunn, M, and Omerod, D, 'The Legality of Boxing' (1995) 15(2) *Legal Studies* 192.

Protection of sport's image

Many sports are now dependent on the money received from television and commercial sponsorship, to encourage the influx of new young players at the junior levels. These sports cannot allow themselves to be perceived as unduly violent by the public. If a sport is so perceived, sponsors may no longer wish to be associated with it and the sport can lose its attraction as a healthy pastime. This can further lead to players not taking it up the sport and ultimately, to fans failing to attend. It is in many governing bodies' interests to encourage a clean and healthy sport.

For example in Australia the Australian Football League (AFL), the governing body of Australian Rules Football, was finding it extremely difficult to recruit young players to the game in the light of the large number of mass fights which were perceived to occur during the game. In 1994 shortly before the prestigious Finals Series began the AFL added to the disciplinary rules the 'Melée Rule', which placed the emphasis on the clubs to clamp down on this kind of mass player violence.

Where four or more players are involved in an incident which in the opinion of the AFL's disciplinary Commission is likely to prejudice the interests or reputation of the AFL, the clubs whose players were involved in the brawl will be liable to a fine of up to A$50,000.[18] Since the introduction of this rule the mass brawls associated with the game have all but disappeared and Australian Rules continues to flourish.

Winning at all costs

As a motivating factor the 'win at all costs' mentality is of growing importance. As more money and prestige are associated with sport, winning, rather than taking part becomes the most important reason for participation. Sport becomes a business with associated career paths instead of being just a game.[19] The professional players lead the way in this but those at the lower levels, who watch the stars, are quick to follow their lead. This is true for tactics, clothing, litigiousness and the desire to win. Participants at all levels see how the elite levels achieve success and copy it hoping for similar success. The culture of 'win at all costs' filters down to all levels of the game.

To ensure that sport continues to be played in a socially acceptable way means that the players must also work to ensure that the game is played in accordance with the values that make sport acceptable to society in the first place. If these values are ignored society will begin to assert its own regulatory

---

18 The 'Melée Rule' was circulated to the clubs as an additional disciplinary rule in 1994.

19 For example, in July 1996, Fabrizio Ravenelli's wages at Middlesborough FC were reputed to be in the region of £30,000 per week, *The Times*, 23 July 1996. In America in the same month, Michael Jordan resigned for the Chicago Bulls basketball team for around £18m for one season, *The Times*, 19 July 1996.

mechanisms to ensure that the games are played in the way that it wants to see them played.

Combat Sports

The legal status of combat sports is a difficult subject for both the law and legal theory. The law must try to justify why behaviour which in any other walk of life would be considered to be clearly illegal should in combat sports be considered legal. The law is further confused by its lack of a definition of sport.[20] Although sports are to be encouraged for all the benefits that they bring, is fighting really a benefit to modern society? Can hitting another person with fists, feet or sticks truly be considered to be sport?

Jurists are placed in a further dilemma over the status of combat sports, depending on whether a libertarian or paternalistic stand is taken. If the former viewpoint is adhered to, everybody should be allowed to do as they wish with their body. As John Stuart Mill stated:

> The only purpose for which power can rightfully be exercised over any member of a civilised community against his will is to prevent harm to others ... His own good either physical or moral is not a sufficient warrant. He cannot rightfully be compelled to do or forebear because it will be better for him to do so, because it will make him happier, because in the opinions of others, to do so would be wise or even right.[21]

Provided that full and informed consent is present, an adult should be free to act as he wishes if he does not cause non-consensual harm to another. Thus all combat sports that are voluntarily participated in should be lawful.

Following a more paternalistic viewpoint a person should not be allowed to inflict harm on himself or others. This was the dominant theory behind the decision in *R v Brown*.[22] However whereas the behaviour in *R v Brown* was held to be unlawful, fighting for sport can have a quite different legal status.

Boxing

Boxing occupies an anomalous position in English law. There is no doubt that boxing is lawful and that the participants are immune from both criminal and civil legal actions despite the potentially fatal injuries which can be inflicted. Much modern discussion is focused on whether boxing is a sport[23] and whether this immunity can be justified in modern society.

---

20 See Gardiner, S, 'Sport: A Need for a Legal Definition?' (1996) 4(2) *Sport and the Law Journal* 31.

21 Hart, HLA, *Law, Liberty and Morality* (1963), Oxford University Press, Chapter 1.

22 [1993] 2 WLR 556 and below, p 464.

23 See further discussion in Chapter 1.

The basis for boxing's immunity from the law is itself quite confused.[24] The leading case of *R v Coney*,[25] did not hold that boxing was lawful but that prize-fighting was unlawful. Prize-fights were contests where the protagonists fought, often bare-knuckle, for an unlimited period until one could no longer continue, usually for money. Sparring, on the other hand, was where the protagonists fought as a test of skill. Gloves were usually used and the object was to score more points from direct hits than your opponent, rather than simply beat him into submission.[26] After the advent of the Marquis of Queensbery's rules in 1865, sparring effectively became the boxing that we see today. It is only this form of fighting, where the object is to score more points than your opponent rather than render him physically incapable of continuing, that appears to be subject to immunity from prosecution:

R v Coney (1882) 8 QBD 534

Cave J: ... [a] blow struck in anger or which is likely or intended to do corporal hurt, is an assault but that a blow struck in sport and not likely or intended to cause bodily harm, is not an assault and that, an assault being a breach of the peace and unlawful, the consent of the person struck is immaterial. If this view is correct a blow struck in a prize-fight is clearly an assault; but playing with single-sticks or wrestling do not involve an assault; nor does boxing with gloves in the ordinary way.[27]

Matthew J: ... [no] consent can render that innocent which is in fact dangerous. This is as true of a prize-fight, as it is of a duel. The fists of a trained pugilist are dangerous weapons which they are not at liberty to use against each other.[28]

Stephen J: ... [the] consent of the person who sustains the injury is no defence to the person who inflicts the injury, if the injury is of such a nature or is inflicted under such circumstances, that its infliction is injurious to the public as well as to the person injured. But, the injuries given and received in prize-fights are injurious to the public, both because it is against the public interest that the lives and the health of the combatants should be endangered by blows and because prize-fights are disorderly exhibitions, mischievous on many obvious grounds. Therefore the consent of the parties to the blows which they mutually receive does not prevent those blows from being assaults ... In cases where life and limb are exposed to no serious danger in the common course of things, I think that consent is a defence to a charge of assault, even where considerable force is used, as, for instance, in cases of wrestling, single-stick, sparring with gloves, football and the like.[29]

Hawkins J: ... [it] is not in the power of any man to give an effectual consent to that which amounts to or has a direct tendency to create, a breach of the peace;

---

24 See Parpworth, N, 'Boxing and Prize Fighting: The Indistinguishable Distinguished?' (1994) 2(1) *Sport and the Law Journal* 5.

25 [1882] 8 QBD 534.

26 Hawkins J, 554.

27 *Ibid*, 539.

28 *Ibid*, 547.

29 *Ibid*, 549.

so as to bar a criminal prosecution ... He may compromise his own civil rights but he cannot compromise the public interest ... every fight in which the object and the intent of each of the combatants is to subdue the other by violent blows, is or has a direct tendency to, a breach of the peace and it matters not, in my opinion, whether such fight be a hostile fight begun and continued in anger or a prize-fight for money or other advantage. In each case the object is the same and in each case some amount of personal injury to one or both of the combatants is a probable consequence ... I have no doubt then, that every such fight is illegal ... The cases in which it has been held that persons may lawfully engage in friendly encounters not calculated to produce real injury to or to arouse angry passions in either, do not in the least militate against the view that I have expressed; for such encounters are neither breaches of the peace nor are they calculated to be productive thereof.[30]

Pollock B: ... [neither] can the combatants in a prize-fight give consent to one another to commit that which the law has repeatedly held to be a breach of the peace. An individual cannot by such consent destroy the right of the Crown to protect the public and keep the peace.[31]

These extracts show that although the aim of the House was to outlaw prize-fights, the reasons for them so doing are not what might first be expected. Only Stephen J concentrates on the dangerous nature of prize-fighting and the degree of injury inflicted by the protagonists on one another The House was more concerned that prize-fights encouraged disorderly groups of gamblers whose spectating caused a breach of the peace. Prize-fighting was illegal as the blows struck could not be consented to because the protagonists could not consent to acts which would cause a breach of the peace. The fact that an opponent may be severely injured or even killed appeared to have little bearing on the reasoning of the House.

Whilst prize-fighting was banned, sparring was allowed to flourish and become modern day boxing. But just how different is boxing from the prize-fights of old? Money is paid to the fighters, who often knock each other out. Although the aim of boxing is to score more points that your opponent, through both attack and defence, the surest way to prevent your opponent from scoring further points is to knock him out.[32] One of the reasons for allowing sparring to flourish was because the House held that when sparring for sport as opposed to prize-fighting the intent to, and likelihood of, injury was unlikely. Is modern boxing really that different from the prize-fights that the House was intent on banning?

However since *R v Coney*, prize-fighting has been considered to be contrary to the public interest and therefore illegal, whilst sparring for points as a test of skill is by implication considered to be legal. In a line of cases

30 *Ibid*, 553.

31 *Ibid*, 567.

32 Law Commission Consultation Paper No 139, para 12.35.

stretching from *R v Orton*[33] to *R v Brown*,[34] the legality of boxing has not been seriously disputed. Following *R v Brown*, whatever the arguments for and against its legality, boxing is now so firmly entrenched in our society that the only way its status can be changed is by Parliament. This view has also been endorsed by the Law Commission.[35] Despite the repeated infliction of blows to which no other section of the community could legally consent and the potential for serious and occasionally fatal, injury, boxing will remain lawful for the foreseeable future.[36]

Boxing causes such problems for the law and for jurists because its object is to deliberately inflict force on your opponent which if inflicted anywhere else would amount to a series of unlawful batteries. Elsewhere in sport the force applied is usually incidental to the object of the game rather its sole purpose. The extent of the immunity is not unlimited. It covers only that which occurs within the normal course of the contest or within the rules, ie repeated blows below the belt or head butts would not be immune from prosecution. In this way the law has at least tried to ensure that boxing does not degenerate entirely into the prize-fights of old.

Martial arts

Whereas a properly conducted boxing match is immune from the operation of the law, the same status is not automatically granted to other combat sports. Participants in popular sports as yet unrecognised by the Sports Council are still, theoretically at least, open to the possibility of legal action arising from injuries caused in the course of a bout.[37] Sports such as these are technically a series of illegal batteries:

Law Commission Consultation Paper No 134

It has been pointed out that some forms of martial arts recently introduced into this country, including Thai boxing, kick boxing and full contact karate, may be equally or more dangerous than (traditional) boxing. Under the present law and under proposals made later in this Paper, serious injuries deliberately inflicted during such contests would appear, in the absence of an express exemption such as that enjoyed by boxing, to be plainly criminal. The legal status of these sports is thus at present controversial and we would welcome further comment about these activities. At the moment we are minded to think that they, like boxing, should be the subject of special consideration by Parliament.

---

33   (1878) 39 LT 293

34   [1993] 2 WLT 556.

35   Law Commission Consultation Paper No 139, para 12.38.

36   For a more detailed discussion of these issues see *ibid*, Gunn, M, and Omerod, D (1995); and Sutcliffe, P, 'The Noble Art', *Total Sport*, February 1996, p 92, and above, pp 108–18.

37   For further discussion see Farrell, R, 'Martial Arts and the Criminal Law' (1994) 2(2) *Sport and the Law Journal* 29 and 'Consent to Violence in Sport and the Law Commission – Part Two' (1996) 4(1) *Sport and the Law Journal* 5.

The Sports Council does operate a recognition process for both sports activities and their governing bodies, however, this is used only to decide whether they should receive funding or not. At present there is no mechanism, either legal or from the world of sport, by which sports can be judged to be lawful or not, except on a case by case basis. This can create much confusion over the status of an activity. Certain martial arts, such as taekwondo and karate, are recognised by the Sports Council. However only boxing is immune from prosecution. This leaves the martial arts in the peculiar position of being actively encouraged by the State yet open to condemnation by society for being too violent:

Law Commission Consultation Paper No 139

[Our] proposals in this paper will provide no protection from the criminal law in relation to those who cause injuries to those who consent to injury or the risk of injury in the course of unrecognised activities of the type we have described, because they will not have the protection afforded to lawful sport. We see no reason why there should be any such protection under any new regime for the recognition of sports and martial arts unless those who are involved in the activity are willing to submit it to the discipline of a recognition procedure and to achieve the designation of a 'recognised sport'. From what we have described in this section, serious attention needs to be given to ensuring that the element of risk in some of these activities is both controllable and containable and until this is done those who cause injuries intentionally or recklessly while participating in them will and should have no defence if a criminal prosecution is brought against them because they are not participating in a 'recognised sport'.

Later in Law Commission Consultation Paper No 139, the Law Commission proposes that a recognition system for lawful sports should be established:

It appears to us that if formal machinery were to be brought into existence to examine the rules and organisation of all those sports and martial arts activities in the course of which there is a risk of physical injury at the hands of another, this would go a long way towards resolving some of the difficulties that we identified in Part XII of this paper. It would also serve to meet the desirable policy aim that people ought to be free to participate in whatever sporting activities they choose, provided that the risks involved in those activities are properly controllable and containable. If the rules of a recognised lawful sport permit the intentional infliction of injury or even of serious injury, then the infliction of such injury should be sanctioned by the criminal law and it should be for the expert recognition body to ensure that such risks are appropriately controlled. Similarly, if a criminal court is faced with an allegation that serious disabling injury was caused by reckless conduct on a sportsfield, it will be very much easier for it to determine whether the risk of causing such injury was a reasonable one for the defendant to take if it has access to the rules of the sport which have been approved by the appropriate recognition body.

... [It] is our firm view, however, that if recognised sports are to enjoy the benefit of a partial exemption from the ordinary rules of the criminal law then the appropriate recognition machinery will have to be created to satisfy the courts and Parliament that the governing bodies of recognised lawful sports can be trusted to regulate their sports effectively.

As to the martial arts activities that are not at present recognised by the Sports Council, The intentional infliction of injury in the course of such activities would be *prima facie* unlawful if our present proposals were implemented unless the activity and a recognisable governing body qualified for recognition. The Central Council for Physical Recreation told us that there was no reason why such activities should not qualify for recognition if those responsible for them made an effort to comply with such requirements as were laid down by the recognition body. It considered it would be wrong to set out a list of 'recognised' types of activity in a schedule to an Act of Parliament. The recognition body would be able to look at developing rules and practices and to recognise or, if necessary, de-recognise an activity depending on whether its rules and its performances measured up to its criteria for recognition. This is also the way we envisage that the recognition body will proceed.

The effect of our provisional proposals would be ... that if people wished to continue to organise and take part in sporting or martial arts activities to which the proposed recognition body is not willing to give the accolade of recognition, then the criminal law would not extend any exemption to those who inflicted injuries on others during the course of such activities and those who were responsible for organising them might be found guilty as accomplices in any offences that were committed. Even if it is now the case that such activities qualify as unlawful prize fights in themselves, the intentional or reckless infliction of injury in the course of them would constitute a criminal offence and the present obscurity and consequential unenforceability of the criminal law in this area would be removed.

... We therefore provisionally propose that in the context of our other proposals:

> the expression 'recognised sport' should mean all such sports, martial arts activities and other activities of a recreational nature as may be set out from time to time in a list to be kept and published by the UK Sports Council (or other such body proposed by the responsible minister) in accordance with a scheme approved by the appropriate minister for the recognition of sports and the rules of a recognised sport should mean the rules of that sport as approved in accordance with the provisions of such a scheme.

The Sports Council currently operates a system of recognition for activities and governing bodies for the purpose of funding. Many of its criteria are not strictly relevant for the purpose of deciding whether a sport should be exempt from the criminal law but they could be used as a basis from which such machinery could be developed. The Law Commission would wish to concentrate on issues of safety, the avoidance of risk and the procedures in place to achieve these.

The Law Commission concludes its discussion by identifying a potential recognition body, the new UK Sports Council, which in conjunction with the appropriate Minister for Sports would develop a scheme which would determine whether a particular activity should be recognised as lawful. A court would then simply have to consult the register of recognised sports to determine the legality or otherwise of a defendant's acts. The acts would either be criminal per se if the sport was not recognised or criminal if outside of the rules of how that sport should be played.

These proposals are still being considered. If implemented they would be a major clarification of the scope of the law in relation to sport.

THE CRIMINAL LAW – AIMS

In controlling acts of sportsfield violence, the criminal law has the same aims as when it seeks to control all other forms of violence; to protect the individual from harm, to uphold the values of society and to punish perpetrators in a way which will deter them and others from following a similar course of conduct in the future.[38] Where sportsfield violence is concerned, the potential for provoking crowd disturbance is also taken into consideration. Where this latter is a possibility, players can be bound over to keep the peace as a means of controlling their future behaviour. It is not just the effect on other participants that is taken into consideration, it is the effect of the incident on society as a whole.

For example on 12 October 1996, Mark Bosnich, Aston Villa FC's goalkeeper, made a Nazi-style salute at the supporters of Tottenham Hotspur FC. The gesture was made in response to taunts from the Tottenham fans regarding an incident involving Bosnich and the German player Jurgen Klinsman when the latter was a player at Tottenham. Bosnich had not taken into account the fact that Tottenham has a large minority of Jewish fans, many of whom were incensed by the gesture. Bosnich was later fined by the Football Association (FA). The incident was also investigated by the police for public order offences.[39] Players must not only control their behaviour in relation to other players but in relation to anyone who may be affected by their actions.

The criminal law also purportedly aims at finding consistency of approach to acts of violence in all walks of life. The criminal law is supposed to treat all assaults in the same manner, whether they are committed on the field of play or in the street. This aim is rarely fulfilled where sportsfield violence is concerned.

---

38 See further, Clarkson, C and Keating, H, *Criminal Law: Text and Materials*, 3rd edn (1994), London: Sweet & Maxwell, Part 1.

39 *The Times*, 16 November 1996.

THE CRIMINAL OFFENCES

Breach of the Peace

A breach of the peace occurs where there is a threat to a person or his property.[40] The powers arise under the s 115 of the Magistrates' Courts Act 1980 and the Justices of the Peace Act 1361. After hearing a complaint, the magistrates can bind over the defendant to keep the peace. A bind over is a promise of good behaviour. A surety is paid into court either by the defendant or on his behalf where it is held for a specified period of time. If during that time the bind over is breached, either the surety is lost or the defendant can be sent to prison or both. Examples of cases involving sport follow:

R v Coney (1882) 8 QBD 534

Two men were involved in a prize-fight at which a large and noisy crowd had gathered to watch and gamble. Held, that the protagonists were causing a breach of the peace by encouraging noisy disturbances in the crowd. Further, the crowd was aiding and abetting them in that breach.

Butcher v Jessop [1989] SLT 593

Several professional footballers became involved in a goal mouth fight during Glasgow Rangers FC v Glasgow Celtic FC Scottish Premier Division match. Held, *inter alia*, that because of the history of sectarian violence between rival fans (Rangers and Celtic are traditionally Glasgow's Protestant and Catholic teams respectively), the players' behaviour was likely to cause a serious breach of the peace, in the form of crowd disturbance. Two of the players were bound over.

Common Assault

Common assault is now governed by s 29 of the Criminal Justice Act 1988 which states that it is a summary offence, ie triable only in the magistrates' courts. The offence can be committed in either of two ways; by a technical assault or a battery. Assault is an act which causes the victim to apprehend the immediate infliction of unlawful personal force. Battery is the actual infliction of unlawful force to the body of another.[41] These two offences are only used where little or no harm is caused to the victim. As a result, they are rarely used to control sportsfield violence, as where little or no injury is caused, the incident will usually be adequately controlled by either the sport's internal disciplinary mechanism or the law on consent.[42]

---

40   *R v Howell* (1982) 73 Cr App R 31.
41   *Fagan v MPC* [1969] 1 QB 439.
42   See below, p 464.

The *mens rea* for common assault is intention or recklessness as to the touching.[43] Both of these words have specific legal meanings. Intention is difficult to prove without a confession. It can only be inferred from the evidence available. After many confusing statements of the law,[44] the Court of Appeal has laid down guidelines stating how and when intent can be inferred:

R v Nedrick (1986) 83 Cr App R 267

In the context of a murder trial, Lord Lane CJ gave the following guidelines on the definition of intention:

> If [the defendant] did not appreciate that death or serious harm was likely to result from his act, he cannot have intended to bring it about. If he did but think that the risk to which he was exposing the person killed was only slight, then it may be easy for the jury to conclude that he did not intend to bring about that result. On the other hand, if the jury are satisfied that at the material time the defendant recognised that death or serious harm would be virtually certain (barring some unforeseen intervention) to result from his voluntary act, then that is a fact from which they may find it easy to infer that he intended to kill or do serious bodily harm, even though he may not have had any desire to achieve that result.[45]

Without a confession, the jury can only infer intent from the evidence and they should only infer that intent when the outcome was a virtually certain consequence of the action. This definition is in line with the evidential provisions laid down in statute:

Section 8 of the Criminal Justice Act 1967

A court or jury in determining whether a person has committed an offence:

(a) shall not be bound in law to infer that he intended or foresaw a result of his actions by reason only of its being a natural and probable consequence of those actions; but

(b) shall decide whether he did intend or foresee that result by reference to all the evidence, drawing such inferences from the evidence as appear proper in the circumstances.

Recklessness is defined as when the perpetrator of the act appreciated that there was a risk involved with his act yet went on to take that risk.[46] For battery the risk to be taken is the risk of touching the victim. This is a very problematical test to apply to sport. Every participant in a contact sport knows that there is a risk of the application of force almost every time that an opponent is challenged. Does this mean that an offence is committed in these circumstances? Often the only way that players are not guilty of offences

---

43 *R v Savage; R v Parmenter* [1992] 1 AC 699.

44 Culminating in *Hancock & Shankland* [1986] AC 455.

45 (1986) 83 Cr App R 267, *per* Lane CJ, 270.

46 *Cunningham* [1957] 2 QB 396.

every time that they play is through the concept of consent[47] and because little or no injury is inflicted.

Section 47 of the Offences Against the Person Act 1861

Section 47 of the Offences Against the Person Act 1861 states that:

> Whosoever shall be convicted ... of any assault occasioning actual bodily harm shall be liable ... to be imprisoned.

The *mens rea* for s 47 is either an intention that force is applied or recklessness as to whether force will be applied to the person of another. The *actus reus* is that actual bodily harm be occasioned to the victim. Actual bodily harm is any harm that is calculated to interfere with the health or comfort of the victim.[48] This is the most common charge for perpetrators of sportsfield violence. It can cover a wide range of injuries and in addition the requirement that the harm be only occasioned and not intended or foreseen can make it relatively easy for a participant to commit this offence. Examples of cases involving sport follow:

R v Birkin [1988] Crim LR 854

Following a late tackle in a football game, the defendant struck the tackler in the face, breaking his jaw in two places. The defendant pleaded guilty and in mitigation stated that it was a spur of the moment action, with the degree of injury caused neither intended nor expected. Held that incidents such as this could not be tolerated on or off the field. The original sentence of eight months was reduced to six months in custody.

R v Lincoln (1990) 12 Cr App R (S) 250

The victim stood in front of the defendant whilst the latter took a throw in during a football match. After taking the throw the defendant ran past the victim and said 'Nobody does that to me' and then punched the victim, breaking his jaw in two places. The defendant was convicted after trial and appealed against the four month prison sentence. Held that the spur and heat of the moment nature of the act, that the defendant was of previous good character, had been provoked, would be likely to lose his job and had been banned from playing football for a year should all be taken into account when computing the sentence. However as this was a serious matter and the provocation was only slight, the sentence would only be reduced from four months to 28 days.

R v Davies [1991] Crim LR 70

Following a collision in a football match, as the players took up their positions for a free kick, one of the players involved in the collision went up to the other and struck him in the face. Although able to play on for the rest of the game, it

---

47 See below, p 464.
48 *Miller* [1954] 2 QB 282.

was subsequently found that the victim had a fractured cheekbone. Held that it was an offence of the utmost seriousness if in the course of a game of football there should be an unprovoked and deliberate assault of this kind. As injury had resulted a sentence of six months was entirely justified.

Section 20 of the Offences Against the Person Act 1861

The *mens rea* of s 20, says that:

Whosoever shall unlawfully and maliciously wound or inflict any grievous bodily harm upon any other person ... shall be guilty of ... an offence,

in that there must be intention or recklessness as to whether force is inflicted on the victim plus at the time that the act is committed the defendant must foresee some harm as the result of his action. He need not foresee either a wound or grievous bodily harm, just some harm.[49] The result of the infliction of the force must be either a wound or grievous bodily harm. A wound is when the continuity of the skin is broken.[50] Grievous bodily harm means really serious harm.[51] Examples of cases involving sport follow:

R v Billinghurst [1978] Crim LR 553

In an off the ball incident during a rugby union match, the defendant punched the victim and fracturing his jaw in both places. The only issue at trial was whether there was consent. Held, that players are deemed to consent only to force of a kind which could be reasonably expected to happen during a game. There is no unlimited licence to use force in the game. In directing the jury the judge said that they may consider decisive whether the force used was in the course of play or outside the course of play. As a man of good character, the defendant was sentenced to nine months, suspended for two years.

R v Gingell [1980] Crim LR 661

The defendant, following an incident in a rugby union match, pleaded guilty to having punched a player, who was lying on the floor, repeatedly in the face, fracturing his nose, cheekbone and jaw. Held, that even if the original blow was provoked, there was no excuse for the following blows. The sentence was reduced from six to two months imprisonment.

R v Chapman (1989) 11 Cr App R (S) 93

The defendant's brother was involved in a scuffle with the victim following a tackle in a football match. As the victim lay on the ground, the defendant kicked him in the head, causing swelling and a laceration which required five stitches. Held, that because of the early plea of guilty, the sentence should be reduced from 18 to 12 months, with the balance suspended.

---

49 *Savage* [1992] 1 AC 699.
50 *Moriarty v Brooks* (1834) 6 C&P 684.
51 *DPP v Smith* [1961] AC 290.

The offences under ss 20 and 47 are the most frequently used to punish sportsfield violence. The cases listed above demonstrate that the courts clearly consider during-the-play violence to be a serious breach of the law. The severity of the sentence can be reduced significantly by a plea of general and more sports specific, mitigation. The general mitigation includes the willingness of the defendant to co-operate with the police, his remorse at the incident, the speed in which a plea is entered and good character of the defendant.[52]

More importantly, however, is the growing use of sports specific mitigation such as a claim that the incident took place in the heat of the moment or that the defendant experienced a degree of provocation from his victim or the fact that some degree of contact is permissible in many sports. Taken together, this means that sports cases, despite the statements of the judges to the contrary, will usually be treated less severely than non-sports cases. However it is usually only incidents that are completely beyond the scope of the game itself, which will feel the full force of the law.

Section 18 of the Offences Against the Person Act 1861

> Whosoever shall unlawfully and maliciously by any means whatsoever wound or cause any grievous bodily harm to any person, with intent ... to do some grievous bodily harm to any person ... shall be guilty of an offence.

For the purposes of sportsfield violence, only this part of s 18 is relevant. The wounding or grievous bodily harm must be caused with intent to wound or cause grievous bodily harm. Again, the main requirement is that there be an assault or a battery. As this is the most serious of the assault offences, there is a further requirement that the defendant actually intends that the result of his action will be either a wound or grievous bodily harm, not just the initial unlawful touching. Cases involving s 18 will be unusual in sport as even where the players intend to criminally assault each other, it will be a rare case indeed where they also intend to cause the very high degree of injury necessary for this offence. Examples of cases involving sport:

R v Lloyd [1989] Crim LR 513

In the course of a rugby union game, the victim was tackled. As he lay on the ground, the defendant kicked him in the face with such force that he had to spend four days in hospital with a fractured cheekbone. Held that although forceful contact within the rules was allowed, the game was not a licence for thuggery. The victim had not provoked the defendant and as on-field violence needs as much discouragement as violence on the terraces a sentence of 18 months was appropriate.

---

52 See below, p 503.

R v Johnson (1986) 8 Cr App R (S) 343

The defendant was legitimately tackled by the victim in a game of rugby union. As they grappled for the ball, the defendant bit the victim's ear lobe and tore it away. Held that despite the heat of the moment and defendant's previous good character, on-field violence needs discouraging as much as violence committed elsewhere. Therefore a sentence of six months was justified.

R v Blissett, The Independent, 4 December 1992

During the course of a professional football match, the defendant and victim both jumped to head the ball. In the course of the challenge, the victim sustained a fractured cheekbone and eye-socket, the result of which resulted in the victim being unable to play competitive football in the future. Although sent off for the challenge the defendant was cleared both by an FA inquiry and the court. The court relied heavily on the evidence of Graham Kelly, the FA Chief Executive, who claimed that this was the kind of challenge which on average would occur around 50 times per game. The defendant was acquitted.

These cases highlight the conflict present in bringing cases of sportsfield violence before the criminal courts. On the one hand, the courts are at pains to point out that sportsfield violence is just as serious as the violence committed in any other walk of life. However evidence such as that put forward by Kelly seems to suggest that if a certain type of act is committed regularly enough it will become legitimised and as such immune from both internal disciplinary and criminal sanctions.

Homicide

Homicide is the unlawful killing of a living person under the Queen's peace.[53] It can be subdivided into two distinct offences, murder and manslaughter. The distinction between these two offences is in the mens rea. The mens rea for murder is either the intent to kill or intent to cause grievous bodily harm to a person who then dies.[54] So far there have been no sports related cases which have resulted in a conviction for murder. In most sports it would be very hard to prove murder, unless something really out of the ordinary occurred.

There are several ways in which manslaughter can be committed. However the only one which is relevant to sport is constructive or unlawful act manslaughter:

R v Church [1966] 1 QB 59

[I]n relation to manslaughter, a degree of mens rea has become recognised as essential ... [A]n unlawful act causing the death of another cannot, simply because it is an unlawful act, render a manslaughter verdict inevitable. For

---

53   *Beckford* [1988] AC 130.
54   *Cunningham* [1982] AC 566.

such a verdict inexorably to follow, the unlawful act must be such as all sober and reasonable people would inevitably recognise must subject the other person to, at least, the risk of some harm resulting therefrom, albeit not serious harm.

Death is neither intended nor even necessarily expected. All that must be foreseen for a charge of manslaughter is that some injury would occur to the victim as a result of the unlawful act, which in a sports situation, will usually be the commission of either a s 47 or s 20 assault. If death results from a s 18 assault, the defendant will be charged with murder.[55] The *mens rea* for manslaughter is the same as for the unlawful act committed plus the requirement that some physical harm be the likely result of the act. Examples of cases involving sport follow:

R v Moore (1898) 14 TLR 229

The goalkeeper in a football match was in the process of clearing the ball when the defendant jumped, with his knees up against the back of the victim, which threw him violently forward against the knee of the goalkeeper. The victim died a few days later from internal injuries. In summing up the judge said that the rules of the game were quite immaterial and it did not matter whether the defendant broke the rules of the game or not. Football was a lawful game but it was a rough one and persons who played it must be careful not to do bodily harm to any other person. No one had a right to use force which was likely to injure another and if he did use such force and death resulted the crime of manslaughter had been committed. A verdict of guilty was returned.

R v Hardy, The Guardian, 27 July 1994

Following a ruck in a rugby union match, there was a brawl between the players of both sides. During the course of this brawl, the defendant punched the deceased on the jaw. The deceased fell and hit his head on the ground, which was still very hard from a recent frost. The deceased died two days later. The defendant was acquitted on grounds of self-defence, as he claimed that he only threw the punch as he was being hit from behind.

These two cases, together with *R v Bradshaw* discussed earlier, are examples of how difficult it is to succeed on a manslaughter charge. Only *Moore* was convicted. *Bradshaw* was considered to have caused the death by accident, whilst Hardy was considered to have acted in lawful self-defence. The severity of the injuries caused is unlikely to be repeated except in the most extreme of cases. However the evidential problems surrounding cases such as these will also mean that it is unlikely that the Crown Prosecution Service will proceed with a prosecution in the first place.[56]

---

55 *Cunningham* [1982] AC 566.

56 See below, p 470.

Defences

According to the provisions discussed above, every time that a participant in a contact sport touches a fellow player, a battery is committed. With recklessness being an acceptable form of *mens rea* for batteries, every time that a player consciously runs the risk that an opponent may be touched during the game, an offence is committed. This is clearly an untenable situation. If this was the usual way that sports batteries were dealt with by the courts, nobody would play sport as the risk of conviction would be too great. Sport itself would be unable to continue in the forms that we presently know it. The two defences most commonly used to charges of sportsfield violence are consent and self-defence. It is the use of the former concept that allows sport to continue to flourish.

Consent

The concept of consent is used to ensure that many minor assaults and batteries committed in sports are never considered for prosecution. Although there are no cases involving participants which give direct and detailed guidance on this issue, the case of *R v Brown*, which involved sadomasochistic conduct and two recent Law Commission Consultation Papers, numbers 134 and 139, do set out how the criminal law perceives the role of consent in sport:[57]

R v Brown [1993] 2 WLR 556

The defendants were charged with offences under ss 20 and 47 of the Offences Against the Person Act 1861. The activities giving rise to the charges involved sadomasochistic homosexual conduct. The only defence that was raised was that of consent. It was held by the House that victims cannot consent to the deliberate infliction of injuries amounting to actual bodily harm or wounding. In relation to sport and consent, the House said:

> Some sports, such as the various codes of football, have deliberate bodily contact as an essential element. They lie at a mid-point between fighting, where the participant knows that his opponent will try to harm him and the milder sports where there is at most an acknowledgment that someone may be accidentally hurt. In the contact sports each player knows and by taking part agrees that an opponent may from time to time inflict upon his body (for example by a rugby tackle) what would otherwise be a painful battery. By taking part he also assumes the risk that the deliberate contact may have unintended effects, conceivably of sufficient severity to amount to grievous bodily harm. But he does not agree that this more serious form

57 For further discussion see, Bibbings, L and Alldridge, P, 'Sexual Expression, Body Alteration and the Defence of Consent' (1993) 20 *Journal of Law and Society* 356, McArdle, D, 'A Few Hard Cases? Sport, Sadomasochism and Public Policy in the English Courts' (1995) 10(2) *Canadian Journal of Law and Society* 109.

of injury may be inflicted deliberately. This simple analysis contains a number of difficult problems, which are discussed in a series of Canadian decisions, culminating in *Cicarelli* on the subject of ice hockey, a sport in which the ethos of physical contact is deeply entrenched. The courts appear to have started with the proposition that some level of violence is lawful if the recipient agrees to it and have dealt with the question of excessive violence by enquiring whether the recipient could really have tacitly accepted a risk of violence at the level which actually occurred ... [In the present appeal] what we need to know is whether, notwithstanding the recipient's implied consent, there comes a point at which it becomes too severe for the law to tolerate. Whilst common sense suggests that this must be so and that the law will not license brutality in the name of sport, one of the very few reported indications of the point at which tolerable harm becomes intolerable violence is in the direction to the jury given by Bramwell LJ in *Bradshaw* that the act (in this case a charge at football) would be unlawful if intended to cause 'serious hurt'.[58]

AG's Reference (No 6 of 1980) [1981] QB 715

The Attorney General asked the Court of Appeal for clarification of the law relating to consent to injuries sustained in a street fight. Held that:

[It] is not in the public interest that people should try to cause or should cause each other bodily harm for no good reason. Minor struggles are another matter. So, in our judgment, it is immaterial whether the act occurs in private or in public; it is an assault if actual bodily harm is intended and/or caused. This means that most fights will be unlawful regardless of consent. Nothing which we have said is intended to cast doubt on the accepted legality of properly conducted games and sports, lawful chastisement or correction, reasonable surgical interference, dangerous exhibitions etc. These apparent exceptions can be justified as involving the exercise of a legal right, in the case of chastisement or as needed in the public interest, in the other cases.[59]

Law Commission Consultation Paper No 134

... [The] role of consent in the case of sport is different from the role that it plays in, for instance, sadomasochistic encounters of the type that were in issue in *Brown*. In the latter case, the victim has consented to a specific course of conduct designed to produce physical contact or even injury and the primary question is simply whether his consent to that particular injury is a defence to a charge of inflicting that injury. In most sports and games, however, the most that the victim has consented to is the risk of incurring a particular type of injury in the course of the game.

The best that we can do, therefore, is to say that the present broad rules for sports and games appear to be: (i) the intentional infliction of injury enjoys no immunity; (ii) a decision as to whether the reckless infliction of injury is

---

58 [1993] 2 WLR 556, *per* Lord Mustill, 592.
59 [1981] QB 715, *per* Lord Lane CJ, 719.

criminal is likely to be strongly influenced by whether the injury occurs during actual play or in a moment of temper or over-excitement when play has ceased or 'off the ball'; (iii) although there is little authority on the point, principle demands that even during play injury that results from risk-taking by a player that is unreasonable, in the light of the conduct necessary to play the game properly, should also be criminal.

Consent in sport is not expressly given. Participants do not say before taking part in a game that they accept that they may be injured as a result of playing. Instead consent is implied by a person's participation in sport. The closest legal analogy to this is the implied consent involved in everyday life. Contact with other people is inevitable simply by the social nature of our existence. These contacts are not unlawful. There is an implied consent to ordinary contact such as bumping into other people on the street, which is a part of modern life.[60] In sport this would mean that for example tackles in contact sports or blocking in basketball would all be legal because of the implied consent of the participants.

It is accepted by the law that generally players can consent to some degree of contact in the name of sport but not to the deliberate infliction of actual bodily harm or greater. Only in the fighting sports can a participant consent to the deliberate infliction of an injury causing battery.[61] Participants can consent to the risk that deliberate contact, which is part of the game, may produce unintended injuries of a serious kind. This is because although the courts have held that sport does not have a licence for thuggery,[62] they appreciate that some harm may occur accidentally in the normal course of many sports. This means that off the ball violence is rarely tolerated by the law.[63] Neither, on the face of it, will on the ball violence. There are number of practical difficulties involved with this form of sportsfield violence which will be discussed later.[64]

The result of the decision in *R v Brown*,[65] is that the rules of consent operate inconsistently in relation to sporting activities. First, boxers are immune from criminal liability, despite the deliberate infliction of injury, as long as the participants fight within the rules. Secondly in most other sports a player cannot consent to the infliction of deliberate injury although he can consent to the accidental risk of harm resulting from force applied in accordance with the rules of the game. Finally some sports such as the more modern and violent martial arts are not recognised by the law and consent does not extend to them in any form.

---

60 *Collins v Willcock* [1984] 1 WLR 1172.
61 For a fuller discussion of the law relaying to boxing and combat sports, see above p 450.
62 *Lloyd* [1989] Crim LR 513.
63 *Ferguson v Normand* [1995] SCCR 770.
64 See below, p 468.
65 See above, p 464.

Sport is treated differently from other activities as it is considered to be a socially acceptable activity, promoting physical fitness, team spirit and discipline. However it fails to address several important issues. What do participants in sport believe that they consent to? Is it as straightforward as the law considers or should it pay more attention to the playing culture of a sport?[66] Should the same rules apply to all sports? Is it still socially acceptable to allow fighting sports, where the deliberate infliction of harm, if not the aim of the sport, is still a necessary by-product of it?

In sport, serious injury is usually inflicted on the strength of implied consent to the risk of injury. The extent of a risk that a player is allowed to run is decided by the House of Lords, who give guidelines on the behaviour that they feel is acceptable to society. This method of acceptance can also mean that the legality of a sport depends on its acceptability to the House of Lords. Boxing is legal[67] though some of the more violent modern martial arts continue to find themselves outside of the law.

For this reason the Law Commission has set down a series of recommendations outlining how consent should operate in sport, alongside a more formal method of deciding when an activity should be classified as a sport.[68] Although consent can operate to ensure immunity from prosecution, its boundaries are by no means settled, neither in the sports to which it applies nor to the extent of injury to which consent may be given.

Self-defence

A person who is being, or believes that they are about to be, attacked can use reasonable force to repel the attacker. This defence can be relied upon by either the victim or somebody who is using force to protect the victim. The use of force must be necessary to prevent a sufficiently specific or imminent attack. Pre-emptive strikes are allowed; the victim does not have to wait to be hit before defending himself. The only limit on the force that can be used is that it must be reasonable in the circumstances. There is no requirement of proportionality in the response.[69] As long as the victim uses only the force that he instinctively believed was necessary to avert the attack, that will be evidence of the reasonableness of the response.[70]

The victim is judged on the facts as he honestly believes them to exist.[71] There is no requirement that the belief be reasonable, just that it was honestly

---

66 See below, p 480.

67 Parpworth, N, 'Parliament and the Boxing Bill' (1996) 4(1) *Sport and the Law Journal* 24, shows how many legislators look favourably on boxing through past involvement in the sport.

68 See above, p 453.

69 *Palmer v R* [1971] AC 814.

70 *Whyte* [1987] 3 All ER 416.

71 *Beckford v R* [1988] AC 130.

held by the victim. If the response is reasonable, the victim has a defence. If there was no honestly held belief in the need for self-defence or the force used was excessive, the defence will fail.[72] Self-defence is a complete defence to a crime resulting in the victim receiving no punishment for his actions, as it operates to legalise the act.

In sport, self-defence is only likely to be an issue in off the ball incidents. If the incident is on the ball, the defence of consent or a claim of accident will usually be more appropriate. In *R v Hardy*,[73] the defendant was acquitted of manslaughter on the grounds of self-defence. He claimed that he was receiving repeated blows to the back of the head and neck and that the only way that he believed that he could prevent further blows was to hit his assailant. The unforeseen consequences of the act did not affect the operation of the defence.

A player can use force to repel an attack which is being carried out on either himself or another player. The difficulty is in trying to distinguish between genuine self-defence and retaliation. Retaliation would appear to be inconsistent with self-defence. The former is an intentional battery, whilst the latter is a lawful act committed only because of the apprehension of danger to oneself. The problem for the criminal courts is to distinguish between the two. In the heat of the moment it would be hard enough for a referee to do this, let alone a jury many months after the incident occurred. The argument then becomes whether the players are consenting to violent responses to violent play or acting in legitimate self-defence. Without a ruling on playing culture, the courts are at present more at ease with the concept of self-defence in these circumstances.

Problems with Using the Criminal Law

Despite the gravity of injury which can be inflicted as a result sportsfield violence, comparatively few cases ever reach the courts. There are many possible reasons for this phenomenon though none as yet have been fully explored or explained. The following theories could explain why so few injured players choose to use the criminal law to achieve justice for themselves.

Not reporting the incident

The most important filter on the number of prosecutions brought, is the initial lack of reporting of incidents by the victims to the police. The reasons why victims choose not to report an incident may include the lack of severity of

---

72 *Williams* [1987] 3 All ER 411.
73 See above, p 463.

injury, as most injuries are of a relatively minor nature; that minor injuries and fouls are simply treated by the players as part of the game; that these issues are more easily sorted out on the pitch as revenge attacks can take place more immediately; that the governing body will adequately punish the perpetrator and that this form of punishment is more relevant and immediate; the victim not wanting to be seen as a complainer, ie keep the problems of the sport within the game.

Many of these issues can be seen at work in an incident involving two professional footballers, which saw a challenge by John Fashanu of Wimbledon FC cause multiple fractures of the cheekbone and eye socket of Tottenham Hotspurs FC's Gary Mabbutt. At first Mabbutt decided to take no action over the incident.[74] However he later said that he had made a complaint to the FA because he wanted to 'highlight the type of injuries that have been caused, in general, by elbows'.[75] The FA took no action over the incident as the video evidence of the incident was inconclusive on the issue of intent. No legal action was taken despite the fact that Mabbutt had seven fractures to his face and was unable to play for a full season.

This highlights that it is not just in the amateur sphere that it is difficult to prove a case. Even where there is extensive media coverage and analysis of an incident it can be impossible to prove a case, as well as being difficult to persuade the victim to be involved in an action from the outset. It is difficult for the police and the CPS to formulate a coherent prosecution policy when no significant number of complaints are made in the first place.

The police

In general, the police are more concerned with crowd control than on-field violence. Again a number of reasons can be put forward for this. First there is usually an alternative form of punishment for violent play which is exercised by the governing body of the sport concerned. Secondly the incident is often not serious in that there is neither a serious injury nor a breach of the peace. As a result of this, there is rarely likely to be a threat to the public in general or to public order and safety. Therefore the police will usually leave an incident to be penalised by the sport, rather than burden the courts unnecessarily with a large number of minor cases. This changes when there is either a serious injury or a potential breach of the peace, as can be seen from the above cases. Such prioritising of different incidents by the police, coupled with the lack of reporting of incidents by the victims, means that very few cases are ever passed on to the CPS.

---

74   *The Times,* 27 November 1993.
75   *The Times,* 4 December 1993.

The Crown Prosecution Service

Many of the same arguments apply to the CPS. If it receives very few cases it cannot form a coherent policy on them. The CPS applies the standard two stage test which it must satisfy before a prosecution will be brought against any defendant. First that there is 'enough evidence to provide a 'realistic prospect of conviction' against each defendant on each charge'.[76] Secondly that the prosecution is in the public interest.[77]

To satisfy the first test there are many evidential obstacles to negotiate. First there are problems with trying to prove the *mens rea* of the offence. Proving intent in a situation where the player appears to be playing within the rules will be virtually impossible unless the factual basis of the action is a fight.[78] Proving recklessness can be equally difficult, especially where a player is playing within the rules or where the working culture of his particular sport is especially physical, such as in ice hockey. The problem then becomes where to draw the line which establishes exactly what kind of behaviour is also criminal. Unless the incident is either off the ball or a fight, the establishment of a culpable mental state is the first major evidential problem.[79]

Secondly is the problem of who is to give evidence. Players and spectators are often biased in favour of their player whether consciously or otherwise. This can place an enormous burden on the officials as impartial witnesses. Where those present at the incident are likely to be biased the match officials can suddenly be thrust into a position similar to that of an expert witness. Too much weight could then be placed on their testimony especially as testifying is not a formal part of their role of match official. A further problem is that all of the evidence that is being given is opinion evidence. In some cases many experts are called, often of legally dubious expert standing.[80] All of these issues simply help to confuse a jury in this already difficult field.

The second test is more easily satisfied in that it is clearly in the public interest to prosecute all acts of unnecessary violence no matter where they occur. The problems inherent in most sports prosecutions are so great that a prosecution will rarely be brought. The public interest against a prosecution may include that violent players pose little threat to society; that it will overload the courts with minor cases; that it will change the nature of the sport; that there is an alternative punishment mechanism in existence; that cases are, from an evidential point of view, very difficult to prove and have a markedly low conviction rate.

---

76 The Code for Crown Prosecutors, para 5.1.

77 The Code lists at paras 6.4 and 6.5 the factors which should be taken into consideration when deciding whether a prosecution is in the public interest.

78 See the problems encountered by the prosecution in *R v Blissett*, above, p 462.

79 See the discussion on Gary Mabbutt, above, p 469.

80 See *R v Blissett*, above, p 462, especially the testimony of FA Chief Executive, Graham Kelly.

Thus even when there is enough evidence on which to base a prosecution a case can still fail to satisfy the public interest test. Violence in general is not in the public interest but when conducted as part of lawful sport, it takes on a different aspect. It then appears to be at least tolerated instead of illegal.

Guidelines on prosecution

One solution to this problem of inconsistency could be to introduce a series of guidelines.[81] These could describe in detail the type of foul play which the law would want eliminated from sport. The following could be factors which are taken into account when deciding whether to prosecute a violent player: the gravity of the injury inflicted; the type of available evidence; what charges ought to be proffered; whether certain sports or certain fixtures should be targeted as potential sources of violence or breaches of the peace.

In Scotland this has been partly achieved by the Lord Advocate issuing instructions to the Scottish Chief Constables in early 1996.[82] The instructions begin by defining the usual roles of the police and governing bodies of sport. The former's first priority at sports fixtures is to be crowd control, whilst the latter will have initial control of player behaviour.[83] They call for the best evidence, especially video evidence, to be used wherever possible[84] and for the prosecutors to take into account any punishment imposed by the governing body when deciding to prosecute a player.[85]

Where discussing the nature of the attack on a player, the instructions state only that the police should investigate an incident which is 'well beyond' that which would be considered normal play in that sport.[86] This raises a number of problems relating to on-field violence, not the least of which is the definition of what is normal play and what is well beyond it. It is also unclear who is to decide the meaning of these terms: the police or those intimately involved with the administration and playing of sport. Further on this matter is the problem of the purpose of these instructions. If they are to guide the police, they are so broadly phrased that they merely remind the police to use the discretion already available to them in any situation. If they are to control violent play, the terms are so vague that players will be left in the same position as they are currently, not knowing whether a particular incident will lead to prosecution.

---

81 For a more detailed discussion of this argument see, James, M, 'The Prosecutor's Dilemma' (1995) 3(3) *Sport and the Law Journal* 60.

82 See also Miller, S, 'Criminal law and sport in Scotland: The Lord Advocate's instructions of 10th July 1996 to Chief Constables' (1996) 4(2) *Sport and the Law Journal* 40 and James, M and Gardiner, S, 'Touchlines and Guidelines' [1997] Crim LR 38.

83 Paragraphs 1 and 2.

84 Paragraph 7.

85 Paragraph 8.

86 Paragraph 3.

These are common sense guidelines, drawing attention to off the ball incidents. They do not help where the incident was on the ball. Many serious injuries occur as the result of on the ball challenges.[87] It is here that the police and prosecutors need more guidance as to when to get involved. Where an off the ball incident is involved, action should be much more clear cut. It is the borderline cases where the assistance is required.

Inconsistency

There are three areas of inconsistency where prosecutions for sportsfield violence is concerned. These are the lack of consistency of approach to on and off the ball incidents; to similar types of incident committed in different sports and between sporting and non-sporting incidents.

On the ball incidents are virtually never prosecuted, despite the gravity of injury that can be inflicted. The evidential problems associated with these incidents results in these cases never reaching court. Most reported cases which have involved sport, are centred around an off the ball incident such as a fight. The law is much more capable of dealing with the latter than the former, as was discussed above.

Some sports have a much higher incidence of conviction than others. For example most of the reported cases involve football or rugby whereas ice hockey, despite its highly physical nature, is rarely involved with the law.[88] At the other extreme, boxing is immune from prosecution, allowing its participants to inflict injury with impunity. The problem arises because each of the different sports permits a different level of contact. For this reason the law must not only look at the rules of a sport but also to its playing culture.[89] It is only after examination of the way in which a sport is actually played that it can be decided whether or not a particular incident was a criminal assault or simply part of the particular game.

Finally the prosecution rate for sports assaults is far below what would be expected for any other type of assault. The majority of incidents are not reported to the police and those that are will rarely be passed on to the CPS. The few cases that are prosecuted receive much more lenient sentences than would the same degree of violence committed anywhere else. Players who commit acts of violence will almost without fail be given a much lower sentence than those who commit crime elsewhere. Sport is treated as an unofficial mitigating factor, whether or not it should be in the circumstances. This could send mixed messages to the public; if violence on the sportsfield will be tolerated by the law, then it will be elsewhere too.

---

87   For example, the incidents involving *Mabbutt*, see above, p 469, and *Uzzell*, see above, p 462.

88   The 1996/97 season did see a number of high profile brawls in the Super League, one of which saw the Great Britain captain, Shannon Hope, investigated by the police for an injury inflicted on Jamie Leach of Sheffield Steelers, *The Times*, 31 December 1996.

89   See below, p 480.

Effectiveness versus Symbolism

The discussion must now focus on whether the criminal law is an effective control mechanism for incidents of sportsfield violence or whether its use is merely symbolic, prosecuting only very serious injuries or the most well-known defendants. If the aim of the criminal law is to control sportsfield violence then it is failing. Incidents of participator violence are still common in contact sports throughout the country. The criminal law is used too erratically and inconsistently to be of true value as a control mechanism. This can lead to the problem that when a conviction is secured, many of those associated with the sport feel that the guilty player has been very harshly and unfairly treated, as was witnessed by the reactions of both his club and its supporters on the release of Duncan Ferguson.

Ferguson had been imprisoned for three months for head butting John McStay in a Scottish Premier Division football match.[90] In the first match following his release from prison, Ferguson played for Everton FC's reserve team.[91] A fixture such as this would usually attract around 1,000 spectators. Ferguson's return was saluted by a Scottish pipe band and banners proclaiming his innocence in front of a crowd of 10,432. For the law to command the respect necessary to control sportsfield violence, it must ensure that players who are punished are not treated as returning heroes in this way, otherwise its position as a control mechanism will be seriously undermined.

If the criminal law is not actually controlling sportsfield violence, can it be said to be having a symbolic effect on players? The answer in all probability is no. Participants believe themselves to be at little or no risk from prosecution. If they do not believe in the threat of criminal sanctions it will not affect their play. What participants are doing is reacting to a playing situation in the heat of the moment. Most players do not intend to injure their opponent; they are simply playing to win. Where the only truly considered consequence is the thought of winning, the criminal law is rarely, if ever, going to be an effective deterrent unless it takes a more defined and proactive role. Otherwise it will continue to be seen as an ineffective knee jerk response to an incident.

It could be said that the symbolism instead attaches to the law, not to sport. The use of the criminal law, though inconsistent, must take place on some level if the law is going to retain any semblance of authority over sport. Thus, although it may not act as a deterrent, it may in fact symbolise the potential power that the law can exert over sport. If the law is then to play a more proactive role in controlling sportsfield violence in the future, it can then point to a history of involvement in past incidents.

---

90 *Ferguson v Normand* [1995] SCCR 770.

91 For a fuller description of the celebrations surrounding Ferguson's first game, see *The Times*, 8 December 1995.

In conclusion, the criminal law can be seen, in its present form to be a cumbersome and inconsistent control of sportsfield violence. It appears not to be taken seriously, rightly or wrongly, by those involved in sport. When it does get involved it is considered to be arbitrary and unfair. Although nobody can argue against its use for off the ball incidents, it is not an effective control of generally violent play or violent sports.

TORT LAW[92]

The role of the law of tort is to compensate those who have suffered loss as a result of the fault of another. Tort establishes who should bear the loss, who should be compensated, how much should be paid in damages and under what circumstances. It is there to compensate those who are caused damage, either physically of financially, by the actions of another person.

Where sport is concerned, tort can be used by an injured player to receive compensation for pain and suffering caused by the injuries resulting from an act of sportsfield violence and also for lost income, whether from the playing of sport or from a non-sports related job. Tort is not generally used to punish directly the perpetrators of sportsfield violence but to compensate victims for their losses. However the natural corollary of forcing a perpetrator of violence to pay compensation to the victim is that the former is also financially punished. In this way the law of tort can be used to control sportsfield violence by the threat of having to pay a large amount of damages to the participant who has been injured.

Under English law every person's body is inviolate. It has long been established that any touching of another person, however slight, may amount to a battery, though as in the criminal law, allowance is made for the normal touchings of everyday life.[93] However unlike the criminal law, tort does not distinguish between different degrees of injury. It totally prohibits the first and lowest degree of touching. The effect is that everybody is protected not only against physical injury but against any form of physical molestation.

BATTERY

The most basic cause of action that a plaintiff can rely on is trespass to the person or battery. This is broadly the same as the criminal offence of the same

---

92 See generally, *Winfield & Jolowicz on Tort*, 14th edn (1994), London: Sweet & Maxwell, Chapter 1.

93 *Collins v Willcock* [1984] 3 All ER 374.

name.[94] The harm must be directly inflicted, ie actual force applied to the person.[95]

Following the decision in *Letang v Cooper*,[96] an action must be framed in either trespass (battery) or negligence. There is no such thing as a negligent battery.[97] The force must be applied intentionally.[98] The *mens rea* for a civil battery is narrower than for its criminal equivalent. Once the force is applied, it is undecided whether the defendant is liable for all reasonably foreseeable injury[99] or for all injuries which are the direct consequence of his actions.[100] The only reported decision on this issue is *Williams v Humphrey*.[101] The plaintiff was pushed into a swimming pool and damaged his ankle. The court appear to have held that the defendant will be liable for all the injuries resulting from the battery, even though they were neither intended nor foreseen, ie the directness test is being used.

A further possible requirement of battery is hostility. It has been held[102] that the touching must be hostile. However this has not been explained by the courts. Further it does not cover all potential batteries. Some, such as a tackle in rugby, could not be classed as a hostile as they are simply part of the game. The explanation put forward in *Collins v Wilcock* is a circular one. An act is hostile if it is unlawful, where the unlawfulness of the act depends on the accompanying hostility. In *F v West Berkshire Area Health Authority*,[103] that hostility was a part of the tort was criticised. To establish a civil battery, the plaintiff would appear to have to prove intent as to the initial touching and that the injury was a consequence of the touching, whilst there is debate over the need for hostility to also be present.

Only in very rare cases will battery be the chosen cause of action of a victim. The same problems arise here as did for the criminal assaults. It is very hard to prove intent in relation to sportsfield violence. The perpetrator of the injury will usually claim that what he did was part of the game and either unintentional or consented. In tort there is no standard of recklessness for batteries. Instead victims will bring an action for negligence.

---

94   See above, p 457.

95   *Scott v Shepherd* (1773) 2 W Bl 892.

96   [1965] 1 QB 232.

97   But see below *Williams v Humphrey*, fn 101.

98   *Wilson v Pringle* [1987] QB 237 and *Fagan v MPC* [1969] 1 QB 439.

99   *The Wagon Mound (No 1)* [1961] AC 388.

100 *Re Polemis and Furness Withy & Co* [1921] 3 KB 560.

101 *The Times*, 20 February 1975. *Winfield & Jolowicz on Tort*, 14th edn (1994), p 61 and *Street on Torts*, 9th edn (1993), London: Butterworths, p 19, n 11.

102 *Fowler v Lanning* [1959] 1 QB 426.

103 [1990] 2 AC 1.

NEGLIGENCE

Where a player seeks compensation for injury on the sportsfield, he will usually rely on an action in negligence. This means that the victim is claiming that the perpetrator dropped below the standard of care expected from other sports participants and that this negligent act has resulted in injury to the victim. The victim can claim for his injuries and any consequential financial loss. The starting point for any discussion of negligence is Lord Atkin's famous statement of the neighbour principle:

Donoghue v Stevenson [1932] AC 562

In English law there must be and is, some general conception of relations giving rise to a duty of care, of which the particular cases found in the books are instances. The liability for negligence, whether you style it such or treat it as in other systems as a species of culpa, is no doubt based upon a general public sentiment of moral wrongdoing for which the offender must pay. But acts or omissions which any moral code would censure cannot in a practical world be treated so as to give a right to every person injured by them to demand relief. In this way, rules of law arise which limit the range of complaints and the extent of their remedy. The rule that you are to love your neighbour becomes, in law, you must not injure your neighbour; and the lawyer's question, Who is my neighbour? receives a restricted reply. You must take reasonable care to avoid acts or omissions which you can reasonably foresee would be likely to injure your neighbour. Who, then, in law is my neighbour? The answer seems to be – persons who are so closely and directly affected by my act that I ought reasonably to have them in contemplation as being so affected when I am directing my mind to the acts or omissions which are called into question.[104]

From here the legal tests involved with claiming compensation for injuries on the sportsfield can be formulated. The injured plaintiff must first establish that the other players owe him a duty to take care not to injure him in the course of play. Secondly that the defendant's play was of such a degree of negligence that the duty was breached and thirdly, that the plaintiff suffered reasonably foreseeable injury and loss as a result of that injury.

When applied to sport, there are several problems with the neighbourhood test. First how badly must the game be played before a player's actions become negligent? What is the standard of care against which a player is to be measured? Secondly what must be the *mens rea* of the player towards his opponent? Finally what is the role of consent in preventing a successful action?

---

104 *Per* Lord Atkin, 580.

Condon v Basi [1985] 1 WLR 866

It is said that there is no authority as to what is the standard of care which covers the conduct of players in competitive sports generally and, above all, in a competitive sport whose rules and general background contemplate that there will be physical contact between the players but that appears to be the position. This is somewhat surprising but appears to be correct. For my part, I would completely accept the decision of the High Court of Australia in *Rootes v Shelton* [1968] ALR 33. I think that it suffices, in order to see the law which has to be applied, to quote briefly from the judgment of Barwick CJ and from the judgment of Kitto J. Barwick CJ said at p 34:

> By engaging in a sport or pastime the participants may be held to have accepted risks which are inherent in that sport or pastime: the tribunal of fact can make its own assessment of what the accepted risks are: but this does not eliminate all duty of care of the one participant to the other. Whether or not such a duty arises and if it does, its extent, must necessarily depend in each case upon its own circumstances. In this connection, the rules of the sport or game may constitute one of those circumstances: but, in my opinion, they are neither definitive of the existence nor of the extent of the duty; nor does their breach or non-observance necessarily constitute a breach of any duty found to exist.

Kitto J [at p 37]:

> ... [in] a case such as the present, it must always be a question of fact, what exoneration from a duty of care otherwise incumbent upon the defendant was implied by the act of the plaintiff joining in the activity. Unless the activity partakes of the nature of a war or of something else in which all is notoriously fair, the conclusion to be reached must necessarily depend, according to the concepts of the common law, upon the reasonableness, in relation to the special circumstances, of the conduct which caused the plaintiff's injury. That does not necessarily mean the compliance of that conduct with the rules, conventions or customs (if there are any) by which the correctness of the conduct for the purposes of the carrying on of the activity as an organised affair is judged; for the tribunal of fact may think that in the situation in which the plaintiff's injury was caused a participant may do what the defendant did and still not be acting unreasonably, even though he infringed the 'rules of the game'. Non-compliance with such rules, conventions or customs (where they exist) is necessarily one consideration to be attended to upon the question of reasonableness; but it is only one and it may be of much or little or even no weight in the circumstances.

I have cited from those two judgments because they show two different approaches which, as I see it, produce exactly the same result. One is to take a more generalised duty of care and to modify it on the basis that the participants in the sport or pastime impliedly consent to taking risks which otherwise would be a breach of the duty of care. That seems to be the approach of Barwick CJ. The other is exemplified by the judgment of Kitto J, where he is saying, in effect, that here is a general standard of care, namely the Lord Atkin approach that you are under a duty to take all reasonable care taking account of the circumstances in which you are placed; which, in a game of football, are quite different from those which affect you when you are going for a walk in the countryside.

For my part I would prefer the approach of Kitto J but I do not think it makes the slightest difference in the end if it is found by the tribunal of fact that the defendant failed to exercise that degree of care which was appropriate in the circumstances or that he acted in a way to which the plaintiff cannot be expected to have consented. In either event there is liability.

Having set out the test, which is the test which I think was applied by the county court judge, I ought to turn briefly to the facts, adding before I do so that it was submitted by counsel on behalf of the defendant that the standard of care was subjective to the defendant and not objective and if he was a wholly incompetent football player, he could do things without risk of liability which a competent football player could not do. For my part, I reject that submission. The standard is objective but objective in a different set of circumstances. Thus there will of course be a higher degree of care required of a player in a First Division match than of a player in a local league football match ...

It is not for me in this court to define exhaustively the duty of care between players in a soccer football game. Nor, in my judgment, is there any need because there was here such an obvious breach of the defendant's duty of care towards the plaintiff. He was clearly guilty, as I find the facts, of serious and dangerous foul play which showed a reckless disregard of the plaintiff's safety and which fell far below the standards which might reasonably be expected in anyone pursuing the game.

The appeal was dismissed and an award of £4,900 made to the plaintiff.

This case raises a number of important theoretical questions in relation to the proposed variable standard of care for players of differing abilities, the operation of the playing culture as a partial defence and the position of reckless disregard as an alternative standard of care. The first point that it makes is in relation to the use of negligence as a cause of action for sportsfield violence.

The negligence standard

In *Condon v Basi*, the Court applied the ordinary principles of negligence to participants in sport. The Court preferred the approach of Kitto J, where a generalised duty of care is used and all of the relevant circumstances are taken into account. a participant will be liable for an injury caused as a result of his failing to take reasonable care to avoid injuring other players. The same test will be used regardless of whether the parties are playing tennis or ice hockey. Only the relevant circumstances will change, involving the different degrees of force necessary to play different sports.

This test would appear to be straightforward in its operation. Courts are well accustomed to applying the duty of care to unusual situations. However its operation is not that simple. So much in sport takes place in the heat of the moment that it is difficult for a court to draw a distinction between simply playing the game and culpably careless play. The Court tried to make some allowance for this by introducing the notion of the variable standard of negligence but as a result of their lack of clarity, the Court simply confused this area further.

The variable standard

The first potential area of confusion that results from the decision in *Condon v Basi*, is where the court held that players in a higher league owed a higher standard of care to their opponents than did players in lower leagues. This is in direct conflict with the general test laid down in *Nettleship v Weston*,[105] where it was held that a learner driver is to be judged by the standard of the ordinary reasonably competent driver, ie all persons must be judged by the same basic standard, that of the ordinary reasonable participant in the particular activity. This aspect of the court's reasoning has since been criticised as being incorrect:

Elliott v Saunders (1994) unreported

During the course of a First Division professional football match, the plaintiff and defendant collided whilst both were challenging for a loose ball. The defendant's foot bounced off the top of the ball and came into contact with the knee of the plaintiff. The defendant's studs caught the plaintiff's knee in such a way as to cause such serious injury to the plaintiff that he was unable to continue his career as a professional footballer. The plaintiff's argument was that the defendant deliberately broke the rules of the game by going either recklessly or negligently for his legs rather than the ball and that the defendant had not exercised that duty of care owed towards the plaintiff in all the circumstances.

In the course of his judgment, Drake J found that *Saunders* had not breached his duty but had merely been attempting to make a legitimate challenge. His reasoning was partly based on the fact that the referee had awarded a free kick against Elliott at the time the challenge was made. Drake J further held that the test to be used was that of negligence in all the circumstances, as stated by Kitto J in *Rootes v Shelton* and that the variable test put forward in *Condon v Basi* was incorrect. The plaintiff's claim was dismissed.[106]

Drake J held that all participants must be judged by the standard of the ordinary reasonable player. Instead of a variable standard, the generalised duty of care is to be used. The particular circumstances of the incident, the rules and playing culture of the sport in question will then be relevant in

---

105 [1976] 2 QB 691.

106 Unreported decision of the High Court, 1994. See further, Felix, A, and Gardiner, S, '*Elliott v Saunders:* Drama in Court 14' (1994) 2(2) *Sport and the Law Journal* 1.

deciding whether or not that duty has been breached. This reasoning has subsequently been followed in another case where for the first time involving professional participants the plaintiff's claim was successful.[107]

The playing culture

The second area of confusion relates to what can be termed as the playing culture[108] of sport. At the end of the quote from Kitto J's judgment in *Rootes v Shelton* above, he mentions the 'rules, conventions or customs' of a sport. Despite its use of the quotation, the court makes no further mention of role of the playing culture theory in negligence actions. The playing culture of a sport is important because it can define the particular types of conduct that players expect from participation. It extends not only to play which is within the rules of the game but to minor infractions of the rules which are accepted as being part of the playing of the game. The playing culture could be used to define the limits of lawful conduct in a sport and the extent to which consent can legitimise certain common non-dangerous types of play.

In the course of his judgment in *Elliott v Saunders*, Drake J[109] accepts the Canadian formulation of the playing culture that 'a frequent or familiar infraction of the rules of a game can fall within the ordinary risks of the game accepted by all the participants'.[110]

Although this argument is accepted, the judge does not go on to expand it in any way as he felt that it would not assist with the case before him. His comments are obiter dicta and therefore not binding on future courts.

In other jurisdictions the notion of the playing culture of sport is well established. In the USA and Australia it is particularly well developed:

American Restatement of Torts[111]

Taking part in a game: Taking part in a game manifests a willingness to submit to such bodily contacts or restrictions of liberty as are permitted by its rules or usages. Participating in such a game does not manifest consent to contacts which are prohibited by the rules or usages of the game if such rules or usages are designed to protect the participants and not merely to secure the better playing of the game as a test of skill. This is true, although the player knows that those with or against whom he is playing are habitual violators of such rules.

---

107 *McCord v Cornforth & Swansea City*, unreported decision of the High Court, 1996. McCord received £250,000 damages for the injury that brought his career to a premature end.

108 See further, Gardiner, S, 'Not playing the Game; is it a Crime?' [1993] *Solicitors Journal* 628, Grayson, E and Bond, C, 'Making foul play a crime' [1993] *Solicitors Journal* 693 and Williams, G, 'Consent and Public Policy' [1962] *Criminal Law Review* 74.

109 *Ibid*, n 106, p 7.

110 *Mattheson v The Governors of Dalhusey University and College* (1983) 57 NSR (2nd) 56; 25 CCLT 91 (SC).

111 2nd edn (1965), p 86.

McNamara v Duncan [1971] 26 ALR 584

It was found by the court that the defendant had intentionally hit the plaintiff during the course of an Australian Rules Football match. It was argued by counsel for the defence that the blow was of the sort that a person playing Australian Rules must expect and was as such part of the game. It was held that:

> The striking was an infringement, a serious infringement, of the rules. The risk of being injured by such an act is not part of the game, if the game is being played according to the rules. But counsel [for the defendant] says that this sort of thing, even if not within the rules, is bound to happen from time to time and the plaintiff must be treated as having accepted the risk that it would happen. The thesis is that a little bit of foul play is a common, if not invariable, concomitant of a game of football (or at least Australian Rules Football) and no legal right arises in a player who is injured thereby.

> I do not think it can be reasonably held that the plaintiff consented to receiving a blow such as he received in the present case. It was contrary to the rules and deliberate. Forcible bodily contact is of course part of Australian Rules Football, as it is with other codes of football but such contact finds justification in the rules and usages of the game. *Winfield on Tort* (8th edn, p 748) says in relation to a non-prize-fight, 'a boxer may consent to accidental fouls but not to deliberate ones'. *Street on Torts* (4th edn, p 75) deals with the presumed ambit of consent in cases of accidental injury: 'A footballer consents to those tackles which the rules permit and, it is thought, to those tackles contravening the rules where the rule infringed is framed to maintain the skill of the game; but otherwise if his opponent gouges out an eye or perhaps even tackles against the rules and dangerously. Prosser in *Law of Torts* (3rd edn, p 103) says, 'One who enters into a sport, game or contest may be taken to consent to physical contacts consistent with the understood rules of the game'.

Sports and games differ in their objects and in what is expected of the actors. In the game of Australian Rules Football, deliberate injury, in the sense of something done solely or principally with a view to causing sensible hurt, is not justified by the rules and usages of the game, Sensible hurt, produced as a result of intentional acts, is on the other hand an inevitable concomitant of ordinary play.

These two extracts show how the court can develop a broad general notion of playing culture which can apply to all sports. Until the playing culture argument is more fully developed in England, the courts are left without sufficient guidelines on when a player has breached the duty of care following an incident sportsfield violence.

Reckless disregard

The main alternative theory to that of using simple negligence is the test of reckless disregard. Reckless disregard has yet to be formally accepted as a tortious standard in English law and has been expressly rejected in

Australia.[112] However in all bar one of the States in America that have ruled on this issue, it is the recognised standard for sports violence. Only Wisconsin, following the case of *Lestina v West Bend Mutual Insurance Company*,[113] uses the ordinary standard of negligence. The reason why there is so much discussion centred around this concept is the possibility that reckless disregard more accurately reflects the actual state of mind of the perpetrator of the violent act than does simple negligence.

This test was first mentioned in English law in relation to participants in sport injuring spectators.[114] It was held that a spectator accepts the risk of a lapse of judgment or skill in a competitor who is going all out to win but does not accept the risk of a participant having a reckless disregard for his safety. In *Condon v Basi*, the trial judge stated that he was not prepared to formulate a specific duty for football games but that the defendant had been guilty of dangerous foul play and having a reckless disregard for the plaintiff's safety.[115] In *Elliott v Saunders*, Drake J held that the ordinary negligence standard used in *Condon v Basi* was applicable, whilst going on to hold that the defendant was not guilty of dangerous and reckless play and was therefore not in breach of the duty of care owed to the plaintiff. Whether a new standard of care can be read into these judgments is open to discussion. Both statements are strictly *obiter dicta*, as both were unnecessary for deciding the case because the negligence standard was applied in both cases. Whilst both judges professed to be using the ordinary standard of negligence, both appear to give judgment in terms of a lower standard of reckless disregard or reckless and dangerous play, being applicable to sports participants.

It is argued that reckless disregard is a more appropriate standard for sportsfield violence.[116] The test is said to be more workable as it allows for a greater degree of culpability before liability attaches than does simple negligence. Less pressure is put on the players to change their style of play simply because of the threat of a civil action hanging over them. Players rarely intend to commit acts of violence and because most injuries come about through actions committed in the heat of the moment, with no thought of the outcome of the act apart from, for example, who is going to gain the advantage or win the game, they should have to adhere to a lower standard of care than other people, ie instead of having to fall below the standard of the ordinary reasonable sports participant, they must act with reckless disregard to the safety of their fellow players.

---

112 *Frazer v Johnstone* [1990] ATR 81–056.

113 501 NW 2d 28.

114 *Wooldridge v Sumner* [1963] 2 QB 43.

115 [1986] 1 WLR 866, 868.

116 See Felix, A, 'The Standard of Care in Sport' (1996) 4(2) *Sport and the Law Journal* 32, for a more detailed discussion of this problem.

It has been argued that reckless disregard is potentially the more workable test for sports cases as it concedes that players are often more concerned with playing the game than wondering about the possibility of legal action. If they are playing to win, it is unlikely that they are fully considering the consequences of their actions. Reckless disregard allows more leeway to players, punishing only a high degree of negligent and dangerous play as opposed to simple negligence which can be too easy to satisfy, especially in contact sports. However in reality there is unlikely to be much practical difference between reckless disregard and negligence in all the circumstances. If the latter is applied taking into account the playing culture, accepted styles of play and the heat of the moment as relevant circumstances, then sports participants are likely to receive just as effective protection using negligence in all the circumstances as the test, as they would under the doctrine of reckless disregard.

VICARIOUS LIABILITY

In the majority of injurious situations, the participant who has caused the harm will be the most obvious defendant to the action. However in certain circumstances, particularly where the participants are paid by their clubs and are therefore employees, a second defendant may be sued for the same act of the perpetrator. This second defendant will be the employer of the perpetrator and sued by virtue of the doctrine of vicarious liability.

An employer can be vicariously liable for the acts of an employee without any wrongdoing on the part of the employer. The theory behind this doctrine is that the employer is considered to be responsible for the acts of an employee who commits a tort in the course of the employment. It also provides a source from which the plaintiff is more likely to successfully receive compensation; the company as opposed to the employee.

Vicarious liability of the employer must be distinguished from direct liability. An employer is directly liable to a plaintiff when it is the employer who has committed the tort. The employer is vicariously liable when an employee has committed a tort in the course of the employment. Therefore to found a claim of vicarious liability, it must be established first who is an employee and secondly which acts are in the course of the employment.

Who is an Employee?

An employee must be distinguished from an independent contractor. The former has been described as an integral part of the business[117] whilst the latter is a self-employed person working for a business. Although this is not a perfect test, it does provide a useful starting point:

> *Ready Mix Concrete (South East) Ltd v Minister of Pensions and National Insurance* [1968] 1 All ER 433
>
> A contract of service exists if the following three conditions are fulfilled:
>
> The servant agrees that, in consideration of a wage or other remuneration, he will provide his own work and skill in the performance of some service for his master.
>
> – He agrees, expressly or impliedly, that in the performance of that service he will be subject to that other's control in a sufficient degree to make that other master.
>
> – The other provisions of the contract are consistent with its being a contract of service.

Thus a sports participant who is paid to play for a team can be considered to be an employee. If the participant commits a tort in the course of this employment with a club, the club can be held vicariously liable.

Course of Employment

To establish whether an act was committed within the course of an employee's employment, the court will first look to whether the act was within the scope of activities included in or incidental to the employment.[118] If the employee was acting for his own purposes, as opposed to for the benefit the employer, the act will not be within the course of employment. If the defendant employee has 'gone off on a frolic of his own'[119] the employer will not be liable for the damage caused:

> *Poland v Parr & Sons* [1927] 1 KB 236
>
> The question is whether the act is one of the class of acts which the servant is authorised to do ... His mode of doing [the act] was not, in my opinion, such as to take it out of the class. He was therefore doing an authorised act for which the respondents are responsible.[120]

---

117 [1952] 1 TLR 101, *per* Denning LJ.

118 *Ruddiman v Smith* (1889) 60 LT 708.

119 This phrase has been consistently used in situations of vicarious liability since the last century. It was first recorded in *Joel v Morrison* (1834) 6 CD 501, 503 *per* Parke B, and is used today to describe actions of employees that are unauthorised by an employer.

120 *Per* Atkin LJ, 245.

A participant is authorised to play the sport according to the rules or more likely to play within the playing culture of the particular game. Certain elements of foul play will be tolerated as within the course of employment if they are committed in the furtherance of the employer's objectives, ie to win the game. If the act is of a purely personal nature then the employer will not be liable. For example if a participant commits a tort when making a tackle, whether or not that tackle is within the rules of the game, the employer will be vicariously liable for the damage as the act is for the benefit of the employer and within the course of the employment. That is merely an improper method of performing an authorised act. If on the other hand a participant simply punches or attacks an opponent, he will be acting outside of the scope of his employment. The act is unauthorised and the employer is not responsible for it.

An example of when an employing club would not be liable for the actions of one of its players would be when Eric Cantona of Manchester United FC kicked Crystal Palace fan Matthew Simmons. Cantona had just been sent from the field of play. As he made his way towards the dressing rooms, he was verbally abused by Simmons. Cantona performed a kung-fu style kick at Simmons's chest.[121] This was clearly not an act authorised by his contract of employment with the club. 'The act of assault by [the employee] was done by him in relation to a personal matter affecting his personal interests.'[122]

Despite expressly prohibiting certain ways of performing in the course of employment, an employer can still be liable for an employee who acts in such a way if the act is for the benefit of the employer.[123] An employer of rugby players, for example, would still be liable for the high tackles of the employees but not for injuries resulting from fights.[124]

An employer can be vicariously liable for both the negligent and intentional wrongs of the employee. Such liability only covers improper modes of doing authorised acts, not acts which are outside of the scope of employment.

Although the doctrine of vicarious liability can enable an injured participant to sue the potentially richer employing club, it can only be applied where there is a relationship of employer and employee. This means that it cannot be used by the vast majority of unpaid sports participants in this country.

---

121 *The Times*, 26 January 1995. See also above, p 139.
122 *Warren v Henlys* Ltd [1948] 2 All ER 935, *per* Hilbery J.
123 *Rose v Plenty* [1976] 1 WLR 141.
124 See *Bugden v Rogers* below, p 514.

DEFENCES

Consent

Consent is only a defence to trespasses against the person. An effective consent is not an automatic bar to a claim in negligence. The act to which the plaintiff consents is one of a range of acts anticipated in advance of their occurrence. In tort, 'One who has invited or assented to an act being done towards him cannot, when he suffers from it, complain of it as a wrong'.[125]

The same basic rules of consent apply to the civil law as do to the criminal law.[126] Consent is implied from a player's conduct, such as participation in a sport, rather than being given expressly. There is no direct authority on the extent to which you can consent for the law of tort. However it is possible that a player may be able to consent to more injury being inflicted on him under the civil law than the criminal law, ie a participant may be prosecuted for an act that could not result in a civil action because of the victim's consent. In *R v Coney*, Hawkins J said, 'It may be that consent can in all cases be given so as to operate as a bar to a civil action; upon the ground that no man can claim damages for an act to which he himself was an assenting party'.[127]

Provided that the victim has given what amounts to a full and informed consent to the activity in question, he will be unable to sue the perpetrator for the injuries which result. It is possible that for the purposes of the civil law, as long as the victim's consent is freely given the perpetrator will be completely immune. This would apply to all sports, not just boxing.

Players do not consent to force which goes beyond that which is normally expected, even if such conduct is a regular occurrence in that sport. Nor do they consent to blows which are out of all proportion to the normal run of the game, only to those which are a legitimate part of the game or at most part of the playing culture.[128] The problem for the law is where the line between playing the game and assaulting your opponent is to be drawn. Some, but not all, conduct beyond the rules is lawful. There are no guidelines describing who is to be responsible for defining the playing culture. Only when this issue is decided can the full extent of players' consent be explored.

A further aspect of violent play which has not been fully explored is the concept of unnecessary roughness. This covers actions which are technically within the playing rules of a sport but which use more force than is necessary to achieve the intended aim. The victim can be injured, sometimes deliberately, by what is seen by the sport as legitimate force. This could in

---

125 *Smith v Baker* [1891] AC 325, *per* Lord Herschell, 360.
126 See above, p 464.
127 (1882) 8 QBD 534, 553.
128 See above, p 480.

effect give players a license to inflict injury as long as what they do is within their sport's rules. The law could clearly not sanction this kind of deliberately inflicted injury but at present it is ill equipped to deal with such incidents.

Volenti non fit injuria [129]

Volenti non fit injuria means that no harm is done to one who has assumed the risk of injury. As a modern defence it sits somewhat uncomfortably and confusingly between contributory negligence and consent. To be able to raise this defence a defendant must show that the plaintiff voluntarily assumed a risk which was known about in advance.

In *Rootes v Shelton*,[130] the court held that *volenti* operated to exclude the duty of care. This cannot be the position. Instead volenti operates to exonerate a defendant from liability for what would otherwise be, an actionable breach of duty. In the majority of sports situations, consent or contributory negligence will be more appropriate defences.

Self-Defence

The same rules apply for tort as for the criminal law.[131] A victim can use such force as is reasonable in the circumstances to prevent an attack on himself or another. Where sport is concerned, this defence is only likely to be raised for off the ball incidents such as fights. For on the ball assaults, consent will usually be a more relevant defence.

PROBLEMS WITH THE USE OF TORT

Evidential Difficulties

The evidential problems encountered in bringing a civil action are very similar to those associated with criminal actions. It is extremely difficult to prove the state of mind of a player who is caught up in the heat of the moment. Many actions will either not be brought or will fail, because of the difficulties associated with drawing a distinction between playing the game and intending to injure an opponent.

The type of evidence relied upon can be quite controversial. Where possible, video evidence is used, however, this is rarely conclusive. On the one

---

129 See further, Salmond and Heuston, *The Law of Torts*, 20th edn (1992), London: Sweet & Maxwell, pp 485–94.

130 [1968] ALR 33.

131 See above, p 467.

hand, in *Elliott v Saunders* several of the witnesses said that the position of the cameras used to film the incident gave a distorted view of the scene, making it impossible to say whether the incident was intentional. On the other, all interpretations of both the incident itself and the accompanying video are merely opinion. This can lead to many experts being called upon to analyse the incident, each giving a different and inconclusive opinion on the play.[132] In the vast majority of sporting contests where sports injuries occur, no video evidence is available and the testimony of players, officials and spectators is required. Actions are very difficult to prove, even where on the face of it, the plaintiff does appear to have a strong case.

Legal Problems

It is rare for injuries to be inflicted deliberately in sport. Actions will usually be brought under the head of negligence rather than trespass to the person. Although technically there are fewer obstacles to proving the former cause of action, there is much confusion over the state of the law of negligence and sportsfield violence.

In the field of negligence there is potential confusion over the standard of care to be used. One school of thought favours the approach of using negligence but taking into consideration all of the circumstances of the case. The other is based around the concept of reckless disregard for the safety of other players. The latter requires a greater degree of carelessness than the former and is said to suit better the sporting environment. English judges appear to favour the use of the ordinary negligence test.[133] If it is accepted that some force will be applied to participants, is simple negligence a workable standard? To establish negligence in a participant is a comparatively low and potentially straightforward standard for the plaintiff to prove. Misjudgments are an integral part of sport and the way that it is played. If nobody ever made mistakes, sport would lose one of its most interesting facets. It is also very hard to discourage negligence. No player wants to play badly or negligently; quite the opposite is true. Negligence as a control of sportsfield violence has little deterrent effect and can really only be said to be useful as a compensatory mechanism.

There is a further problem with defining the degree of force that a player can consent to in the name of sport. Players in some sports consent to a high degree of force being applied to them as part of the game. They also undoubtedly consent to some force which is beyond the rules but within the playing culture as discussed above. In England there has been very little

---

132 In *Elliott v Saunders*, see above, n 1 and p 479, 12 'experts' were called to interpret the incident, none of whom had played or officiated in the game in question.

133 *Condon v Basi* above, p 477, and *Elliott v Saunders*, see above, n 1 and p 479.

judicial discussion of this concept. Although accepted as part of the law by Drake J in *Elliott v Saunders*[134] there has been no detailed discussion of its application or definition as there has been in other common law jurisdictions.

Without further definition, the courts are left with little guidance in respect of the legality of behaviour that goes beyond the playing rules of a sport. This lack of a definition leaves unanswered several other questions such as; who is to decide the extent of the playing culture of a sport, the courts, police, players or governing body? How much violence can it allow: anything which is reasonable to achieve the goals of a game or only up to a certain level of injury? Until these issues are decided the courts will continue to have difficulty in precisely defining the duty of care for sports participants.

Finally there is confusion about the extent of the injuries which a breach of duty extends to. If the cause of action is battery and directness is the limit of damage, then you are liable for all injury resulting from any unlawful assault, even if it was part of the game. This is a problem for many sports where intentional contact is a natural, sometimes integral, part of the game. Although not within the rules, some forms of deliberate contact are such an inherent part of the way that a particular sport is played that it can be said to be part of that sport's working culture. For example, pushing in football or basketball. Technically, a plaintiff could claim for any injury, caused by any foul, rather than only for those which are reasonably foreseeable, as per negligence. Without some limitations, participants could find their personal liability to be extremely far reaching.

Procedural Problems

It has long been considered that the present system of civil justice in this country is in need of overhaul. The cost of bringing an action, the length of delay between the incident causing injury and the trial and the complexity of the trial itself, have all provoked criticism. Injuries from sportsfield violence are no exception to this phenomenon. The time from the date of injury to payment of compensation will be around four years, during which time the victim can do little but wait.

The present Master of the Rolls, Lord Woolf, is in the process of overseeing a wholesale restructuring of civil procedure. It is hoped that his proposals, contained in the Woolf Report on Civil Justice, will remedy the defects in the present system, reducing delays and making it easier for plaintiff's to bring a successful action.[135]

Problems could be raised by allowing solicitors to charge conditional fees. This is the system whereby the solicitor will only receive a fee for the work

---

134 Unreported case (1994), see above, p 479.
135 *Access to Justice: Final Report*, 1996, London: HMSO.

done on a case if the case has a successful conclusion. This may lead to solicitors taking more chances on cases with a lower chance of success, which in turn could lead to more, rather than fewer, and more complicated, sports cases coming before the courts.

All cases are complicated by the possibility of an impecunious defendant. It does not matter how good the victim's case is, if the defendant does not have the means to meet the order. If the defendant is neither wealthy, nor insured, a victim may find that a civil action for damages is simply an expensive method of establishing who was at fault.

Otherwise as with the criminal law the law of tort is potentially opening itself up to a plethora of small claims, which may be more capably dealt with outside the scope of the legal system. Until there are changes, the victims of sportsfield violence will continue to go without compensation for their injuries.

EFFECTIVENESS IN CONTROLLING VIOLENCE

Can the civil law really be said to control violence when many participants do not consider whether their actions are wrong until after the act has taken place? If participants do not consider the non-sporting consequences of their actions then the law is not operating as an effective control mechanism. Its infrequent use also suggests that in general participants do not consider the courts a legitimate forum for these issues.

More important is the problem that whereas society may feel little compulsion to punish sports violence, it will invariably feel the need to compensate those who are injured by the fault of others. Although tort may have a better claim to be involved in issues of sports violence, it is no more effective as a control than the criminal law. Both are so rarely used that they cannot be said to be effective control mechanisms for sports violence. This leads to players not even contemplating the possibility of recovering compensation for many sports related injuries. It also means that as violent players do not expect to be sued for their conduct, they are under no compulsion to change their style of play. When the law is used, there is often as much sympathy for the defendant as there is for the plaintiff.[136] As with the criminal law, it is time for the civil law to either assert its powers or allow sport to sort produce its own effective mechanisms of control and compensation.

---

136 See the discussion on *Duncan Ferguson* above, p 473.

LIABILITY OF MATCH OFFICIALS FOR PLAYER VIOLENCE AND INJURIES

Until 1996 little, if any, judicial thought had been given to the potential liability of match officials for injuries suffered by players under their control. The following case has the potential to create a massive new area of liability for officials and in all probability, coaches too:

Smoldon v Nolan & Whitworth, The Times, 18 December 1996

The plaintiff was playing in the front row of the scrum in an under-19s colts rugby fixture. During the course of the game, the scrum had collapsed what was found to be an abnormally high number of times. In colts fixtures, a special procedure for engaging the scrum was part of the rules. This was supposed to ensure greater safety for the players involved in scrums at junior levels. It was found by the court that the referee had not enforced the correct procedure for engagement and that this was one of the reasons for the high number of collapsed scrums. In one of the collapsed scrums, the plaintiff suffered a broken neck, leaving him paralysed.

The court held that the law was as stated in *Condon v Basi* and *Elliott v Saunders;* namely that the standard of care is that of negligence in all the circumstances. The duty imposed on the referee is to exercise that degree of care for the safety of the players which is appropriate in the circumstances. There are no grounds of public policy which operate to exclude liability in the case of sports officials.

The role played by the rules of the game, especially by the special rules relating to the engagement of scrums, was only evidence from which could be drawn the inference that the referee had breached his duty. The court held that the referee had failed to exercise reasonable care and skill in the prevention of collapses by sufficient instruction to the front rows and in the use of the special engagement procedures for colts.

Following this decision, a previously unexplored area of liability has been opened up. Although the judge explained that his was a decision on the particular facts of the case and not of general applicability to other levels of the sport, the effect of the decision could be that if a referee negligently allows breaches of the safety rules, as opposed to merely the playing rules, of a game then a player who is injured as a result of those breaches may bring a civil action against the referee.

The consequences of this decision are potentially very far reaching. If a referee failed to send a player off for an offence and later that player caused an injury to another, the referee could be held partly liable for the defendant committing the foul, since if he had followed the rules correctly, the defendant would not have been on the field of play to commit the foul in the first place. A further problem for referees could arise from the state of the playing surface. If a pitch was too wet, too hard or uneven and he should not have allowed the game to proceed, any player injured by the referee negligently allowing the game to be played on an unplayable or otherwise unsafe surface, could again find themselves liable for the consequent injuries.

The true extent of this decision will only be seen over time when other cases are brought before the court. This area of liability could be the most devastating for sport. The immediate outcome of the decision is that referees will want to be insured before taking to the field. Others may see the risk as too great to run just to be involved with sport. Part of the fun element will be removed from sport.

A further unexplored area which could grow from the *Smoldon v Whitworth* decision is the liability of coaches. If a referee can be liable for the negligent application of the rules of a game, then by analogy, a coach could be liable for the negligent supervision of a player or for inappropriate training methods or tactics. The greatest area for growth could be where players are asked or even forced to play whilst still recovering from injury. Any exacerbation of the injury could be at least partly the fault of the coach especially if the true nature of the injury is kept from the player to encourage him to play on. Once the law is involved in sport, as it now is, it will become increasingly hard to control it as it is applied to new situations.

SPORTS PUNISHMENTS

The last form of regulation of sportsfield violence are the various mechanisms from within particular sports themselves. There are two main systems of control within sports; those which are concerned with minor breaches of the rules and result in during the game penalties and those which involve major breaches of the rules and lead to the use of the sport's internal disciplinary mechanism. The basic aim of both forms of sanction is to uphold the rules, to make the game worthwhile to play and to protect players and sporting values. The following is a brief, general outline of how sports disciplinary mechanisms operate. It must be stressed that no particular sport is detailed and that this is simply an overview.

AIM OF PUNISHMENTS

During the Game

Match penalties are there to ensure that players play their respective sports by the letter of the rules and in the spirit in which it was intended to be played. These are instant punishments designed to deter certain forms of behaviour and to ensure that the game is played properly. The most basic form of punishment is usually some form of losing possession or points depending on the sport in question.

Changes in the laws of sports can be used to clamp down on various forms of violence within a particular sport. For example in football, changes in the rules have lead to it becoming contrary to the rules to barge the goalkeeper or tackle from behind. In rugby union, changes in the scrummage rules have made this most dangerous aspect of rugby much safer. However the laws cannot be changed too frequently as this can lead to a situation where uncertainty is created amongst both players and officials, which can lead to a decrease, as opposed to an increase, in participant safety.

Disciplinary Sanctions

The aim of internal disciplinary penalties is twofold. These sanctions are usually reserved for the more serious forms of on-field conduct and so the penalties are more severe. Disciplinary sanctions are also there to ensure that the game is played properly. They are there not only to deter those who seriously transgress the rules but also to punish them. By banning a player from playing his chosen sport or by fining him, the governing body is showing that certain forms of behaviour are not acceptable within their sport; that those who indulge in such behaviour will be punished and everyone else should be deterred from acting in the same manner as the player who is before the tribunal.

Changes in the penalties can be used to eradicate certain forms of unwanted behaviour in sport. For example several years ago in rugby league, there was perceived to be a problem with high tackling. The Rugby Football League's (RFL) disciplinary tribunal handed down a number of severe sentences to those who continued to tackle too high. The result was a massive decline in the number of high tackles and the number of injuries that occurred as a result of them.

TYPES OF CHARGE

During the Game

These penalties are simple and quickly imposed on the perpetrator. They are designed to deter future similar behaviour and to punish the offender immediately. At the bottom end of the scale are punishments which simply result in loss of possession. Punishments then increase to a free attempt to score, loss of points or the awarding of points to the opposition. Finally for the most serious on-field offences and usually combined with one of the foregoing penalties, a player may be formally warned that his conduct is seriously contrary to the rules before finally being removed from the game for part or all of the remaining playing time.

These punishments are mainly to ensure that the game flows and is played according to its rules. They also play an important role in controlling violence and other rule infractions. If a match official ensures that the game is played strictly according to the rules, all forms of foul play will be penalised. The natural corollary of this is that violent foul play will be punished and the perpetrators will be deterred from breaking the rules in the first place. They are also important in improving the safety aspect of sport by discouraging foul play. If the acts of dangerous foul play are prevented from occurring, the likely incidence of injury from foul play will also be reduced.

In field hockey a 'sin bin' is used to diffuse potentially volatile situations. A player can be sent from the field of play for up to 10 minutes as a final warning before being removed from the game altogether. In this way it is hoped that players will calm down enough that they will continue to play the game rather than be overcome by the passion of the moment.

Disciplinary Sanctions

These are entirely at the discretion of the particular governing body. They usually take the form of either banning a player from the particular sport or fining him. One problem with these sanctions can be their archaic nomenclature. Phrases such as 'bringing the game into disrepute' and 'ungentlemanly conduct' are used to describe what should perhaps be better described as brutal, dangerous or violent play.

This apparent lack of acceptance of violence for what it is can lead players to consider that what they are doing is not really violent but simply in excess of the playing rules of a game or unfair. It can be seen as the sport itself playing down the severity of the conduct. Without an acceptance that violent play is unwanted, players are not going to be deterred from repeating the behaviour in the future unless the disciplinary tribunals act to the fullest of their powers.

Some sports, such as football, have a 'totting up' procedure for their disciplinary sanctions. If a player is cautioned or sent off, his behaviour is graded on a points scale. When he reaches various points levels during the season, he will be banned for a predetermined number of games. This is a further method by which on-field conduct is controlled by the governing body, through its position as an overseer for the entire sport.

EFFECTIVENESS

Internal sports punishment is potentially the most effective method for controlling sports violence. It is a more immediate and direct form of punishment. Players play sports because they want to, whether for Corinthian or financial reasons. If their right to play a particular sport is removed, so is the opportunity to repeat the offence in the future. If they are prevented from playing, they can no longer be a threat to other players. The more often they are violent, the longer could be the ban until the stage is reached where either the player learns his lesson or he is banned indefinitely or for life.

For example in Scotland, Jason Fayers, a prop at the Edinburgh Academicals club, was banned for four years by the Scottish Rugby Union after being found guilty of foul play. The victim of his punch was required to have two metal plates in his mouth to correct his broken jaw. The length of the ban was partly determined by Fayers's previous poor disciplinary record.[137] In rugby league, Bramley's Dean Hall was banned for 15 months for elbowing an opponent.[138] Again his previous disciplinary record was taken into account when determining the appropriate length of ban. Bans of this kind are the clearest indication to the law enforcement agencies that sport is trying to get its own house in order rather than wait for the law to do it for them.

Governing bodies are quite willing to ban participants for considerable periods of time for taking performance-enhancing drugs. The only obstacle for the governing body is usually one of detecting this type of cheating in the first place. Where during the game violence is at issue, there is a much lesser problem over detection. The use of unnecessary violence is just as much cheating as the use of performance-enhancing drugs. It is arguable that violence is worse as it affects the health of other players and not just the one player in question. As both are forms of cheating, there is no reason why violence could not be punished more severely than at present even if not necessarily at the same levels as for drug violations.

Delays can be kept to a minimum if the disciplinary tribunal is efficiently run. This would ensure a clear connection between the violent incident and the penalty. This has been quite successfully achieved by the RFL in this country, where a player will be brought before the disciplinary tribunal the Thursday following the incident. In football, a wait of over a month can be expected if the player requests a personal hearing.

This length of delay can lead to players being able to 'play the system'. A player's ban can be made to fall at a more convenient time of the season for both the player and the team. For example, in the weeks prior to the English Football League's 1996 Coca Cola Cup Final, one of the footballers likely to be

---

137 *The Times,* 15 October 1996.
138 *Daily Telegraph,* 26 June 1996.

involved in the game, Ugo Ehiogu of Aston Villa FC, was approaching the number of disciplinary points for a season which would have resulted in a playing ban. He was booked in what would have been the last game in which he could receive disciplinary points and still serve the obligatory one match ban before the Final.

The match referee classified the offence as ungentlemanly conduct, worth two disciplinary points, as opposed to violent conduct, which is worth three points. This left Ehiogu one point below the banning limit, which would have meant that he was likely to pass the points level for a ban during the period which would result in his missing the Final.

In an unusual step, the Aston Villa FC manager, Brian Little, claimed that the whole disciplinary system needed looking at if the foul committed by his player was worth only two disciplinary points. It was even rumoured that Ehiogu would play a reserve team game in which he could commit a foul which would push him over the disciplinary threshold.[139] In the event, the foul was eventually upgraded and Ehiogu served his ban in time to play in the Final. However if the FA's disciplinary mechanism was more expedited than it is at present, this would never have been an issue as the player would have been banned from the day after he reached the requisite number of points. Instead players are able to play the system to an extent which will allow them to serve a ban when it is more convenient for them and their club.

A disciplinary tribunal constituted on a sounder legal basis would also guarantee players the natural justice and fairness of procedure that they would expect from a court.[140] This would extend to more appropriately phrased charges rather than the archaic nomenclature currently used by most governing bodies.

The major problem with disciplinary tribunals is that many of them are ineffective and underused at present. Bans are often too short, fines are too small and players continue to act as they always have done. Additionally the different tribunals have vastly different procedures even within the same sport. If a player participates in a number of sports, he is likely to come across a variety of different procedures all of which will look on a particular form of violence in a different way. The lack of consistency within the same sport and throughout sport as a whole is the main obstacle to sports disciplinary tribunals playing an even greater role in the controlling of sportsfield violence.

In the US, this led to the Sports Violence Act of 1980 being introduced before Congress.[141] Its aim was to 'deter and punish, through criminal penalties, the episodes of excessive violence that are increasingly

---

139 See further, *The Times*, 5 March 1996.

140 See further above, Chapter 4.

141 126 Cong Rec E3711–12 (daily ed, 31 July 1980). See also, Langevin, M, 'A Proposed Legislative Solution to the Problem of Violent Acts by Participants during Professional Sporting Events: The Sports Violence Act of 1980' (1981) 7 *University of Daytona Law Review* 91.

characterising professional sports'. The maximum penalty would have been a $5,000 fine; the Act would only have applied to professional sports and would have been federal, thus avoiding the problems of enactment in separate State jurisdictions. Although it never became law, the Act does highlight the potential for interference in sport by the law, if sport does not treat incidents of violence with sufficient seriousness.

LEGAL STANDING OF SPORT'S PUNISHMENTS – THE RELATIONSHIP BETWEEN DISCIPLINARY AND LEGAL SANCTIONS

In England there is no formal relationship between criminal law punishments, tortious compensation and a sport's internal disciplinary mechanism. This lack of guidance can lead to serious problems for the perpetrator of a violent act committed on the field of play. A participant can face some form of disciplinary action from any of the following bodies: the criminal law, the civil law, the match official, his club, the national team and the governing body. Even in Scotland, where there are guidelines as to when the criminal law should be used, there is nothing to say whether any of the other forms of control could or should also be resorted to. The only mention made of the tribunal's concurrent jurisdiction in the Lord Advocate's instructions states that the Procurator Fiscal should take into account any sports related punishment that the player has received when deciding whether to also prosecute.[142]

This problem of double jeopardy is great. It is a problem which is also present in other professions, such as the medical and legal professions, where an internal tribunal can punish a wrongdoer as can the courts. However it is sport where those punished seem to complain the most about the operation of two concurrent punishment mechanisms.

Receiving more than one punishment can lead to a feeling of injustice amongst a player's club and its supporters. Before Duncan Ferguson's appeal to the Scottish Football Association (SFA) against his 12 match ban for butting a fellow player, his lawyer Blair Morgan said, 'Our case will be based upon the belief that Duncan has been punished once [by the criminal courts] already and that to impose a second form of punishment would be very unfair'.[143] After the appeal was dismissed, the Everton FC chairman Peter Johnson summed up the feeling at the club by saying, 'Even muggers don't get punished twice'.[144]

---

142 Paragraph 8.
143 *The Guardian*, 7 November 1995.
144 *The Guardian*, 9 November 1995.

These statements clearly show the Everton club's view on the subject. It was unfair for the player to be punished twice. This was not the view of the court. Although the ban was later overturned, it was not on the grounds of double jeopardy but because the SFA had not applied its own rules correctly when punishing Ferguson. As far as the courts are concerned, the criminal law operates in all of society's activities and the additional punishment is the one imposed by a private body which has no effect on the operation of the law.

The problem remains for players who are eventually acquitted by the courts. Which action should be taken first? The disciplinary tribunal's action, which is fairly swift, or the legal action, which can take many months to get to court, and how should the different mechanisms interact to be the most effective way of controlling violence? If the higher criminal standard of proof is not satisfied should a player still be disciplined by his sport, as was William Hardy? Hardy was banned by the Middlesex Rugby Football Union for 120 days for retaliating. Although the ban was imposed retrospectively, so that Hardy did not miss any further games, it is still registered against his name for an incident in which the law considered him to have acted in lawful self-defence.

A further problem in this area concerns the extraterritorial nature of some governing bodies' powers. They are able to impose penalties for misconduct that has no connection with the playing of the particular game. Not only are the players subject to double jeopardy but they are also being punished by a body that has extremely wide powers of control over their non-sporting life too.[145]

In general a governing body's decisions are not susceptible to judicial review. This is because the law treats domestic sporting activities as private activities. Only public activities and bodies are susceptible to actions of judicial review. Once the governing body has ruled that a player should be fined or banned, he cannot appeal against that decision in the ordinary courts, only in the internal appeals structure.[146] In Scotland, Duncan Ferguson[147] successfully challenged the validity of the ban handed down to him by the SFA. Under the SFA's regulations, bans could only be handed down in addition to penalties given by the referee. Ferguson's action was unseen by the referee and consequently went unpunished during the game. There was no punishment for it to be additional to and the 12 match ban was *ultra vires* and overturned.

This is a very rare example of judicial interference with a governing body's decision. Although the courts were willing to hear Ferguson's action, it was

---

145 See above, Chapter 1.

146 See above, Chapter 4.

147 *Ferguson v SFA*, unreported, 1995. See also Duff, A, 'The Road to Consistency' (1996) 4(1) *Sport and the Law Journal* 15.

only in relation to the fact that the SFA had not followed its own procedure. If he had been claiming that the punishment was unfair or too long, it is unlikely that the court would have interfered with the exercise of a private body's internal powers.[148]

A further problem could exist if English courts declared unlawful the rules of an international sport. This could lead to different rules being used in different countries or in the case of the UK, in different parts of the same country. Although the declaration of an established sport's rules as unlawful is highly unlikely, as boxing has shown on numerous occasions, it could lead to some modern sports not being granted lawful status in this country.[149]

ALTERNATIVE PROCEDURES

Legal Recognition of Disciplinary Tribunals

If the disciplinary tribunals were to operate within a formally recognised legal structure, with powers either established through a statute or an extension of the power of judicial review, then all sports tribunals would have to follow a legally sound procedure. The penalties that they hand down would then have a better legal grounding. They would also be susceptible to judicial review. This would provide players with an important safeguard in that when disciplinary tribunals were exercising their increased powers they would have to do so within a strict set of legal criteria. Those that failed to follow these criteria would have their decisions overturned on appeal, either internally or to the High Court.

A Sports Court?

The idea of a dedicated Sports Court has received some support, though more from American than British writers.[150] It would operate as a specialist tribunal along the lines of, for example, the Employment Appeals Tribunal. However it could create as many problems as it solves. It would raise questions such as what actions would it have jurisdiction over, who would fund it and who would sit on it. A dedicated sports court could be an effective form of alternative dispute resolution but from a practical point of view, the argument is not very convincing.[151]

---

148 *Law v National Greyhound Racing Club Limited* [1983] 3 All ER 300.

149 See the discussion above, p 453, relating to the legality of martial arts.

150 See, Langevin, M, *ibid*, n 5 and DiNicola, R and Mendeloff, S, 'Controlling Violence in Professional Sports: Rule Reform and the Federal Sports Violence Commission' (1983) 21 *Duquesne Law Review* 843; and below, Chapter 11.

151 See Chapter 4.

CONCLUSION

Injuries from violence in sport are a perennial problem. For years they were treated as part of the game, whether they were deliberately inflicted or not. Now a combination of increased financial rewards and greater awareness of legal rights means that participants are more willing than ever to take action over injuries which are the result of someone else's fault.

There are only three mechanisms that sports participants can presently use to control sportsfield violence; the criminal law, tort law and disciplinary tribunals. None of these are particularly well adapted to cope with issues of sports violence. None of them are used to their full potential. They are often clumsy and inefficient, overlap with each other and produce injustices for the victim and perpetrator alike. This position needs formalising so that injuries are properly compensated and violent players effectively and consistently punished. The remedies and punishments available following these types of incidents are considered in the next chapter.

CHAPTER ELEVEN

THE LEGAL AND NON-LEGAL REMEDIES AND CONSEQUENCES OF SPORTSFIELD VIOLENCE

This chapter explores the issues that arise following an incident of sportsfield violence. It examines the different types of punishment that a perpetrator may receive and the different ways in which an injured player may try to claim compensation. The chapter will work through the criminal law and the solutions that it proposes, civil law issues of negligence and battery and the degree of compensation that an injured player may receive, as well as the powers of punishment that can be exercised by a typical governing body. A brief analysis of the different forms of insurance currently available to sports participants will be made, before finally examining several comparative approaches to how players can be compensated for the injuries they suffer during a game.

WHY DO PLAYERS NEED TO GO TO COURT TO CLAIM COMPENSATION?

The first issue to be discussed in relation to injured players receiving compensation for their injuries, is why resort to such a long and complex method such as the law in a situation where there is a high degree of probability that some form of injury or another will be received by participation in sport? The types of injury and risk thereof vary from sport to sport, for example pulled muscles in all sport, crashes in motor sport and fractures in contact sports. A risk of injury is present by participation in almost all sport. The question why do players need to go to court to claim compensation, can be answered in two sections: whether a sports participant is an employee and whether or not the participant is insured.

EMPLOYEE STATUS

In most situations where an employee is injured in the course of his or her employment, the employer must have insurance cover to compensate the injured party for their injuries. The Employer's Liability (Compulsory Insurance) Act 1969 imposes a duty on almost all non-public employers to take out and maintain a policy of insurance against liability for bodily injury and disease sustained during the course of the employee's employment. The Act applies to sports clubs as it does to all other employers. The injured person must simply show that they were an employee injured in the course of their employment.[1]

Further duties are imposed on the employer at common law, creating liability where a safe system of work is neither provided nor operated by the employer.[2] The Health and Safety at Work Act 1974 imposes a generalised duty on employers to ensure as far as is reasonably practicable the safety of their employees. This Act allows for regulations to be passed to cover specific situations such as the operation of machinery.[3]

Where sportsfield violence is at issue, this type of civil action is often inappropriate. The perpetrator of the injury, the opposing player, is not under the control or management of the injured player's employer. By analogy to the industrial employers type of liability, it is not one of the injured player's employer's machines that has caused the injury but that of another employer. Thus the most common route for recovering compensation for workplace related injuries is closed.

There is a further problem over the definition of who is a worker where sports participants are concerned. This problem is compounded by the high number of low paid, part-time participants in many sports. Are these players also to be classed as workers and if so what rights do they have?[4]

The final problem with employer's liability related claims is that the vast majority of all sports participants in the UK receive no payment at all. They are either amateurs or simply compete for fun or leisure purposes. This category of participants are clearly not employees of any description. They will have to pursue an alternative cause of action to receive compensation.

INSURANCE STATUS

The closest to a guarantee of receiving compensation for injuries suffered on the sportsfield is through insurance. The different available schemes are discussed in more detail later in this chapter.[5] The most important problem related to insurance and sportsfield injuries is that very few participants ever take out a policy. Those that do are often inadequately covered. If a participant cannot claim compensation from his employer and is not covered by a policy of insurance, he is left with only one realistic option, the law. The only reasonable methods by which participants can receive compensation for their injuries is through either the criminal courts or by one of the traditional tort causes of action, negligence or trespass to the person.

---

1   See above, Chapter 7.

2   *Bux v Slough Metals* [1974] 1 All ER 262.

3   Section 47(2).

4   For more detail, see above, Chapter 7.

5   See below, p 523.

CRIMINAL LAW – PUNISHMENTS

The sentences available to a court following the conviction of an offender are supposed to be calculated following the same criteria for all offences regardless of whether the assault was committed on the sportsfield or not. There is still a great deal of inconsistency between how sports crimes and 'real life' crimes are treated. An offence committed on the sportsfield will be treated with a degree of leniency not otherwise shown to violent offenders.

The fact that an offence was committed during the course of a sports fixture is not formally acknowledged as a mitigating factor in sentencing. Offences was committed as the result of a momentary loss of self-control or in the heat of the moment is discussed more fully below. Perhaps more important to the discussion is the fact that a sportsfield offender will receive a lower sentence than that imposed on any other type of offender. Despite the gravity of the injuries often inflicted, the sportsfield offender will generally receive a sentence of around a third of that imposed on other offenders. The following are examples of the kind of sentence that a sportsfield offender might expect to receive:

R v Lloyd (1989) 11 Cr App R (S) 36

Kicked a prone player in the face in a rugby union match, fracturing his cheekbone. Convicted of causing grievous bodily harm with intent. Sentence: 18 months' imprisonment.

Attorney General's Reference (No 27 of 1983) (1994) 15 Cr App R (S) 737

Head butted an opponent in a football match, shattering his cheekbone and eye socket and causing a laceration to his face. Pleaded guilty to causing grievous bodily harm with intent. Sentence: six months' imprisonment.

R v Chapman (1989) 11 Cr App R (S) 93

Kicked a prone player in a football match, causing swelling and a laceration. Pleaded guilty to unlawful wounding. Sentence: 12 months' imprisonment, with a further six suspended.

R v Shervill (1989) 11 Cr App R (S) 284

Kicked a prone player in a football match, causing a wound that required stitching. Pleaded guilty to unlawful wounding. Sentence: two months' imprisonment.

These cases and those below show that there is a considerable degree of inconsistency between how the courts treat different cases of sports violence. Sentences are not particularly lengthy, with 18 months being the longest term of imprisonment imposed. In the first two of the cases listed below, the assaults took place in similar circumstances, two players both threw punches at opponents, causing similar serious injuries. Both defendants also ran similar defences to their charges. In one case the defendant was eventually sentenced to four months' imprisonment, whilst in the other, a mere 28 days in prison was the final verdict. The courts seem to believe that violence in sport should be regarded as criminal but not too criminal.

The following arguments have been put forward to justify either a less severe sentence or an acquittal following prosecutions for on-field violence. These arguments are often submitted by the defence as mitigating circumstances and could go some way to explain the generally low sentences imposed by the courts.

Seriousness of the Injury Neither Intended nor Expected

R v Birkin [1988] Crim LR 854

The appellant had been playing football when an opponent made a late tackle on him. After the tackle, the appellant ran a few steps with the victim before striking him with a blow which broke his jaw in two places. The appellant pleaded guilty to assault occasioning actual bodily harm and was sentenced to eight months' imprisonment.

On appeal, it was held that violence such as this, whether on or off the field of play, must result in an immediate custodial sentence. However as the incident had taken place *on the spur of the moment* and that *the seriousness of the injury was neither intended nor expected,* the sentence should be reduced to six months (emphasis added).

Actions in the Heat of the Moment

R v Lincoln (1990) 12 Cr App R (S) 250

The appellant and victim were on opposing sides in a football match. As the appellant went to take a throw in, the victim took up a position directly in front of the appellant to restrict his ability to throw the ball as far. The appellant took the throw in and after running a few paces together said to the victim 'Nobody does that to me' and punched the victim, breaking his jaw in two places. The appellant was found guilty of assault occasioning actual bodily harm and sentenced to four months imprisonment.

On appeal, it was accepted by the court that there was *only one blow* and that was *struck on the spur of the moment and in the heat of the moment.* It was also accepted that the appellant had suffered a *momentary loss of control in circumstances where he had considered that he had received a degree of provocation.* As such, the court reduced the sentence to one of 28 days' imprisonment[6] (emphasis added).

---

6   See also *R v Birkin,* above.

Imposition of a Playing Ban where the Incident Occurred during Actual Play

R v Goodwin (1995) 16 Cr App R (S) 885

The incident took place during an amateur rugby league match. The victim was running towards the appellant with the ball. Just before reaching him, the victim chipped the ball over the appellant's head. The victim went to run past the appellant to retrieve the ball. However instead of tackling the victim, the appellant elbowed him in the face, causing him to suffer a fractured cheekbone which extended to the jaw, a fractured palate and two fractured molars. The appellant was convicted of inflicting grievous bodily harm and was sentenced to six months' imprisonment.

The court held that an important consideration is *whether the criminal violence occurred at or about the time that one or other of the parties was playing the ball*. Clearly, if the assault occurred then rather than when the ball was being played elsewhere on the field it may be possible to take a less serious view of the offence as in such circumstances, the claim that the seriousness was unintentional and unexpected may be made with more justification.

Further, *as the appellant had been prohibited from playing rugby league for 14 months and had thereby lost an opportunity to play the game professionally*, the sentence was reduced to one of four months' imprisonment (emphasis added).

Involuntary Reflex

The only reported use of the 'involuntary reflex' defence is in an American case. However, with the similarities between the English and American legal systems, it is worthy of consideration:

State v Forbes No 63280 (Minn Dist Ct, dismissed 12–9–75)

The defendant and victim were both professional ice hockey players in America's National Hockey League. Following an on-ice fight, both were sent to the penalty box or sin bin for seven minutes. On returning to the ice at the completion of the penalties, angry words were exchanged. The defendant then hit the victim in the face with the butt end of his stick. The stick caught the victim in the right eye and caused him to fall to the ice. The defendant then jumped on to the victim and continued to punch him and pummel his head on the ice until another player pulled them apart.

The victim suffered a fractured eye socket and required 25 stitches to close facial cuts. He later required further surgery to correct double vision. The defendant was charged with aggravated assault by use of a dangerous weapon.

At trial, the defendant raised the defence of *involuntary reflex*. The basis of this defence was that as ice hockey players are trained from a very early age to use violence as part of the game strategy, *such violence when used is an instinctive reflex action.* There can therefore be no criminal assault as the necessary *mens rea* is missing. The jury was hung 9–3 in favour of prosecution and a mistrial was declared. The defendant was not retried (emphasis added).

This defence has not yet been used during a British trial. If it can be considered to be a species of automatism,[7] then the law could be faced with a serious problem of having to judge not only the acts of a player but the training methods and game strategies of an entire sport.

Self-Defence

Self-defence is will usually only be a defence to off the ball assaults. As far as on the ball assaults are concerned, use of self-defence may look more like retaliation as opposed to trying to prevent further attack on oneself:

R v Hardy, The Guardian, 27 July 1994

Following a ruck in a rugby union match, there was a brawl between the players of both sides. During the course of this brawl, the defendant punched the deceased, knocking him out. The deceased fell and hit his head on the ground, which was still very hard following recent frosts. The deceased died two days later. The defendant was charged with manslaughter.

The prosecution alleged that the defendant had joined in a free-for-all, during which he had deliberately punched the deceased. The defendant claimed that after seeing team-mates be hit and after receiving at least two blows to the back of his head he had struck out at his assailant in *self-defence.* He had lashed out at whoever was attacking him from behind but only *for his own protection.*

The jury returned a verdict of not guilty (emphasis added).

CRIMINAL LAW – COMPENSATION

There are two mechanisms available to an injured sports participant within the criminal law which can enable him to receive compensation. The first, the Criminal Injuries Compensation Scheme, allows for an award of compensation on proof by the victim that the injuries suffered were the result of a crime of violence. The second, the compensation order, can be awarded by the trial court on conviction of the offender.

---

7   Automatism is the state where an act is not willed or committed voluntarily, by the defendant. See also, *Bratty v AG for Northern Ireland* [1963] AC 386, *per* Lord Denning, 409.

CRIMINAL INJURIES COMPENSATION SCHEME

Background

The following is a brief outline describing the circumstances in which a claim can be made under the Criminal Injuries Compensation Scheme (CICS) and the basic procedure which must be followed.[8] The CICS is a State run compensation system for the physically injured victims of crimes of violence. It does not extend to compensation for purely property damage. The CICS provides compensation for the blameless victims of crimes of violence whose potential civil claims are, effectively, worthless either because the offender is unknown or has insufficient means to pay compensation or against whom there is insufficient evidence to secure a conviction. The CICS applies to sportsfield violence as it does to all victims of violent crimes.

State compensation for criminal injuries began in 1964. Over the years it has been refined and developed. Originally compensation awards were based on the common law scales applicable in tort cases. This has now been replaced by an enhanced tariff scheme which is in statutory form. The Criminal Injuries Compensation Act 1995 states the law as it applies to all claims received by the Criminal Injuries Compensation Authority (CICA) after 1 April 1996. It is the new procedure under the Act which will be examined below.

Application Procedure

If a victim considers that their injuries were the result of a crime of violence, they must complete a claim form and return it to the CICA. The application must give details of the offence committed, together with whether and how the circumstances were reported to the police; the extent of the injuries suffered and the treatment received; loss of earnings and other expenses; and particulars of any previous claims made to the Authority.

The application is dealt with by a claims officer, whose first job is to decide whether the applicant is eligible for a payout. In coming to this conclusion, the officer will have to decide whether the injury was the result of a crime of violence and check that the applicant has followed the rules relating to the application procedure, most especially whether the incident was reported to the police. If the applicant is eligible, the officer then decides the applicable tariff for the injuries suffered. A payout can then be made.

To be eligible, the applicant must have suffered personal injury, either physical, mental or a disease, from a crime of violence. Although there is no definition of a crime of violence, the implication from the decided cases is that

---

8   For a more detailed review of the operation of the Scheme see, Miers, D, *State Compensation for Criminal Injuries*, 2nd edn (1997), London: Blackstones.

there must be an unlawful physical act by the offender that causes injury to the applicant. The burden of proof of these issues lies with the applicant, who must be able to prove his case on the balance of probabilities ie to the civil, not the criminal, standard of proof. Neither a prosecution nor a conviction are necessary preconditions of an award, though obviously their existence may assist the applicant greatly.

For an application to be successful, the applicant must also satisfy four further conditions. First the application must be made within two years of the incident which gave rise to the criminal injury. Secondly the award must be for a total amount of compensation in excess of the minimum level, currently £1,000. Thirdly the applicant must without delay take all reasonable steps to inform the police of the circumstances of the injury, co-operate with them in bringing the offender to justice and give all parties concerned with the application all reasonable assistance with the application. Finally, the applicant's conduct before, during and after the injury causing incident can be taken into account when deciding whether the applicant is deserving of an award or whether the award ought to be reduced or denied. In relation to this last condition the most relevant conduct is whether the applicant has any previous convictions. This is to ensure that the applicant is 'deserving'. In respect of a CICS payout, deserving effectively means that the applicant has not brought the injury upon himself by, for example, keeping company with known violent criminals.

The amount of compensation payable is determined by examining the tariff of injuries appended to the CICS. This details 310 injuries and the amounts payable to those who have received them. If an applicant is off work for more than 28 weeks as a result of the criminal injury, he can further claim for lost earnings and any additional medical treatment.

Where an applicant disagrees with any of the findings of the claims officer, the application will be reviewed by a more senior officer. If there is further disagreement, the applicant can appeal to the Criminal Injuries Compensation Appeals Panel. If the appeal concerns an application made outside of the two year limitation period or whether an old claim ought to be reopened because, for example, the applicant's condition has deteriorated, the appeal is made on the documents alone. If the appeal concerns a dispute over the value of the compensation award, there will be an oral hearing, during which the claim will be heard afresh before two members of the Panel. The procedure at an oral hearing is kept as informal as possible to ensure that all parties are better able to understand the proceedings.

The main problem for the victims of sportsfield violence in making a claim under the CICS is their reluctance to bring the police into any incident. As seen above, the applicant must co-operate with the police and prosecuting authorities when making an application. In sport, it will usually be relatively straightforward to determine the identity of the offender. If the applicant does not co-operate with the police on this issue, then his claim is doomed.

COMPENSATION ORDERS[9]

Section 35 of the Powers of Criminal Courts Act 1973

(1) ... [A] court by or before which a person is convicted of an offence ... may ... make an order requiring him to pay compensation for any personal injury, loss or damage resulting from that offence ... or to make payments for funeral expenses or bereavement in respect of a death resulting from any such offence ... and a court shall give reasons, on passing sentence, if it does not make such an order in a case where this section empowers it to do so.

(1)(a) Compensation under subsection (1) above shall be of such amount as the court considers appropriate, having regard to any evidence and to any representations that are made by or on behalf of the accused or the prosecutor ...

(4) In determining whether to make a compensation order against any person and in determining the amount to be paid by any person under such an order, it shall be the duty of the court:

(a) to have regard to his means so far as they appear or are known to the court.

A compensation order can be made in respect of any personal injury suffered as a result of a criminal offence, following the conviction of the offender. In the magistrate's court, the maximum amount payable in compensation is limited to £5,000 per conviction.[10]

To be eligible for a compensation order, a victim must supply detailed information of his losses and especially the injuries that he suffered.[11] Depending on the size of the compensation awarded, the judge will usually either follow the tariff in the CICS or the Judicial Studies Board Guidelines.[12] When making a compensation order, the court should disregard any potential CICS claim, as any award made under the Scheme will be reduced to reflect the award made by way of a compensation order.

Compensation orders should only be made if it is realistic that the offender has the means available or will have such means, to pay the compensation within a reasonable period of time. The period during which the compensation order should be paid, if being paid by instalment, can be as long as two years or three in exceptional circumstances.[13]

---

9   See further Archbold, *Pleadings and Procedure* (1997), London: Sweet & Maxwell, sections 5–369.

10   Section 40 of the Magistrates' Courts Act 1980.

11   *R v Cooper* (1982) 4 Cr App R (S) 55.

12   The 'Guidelines on the Assessment of General Damages in Personal Injuries Cases' are the official guidelines used by judges to determine the amount of damages in personal injury cases.

13   *R v Olliver & Olliver* (1989) 11 Cr App R (S) 10.

The rationale behind compensation orders is that it allows the trial court to determine quickly the question of compensation for the injured victim, without the need for any further rehearing. An offer of compensation from the offender also allows him the opportunity to be seen to be expressing some remorse for his actions. The main drawback with compensation orders, for a victim, is that, unlike tortious damages or a CICS award, they are means tested. Whereas damages calculated under the law of tort and CICS compensation awards are based on the gravity of the injury inflicted on the victim, the criminal courts will also look to the ability of the defendant to pay the compensation order. This can lead to a dramatic reduction on the size of any award. However the possibility of a CICS award can still be explored by the victim.

PROBLEMS INHERENT WITH PURSUING A CLAIM THROUGH THE CRIMINAL LAW

For a victim seeking compensation through the criminal law procedures, there are a number of problems to be overcome before an award can be made. From a practical point of view is the basic fact that a lower amount of compensation is payable through the two criminal law procedures. From a procedural point of view, there is the difficulty that to receive a compensation payout, a victim must be prepared to proceed with a prosecution against the offending sports participant.

Undervaluation of the Compensatory Award

When a victim seeks compensation for a sportsfield injury, he will receive different sums depending on which compensatory mechanism he uses. In most cases, the highest award would come from a successful tort action against the perpetrator, as in the civil law, there are very few limits on the type of loss that an injured victim can claim for.

The two criminal mechanisms will both lead to lower payouts, though for different reasons. The CICS award will usually be the second highest of the claims. The tariff award is based on payments made on the common law scale, which includes a small percentage in relation to lost earnings. However a victim cannot claim for lost earnings or medical expenses until he has spent at least 28 weeks away from work. The victim is further debarred from claiming for damage to any property caused by the crime. In a civil claim, the victim would be able to claim medical and earnings related losses from the date of the injury, as well as compensation for any property damage caused.

The main drawback of the compensation order is that it is means tested as against the offender. Although a civil award can be said to be means tested in as much as if the defendant does not have the money he cannot pay, where a compensation order is concerned, the defendant's lack of funds will mean that the victim may receive well below the compensation award that could be expected from either of the other two sources. Thus, although the criminal law mechanisms do at least provide a degree of compensation for a victim, it is much less than could be expected from a traditional tort payout or insurance claim.

Co-operation with the Prosecuting Authorities

The second problem with claiming compensation through the criminal law mechanisms, is the requirement that the victim cooperate fully with the prosecuting authorities. It is a condition of any CICS claim that the victim both reports the crime of violence to the police and cooperates, where appropriate, with the investigation of the incident and the prosecution of the offender. This requirement is even more obvious in relation to a compensation order, which is only available following the conviction of the offender.

Cooperation with the authorities can be a problem for a victim in a situation where, for example, there is an on-going relationship with the offender. In sport, this could be where the two parties play in the same league and will play against each other on a regular basis. Other victims, although aggrieved at their injuries and wanting compensation, do not feel that the criminal law is an appropriate mechanism to resolve their dispute. This could be either because it is felt that the use of the criminal law is too severe a punishment or that the dispute could be more effectively resolved by the governing body or by the participants themselves during the present or a later, game.

Whichever way it is viewed, participants in sport rarely use the compensation mechanisms available to them through the criminal law. Many would rather forego the chance of compensation than bring a criminal action against a fellow participant.

COMPENSATION UNDER THE LAW OF TORT[14]

There are a number of remedies available to a victim of a tort. In relation to sportsfield violence, the only relevant claim would be for damages. The aim of a claim for damages is to fully compensate the victim for the losses that are incurred as a result of the tort.

---

14 See further, *Winfield and Jolowicz on Tort*, 14th edn (1994), London: Sweet & Maxwell, Chapter 23.

Damages can be a gamble for both parties to an action. The court can accurately determine pre-trial losses, however, the plaintiff's future losses are much more a matter of speculation. If the plaintiff recovers more fully than expected, there is a risk of over-compensation; if the condition degenerates, there is a risk of under-compensation. This problem arises as the court will, in general, award the plaintiff a lump sum in advance, as compensation. In recent years, there has been a growing trend towards the use of structured settlements for serious injuries. Instead of paying a one-off lump sum to the plaintiff, a structured settlement makes a series of periodic payments, usually by way of a life assurance policy, to the injured party. These can be devised in such a way as to take account of such problems. However their operation is usually only a viable alternative to traditional damages awards in instances of catastrophic injury.[15]

The two causes of action that have been examined, trespass to the person and negligence, have one distinct difference between when an action for damages can be pursued. For an action in negligence, the plaintiff must prove that he has suffered physical and/or property damage.[16] An action in trespass to the person is actionable *per se*, without proof of injury.[17] Obviously, in an action for trespass, the lack of actual injury caused is likely to lead to only a small award in damages to the plaintiff, to show the court's displeasure at the trespass.

There are three different types of damages that can be claimed in a tortious action: compensatory; aggravated and exemplary damages. The two latter categories are only rarely awarded in English courts. The plaintiff's main claim will be for compensatory damages. The aim of compensatory damages is to compensate the plaintiff, as far as is financially possible, with an amount which will put him in the same position that he was before the tort occurred.

Compensatory Damages

Compensatory damages will usually be the plaintiff's largest and only, claim from the defendant. They can be split into two further sub-categories of special and general damage.

Special damage is the category of losses that are precisely quantifiable pre-trial. This head of damage will include pre-trial loss of earnings, medical expenses and damage caused to any personal property as a result of the tort.

General damage on the other hand, cover those losses which are more speculative in nature or incapable of exact calculation. The most common and

---

15 See further, Markesinis, B, and Deakin, S, *Tort Law*, 3rd edn (1994), Oxford: Clarendon, pp 705–08, Lewis, R, 'Legal Limits on the Structured Settlement of Damages' (1993) *Cambridge Law Journal* 470 and the Damages Act 1996.

16 *Donoghue v Stevenson* [1932] AC 562 and above, p 476.

17 *Letang v Cooper* [1965] 1 QB 232.

usually the most important claims which come under this heading are: compensation for the pain and suffering caused by the injury; loss of amenity, which is compensation for being unable to do certain things that could previously be done as a result of the injury; loss of future earnings and any loss of future earnings capacity, such as not getting promoted or not being able to follow equally remunerative employment as a result of the injury.

Aggravated Damages

This head of damage is a sub-species of compensatory damages that is often confused with the exemplary damages discussed in the next section. However aggravated damages are not awarded to punish the defendant. They are awarded instead to reflect the greater degree of damage caused to the plaintiff by the circumstances in which the injury was inflicted. As Lord Hailsham has said:

> In awarding aggravated damages the natural indignation of the court at the injury on the plaintiff is a perfectly legitimate motive in making a generous rather than a more moderate award to provide an adequate solution. But that is because the injury to the plaintiff is actually greater and as the result of the conduct exciting the indignation demands a more generous solution.[18]

Aggravated damages can be awarded for the damage caused to one's pride or for the humiliation suffered during the commission of the tort. The circumstances in which the tort was committed and which may lead to an award of aggravated damages are varied. The most common in a sports setting would be that the tort was committed in public in front of a large audience or whilst being broadcast on television or the frustration at being unable to continue to play one's chosen sport. Any of these factors could lead to the court to consider that the damage suffered was more serious than the simple infliction of an injury.

Exemplary Damages

Exemplary damages are purely punitive in nature. They are awarded only very rarely by English courts. They are best described as a civil fine, which is payable to the plaintiff, instead of the State. English courts do not like to award exemplary damages as they feel that it creates a windfall effect, leading to over-compensation of the plaintiff. ie exemplary damages reward the plaintiff for a loss that has not been suffered.

Exemplary damages should only be awarded in two cases. The first category, which is not appropriate to sports situations, is following

---

18 *Cassell & Co Ltd v Broome* [1972] 1 All ER 801.

unconstitutional behaviour by officials of the State or local government. The second is where the defendant has committed the tort in a manner in which he knows that he will make a profit from it's commission. The exemplary damages award will take the profit element from the defendant and award it to the plaintiff.

Rookes v Barnard [1964] 1 All ER 367

Cases in the second category are those in which the defendant's conduct has been calculated by him to make a profit for himself which may well exceed the compensation payable to the plaintiff ... it is necessary for the law to show that it cannot be broken with impunity. This category is not confined to moneymaking in the strict sense. It extends to cases in which the defendant is seeking to gain at the expense of the plaintiff some object – perhaps some property which he covets – which either he could not obtain at all or not obtain at a price greater than he wants to put down. Exemplary damages can be awarded whenever it is necessary to teach a defendant that tort does not pay.

[The following] considerations ... should always be borne in mind when awards of exemplary damages are being considered. Firstly, the plaintiff cannot recover exemplary damages unless he is a victim of the punishable behaviour. The anomaly inherent in exemplary damages would become an absurdity if a plaintiff, totally unaffected by some oppressive conduct which the jury wished to punish, obtained a windfall in consequence ... Thirdly, the means of the parties, irrelevant in the assessment of compensation, are material in the assessment of exemplary damages. Everything which aggravates or mitigates the defendant's conduct is relevant.[19]

Thus, the injury causing situations associated with sport where exemplary damages are appropriate are likely to be limited. Their similarity with a criminal fine is highlighted by the fact that they, unlike other categories of damages, are means tested.

Bugden v Rogers (1993) ATR 81–246

The plaintiff was a professional rugby league footballer with the Cronulla club. The defendant Bugden was a professional rugby league player with the Canterbury-Bankstown club (the club). The plaintiff's jaw was broken following a high tackle by Bugden in a match played between the two clubs.

Dental work and the insertion of a plate had been required, with further dental work and surgery being necessary. The plaintiff experienced pain and distress and continued to suffer the inconvenience of an insensitive lower lip and chin, difficulty in opening his mouth wide and a 'clicking' when chewing. He also experienced feelings of anger and frustration about not being able to play football and about the manner in which he had been injured and publicly humiliated. The plaintiff sued Bugden and the club for damages in assault.

The trial judge rejected Bugden's claim that the injury occurred when Bugden's shoulder came into contact with the plaintiff's jaw while Bugden was

---

19 *Per* Lord Devlin, 410. See also, *AB v South West Water Services* [1993] 1 All ER 609.

executing a legitimate 'smother tackle'. The trial judge found that Bugden, clearly aimed for the plaintiff's head, had deliberately struck him with his outstretched forearm with the intention of hurting him and that this was contrary to the rules of the game.

The assault was thereby proved and judgment was entered against Bugden for compensatory damages in the sum of $68,154.60 which included general damages for pain, suffering and loss of amenities in the sum of $25,000.

The trial judge held that the club was vicariously liable for the assault because the actions of Bugden constituted a mode, albeit an improper one, of acting within the scope of his employment. His Honour held that Bugden's employment contract authorised him to use force to tackle an opposing player. The club's argument that it had only authorised the use of force by way of legitimate tackles was considered not sufficient to exclude its liability.

The plaintiff's alternative claim of vicarious liability, that the club had impliedly authorised the assault, was rejected. The basis for this claim was that before the game, Bugden's coach had 'revved up' the players and told them to stop three players, one of whom was the plaintiff. In addition, the club had not punished Bugden for the incident nor criticised his conduct.

By the end of the season the plaintiff was playing in the Cronulla reserve team. He then contracted to play football in England in the off-season and to play with the Illawarra club in the following season. The plaintiff broke his leg in his first game in England. This injury prevented him from playing with Illawarra. His claim that, because he would not have signed to play in England if his jaw had not been broken, he should recover his lost earnings as a footballer with the Illawarra club was rejected.[20]

The plaintiff's claim for aggravated damages appeared to have been overlooked by the trial judge and his claim for exemplary damages was rejected on the grounds that Bugden had been punished by the 14 week suspension imposed on him by the Rugby League in respect of the incident and that that the award would necessarily be small having regard to Bugden's employment as a police constable and his limited capacity to pay. If not for these factors, the trial judge would have regarded this as an appropriate case for an award of exemplary damages. It appeared that the trial judge failed to consider whether exemplary damages should have been awarded against the club.

Each of the three parties appealed against aspects of the decision.

Held: the award of damages would be increased against both parties to include aggravated damages of $8,000 ... and the award was further increased against Bugden but not against the club to include exemplary damages of $7,500.

(1) The appeal against liability would be dismissed. The trial judge's conclusion that the plaintiff's jaw was broken by a deliberate head-high tackle could not be disturbed. The finding was based not only upon videotape film and photographs but also upon the credibility of several witnesses. It was not established that the trial judge misused his advantage

---

20 As being too remote from the original injury which caused the loss.

in seeing or hearing the witnesses or that his conclusions were at variance with objective facts reliably established thereby. On the contrary, the videotape evidence and the photographic evidence amply supported his Honour's conclusion.

(2) The finding that the club was vicariously liable was correct on the facts ... There was no suggestion that Bugden acted from animosity towards the plaintiff or in furtherance of his own interests; he did what he did in the course of playing for the club and it could only be seen as intended to assist and in fact assisting, the club to defeat Cronulla and as doing so by achieving a result (stopping the plaintiff's progress) which could have been achieved by the proper mode of a legitimate tackle. Bugden had achieved it by the improper mode of an illegitimate tackle. Although it was not established that the illegitimate tackle had been authorised by the club, the risk that motivation would, in some, lead to the adoption of illegitimate means was plain. An employer which encouraged action close to the line would, in an appropriate case, have to bear the consequences over the line.

(3) No reason was shown for interfering with the award of general damages.

(4) The trial judge correctly declined to award damages for the plaintiff's loss of earnings with the Illawarra club. There was no evidence that the broken leg was related to the consequences of the jaw injury and such a relationship could not be inferred. Once the plaintiff had arrived at a state of fitness which he considered sufficient to enable him to return to first grade football he, like every other player, faced all the risks of injury arising in such play.

(5) The plaintiff was entitled to an additional award for aggravated damages for the injury to his feelings. The emotional impact of the plaintiff's realisation that he had been the public victim of a deliberate assault and its contribution to his frustration and anger was not reflected in the award of general damages.

(6) The trial judge erred in rejecting the claim for exemplary damages against Bugden. The matters which lead the trial judge to refuse to award exemplary damages were relevant. However in referring to Bugden's earnings as a police constable the trial judge overlooked his earnings as a footballer. While his match payments ceased during his period of suspension, Bugden continued to receive his playing fees and remained in the game after he had taken the plaintiff out of the game. Notwithstanding the deterrent effect of the suspension, the tackle was deliberate, intended to hurt and unnecessary.

(7) No exemplary damages would be awarded against the club, although this was a borderline case. The evidence stopped short of establishing that the club had encouraged or incited Bugden to engage in unlawful conduct on the field. A club seeking to motivate its players and in particular to direct their efforts against particular opposing players ran the risk that it would be found to have authorised or induced illegitimate action, in which case an award of exemplary damages in the order of $150,000 may not have been inappropriate.

PROBLEMS WITH TORTIOUS COMPENSATION AWARDS

Procedural Difficulties

The civil justice system in England is, at present, slow and expensive. Although this is not a sports specific problem, it is a significant inhibitor of many potential civil actions. If Lord Woolf's proposals relating to the speeding up of civil claims are introduced, an increase in the number of sports related claims could be seen in the near future.[21]

Aside from these basic problems relating to civil procedure, there are further serious problems relating to the proving of a tortious action involving sportsfield violence. Although off-the-ball incidents are relatively straightforward to prove, proving a case involving an on-the-ball incident is much more difficult. Unless the incident is as blatant as the court found the assault in *Bugden v Rogers*[22] it is more likely that confused opinion will cloud the arguments, as happened in *Elliott v Saunders*.[23]

Finally, connected with the procedural difficulties, is the degree of tactics and brinkmanship inherently involved with bringing a civil action. For example, Glasgow Rangers FC player, Ian Durrant, had his case settled at the door of the court after four years of negotiation. He received an estimated £225,000 plus legal expenses from Aberdeen FC for a tackle by their former player, Neil Simpson. Durrant had been unable to play for three years. There was no real reason why the case could not have been settled at an earlier date. Other players, such as Paul Elliott have not been so lucky. After his unsuccessful action, he was left with a legal bill estimated to be in the region of £750,000 or roughly the equivalent to that which he received by way of an insurance payout. Whilst participants and their lawyers are able to play on the inherent difficulties of bringing a sportsfield violence action, many injured victims will continue to go either uncompensated or receive a smaller award than their injuries require.

Legal Difficulties

Where an action is brought in negligence, there is a significant danger that any damages awarded will be reduced considerably if any contributory negligence of the victim can be proved. In more extreme cases, the award may be completely extinguished by the operation of the defences of either consent or *volenti non fit injuria*. If either of these defences can be successfully raised, the plaintiff will receive no compensation. The operation of these defences can

---

21 'Access to Justice', Final Report, 1996, London: HMSO.
22 See above, p 514.
23 (1994) unreported decision of the High Court.

be particularly problematic if the injury causing incident occurred as part of the legitimate playing of the game, such as an on-the-ball challenge. In sports where a degree of physical contact is an expected an necessary part of the playing of the game, a reduction in the amount of damages payable is a real risk.

Linked to this, is the problem of unnecessary roughness. As the courts have spent comparatively little time examining the role of the law in sports situations, the deliberate use of too much force has not yet been addressed. If the courts wish to clamp down on the use of deliberate violence against fellow participants, they must address this conceptual difficulty sooner, rather than later.[24]

Difficulties with Quantification and Payment of the Award

Where the injured participant is unable to continue playing sport or must play at a lower level, it is virtually impossible to quantify the loss to him. Although the court will obviously calculate an appropriate sum, a compensatory award can never really replace the inability to play sport.

A further difficulty related to payment of the award is that the defendant may be unable to pay the compensation to the plaintiff where the former is not covered by insurance. This can lead to a somewhat hollow victory. For example, in *Smoldon v Whitworth*,[25] the plaintiff's action would have been an irrelevancy if Whitworth had not been covered by the Rugby Football Union's own insurance scheme. His job as a schoolteacher could never have provided the funds for the £1 million settlement. In the *Smoldon* case itself, the original claim was for considerably more than £1 million but it was reduced to the maximum payable under the Rugby Football Union's insurance scheme, as it was known that Whitworth would be unable to meet any greater claim out of his own pocket. Thus, where a defendant is uninsured or has limited means, a civil action can be barely worth pursuing.

Finally, only rarely will there be an element of personal liability specifically payable by the defendant, incorporated into the award. This could be a problem at the professional level where the employing club may pay the award on the player's behalf. If the player has paid nothing then there cannot be said to have been a punishment or a concomitant deterrent effect. This can be overcome, as it was in *Bugden v Rogers*.[26] However this was a rare instance of personal exemplary damages being awarded against a sports participant.

---

24 See for example the Tatum and Stingley incident, above, p 447.
25 See above, p 491.
26 See above, p 514.

NATIONAL GOVERNING BODY PUNISHMENTS

At present, no British governing body operates a compensation system for the benefit of those injured whilst playing sport. Although most either provide some form of insurance or advise as to the merits of various insurance schemes, governing bodies do not appear to consider compensation for injury to be a particularly important aspect of their brief. However most do have some form of internal disciplinary mechanism. This can take many forms but is usually, to a greater or lesser degree, quasi-judicial in its operation. This section will examine the various punishments that can be imposed on the perpetrators of sportsfield violence by the officials in charge of the game, the club of the perpetrator and the sports governing body.

Penalties during the Game

Penalties imposed by the game officials can take many forms, depending on the type of foul committed, the severity of harm inflicted and the sport in question. These forms of punishment are imposed following a perpetrator's breach of one of the rules of the particular sport. The penalties imposed can take on a wide variety of forms. The following are some of the basic categories of during the game penalties.

Loss of possession

For a relatively minor infringement involving physical contact, the victim's team may be awarded control of the game when play restarts. This is variously termed a free kick or free hit, depending on the sport.

Free opportunity to score

Where there has been a more serious infringement of the laws, the victim's team may be awarded to score points, either unopposed or with minimal opposition. For example, a penalty in rugby or football or a free throw in basketball.

Official warnings

Where there has been deliberate foul or dangerous, play, the game officials may have the power to formally warn the perpetrator about the misconduct. An official warning is often coupled with a warning that if similar behaviour is repeated, the participant will not be allowed to continue to play. Football's yellow card for an official warning is probably the best known of these, however, similar cards are also used in field hockey and rugby union. In basketball, the officials keep a separate count of a participant's personally accumulated fouls.

Ejection from the game

For the most serious offences, officials may have the power to remove the player from the game for all or part of the remainder of the game's duration. Rugby league, ice hockey and field hockey, all have 'sin bins' in operation. Where a player has seriously breached the rules, they can be removed for, usually, 10 minutes of playing time. If the offence is particularly serious or worthy of a second official warning in one game, the participant may be removed from the game for all of the remainder of the playing time.

These during the game punishments have the advantage of being imposed instantaneously on the offender. They can be used not only to punish an offender but also to defuse a potentially volatile situation, for example, where a game is becoming excessively violent. These during the game sanctions have the added advantage of being immediately effective. In this respect, players can easily relate the crime to the punishment. The strict enforcement of such match penalties can prevent much violent play and the potential legal actions that are parasitic on such play.

Punishment Imposed by a Player's Club

Where professional sport is concerned, most clubs will be able to punish their players for violent conduct. The playing contract may even include a clause to the effect that a player can be fined for conduct which usually falls under the catch all phrase of 'bringing the game into disrepute'. Occasionally, contracts include a more specific clause relating to the player's on-field conduct. A provision of this kind may allow a club to withhold a player's wages for his on-field behaviour or in extreme cases, cancel the contract altogether.

There are several drawbacks with this form of punishment. Firstly and most importantly, is the highly variable nature of such clauses. These can vary not just as between different clubs or sports but also between different players at the same club. Secondly, they are obviously inapplicable where there is no contract between the employing club and the offending player. Without such a contractual provision, the player cannot be fined by his club. Finally, there is a serious conflict of interest for the club. Clubs do not want to ban and fine their best players, even when they are violent; they want the stars to play. Clubs will further not want to scare off potential new players from playing for a club with a strict disciplinary policy. Thus, this particular form of punishment, although a possibility, is not the best of deterrents for violent players.

Internal Disciplinary Tribunal Punishments

Where an offence is considered to be particularly serious by a governing body, provisions can exist that allow for the governing body itself to specifically review the incident and punish the offender either additionally to any penalty already imposed by the match officials or for the first time if no during the game action was taken.[27] The internal disciplinary tribunal will usually be, to a greater or lesser extent, quasi-judicial in its procedure. However procedures differ both between different sports and between the same sport in the different regional jurisdictions of the United Kingdom.

In outline, the same basic mechanism exists for most sports. A player will be informed of the fact that has been charged and must appear before the tribunal. At the hearing, evidence of the charge will be put to the tribunal, using where possible, video or photographic evidence. The offender will be allowed to make representations to the panel to either justify or excuse his actions. These representations may be made by the player himself or a representative. This representative may be from the sport's players' association, the player's club or in some circumstances may be the player's lawyer. When all relevant representations have been made, the tribunal will then retire to make its judgment.

If the offence is proved against the offender, the punishment will usually take the form of a playing ban, fine or both. In each sport, there are rules stating the maximum penalties that can be imposed for each different offence. Some sports have a tariff system, where for each offence, there is a pre-determined punishment to be imposed on the offender. Other tribunals simply use their own previous decisions as guidelines for the penalty to be imposed. Whatever the actual system in place, for many sports there is an effective, if not always effectively used, punishment system in place to penalise violent conduct.

In most instances of sports violence, the penalties imposed by the disciplinary tribunal are considered to be an adequate form of punishment, by both players and administrators alike. However when compared to the potential punishments that can be handed down by the criminal courts, the tribunal's punishments can be said to be somewhat lenient. This is the main criticism of reliance on these tribunal's as the sole source of punishment for on-field violence. It is not the case that the tribunals are lacking in powers, it is much more the case that they do not often use their existing powers to their full extent.

---

27 *Ferguson v SFA*; see further, Duff, A, 'Own Goal' (1996) 4(1) *Sport and the Law Journal* 12. Ferguson had his ban overturned as the SFA's rules only allowed the disciplinary tribunals to punish a player in addition to the punishment imposed by the match official. As Ferguson had not been punished during the game, the SFA's punishment was not in addition to anything and, therefore, *ultra vires*.

In both rugby codes, steps have been taken in the past season to address this apparent leniency in their internal punishment structures. The Scottish Rugby Union has banned one player for four years following an on-field fight.[28] The Rugby Football League is also continuing its fight to eradicate sportsfield violence in its sport by the use of probably the most efficient disciplinary tribunal in Britain and an effective use of short, medium and long term bans.[29] At present, other governing bodies have been slow to follow this lead.

The only other drawback of the disciplinary tribunal system is its inability to award compensation to the injured victims. Some players associations, most notably the Professional Footballers' Association (PFA), do provide a good degree of cover for their members. However the PFA only represents a tiny minority of those who play football every week.[30] Most victims must still look outside of their sport to find adequate compensation mechanisms. This will mean either turning to insurance policies or more often, to the civil law.

Other Forms of Punishment

There are a number of peripheral methods by which a perpetrator of sportsfield violence can be punished. These can originate from a variety of different sources. A player may be dropped from representative sides, such as from playing for his national team. This sanction can show either the coach's or the governing body's, disapproval of the violent conduct and that it will not be tolerated at the highest level of competition.

A player may also be relieved of a position of responsibility, such as having his club or representative side's captaincy removed from him. This can again show a high degree disapproval of the conduct by such a public condemnation of the violent conduct.

If either of the above penalties are imposed on a player or if a player is banned from playing his sport, it has the potential to lead to heavy financial loss. This can take the form of lost wages, where a player is paid on a pay per play basis. It could also mean that the player is unable to qualify for certain bonus payments, if he is not in the team's starting line up because of a ban. It may also lead to the cancellation of lucrative sponsorship deals if a company feels that it is more likely that its reputation will be damaged by association with a violent player.

For a non-professional participant, some of these consideration's clearly do not apply. However being dropped from a team can have a detrimental effect

---

28 Jason Fayers, see *The Times*, 15 October 1996.

29 For example, Dean Hall of Bramley was banned for 15 months for elbowing an opponent, *Daily Telegraph*, 29 June 1996; Bobby Goulding of Saint Helens and Great Britain was banned for six matches for a high tackle, *The Times*, 21 February 1997.

30 See further, Taylor, G, 'Why the Duty of Care is Paramount', *The Sunday Times*, 23 March 1997.

on a young player's future playing prospects and can take away the sheer enjoyment of participating in one's chosen sport. All of these forms of punishment, although not specifically taken into consideration when a player is punished by more conventional means, are all important when the effect of punishment as a whole is assessed.

Problems Associated with Non-Legal Punishments

Although there are a number of methods by which a perpetrator of sportsfield violence can be punished, none of the mechanisms are without their difficulties. The most obvious criticism is that the use of such non-legal punishments allows sportsfield violence to be treated differently from other forms of violence. This criticism seems all the more pertinent when comparatively lenient fines and playing bans are imposed for what can be considered to be serious, violent assaults.

A further fault with these forms of punishment is their lack of consistency. There is no consistency of approach between different sports, each considering different types of foul play to be more or less serious depending on the sport being played; a legitimate strategy in one sport is a clear foul in another. There is often a degree of inconsistency in how the same sport treats different incidents. This is one of the most common criticisms of the disciplinary tribunal system.

Finally, there is no provision for compensation to be awarded by these internal tribunals. Although the punishment structure may prove to be an adequate alternative to criminal sanctions, most participants injured whilst playing sport will have little option but to sue the aggressor in the civil courts. In this respect, the internal mechanisms are only doing half of the job. However the present structures in place in most sports are a good foundation from which can be built more effective non-legal methods of controlling sportsfield violence.

INSURANCE

Outside of the three main punishment and compensation mechanisms discussed above, the criminal law, tort law and disciplinary tribunals, insurance is the only other significant controlling mechanism for sportsfield violence. Potentially, insurance could become by far the most important method by which injuries sustained from sportsfield violence are compensated. However, at present, very few participants outside of the very highest levels of sport are covered by anything approaching adequate insurance cover.

The most important practical advantage of insurance cover is that it can guarantee some level of compensation, as opposed to the comparative lottery of a tort action. However there are also a number of disadvantages of such a scheme, especially if it is implemented on a voluntary, as opposed to a compulsory, basis. The following is a brief outline of the different types of insurance cover currently available to sports participants. The extent of cover provided by any particular insurance scheme will depend partly on the terms of the policy purchased and partly on the sum paid by way of a premium.

Personal Liability or Personal Accident Insurance

Personal liability insurance schemes cover the insured participant for injuries caused by him to another participant. Such schemes will usually cover all non-intentionally inflicted injuries. Intentionally inflicted injuries will usually be specifically excluded by the policy. Where such an injury is inflicted deliberately by the policy holder, the injured party will have to use the normal legal routes, of the civil or criminal law, to recover compensation.

Personal Injury Insurance

Personal injury insurance is effectively the opposite of personal liability insurance. These schemes cover situations where the insured party himself has been injured whilst participating in sport. These schemes are often very wide in the type of injuries which they cover. Depending on the actual scheme preferred by the insured, such a scheme can cover injuries received through participation in sport, training and travelling to and from a match or training session. This type of policy is the closest that an injured participant can get to a guarantee of a compensation payout.

Comprehensive and No Fault Insurance

Comprehensive insurance cover is, in effect, a combination of personal liability and personal injury insurance. A comprehensive scheme would be similar to that currently in operation for motor vehicles. A comprehensive scheme would ensure that an injured participant would be able to receive compensation and an injury causer would be able to make a full compensation payment to his victim. Such a scheme would cover any injuries suffered by participation, training and travelling, except those deliberately inflicted. For such an injury, a legal action would still usually be necessary.

No fault insurance is a much touted system of compensation for injuries suffered during sports participation. The advantages of such a scheme are attractive and obvious. There would be a guaranteed payout to any participant, for any injury, regardless of the cause of the injury. Such a payout could be made from a mass insurance policy or a central fund, which covered all participants, either in a given sport or in all sports. If a workable administration system could be established, no fault insurance could be the main compensation mechanism for sportsfield injuries in the future.

Problems and Discussion Points Relating to Insurance Schemes

Despite the apparently attractive nature of the various insurance schemes, they are not without their own, quite specific, problems and disadvantages. If insurance is going to play are more important and effective role in this area, it must address some fundamental issues. Although none of these issues should mean that insurance is discounted as a means of compensation, they do show that before its introduction on a wider scale, a fair and effective system must be devised.

Should Insurance be Compulsory?

Insurance can only be an effective compensatory mechanism for sports injuries if one of the schemes discussed above is made compulsory. If some form of insurance is not compulsory, then an injured participant will still run the risk that the causer of the injury was uninsured, thus leaving the victim with only a legal claim to pursue. Alternatively, without compulsory personal injury insurance, the victim will not even have his own policy to claim from.

Thus, it would appear that making insurance cover compulsory is essential. However, as discussed below, compulsory insurance is itself not free from serious disadvantages.

Additional Expenditure

Whether or not insurance is made compulsory, the burden of the additional expense of most insurance schemes will, in some way or another, fall on the participant. This will have the obvious effect of making some sports, especially those most commonly participated in, much more expensive to play. For example, overall, footballers at all levels suffer the most injuries per season, whilst rugby union players suffer the most serious injuries.[31]

Participants in these two sports could expect to have relatively high premiums. So also could those whose sport requires expensive equipment or a relatively dangerous playing arena. The value of premiums to be paid could have an impact on both overall participation in a sport and its demographic

---

31   See 'Sport's Risky Business', *Daily Telegraph,* 12 April 1997.

makeup. Compulsory insurance could, in other words, produce a degree of financial elitism in sports participation. One proposed method of controlling spiralling premiums is for teams or national governing bodies to purchase block cover. This would greatly decrease the premium to be paid, whilst at the same time greatly increase the degree of cover for sports participants.[32]

Increased Reckless Play

The possibility that the introduction of compulsory insurance in sport will actually lead to an increase in reckless play cannot be discounted. If participants know that when they cause injury to another participant, the injured player will be fully compensated by an insurance policy, part of the deterrent effect of legal action is removed. Thus if compulsory insurance was to be introduced, it should really only be done so alongside a complete overhaul of the punishment structure of sportsfield violence. A trade off of full compensation for removal of the deterrent effect, may to lead to an increase in the number of sports related injuries, as opposed to the hoped for decrease.

Malingering

This is, possibly, more likely to be a problem at the elite levels of sport. If a participant is receiving full compensation and full pay from an insurance policy, there is less incentive for him to regain full fitness. From a different perspective, it may be in a club's interests to allow the player to take longer than is necessary to recuperate as they will not have to pay his wages as this will be covered by the compensation claim. In an era when many teams at all levels of sport are teetering on the brink of financial difficulties, there may have to be tight control over a participant's continued need for recuperation time.

Continued Legal Actions between Insurers

The introduction of compulsory insurance may not see the desired removal of civil litigation form sports, as it introduces an additional group of potential plaintiffs and defendants; the insurers. Insurance companies may wish to challenge a payment on the grounds that because of the perpetrator's fault element, his insurers should pay, not the victim's. This could lead to insurers suing each other through the participants in order to claim indemnities off other insurance companies. Again, the law would be continuing to play a role that sport felt was no longer necessary.

---

32   See above, p 524.

No Fault Insurance

Again, the criticisms of this type of scheme relate more to the administration of such a scheme, as opposed to any fundamental objection to its introduction. It must be decided whether such a scheme should cover all sports or whether each sport should establish and administer its own scheme. The source of funding must be pinpointed, as must whether the scheme should apply to an entire sport or whether there should be a distinction between professional and amateur participants. A further distinction could be made between school sports and other participants and whether the former should be covered by such a general scheme or a more specific scheme for children.

None of these problems are insurmountable. However they are important issues that must be addressed before no fault insurance can be introduced effectively and efficiently.

COMPARATIVE APPROACHES

The other major common law jurisdictions, Australia, New Zealand, Canada and the United States, all operate broadly similar principles of both punishment and compensation to incidents of sportsfield violence as are used in the United Kingdom. Each of these jurisdictions does have its own individual characteristics, some more significant than others. These more specific differences are discussed in more detail below.

Criminal Law

One basic difference between English law's response to sportsfield violence and that of the other jurisdiction's is that, with the notable exception of Canada, there are virtually no criminal prosecutions for on-field conduct. Although prosecutions are not unheard of, they are extremely rare. For example, in America, there has been only one prosecution involving a professional sports participant,[33] and very few reported cases even at the amateur level. That case was declared a mistrial after the jury were unable to agree on a verdict. The prosecutor felt unable to proceed with a retrial as it was his belief that it would be virtually impossible to secure a conviction against a professional player.

Conversely, in Canada, there has been a number of prosecutions for during the game violence in ice hockey. These have occurred at all levels of the game, though securing a conviction has at times been difficult. In the professional National Hockey League, the most notorious incident involved

---

33 *State v Forbes*, above, p 505.

Ted Green of the Boston Bruins and Wayne Maki of the St Louis Blues. Both were prosecuted and acquitted:

> *R v Green* **(1970) 16 DLR (3d) 137 (Prov Ct);** *R v Maki* **(1970) 14 DLR (3d) 164 (Prov Ct)**
>
> During the course of a National Hockey League exhibition match, the players had become involved in a series of incidents associated with the play. Green skated past Maki and either pushed or punched him in the face with a gloved hand. Maki responded with a vertical chopping blow with his stick on to Green's head, causing him injury.
>
> Green was charged with common assault, Maki with assault causing bodily harm. Both were acquitted. Green, on the grounds that this was the kind of contact that was expected in professional ice hockey and, therefore, impliedly consented to. Maki, on the grounds that he was acting in self-defence to an unprovoked attack.

Although they were acquitted, these cases show that the courts are prepared to examine the behaviour of some of the highest paid sportsmen in the world. The junior levels have not escaped the courts' censure.[34] In these cases a variety of injuries have been inflicted, some resulting in conviction. However where conviction does result, the courts have generally not imprisoned the offender but instead either fined or conditionally discharged them, the condition being that no further sport is played for a set period of time.[35]

The Canadian courts have generally ruled that violence should not be an acceptable part of ice hockey. It is generally considered that participants would rather leave the resolution of disputes to their governing body or to take retaliatory measures on the ice, as fighting is 'part of the game.'[36] This may explain why relatively few cases have reached the courts and resulted in conviction. However, Canada is the only other common law jurisdiction that regularly entertains criminal prosecutions of during the play violent conduct.

Tort Law

This lack of use or reported use, of the criminal law does not extend itself to the civil law. In Australia, a test similar to that used to establish liability in English law has been developed. Australian law has simply developed the test of 'negligence in all the circumstances' to apply more specifically to sports torts.[37]

---

34 See for example, *R v Langton* (1976) 32 CRNS 121 (Sask CA); *R v Watson* 26 CCC 2d 150 (Ont Prov Ct).

35 For more detail on this area, see Barnes, J, *Sports and the Law in Canada*, 2nd edn (1995), Toronto: Butterworths.

36 *R v Henderson* [1976] 5 WWR 119, at 123. See also, White, D, 'Sports Violence as Criminal Assault: Development of the Doctrine by Canadian Courts' [1986] Duke LJ 1030.

37 See *Johnstone v Frazer* [1990] ATR 81–056 and *Bugden v Rogers*, above, p 514.

In America and Canada, however, the 'reckless disregard' standard[38] is used in all bar one State. This standard allows sports participants to show a greater degree of disregard for the safety of their fellow participants before civil liability is imposed on their behaviour. In the odd State out, Wisconsin, the ordinary negligence standard, which takes into account the specific circumstances in which the negligent act took place, is used to establish liability.[39] This test is very similar to that put forward by Drake J in *Elliott v Saunders*.[40]

New Zealand differs quite dramatically to the other common law countries in its approach to compensation for personal injury. In the early 1970s, New Zealand moved away from the traditional notion of how tortious damages should be claimed for personal injury. The common law scheme was replaced by what is, in effect, a 24 hour, State sponsored insurance policy. The most recent incarnation of the legislation, the Accident, Compensation, Rehabilitation and Insurance Act 1982, together with a large number of accompanying regulations, establishes the basis of the no fault compensation scheme. At the same time, the Act abolished the right of action to sue a potential defendant for damages for the injuries inflicted.

Any person who is accidentally injured in New Zealand, including during participation in sport, can claim under the Act. Although the quantum of compensation awarded under the Act is much less than that which could have been received through a tort action, this system has the advantage of guaranteeing payout in a very short time. Most claims are met within a month of submission of the claim form.

The cost of administering the system has lead to a gradual erosion of the claims that will be met under the Act. Further, the Act fails to adequately compensate high earners, including professional sports participants. In the future, it is possible that civil actions may be brought for exemplary damages to make up some of the difference between the compensation awarded under the Act and that which would have been awarded by a tort action.

The Sporting Injuries Insurance Act 1978 of New South Wales, Australia

In New South Wales, the introduction of the Sporting Injuries Insurance Act 1978 has guaranteed a level of compensation to all registered players of authorised sports in the State. The Act established a framework through which a payment fund is administered. Premiums are levied on organisations

---

38 See above, p 481.

39 *Lestina v West Bend Mutual Insurance Company* 501 NW 2d 28.

40 See above, p 479.

who wish to be registered and covered by the Act. The size of the premium is determined by the number of players of the sport and how great the likelihood of injury is considered to be.

Players must be registered with the sports organisation, which must be registered with the fund administrators. Any registered player who is injured in the course of an event which has been sanctioned by the registered organisation, can claim for compensation from the fund. Compensation can only be claimed for the injuries sustained during the sport and for any further losses relating to the playing of the sport. It does not cover lost earnings from non-sports related employment. This ensures that the fund can pay as much compensation for injuries to the maximum possible number of applicants. Any additional losses must be recovered either under the applicant's own insurance policy or by way of a civil action.

Waiver Clauses

In most of the States in the USA, waiver clauses are used by potential defendants to exclude their liability. By these, a potential plaintiff must sign a release form that states that if he or she is negligently injured during the course of the activity, they will not sue the person at fault. These waiver clauses are contacts which realign the duties imposed on the parties. If a waiver clause is signed, the injured party does not have a tortious right of action against the perpetrator.

The only limit on this type of clause is that it must not be contrary to public policy.[41] Generally where sports are concerned, it will only be contrary to public policy where the waiver must be signed by the parent in respect of injuries that might be caused to a minor.[42] So, in most of the States in the USA, participants can waive their right to sue for injuries caused through participation in sport in advance.

Such terms are, however, unlawful in this country.

Sections 1 and 2 of the Unfair Contract Terms Act 1977

(1) For the purposes of this Part of this Act, 'negligence' means the breach ...

    (b) of any common law duty to take reasonable care or exercise reasonable skill (but not any stricter duty);

(2) A person cannot by reference to any contract term or to a notice given to persons generally or to particular persons exclude or restrict his liability for death or personal injury resulting from negligence.

The result of this piece of legislation is that nobody can waive their right to sue for negligently inflicted injuries under English law. The only way that

---

41 *Tunkl v Regents of the University of California* 20 Cal 2d 92.

42 *Wagenblast v Odessa School District and Vuillet v Seattle School District* 119 Wash 2d 845.

potential defendants can escape liability is if they can rely on the doctrine of assumption of risk.[43]

Each of these different systems has its own particular merits and demerits. However none appears to work perfectly where sports injuries are concerned. What they do provide for the English system, are alternatives which can be examined and refined and later, perhaps, applied to our own system. By these means, it may become possible to avoid the need for lengthy and expensive trials, whilst guaranteeing the injured party some measure of compensation.

THE FUTURE

The present systems of punishment and, perhaps to an even greater degree, compensation for sportsfield injuries are ill-equipped to cope with the demands currently being put on it. A number of proposals have been put forward in recent years to cope with this growing problem. In the field of compensation, the various insurance schemes discussed above, especially no fault insurance, have been advocated as ways of ensuring fairness to those injured through the fault of another in sport. Others have argued for greater powers of internal mechanisms and greater control of those powers by the courts through the judicial review procedure.[44] Three of these propositions, a Sports Appeals Tribunal, arbitration and risk management schemes, are briefly discussed below.

Sports Appeals Tribunal

A dedicated Sports Appeal Tribunal (SAT) could have jurisdiction to deal with a wide range of sports related matters. It would not have to be limited to cases involving sportsfield violence alone, however, it can be envisaged that disputes relating to compensation and punishment would form at least part of its jurisdiction. The SAT could be run along similar lines to the Employment Appeals Tribunal or the Commercial Courts, effectively being a final court of appeal for the internal disciplinary tribunals of individual sports.

In the USA, there has been an attempt to introduce a more formal method of punishing those guilty of during the game violence than those already on offer by the governing bodies of sport.[45] In 1981, Representative Ronald Mottl proposed The Sports Violence Arbitration Act 1981.[46] The purpose of the

---

43 See above, p 487.

44 See above, Chapter 4.

45 DiNicola, R and Mendeloff, S, 'Controlling Violence in Professional Sports: Rule Reform and the Federal Professional Sports Violence Commission' (1983) 21 *Duquesne Law Review* 843.

46 (1981) 127 Cong Rec H8759.

proposed Sports Court was to impose fines on clubs, holding them liable for the conduct of their players. It could further fine and suspend the player for the violent conduct. The court was to be made up of people with a knowledge of the particular sport before it.

In this way, the court could deter and punish excessive violence in professional sports through the application of systematised punishments. Amateur sports were not covered by the legislation. It was believed that a federal law was required for professional sports, as most teams are in different States and the multitude of jurisdictions would ensure that most prosecutions would fail from a procedural point of view. The Sports Violence Arbitration Act would bypass these problems by being imposed from above the State legislatures, through federal law.

The Act is open to criticism, in that the terms that it uses are not clearly defined. Depending on why one participates in sport, the competitive goals will change. These can range from participation to winning to earning a living. Excessive force is not a term used elsewhere in the law. Its use here could lead to confusion between the operative standards for this Act and other related assault Acts. It does not state the level of payment, whether this should be a salary, match fee or expenses, that is required to activate the law.

Apart from these problems of terminology, the Act was not given the wholehearted support of the sport community. Many saw this not as a beneficial piece of legislation but as an unwarranted legal encroachment on their sports. From a less self-interested point of view, it is also of only marginal significance. Any control in this area must include non-professional players. That is the sector where the majority of participants play their sport and also where the majority of injuries occur. However the Act did draw attention to the problem of sportsfield violence in the USA. Similar legislation would probably meet the same fate here but would again raise the profile of the problem.

Arbitration

Arbitration is a growing mechanism for dispute resolution in sport. The International Olympic Committee's Court of Arbitration for Sport (CAS), based in Lausanne and Sydney is the most important of these, though others in Australia and the UK are beginning to develop.[47]

These mechanisms will arbitrate any dispute as between a participant and their governing body. Presently, their jurisdictions are not wide enough to cover the kind of problems discussed in this chapter. However as a model on

---

47 The Central Council of Physical Recreation is currently establishing an arbitration panel. For more details of the Australian procedure see, Doyle, B, 'The Anzsla Dispute Resolution Service' (1995) 3(3) *Sport and the Law Journal* 38.

which an arbitration mechanism could be developed, the CAS is a good example.[48]

Development of Risk Management Strategies

Risk management for sportsfield violence is, as yet, a largely unexplored preventative measure. Risk management would operate on the age old theory that prevention is better than cure. It is advice given to and methods used by those involved in a potentially dangerous situation, so that they may take action to ensure that the danger either does not arise or arises on a less frequent or less serious basis.[49]

Risk management essentially sets out to identify, evaluate and control the risks involved with sports participation. It is a more defensive way of participating in sports. It is a commitment by a sports program to participant health and safety. The overall purpose of any risk management program is to decrease the risk of injury to participants, the institution of loss reduction and injury prevention programmes and the shifting through transfer mechanisms of those losses which cannot be controlled by other means. In essence, risk management is a form of loss control.

Risk can be defined as anything which injuriously affects a participant. There are two types of risks that arise through participation in sport: inherent risks and unacceptable risks. Inherent risks are those that are considered to be a part of the game. They are inevitable and acceptable risks, resulting from the participant's decision to participate in sports. For example, a rugby player who breaks his wrist in the normal course of the game.

An unacceptable risk is one that is not an inherent risk of the sport. For example, an unacceptable risk is taken when a participant, who is clearly injured and wants to take no further part in the game, is forced to continue playing by the coach, which in turn causes the injury to become a permanent disability.

Instead of relying on the reactive nature of the legal actions and internal disciplinary tribunals, a pro-active stance against sportsfield violence could be taken. This could take any of a wide variety of forms. These could include the encouragement of fair play in sport, the dissemination of information relating to commonly occurring sports injuries, the publishing of internal disciplinary punishments in advance in a tariff form, compulsory insurance schemes or better coaching of physical contact techniques in sport.

The use of any of these risk management techniques could lead to a dramatic reduction in the incidence of sportsfield violence. If the number of

---

48 See above, Chapter 4.

49 For further detal of this subject see, Greenberg, M, and Gray, J, 'Designing and Implementing a Sports Based Risk Management Programme' (1997) 5(2) *Sport and the Law Journal* 49.

injuries can be reduced, the concomitant requirement for legal intervention to punish or compensate those involved could also be reduced. The use of risk management techniques to control unnecessary sports injuries may help sport to avoid serious accidents becoming more commonplace. It may also help to slow down the advance of the law into the sports arena by making its use unnecessary.

The following is an example of the measures that can be taken and which could be found in a risk management or risk reduction programme:

- Inspect the premises periodically and thoroughly to ensure that there are no potentially dangerous defects present.
- Place warnings or protective devices at the site of any hazard and be sure that such warnings are understood by the participants.
- Explain the inherent risks involved in participation to the participants so that they are aware of the dangers.
- Inform the participants of their potential liability should they flagrantly violate a rule and injure another as a result.
- Never instruct a participant to commit an act which is outside the scope of rules and customs of the game.
- Guarantee that your instructors or coaches are qualified to perform their duties by reviewing their qualifications and providing continuing education opportunities.
- Make sure that participants receive proper instructions regarding their sports and the equipment used in that sport.
- Have a qualified coach or instructor supervise all practices and contests.
- Clearly outline medical procedures and rules to be utilised should an accident occur and have qualified personnel on hand at events and contests if needed.
- Thoroughly inspect all equipment used on a regular basis and make sure that it complies with sport or industry standards.
- Investigate the feasibility of obtaining liability insurance for your programme.
- Buy quality equipment from reliable suppliers and keep up to date with changes in the sport.
- Select competition and activities that are appropriate for your participants.
- Athletic associations should incorporate to protect their assets.
- Form a risk management committee and appoint a risk manager to apportion and share risk managing responsibilities.
- Develop and implement guidelines regarding the safe and proper conduct of participants and coaches.
- Provide detailed medical emergency procedures.
- Develop procedures to document and investigate injuries to participants.
- Involve parents or guardians and the media in keeping aware of the need for a risk management programme.

CHAPTER TWELVE

SPECTATORS, PARTICIPANTS AND STADIUMS

INTRODUCTION

For thousands of years people have gathered together to watch sporting events. On the most simplistic level, such a gathering would have been in any place suitable for the event to be staged and formal, permanent arrangements would not have been considered. Even today, golf's Open Championship has no permanent home. Rather, it is shared amongst a number of links courses in England and Scotland with makeshift stands being constructed for the event. As society has developed, more organised and permanent structures have evolved from which to view and participate in major sporting events. The word 'stadium' derives from an ancient Greek measure of length, roughly the equivalent of a furlong which was used as the standard distance for foot-races. As buildings were erected from which to view the racing, they also became known as 'stadiums'.[1]

Many stadiums and venues are now inextricably linked in the eyes of the public with a particular sport; The Currah and Aintree with horse racing, Crystal Palace with athletics, St Andrew's with golf and Lord's with cricket. On a national level our sporting teams have also become associated with particular venues such as The National Stadium Cardiff, Murrayfield, Wembley and Hampden Park. On a club level, Ibrox, Anfield and Old Trafford form part of the footballing folklore of Glasgow Rangers, Liverpool and Manchester United respectively. In effect the stadium has become synonymous with, and part of the sporting identity of, the club.[2] Many stadiums are situated in large cities so that they are accessible to spectators and are by their nature enclosed venues whereby the sporting event is divorced from its surroundings. This is necessary not only for the obvious reason, that it allows for the efficient collection of revenue, but also because inter alia it allows for safety of spectators within a controllable environment.

Some sporting events such as the Round the World Yacht Race do not lend themselves to spectator participation and so perhaps have fallen outside what we now term stadium or arenas. However it is vital that they should be

---

1 The plural of stadium is often referred to as 'stadia'. Whilst this is the correct plural when referring to measures of distance, it is less appropriate when referring to sports grounds. The Oxford English Dictionary prefers the plural 'stadiums' and this will be adopted for the purpose of this chapter.

2 See Bale, B 'Playing at Home: British Football and a Sense of Place' in Williams, J and Wagg, S (ed), *British Football and Social Change: Getting into Europe* (1991), Leicester University Press.

included in any legal discussion for tragedies that befall such sporting events are often as a result of factors comparable to those relevant in conventional stadium 'disasters'.

It would also be wrong to consider only spectator safety because while incidents concerning spectators are rightly an important element of any discussion of sporting venues and the law, they are but one consideration in a complex interaction involving owners, players, spectators, police and local residents. As it will be seen, issues of law even extend to those spectators watching an event from the comfort of their own living rooms.[3]

PARLIAMENT AND STADIUM SAFETY

Although on most occasions when the law becomes involved in sport the effects and implications are relatively minor, it is natural that much of the attention is drawn to major sporting disasters where there is injury and loss of life. These occurrences make up a fraction of the law's involvement in sport yet receive a high proportion of coverage. The latest in a long list of stadium disasters occurred at Hillsborough during an FA Cup semi-final between Liverpool and Nottingham Forest at Sheffield Wednesday's ground on 15 April 1989, as a result of which, 96 lives were lost. The Hillsborough disaster is discussed in more detail later. It is pertinent at this stage to cite the words of Lord Justice Taylor whose opening words in his final report read 'It is a depressing and chastening fact that mine is the ninth official report covering crowd safety at football grounds. After eight previous reports and three editions of the Green Guide, it seems astounding that 96 people could die from overcrowding before the very eyes of those controlling the event'.[4] This comment is one in a long line of indictments of our ability to ensure the safety of the public at sporting events but is perhaps more chilling when compared with the comment of Mr Justice Popplewell, the author of the eighth report[5] in 1986 that 'almost all the matters into which I have been asked to inquire and almost all the solutions I have proposed have been previously considered in detail by many distinguished inquiries over a period of 60 years'.[6]

The first government report into ways of controlling and ensuring the safety of spectators, the Shortt Report,[7] was commissioned following concerns over crowd control highlighted by the massive overcrowding of Wembley

---

3 *Alcock v Chief Constable of South Yorkshire* [1991] 1 WLR 814.

4 The Hillsborough Stadium Disaster (Final Report) Cm 962, p 4.

5 Committee of Inquiry into Crowd Safety and Control at Sports Grounds (Final Report) Cm 9710.

6 At p 10.

7 Cm 2088 (1924).

Stadium for the 1923 FA Cup Final. It was the first time the stadium had hosted the final. However it would be wrong to assume that this was the first occasion that safety at sports stadiums had been called into question. Indeed there is considerable evidence of stadium inadequacies prior to 1923. Stands had collapsed causing injury at the Cheltenham National Hunt Festival in 1886,[8] Ewood Park in Blackburn in 1896[9] and at Ibrox in Glasgow in 1902 where 26 people were killed at a Scotland v England international.

The Shortt Report 1924 highlighted a lack of apportionment of responsibility between the police and the ground authority. It suggested that responsibility should lie in the hands of a single, competent officer. It also recommended the increased use of stewards. Issues such as police responsibilities and adequate stewarding would again come under the microscope following Hillsborough. The report also observed: 'We have been somewhat surprised to find that in many cases little or no precaution has been taken against the risk of fire in stands. We do not suppose that either the risk or the consequences of fire would be so serious in an open stand as in a closed building but we consider it most important that adequate arrangements should be made to deal with any outbreak which might occur.'[10] The tragic consequences of inadequate fire precaution became apparent following the Bradford City fire disaster in 1985, where the Main South Parade Stand was razed to the ground in nine minutes and 56 people died.

If these issues could be identified in 1923 then why were adequate measures not taken in the intervening years to prevent the later disasters? One reason which is particularly pertinent to the Shortt Report is the unwillingness to view the events as a matter of governmental responsibility. The report 'anaemically'[11] concluded 'We are assured that these governing bodies are only too anxious to secure that their sport is carried on under conditions which will promote the public safety and we feel at this stage it is safe to leave the matter to them'.[12]

A good example of Parliament's inability or disinclination to act was the response to the Moelwyn Hughes Report of 1946.[13] The report followed the disaster at Bolton Wanderers' ground in that year.[14] Here a crowd of 85,000, far exceeding anything experienced or expected, had crammed into Burnden Park. Two barriers collapsed resulting in the death of 33 people. The Moelwyn Hughes Report recommended mechanical means of counting those entering the ground, scientific calculations of maximum attendances and inspections of

---

8   *Francis v Cockerell* [1870] 5 QB 501.
9   *Brown v Lewis* [1896] 12 TLR 455.
10   Cm 2088, para 40.
11   The description given by the Moelwyn Hughes Report, Cm 6846 (1946).
12   Paragraph 47.
13   Cm 6846.
14   *The Guardian*, 9 March 1996.

enclosures. The report concluded 'No ground of any considerable size should be opened to the public until it has been licensed by, I suggest as an appropriate licensing authority, the local authority. The issue of the licence would depend upon satisfying the authority as to the construction and equipment of the ground, its compliance with regulations and the proposed maximum figures of admission to the different parts'.[15]

The issues raised by the Hughes Report in 1946 were finally addressed by the Safety of Sports Grounds Act 1975 following another disaster at Ibrox. The recommendations of the Moelwyn Hughes Report were not implemented. The reasons for this are unclear. Cost cannot be ignored as a factor. As the report concluded, 'Compliance with the recommendations of this report will cost money. They will involve grounds in a loss of gate money ... The insurance for greater safety for the public demands a premium'.[16]

Another important factor is the complexity of the issues involved. As the Lang Report 1969 commented 'The working party was dealing with a subject which has been discussed almost *ad nauseam* during recent years. Not unexpectedly the working party has not found a single simple solution for a problem which is often due to a combination of factors'.[17] The Lang Report was commissioned to look into what was considered to be an increasing problem at football grounds: that of crowd behaviour. Subsequent major disasters such as Bradford and Hillsborough have highlighted that whilst hooliganism remains a worrying social condition it is in most instances a distinct problem from that of stadium safety.[18]

The Wheatley Report 1971[19] was commissioned following the disaster at Ibrox Park where inadequate stairways and handrails caused the death of 66 spectators. The report is of great significance as it was the first of the reports to directly spawn an Act of Parliament, the Safety of Sports Grounds Act 1975. In his report Lord Wheatley was conscious of both the history of recommendations such as his and the economic arguments against imposing stringent safety conditions. He dismissed such misgivings emphatically:

The Wheatley Report

I recognise that a decision to introduce a licensing system for grounds along the lines I have recommended may cause anxiety to some football clubs and football administrators. As I see it, their misgivings are associated with a fear that such stringent conditions may be attached to the granting of a licence that many clubs may not be able to afford the cost and some may have to go out of business ... My answer to that is this. My task is to consider the problem of

15   The Moelwyn Hughes Report, p 11.

16   *Ibid*, p 12.

17   *Ibid*, p 3.

18   The Heysel Stadium disaster is an unusual example of where the issues of crowd management and crowd disturbances were both integral factors.

19   Cm 4952.

crowd safety at the grounds. Clubs which charge the public for admission have a duty to see that their grounds are reasonably safe for spectators. That is a primary consideration. It is accordingly necessary that some standards should be imposed and observed. This has been recognised by the football authorities themselves ... I have canvassed all the alternatives that have been proposed or which I personally thought were reasonable to consider and the one I decided was best to meet the situation in the interest of the public is a licensing system by a local authority. There is nothing new in this proposal. It has been mooted for almost 50 years. It can come as no surprise to the football world and in the light of happenings over the years the demand for an independent appraisal and determination of the safety of grounds becomes almost irresistible. I certainly cannot resist it.[20]

Other reports such as the Harrington Report,[21] The McElhone Report[22] which looked at *inter alia* the consumption of alcohol, and the Department of the Environment Working Group 1984 which was commissioned following violence by football supporters in Luxembourg in 1983 and France in 1984, all focused on what was perceived to be an increase in football crowd violence. None of these reports resulted directly in legislation.

Justice Popplewell's Report published in the aftermath of the Bradford City fire disaster concluded 'A study of all these reports (and there are numerous reports and discussion papers by other bodies) shows that the following are measures which have been frequently recommended: closed Circuit Television; membership cards; segregation; more seating at football grounds; encouragement of supporters clubs; a ban on alcohol; involvement of the clubs with the community and heavier penalties. I too shall argue for these and related measures'. He added wisely, 'It is to be hoped they will be more vigorously pursued by the appropriate bodies than in the past'.[23]

Whilst the Popplewell Report is often perceived as being an inquiry into the Bradford Fire Disaster, its terms of reference were in fact wider. On the same day as the Bradford fire disaster, one supporter was killed and another 200 injured in violent clashes between rival supporters of Birmingham City and Leeds United at St Andrew's and football violence was a high-profile issue. Justice Popplewell was asked to inquire into both these events.

This tendency to amalgamate issues of crowd management and crowd disturbances set a dangerous precedent. The incident at the Hysel Stadium before the 1985 European Cup Final between Liverpool and Juventus where 39 supporters were killed was also considered by Justice Popplewell. The incident represents a rare occurrence where fighting spectators (crowd

---

20 Paragraphs 66 and 67.
21 *Soccer Hooliganism: A Preliminary Report* (1968), Bristol: John Wright and Sons Ltd.
22 *Report of the Working Group on Football Crowd Behaviour*, Scottish Education Department, HMSO 1977.
23 At p 16.

disturbance) caused a concentration of people causing a wall to collapse (crowd management). Bradford and subsequently Hillsborough were disasters caused by an inability to house large numbers of people in safety and crowd disturbance played little if any part. One of the most significant developments following Hillsborough was the government's ill-fated attempt to introduce a membership system: a means of curbing crowd disturbances. Measures aimed at curbing crowd violence such as controlling the consumption of alcohol, increasing police powers of arrest and courts powers to punish, are very different from the measures needed to manage large numbers of spectators in an enclosed space. This calls for good stadium design, adequate safety margins and good stewarding.

Adequate safety measures cost money and although the Taylor Report 1990 and the government's resolve in pursuing all seater stadiums showed a refreshing departure from the recommendations of earlier reports, the government's financial assistance in achieving these aims could hardly be described as largess. It was decreed by the Football Licensing Authority that all first and second division clubs should be all seater by 1994 with third and fourth division clubs given until 1999. With less wealthy clubs such as Aldershot and Maidstone vanishing in 1992 because of financial problems, it was clear that clubs in the lower divisions could not cope with the financial burden. David Mellor, the National Heritage Secretary, announced subsequently that only those clubs outside the Premier League with crowds above 10,000 would have to shut down their terracing. In 1990 the government had reduced its take from the Pools Betting Levy by 2.5% and in 1993 this was reduced further to release £100 million more over five years to assist the clubs. Most of the money was earmarked for third and fourth division clubs. It was estimated that the Premier League needed approximately £200 million to fulfil the recommendations.[24] The Football Trust which administered the distribution of moneys to the clubs offered a maximum rebuilding grant of £2 million to each Premiership club.

During the 1980s, deaths occurred at football grounds around the world from Columbia to Nigeria.[25] In Britain the desire to address issues of safety in the light of the Popplewell and Taylor Reports is indicative of a more paternal approach towards spectator safety and, it has been suggested, British sporting grounds have never been as safe. However if Parliament continues to rely on the Green Guide, the advisory document detailing safety standards and specifications for sports grounds, rather than extending the safety legislation, then the onus of ensuring spectator safety rests with individual sporting clubs. A Channel 4 *Dispatches*[26] programme has highlighted that many of the Green Guide recommendations such as minimum corridor widths and adequate

---

24 Heatley, M and Ford, D, *British Football Grounds Then and Now* (1994), Shepperton: Dial Press.

25 *Ibid.*

26 'An Accident Waiting to Happen.' Originally broadcast on 12 October 1994.

means of egress are not implemented by English football clubs. This lack of a safety culture brings into question the effectiveness of recommendations which lack criminal sanctions.[27]

STADIUMS AND NEIGHBOURS

Despite comments thus far that would suggest that legal issues relating to sporting venues are contained within the stadium, one would need only to speak to residents living near to major sporting venues to appreciate that whilst the sporting action may be contained, legal issues, like spectators, tend to spill over and affect the surrounding environment. Legal protection for those outside the stadium is important for two principal reasons.

First because in order to arrive at and depart from the stadium, spectators need to pass through residential areas. Large numbers of fans need to be managed in such a way as to avoid encroaching on the safety and peaceful enjoyment of the property of local residents.

Secondly because what goes on inside the stadium directly impacts on those outside. Sir Garfield Sobers's six sixes in an over off Malcolm Nash at the St Helen's ground in Swansea is rightly recognised as an historic sporting moment, in no small measure because of the power and timing of some of Sobers's hits from long off to square leg, two of which cleared not only the boundary ropes but also the ground itself.[28] From a legal perspective such shots could have caused injury to property and persons and it is not beyond the realms of possibility that a passer by could have been killed. This problem is even more evident at the village green level where cricket grounds are often situated next to the highway or adjoining property where there is little or no protection.[29]

A less tangible concern but one which may impact on a greater number of local residents is the level of noise emanating from the stadium. This noise may be particularly acute if the stadium in question hosts motor or speedboat racing for example, although these event tend to be held in less built up areas.[30]

---

27 See Taylor, I, 'English Football in the 1990's: Taking Hillsborough Seriously?' in Williams, J and Wagg, S (ed), *British Football and Social Change: Getting into Europe* (1991), Leicester University Press.

28 Although such feats of hitting are rare, Sobers achievement was repeated by Ravi Shastri off of the bowling of Tilak Raj in the 1984–85 Ranji Trophy and almost by Frank Hayes of Lancashire against Glamorgan in 1977 off the unfortunate Malcolm Nash (his second boundary was a four).

29 In a club game between Bath Cricket Association and Thornbury in 1902, Billy Hyman hit 359 runs in 100 minutes. Fortunately for local residents, even at club level, such Herculean feats are rare.

30 However, in more recent years Parliament has begun to take an interest in the noise pollution caused by motor racing circuits. See *The Times*, 22 April 1995.

THE ARRIVAL AND DEPARTURE OF SPECTATORS

The problems of spectators as they arrive and leave sporting venues can be dealt with briefly. Any physical or property damage sustained by local residents will usually be dealt with by the criminal law or by claims in tort.

Sport-specific criminal provisions are discussed in more detail later. General criminal provisions aimed at crowd control are contained in the Public Order Act 1986 and the Criminal Justice and Public Order Act 1994, examples of which are given below.

Section 4 of the Public Order Act 1986

(1) A person is guilty of an offence if he–

  (a) uses towards another person threatening, abusive or insulting words or behaviour, or

  (b) distributes or displays to another person any writing, sign or other visible representation which is threatening, abusive or insulting,

with intent to cause that person to believe that immediate unlawful violence will be used against him or another by any person or to provoke the immediate use of unlawful violence by that person or another or whereby that person is likely to believe that such violence will be used or it is likely that such violence will be provoked.

(3) A constable may arrest without warrant anyone he reasonably suspects is committing an offence under this section.

Section 5 of the Public Order Act 1986

(1) A person is guilty of an offence if he–

  (a) uses towards another person threatening, abusive or insulting words or behaviour or disorderly behaviour, or

  (b) displays any writing, sign or other visible representation which is threatening, abusive or insulting,

within the hearing or sight of a person likely to be caused harassment, alarm or distress thereby.

(4) A constable may arrest a person without warrant if–

  (a) he engages in offensive conduct which the constable warns him to stop, and

  (b) he engages in further offensive conduct immediately or shortly after the warning.

Section 60 of the Criminal Justice and Public Order Act 1994

(1) Where a police officer of or above the rank of superintendent reasonably believes that–

  (a) incidents involving serious violence may take place in any locality in his area, and

  (b) it is expedient to do so to prevent their occurrence,

he may give authorisation that the powers to stop and search persons and vehicles conferred by this section shall be exercisable at any place within that locality for a period not exceeding twenty four hours.

(4) This section confers on any constable in uniform power–

    (a) to stop any pedestrian and search him or anything carried by him for offensive weapons or dangerous instruments,

    (b) to stop any vehicle and search the vehicle, its driver and any passenger for offensive weapons or dangerous instruments.

(5) A constable may, in the exercise of those powers, stop any person or vehicle and make any search he thinks fit whether or not he has any grounds for suspecting that the person or vehicle is carrying weapons or articles of that kind.

In tort, claims against the stadium owners may prove problematic since, generally speaking, owners are not responsible for the actions of spectators outside the stadium. In *AG v Corke*[31] the defendant was held responsible under the principle in *Rylands v Fletcher*[32] for the nuisance created off his land by travellers staying on the land. The principle in *Rylands v Fletcher* is a variation on the tort of nuisance as it imposes strict liability for foreseeable damage caused by the escape from the defendant's land of things accumulated or brought there by the defendant which amounts to a non-natural use of the land.[33] Had this principle continued to be applied to human beings it may have proved to be a means by which local residents could have sought redress from stadium owners. Subsequent decisions suggest that the rule is not applicable in these circumstances.[34]

NEIGHBOURS AND SPORTING EVENTS

The law relating to damage outside the stadium caused by the activities inside the stadium has resulted in many of the most famous sporting legal cases. It is a possibility in many sports that a ball may be hit out of the stadium. In football a defender's desperate clearance from an onrushing forward, in rugby a kick into touch to move play up-field. Incidents of these types of projectiles causing harm are rare. Much more likely, although not exclusively, is the

---

31 [1933] Ch 89.

32 [1886] LR 3 HL 330; [1861–73] All ER Rep 1.

33 *Cambridge Water v Eastern Counties Leather Plc* [1994] 1 All ER 53.

34 *Smith v Scott* [1973] Ch 314, *Matheson v Northcote College Board of Governors* [1975] 2 NZLR 106.

potential damage from a golf ball[35] or a cricket ball.[36] Not only is a cricket ball hard but, by awarding six runs for a shot which clears the boundary, the game encourages big hits and potential danger. Any liability for such an occurrence is likely to be based on the torts of negligence and nuisance.

Negligence can be defined as the breach of a duty to take care, owed by the defendant, which causes harm to the plaintiff. Private nuisance occurs where the use by the defendants of their land results in unreasonable interference with the plaintiff's enjoyment of their land. As nuisance requires the plaintiff to have an interest in land it follows that this tort can only be invoked by those with an interest in land in the vicinity of the stadium[37] whereas a claim in negligence can be made by property owners or unfortunate passers by.

In *Bolton v Stone and Others*[38] a visiting cricketer struck a six which had cleared the boundary, 75 feet from the wicket, a 17 foot fence and had travelled a further 100 yards before striking the plaintiff standing on the highway. The cricket ground had been used for 90 years and evidence from the last 30 revealed only six incidents of escaped balls with no damage having been caused by any. The House of Lords allowed the appeal on the basis that the likelihood of injury occurring was so slight that a reasonable man would be justified in ignoring it:

Bolton v Stone [1951] 1 All ER 1078

Lord Reid: This case, therefore, raises sharply the question what is the nature and extent of the duty of a person who promotes on his land operations which may cause damage to persons on an adjoining highway. Is it that he must not carry out or permit an operation which he knows or ought to know clearly can cause such damage, however improbable that result may be or is it that he is only bound to take into account the possibility of such damage if such damage is a likely or probable consequence of what he does or permits or if the risk of damage is such that a reasonable man, careful of the safety of his neighbour, would regard that risk as material? I do not know of any case where this question has had to be decided or even where it has been fully discussed. Of course there are many cases in which somewhat similar questions have arisen but, generally speaking, if injury to another person from the defendants' acts is reasonably foreseeable the chance that injury will result is substantial and it does not matter in which way the duty is stated. In such cases I do not think

---

35   In *Castle v St Augustines Links Ltd and Another* [1922] 38 TLR 615. Here a taxi driver was successful in an action for nuisance (although today would most probably be brought under the tort of negligence) against a golf club, when a golfer's wayward tee shot from the 13th tee smashed through the window of the plaintiff's taxi resulting in the loss of an eye. Williamson, DS, 'Some Legal Aspects of Golf' (1995) 3(1) *Sport and the Law Journal*.

36   For example see (1996) 39 *Legal Times* 24.

37   *Hunter and Others v Canary Wharf Ltd; Hunter and Others v London Docklands Development Corporation* [1997] NLJ 634.

38   [1951] 1 All ER 1078.

that much assistance is to be got from analysing the language which a judge has used. More assistance is to be got from cases where judges have clearly chosen their language with care in setting out a principle but even so, statements of the law must be read in light of the facts of the particular case. Nevertheless, making all allowances for this, I do find at least a tendency to base duty rather on the likelihood of damage to others than on its foreseeability alone.

The definition of negligence which has, perhaps, been most often quoted is that of Alderson B in *Blyth v Birmingham Waterworks Co* ... I think that reasonable men do, in fact, take into account the degree of risk and do not act on a bare possibility as they would if the risk were more substantial. A more recent attempt to find a basis for man's legal duty to his neighbour is that of Lord Atkin in *Donoghue v Stevenson*: 'You must take reasonable care to avoid acts or omissions which you can reasonably foresee would be likely to injure your neighbour.' Parts of Lord Atkin's statement have been criticised as being too wide but I am not aware that it has been stated that any part of it is too narrow. Lord Atkin does not say 'Which you can reasonably foresee could injure your neighbour': he introduces the limitation 'would be likely to injure your neighbour'. Lord Macmillan said in *Bourhill v Young* that 'The duty to take care is the duty to avoid doing or omitting to do anything the doing or omitting to do which may have as its reasonable and probable consequence injury to others and the duty is owed to those to whom injury may reasonably and probably be anticipated if the duty is not observed'.

Lord Thankerton in *Glasgow Corpn v Muir*, after quoting this statement, said:

> In my opinion, it has long been held in Scotland that all that a person can be held bound to foresee are the reasonable and probable consequences of the failure to take care, judged by the standard of the ordinary reasonable man ... The court must be careful to place itself in the position of the person charged with the duty and to consider what he or she should have reasonably anticipated as a natural and probable consequence of neglect and not to give undue weight to the fact that a distressing accident has happened ...

The law of Scotland does not differ in this matter from the law of England. There are other statements which may seem to differ but which I do not think are really inconsistent with this. For example in *Fardon v Harcourt-Rivington* Lord Dunedin said 'This is such an extremely unlikely event that I do not think any reasonable man could be convicted of negligence if he did not take into account the possibility of such an occurrence and provide against it ... people must guard against reasonable probabilities but they are not bound to guard against fantastic possibilities'.

I doubt whether Lord Dunedin meant the division into reasonable probabilities and fantastic possibilities to be exhaustive so that anything more than a fantastic possibility must be regarded as a reasonable probability. What happened in that case was that a dog left in a car broke the window and a splinter from the glass entered the plaintiff's eye. Before that had happened it might well have been described as a fantastic possibility and Lord Dunedin did not have to consider a case nearer the border-line. I do not think it necessary to discuss other statements which may seem to be at variance with the trend of authority which I have quoted because I have not found any which is plainly inconsistent with it and I have left out of account cases where the defendant clearly owed a duty to the plaintiff and by his negligence caused damage to the plaintiff. In such cases questions have arisen whether damages can only be recovered in respect of consequences which were foreseeable or were natural and probable or whether damages can be recovered in respect of all consequences, whether foreseeable or probable or not but remoteness of damage in this sense appears to me to be a different question from that which arises in the present case.

Counsel for the respondent in the present case had to put his case so high as to say that, at least as soon as one ball had been driven into the road in the ordinary course of a match, the appellants could and should have realised that that might happen again and that, if it did, someone might be injured and that that was enough to put on the appellants a duty to take steps to prevent such an occurrence. If the true test is foreseeability alone I think that must be so. Once a ball has been driven on to a road without there being anything extraordinary to account for the fact, there is clearly a risk that another will follow and if it does there is clearly a chance, small though it may be, that somebody may be injured. On the theory that it is foreseeability alone that matters it would be irrelevant to consider how often a ball might be expected to land in the road and it would not matter whether the road was the busiest street or the quietest country lane. The only difference between these cases is in the degree of risk. It would take a good deal to make me believe that the law has departed so far from the standards which guide ordinary careful people in ordinary life. In the crowded conditions of modern life even the most careful person cannot avoid creating some risks and accepting others. What a man must not do and what I think a careful man tries not to do, is to create a risk which is substantial. Of course, there are numerous cases where special circumstances require that a higher standard shall be observed and where that is recognised by the law but I do not think that this case comes within any such special category.

Lord Radcliffe: I can see nothing unfair in the appellants being required to compensate the respondent for the serious injury that she has received as a result of the sport that they have organised on their cricket ground at Cheetham Hill but the law of negligence is concerned less with what is fair than with what is culpable and I cannot persuade myself that the appellants have been guilty of any culpable act or omission in this case ...

If the test whether there has been a breach of duty were to depend merely on the answer to the question whether this accident was a reasonably foreseeable risk, I think that there would have been a breach of duty, for that such an accident might take place some time or other might very reasonably have been present to the minds of the appellants. It was quite foreseeable and there would have been nothing unreasonable in allowing the imagination to dwell on the possibility of its occurring. There was, however, only a remote, perhaps I ought to say only a very remote, chance of the accident taking place at any particular time, for, if it was to happen, not only had a ball to carry the fence round the ground but it had also to coincide in its arrival with the presence of some person on what does not look like a crowded thoroughfare and actually to strike that person in some way that would cause sensible injury.

Those being the facts, a breach of duty has taken place if they show the appellants guilty of a failure to take reasonable care to prevent the accident. One may phrase it as 'reasonable care' or 'ordinary care' or 'proper care' – all these phrases are to be found in decisions of authority – but the fact remains that, unless there here has been something which a reasonable man would blame as falling beneath the standard of conduct that he would set for himself and require of his neighbour, there has been no breach of legal duty and here, I think, the respondent's case breaks down. It seems to me that a reasonable man, taking account of the chances against an accident happening, would not have felt himself called on either to abandon the use of the ground for cricket or to increase the height of his surrounding fences. He would have done what the appellants did. In other words, he would have done nothing. Whether, if the unlikely event of an accident did occur and his play turn to another's hurt, he would have thought it equally proper to offer no more consolation to his victim than the reflection that a social being is not immune from social risks, I do not say, for I do not think that that is a consideration which is relevant to legal liability.[39]

The fact that the ball had left the ground previously and the chances of it doing again had been guarded against to some extent by the fencing, shows that the decision was not based on foreseeability alone. The House of Lords was able to look at the history of cricket balls leaving the ground and concluded that there were some foreseeable risks that it was possible to ignore.

It is interesting to note that Mrs Stone's action was taken against those responsible for the ground and not the batsman. It will be no defence in this type of situation for those in control the ground to shift responsibility onto the players. The onus remains with those who control the cricket ground or driving range to take action should the occurrence of balls leaving the ground reach an unacceptable level. The difficulty will be to set such a level.

The law is clear that the level of duty owed by sportsmen will be that of the reasonable sportsman with the level of skill and knowledge of the plaintiff. It is in this way that we can require a higher level of skill from doctors and other professionals. Clearly then we cannot expect a child to have the knowledge and experience of a reasonable adult. It is possible that a professional sportsman may be liable in circumstances where a child who hits a ball from a playground cage may not. The potential liability of the owners of the stadium will depend on their assessment of the likelihood of risk taking into account the age and skill of the participants.

In *Hilder v Associated Portland Cement Manufacturers Ltd*[40] the defendant landowners allowed children to play on their land their situated adjacent to a

---

39 At p 1084.
40 [1961] 1 WLR 1434.

highway. During a game of football the ball was kicked over a small fence onto the highway. The husband of the plaintiff was killed as a result of avoiding the ball:

Hilder v Associated Portland Cement Manufacturers Ltd [1961] 1 WLR 1434

Ashworth J: In my judgment, a reasonable man would come to the conclusion that there was a risk of damage to persons using the road and that risk was not so small that he could safely disregard it. While it is true that a football itself is unlikely to damage a person or vehicle on the road in the way that might occur with a cricket ball or a golf ball, I think that the sudden appearance of a football in front of a cyclist or motor-cyclist is quite likely to cause him to fall or to swerve into the path of another vehicle and in either event sustain serious injury ... Accordingly, I find that the defendants failed to take reasonable care in all the circumstances and that this failure unhappily caused the death of the deceased. The claim in negligence therefore succeeds.[41]

It can be seen that it is often difficult to predict when liability will be imposed: *Bolton* and *Hilder* are difficult to distinguish. No reference is made in *Hilder* to the frequency with which the football left the field. It may well be that the reasonable man, with the knowledge that it is one of the objectives of the game of cricket to hit the ball off the playing field, may conclude that *Bolton* posed a greater risk than *Hilder*. The next extract is from *Overseas Tankship (UK) Ltd Miller SS Co Pty*,[42] commonly known as *The Wagon Mound (No 2)*. This is not a sporting case but is the leading case in this area where Lord Reid made it clear that just because a likelihood is remote does not mean that one has carte blanche to ignore it:

Overseas Tankship (UK) Ltd Miller SS Co Pty [1966] 2 All ER 709 Privy Council

Lord Reid: It does not follow that, no matter what the circumstances may be, it is justifiable to neglect a risk of such a small magnitude. A reasonable man would only neglect such a risk if he had some valid reason for doing so, eg that it would involve considerable expense to eliminate the risk. He would weigh the risk against the difficulty of eliminating it. If the activity which caused the injury to Miss Stone had been an unlawful activity there can be little doubt but that *Bolton v Stone* would have been decided differently. In their Lordships' judgment *Bolton v Stone* did not alter the general principle that a person must be regarded as negligent if he does not take steps to eliminate a risk which he knows or ought to know is a real risk and not a mere possibility which would never influence the mind of a reasonable man. What that decision did was to recognise and give effect to the qualification that it is justifiable not to take steps to eliminate a real risk if it is small and if the circumstances are such that a reasonable man, careful of the safety of his neighbour, would think it right to neglect it.[43]

---

41 At 1438.
42 Privy Council [1966] 2 All ER 709.
43 At p 718.

It would seem that foreseeability and likelihood are part of a larger equation. Whereas the ground owner may be justified in ignoring a foreseeable risk of a rare occurrence if the outcome would cause limited damage, he may not be at liberty to ignore the same risk if the possible outcome is more serious. Does the law adequately protect the likes of Mrs Stone? It is important to note that, in *Bolton*, Lord Reid was of the opinion that the cost of remedial measures should not be taken into account when considering the standard of duty owed by the ground owners, however in *The Wagon Mound* he appeared to conclude that the cost of prevention was a factor to be considered. It would be judicious for stadium owners to take all low cost safety precautions.

In the above cases liability centred on the tort of negligence however as the courts have stated the likelihood of someone being injured is remote. Most wayward tee shots or six-hits will injure no one. However for people dwelling beside stadiums and grounds the fear of damage to person and property can undermine the enjoyment of that property. In *Miller v Jackson*[44] the defendant cricket club had played cricket on a small ground for many years. A small housing estate was built on land abutting the cricket field so that, despite there being a boundary fence, some balls were bound to be hit into the houses or their gardens. The plaintiffs sued in nuisance and negligence in respect of cricket balls being hit into their garden:

Miller v Jackson [1977] 3 All ER 338 CA

Geoffrey Lane LJ: ... have the plaintiffs established that the defendants are guilty of nuisance or negligence as alleged? The evidence ... makes it clear that the risk of injury to property at least was both foreseeable and foreseen. It is obvious that such injury is going to take place so long as cricket is being played on this field ... It is true that the risk must be balanced against the measures which are necessary to eliminate it and against what the defendants can do to prevent accidents from happening ... In the present case, so far from being one incident of an unprecedented nature about which complaint is being made, this is a series of incidents or perhaps a continuing failure to prevent incidents from happening, coupled with the certainty that they are going to happen again. The risk of injury to person and property is so great that on each occasion when a ball comes over the fence and causes damage to the plaintiffs, the defendants are guilty of negligence.

In circumstances such as these it is very difficult and probably unnecessary, except as an interesting intellectual exercise, to define the frontiers between negligence and nuisance: see Lord Wilberforce in *Goldman v Hargrave*.

Was there here a use by the defendants of their land involving an unreasonable interference with the plaintiffs' enjoyment of their land? There is here in effect no dispute that there has been and is likely to be in the future an interference with the plaintiffs' enjoyment of No 20 Brackenridge. The only question is whether it is unreasonable. It is a truism to say that this is a matter of degree.

---

44 [1977] 3 All ER 338 CA.

What that means is this. A balance has to be maintained between on the one hand the rights of the individual to enjoy his house and garden without the threat of damage and on the other hand the rights of the public in general or a neighbour to engage in lawful pastimes. Difficult questions may sometimes arise when the defendants' activities are offensive to the senses, for example, by way of noise. Where, as here, the damage or potential damage is physical the answer is more simple. There is, subject to what appears hereafter, no excuse I can see which exonerates the defendants from liability in nuisance for what they have done or from what they threaten to do. It is true that no one has yet been physically injured. That is probably due to a great extent to the fact that the householders in Brackenridge desert their gardens while cricket is in progress. The danger of injury is obvious and is not slight enough to disregarded. There is here a real risk of serious injury.

There is, however, one obviously strong point in the defendants' favour. They or their predecessors have been playing cricket on this ground (and no doubt hitting sixes out of it) for 70 years or so. Can someone, by building a house on the edge of the field in circumstances where it must have been obvious that balls might be hit over the fence, effectively stop cricket being played? Precedent apart, justice would seem to demand that the plaintiffs should be left to make the most of the site they have elected to occupy with all its obvious advantages and all its equally obvious disadvantages. It is pleasant to have an open space over which to look from your bedroom and sitting room windows, so far as it is possible to see over the concrete wall. Why should you complain of the obvious disadvantages which arise from the particular purpose to which the open space is being put? Put briefly, can the defendants take advantage of the fact that the plaintiffs have put themselves in such a position by coming to occupy a house on the edge of a small cricket field, with the result that what was not a nuisance in the past now becomes a nuisance? If the matter were res integra, I confess I should be inclined to find for the defendants. It does not seem just that a long established activity – in itself innocuous – should be brought to an end because someone chooses to build a house nearby and so turn an innocent pastime into an actionable nuisance. Unfortunately, however, the question is not open. In *Sturges v Bridgman* this very problem arose ... That decision involved the assumption, which so far as one can discover has never been questioned, that it is no answer to a claim in nuisance for the defendant to show that the plaintiff brought the trouble on his own head by building or coming to live in a house so close to the defendant's premises that he would inevitably be affected by the defendant's activities, where no one had been affected previously: see also *Bliss v Hall*. It may be that this rule works injustice, it may be that one would decide the matter differently in the absence of authority. But we are bound by the decision in *Sturges v Bridgman*; it is not for this court as I see it to alter a rule which stood for so long.

Lord Denning MR (dissenting): In support of the case, the plaintiffs rely on the dictum of Lord Reid in *Bolton v Stone:* 'If cricket cannot be played on a ground without creating a substantial risk, then it should not be played there at all.' I would agree with that saying if the houses or road was there first and the cricket ground came there second. We would not allow the garden of Lincoln's Inn to be turned into a cricket ground. It would be too dangerous for windows and people. But I would not agree with Lord Reid's *dictum* when the cricket ground has been there for 70 years and the houses are newly built at the very edge of it. I recognise that the cricket club are under a duty to use all reasonable care consistent with the playing of the game of cricket but I do not think the cricket club can be expected to give up the game of cricket altogether. After all they have their rights in their cricket ground. They have spent money, labour and love in the making of it: and they have the right to play upon it as they have done for 70 years. Is this all to be rendered useless to them by the thoughtless and selfish act of an estate developer in building right up to the edge of it? Can the developer or a purchaser of the house say to the cricket club: 'Stop playing. Clear out.' I do not think so. And I will give my reasons ...

The case was pleaded in negligence or alternatively nuisance. That was, I think, quite right, having regard to the decision of the House of Lords in *Bolton v Stone*. Miss Stone had just stepped out of her garden gate on to the pavement when she was hit by a cricket ball ... Miss Stone did seek to put her case on the doctrine of *Rylands v Fletcher*. She suggested that a cricket ball was a dangerous thing which the defendants had brought on to the cricket ground and it had escaped. That suggestion was dismissed by the House of Lords out of hand ... She also suggested that the club were liable in nuisance: but this was not pressed in the House of Lords, because nuisance was not distinguishable from negligence. Lord Porter remarked that 'in the circumstances of this case nuisance cannot be established unless negligence is proved'.

In our present case, too, nuisance was pleaded as an alternative to negligence. The tort of nuisance in many cases overlaps the tort of negligence. The boundary lines were discussed in ... *The Wagon Mound (No 2)* and *Goldman v Hargrave*.

But there is at any rate one important distinction between them. It lies in the nature of the remedy sought. Is it damages? Or an injunction? If the plaintiff seeks a remedy in damages for injury done to him or his property, he can lay his claim either in negligence or nuisance. But if he seeks an injunction to stop the playing of cricket altogether, I think he must make his claim in nuisance. The books are full of cases when an injunction has been granted to restrain the continuance of a nuisance. But there is no case, so far as I know, where it has been granted so as to stop a man being negligent. At any rate in a case of this kind where an occupier of a house or land seeks to restrain his neighbour from doing something on his own land, the only appropriate cause of action on which to base the remedy of an injunction is nuisance: see the report of the Law Commission on Civil Liability For Dangerous Things and Activities, Law Commission Report No 32 (1970) p 25. It is the very essence of a private nuisance that it is the unreasonable use by a man of his land to the detriment of his neighbour. He must have been guilty of the fault, not necessarily of negligence but of the unreasonable use of the land: see *The Wagon Mound (No 2)*, by Lord Reid.

It has been often said in nuisance cases that the rule is *sic utere tuo ut alienum non laedas*. But that is a most misleading maxim. Lord Wright put it in its proper place in *Sedleigh-Denheld v O'Callaghan*:

[It] is not only lacking in definiteness but is also inaccurate. An occupier may make in many ways a use of his land which causes damage to the neighbouring landowners and yet be free from liability ... a useful test is perhaps what is reasonable according to the ordinary usages of mankind living in society or more correctly in a particular society.

I would, therefore, adopt this test. Is the use by the cricket club of this ground for playing cricket a reasonable use of it? To my mind it is a most reasonable use. Just consider the circumstances. For over 70 years the game of cricket has been played on this ground to the great benefit of the community as a whole and to the injury of none. No one could suggest that it was a nuisance to the neighbouring owners simply because an enthusiastic batsman occasionally hit a ball out of the ground for six to the approval of the admiring onlookers. Then I would ask: does it suddenly become a nuisance because one of the neighbours chooses to build a house on the very edge of the ground in such a position that it may well be struck by the ball on the rare occasion when there is a hit for six? To my mind the answer is plainly No. The building of the house does not convert the playing of cricket into a nuisance when it was not so before. If and in so far as any damage is caused to the house or anyone in it, it is because of the position in which it was built. Suppose that the house had not been built by a developer but by a private owner. He would be in much the same position as the farmer who previously put his cows in the field. He could not complain if a batsman hit a six out of the ground and by a million to one chance it struck a cow or even the farmer himself. He would be in no better position than a spectator at Lord's or the Oval or at a motor rally. At any rate, even if he could claim damages for the loss of the cow or the injury, he could not get an injunction to stop the cricket. If the private owner could not get an injunction, neither should a developer or a purchaser from him.

It was said, however, that the case of the physician's consulting-room was to the contrary: *Sturges v Bridgman*. But that turned on the old law about easements and prescriptions and so forth. It was in the days when rights of property were in the ascendant and not subject to any limitations except those provided by the law of easements. But nowadays it is a matter of balancing the conflicting interests of the two neighbours. That was made clear by Lord Wright in *Sedleigh-Denfield v O'Callaghan*, when he said 'A balance has to be maintained between the right of the occupier to do what he likes with his own and the right of his neighbour not to be interfered with'.

In this case it is our task to balance the right of the cricket club to continue playing cricket on their cricket ground as against the right of the householder not to be interfered with. On taking the balance, I would give priority to the right of the cricket club to continue playing cricket on the ground, as they have done for the last 70 years. It takes precedence over the right of the newcomer to sit in his garden undisturbed. After all, he bought the house four years ago in mid-summer when the cricket season was at its height. He might have guessed that there was a risk that a hit for six might possibly land on his property. If he finds that he does not like it, he ought, when cricket is played, to sit on the other side of the house or in the front garden or go out: or take advantage of the offers the club have made to him of fitting unbreakable glass and so forth. Or if he does not like that, he ought to sell his house and move elsewhere. I expect there are many who would gladly buy it in order to be near the cricket field and open space. At any rate he ought not be allowed to stop cricket being played on this ground.

This case is new. It should be approached on principles applicable to modern conditions. There is a contest here between the interest of the public at large; and the interest of a private individual. The public interest lies in protecting the environment by preserving our playing fields in the face of mounting development and by enabling our youth to enjoy all the benefits of outdoor games, such as cricket and football. The private interest lies in securing the privacy of his home and garden without intrusion or interference by anyone. In deciding between these two conflicting interests, it must be remembered that it is not a question of damages. If by a million to one chance a cricket ball does go out of the ground and cause damage, the cricket club will pay. There is no difficulty on that score. No, it is a question of an injunction. And in our law you will find it repeatedly affirmed that an injunction is a discretionary remedy. In a new situation like this, we have to think afresh as to how discretion should be exercised. On the one hand, Mrs Miller is a very sensitive lady who has worked herself up into such a state that she exclaimed to the judge: 'I just want to be allowed to live in peace ... Have I got to wait until someone is killed before anything can be done?' If she feels like that about it, it is quite plain that, for peace in the future, one or other has to move. Either the cricket club has to move: but goodness knows where. I do not suppose for a moment there is any field in Lintz to which they could move. Or Mrs Miller must move elsewhere. As between their conflicting interests, I am of opinion that the public interest should prevail over the private interest. The cricket club should not be driven out. In my opinion the right exercise of discretion is to refuse an injunction; and, of course, to refuse damages in lieu of an injunction. Likewise as to the claim for past damages. The club were entitled to use this ground for cricket in the accustomed way. It was not a nuisance, nor was it negligent of them so to run it, nor was the batsman negligent when he hit the ball for six. All were doing simply what they were entitled to do. So if the club had put it to the test, I would have dismissed the claim for damages also. But as the club very fairly say that they are willing to pay for any damage, I am content that there should be an award of £400 to cover any past or future damage. I would allow the appeal, accordingly.[45]

The judgments given by the Court of Appeal tend to muddy the waters rather than clear them.[46] The two issues at stake were whether there was liability in negligence or nuisance by the cricket club in allowing balls to be struck regularly into neighbouring gardens and if there was liability, what would be the appropriate remedy. On the second issue the appellant sought an injunction: a discretionary remedy to prevent recurrence of the tortious act. They had been offered compensation by the club which was also prepared to

---

45 *Ibid*, 342.

46 See Parpworth, N, 'Lord Denning and the "Other Cricket Ball Case"' (1994) 2(2) *Sport and the Law Journal* 4 and 'A Further Cricket Ball Case: *Lacey v Parker and Bingle*' (1994) 2(3) *Sport and the Law Journal* 9.

undertake preventative measures such as the installation of safety glass. A fence had already been erected and expert advice had suggested weather conditions would make a higher fence unviable. However damages would be unsatisfactory in these circumstances. What the appellant wanted was an end to the nuisance of cricket balls landing in her garden.

Geoffrey Lane and Cumming-Bruce LJJ thought that there was liability on the part of the cricket club, Lord Denning thought not. Geoffrey Lane LJ was prepared to grant an injunction Lord Denning and Cumming-Bruce were not. The public interest, thought Geoffrey Lane LJ, could not be put before the rights of individuals to quiet enjoyment of their land. Lord Denning on the other hand thought that the public interest was such a vital consideration that it made the playing of cricket and the inevitable six hits into neighbouring gardens a reasonable activity which did not therefore attract liability in the first place. Cumming-Bruce LJ did not invoke the public interest to deny liability but considered it a factor in his refusal to grant an injunction. Geoffrey Lane LJ, whilst sympathetic toward the respondents' argument that the club had existed long before the housing estate was built, felt bound by precedent to disregard this consideration whereas the fact that the appellant had come to the nuisance appeared to be an important factor in Lord Denning denial of liability. Cumming-Bruce LJ appearing to take a middle line felt that coming to the nuisance was an important factor in refusing the injunction.

Some of the issues that had concerned the Court of Appeal in Miller resurfaced in a different guise in *Kennaway v Thompson*.[47] Here the plaintiff lived in a house next to a lake on which there were water sports. The club had begun racing on the lake some 10 years before the plaintiff built and occupied her house adjoining the lake. She had always lived in the vicinity and had inherited the land from her father. Over the years immediately prior to and after this the use of the lake and the noise level increased considerably. In the Court of Appeal the defendants, a motor boat racing club, accepted that some of their activities caused a nuisance. The judge had awarded damages but refused an injunction. The Court of Appeal granted an injunction and applied the principle in *Shelfer v City of London Electric Lighting Co*:[48]

Kennaway v Thompson [1981] QB 88 CA

Lawton LJ: Counsel for the plaintiff has submitted that the judge misdirected himself. What he did, it was said, was to allow the club to buy itself the right to cause a substantial and intolerable nuisance. It was no justification to say that this was for the benefit of that section of the public which was interested in motor boat racing. Once the plaintiff had proved that the club caused a nuisance which interfered in a substantial and intolerable way with the use and enjoyment of her house she was entitled to have it stopped by injunction.

---

47   [1981] QB 88 CA.
48   [1895] 1 Ch 287.

Counsel for the defendant submitted that this court should not interfere with the exercise of the judge's discretion. He was entitled to take into account the effect which an injunction would have on the club and on those members of the public who enjoyed watching or taking part in motor boat racing.

Counsel for the plaintiff based his submissions primarily on the decision of this court in *Shelfer v City of London Electric Lighting Co*. The opening paragraph of the headnote, which correctly summarises the judgment, is as follows:

> Lord Caims's Act (21 and 22 Vict c 27), in conferring upon Courts of Equity a jurisdiction to award damages instead of an injunction, has not altered the settled principles upon which those courts interfered by way of injunction; and in cases of continuing actionable nuisance the jurisdiction so conferred ought only to be exercised under very exceptional circumstances.

... in a much-quoted passage, Lindley LJ said:

> ... ever since Lord Caims's Act was passed the Court of Chancery has repudiated the notion that the Legislature intended to turn that Court into a tribunal for legalising wrongful acts; or in other words, the courts has always protested against the notion that it ought to allow a wrong to continue simply because the wrongdoer is able and willing to pay for the injury he may inflict. Neither has the circumstance that the wrongdoer is in some sense a public benefactor (eg a gas or water company or a sewer authority) ever been considered a sufficient reason for refusing to protect by injunction an individual whose rights are being persistently infringed.'

Smith LJ, in his judgment, set out what he called a good working rule for the award of damages in substitution for an injunction. His working rule does not apply in this case. The injury to the plaintiff's legal rights is not small; it is not capable of being estimated in terms of money save in the way the judge tried to make an estimate, namely by fixing a figure for the diminution of the value of the plaintiff's house because of the prospect of a continuing nuisance; and the figure he fixed could not be described as small. The principles enunciated in *Shelfer's* case, which is binding on us, have been applied time and time again during the past 85 years. The only case which raises a doubt about the application of the *Shelfer* principles to all cases is *Miller v Jackson*, a decision of this court ... We are of the opinion that there is nothing in *Miller v Jackson* binding on us which qualifies what was decided in *Shelfer*. Any decisions before *Shelfer's* case (and there were some at first instance as counsel for the defendants pointed out) which give support for the proposition that the public interest should prevail over the private interest must be read subject to the decision in *Shelfer's* case.

It follows that the plaintiff was entitled to an injunction and that the judge misdirected himself in law in adjudging that the appropriate remedy for her was an award of damages under Lord Cairns's Act. But she was only entitled to an injunction restraining the club from activities which caused a nuisance and not all of their activities did. As the judge pointed out and counsel for the plaintiff accepted in this court, an injunction in general terms would be unworkable.

Our task has been to decide on a form of order which will protect the plaintiff from the noise which the judge found to be intolerable but which will not stop the club from organising activities about which she cannot reasonably complain.

When she decided to build a house alongside Mallam Water she knew that some motor boat racing and water skiing was done on the club's water and she thought that the noise which such activities created was tolerable. She cannot now complain about that kind of noise provided it does not increase in volume by reason of any increase in activities. The intolerable noise is mostly caused by the large boats; it is these which attract the public interest.

Now nearly all of us living in these islands have to put up with a certain amount of annoyance from our neighbours. Those living in towns may be irritated by their neighbours' noisy radios or incompetent playing of musical instruments; and they in turn may be inconvenienced by the noise caused by our guests slamming car doors and chattering after a late party. Even in the country the lowing of a sick cow or the early morning crowing of a farmyard cock may interfere with sleep and comfort. Intervention by injunction is only justified when the irritating noise causes inconvenience beyond what other occupiers in the neighbourhood can be expected to bear. The question is whether the neighbour is using his property reasonably, having regard to the fact that he has a neighbour. The neighbour who is complaining must remember, too, that the other man can use his property in a reasonable way and there must be a measure of 'give and take, live and let live'.

Understandably the plaintiff finds intolerable the kind of noise which she has had to suffer for such long periods in the past; but if she knew that she would only have to put up with such noise on a few occasions between the end of March and the beginning of November each year and she also knew when those occasions were likely to occur, she could make arrangements to be out of her house at the material times. We can see no reason, however, why she should have to absent herself from her house for many days so as to enable the club members and others to make noises which are a nuisance. We consider it probable that those who are interested in motor boat racing are attracted by the international and national events, which tend to have the larger and noisier boats. Justice will be done, we think, if the club is allowed to have, each racing season, one international event extending over three days, the first day being given over to practice and the second and third to racing. In addition there can be two national events, each of two days but separated from the international event and from each other by at least four weeks. Finally there can be three club events, each of one day, separated from the international and national events and each other by three weeks. Any international or national event not held can be replaced by a club event of one day. No boats creating a noise of more than 75 decibels are to be used on the club's water at any time other than when there are events as specified in this judgment. If events are held at weekends, as they probably will be, six weekends, covering a total of 10 days, will be available for motor boat racing on the club's water. Water skiing, if too many boats are used, can cause a nuisance by noise. The club is not to allow more than six motor boats to be used for water skiing at any one time. An injunction will be granted to restrain motor boat racing, water skiing and the use of boats creating a noise of more than 75 decibels on the club's water save to the extent and in the circumstances indicated.[49]

As Lawton LJ stated, actions of this kind depend to a degree on the reasonableness of the activities undertaken: it is a matter of give and take. The facts of *Kennaway* lend themselves more readily to a give and take solution than Miller. In Kennaway the club admitted that the extra activity of recent years amounted to a nuisance so liability was less of an issue than the appropriate remedy. The plaintiff had, in a sense, come to the nuisance for although she had lived in the area all her life, the land beside the lake on which she now lived had been inherited from her farther approximately 10 years after the club had commenced activities on the lake. The court was able to reach a compromise solution therefore by granting the injunction to limit activities above and beyond that which the plaintiff was deemed to have accepted as normal when coming to the lake. This logic would not have been easy to apply in Miller. It would not have been possible to grant an injunction limiting the number of sixes every season. It could be argued that the courts have reached a level on consistency by granting an injunction only where the level of activity extends beyond what the plaintiff is deemed to have accepted in coming to the nuisance.

In *Tetley v Chitty*[50] the local authority had granted permission to a go-karting club to use land in a residential housing area. McNeill J held that the noise generated by go-karting activities was an ordinary and natural consequence of the operation of go-karts on the council's land. In the same way as it would be difficult to play cricket without hitting sixes it would be difficult to run a go-karting club without noise. The difference however would lie in the frequency of the nuisance. McNeill J granted an injunction against the local authority's allowing use of the land for the purpose which gave rise to a nuisance, effectively terminating the activity in that area.

It is important to note that the local authority, as landlord, was liable for allowing the nuisance committed by its tenants. McNeill J cited the headnote from *White v Jameson*[51] which states 'Where the occupier of lands grants a licence to another to do certain acts on the land and the licencee in doing them commits a nuisance, the occupier may be made a defendant to the suit to restrain the nuisance'. The owners of sporting stadiums will not avoid liability merely because they are not legally the party controlling the sporting function.

---

49   *Ibid*, 332.
50   [1986] 1 All ER 663.
51   [1874] LR 18 Eq 303.

SPECTATOR SAFETY

Parliament's efforts to protect spectators at sporting events represents but a fraction of the law in this area. The issue of stadium disasters will be considered in more detail with an analysis of the issues raised by the Hillsborough disaster but legal issues can be spawned from less tragic circumstances. Incidents such as a collapsed seat, the spectator struck by the ball from a speculative and errant goal attempt or an altercation between rival supporters illustrate just as effectively the law's intervention in sport. Whilst most sports spectators return from their chosen event with no more injury than the pain of their team's demise, a minority will consider recourse to law. Their reason is likely to fall into one of three categories. The first but least frequent occurrence would be an injury caused by the overspill of occurrences taking place on the pitch. The second is injury caused by the stadium itself. This would cover both defective premises and faulty safety procedures. The third are those injuries inflicted by other spectators.

OVERSPILL FROM THE AREA OF PLAY

One only need consider the clamour for tickets at major sporting events to appreciate that two of the most important reasons for attending certain sporting functions are the intensity and importance of the competition. This is particularly so of top level professional sport where the participants are performing to the maximum of their endeavours. Such extremes of performance, if misjudged, can result in balls, pucks, cars and even the participants themselves coming into contact with spectators.

An early case that examined the issue of liability was *Hall v Brooklands Auto Racing Club*.[52] Brooklands owned a two mile oval racing track which held regular races. Spectators paid to gain access to the track and were provided with stands from which they could view. The race track itself was partitioned from the spectators by railings and spectators preferred to stand just outside the railings rather than sit in the stands. During one long distance race two of the competing cars touched causing one of them to be catapulted into the railings. Two spectators were killed and many others injured. The Court of Appeal allowed an appeal against the findings of a special jury at first instance that the club had failed to provide adequate safety facilities:

Hall v Brooklands Auto Racing Club [1933] 1 KB 205

Greer LJ: In my judgment both parties must have intended that the person paying for his licence to see a cricket match or a race, takes upon himself the risk of unlikely and improbable accidents, provided that there has not been on

---

52 [1933] 1 KB 205.

the part of the occupier a failure to take reasonable precautions. I do not think it can be said that the content of the contract made with every person who takes a ticket is different. I think it must be the same and it must be judged by what any reasonable member of the public must have intended should be the term of the contract. The person concerned is sometimes described as 'the man in the street' or 'the man in the Clapham omnibus' ... Such a man taking a ticket to see a cricket match at Lord's would know quite well that he was not going to be encased in a steel frame which would protect him from the one in a million chance of a cricket ball dropping on his head. In the same way, the same man taking a ticket to see the Derby would know quite well that there would be no provision to prevent a horse which got out of hand from getting amongst the spectators and would quite understand that he himself was bearing the risk of an such possible but improbable accident happening to himself. In my opinion, in the same way such a man taking a ticket to see motor races would know quite well that no barrier would be provided which would be sufficient to protect him in the possible but highly improbable event of a car charging the barrier and getting through to the spectators.[53]

It is interesting to note that the cause of action in this instance was breach of contract with the club in breach of an implied term to ensure that the spectators were safe. Greer LJ held that there was an implied term whereby the plaintiff agreed to take the risk of this kind of accident occurring.[54] Today such an action would be brought in negligence (an area of law which has developed considerably since 1933) or under the Occupiers' Liability Act 1957, rather than in contract. The Occupiers' Liability Act 1957 will be discussed in more detail later. It is appropriate where an action is commenced against the occupier rather than the participant. The Act provides that a common duty of care is owed 'to take such care as in all the circumstances is reasonable to see that the visitor will be reasonably safe in using the premises for the purpose for which he is invited or permitted by the occupier to be there'.[55] An action in negligence in those circumstances would also be appropriate. Negligence is wider in scope and is applicable should the action be maintained against the participant.

The principle enunciated in *Hall v Brooklands Auto Racing Club* was applied in *Murray and Another v Harringay Arena Ltd*.[56] There a six year old spectator was injured by a puck hit out of the playing area during an ice hockey match. The Court of Appeal held that the defendants, by installing nets at both ends of the rink only, had satisfied their duty in that the limited netting was in conformity with other ice hockey rinks. The child's injury, as a result of something incidental to the game, was held to be a risk the spectator accepted. Again this case was decided on contractual grounds with the two competing

---

53 *Ibid*, 223.
54 *Ibid*, 224.
55 Section 2(2).
56 [1951] 2 KB 529.

implied terms, first that it was implied into the contract that the occupier would take reasonable precautions to ensure safety and secondly that there was an implied term whereby the visitor would accept all risks beyond what was reasonable for the occupier to protect against. Singleton LJ commented 'It may strike one as a little hard that this should apply in the case of a six year old boy'[57] but considered it right that the implied term should be consistently applied. This works with contractual matters but gives rise to difficulties in negligence where the courts are more inclined to distribute fault by contributory negligence rather than to deny any recovery on the grounds that the plaintiff had accepted the risk. This is an important legal distinction. The concept of contributory negligence allows the court to find liability and apportion culpability. However if the plaintiff has accepted the risk, the concept of *volenti non fit injuria*, then there is no liability and the defendant escapes entirely.

This question was resolved in *Wooldridge v Sumner*[58] where the plaintiff, an official photographer, was injured at a horse show when a horse being galloped around the arena went out of control plunging through a bordered area and struck him. The facts differed materially from the above cases in two ways. First the plaintiff was not a paying spectator, which meant that the issue could not be resolved in terms of implied contractual terms. Secondly it was acknowledged that no fault could be attributed to the occupiers of the arena and so the action was brought against the owners of the horse through the negligence of their servant, the rider.

One of the issues raised by the defendants was *volenti*: that the plaintiff had volunteered to accept the inherent risk of injury. This would seem to be compatible with the earlier plaintiff's implied contractual term to assume the risk. However *volenti* is a defence to negligence and implies that a *prima facie* case of negligence has been established. Under the old contractual actions, liability had always been denied on the basis that there had not been a breach of contact by the defendant in the first place. One of the problems facing the court was whether liability was to be denied on the basis that there was no prima facie negligence or whether there was *prima facie* negligence but with the successful defence of *volenti*.

Sellers LJ considered the plaintiff's claim that the horse had been ridden too fast:

Wooldridge v Sumner [1963] 2 QB 43

Sellers LJ: In my opinion 'too fast' in these circumstances would only be an error of judgment of a highly competent rider all out to succeed. It is no doubt a misfortune for a skilled batsman to be bowled or caught in a supreme effort to hit a six. It is also a misfortune if, on the other hand, he succeeds in hitting a six and the ball hits someone over the boundary. The three-quarter who dives

---

57 *Ibid*, 536.
58 [1963] 2 QB 43.

at speed over the line for a try at Twickenham or on occasions at Wembley or the opponent who dives into a tackle to prevent a try may and sometimes does roll over and come into heavy contact with the surrounding barrier sometimes to his own hurt and to the possible injury of an adjacent spectator. No court or jury would, I think, condemn such endeavour as negligent.[59]

On the issue of *volenti* he continued:

> In my opinion a competitor or player cannot in the normal case at least of competition or game rely on the maxim *volenti non fit injuria* in answer to a spectator's claim, for there is no liability unless there is negligence and the spectator comes to witness skill and with the expectation that it will be exercised. But provided the competition or game is being performed within the rules and the requirement of the sport and by a person of adequate skill and competence the spectator does not expect his safety to be regarded by the participant.[60]

It would appear that volenti is unlikely ever to feature in sports spectator injury cases as legal issues would revolve around the establishment of negligence rather that defences to negligence. The spectator struck by a puck, ball or car, as long as it was done so as an accepted part of the game, is subject to a lower standard of duty owed by the plaintiff and will have impliedly accepted that lower standard.

At the other end of the spectrum, incidents where spectators are injured as a result of deliberate actions outside of the rules of the game will be subject to both the criminal and civil law. The infamous incident of Eric Cantona kicking a spectator following his dismissal during Manchester United's FA Cup match against Crystal Palace at Selhurst Park in 1995, resulted in a criminal conviction for assault.[61]

It is in between these two extremes that the law is a little less clear. When will the actions of the participant fall below this lower standard of duty?

Wooldridge v Sumner [1963] 2 QB 43

Sellers LJ: If the conduct is deliberately intended to injure someone whose presence is known or is reckless and in disregard of all safety of others so that it is a departure from the standards which might reasonably be expected in anyone pursuing the competition or game, then the performer might well be held liable for any injury his act might cause. There would, I think, be a difference, for instance, in assessing blame which is actionable between an injury caused by a tennis ball hit or a racket accidentally thrown in the course of play into the spectators at Wimbledon and a ball hit or a racket thrown into the stands in temper or annoyance when play was not in progress.[62]

---

59 *Ibid*, 53.

60 *Ibid*, 56.

61 Gardiner, S, 'Ooh Ah Cantona: Racism as Hate Speech' [1996] 23 CMJ 23. See also the Bosnich 'Nazi salute' incident, *The Times*, 16 November 1996.

62 *Wooldridge v Sumner* [1963] 2 QB 43, at 57.

Diplock LJ in Wooldridge was of the opinion that there would be no breach of duty 'unless the participant's conduct is such as to evince a reckless disregard of the spectators safety'.[63] This test was also adopted by Lord Denning in *Wilks v Cheltenham Homeguard Motor Cycle and Light Car Club*.[64] R Phillimore and Edmund Davies LJJ in that case preferred 'reasonable care in all the circumstances'.

It might appear that there would be no remedy even to a spectator who deliberately positions himself in such a place in a cricket ground that only a totally miss-hit six could cause him harm because as Diplock LJ stated in *Wooldridge* 'the duty which [the participant] owes is a duty of care, not a duty of skill'.[65] He continued 'It may well be that a participant in a game or competition would be guilty of negligence to a spectator if he took part in it when he knew or ought to have known that his lack of skill was such that even if he exerted to the utmost he was likely to cause injury to a spectator watching him'. It would seem that the judiciously located spectator struck by a miss-hit six from an England international would be unsuccessful in his action but the same spectator struck by a similarly miss-hit six from an incompetent cricketer, unable to do any better, may well be successful.

Sellers LJ's notion of actions within the rules of the game also causes problems. Singleton LJ in Murray spoke of the breach of ice hockey rules of a participant who deliberately hits the puck out of the rink when pressed and the two minute penalty it invoked but did not seem to consider it negligent. Yet in the criminal case of *R v Kirk*[66] a Scottish professional footballer was convicted of culpably and recklessly kicking a ball into a crowd of spectators injuring a young girl. There was no breach of football rules in such action but he was convicted because it was done out of anger, which the court found unacceptable, rather than in an effort to gain time.

It appears unsatisfactory that the law should allow a football to be kicked into the spectators (with resulting injuries) with impunity as long as it was done within a normal footballing context whilst the participant who kicks the ball out of frustration, with the same force and accuracy, should be held legally responsible for his actions. This is particularly so as it could well be argued that football spectators expect such behaviour. Utilising such considerations as the rules of the game or the mental state of the participant may satisfy a test of reckless disregard. Such a test does not take into account the subjective element of the lower standard of duty which may be expected of the participant and therefore, a test of 'reasonable care in all the circumstances' is to be preferred.

---

63 *Ibid*, at 68.
64 [1971] 1 WLR 668.
65 *Ibid, Wooldridge*, 68.
66 Unreported, *Daily Telegraph*, 17 October 1995.

STADIUM SAFETY

The first recorded example of stadium occupiers being held liable for a defective stand was *Francis v Cockrell*[67] where part of a stand collapsed at the Cheltenham National Hunt Festival. The court upheld a claim for damages against the occupiers even thought it was builders with whom the occupiers had contracted to build the stand who were negligent. The courts held that a contract existed between the spectator and the occupier with an implied term ensuring a reasonable standard of safety. Today a cause of action would most likely lie in negligence, occupiers' liability or under one of the sports-specific Acts which have proliferated in recent years.

Occupiers of stadiums and sporting clubs quickly became aware of their potential liability for stadium defects. Football clubs and bodies which initially existed in legal form as unincorporated associations soon became incorporated as limited companies. In *Brown v Lewis*[68] the court held that members of the club committee were individually liable for £25 damages following the collapse of a stand at Blackburn Rovers Football Club. By this time the benefits of incorporation were widely known. Incorporation brings into being an entirely separate legal entity which means that liability in most cases will be limited to the club and its resources, the membership being protected by the 'veil of incorporation'.[69] It was not long before most sporting clubs took advantage of this. More recently, sporting clubs, like other commercial enterprises, have sought to exploit the benefits of limited liability by hiving off areas of business into separate subsidiary companies under the general umbrella of a holding or parent company. This has the effect of divorcing the liability of smaller economic units from the whole. The primary motive for this exercise is clearly not to avoid liability for injured spectators, however it must form part of a greater design to ensure clubs' solvency. To this end sporting clubs may often not own their own ground. Although from a legal perspective the ground will be owned by a different person, that person will often be another company with some of the same directors and shareholders as the club itself. An attempt was made by Lord Denning[70] to start a trend of considering groups of companies as a whole but this movement has fallen from favour in recent years.[71] This does not mean that other companies in a group will not be liable, as the courts have construed the Occupiers' Liability Acts so that it is possible for there to be multiple occupancy of premises:[72]

---

67   [1870] QB 501.

68   [1886] 12 TLR 455.

69   *Salomon v Salomon & Co Ltd* [1897] AC 22 HL.

70   *DHN Food Distributors Ltd v Tower Hamlets LBC* [1976] 1 WLR 852.

71   *Woolfson v Strathclyde Regional Council* [1978] SLT 159; *Adams v Cape Industries Plc* [1990] 2 WLR 657.

72   *Wheat v Lacon* [1966] 1 All ER 582.

Section 2 of the Occupiers' Liability Act 1957

(1) An occupier of premises owes the same duty, the 'common duty of care', to all his visitors, except in so far as he is free and does extend, restrict, modify or exclude his duty to any visitor or visitors by agreement or otherwise.

(2) The common duty of care is a duty to take such care as in all the circumstances of the case is reasonable to see that the visitor will be reasonably safe in using the premises for the purposes for which he is invited or permitted by the occupier to be there.

(3) The circumstances relevant for the present purpose include the degree of care and of want of care, which would ordinarily be looked for in such a visitor, so that (for example) in proper cases–

    (a) an occupier must be prepared for children to be less careful than adults; and

    (b) an occupier must expect that a person, in the exercise of his calling, will appreciate and guard against any special risks ordinarily incident to it, so far as the occupier leaves him free to do so.

(4) In determining whether the occupier of the premises has discharged the common duty of care to a visitor, regard is to be had to all the circumstances, so that (for example)–

    (a) where damage is caused to a visitor by a danger of which he had been warned by the occupier, the warning is not to be treated without more as absolving the occupier of liability, unless in all the circumstances it was enough to enable the visitor to be reasonably safe; and

    (b) where damage is caused to a visitor by a danger caused by the faulty execution of any work of construction, maintenance or repair by an independent contractor employed by the occupier, the occupier is not to be treated without more as answerable for the danger if in all the circumstances he had acted reasonably in entrusting the work to an independent contractor and had taken such steps (if any) as he reasonably ought in order to satisfy himself that the contractor was competent and that the work had been properly done.

(5) The common duty of care does not impose on an occupier any obligation to a visitor in respect of risks willingly accepted as his by the visitor (the question whether a risk was so accepted to be decided on the same principles as in other cases in which one person owes a duty of care to another).

The 1957 Act lays down in statutory form the standard of duty required of all sporting clubs inviting spectators on to their premises. The standard is similar to that for common law negligence. The occupier must also take into account that child supporters may be owed a higher duty than adults.

Following *White v Blackmore*[73] it appeared that s 2(1) allowed occupiers to avoid liability by warning notices. In that case the deceased was a competitor at a 'jalopy' meeting. Having competed in one race he watched another. In

---

73 [1972] 2 QB 651.

that race a car ran into a safety rope which, because it had been staked negligently, pulled at a rope segregating spectators, causing the deceased to be catapulted into the air sustaining injuries from which he died. The Court of Appeal held that warning notices placed at the entrance to the venue stating that the organisers would not be liable for accidents to spectators however caused had effectively excluded liability.

The Unfair Contract Terms Act 1977, which applies to business liability only, appears to have closed this loophole. Section 2(1) of the Act prevents the exclusion or restriction of liability by contractual term or notice for death or personal injury resulting from negligence. Section 2(2) extends this by stating that liability for other loss or damage caused by negligence can only be excluded or restricted where reasonable.

It is important to note that the duty is only owed to a visitor who is 'using the premises for the purposes for which he is invited or permitted to be there'.[74] Injury sustained through standing on a faulty seat which subsequently collapses or whilst running on the field of play to celebrate victory may transform the visitor into a trespasser for 'when you invite a person into your house to use the staircase, you do not invite him to slide down the banisters'.[75]

Trespassers such as these or spectators who have gained entry to a sporting event unlawfully are considered to be owed a lesser duty than lawful visitors. Until relatively recently[76] the law has had little truck with trespassers at all. Now they are governed by the Occupiers' Liability Act 1984. However the 1984 Act is unlikely to have an important impact in the sporting context as s 3(a) states the duty is only owed where the occupier 'is aware of the danger or has reasonable grounds to believe it exists'. In the 1960s and 1970s one could have envisaged a scenario of supporters gaining access to derelict stands that littered our sports grounds and sustaining injury but with the general improvement in sporting facilities this now seems an unlikely occurrence.

In the area of stadium safety prevention is clearly better than cure and in 1975, Parliament enacted the Safety of Sports Grounds Act. The Act introduced a system of licensing of major sports grounds by local authorities. Section 1 of the Act as amended by s 19 of the Fire Safety and Safety of Places of Sports Act 1987 states 'The Secretary of State may by order designate as a sports ground requiring a certificate under this Act (in this Act referred to as a 'safety certificate') any sports ground which in his opinion has accommodation for more than 10,000 spectators'. The certificate is appropriate

---

74 Section 2(2).

75 *The Carlgarth* [1927] P 93, 110, *per* Scrutton LJ.

76 In 1972 the House of Lords in *British Railways Board v Herrington* [1972] AC 877 held that trespassers were owed a duty of 'common humanity'.

for a number of activities during an indefinite period or individual occasion.[77] Section 2 explains that 'a safety certificate shall contain such terms and conditions as the local authority consider necessary or expedient to secure reasonable safety at the sports ground when it is in use for a specified activity or activities and the terms and conditions may be such as to involve alterations or additions to the sports ground'. If the local authority believes that the ground or parts of the ground are a serious risk to spectator safety then they are empowered under s 10 to prohibit or restrict admission and direct the holder of the licence as to the steps that must be taken before the order will be lifted.

The local authority's licensing duties in relation to designated football matches are now overseen by the Football Licensing Authority. The duties and powers of this body are contained in the Football Spectators Act 1989. The Secretary of State's criteria for labelling designated football matches is unclear but will be no less stringent than under the provisions of the 1975 Act. The Football Licensing Authority has the power to grant licences[78] as well as 'keeping under review the discharge by local authorities of their function under the Safety of Sports Grounds Act 1975'.[79] This supervisory role was recommended by Lord Justice Taylor following his critical analysis of the local authority's performance of its functions under the 1975 Act.

A licensing system also operates for those sports grounds that are undesignated but provide covered accommodation in stands for 500 or more spectators. This system is provided for by the Fire Safety and Safety of Places of Sport Act 1987. Again the system is operated by the relevant local authority which has the power to issue a certificate for a regulated stand containing 'such terms and conditions as the local authority considers necessary'.[80]

Whilst the Acts put in place a structure for the certification of sports grounds they are couched in general terms and do not specify minimum safety measures. Reference therefore must be made to the Guide to Safety at Sports Grounds, known as the 'Green Guide'. The Green Guide is not a statutory provision but it forms the basis of local authority enforcement of a safety standard and could be adopted by the courts as the benchmark for safety standards. The Green Guide specifies such details as the capacity of stands, evacuation procedures and fire safety as well as general conditions and maintenance.

In its present form, the Green Guide is not without its critics. A joint executive of local authorities, the FA, the Football League and the Sports Council have criticised the latest Green Guide, revised following the Taylor

---

77 Section 1(3).
78 Section 10.
79 Section 13(1).
80 Section 27(1).

Report. As well as questioning its ability to serve as both the minimum standard for existing stadiums and the blueprint for new ones. The Joint Executive reported:

Ground Safety and Public Order. Report No 1 of the Joint Executive on Football Safety

The Taylor Report recommended that although some aspects of the guide should become mandatory requirements in safety certificates, the guide should remain a non-mandatory set of guidelines. Lord Justice Taylor felt that sports grounds varied greatly in their layout and fixtures and it should be open to local authorities to deviate in some respects at some grounds from the guide's recommendations. We recognise that in the assessment of new grounds, it might be necessary for interpretation to be used where the standards of the guide cannot feasibly be met in their entirety by a club. Nevertheless, we feel that minimum standards should be enforced but with clearly established procedures for standards to be 'waived' in special circumstances.[81]

CROWD DISTURBANCE, MANAGEMENT AND SPECTATOR SAFETY

The issues of crowd management and crowd disturbances have been responsible for more debate, media coverage, parliamentary time and official reports than any other stadium safety issue. Indeed an analysis of official reports has shown a concerning trend to amalgamate these issues when, in fact, they are quite separate sporting problems. It is ironic that the introduction of all seater stadiums, arguably the most important factor in reducing crowd disturbances in recent years, was recommended by the Taylor Report into the Hillsborough Disaster where hooliganism was not a major issue.

Although it has often been said that crowd control is the responsibility of the clubs and their stewards, it has equally been acknowledged that, in many instances, the police do assume de facto control as part of their policing duties. This debate as to the role of the police in crowd management formed an important part of the Taylor Report considered later. In *Harris v Sheffield United Football Club*[82] the club argued that by fulfilling their policing duties the police were doing no more than was required of them under their public duty and the club were not liable to pay for 'special police services' under s 15(1) of the Police Act 1964. In the High Court, Boreham J considered the extent of the police's duty:

---

81   Ground Safety and Public Order. Report No 1 of the Joint Executive on Football Safety 1991, London: ACC Publications.

82   [1987] 2 All ER 838.

Harris v Sheffield United Football Club **(unreported) QBD 26 March 1986**

Boreham J: ... the police were not discharging their own duty to the public; they were in fact discharging the club's duties to the spectators whom the club invited to the ground. The club chose to invite large numbers to their private premises; it was the club's duty to provide for their safety, health and comfort. They could have employed a security firm as banks and others have to do to protect their interests; they chose to request the police to perform those duties knowing that the police expected payment ... the police within the ground provided services which it was not within the scope of their public duty to perform. For instance, they assisted in crowd management and in the enforcement of such ground regulations as refused entry to those who tried to enter without paying or prohibited spectators encroaching on parts of the ground which their entry fee did not entitle them to enter. It may be ... that the maintenance of law and order was the predominant aim but there were other services performed.[83]

The Court of Appeal did not examine this issue to the extent of Boreham J but in rejecting the club's arguments Neill LJ did say 'The club has responsibilities which are owed not only to its employees and the spectators who attend but also to the football authorities to take all reasonable steps to ensure that the game takes place in conditions which do not occasion danger to any person or property. The attendance of the police is necessary to assist the club in the fulfilment of this duty'.[84] This seems to suggest that crowd management assistance from the police is something for which the club is paying although the legal division of responsibility between the police and the club for crowd management has yet to be satisfactorily defined. There may be circumstances where an injured spectator has recourse to the club, with the club having recourse subsequently, to the police.[85]

Much of the recent sports related legislation has been aimed at dealing with the problems associated with football hooliganism. It has long been possible for convicted hooligans to have restrictions placed on their attendance at matches and football clubs are now taking a more active stance by banning convicted hooligans from their grounds.[86] The police have powers to arrest spectators for committing a wide range of criminal offences. The remainder of this exposition will concentrate on sports-specific law.

Parliament has adopted a dual approach to the problem of football hooliganism. The first approach is to increase the powers of the police and the courts to punish hooliganism. Principally, this has been achieved through the

---

83   QBD 26 March 1986.
84   [1987] 2 All ER 838, 847.
85   The Hillsborough Disaster, see below, p 577.
86   *Bristol City v Milns* (1978) *Daily Telegraph*, 31 January and *R v Clark and Others* (1985) *Daily Telegraph*, 10 April.

Football (Offences) Act 1991:[87]

Football (Offences) Act 1991

1   Designated football matches

(1) In this Act a 'designated football match' means an association football match designated or of a description designated, for the purposes of this Act by order of the Secretary of State.

(2) References in this Act to things done at a designated football match include anything done at the ground–

   (a) within the period beginning two hours before the start of the match or (if earlier) two hours before the time at which it is advertised to start and ending one hour after the end of the match; or

   (b) where the match is advertised to start at a particular time on a particular day but does not take place on that day, within the period beginning two hours before and ending one hour after the advertised starting time.

2   Throwing of missiles

It is an offence for a person at a designated football match to throw anything at or towards–

(a) the playing area or any area adjacent to the playing area to which spectators are not generally admitted; or

(b) any area in which spectators or other persons are or may be present, without lawful authority or lawful excuse (which shall be for him to prove).

3   Indecent or racist chanting

(1) It is an offence to take part at a designated football match in chanting of an indecent or racist nature.

(2) For this purpose–

   (a) 'chanting' means the repeated uttering of any words or sounds in concert with one or more others; and

   (b) 'of a racist nature' means consisting of or including matter which is threatening, abusive or insulting to a person by reason of his colour, race, nationality (including citizenship) or ethnic or national origins.

4   Going onto the playing area

It is an offence for a person at a designated football match to go onto the playing area or any area adjacent to the playing area to which spectators are not generally admitted, without lawful authority or lawful excuse (which shall be for him to prove).

---

87 For an analysis of arrests under the Act and in particular the effectiveness of s 3, see Greenfield, S and Osborn, G, 'When the Whites go Marching in? Racism and Resistance in English Football' (1996) 6 *Marquette Sports Law Journal* 315 and Gardiner, S, 'Ooh Ah Cantona: Racisim as Hate Speech' [1996] 23 CJM 23.

Whilst s 1(2)(a) would appear to be of long enough duration to cover early arrivals and late leavers it is difficult to envisage when s 1(2)(b) would be invoked. If a match was not going to take place that day it is unlikely spectators would be admitted to the ground in the first place. Equally, whilst it is possible to envisage occasions on which spectators might spill over onto the playing area it is difficult to envisage a lawful excuse for the throwing of missiles. Also it is odd that the legislation should be limited to racist chanting rather than a wider definition including racist abuse from one spectator.

Section 4 makes it a specific offence to go onto the playing area. In the earlier case of *Cawley v Frost*[88] a spectator was charged with using threatening words and behaviour in a public place contrary to s 5 of the Public Order Act 1956 when supporters clashed on the speedway track between the stand and the pitch. The issue arose as to whether the speedway track was a public place. The Court of Appeal held that the stadium was a public place in its entirety allowing incidents that happen on the pitch to be subject to public order offences. Section 4 extends the law by disposing of any requirement for a further criminal act to take place on the pitch.

Other legislative provisions of recent years have been aimed at preventing disruption rather than dealing with its aftermath. The means by which hooligans can be prevented from attending football matches in England and Wales were discussed earlier. Part 3 of the Football Spectators Act 1989 is important because it allows courts to impose restriction orders preventing spectators convicted of relevant offences[89] from attending designated matches outside England and Wales. In this way the law impacts on the actions and freedoms British citizens even outside of its own jurisdiction. The restriction can last between two and five years.[90]

Alcohol has long been identified by politicians as a major cause of football hooliganism. The main provisions are now contained in the Sporting Events (Control of Alcohol etc) Act 1985. The legislation also acknowledges that although alcohol consumed at matches could prove problematical, drunkenness before matches also needed to be addressed. As Lord Justice Taylor recognised, the match was only a part, albeit a central part, of a Saturday afternoon's recreation which, for many supporters, began with the consumption of alcohol in pubs close to the ground or on the journey to the ground. Therefore much of the drunkenness was a result of drinking prior to the match:

88　(1971) 64 CHR 20.

89　Those listed in Schedule 1 of the Act, including offences under the Football Spectators Act 1989; the Sporting Events (Control of Alcohol) Act 1985; s 5 of the Public Order Act 1986; s 12 of the Licensing Act 1872; s 91(1) of the Criminal Justice Act 1967; and s 4 or s 5 of the Road Traffic Act 1988.

90　The five year restriction applies where the person has been sentenced in respect of an offence to a period of imprisonment taking immediate effect: s 16(2)(a).

Sporting Events (Control of Alcohol etc) Act 1985

1   Offences in connection with alcohol on coaches and trains

(1) This section applies to a vehicle which–

(a) is a public service vehicle or railway passenger vehicle; and

(b) is being used for the principle purpose of carrying passengers for the whole or part of a journey to or from a designated sporting event.

(2) A person who knowingly knowingly causes or permits intoxicating liquor to be carried on a vehicle to which this section applies is guilty of an offence–

(a) if the vehicle is a public service vehicle and he is the operator of the vehicle or the servant or agent of the operator; or

(b) if the vehicle is a hired vehicle and he is the person to whom it is hired or the servant or agent of that person.

(3) A person who has intoxicating liquor in his possession while on a vehicle to which this section applies is guilty of an offence

(4) A person who is drunk on a vehicle to which this section applies is guilty of an offence.

2   Offences in connection with alcohol, containers, etc at sports grounds

(1) A person who has intoxicating liquor or an article to which this section applies in his possession–

(a) at any time during the period of a designated sporting event when he is in any area of a designated sports ground from which the event may be directly viewed; or

(b) while entering or trying to enter a designated sports ground at any time during the period or a designated sporting event at that ground,

is guilty of an offence.

(2) A person who is drunk in a designated sports ground at any time during the period of a designated sporting event at that ground or is drunk while entering or trying to enter such a ground at any time during the period of a designated sporting event at that ground is guilty of an offence.

(3) This section applies to any article capable of causing injury to a person struck by it, being–

(a) a bottle, can or other portable container (including such an article when crushed or broken) which–

(i) is for holding any drink; and

(ii) is of a kind which, when empty, is normally discarded or returned to or left to be recovered by, the supplier; or

(b) part of an article falling within paragraph (a) above.

Section 1 applies not only to the person in possession of the alcohol but also to the person who permits the alcohol to be carried on a public service vehicle. Section 1(2)(a) makes it clear that the offence will be committed by coach operators or the railway authorities and their staff. Although being drunk at the ground,[91] taking alcohol to the ground[92] and being in possession of alcohol whilst viewing the match, are all offences,[93] it is not an offence to drink alcohol before entering the ground nor to drink at the club's bars. It could be argued that the consumption of alcohol at a public house near the ground is a more effective measure of a person's intoxication than his mere possession of alcohol. Clearly the measures are aimed at preserving the individual right to moderate consumption of alcohol as well as protecting the business interests of public houses and restaurants but it is uncertain as to how effective the provisions will prove. Effective enforcement of these measures at a Premier League football match where there may be in excess of 30,000 people is impossible. The Act makes no attempt to define 'drunk', unlike the road traffic provisions relating to drinking and driving, and so even extremely intoxicated but discreet supporters should evade detection. The only time that drunkenness is likely to be observed is if the spectator's behaviour is such as to draw the attention of the police. At this stage it is likely that other offences such as public order offences would have been committed thus negating the need for the Act. The main benefit of the Act may be to enable the police to filter out a small percentage of the most visibly or audibly drunk prior to admission.

Segregation of the rival spectators has been a principal means by which crowd disruption has been avoided. It was one of the most effective weapons in the armoury of the police in ensuring that football's Euro '96 was relatively trouble free within the confines of the stadiums. However no matter how well seating allocation is handled by the clubs, their efforts could be undermined by ticket touts selling tickets indiscriminately, to various parts of the ground. This problem is now dealt with by s 166 of the Criminal Justice and Public Order Act 1994.[94] The section makes it a criminal offence 'for an unauthorised person to sell or offer or expose for sale a ticket for a designated football match in any public place or place to which the public has access or, in the course of a trade or business, in any other place'.[95]

Finally while considering preventative measures, it is necessary to consider the issue of identity cards. A national membership scheme, the brainchild of the Thatcher government, was enacted in the Football Spectators Act 1989[96] but no order was ever made to bring the relevant sections into force

---

91   Section 2(2).

92   Section 2(1)(b).

93   Section 2(1)(a).

94   Bitel, N, 'Ticket Rights' (1993) 1(1) *Sport and the Law Journal*; Bitel, N, 'Not Quite the Ticket' (1995) 3(1) *Sport and the Law Journal*; Greenfield, S and Osborn, G, 'Criminalising Football Supporters: Tickets, Touts and Criminal Justice and Public Order Act 1994' (1995) 3(3) *Sport and the Law Journal*; Farrell, R, 'Ticket Rights – and Wrongs' (1994) 2(1) *Sport and the Law Journal*.

95   Section 166(1).

96   Part 1, ss 2–7.

and the provisions have lain dormant on the statute books. In essence the intention of the scheme was to register football spectators and issue them with identity cards authorising the attendance at designated football matches. A conviction for a relevant offence would result in membership being withdrawn. The measures were roundly condemned by interested parties and following criticism by Lord Justice Taylor[97] the government reluctantly backed down. The main planks of criticism were that the scheme was logistically unworkable and that it was an affront to individual liberty. It is a pity however that a more formalised system for barring spectators following conviction could not have been salvaged from the wreckage.

PARTICIPANT SAFETY

In the clamour to consider public safety, the safety of the participant is often overlooked. The law relating to injuries inflicted by other players is dealt with in Chapters 10 and 11. However two facets of player safety are relevant here because they arise specifically as a result of activities within stadiums; injuries caused by spectators and injuries caused by the stadium itself.

Whilst intra-spectator violence has become a familiar if unacceptable sight at many large sporting occasions, spectator violence towards players is relatively rare. The Cantona incident and the stabbing of Monica Seles at a tennis tournament in Hamburg in April 1993 has served to heighten awareness of a further situation where the law, reluctantly, may become involved in sporting issues. The stabbing was particularly shocking because tennis is not a sport usually associated with violent spectators and subsequently many of the participants took the precaution of turning the chairs to face the spectators. This measure seems to have died out as the shock of the Seles incident recedes and today tennis players and spectators retain the same degree of proximity as always (albeit with heightened security).

Being within touching distance of sporting heroes remains an intimacy that many other nations have relinquished. It is precisely in order to protect this intimacy at sports events that laws have been introduced to outlaw racist chanting, the throwing of missiles, running onto the playing area and being drunk at certain sporting occasions. What is most likely to change the relationship between player and spectator would be successful legal action brought by players against the owners of sporting venues. The more frequent the attacks on players the more likely that courts will be prepared to conclude that stadium owners are negligent by ignoring a foreseeable risk to players safety.

97 Final Report, p 65.

Player safety is recognised by the sports governing bodies as highly important and these sports have developed standard protective clothing and other safety measures to ensure that players remain safe. Injuries caused by deficiencies in the stadium or playing area, because they are much rarer, attract less attention. The lower parts of rugby posts are sometimes padded but often collisions with the stadium are considered to be a risk the players must accept. With top sportsmen's careers being increasingly well paid but brief, players may feel more inclined to pursue claims for injuries of this nature more energetically. There is no legal reason why a player should not bring an action against the ground-owner, club or governing body for injuries sustained as a result of a frozen pitch or a slippery surface.[98]

In an unreported case,[99] a long jumper was successful in an action for negligence against a local authority, the owners of an athletics stadium, for a knee injury sustained when jumping in a local competition. His claim that his leg was twisted as a result of jumping into wet sand was upheld in the county court. Cases such as this emphasise the importance of stadium owners fulfilling their duty to provide sporting surfaces that in all the circumstances afford athletes reasonable safety.

The Occupiers' Liability Act 1957 places such a duty on the occupiers of premises to all visitors. This would cover all participants irrespective of whether they were 'home' or 'away' players. The limitations of these provisions were exposed in *Sims v Leigh Rugby Club*.[100] The plaintiff was a winger for Oldham Football Club and was involved in an 'away' rugby league match against Leigh. In attempting to score a try, the plaintiff was bundled over the touch line which, he alleged, resulted in his colliding with a concrete wall more than seven feet from the touchline. The plaintiff sustained a broken leg and brought an action against the 'home' club for a breach of their duty under the Occupiers' Liability Act 1957. Wrangham J in the High Court rejected the plaintiff's claim because, on the balance of probabilities, the injuries were sustained as a result of the tackle rather that on the collision with the wall. Comments made obiter should be of great interest to all stadium occupiers and the standard of duty required of them under the Act:

Sims v Leigh Rugby Club [1969] 2 All ER 923

Wrangham J: Now what did the defendants actually do? The answer to that is, it provided a playing field which complied in all respects so far as the evidence goes with the requirements of the governing body of the game. The governing body of the game is the Rugby Football League and that league directs through a council which consists of representatives of each club. They have made (I do not know when) bylaws which govern the layout of the playing fields which clubs are to provide for the games they play. One of those rules is that there

---

98 On the effects of playing on artificial surfaces, see *The Times*, 4 November 1996.

99 *The Times*, 10 July 1996.

100 [1969] 2 All ER 923.

shall be a distance of not less than seven feet from the outside of the touch line to the ringside. This concrete post was seven feet three inches from the touch line. Therefore it complied with the bylaw of the governing body of the game. Nevertheless, it is said that the defendant which I suspect operates through a committee, ought to have been wiser than the governing body of this game and ought to have said to itself: 'although the governing body consider the barrier between the playing pitch and the spectator's area may be near the touch line as seven feet, we think it ought to be much further off and therefore we will set our barrier not at seven feet but much further away'. And it is said that the defendant ought to have assumed this greater wisdom although it had not got one jot or one tittle of evidence to support its opinion, because it is common ground that a serious accident arising from the too great proximity of the barrier to the touch line has not been known at all. No one has been able to assist me with evidence of a single case arising from a barrier being too close to the touch line. It is true that on quite a number of occasions players have stopped themselves at the barrier; they have run into the barrier in that sense and only just stopped themselves at it, perhaps even had to hurdle the barrier because they were running so fast that they could not stop themselves in time. But no one has suggested that, apart from this unfortunate accident, a single accident has been caused in this way. So that it amounts to this, that it is said that the defendant was unreasonable because it did not set up its opinion against that of the governing body of the sport, although such evidence as there was entirely supported the view of the governing body of the sport. I think that is wholly unreasonable criticism to make of the defendant.[101]

Even if his Lordship had been convinced that there was a breach of duty, the plaintiff would still have fallen at the final hurdle:

The matter perhaps does not quite stop there, for by s 2(5) of the Occupiers' Liability Act 1957 it is provided that a duty of care does not impose on an occupier any obligation to a visitor in respect of risk willingly accepted by the visitor. Now, it is not in dispute, of course, that anyone accepts employment as a professional footballer by a club playing under the rules of the Rugby Football League willingly accepts the risk of playing football, risks which are by no means small because it is a game involving great physical effort by one side an the other. It seems to me that a footballer does not merely accept the risks imposed by contract with the players on the other side. He willingly accepts all the risks of playing a game on such a playing field as complies with the bylaws laid down by the governing body of the game. I am sure that footballers who go to the Leigh ground, go to that ground willingly accepting the risks that arise from playing the game under the rules of the league, on a ground approved by the league.[102]

Thus it would appear that liability revolves around compliance with the rules of the governing body of the sport. In the unlikely event that the court considers the standards of the governing body to be inadequate, the

101 At pp 926–27.
102 At p 927.

participant will still be held to have accepted the risks inherent in the stadium. The conclusion reached by the judge, that accidents involving collisions with partitions, walls or advertising hoardings are extremely rare, is nonsensical.[103] Keen observers of cricket, rugby union, rugby league, football, boxing or basketball will be all too familiar with the image of participants crashing into hoardings, etc after leaving the arena of play. It is suggested that Wrangham J's approach of considering injuries in rugby league is too narrow. Ayrton Senna's death when he crashed into a tyre wall at the 1994 San Marino Grand Prix at Immola serves to highlight the importance of boundary walls and fences and the danger to sportsman should they prove inadequate. Although injuries of this kind may be rare, they are nevertheless frequent enough to put occupiers on notice that injuries are more that an unlikely eventuality.

The judgment assumes that standards set by governing bodies are adequate. In this instance, seven feet may well have been a reasonable distance but to assume as much is an abdication of the responsibilities of the court. Equally the judgment is of little use to the providers of recreational sporting facilities whose standards would not be governed by sporting bodies. In order for the law to be comprehensive, courts would need to start with the rebuttable presumption that, confronted with an injured participant, safety measures were inadequate.

Even if the plaintiff managed to overcome this hurdle he would still be faced with the view that, in continuing with his participation, he had accepted the risks of playing in an arena in conformity with the rules of the governing body. This is not broad enough to encompass the problems encountered by the recreational sportsman who is entitled to assume that adequate measures have been taken to assure his safety.

On a professional sporting level, the judgment fails to take into account the sportsman as employee. Faced with an ultimatum of play or dismissal many professional sportsmen, reluctantly, may decide to continue. The courts have often acknowledged this imbalance of power in the contacting relationship between employer and employee and, it is submitted, the judge was wrong in the circumstances to conclude that the plaintiff had 'willingly' accepted the risk.

A potential source of liability in instances such as Sims but which was not raised in that case, is the employers statutory duty under the Health and Safety at Work Act 1974:

---

103 See the contradictory comments of Sellers LJ in *Wooldridge v Sumner* [1963] 2 QB 43, 53.

Health and Safety at Work Act 1974

2   General duties of employers to their employees

(1) It shall be the duty of every employer to ensure, so far as it is reasonably practicable, the health, safety and welfare at work of all his employees.

(2) Without prejudice to the generality of an employer's duty under the preceding subsection, the matters to which the duty extends include in particular–

> (a) the provision and maintenance of plant and systems of work that are, so far as is reasonably practicable, safe and without risks to health;

> (e) the provision and maintenance of a working environment for his employees that is, so far as is reasonably practicable, safe, without risks to health and adequate as regards facilities and arrangements for their welfare at work.

3   General duties of employers and self-employed to persons other than their employees

(1) It shall be the duty of every employer to conduct his undertaking in such a way as to ensure, so far as is reasonably practicable, that persons not in his employment who may be affected thereby are not thereby exposed to risks to their health and safety.

Section 2 covers 'home' players whilst s 3 covers visiting players. Section 2 would also cover home players in actions against their own employers for a failure to provide a safe system of work Although the stadium would not be under the control of the visiting employer, his duty towards his employees is non-delegable. While he may delegate the operation of the system of work he cannot avoid liability should that system prove inadequate.[104]

THE HILLSBOROUGH DISASTER

The Football Association on 20 March 1989 had decided to hold that year's FA Cup semi-final between Nottingham Forest and Liverpool at the Hillsborough Stadium in Sheffield. The date for the match was fixed for 15 April. The match was to be policed by the South Yorkshire Constabulary. The police had agreed to perform this function on the condition that the ticket allocation was the same as in the corresponding semi-final between the two clubs seven years earlier. The Liverpool supporters were unhappy with this arrangement as they were allotted 24,256 places as against 29,800 for Nottingham Forest despite the latter's smaller average home attendance. To accommodate the Liverpool supporters at the larger end of the ground, argued the police, would involve rival supporters crossing paths and the consequent risk of crowd disturbance. Eventually Liverpool reluctantly agreed.

---

104 *McDermid v Nash Dredging Ltd* [1987] AC 906.

The stand allocated to Liverpool supporters is known as the West Stand or Leppings Lane end. It held 4,456 seated supporters behind terracing and the total capacity was stated as 10,100. It was fenced by eight foot high fences mounted on low walls. As well as having crush barriers running parallel with the goal line, the stand also had further barriers running at right angles. These were installed following the 1981 FA Cup semi-final between Tottenham Hotspurs and Wolverhampton Wanderers where crushing occurred and a disaster was prevented by hundreds of supporters climbing onto the pitch. At the time, the police had advised that the capacity in the Leppings Lane end was too high but, tragically, this warning was ignored.

The effect of the crush barriers was to create seven pens. They had been constructed in stages in a piecemeal fashion. The south and east sides of the ground accommodating 29,800 were accessed though 60 turnstiles whilst the north and west sides with a capacity of 24,256 were accessed solely from the Leppings lane end where there were only 23 turnstiles. Of those 23 turnstiles, seven (labelled A – G) provided access to the Leppings Lane terraces. Supporters gaining access through one of these turnstiles would find themselves on a walled concourse containing one exit gate, gate C. Supporters could then choose to access pens one and two or six and seven by walking around the outsides of the stand and gaining access from the sides. This would not have been obvious to the first-time visitor who would not have been helped by the poor signposting and lack of information on the tickets. A supporter unfamiliar with the ground would naturally have used the tunnel under the centre of the stand signposted 'standing'. This tunnel gave access to the two central pens, three and four.

The policing arrangements were under the supervision of Superintendent Duckenfield who had recently assumed this supervisory responsibility. He had 1,122 police officers at his disposal on that day: 38% of the total South Yorkshire force. The police were operating under their own 'Standing Instructions for the Policing of Football Grounds'. In addition Sheffield Wednesday FC provided 376 stewards and gate men.

A computerised turnstile system ensured that, at any time an accurate count could be made of the number of supporters in any section of the ground and appropriate warnings given if a section neared capacity. In the west terracing this would mean a warning would be given when capacity reached 85% of the total 10,100. There were no means of monitoring the capacity of any individual pen. The crowd could be observed through five cameras with zoom facility which relayed pictures to the police control room. The cameras gave good views of the terracing and the turnstiles.

On the day of the match all the turnstiles were opened at midday. There was some debate amongst police officers whether the pens on the west terrace should be filled one by one but it was decided that the option should be left to supporters who would find their own level. At 2 pm it was observed that the

Nottingham Forest end contained many more supporters than the Liverpool end where the central pens, three and four, were filling but pens one and two at one end and six and seven at the other were relatively empty. Although it was suggested that the Liverpool supporters had arrived in Sheffield in plenty of time but were reluctant to enter the ground, many did arrive late. There were roadworks on the M62; many coaches were pulled off the road and searched by police; and coaches were still queuing for the coach park half an hour before the kick off.

In the half hour preceding the three o'clock kick off, conditions worsened significantly. Pens three and four appeared full to the point that the numbers exceeded those recommended by the Green Guide although the pens at either end had spare capacity. The numbers of people attempting to gain access to the stand before kick off were concerning police officers on the ground. Pressure was building both at the turnstiles and on the concourse as 5,000 supporters congregated.

With eight minutes to go before kick off and crowd congestion reaching a critical level permission was sought and obtained by officers on the ground to open exit gate C to relieve the pressure. Most of the supporters headed through the tunnel into the central pens. Although central control were unaware of it, there was evidence that some police officers had realised that the crush at the front of the pens was causing distress. Others however, unaware of what was happening, refused to allow worried fans to climb the front fence for fear of a pitch invasion. The pressure in pen three was now so great that two spans of crush barrier at the front gave way. This caused some supporters to fall and cause an increase in pressure on those at the front. Unlike normal football crowds the mass of supporters in the central pens could not step back after the initial surge. Lord Justice Taylor captured the horror of the moment when he wrote 'The pressure stayed and for those crushed breathless by it, standing or prone, life was ebbing away. If no relief came in four minutes there would be irreversible brain damage; if longer, death'.[105]

Still the desperation of the moment went unrecognised. When a senior police officer saw the crowding he underestimated the gravity of the situation. When fans began to spill out of the pens, the immediate police reaction was to call up extra officers and dogs to prevent a pitch invasion. This ignorance of the situation was shared by many of the supporters at the back of the terrace. Lord Justice Taylor commented 'Behind them, there were still many unaware of the crisis, watching the game. The football continued to joyous shouting and singing round the rest of the ground while those crushed and trapped slowly expired'.[106] At five and a half minutes past three a senior police officer ran on to the pitch and instructed the referee to stop the match.

---

105 Interim Report, para 77.
106 Interim Report, para 79.

As attempts by police and supporters were made to rescue injured fans the enormity of what had happened became clear:

The Hillsborough Stadium Disaster (Interim Report)

It was truly gruesome. The victims were blue, cyanotic, incontinent; their mouths open, vomiting; their eyes staring. A pile of dead bodies lay and grew outside gate three. Extending further and further on to the pitch, the injured were laid down and attempts made to revive them. More and more walking survivors flooded out on to the pitch as the players left. The scene was emotive and chaotic as well as gruesome. As the enormity of the disaster was realised, many of the fans milling about were bitter and hostile to the police, blaming them for what had happened. Officers were confronted, abused, spat on and even assaulted. A small number of hysterical fans had to be subdued.[107]

Efforts were made by the fire brigade, the ambulance service, St John's ambulance brigade, medical staff in the ground and the supporters themselves to assist in the rescue operation. Senior FA officials went to the police control room for information and were told that exit gate C had been forced open by incoming supporters. Graham Kelly, Chief Executive of the FA, repeated this information on television a little later. Television cameras were at the ground to record the match for later broadcasting. BBC's Grandstand programme was interrupted to show pictures of the aftermath of the disaster, multiplying the impact of the tragedy. The code of ethics adopted by television authorities which prevent the broadcasting of suffering by recognisable individuals prevented an even more painful scenario of friends and relatives viewing the suffering of those they knew.

The ground gymnasium was converted to a temporary mortuary and scenes of distress continued there with relatives attempting to revive deceased relatives and others desperately searching for missing friends and relatives:

The Hillsborough Stadium Disaster (Interim Report)

... [the pathologists] found that 88 of the victims were male and seven female. Thirty eight were under 20 years of age, 39 were between 20 and 29 years and only three were over 50. In virtually every case the cause of death was crush asphyxia due to compression of the chest wall against other bodies or fixed structures so as to prevent inhalation. In all but nine cases that was the sole cause. In one, pressure on the chest had been so great as to crush the aorta; in six cases there were also injuries to the head, neck or chest; in the remaining two cases, natural disease was a contributory factor. In 18 cases bones were fractured. Thirteen of those were rib fractures. However one was a fractured femur, one a fractured radius and the remaining three involved fractures of bones and cartilages round the voice box. These injuries suggest the victims may have been trodden while on the ground.[108]

---

107 Interim Report, para 83.
108 Interim Report, para 109.

This represents only the tip of the iceberg. As Coleman *et al* have stated in their report produced for Liverpool City Council, the grief and suffering extended far beyond the confines of the stadium:

Hillsborough and After: The Liverpool Experience

The officially-recorded statistics show that 95 people died, 400 received hospital treatment and 730 were injured. These statistics do not and cannot record the full extent of the disaster and its victims. It is clear from the experiences of many concerned with counselling survivors since the disaster that an inestimable number of people received actual physical injury but did not seek immediate medical help. Claims for compensation made to the Hillsborough Disaster Appeal Fund provide no more concrete or substantive indication of the numbers involved as a further inestimable number of people have declined to pursue claims for a range of reasons. In addition to the 'hidden figure' of physical injury is the massive number of people, many of whom were not at Hillsborough, who have suffered severe mental anguish and debilitating trauma. Again the evidence suggests that a substantial number have suffered alone and, typically, have refused to speak with anyone about their experiences. Others, however, cannot stop talking about their experiences as the disaster has come to dominate their lives. Recurrent nightmares and fundamental changes in behaviour are further, regular long-term effects endured by survivors, friends and relatives. Thus any attempt to establish the real 'extent' of the Hillsborough disaster is impossible if not futile. It remains apparent, however, that several thousand people have been deeply affected and it will be a long time before recoveries from physical and mental injuries will be made. For some, 'full recovery' will never be possible.[109]

THE INQUIRY

Two days after the disaster, Lord Justice Taylor was appointed to conduct an inquiry into the incidents at Hillsborough. His terms of reference were 'To inquire into the events at Sheffield Wednesday football ground on 15 April 1989 and to make recommendations about the needs of crowd control and safety at sports events'.[110]

The Stadium

Lord Justice Taylor was particularly critical of the layout and capacity of the Leppings Lane end. Following the crushing that occurred at the 1981 semi-final, additional fencing was erected which, in effect, segregated the terrace into three sections. Pens three and four formed the central section. Within the

---

109 A report from the Centre for Studies in Crime and Social Justice, prepared for Liverpool City Council, p 2.
110 *Ibid*, p 1.

central section modifications were made to the layout with a number of barriers being removed. Although extensive modifications had been made, compensatory safety measures had not. Access to the central section could still be made through any of the turnstiles for that terrace. Although the turnstiles had been computerised therefore, the system could give no information as to the number of supporters in any particular section.

Under s 1 of the Safety at Sports Grounds Act 1975 as amended by the Fire Safety and Safety of Places of Sport Act 1987, Hillsborough had been designated as a stadium requiring a safety certificate in 1979. Section 2(2)(a) of the 1975 Act as originally enacted[111] stated that the safety certificate 'shall specify the maximum number of spectators to be admitted to the stadium'. However s 2(2)(b) stated merely that a safety certificate 'may specify the maximum number to be admitted to different parts of it'. The certificate for Hillsborough did not contain maximum numbers for the pens at the Leppings Lane end and although evidence showed that engineers were aware that the alterations to the terrace would impact on spectator numbers no alterations were made to the certificate.

Although s 2(2) had been repealed by s 19 of the Fire Safety and Safety of Places of Sports Act 1987, it was still effective because s 19 gave power to the Secretary of State to lay down terms and conditions for the granting of a certificate and, as no order had been made, the Home Office had recommended that certificates continued to granted in accordance with the repealed section. According to s 2(2) of the 1975 Act, terms and conditions would include those relating to 'the number, strength and situation of any crush barriers'[112] and although it was not a mandatory requirement under the Act to specify capacity of the particular sections of the terrace there was a breach of the provisions in not amending the certificate to reflect the lowering of overall capacity.

Enforcing the Safety Provisions

Another weakness of the provisions became evident when the Inquiry considered how the local authority exercised their supervisory duties under the Act. The Officer Working Party, formed to comply with the regulations, was informal with no chair or record of decisions. The report commented that 'the attention given to this important licensing function was woefully inadequate'.[113] This illustrates the valuable point that the best intentions of Parliament can be thwarted by inadequate application.

---

111 Before it was amended by s 19 of the Fire Safety and Safety of Places of Sport Act 1987.
112 Section 2(2)(iii).
113 Interim Report, para 158.

Crowd Control and the Role of the Police

On the issue of crowd control, Lord Justice Taylor concurred with Justice Popplewell's earlier report that 'it cannot be too strongly emphasised that it is upon the club or the occupier of the ground who is putting on the function, that the primary or continuing obligation rests'.[114] This causes certain problems. *Harris v Sheffield United Football Club* suggests that the money paid to police is for more than normal policing duties. On the assumption that both stewards and police will be present, how will their functions, in fact, be divided? Justice Popplewell acknowledged the reality of the police's *de facto* control but this does not resolve the problem of legal responsibility. In the interim report Lord Justice Taylor concludes:

The Hillsborough Stadium Disaster (Interim Report)

There remains, however, the question of whether there are some grounds or parts of grounds where the club may need to rely on the police (whom they pay to attend) to control the filling of pens and monitoring them for overcrowding. In other words, whilst the duty to in law to insure safety rest upon the club, they may need and by arrangement be entitled, to employ the police as their agents in certain circumstances.[115]

It would appear that Lord Justice Taylor is concluding that clubs owe a non-delegable duty to spectators, the running of which may be delegated to the police. This would mean that an injured spectator's recourse in law would be with the club but would not resolve the legal position regarding the police's legal obligation to the club. Lord Justice Taylor's solution was a Written Statement of Intent:

The Hillsborough Stadium Disaster (Final Report)

I therefore repeat my recommendation that there should be a written document setting out the respective functions of club and police for crowd safety and control 'and in particular for the filling of each self-contained pen or other terraced area and the monitoring of spectators in each such pen or area to avoid overcrowding'. The aim should be for the club through its stewards to perform all those functions of controlling spectators of which they are capable having regard to the quality of the stewards, the layout of the ground and the nature of the match. Where they are not able to discharge any such function the police should perform it. As the proportion of seating at grounds increases, control by stewards should become the norm.

In making interim recommendation four,[116] I used the phrase 'written agreement'. This led to anxiety that what was required was a binding legal contract which would deprive the police of any flexibility in response to circumstances of the day. My intention was not to shackle either party by a

---

114 Paragraph 4.13.
115 Paragraph 165.
116 Interim Report, p 57.

binding contract; it was simply to have a document setting out how the functions were to be divided so that no misunderstanding would arise whereby one party thought that the other had undertaken some duty or vice versa. I am content that the document be referred to simply as a 'statement of intent', so it can be subject to alteration without breach of contract should circumstances so demand.[117]

However the agreement is titled or phrased there may in fact be legal implications for such a document. There is clearly a contract between the club and the police and, according to Harris, this can be for the provision of a crowd control function. It is possible that a Statement of Intent could be used to evidence terms as to the extent of the police's contractual obligation.

THE LEGAL IMPLICATIONS

Civil Actions

Potential litigants could be divided into three categories: those physically injured in the crush at the Leppings Lane end; friends and family of those who died who were now suffering psychiatric injury as a result; and police officers who also suffered psychiatric illness as a result of witnessing the horrific scenes. The civil actions taken by victims against the police gave rise to important legal issues that have had repercussions extending far beyond the sporting context. It was one thing to establish that the police were negligent in their actions but entirely another to establish that they owed a duty to the 'indirect' victims, ie those who did not suffer directly as a result of the alleged negligence.

There was little doubt that those who were injured would be able to claim. More contentiously, the South Yorkshire Police Force's insurers advised them to settle claims with police officers who had suffered psychiatric illness. It was asserted on behalf of the officers that 'they accept the reasonable risks of their service but they should not be expected to deal with the appalling consequences of the negligent actions of others'.[118] In the light of earlier claims by relatives and friends the compensation awarded to police officers became a controversial issue.[119]

The fact that the police officers were successful in their claim reflects a gradual shift in attitude by the courts toward claims for psychiatric injury. Originally psychiatric injury could only be claimed successfully as an adjunct

---

117 Final Report, paras 213 and 214.

118 *The Guardian*, 4 June 1996.

119 *Ibid*. As the Chairman of the Hillsborough Family Support Group commented 'Obviously we accept that these police officers are human beings and they have human emotions the same as everyone else ... but these officers chose to be police officers. We did not choose to be victims'.

to physical injury.[120] There were two reasons for this. First there was the difficulty in substantiating a claim for psychiatric injury. The courts seemed concern over the possibility of false claims. Secondly there was the floodgates argument. This meant that the courts feared that anyone witnessing injury could claim resulting in the courts being inundated with claims. The importance of this has been over emphasised. The courts have always found ways of limiting the scope of such claims with tests of foreseeability and proximity. This caution is probably more out of a fear of indeterminate liability, where it is not known how many claimants may exist, rather than a multitude of claims where the court would readily find liability should the claim satisfy the necessary legal requirements.

Any concessions that the courts have made to claims for psychiatric illness have been made most circumspectly. Claims will be entertained only from applicants within a close familial proximity to the primary victims[121] with more distant relatives and friends considered by the courts to have the 'reasonable phlegm'[122] to overcome such a vicissitude. It is a general principle of negligence that the injury must have been foreseeable by the defendant.[123] It has been successfully argued that although liability toward the primary victim has been established, liability cannot be extended to secondary victims because such an eventuality could not have been foreseen as a consequence of the tortfeasor's action.

Other ways of restricting claims have been to limit them to those who have personally witnessed the shocking scene rather than those told second hand.[124] The additional requirement that the secondary victim should suffer injury at approximately the same time as the injury to the primary victim have been relaxed following *McLoughlin v O'Brian*.[125] In that case the plaintiff was informed of a road accident involving her husband and children approximately one hour after the incident. At the hospital she was told that one child was dead and she saw the other injured members of her family. The House of Lords, relaxing the definition of proximity in time, gave judgment in favour of the plaintiff. Although she had not witnessed the accident she had come to it in the immediate aftermath and this was sufficient to establish a claim.

Following the Hillsborough disaster, claims were brought by a number of plaintiffs. By the time the cases reached the House of Lords that number had

---

120 *Victorian Railways Commissioners v Coultas* [1888] 13 App Cas 222.

121 *Page v Smith* [1995] 1 WLR 644.

122 *Alcock v Chief Constable South Yorkshire* [1991] 1 WLR 814. Reported *sub nom Jones v Wright* [1991] 1 All ER 353 *per* Hidden J, 839c.

123 *The Wagon Mound (No 2)* [1967] 1 AC 617.

124 *Hambrook v Stokes Bros* [1925] 1 KB 141.

125 [1983] AC 410.

been reduced to 10. They represented a range of familial relationships. Two were at the ground whilst others saw the horror unfold on television or listened to it on radio. All the appeals failed:

Alcock v Chief Constable of the South Yorkshire Police [1991] 1 WLR 814

Lord Keith: It was argued for the appellants in the present case that reasonable foreseeability of the risk of injury to them in the particular form of psychiatric illness was all that was required to bring home liability to the respondent. In the ordinary sense of direct physical injury suffered in an accident at work or elsewhere, reasonable foreseeability of the risk is indeed the only risk that need be applied to determine liability. But injury by psychiatric illness is more subtle ... In the present type of case it is a secondary sort of injury brought about by the infliction of physical injury or the risk of physical injury, upon another person. That can affect those closely connected with that person in various ways. One way is by subjecting a close relative to the stress and strain of caring for the injured person over a prolonged period but psychiatric illness due to such stress and strain has not so far been treated as founding a claim in damages. So I am of the opinion that in addition to reasonable foreseeability liability for injury in the particular form of psychiatric illness must depend in addition upon a prerequisite relationship of proximity between the claimant and the party said to owe the duty.[126]

Their Lordships went on to explain that there were two elements to the concept of proximity: proximity of love and affection and spatial proximity:

Lord Keith: As regards the class of persons to whom a duty may be owed to take reasonable care to avoid inflicting psychiatric illness through nervous shock sustained by reason of physical injury or peril to another, I think it sufficient that reasonable foreseeability should be the guide. I would not seek to limit the class be reference to particular relationships such as husband and wife or parent and child. The kinds of relationships which may involve close ties of love and affection are numerous and it is the existence of such ties which lead to mental disturbance when the loved one suffers a catastrophe. They may be present in family relationship or those of close friendship and may be stronger in the case of engaged couples than in that of persons who have been married to each other for many years. It is common knowledge that such ties exist and reasonably foreseeable that those bound by them may in certain circumstances be at real risk of psychiatric illness if the loved one is injured or put in peril. The closeness of the tie would, however, require to be proved by the plaintiff, though no doubt being capable of being presumed in appropriate cases.[127]

On the issue of spatial proximity, Lord Ackner explained:

Lord Ackner: It is accepted that the proximity to the accident must be close both in time and space. Direct and immediate sight or hearing of the accident is not required. It is reasonably foreseeable that injury by shock can be caused to

---

126 *Ibid*, 913.
127 *Ibid*, 914.

the plaintiff, not only through the sight and hearing of the event but of its immediate aftermath. Only two of the plaintiffs before us were at the ground. However it is clear from *McLoughlin's* case that there may be liability where subsequent identification can be regarded as part of the 'immediate aftermath' of the accident. Mr Alcock identified his brother-in-law in a bad condition in the mortuary at about midnight, that is some eight hours after the accident. This was the earliest of the identification cases. Even if this identification could be described as part of the 'aftermath', it could not in my judgment be described as part of the immediate aftermath. *McLoughlin's* case was described by Lord Wilberforce as being upon the margin of what the process of logical progression of case to case would allow. Mrs McLoughlin had arrived at the hospital within an hour or so after the accident. Accordingly, in the post-accident identification cases before your Lordships there was not sufficient proximity in time and space to the accident.[128]

Finally the court addressed the issue of those friends and relatives who witnessed the disaster on television. Lord Ackner was of the opinion that it was indeed possible to suffer psychiatric illness as a result of viewing pictures on the television and therefore there was a possibility of recovering damages for that shock. However the Chief Constable would have been aware of the television restriction on showing pictures of individual suffering and 'although the television pictures certainly gave rise to feelings of the deepest anxiety and distress, in the circumstances of this case there were no such pictures'.[129]

Whilst many of the claimants satisfied one of the elements of a successful claim none of them satisfied all the elements. The case can be criticised for setting arbitrary and artificial limits on who can claim. However the repercussions of extending the boundaries of liability are enormous and in an area such as nervous shock objective judgments will always have to be made to limit the claims.

THE LEGISLATION

Stadium Safety

Lord Justice Taylor's most important recommendation: that of all seater football stadiums,[130] has ensured not only a reduction in football hooliganism but, most importantly, there has been no repetition of the Hillsborough disaster. The effect of all seater stadiums has also reduced the importance of ground capacity at football matches but other sporting grounds are not so

---

128 *Ibid*, 921.
129 *Ibid*, 921.
130 The Hillsborough Stadium Disaster (Final Report) Cm 962, p 12.

well protected. The enactment of the Fire Safety and Safety of Places of Sport Act 1987 is to be applauded for its attempt to broaden the scope of the safety legislation to cover all sports grounds. However as it has been seen this was achieved at the expense of the original s 2 of the Safety of Sports Grounds Act 1975 which enshrined in statute the need for safety certificates to identify ground capacity and the option of stating stand or pen capacity. Section 27 of the Fire Safety and Safety of Places of Sport Act 1987 which deals with the contents of safety certificates for stands at undesignated matches states 'A safety certificate for a regulated stand shall contain such terms and conditions as the local authority consider necessary or expedient to secure reasonable safety'. The local authority can call upon the latest edition of the Green Guide but the Taylor Report advised against incorporating its provisions into statute. The Taylor Report highlighted the cursory adherence to the legislation by the local authority when that legislation merely gives a discretion rather than instruction. It is difficult to see, outside of football, any direct improvement in safety legislation and it is hoped that the disaster has not just transferred the problem to another sport.

Crowd Disturbances

The legislation spawned as a direct consequence of the Report is aimed not at the causes of the Hillsborough disaster but more at the problems of crowd disturbances. The restrictions on spectators travelling overseas under Part 3 of the Football Spectators Act 1989 and the provision contained within the Football (Offences) Act 1991 continue the trend of previous reports into stadium disasters of combining provisions relating to crowd management and crowd disturbance. Only time will time whether the priority given to dealing with crowd disturbances has been to the detriment of those relating to crowd management.

The whole Hillsborough affair is far from settled. A government announcement of a new inquiry into the disaster raises the possibility of further legal repercussions. The inquiry will address inter alia issues relating to the conduct of the police and it is hoped that the role and responsibility of the police will be examined and clarified.

INDEX